MODERN

DATABASE

MANAGEMENT

SIXTH EDITION

JEFFREY A. HOFFER
University of Dayton

MARY B. PRESCOTT
University of Tampa

FRED R. McFADDEN
University of Colorado—Colorado Springs

Prentice
Hall

Upper Saddle River, New Jersey 07458

EXECUTIVE EDITOR: Bob Horan
SENIOR EXECUTIVE EDITOR: David Alexander
PUBLISHER: Natalie Anderson
PROJECT MANAGER: Lori Cerreto
EDITORIAL ASSISTANT: Maat Van Uitert
MEDIA PROJECT MANAGER: Joan Waxman
SENIOR MARKETING MANAGER: Sharon Turkovich
MARKETING ASSISTANT: Scott Patterson
MANAGING EDITOR (PRODUCTION): Cynthia Regan
PRODUCTION EDITOR: Michael Reynolds
PRODUCTION ASSISTANT: Dianne Falcone
PERMISSIONS SUPERVISOR: Suzanne Grappi
ASSOCIATE DIRECTOR, MANUFACTURING: Vincent Scelta
PRODUCTION MANAGER: Arnold Vila
DESIGN DIRECTOR: Patricia Smythe
INTERIOR DESIGN: Lee Goldstein
COVER DESIGN: Steven Frim
COVER PAINTING: Steven Frim
ILLUSTRATOR (INTERIOR): Electragraphics
ASSOCIATE DIRECTOR, MULTIMEDIA PRODUCTION: Karen Goldsmith
MANAGER, MULTIMEDIA PRODUCTION: Christy Mahon
PRINT PRODUCTION LIAISON: Ashley Scattergood
COMPOSITION: UG / GGS Information Services, Inc.
FULL-SERVICE PROJECT MANAGEMENT: UG / GGS Information Services, Inc.
PRINTER/BINDER: R. R. Donnelley, Willard

Library of Congress Cataloging-in-Publication Data

Hoffer, Jeffrey A.,
    Modern database management / Jeffrey A. Hoffer, Mary B. Prescott, Fred R.
McFadden.—6th ed.
    p.   cm.
    Includes bibliographical references and index.
    ISBN 0–13–033969–5
    1. Database management.   I. Hoffer, Jeffrey A.   II. Prescott, Mary B.
    III. Title
QA76.9.D3 M395 2001
005.74—dc21
                                                    2001036826

Credits and acknowledgments borrowed from other sources and reproduced, with permission, in this textbook appear on page 626.

10 9 8 7 6 5 4 3 2 1
ISBN 0–13–033969–5

To Patty, for her sacrifices, encouragement, and support.
To my students, for being receptive and critical, and for challenging me to be
a better teacher.

—J.A.H.

To Larry, Mike, and Ivan. Their love and support provide a foundation to
my life, which makes efforts such as writing this book possible. And to Jeff
and Fred, who gave me the opportunity to write with them and patiently
provided invaluable guidance along the way.

—M.B.P.

In memory of my valued colleague Daniel Couger.

—F.R.M.

Brief Contents

Contents

2   Database Development Process   34

Part II   Database Analysis

PART II OVERVIEW   74

4   The Enhanced E-R Model and Business Rules   127

Part III   Database Design

6   Physical Database Design and Performance

Part IV   Implementation

Part V Advanced Database Topics

Preface

This text is designed for an introductory course in database management. Such a course is usually required as part of an information systems curriculum in business schools, computer technology programs, and applied computer science departments. The Association of Information Technology Professionals (AITP), Association for Computing Machinery (ACM), and International Federation of Information Processing Societies (IFIPS) curriculum guidelines (for example, IS '97) all outline this type of database management course. Previous editions of our text have been used successfully for more than 15 years at both the undergraduate and graduate levels, as well as in management and professional development programs.

This text represents an extensive revision and updating of the fifth edition of *Modern Database Management*. These revisions are necessary to accommodate the technical, managerial, and methodological changes occurring at an ever-increasing pace in this field. However, we have endeavored to retain the best features of our previous editions. We have made every effort to justify the title *Modern Database Management*, which was introduced in the fourth edition.

In this sixth edition we have changed the order of authorship because of the reduced involvement of Fred McFadden as he eases into retirement. Fred has reviewed every page of the manuscript and provided sage guidance on the direction of the revisions. Fred McFadden is the "father" of this text, and his words and ideas will always be present on its pages.

New to This Edition

The sixth edition of *Modern Database Management* updates and expands materials in areas undergoing rapid change due to improved managerial practices, database design tools and methodologies, and database technology. The themes of the sixth edition reflect the major trends in the informations systems field and the skills required of modern information systems graduates:

- Web-enabled systems design and programming within an overall client/server architecture for systems
- Large-scale databases and data warehouses
- Clarifying system requirements through thorough system modeling and design
- Criticality of database performance in an increasingly on-line environment
- SQL as a standard for database querying

In all the chapters, new screen captures are included to reflect the latest database technologies and a new Web Resources section lists Websites that can provide the student with the information on the latest database trends and expanded background details on important topics covered in the text. The major structural changes to the text are:

- The two object-oriented database chapters are now adjacent chapters, and have been moved to the end of the text, where they are presented as a continuous coverage of this emerging database technology and where they do not break up the natural flow among the other chapters.
- The client/server section of the book has been extensively rewritten and now emphasizes the Internet, intranet, and extranet as implementations of a client/server architecture.
- SQL is now covered in more depth and in two chapters.
- The data warehousing chapter has been significantly rewritten and moved forward as a chapter in the implementation section of the book, representing the explosive growth of this form of database.

The following presents a chapter-by-chapter description of the major changes in this edition. Each chapter description presents a statement of the purpose of that chapter, followed by a description of the changes and revisions that have been made since the fifth edition. Each paragraph concludes with a description of the strengths that have been retained from the fifth edition.

Part I: The Context of Database Management

Chapter 1: The Database Environment   This chapter discusses the role of databases in organizations and previews the major topics in the remainder of the text. The chapter introduces a revised classification scheme that now recognizes the four types of databases outlined in the fifth edition—personal, work group, departmental, and enterprise—and now includes Internet/intranet/extranet databases. The explanation of enterprise databases is expanded to include databases that are part of enterprise resource planning systems and data warehouses. The chapter updates the discussion of the evolution of database technologies from pre-database files to modern object-relational and Web-enabled systems. The chapter continues to present a well-organized comparison of database technology compared to conventional file-processing systems.

Chapter 2: Database Development Process   This chapter presents a detailed discussion of the role of database development within the broader context of information systems development. The chapter explains the process of database development for both structured life cycle and prototyping methodologies. The chapter continues to discuss important issues in database development, including management of the diverse group of people involved in database development and frameworks for understanding database architectures and technologies. The chapter also continues to emphasize the information engineering methodology in database development, including the role of the enterprise data model. Reviewers frequently note the compatibility of this chapter with what students learn in systems analysis and design classes.

Part II: Database Analysis

Chapter 3: Modeling Data in the Organization   This chapter, with a new title, presents a thorough introduction to conceptual data modeling with the entity-relationship model. The new chapter title reflects a refocusing of the chapter on the reason for the entity-relationship model: to unambiguously document the rules of the business that influence database design. The chapter contains a thoroughly updated section on the latest approaches to modeling business rules, which has been moved from Chapter 4. Specific subsections explain in detail how to name and define elements of a data model, which are essential in developing an unambiguous E-R diagram. A new section addresses an issue many students face as they learn data modeling: whether to represent data as attributes or relationships. The chapter continues to proceed from simple to more complex examples, and it concludes with a comprehensive E-R diagram for Pine Valley Furniture Company.

Chapter 4: The Enhanced E-R Model and Business Rules   This chapter presents a discussion of several advanced E-R data model constructs. New to the chapter is an introduction of entity clustering, which is a way to present simpler versions of an E-R diagram. The chapter extensively updates coverage of the GUIDE business rules methodology based on the latest guidelines, and now shows the structure of these guidelines, which will facilitate student understanding. The chapter continues to present a thorough coverage of supertype/subtype relationships.

Part III: Database Design

Chapter 5: Logical Database Design and the Relational Model   This chapter describes the process of converting a conceptual data model to the relational data model. It features an improved discussion of the characteristics of foreign keys and introduces the important concept of a non-intelligent enterprise key. Enterprise keys (also called surrogate keys for data warehouses) are being emphasized as some concepts of object-orientation migrate into the relational technology world. The discussion of functional dependencies and normalization has been somewhat enhanced. The chapter continues to emphasize the basic concepts of the relational data model and the role of the database designer in the logical design process.

Chapter 6: Physical Database Design and Performance   This chapter describes the steps that are essential in achieving an efficient database design. The chapter contains a new emphasis on ways to improve database performance. Several sections have been enhanced with references to specific techiniques available in Oracle and other DBMSs to improve database processing performance. The discussion of indexes has been expanded to include descriptions of types of indexes (primary and secondary indexes, join index, hash index table) that are more widely available in database technologies as techniques to improve query processing speed. The discussion of RAID has been updated to reflect the latest thinking on this important technology. The chapter continues to emphasize the physical design process and the goals of that process.

Part IV: Implementation

Chapter 7: SQL   This chapter presents a thorough introduction to the SQL used by most DBMSs (SQL-92) and introduces the changes that are included in the latest standard (SQL-99). The major change for the sixth edition is that the overall coverage of SQL is expanded and divided into this and the next chapter. This chapter includes more examples of SQL code, using mostly SQL-99 syntax and some Oracle 8i syntax. There is an improved coverage of views, both dynamic and materialized. Chapter 7 explains the SQL commands to create and maintain a database and to program single-table queries. The chapter continues to use the Pine Valley Furniture Company case to illustrate a wide variety of practical queries and query results.

Chapter 8: Advanced SQL   This new chapter continues the explanation of SQL with a careful explanation of multiple-table queries, transaction integrity, data dictionary, triggers and stored procedures, and embedded SQL in other programming language programs. All forms of the OUTER JOIN command are now covered. This chapter illustrates how to store the results of a query in a derived table, the CAST command to convert data between different data types, and the CASE command for doing conditional processing in SQL. The chapter also outlines the new on-line analytical processing (OLAP) features of SQL-99, which are necessary for SQL to be useful as a data access tool for data warehouses. As in Chapter 7, most SQL code illustrations are written using SQL-99 syntax and some Oracle 8i syntax. The chapter continues to contain a clear explanation of subqueries and correlated subqueries, two of the most complex and powerful constructs in SQL.

Chapter 9: The Client/Server Database Environment   This extensively rewritten chapter combines content from two chapters in the fifth edition. The purpose of the chapter is to provide a thoroughly modern discussion of the client/server architecture, applications, middleware, and client database access in contemporary database environments. This chapter lays the technology groundwork for the Internet topics in the remainder of the text. Many figures have been updated to more clearly show the options in multi-tiered networks, including application and database servers, database processing distribution alternatives among network tiers, and browser (thin) clients. Important new topics include security for Web-enabled databases, and ODBC and JDBC connectivity (including a detailed example of code to access a JDBC-compliant database). The chapter continues to contain a discussion of the three-tier client/server architecture, application partitioning, role of the mainframe, use of parallel computer architectures, middleware, and Microsoft Access 2000 Query-by-Example. Symmetric multiprocessing (SMP) and massively parallel processing (MPP) architectures are described and compared.

Chapter 10: The Internet Database Environment   The purpose of this new chapter is to describe the connectivity to databases from Web-based applications. This chapter includes a discussion of scripting languages and embedded SQL in scripts, with examples from ASP and ColdFusion for a shopping cart application (all of the code for these examples appears on the book's Website). The chapter also includes a review of the Internet-related terminology and concepts (such as firewall, proxy server, static and dynamic Web pages, HTML/SGML/XML/XHTML languages, cascading style sheets, Common Gateway Interface, and servlets) necessary to understand connecting a database to a Web page. The role of Web servers and server-side extensions for database connectivity is addressed. Web security and privacy issues are also covered.

Chapter 11: Data Warehousing   This chapter is extensively revised from the fifth edition. Its purpose is to describe the basic concepts of data warehousing, the reasons data warehousing is regarded as critical to competitive advantage in many organizations, and the database design activities and structures unique to data warehousing. Topics include alternative data warehouse architectures, techniques for data transformation and reconciliation, and the dimensional data model (or star schema) for data warehouses. Operational data store; independent, dependent, and logical data mart; and various forms of on-line analytical processing are defined. The most extensive changes to the chapter are in the sections dealing with database design for data marts (the derived data layer), in which the topics of surrogate keys, fact table grain, modeling dates and time, conformed dimensions, factless fact tables, and helper/hierarchy/reference tables are thoroughly explained and illustrated. User interfaces, including on-line analytical processing (OLAP) and data mining, are also described.

Part V: Advanced Database Topics

Chapter 12: Data and Database Administration   This chapter presents a thorough discussion of the importance and roles of data and database administration and describes a number of the key issues that arise when these functions are being performed. This chapter emphasizes the changing roles and approaches of data and database administration, with increasing emphasis on tuning the database and queries for improved performance. It contains a thorough discussion of database backup procedures and data security threats and responses and provides a detailed description of managing data quality. There is a new discussion of transaction integrity properties for better recovery and concurrency control. The chapter continues to emphasize the critical importance of data and database management in managing data as a corporate asset.

Chapter 13: Distributed Databases   This chapter reviews the role, technologies, and unique database design opportunities of distributed databases. There is an expanded and updated coverage of the objectives and trade-offs for distributed databases, data replication alternatives, factors in selecting a data distribution strategy, and distributed database vendors and products. This chapter, along with Chapter 12, provides thorough coverage of database concurrency access controls.

Chapter 14: Object-Oriented Data Modeling   This chapter presents an introduction to object-oriented modeling using the Unified Modeling Language (UML) of Booch, Jacobson, and Rumbaugh. This chapter has been thoroughly updated to illustrate the latest UML notations. Using UML provides an industry-standard notation for representing classes and objects. The chapter continues to emphasize basic OO concepts, such as inheritance and aggregation. The chapter includes an extensive example of an OO data model for Pine Valley Furniture.

Chapter 15: Object-Oriented Database Development   The purpose of this chapter is to show how to translate object-oriented models (explained in Chapter 14) into class, object, relationship, and operation definitions for an object-oriented DBMS. The chapter also introduces the latest format for object defintion language (ODL) and object query language (OQL), the standard language for ODBMSs. The chapter includes an OO database definition using ODL for the Pine Valley Furniture database design of the previous chapter. The chapter concludes with a survey of ODBMSs—both vendors and products.

Appendices

The sixth edition contains four appendices intended for persons who wish to explore certain topics in greater depth.

Appendix A: E-R Modeling Tools and Notation   This new appendix addresses a need raised by many readers—how to translate the E-R notation in the text into the form used by the CASE tool or DBMS used in class. Specifically, this appendix compares the notations of Visible Analyst 7.4, ERwin 3.5.2, Microsoft Access 2000, and Oracle Designer 6.0. Tables and illustrations show the notations used for the same constructs in each of these popular software packages.

Appendix B: Advanced Normal Forms   This appendix presents a description (with examples) of Boyce/Codd and Fourth normal forms. A new, additional example is included on BCNF to show how to handle overlapping candidate keys.

Appendix C: Data Structures   This appendix describes several data structures that often underlie database implementations. Topics include the use of pointers, stacks, queues, sorted lists, inverted lists, and trees.

Appendix D: Object-Relational Databases   This appendix presents a description of object-relational database management systems (ORDBMS). Topics include features of an ORDBMS, enhanced SQL, advantages of the object-relational approach, and a summary of ORDBMS vendors and products.

Pedagogy

A number of additions and improvements have been made to chapter-end materials to provide a wider and richer range of choices for the user. The most important of these improvements are the following:

1. *Review Questions*   This section now includes matching questions previously in the Problems and Exercises. Many new questions have been added to support new chapter material.

2. *Problems and Exercises*   This section has been expanded in every chapter and contains many new problems and exercises to support updated chapter material.

3. *Field Exercises*   This section provides a set of "hands-on" minicases that can be assigned to individual students or to small teams of students. Field exercises range from directed field trips to Internet searches and other types of research exercises.

4. *Project Case*   The Mountain View Community Hospital case continues to be included as a student project. New cases have been written for the new and expanded chapters. In each chapter the case begins with a brief description of the project as it relates to that chapter. The case then presents a series of project questions and exercises to be completed by individual students or by small project teams. This case provides an excellent means for students to gain hands-on experience with the concepts and tools they have studied.

5. *Web Resources*   Each chapter contains a list of URLs for Websites with information useful to supplement the chapter. These Websites cover on-line publication archives, vendors, electronic publications, industry standards organizations, and many other sources. These sites allow students and faculty to find updated product information, innovations that appear since the printing of the book, background information to explore topics in greater depth, and resources for writing research papers.

We have also updated the pedagogical features that helped make the sixth edition widely accessible to instructors and students. These features include the following:

1. **Learning objectives** appear at the beginning of each chapter to preview the major concepts and skills students will learn from that chapter. The learning objectives also provide a great study review aid for students as they prepare for assignments and examinations.

2. **Chapter introductions and summaries** both encapsulate the main concepts of each chapter and link material to related chapters, providing students with a comprehensive conceptual framework for the course.

3. The **chapter review**, which includes the review questions, problems and exercises, and field exercises discussed earlier, also contains **key terms** to test the student's grasp of important concepts, basic facts, and significant issues.

4. A **running glossary** defines key terms in the page margins as they are discussed in text. These terms are also defined at the end of the text in the **glossary of terms**. Also included is an end-of-book **glossary of acronyms** for abbreviations commonly used in database management.

Organization

We encourage instructors to customize their use of this book to meet the needs of both their curriculum and student career paths. The modular nature of the text, its broad coverage, extensive illustrations, and inclusion of advanced topics and emerging issues make customization easy. The many references to current publications and Websites can help instructors develop supplemental reading lists or expand classroom discussion beyond material presented in the text. The use of appendices for several advanced topics allow instructors to easily include or omit these topics.

The modular nature of the text allows the instructor to omit certain chapters or to cover chapters in a different sequence. For example, an instructor who wishes to emphasize data modeling may cover Chapter 14 on object-oriented data modeling along with or instead of Chapters 3 and 4. Another instructor who wishes to cover only basic entity/relationship concepts (but not the enhanced E-R model or business rules) may skip Chapter 4.

Case Tools

Modern Database Management, sixth edition, offers adopters the option of acquiring outstanding CASE tools software packages from Oracle and Visible Systems. Students can purchase this book packaged with the full editions of Oracle Designer, Oracle Forms and Reports (Developer), and Personal Oracle, or with Visible Analyst at a greatly reduced fee. We are proud to offer such highly valued, powerful software packages to students at such a low cost. These packages can be used to draw data models, generate normalized relations from conceptual data models, and generate database defintion code, among other tasks. These tools also are useful in other courses on information systems development.

The Supplement Package

A comprehensive and flexible technology support package is available to enhance the teaching experience:

Instructor's Resource CD-ROM   The Instructor's Resource CD-ROM features the following:

- *Instructor's Resource Manual* provides chapter-by-chapter instructor objectives, classroom ideas, and answers to review questions, problems and exercises, field exercises, and project case questions. The Instructor's Resource Manual is also available in print and from the faculty area of the text's Website.

- *Test Item File* and *Windows PH Test Manager* include a comprehensive set of test questions in multiple-choice, true-false, and short-answer format, ranked according to level of difficulty, and referenced with page numbers and topic headings from the text. The Test Item File is available in print and on the IR CD-ROM in Microsoft Word and as the computerized Prentice Hall Test Manager. Test Manager is a comprehensive suite of tools for testing and assessment. It allows instructors to easily create and distribute tests for their courses, either by printing and distributing through traditional methods or by on-line delivery via a Local Area Network (LAN) server. Test Manager features Screen Wizards to assist you as you move through the program, and the software is backed with full technical support.

- *PowerPoint Presentation Slides* feature lecture notes that highlight key text terms and concepts. Professors can customize the presentation by adding their own slides or editing the existing ones.

- *Image Library* is a collection of the text art organized by chapter. This includes all figures, tables, and screenshots, as permission allows.

- *Accompanying Databases*   Two versions of the Pine Valley Furniture case have been created and populated for the sixth edition. One version is scoped to match the textbook examples. The other version is fleshed out with sample forms, reports, and modules coded in Visual Basic. This version is not complete, however, so that students may create missing tables and additional forms, reports, and modules. A preliminary version of the Mountain View Community Hospital case is also included. Oracle scripts are included to create the tables and insert sample data for both Pine Valley Furniture and Mountain View Community Hospital. Robert Lewis, of the University of South Florida, has created these data sets and applications for us. The database files are available on the Instructor's Resource CD-ROM and on the text Website in the instructor's section.

MyPHLIP Companion Website (http://www.prenhall.com/hoffer)   The Companion Website accompanying *Modern Database Management* includes:

1. Totally new data sets and sample database applications in Access and Oracle for use with the Pine Valley Furniture case and the Mountain View Community Hospital case; provided in the secure Instructor's Area.

2. An interactive study guide with multiple choice, true/false, and essay questions. Students receive automatic feedback to their answers. Responses to the essay questions, and results from the multiple choice and true/false questions can be emailed to the instructor after a student finishes a quiz.

3. Web Resources module includes the Web links referenced at the end of each chapter in the text, to help students further explore database management topics on the Web.

4. PowerPoint presentations for each chapter are available in the student area of the site.

5. A full glossary is available both alphabetically and by chapter, along with a glossary of acronyms.

6. New case studies have been added to the Website. Some are designed to become the basis of semester-long student projects. Others are designed as teaching cases. Additional cases will be added over time.

Acknowledgments

We are grateful to numerous individuals who contributed to the preparation of *Modern Database Management*, sixth edition. First, we wish to thank our reviewers for their detailed suggestions and insights, characteristic of their thoughtful teaching style. Because of the extensive changes made from the fifth edition of *Modern Database Management*, analysis of topics and depth of coverage provided by the reviewers was crucial. Our reviewers include the following:

Cyrus Azarbod, *Mankato State University*

Willard Baird, *Progress Telecom*

Michael Barrett, *Clarion University of Pennsylvania*

Douglas Bock, *Southern Illinois University, Edwardsville*

Sue Brown, *Indiana University*

Traci Carte, *University of Oklahoma*

I-Shien Chien, *Creighton University*

Kevan Croteau, *Francis Marion University*

Sergio Davalos, *Portland, OR*

Monica Garfield, *University of South Florida*

Mark Gillenson, *University of Memphis*

Bernard Han, *Washington State University*

James Harris, *Francis Marion University*

Myron Hatcher, *California State University—Fresno*

James Henson, *Barry University*

Chang Hsieh, *University of Southern Mississippi*

Constance Knapp, *Pace University*

William Korn, *University of Wisconsin—Eau Claire*

Ram Kumar, *University of North Carolina, Charlotte*

Robert Lewis, *University of South Florida*

Kathleen Moser, *Iowa State University*

Heidi Owens, *Portland State University*

David Paradice, Bryan, TX

Fred Prose, Phoenix, AZ

John Russo, *Wentworth Institute of Technology*

Siva Sankaran, *California State University—Northridge*

Werner Schenk, *University of Rochester*

Richard Segall, *Arkansas Sate University*

Maureen Thommes, *Bemidja State University*

Heikki Topi, *Bentley College*

Chelley Vician, *Michigan Technological University*

Charles Wertz, *Buffalo State University*

Surya Yadav, Lubbock, TX

Ahmed Zaki, *College of William & Mary*

Han Zhang, *Georgia Institute of Technology*

We received excellent input from people in industry, including: Todd Walter, Carrie Ballinger, Rob Armstrong, and Dave Schoeff (all of NCR Corp.); Patty Melanson, Kelly Carrigan, and Joanna Frankenberry (all of Catalina Marketing); Don Berndt (University of South Florida); Bernadette Lynch (Oracle Corporation); and Michael Alexander (Open Access Technology, Int'l.).

We also thank Joe Valacich at Washington State University and Joey George at Florida State University for their great insights on the relationship of database development to the overall development of information systems. Their careful attention helps make our book compatible with books used in systems analysis and design courses, such as *Modern Systems Analysis and Design*, by Hoffer, George, and Valacich, and *Essentials of Systems Analysis and Design* by Valacich, George, and Hoffer (Prentice Hall).

We also thank Atish Sinha at the University of Wisconsin, Milwaukee, who authored the original versions of Chapters 14 and 15 on object-oriented database modeling and implementation. We sincerely appreciate his efforts to integrate these chapters into the whole text by using the Pine Valley Furniture and Mountain View Community Hospital cases, to create parallel exercises that contrast OO approaches with entity-relationship and relational approaches, and to provide suggestions concerning all chapters.

This edition of the textbook will be accompanied by more sample database applications that faculty and students can explore than any previous edition. Our thanks for creating these supplements go to Robert Lewis, University of South Florida, for the Pine Valley Furniture and Mountain View Community Hospital cases. We also want to thank Michael Alexander, Open Access Technology, Int'l., for creating the ASP and ColdFusion versions of a basic Internet shopping cart.

Laura Biasci, University of South Florida, created the comparisons of four data modeling case tools notation conventions for Appendix A. We want to thank her for the flurry of late nights and lost weekends incurred while getting the four software programs to work on her computer, so she could compare and capture the notation conventions.

We are also very grateful to the staff and associates of Prentice Hall for their support and guidance throughout this project. In particular, we wish to thank Executive Editor Bob Horan, who coordinated the planning for the text, Associate Editor Lori Cerreto, who kept us on track and made sure everything was complete, Production Editor Mike Reynolds, Senior Marketing Manager Sharon Turkovich, and Marketing Assistant Jason Smith. We extend special thanks to Terri O'Prey at University Graphics Production Services, whose excellent supervision of editing was invaluable.

Jeff and Mary are also thrilled to have had a chance to work with and learn from Fred McFadden. Fred is the "father" of this text and was instrumental in setting its style for clarity, accessibility, careful organization, and mainstream modern content. Fred's student-centered philosophy and disciplined writing set the standard for us. Fred has been extremely helpful in the sixth edition and strongly supportive of the revisions, for which we are very grateful.

Finally, we give immeasurable thanks to our spouses, who endured many evenings and weekends of solitude for the thrill of seeing a book cover hang on a den wall. In particular, we marvel at the commitment of Patty Hoffer, who has lived the lonely life of a textbook author's spouse through six editions. Now, Larry Prescott has shown his support through two editions, including leading several "contemplation excursions" into Tampa Bay. Much of the value of this text is due to their patience, encouragement, and love, but we alone bear the responsibility for any errors or omissions between the covers.

Jeffrey A. Hoffer
Mary B. Prescott
Fred R. McFadden

Part ONE

The Context of
Database Management

An Overview of Part ONE

Part I consists of two chapters that set the context and provide basic database concepts and definitions used later throughout the text. In this part, we portray database management as an exciting, challenging, and rapidly growing field that provides numerous career opportunities for information systems students. Databases continue to become a more common part of everyday living and a more central component of business operations. From the database that stores contact information in your personal digital assistant (PDA) to the very large databases that support enterprise-wide information systems, databases have become the central points of data storage that were envisioned decades ago. Customer relationship management and Internet shopping are examples of two database-dependent activities that have developed in recent years.

Chapter 1 (The Database Environment) provides basic definitions of data, databases, metadata, data warehouses, intranets, extranets, and other terms associated with this environment. We compare databases with the older file management systems they replaced and describe several important advantages that are enabled by the carefully planned use of databases. We describe typical database applications and their characteristics for personal, work group, departmental, enterprise, and Internet/intranet/extranet databases. Enterprise databases include enterprise resource planning systems and data warehouses. We describe the major components of the database environment, which are all described in more detail later in the text. Finally, we provide a brief history of the evolution of database systems, including object-relational and Web-enabled systems, and the forces that have driven and continue to drive their development. The Pine Valley Furniture Company case is introduced and used to illustrate many of the principles and concepts of database management. This case is used in subsequent chapters as a continuing example of the use of database management systems.

Chapter 2 (The Database Development Process) describes the general steps followed in the analysis, design, implementation, and administration of databases. This chapter also describes how the database development process fits into the overall information systems development process. Database development for both structured life cycle and prototyping methodologies is explained. We introduce enterprise data modeling, which sets the range and general contents of organizational databases, and is therefore often the first step in database development. We also present the concept of an information systems architecture that may be used as a blueprint for information systems in organizations. We describe and illustrate information engineering, which is a data-oriented methodology to create and maintain information systems. Issues in database development, including management of the diverse group of people involved in database development and frameworks for understanding database architectures and technologies, are presented.

We describe and illustrate the systems development life cycle in this chapter, as well as the alternative use of prototyping, which is an iterative development process. We describe the importance and use of computer-aided software engineering (CASE) tools and a repository in the information systems development process. We introduce the concept of schemas and a three-schema architecture, which is the dominant approach in modern database systems. Finally, we describe the roles of the various persons who are typically involved in a database development project.

It is essential to gain a clear understanding of the various concepts and definitions presented in Part I. These concepts and definitions are used throughout the remainder of the text. To ensure that an adequate understanding has been gained, answer a number of the review questions and exercises, and ask your instructor to clarify any concepts that remain unclear.

Chapter 1

The Database Environment

LEARNING OBJECTIVES

After studying this chapter, you should be able to:

- Define the following key terms: **database, data, database management system, information, metadata, enterprise data model, enterprise resource planning (ERP) system, extranet, intranet, legacy data, database application, data warehouse, data independence, repository, user view,** and **constraint.**

- Explain why databases will continue to grow in number and into the next century.

- Name several limitations of conventional file processing systems.

- Identify five categories of databases, and several key decisions that must be made for each category.

- Explain at least six advantages of the database approach, compared to traditional file processing.

- Identify several costs and risks of the database approach.

- List and briefly describe nine components of a typical database environment.

- Briefly describe the evolution of database systems.

INTRODUCTION

The past two decades have witnessed enormous growth in the number and importance of database applications. Databases are used to store, manipulate, and retrieve data in nearly every type of organization including business, health care, education, government, and libraries. Database technology is routinely used by individuals on personal computers, by workgroups accessing databases on network servers, and by all employees using enterprise-wide distributed applications.

Following this period of rapid growth, will the demand for databases and database technology level off? Certainly not. In the highly competitive environment of the early 2000s there is every indication that database technology will assume even greater importance. Managers are seeking to use knowledge derived from databases for competitive advantage. For example, detailed sales databases can be mined to determine customer buying patterns as a basis for advertising and marketing campaigns. Many organizations today are building separate databases, called "data warehouses," for this type of decision support application (Lambert, 1996).

Use of databases to support customer relationship management, on-line shopping, and employee relationship management is increasingly important. Databases are fundamental to most information systems now, from small databases used in personal digital assistants and information appliances to the very large databases that support enterprise-wide information systems.

Although the future of databases is assured, much work remains to be done. Many organizations have a proliferation of incompatible databases that were developed to meet immediate needs, rather than based on a planned strategy or a well-managed evolution. Much of the data are trapped in older, "legacy" systems, and the data are often of poor quality. New skills are required to design data warehouses, and there is a critical shortage of skills in areas such as database analysis, database design, data administration, and database administration. We address these and other important issues in this textbook.

A course in database management has emerged as one of the most important courses in the information systems curriculum today. As an information systems professional, you must be prepared to analyze database requirements and design and implement databases within the context of information systems development. You must be prepared as well to consult with end users and show them how they can use databases (or data warehouses) to build decision support systems and executive information systems for competitive advantage. And, the widespread use of databases attached to Websites in order to return dynamic information to users of the Website requires that you understand not only how to attach databases to the Web, but also how to secure those databases so that their contents may be viewed but not compromised by outside users.

In this chapter we introduce the basic concepts of databases and database management systems (DBMS). We describe traditional file management systems and some of their shortcomings that led to the database approach. We describe the range of database applications, from personal computers and digital assistants to workgroup, departmental, and enterprise databases. Next we consider the benefits, costs, and risks of using the database approach. We conclude the chapter with a summary of the evolution of database systems and of the range of technologies used to build, use, and manage databases. This chapter is intended to serve as a preview of the topics in the remainder of the text.

BASIC CONCEPTS AND DEFINITIONS

Database: An organized collection of logically related data.

We define a **database** as an organized collection of logically related data. A database may be of any size and complexity. For example, a salesperson may maintain a small database of customer contacts on her laptop computer that consists of a few megabytes of data. A large corporation may build a very large database consisting of several terabytes of data (a *terabyte* is a trillion bytes) on a large mainframe computer that is used for decision support applications (Winter, 1997). Very large data warehouses contain more than a petabyte of data (a *petabyte* is a quadrillion bytes). (We assume throughout the text that all databases are computer-based.)

Data

Historically, the term *data* referred to known facts that could be recorded and stored on computer media. For example in a salesperson's database, the data would include facts such as customer name, address, and telephone number. This definition now needs to be expanded to reflect a new reality. Databases today are used to store objects such as documents, photographic images, sound, and even video segments, in addition to conventional textual and numeric data. For example, the salesperson's database might include a photo image of the customer contact. It might also include a sound recording or video clip of the most recent conversation with the customer. To reflect this reality, we use the following broadened definition: **Data** consist of facts, text, graphics, images, sound, and video segments that have meaning in the users' environment.

Data: Facts, text, graphics, images, sound, and video segments that have meaning in the users' environment.

We have defined a database as an organized collection of related data. By *organized* we mean that the data are structured so as to be easily stored, manipulated, and retrieved by users. By *related* we mean that the data describe a domain of interest to a group of users and that the users can use the data to answer questions concerning that domain. For example, a database for an automobile repair shop contains data identifying customers (the data items it lists include each customer's name, address, work phone number, home phone number, and preferred credit card number), automobiles belonging to those customers (the data items include make, model, and year), and repair histories for each of those automobiles (e.g., date of service, name of person who worked on vehicle, type of repair performed, and dollar amount of work performed).

Data Versus Information

The terms *data* and *information* are closely related, and in fact are often used interchangeably. However, it is often useful to distinguish between data and information. We define **information** as data that has been processed in such a way that it can increase the knowledge of the person who uses it. For example, consider the following list of facts:

Information: Data that have been processed in such a way as to increase the knowledge of the person who uses the data.

Baker, Kenneth D.	324917628
Doyle, Joan E.	476193248
Finkle, Clive R.	548429344
Lewis, John C.	551742186
McFerran, Debra R.	409723145
Sisneros, Michael	392416582

These facts satisfy our definition of data, but most persons would agree that the data are useless in their present form. Even if we guess that this is a list of persons' names together with their Social Security numbers, the data remain useless since we have no idea what the entries mean. Notice what happens when we place the same data in a context, as shown in Figure 1-1a. By adding a few additional data items and providing some structure, we recognize a class roster for a particular course. This is useful information to some users, such as the course instructor and the registrar's office.

Another way to convert data into information is to summarize them or otherwise process and present them for human interpretation. For example, Figure 1-1b shows summarized student enrollment data presented as graphical information. This information could be used as a basis for deciding whether to add new courses or to hire new faculty members.

In practice, databases today may contain either data or information (or both), according to our definitions. For example, a database may contain an image of the class roster document shown in Figure 1-1a. Also, data are often preprocessed and stored in summarized form in databases that are used for decision support. Throughout this text we use the term *database* without distinguishing its contents as data or information.

Figure 1-1
Converting data to information
(a) Data in context

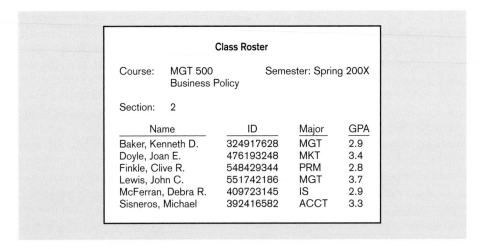

(b) Summarized data

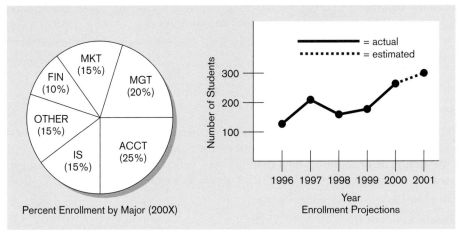

Metadata

Metadata: Data that describe the properties or characteristics of other data.

As we have indicated, data only become useful when placed in some context. The primary mechanism for providing context for data is metadata. **Metadata** are data that describe the properties or characteristics of other data. Some of these properties include data definitions, data structures, and rules or constraints.

Some sample metadata for the Class Roster (Figure 1-1a) are listed in Table 1-1. For each data item that appears in the Class Roster, the metadata show the data item name, the data type, length, minimum and maximum allowable values (where appropriate), and a brief description of each data item. Notice the distinction between data and metadata: Metadata are once removed from data. That is, metadata describe the

Table 1-1 Example Metadata for Class Roster

Data Item			Value		
Name	**Type**	**Length**	**Min**	**Max**	**Description**
Course	Alphanumeric	30			Course ID and name
Section	Integer	1	1	9	Section number
Semester	Alphanumeric	10			Semester and year
Name	Alphanumeric	30			Student name
ID	Integer	9			Student ID (SSN)
Major	Alphanumeric	4			Student major
GPA	Decimal	3	0.0	4.0	Student grade point average

properties of data but do not include that data. Thus, the metadata shown in Table 1-1 do not include any sample data from the Class Roster of Figure 1-1a. Metadata allow database designers and users to understand what data exist, what the data mean, and what the fine distinctions are between seemingly similar data items. The management of metadata is at least as crucial as managing the associated data since data without clear meaning can be confusing, misinterpreted, or erroneous.

TRADITIONAL FILE PROCESSING SYSTEMS

In the beginning of computer-based data processing, there were no databases. Computers that were considerably less powerful than today's personal computer filled large rooms and were used almost exclusively for scientific and engineering calculations. Gradually computers were introduced into the business world. To be useful for business applications, computers must be able to store, manipulate, and retrieve large files of data. Computer file processing systems were developed for this purpose. Although these systems have evolved over time, their basic structure and purpose have changed little over several decades.

As business applications became more complex, it became evident that traditional file processing systems had a number of shortcomings and limitations (described below). As a result, these systems have been replaced by database processing systems in most critical business applications today. Nevertheless, you should have at least some familiarity with file processing systems for the following reasons:

1. File processing systems are still widely used today, especially for backing up database systems.

2. Understanding the problems and limitations inherent in file processing systems can help us avoid these same problems when designing database systems.

In the remainder of this section we describe file processing systems and discuss their limitations by means of a realistic case example. In the next section we use the same case example to introduce and compare database processing systems.

File Processing Systems at Pine Valley Furniture Company

Pine Valley Furniture Company manufactures high-quality, all-wood furniture and distributes it to retail stores nationwide. Among the firm's several product lines are computer desks, entertainment centers, dinette sets, bookcases, and wall units. Customers submit orders to Pine Valley Furniture by any of several means: telephone, mail, fax, or electronic forms via the Internet. The company employs a total of about 100 persons at the present time and is experiencing rapid growth.

Early computer applications at Pine Valley Furniture used the traditional file processing approach. This approach to information systems design focused on the data processing needs of individual departments, instead of evaluating the overall information needs of the organization. The information systems group typically responds to users' requests for new systems by developing (or acquiring) new computer programs for individual applications such as inventory control, accounts receivable, or human resource management. Each application program or system that is developed is designed to meet the needs of the particular requesting department or user group. Thus there is no overall map, plan, or model to guide the growth of applications.

Three of the computer applications based on the file processing approach are shown in Figure 1-2. The systems illustrated are Order Filling, Invoicing, and Payroll. The figure also shows the major data files associated with each application. A *file* is a collection of related records. For example, the Order Filling System has three files:

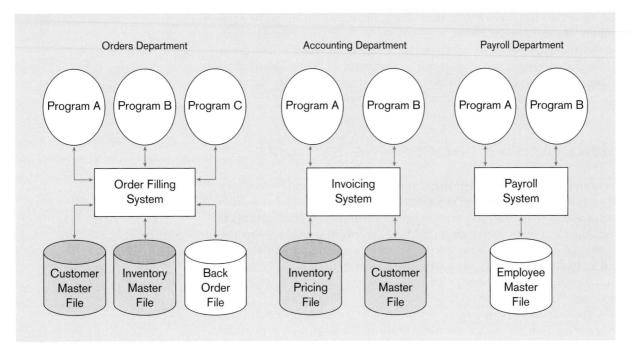

Figure 1-2
Three file processing systems at Pine
Valley Furniture

Customer Master, Inventory Master, and Back Order. Notice that there is duplication of some of the files used by the three applications, which is typical of file processing systems.

Disadvantages of File Processing Systems

Several disadvantages are associated with conventional file processing systems. These disadvantages are listed in Table 1-2 and described briefly below.

Program-Data Dependence File descriptions are stored within each application program that accesses a given file. For example, in the Invoicing System in Figure 1-2, Program A accesses both the Inventory Pricing File and the Customer Master File. Therefore, this program contains a detailed file description for both of these files. As a consequence, any change to a file structure requires changes to the file descriptions for all programs that access the file.

Notice in Figure 1-2 that the Customer Master File is used in both the Order Filling System and the Invoicing System. Suppose it is decided to change the customer address field length in the records in this file from 30 to 40 characters. The file descriptions in each program that is affected (up to five programs) would have to be modified. It is often difficult even to locate all programs affected by such changes. What is worse, errors are often introduced when making changes.

Duplication of Data Since applications are often developed independently in file processing systems, unplanned duplicate data files are the rule rather than the exception. For example, in Figure 1-2 the Order Filling System contains an Inventory Master File, while the Invoicing System contains an Inventory Pricing File. These files undoubtedly both contain data describing Pine Valley Furniture Company's products, such as product description, unit price, and quantity on hand. This duplication is wasteful since it requires additional storage space and increased effort to keep all files up to date. Unfortunately, duplicate data files often result in loss of data integrity since either the data formats may be inconsistent or data values may not agree (or both). Such unplanned and uncontrolled redundancy also can lead to

Table 1-2 Disadvantages of File Processing Systems

Program-data dependence
Duplication of data
Limited data sharing
Lengthy development times
Excessive program maintenance

loss of metadata integrity. For example, the same data item may have different names in different files, or conversely the same name may be used for different data items in different files.

Limited Data Sharing With the traditional file processing approach, each application has its own private files and users have little opportunity to share data outside their own applications. Notice in Figure 1-2, for example, that users in the Accounting Department have access to the Invoicing System and its files, but they probably do not have access to the Order Filling System or the Payroll System and their files. It is often frustrating to managers to find that a requested report will require a major programming effort to obtain data from several incompatible files in separate systems. In addition, a major management effort may also be required since different organizational units may own these different files.

Lengthy Development Times With traditional file processing systems, there is little opportunity to leverage previous development efforts. Each new application requires that the developer essentially start from scratch by designing new file formats and descriptions, and then writing the file access logic for each new program. The lengthy development times required are often inconsistent with today's fast-paced business environment, in which time to market (or time to production for an information system) is a key business success factor.

Excessive Program Maintenance The preceding factors all combine to create a heavy program maintenance load in organizations that rely on traditional file processing systems. In fact, as much as 80 percent of the total information systems development budget may be devoted to program maintenance in such organizations. This of course leaves little opportunity for developing new applications.

It is important to note that many of the disadvantages of file processing we have mentioned can also be limitations of databases if an organization does not properly apply the database approach. For example, if an organization develops many separately managed databases (say, one for each department or business function) with little or no coordination of the metadata, then uncontrolled data duplication, limited data sharing, lengthy development time, and excessive program maintenance can occur. Thus, the database approach, which is explained in the next section, is as much a way to manage organizational data as it is a set of technology for defining, creating, maintaining, and using these data.

THE DATABASE APPROACH

The database approach emphasizes the integration and sharing of data throughout the organization (or at least across major segments of the organization). This approach requires a fundamental reorientation or shift in thought process, starting with top management. Such a reorientation is difficult for most organizations; still, many are making this shift today and learning that information can be used as a competitive weapon.

The Database Approach at Pine Valley Furniture Company

By the early 1990s competition in furniture manufacturing had intensified, and competitors seemed to respond more rapidly than Pine Valley Furniture to new business opportunities. While there were many reasons for this trend, managers felt that the computer information systems they had been using (based on traditional file processing) had become outmoded. The company started a development effort that eventually led to adopting a database approach for the company. This approach is described briefly in this chapter and in greater detail in Chapter 2.

Enterprise Data Model   Pine Valley Furniture Company's first step in converting to a database approach was to develop a list of the high-level entities that support the business activities of the organization. An *entity* is an object or concept that is important to the business. Some of the high-level entities identified at Pine Valley Furniture are the following: CUSTOMER, PRODUCT, EMPLOYEE, CUSTOMER ORDER, and DEPARTMENT.

After these entities were identified and defined, the company proceeded to develop an enterprise data model. An **enterprise data model** is a graphical model that shows the high-level entities for the organization and associations among those entities. A segment of the enterprise data model containing four entities and three pertinent associations is shown in Figure 1-3. The entities shown in this model segment are the following:

Enterprise data model: A graphical model that shows the high-level entities for the organization and the relationships among those entities.

- CUSTOMER   People and organizations that buy or may potentially buy products from Pine Valley Furniture

- ORDER   The purchase of one or more products by a customer

- PRODUCT   The items Pine Valley Furniture makes and sells

- ORDER LINE   Details about each product sold on a particular customer order (such as quantity and price)

The three associations (called *relationships* in database terminology) shown in the figure (represented by the three lines connecting entities) capture three fundamental business rules, as follows:

1. Each CUSTOMER *Places* any number of ORDERs. Conversely, each ORDER *Is placed by* exactly one CUSTOMER.

2. Each ORDER *Contains* any number of ORDER LINEs. Conversely, each ORDER LINE *Is contained in* exactly one ORDER.

3. Each PRODUCT *Has* any number of ORDER LINEs. Conversely, each ORDER LINE *Is for* exactly one PRODUCT.

Places, Contains, and Has are called one-to-many relationships because, for example, one customer places potentially many orders and one order is placed by exactly one customer.

The type of diagram shown in Figure 1-3 is referred to as an *entity-relationship diagram*. Entity-relationship (or E-R) diagrams are of such importance in database applications that we devote two chapters (3 and 4) to this type of model. Chapter 3 describes basic E-R diagrams and data modeling, while Chapter 4 describes advanced data modeling. Both of these chapters also describe the various types of business rules and how they are captured and modeled.

Figure 1-3
Segment from enterprise data model
(Pine Valley Furniture Company)

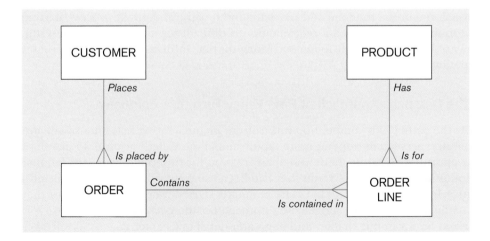

Notice the following characteristics of the enterprise data model:

1. It is a model of the organization that provides valuable information about how the organization functions, as well as important constraints.

2. The enterprise data model stresses the *integration* of data and processes by focusing on entities, relationships, and business rules.

Relational Databases The results of preliminary studies convinced management of the potential advantages of the database approach. The company decided to implement a modern relational database management system that views all data in the form of tables (we describe relational databases in Chapter 5). Figure 1-4 shows the following four tables with sample data: Customer, Product, Order, and Order_Line. Notice that these tables represent the four entities shown in the enterprise data model (Figure 1-3).

Each column of a table represents an attribute (or characteristic) of an entity. For example, the attributes shown for Customer are Customer_ID, Customer_Name, Address, City, State, and Postal_Code. Each row of a table represents an instance (or occurrence) of the entity. An important property of the relational model is that it represents relationships between entities by values stored in the columns of the corresponding tables. For example, notice that Customer_ID is an attribute of both the Customer table and the Order table. As a result, we can easily link an order to its associated customer. For example, we can determine that Order_ID 3 is associated with Customer_ID 1. Can you determine which Product_IDs are associated with Order_ID 2? In subsequent chapters, you will learn how to retrieve data from these tables by using a powerful query language that exploits these linkages.

Implementing Relational Databases The database approach offers a number of potential advantages compared to the older file processing systems. However, few of these advantages will be realized if the organization simply implements a series of stand-alone databases, since this approach does not permit sharing of data by various members of the organization. In fact, stand-alone databases exhibit many of the same disadvantages common to file processing systems.

To facilitate sharing data and information, Pine Valley Furniture Company uses a local area network (LAN) that links employee workstations in the various departments to a database server, as shown in Figure 1-5. To improve intracompany communication and decision making, an Intranet that uses Web-based Internet technology and is only accessible within the company has also been installed. Each employee's workstation may be used as a Web browser, gaining fast access to company information including phone directories, furniture design specifications, electronic mail, and so forth. Or, the workstation may be used as a personal computer and connected to the database server as needed through the local area network.

Pine Valley Furniture Company anticipates adding a Web interface to its business applications, such as order entry, so that more internal business activities can be conducted through its Intranet. They are also planning to become more accessible to their customers through the Internet. Many of the furniture retail outlets that sell their lines of furniture want access through the Internet to determine the availability of furniture pieces in Pine Valley's inventory. Then the retailers can provide this information to their customers. Opening up Pine Valley's inventory information to the retailers raises information security questions that will be addressed in Chapter 12 and platform issues that will be discussed in Chapter 10.

Although the database quite adequately supports daily operations at Pine Valley Furniture Company, managers soon learned that the same database is often inade-

Figure 1-4
Four relations (Pine Valley Furniture Company)
(a) Order and Order_Line tables

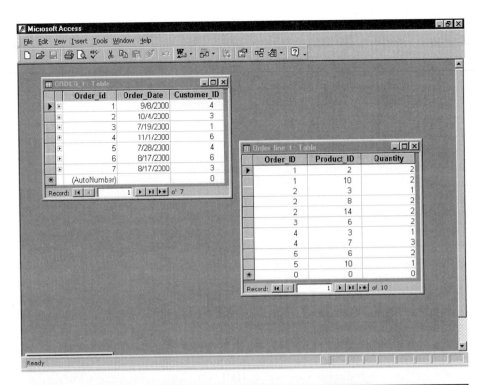

(b) Product and Customer tables

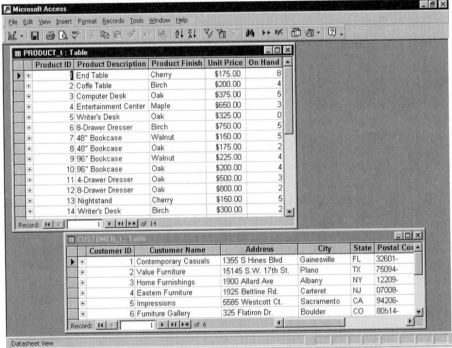

quate for decision support applications. For example, following are some types of questions that cannot be easily answered:

1. What is the pattern of furniture sales this year, compared to the same period last year?

2. Who are our 10 largest customers, and what are their buying patterns?

3. What types of furniture tend to be sold together (for example, tables with chairs)?

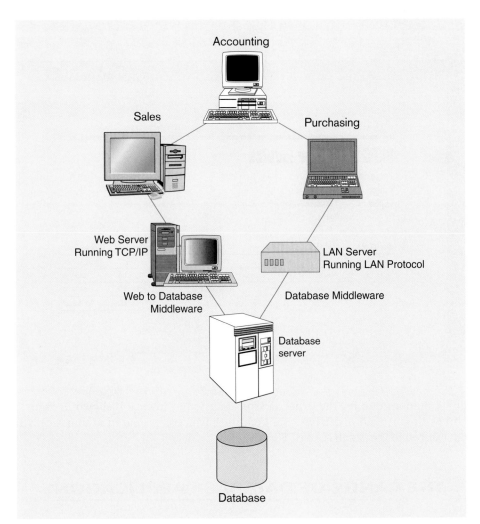

Figure 1-5
Computer system for Pine Valley
Furniture Company

To answer these and other questions, an organization often needs to build a separate database that contains historical and summarized information. Such a database is usually called a *data warehouse,* or in some cases a *data mart.* Also, analysts need specialized decision support tools to query and analyze the database. One class of tools used for this purpose is called *on-line analytical processing* (or *OLAP*) tools. We describe data warehouses, data marts, and related decision support tools in Chapter 11.

A Database Application A **database application** is an application program (or set of related programs) that is used to perform a series of activities on behalf of database users. Each database application performs some combination of the following basic operations:

1. *Create*   Add new data to the database.
2. *Read*   Read current database data (often presented in a useful format on a computer screen or on a printed report).
3. *Update*   Update (or modify) current database data.
4. *Delete*   Delete current data from the database.

One of the important database applications at Pine Valley Furniture creates a customer invoice. When an order is ready to be shipped to a customer, an invoice is prepared that summarizes the items included on the order and computes the total

Database application: An application program (or set of related programs) that is used to perform a series of database activities (create, read, update, and delete) on behalf of database users.

Figure 1-6
Customer invoice (Pine Valley Furniture Company)

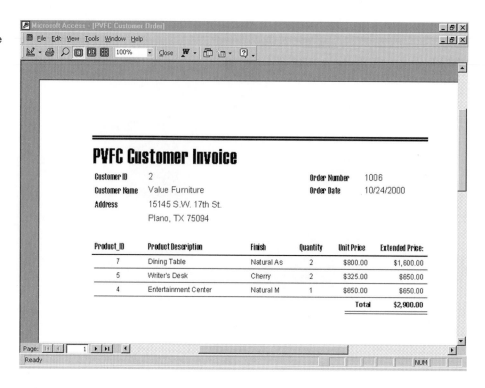

dollar amount due for the order. A typical customer invoice is shown in Figure 1-6. Unless the original order has changed, the invoice is prepared automatically from data stored in the database (see Figure 1-4).

THE RANGE OF DATABASE APPLICATIONS

Databases range from those for a single user with a desktop computer or personal digital assistant to those on mainframe computers with thousands of users. The range of database applications can be divided into five categories: personal databases, workgroup databases, department databases, enterprise databases, and Internet, Intranet, and Extranet databases. We introduce each category with a typical example, followed by some issues that generally arise within the category of use.

Personal Databases

Personal databases are designed to support one user. Personal databases have long resided on personal computers (PCs), including laptops. Recently the introduction of personal digital assistants (PDAs) has incorporated personal databases into handheld devices that not only function as computing devices but also as cellular phones, fax senders, and Web browsers. Simple database applications that store customer information and the details of contacts with each customer can be used from a PC or a PDA, and easily transferred from one device to the other for backup and work purposes. For example, consider a company that has a number of salespersons who call on actual or prospective customers. If each salesperson also has other applications, such as a graphics-intensive sales presentation and a pricing program that helps the salesperson determine the best combination of quantity and type of items for the customer to order, a laptop computer may be appropriate because of storage and performance requirements. If the salespersons only need to keep their contact list, a PDA with a contacts management application that uses a small database may be best. Typical data from a customer contact list is shown in Figure 1-7.

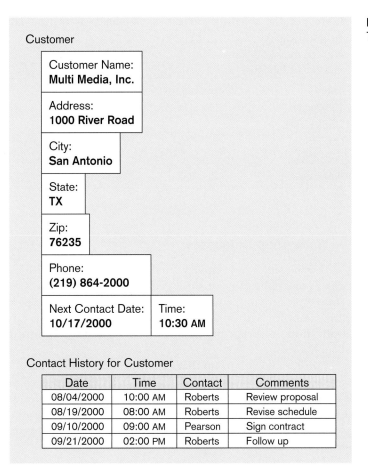

Figure 1-7
Typical data from a personal database

Some of the key decisions that must be made in developing personal databases are the following:

1. Should the application be purchased from an outside vendor or developed within the organization?

2. If the database application is developed internally, should it be developed by the end user or by a professional within the information systems (IS) department?

3. What data are required by the user and how should the database be designed?

4. What commercial database management system (DBMS) product should be used for the application?

5. How should data in the personal database be synchronized with data in other databases?

6. Who is responsible for the accuracy of the data in the personal database?

Personal databases are widely used because they can often improve personal productivity. However, they entail a risk: The data cannot easily be shared with other users. For example, suppose the sales manager wants a consolidated view of customer contacts. This cannot be quickly or easily provided from an individual salesperson's databases. This illustrates a very common problem: If data are of interest to one person, they probably are (or will soon become) of interest to others as well. For this reason, personal databases should be limited to those rather special situations (such as in a very small organization) where the need to share the data among users of the personal database is unlikely to arise.

Table 1-3 List of Software Objects in an Example Workgroup Database

Object Place, Inc.
400 Magnolia St.
Atlanta, GA 02103

Name	Language	Description	Price
123Xtender	Visual Basic	Spreadsheet wrapper	595
DSSObjects	C++	Decision support generator	595
ObjectSuite	Smalltalk	Set of 6 generic objects	5000
OrderObject	Smalltalk	Generic order object	1000
PatientObject	Smalltalk	Generic patient object	1000

Workgroup Databases

A *workgroup* is a relatively small team of people who collaborate on the same project or application or on a group of similar projects or applications. A workgroup typically comprises fewer than 25 persons. These persons might be engaged (for example) with a construction project or with developing a new computer application. A workgroup database is designed to support the collaborative efforts of such a team.

Consider a workgroup that develops both standard and custom objects (or software components) that are sold to software vendors as well as to end users. Table 1-3 is a list of some of the software objects that have been developed recently. Typically one or more persons work on a given object or component at a given time. The group needs a database that will track each item as it is developed and allow the data to be easily shared by the team members.

The method of sharing the data in this database is shown in Figure 1-8. Each member of the workgroup has a desktop computer and the computers are linked by means of a local area network (LAN). The database is stored on a central device called the *database server*, which is also connected to the network. Thus each member of the workgroup has access to the shared data. Different types of group members (e.g., developer or project manager) may have different user views of this shared database. Notice that this arrangement overcomes the principal objection to PC data-

Figure 1-8
Workgroup database with local area network

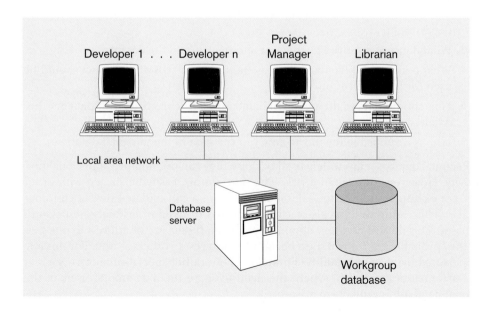

bases, which is that the data are not easily shared (at least data are easily shared within the workgroup). This arrangement, however, introduces many data management issues not present with personal (single-user) databases, such as data security and data integrity with concurrent user data updating. Also, since an organization is composed of many workgroups, and an individual may be part of many different workgroups at the same or different times, it is possible to generate many databases, just as in the situation of personal databases.

In establishing a workgroup database, the organization must answer the same questions that applied to personal databases. In addition, the following database management questions arise:

1. How can the design of the database be optimized for a variety of group members' information requirements?

2. How can the various members use the database concurrently without compromising the integrity of the database?

3. Which database processing operations should be performed at a workstation and which should occur on the server?

Department Databases

A *department* is a functional unit within an organization. Typical examples of departments are personnel, marketing, manufacturing, and accounting. A department is generally larger than a workgroup (typically between 25 and 100 persons) and is responsible for a more diverse range of functions.

Department databases are designed to support the various functions and activities of a department. They are the most common of the five types of databases described in this section. For example, consider a personnel database that is designed to track data concerning employees, jobs, skills, and job assignments. Once the relevant data are stored in the database, users can query the database to obtain answers to questions such as the following:

1. For a particular job classification (such as Software Engineer), what job opportunities exist in the company at the present time?

2. For that same job classification, what skill (or skills) are required?

3. What skills are possessed by a particular employee? Conversely, which employees possess a particular skill (such as C++ programming)?

4. Which employees have held a particular job assignment? Conversely, what is the job history for a particular employee?

5. Which employees are supervised by a particular manager?

Typical questions that must be addressed when designing and implementing department databases (besides those already described) include the following:

1. How can the database and its environment be designed to produce adequate performance, given the large number of users and user transactions?

2. How can adequate security be provided to protect against unauthorized disclosure or distribution of sensitive data?

3. What database and application development tools should be used in this complex environment?

4. Do other departments maintain the same type of data, and if so, how can data redundancy and consistency of data and metadata best be managed?

5. Are the users of the database geographically dispersed or the size of the database so great that data must be stored on several computer systems, thus creating a *distributed database*?

Enterprise Databases

An enterprise database is one whose scope is the entire organization or enterprise (or, at least, many different departments). Such databases are intended to support organization-wide operations and decision making. Note that an organization may have several enterprise databases, so such a database is not inclusive of all organizational data. A single, operational, enterprise database is impractical for many medium to large organizations due to difficulties in performance for very large databases, diverse needs of different users, and the complexity of achieving a single definition of data (metadata) for all database users. An enterprise database does, however, support information needs from many departments. Over the last decade, the evolution of enterprise databases has resulted in two major developments:

1. Enterprise resource planning (ERP) systems
2. Data warehousing implementations

Enterprise resource planning (ERP)
systems: A business management system that integrates all functions of the enterprise, such as manufacturing, sales, finance, marketing, inventory, accounting, and human resources. ERP systems are software applications that provide the data necessary for the enterprise to examine and manage its activities.

Data warehouse: An integrated decision support database whose content is derived from the various operational databases.

Enterprise resource planning (ERP) systems have evolved from the materials requirements planning (MRP) and manufacturing resources planning (MRP-II) systems of the 1970s and 1980s. While MRP systems scheduled the raw materials, component, and subassembly requirements for manufacturing processes, MRP-II systems also scheduled shop floors and product distribution. Next, extension to the remaining business functions resulted in enterprise-wide management systems, or enterprise resource planning systems. All ERP systems are heavily dependent on databases to store the data required by the ERP applications.

While ERP systems work with the current operational data of the enterprise, **data warehouses** collect their content from the various operational databases, including personal, workgroup, and department databases. Data warehouses provide users with the opportunity to work with historical data to identify patterns and trends and answers to strategic business questions. We describe data warehouses in detail in Chapter 11.

Consider a large health care organization that operates a group of medical centers including hospitals, clinics, and nursing homes. As shown in Figure 1-9, each of these medical centers has a separate database (or databases) to support the various operations at that facility. These databases contain data concerning patients, physicians, medical services, business operations, and other related entities.

The databases provide adequate support for most functions at each individual medical center. However, the organization realizes the need for a single, consolidated view of the entire organization; for example, to see the total activities with a single patient or supplier. Operating efficiencies can be achieved, for example, by central ordering of supplies for all medical units and scheduling staff and services across all units. An ERP system makes these approaches possible. Corporate decision making, dealing with external suppliers (such as insurance companies), and reporting to various agencies require compiled historical data and information. To satisfy these requirements, the organization has created a data warehouse that is maintained at the corporate office. Data in the data warehouse are derived by extracting and summarizing data from the individual databases on a periodic basis and transmitting those data by means of a telecommunications network to the corporate data warehouse.

Several questions that often arise in the context of an enterprise database are the following:

1. How should the data be distributed among the various locations in the corporate structure?
2. How can the organization develop and maintain standards concerning data names, definitions, formats, and related issues?

Legacy data: Data contained by a system used prior to the installation of a new system. Often legacy data resides on mainframe systems, which may have been replaced by client/server systems or Web-enabled systems.

3. What actions must be taken in order to successfully integrate numerous systems, including **legacy data** from earlier systems that are desired for analysis.

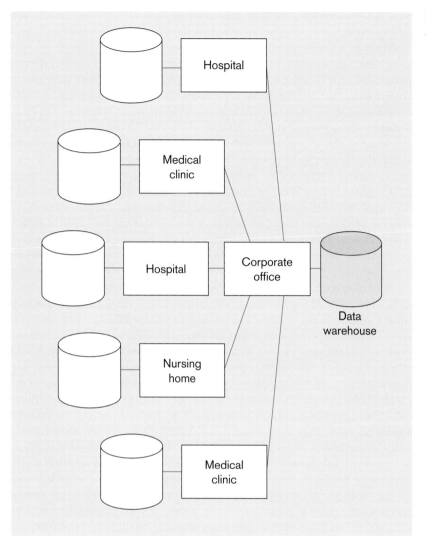

Figure 1-9
An enterprise data warehouse

Internet, Intranet, and Extranet Databases

The most recent change that affects the database environment is the ascendance of the Internet, a worldwide network that connects users of multiple platforms easily through an interface known as a Web browser. Acceptance of the Internet by businesses has resulted in important changes in long-established business models. Very successful companies have been shaken by competition from new businesses that have employed the Internet to provide improved customer information and service, eliminate traditional marketing channels and distribution channels, and implement employee relationship management. Customers configure and order their latest personal computer directly from the computer manufacturer. Bids are accepted for airline tickets and collectables within minutes of submission, sometimes resulting in savings of over 40 percent. Information about open positions and company activities is readily available within many companies.

Each of these applications requires database support and many applications require universal access. The easy connection of multiple platforms allows companies to reorganize their operations and develop new applications faster and at lower cost. A standard interface allows users to be productive with less training and to require less support. Central to the development of useful applications is the ability to attach a database from which current information may be retrieved. When a database is Web-enabled, the Web browser interface allows users to ask unique and specific questions and receive answers based on current information. The answer to the question is automated; there is no need to go through a series of options over the telephone and wait for a human to offer assistance. Web-enabled databases are indispensable to the development of on-line shopping sites. Companies are scrambling to collect information about their customers (purchase patterns, site navigation and duration of stay at each screen, and so forth) in order to improve their customer relationship management (CRM) efforts.

Most of the examples cited above reflect business-to-customer (BtoC) relationships, though some businesses' customers are other businesses. Their interactions are commonly referred to as BtoB relationships. The Internet is used to facilitate BtoC relationships because customers are necessarily external to the business and the capability of the customer to access business data or information is critical to the success of the relationship. Allowing such external access to a business database raises data security and integrity issues that are new to the management of information systems, where data have traditionally been closely guarded and secured within each company. These issues are covered in more detail in Chapters 10 and 12.

Companies have traded information by means of electronic data interchange (EDI) for years. Many companies continue to use their EDI systems to conduct their BtoB business. Some companies, particularly those who are new or did not previously use EDI for intercompany information exchange, have set up **extranets** to conduct their BtoB exchanges. An extranet uses Internet technology, but access to the extranet is not universal as is the case with an Internet application. Rather, access is restricted to business suppliers and customers with whom an agreement has been reached about legitimate access and use of each other's data and information. Typically, these suppliers and customers have access to a part of the company's **intranet**, discussed next. This access facilitates the business relationship by providing faster and more efficient processing or access to information.

As previously mentioned, many companies have used Internet technology to create private networks intended for information management within an organization. In appearance, an intranet page is not distinguishable from an Internet page, but access to the page is limited to those within the organization. Thus, access to company databases is restricted. Intranets may also be able to establish an Internet connection, but that connection will be protected by a firewall, which prevents external users from connecting to the intranet.

Extranet: Use of Internet protocols to establish limited access to company data and information by the company's customers and suppliers.

Intranet: Use of Internet protocols to establish access to company data and information that is limited to the organization.

Summary of Database Applications

A summary of the various types of database applications that we have described in this section is shown in Table 1-4. For each type of database, the table shows the typical number of users, the typical database architecture (client/server architectures explained in Chapter 9), and the typical range of database size.

Table 1-4 Summary of Database Applications (adapted from White, 1995)

Type of Database	Typical Number of Users	Typical Architecture	Typical Size of Database
Personal	1	Desktop/laptop computer, PDA	Megabytes
Workgroup	5–25	Client/server (two-tier)	Megabytes–gigabytes
Department	25–100	Client/server (three-tier)	Gigabytes
Enterprise	>100	Client/server (distributed or parallel server)	Gigabytes–terabytes
Internet	>1000	Web server and application servers	Megabytes–gigabytes

ADVANTAGES OF THE DATABASE APPROACH

The database approach offers a number of potential advantages compared to traditional file processing systems. The primary advantages are summarized in Table 1-5 and described below.

Program-Data Independence

The separation of data descriptions (metadata) from the application programs that use the data is called **data independence**. With the database approach, data descriptions are stored in a central location called the *repository*. This property of database systems allows an organization's data to change and evolve (within limits) without changing the application programs that process the data.

Minimal Data Redundancy

The design goal with the database approach is that previously separate (and redundant) data files are integrated into a single, logical structure. Each primary fact is recorded (ideally) in only one place in the database. For example, the fact that the product with Product_ID 3 is an oak computer desk with a unit price of $375.00 is recorded in one place in the Product table (see Figure 1-4b). The database approach does not eliminate redundancy entirely, but it allows the designer to carefully control the type and amount of redundancy. For example, each order in the Order table (Figure 1-4a) contains a Customer_ID to establish the relationship between orders and customers. At other times it may be desirable to include some limited redundancy to improve database performance, as we will see in later chapters.

Improved Data Consistency

By eliminating (or controlling) data redundancy, we greatly reduce the opportunities for inconsistency. For example, if a customer address is stored only once, we cannot disagree on the stored values. Also, updating data values is greatly simplified when each value is stored in one place only. Finally, we avoid the wasted storage space that results from redundant data storage.

Improved Data Sharing

A database is designed as a shared corporate resource. Authorized internal and external users are granted permission to use the database, and each user (or group of users) is provided one or more user views to facilitate this use. A **user view** is a logical description of some portion of the database that is required by a user to perform some task. For example, each table in the Pine Valley Furniture database (Figure 1-4) can constitute a user view. However, a user view is often a form or report that comprises data from more than one table. For example, the customer invoice (Figure 1-6) also is a user view of the same database; a product catalog available on Pine Valley's Website is another user view.

Increased Productivity of Application Development

A major advantage of the database approach is that it greatly reduces the cost and time for developing new business applications. There are two important reasons that database applications can often be developed much more rapidly than conventional file applications:

1. Assuming that the database and the related data capture and maintenance applications have already been designed and implemented, the programmer

Table 1-5 Advantages of the Database Approach

Program-data independence

Minimal data redundancy

Improved data consistency

Improved data sharing

Increased productivity of application development

Enforcement of standards

Improved data quality

Improved data accessibility and responsiveness

Reduced program maintenance

Data independence: The separation of data descriptions from the application programs that use the data.

User view: A logical description of some portion of the database that is required by a user to perform some task.

can concentrate on the specific functions required for the new application, without having to worry about file design or low-level implementation details.

2. The database management system provides a number of high-level productivity tools such as forms and report generators and high-level languages that automate some of the activities of database design and implementation. We describe many of these tools in subsequent chapters.

Enforcement of Standards

When the database approach is implemented with full management support, the database administration function should be granted single-point authority and responsibility for establishing and enforcing data standards. These standards will include naming conventions, data quality standards, and uniform procedures for accessing, updating, and protecting data. The data repository provides database administrators with a powerful set of tools for developing and enforcing these standards. Unfortunately, the failure to implement a strong database administration function is perhaps the most common source of database failures in organizations. We describe the database administration (and related data administration) functions in Chapter 12.

Improved Data Quality

Concern with poor quality of data is a common theme in database administration today (Ballou and Tayi, 1999). The database approach provides a number of tools and processes to improve data quality. Two of the more important are the following:

Constraint: A rule that cannot be violated by database users.

1. Database designers can specify integrity constraints that are enforced by the DBMS. A **constraint** is a rule that cannot be violated by database users. We describe numerous types of constraints (also called business rules) in Chapters 3 and 4.

2. One of the objectives of a data warehouse environment is to clean up (or "scrub") operational data before they are placed in the data warehouse (Jordan, 1996). We describe data warehouses and the potential for improving data quality in Chapter 11.

Improved Data Accessibility and Responsiveness

With a relational database, end users without programming experience can often retrieve and display data, even when it crosses traditional departmental boundaries. For example, an employee can display information about computer desks at Pine Valley Furniture Company with the following query:

```
SELECT *
FROM PRODUCT
WHERE Product_Name = "Computer Desk";
```

The language used in this query is called Structured Query Language, or SQL (you will study this language in detail in Chapters 7 and 8).

Reduced Program Maintenance

Stored data must be changed frequently for a variety of reasons: new data item types are added, data formats are changed, and so on. A celebrated example of this problem is the well-known "year 2000" problem, in which common two-digit year fields were extended to four digits to accommodate the rollover from the year 1999 to the year 2000.

In a file processing environment, the descriptions of data and the logic for accessing data are built into individual application programs (this is the program-data dependence issue described earlier). As a result, changes to data formats and access methods inevitably result in the need to modify application programs. In a database environment, data are more independent of the application programs that use them. Within limits, we can change either the data or the application programs that use the data without necessitating a change in the other factor. As a result, program maintenance can be significantly reduced in a modern database environment.

Cautions About Database Benefits

This section has identified nine major potential benefits of the database approach. However, we must caution you that many organizations have been frustrated in attempting to realize some of these benefits. For example, the goal of data independence (and therefore reduced program maintenance) has proven elusive due to the limitations of older data models and database management software. Fortunately, the relational model (as well as the newer object-oriented model) provide a significantly better environment for achieving these benefits. Another reason for failure to achieve the intended benefits is poor organizational planning and database implementation—even the best data management software cannot overcome such deficiencies. For this reason, we stress database planning and design in this text.

COSTS AND RISKS OF THE DATABASE APPROACH

As with any business decision, the database approach entails some additional costs and risks that must be recognized and managed when implementing this approach (see Table 1-6).

New, Specialized Personnel

Frequently, organizations that adopt the database approach need to hire or train individuals to design and implement databases, provide database administration services, and manage a staff of new people. Further, because of the rapid changes in technology these new people will have to be retrained or upgraded on a regular basis. This personnel increase may be more than offset by other productivity gains, but an organization should not minimize the need for these specialized skills, which are required to obtain the most from the potential benefits. We discuss the staff requirements for database management in Chapter 12.

Installation and Management Cost and Complexity

A multiuser database management system is a large and complex suite of software that has a high initial cost, requires a staff of trained personnel to install and operate, and also has substantial annual maintenance and support costs. Installing such a system may also require upgrades to the hardware and data communications systems in the organization. Substantial training is normally required on an ongoing basis to keep up with new releases and upgrades. Additional or more sophisticated and costly database software may be needed to provide security and to ensure proper concurrent updating of shared data.

Table 1-6 Costs and Risks of the Database Approach

New, specialized personnel

Installation and management cost and complexity

Conversion costs

Need for explicit backup and recovery

Organizational conflict

Conversion Costs

The term *legacy systems* is widely used to refer to older applications in an organization that are based on file processing and/or older database technology. The cost of converting these older systems to modern database technology—measured in terms of dollars, time, and organizational commitment—may often seem prohibitive to an organization. As will be shown in Chapter 11, the use of data warehouses is one strategy for continuing to use older systems while at the same time exploiting modern database technology and techniques (Ritter, 1999).

Need for Explicit Backup and Recovery

A shared corporate database must be accurate and available at all times. This requires that comprehensive procedures be developed and used for providing backup copies of data and for restoring a database when damage occurs. A modern database management system normally automates many more of the backup and recovery tasks than a file system. We describe procedures for security, backup, and recovery in Chapter 12.

Organizational Conflict

A shared database requires a consensus on data definitions and ownership as well as responsibilities for accurate data maintenance. Experience has shown that conflicts on data definitions, data formats and coding, rights to update shared data, and associated issues are frequent and often difficult to resolve. Handling these issues requires organizational commitment to the database approach, organizationally astute database administrators, and a sound evolutionary approach to database development.

If strong top management support of and commitment to the database approach is lacking, end-user development of stand-alone databases is likely to proliferate. These databases do not follow the general database approach that we have described, and they are unlikely to provide the benefits described earlier.

COMPONENTS OF THE DATABASE ENVIRONMENT

The major components of a typical database environment and their relationships are shown in Figure 1-10. You have already been introduced to some (but not all) of these components in previous sections. Following is a brief description of the nine components shown in Figure 1-10.

Repository: A centralized knowledge base of all data definitions, data relationships, screen and report formats, and other system components.

Database management system (DBMS): A software application that is used to create, maintain, and provide controlled access to user databases.

1. **Computer-aided software engineering (CASE) tools**   Automated tools used to design databases and application programs. We describe the use of CASE tools for database design and development throughout the text.

2. **Repository**   Centralized knowledge base for all data definitions, data relationships, screen and report formats, and other system components. A repository contains an extended set of metadata important for managing databases as well as other components of an information system. We describe the repository in Chapter 12.

3. **Database management system (DBMS)**   Commercial software (and occasionally, hardware and firmware) system used to define, create, maintain, and provide controlled access to the database and also to the repository. We describe the functions of a DBMS in Chapters 12 and 13.

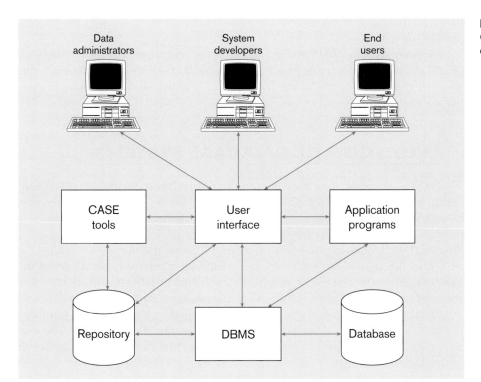

Figure 1-10
Components of the database
environment

4. **Database**   An organized collection of logically related data, usually designed to meet the information needs of multiple users in an organization. It is important to distinguish between the database and the repository. The repository contains *definitions* of data, whereas the database contains *occurrences* of data. We describe the activities of database design in Chapters 5 and 6 and of implementation in Chapters 7 through 11.

5. **Application programs**   Computer programs that are used to create and maintain the database and provide information to users. Key database programming skills are described in Chapters 7 through 11.

6. **User interface**   Languages, menus, and other facilities by which users interact with various system components, such as CASE tools, application programs, the DBMS, and the repository. User interfaces are illustrated throughout this text.

7. **Data administrators**   Persons who are responsible for the overall information resources of an organization. Data administrators use CASE tools to improve the productivity of database planning and design. We describe the functions of data administration in detail in Chapter 12.

8. **System developers**   Persons such as systems analysts and programmers who design new application programs. System developers often use CASE tools for system requirements analysis and program design.

9. **End users**   Persons throughout the organization who add, delete, and modify data in the database and who request or receive information from it. All user interactions with the database must be routed through the DBMS.

With advances in software, the user interface is becoming increasingly user-friendly. Examples of such advances are menu-driven systems, Web-enabled systems, use of a mouse, and voice-recognition systems. These systems promote end-user computing, which means that users who are not computer experts can define their own reports, displays, and simple applications. Of course, in such an environment, database administration must ensure the enforcement of adequate security measures to protect the database.

In summary, the DBMS operational environment shown in Figure 1-10 is an integrated system of hardware, software, and people that is designed to facilitate the storage, retrieval, and control of the information resource and to improve the productivity of the organization.

EVOLUTION OF DATABASE SYSTEMS

Database management systems were first introduced during the 1960s and have continued to evolve during subsequent decades. Figure 1-11 sketches this evolution by highlighting the database technology (or technologies) that tended to be in the forefront during each decade. In most cases the period of introduction was quite long, and the technology was first introduced during the decade preceding the one shown in the figure. For example, the relational model was first defined by E. F. Codd, an IBM research fellow, in a paper published in 1970 (Codd, 1970). However, the relational model did not realize widespread commercial success until the 1980s.

Database management systems were developed to overcome the limitations of file processing systems, described in a previous section. To summarize, some combination of the following three objectives always drove the development and evolution of database technology:

1. The need to provide greater independence between programs and data, thereby reducing maintenance costs
2. The desire to manage increasingly complex data types and structures
3. The desire to provide easier and faster access to data for users who have neither a background in programming languages nor a detailed understanding of how data are stored in databases

1960s

File processing systems were still dominant during this period. However, the first database management systems were introduced during that decade and were used primarily for large and complex ventures such as the Apollo moon-landing project. We can regard this as an experimental "proof-of-concept" period in which the feasibility of managing vast amounts of data with a DBMS was demonstrated. Also, the first efforts at standardization were taken with the formation of the Data Base Task Group in the late 1960s.

Figure 1-11
Evolution of database technologies

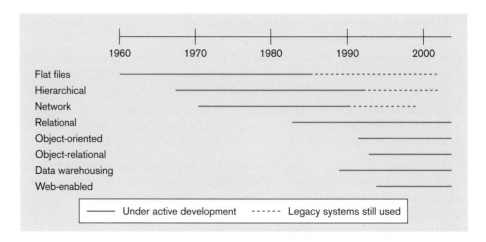

1970s

During this decade the use of database management systems became a commercial reality. The hierarchical and network database management systems were developed largely to cope with increasingly complex data structures such as manufacturing bills of materials that were extremely difficult to manage with conventional file processing methods. The hierarchical and network models are generally regarded as first-generation DBMS. Both approaches were widely used, and in fact many of these systems continue to be used today. However, there are some major disadvantages:

1. Difficult access to data, based on navigational record-at-a-time procedures. As a result, complex programs have to be written to answer even simple queries.

2. Very limited data independence, so that programs are not insulated from changes to data formats

3. No widely accepted theoretical foundation for either model, unlike the relational data model

1980s

To overcome these limitations, E. F. Codd and others developed the relational data model during the 1970s. This model, considered second-generation DBMS, received widespread commercial acceptance and diffusion during the 1980s. With the relational model, all data are represented in the form of tables. A relatively simple fourth-generation language called SQL (for Structured Query Language) is used for data retrieval. Thus the relational model provides ease of access for nonprogrammers, overcoming one of the major objections to first-generation systems.

1990s

The decade of the 1990s ushered in a new era of computing, first with client/server computing, then data warehousing and Internet applications becoming increasingly important. Whereas the data managed by a DBMS during the 1980s were largely structured (such as accounting data), multimedia data (including graphics, sound, images, and video) became increasingly common during the 1990s. To cope with these increasingly complex data, object-oriented databases (considered third generation) were introduced during the late 1980s (Grimes, 1998). We describe object-oriented databases in detail in Chapter 14 and 15.

Since organizations must manage a vast amount of both structured and unstructured data, both relational and object-oriented databases are of great importance today. In fact, some vendors are developing combined object-relational DBMSs that can manage both types of data. We describe object-relational databases in Appendix D.

2000 and Beyond

We are naturally led to speculate what directions database technology will take during the next decade. While there will undoubtedly be some surprises, we can expect several well-established trends to continue:

1. The ability to manage increasingly complex data types. These types include multidimensional data, which have already assumed considerable importance in data warehouse applications. We discuss multidimensional data in Chapter 11.

2. The continued development of "universal servers." Based on object-relational DBMS, these are database servers that can manage a wide range of data types transparently to users. They will become especially important to Internet applications.

3. While fully distributed databases have become a reality, the current trend toward centralization of databases will continue. With communications costs coming down as the volume of data increases, the cost to locate and access centralized data is going down. The lower cost of high-performance computing also encourages centralization.

4. Content-addressable storage will become more popular. With this approach, users can retrieve data by specifying what data they desire, rather than how to retrieve them. For example, a user can scan a photograph and have the computer search for the closest match to that photo.

5. Database and other technologies, such as artificial intelligence and television-like information services, will make database access much easier for untrained users. For example, users will be able to request data in a more natural language, and database technology will anticipate users' data needs based on past queries and relevant database changes.

6. Work on developing data mining algorithms that scale to handle very large data sets will result in organizations being able to efficiently analyze their huge data stores. Improving abilities to discern patterns, trends, and correlations about customers, employees, products, and suppliers will influence their strategic decision making. This capability will also be applied to the large volume of data being collected from Website activity, for example, click-stream analysis (Riggs, 2000).

7. On the other end of the scale, the proliferation of personal data assistants will lead to improved synchronization of small databases and improvement of wireless transmission rates. The Bluetooth wireless standard will greatly accelerate development of wireless PDAs that connect to the Internet. This development will accentuate the importance of protecting data security in an increasingly wireless world.

Summary

The past two decades have witnessed an enormous growth in the number and importance of database applications. Databases are used to store, manipulate, and retrieve data in every type of organization. In the highly competitive environment of the 2000s, there is every indication that database technology will assume even greater importance. A course in modern database management is one of the most important courses in the information systems curriculum.

A database is an organized collection of related data. We define data as known facts or objects that have meaning in the user environment. The term *organized* means that the data are structured so as to be easily stored, manipulated, and retrieved by users. The term *related* means that the data describe a domain of interest to a group of users, and that those users can use the data to answer questions concerning the domain. Information is data that have been placed in a context, or processed and presented in a form suitable for human interpretation.

Metadata are data that describe the properties or characteristics of other data. A database management system is a general-purpose commercial software system used to define, create, maintain, and provide controlled access to the database. A DBMS stores metadata in a repository, which is a central storehouse for all data definitions, data relationships, screen and report formats, and other system components.

Computer file processing systems were developed early in the computer era so that computers could store, manipulate, and retrieve large files of data. These systems (still in use today) have a number of important limitations such as dependence between programs and data, data duplication, limited data sharing, and lengthy development times. The database approach was developed to overcome these limitations. This approach emphasizes the integration and sharing of data across the organization. Advantages of this approach include program-data independence, improved data sharing, minimal data redundancy, and improved productivity of application development.

Database applications can be described in the following categories: personal databases, workgroup databases, departmental databases, enterprise databases, and Internet databases. Enterprise databases today include data warehouses, integrated decision support databases whose content is derived from the various operational databases. Enterprise resource planning (ERP) systems rely heavily on enterprise databases.

Database technology has evolved steadily since it was first introduced during the 1960s. The major objectives driving this evolution have included the desire to provide greater program-data independence, the need to manage increasingly complex data structures, and the desire to provide faster and easier access to all users. Today, both object-oriented and object-relational databases are increasingly being used to satisfy these objectives.

CHAPTER REVIEW

Key Terms

Constraint
Data
Data independence
Data warehouse
Database
Database application

Database management system (DBMS)
Enterprise data model
Enterprise resource planning (ERP) systems
Extranet

Information
Intranet
Legacy data
Metadata
Repository
User view

Review Questions

1. Define each of the following key terms:
   a. data
   b. information
   c. metadata
   d. database application
   e. data warehouse
   f. constraint
   g. database
   h. legacy data

2. Match the following terms and definitions:

   _____ data
   _____ database application
   _____ constraint
   _____ repository
   _____ metadata
   _____ data warehouse
   _____ information
   _____ user view
   _____ data independence
   _____ database

   a. data placed in a context or summarized
   b. application program(s)
   c. facts, text, graphics, images, etc.
   d. integrated decision support database
   e. organized collection of related data
   f. includes data definitions and constraints
   g. centralized storehouse for all data definitions
   h. separation of data descriptions from programs
   i. a rule that cannot be violated
   j. logical description of portion of database

3. Contrast the following terms:
   a. data dependence; data independence
   b. data warehouse; data mining
   c. data; information
   d. repository; database
   e. entity; enterprise data model
   f. data warehouse; ERP system

4. List and briefly describe five categories of databases and give an example of each type.

5. Why has the definition of data been expanded in today's environment?

6. List the nine major components in a database system environment.

7. How are relationships between tables expressed in a relational database?

8. List some key questions that must typically be answered for each of the following types of databases: personal; workgroup; departmental; enterprise; Internet.

9. What does the term *data independence* mean and why is it an important goal?

10. List six potential benefits of the database approach compared to conventional file systems.

11. List five additional costs or risks associated with the database approach.

12. For each decade from the 1960s to the 1990s, list the database technology (or technologies) that was dominant. Indicate the generation generally associated with each technology.

13. As the ability to handle large amounts of data improves, describe three business areas where these very large databases are being used effectively.

Problems and Exercises

1. For each of the following, indicate whether (under typical university circumstances) there is a one-to-many or a many-to-many relationship. Then using the shorthand notation introduced in the text, draw a diagram for each of the relationships.
   a. STUDENT and COURSE (students register for courses)
   b. BOOK and BOOK COPY (books have copies)
   c. COURSE and SECTION (courses have sections)
   d. SECTION and ROOM (sections are scheduled in rooms)
   e. INSTRUCTOR and COURSE

2. Refer to Figure 1-4 and answer the following questions:
   a. What order(s) do we have outstanding for Customer_ID 6? (Give the Order_ID and Order_Date.)
   b. What products are included on Order_ID 2? (Give the Product_ID and Quantity for each item.)
   c. What products are included on Order_ID 2? (Give the Product_ID, Product_Name, and Unit_Price for each item.)

3. Examine the personal database for customer contacts (Figure 1-7). Is the relationship between CUSTOMER and CONTACT HISTORY one-to-many or many-to-many? Using the shorthand notation introduced in the text, draw a diagram showing this relationship.

4. Reread the definitions for data and database in this chapter. Database management systems only recently included the capability to store and retrieve more than numeric and textual data. What special data storage, retrieval, and maintenance capabilities do images, sound, video, and other advanced data types require that are not required or are simpler with numeric and textual data?

5. Table 1-1 shows example metadata for a set of data items. Identify three other columns for these data (that is, three other metadata characteristics for the listed attributes) and complete the entries of the table in Table 1-1 for these three additional columns.

6. In the section on "Disadvantages of File Processing Systems" the statement is made that the disadvantages of file processing systems can also be limitations of databases, depending on how an organization manages its databases. First, why do organizations create multiple databases, not just one all-inclusive database supporting all data processing needs?

Second, what organizational and personal factors are at work that might lead an organization to having multiple, independently managed databases (and, hence, not completely following the database approach)?

7. Consider a student club or organization in which you are a member. What are the data entities of this enterprise? List and define each entity. Then, develop an enterprise data model (such as Figure 1-3) showing these entities and important relationships between them.

8. In the section of this chapter titled "The Range of Database Applications" five different categories of databases are introduced. For each category, a series of key decisions are outlined. Later in the text you will learn how to deal with these and other decisions; however, you should be able to anticipate partial responses for these decisions from your reading of this chapter and your overall familiarity with computer technologies. For the categories and key decisions listed below, explain what choice you think should be made or what factors should be considered in making a choice within any organization.
   a. *Personal database.* Who is responsible for the accuracy of the data in a personal database?
   b. *Workgroup database.* Which database processing operations should be performed at a workstation and which should occur on the server?
   c. *Department database.* How can adequate security be provided to protect against unauthorized disclosure or distribution of sensitive data?
   d. *Enterprise database.* How can the organization develop and maintain standards concerning data names, definitions, formats, and related issues?
   e. *Internet, intranet, or extranet database.* With applets and code modules on different servers and browsers, how can all components have a shared understanding of the meaning of data?

9. One of the biggest challenges of building e-commerce dot.coms has been establishing the ability of customers to receive the merchandise they order over the Web quickly. From what you have learned about databases in this first chapter and your own experience with ordering over the Web, why do you think companies are turning to database solutions to help them improve their supply chain management and expedite the filling and delivery of orders?

Field Exercises

1. Choose an organization with a fairly extensive information systems department and set of information system applications. Investigate whether the organization follows more of a traditional file processing approach or the database approach to organizing data. How many different databases does the organization have? Try to draw a figure, similar to

Figure 1-2, to depict some or all of the files and databases in this organization.

2. For the same organization as Field Exercise 1 or a different organization, talk with a database administrator or designer. What type of metadata does this organization maintain

about its databases? Why did the organization choose to keep track of these and not other metadata? What tools are used to maintain these metadata?

3. For the same organization as Field Exercises 1 or 2 or a different organization, identify, if possible, one database of each of the five types of databases listed in this chapter: personal, workgroup, department, enterprise, and Internet. Does this organization have a data warehouse? If so, how is the data warehouse formed from data in all the other databases? Does this organization use an ERP system?

4. For the same organization as the first three field exercises, determine the company's use of intranet, extranet, or Web-enabled business processes. For each being used, determine the purpose and the database management system that is being used in conjunction with the networks. Ask what the company's plans are for the next year with regard to using intranets, extranets, or the Web in their business activities.

Ask what new skills they are looking for in order to implement these plans.

5. You may want to keep a personal journal of ideas and observations about database management while you are studying this book. Use this journal to record comments you hear, summaries of news stories or professional articles you read, original ideas or hypotheses you create, uniform resource locators (URLs) for and comments about Websites related to databases, and questions that require further analysis. Keep your eyes and ears open for anything related to database management. Your instructor may ask you to turn in a copy of your journal from time to time in order to provide feedback and reactions. The journal is an unstructured set of personal notes that will supplement your class notes and can stimulate you to think beyond the topics covered within the time limitations of most courses.

References

Ballou, D. P. and G. K. Tayi. 1999. "Enhancing Data Quality in Data Warehouse Environments." *Communications of the ACM* 42 (January): 73–78.

Codd, E. F. 1970. "A Relational Model of Data for Large Relational Databases." *Communications of the ACM* 13 (June): 377–87.

Grimes, S. 1998. "Object/Relational Reality Check." *Database Programming and Design* 11:7 (July): 26–33.

Jordan, A. 1996. "Data Warehouse Integrity: How Long and Bumpy the Road?" *Data Management Review* 6:3 (March): 35–37.

Lambert, B. 1996. "Data Warehousing Fundamentals: What You Need to Succeed." *Data Management Review* 6:3 (March): 24–30.

Riggs, S. 2000. "Collecting Webdata." *Teradata Review* 3:1 (Spring): 12–19.

Ritter, D. 1999. "Don't Neglect Your Legacy." *Intelligent Enterprise* 2:5 (March 30): 70,72.

White, C. 1995. "Database Technology: Sorting Out the Options." *Supplement to Database Programming & Design* 8 (December): 41–44, 46.

Winter, R. 1997. "What, After All, Is a Very Large Database?" *Database Programming & Design* 10:1 (January): 23–26.

Further Reading

Date, C. J. 1998. "The Birth of the Relational Model, Part 3." *Intelligent Enterprise* 1:4 (December 10): 45–48.

Hoffer, J. A., J. F. George, and J. S. Valacich. 2002. *Modern Systems Analysis and Design.* 3rd ed. Upper Saddle River, NJ: Prentice Hall.

Ritter, D. 1999. "The Long View." *Intelligent Enterprise* 2:12 (August 24): 58, 63, 67.

 # Web Resources

www.webopedia.com An on-line dictionary and search engine for computer terms and Internet technology.

www.techrepublic.com A portal site for information technology professionals that you can customize to your own particular interests.

www.zdnet.com Another portal site where you can review recent articles on information technology subjects of your choosing.

Project Case

INTRODUCTION

This case is included to provide you an opportunity to apply the concepts and techniques you have learned in each chapter. We have selected a hospital for this case since it is a type of organization that is at least somewhat familiar to most persons and because health care institutions are of such importance in our society today. A segment of the case is included at the end of each chapter in this text. Each segment includes a brief description of the case as it relates to the material in the chapter followed by questions and exercises related to the material.

PROJECT DESCRIPTION

Mountain View Community Hospital is a not-for-profit, short-term, acute care general hospital. It is a relatively small hospital, with some 150 beds at the present time. The basic goal of Mountain View Community is to provide high-quality health care for its surrounding community while containing costs that have been rising in accordance with national trends in recent years.

Mountain View Community has computer applications that support the following areas (among others): patient care administration, clinical services, financial management, and administrative services. Most of these applications have been purchased from outside vendors, but a few have been developed internally. The computer applications are based on the use of client/server technology, such as illustrated in Figure 1-5. Most of the computer applications are implemented using relational database technology. Most of the databases (as well as the applications) are departmental, using the classification introduced in this chapter.

The relational databases at Mountain View Community Hospital contain a number of tables. Two of these tables, with some sample data, are shown in Figure 1. The PATIENT table contains data concerning current or recent patients at the hospital, while the PATIENT CHARGES table contains data describing charges that have been incurred by those patients. These tables have been simplified for this chapter but will be expanded in later chapters.

PROJECT QUESTIONS

1. What are some of the important benefits that Mountain View Community should seek in using databases? Relate your response to the hospital environment, as much as possible.

2. What are some of the costs and risks of using databases that the hospital must manage carefully?

3. At the present time, Mountain View Community is using relational database technology. Although this technology is appropriate for structured data such as patient or accounting data, it is less well suited to complex data such as graphical data and images. Can you think of some types of data maintained by a hospital that fit this latter category? What types of database technology might be better suited to these data types than relational?

4. How are data in the PATIENT and PATIENT CHARGES tables related? That is, how can a user find the relevant charges for a particular patient?

5. What are some ways the hospital could use the Internet?

PROJECT EXERCISES

1. Using the shorthand notation introduced in this chapter, draw a diagram showing the relationship between PATIENT and PATIENT CHARGES.

2. Develop a metadata chart (see Table 1-1) for the data attributes in the PATIENT and PATIENT CHARGES tables. Use at least those columns shown in Table 1-1, but you may include other metadata characteristics that you think are appropriate for the management of data at Mountain View Community Hospital.

3. One of the important database views for the hospital is the Patient Bill. Following is a highly simplified ver-

Figure 1
Two database tables

PATIENT

Patient Name	Patient Number	Patient Address
Dimas, Salena	8379	617 Valley Vista
Dolan, Mark	4238	818 River Run
Larreau, Annette	3047	127 Sandhill
Wiggins, Brian	5838	431 Walnut
Thomas, Wendell	6143	928 Logan

PATIENT CHARGES

Item Description	Item Code	Patient Number	Amount
Room Semi-Priv	200	4238	1600
Speech Therapy	350	3047	750
Radiology	275	4238	150
Physical Therapy	409	5838	600
EKG Test	500	8379	200
Room Semi-Priv	200	3047	800
Standard IV	470	8379	150
EEG Test	700	4238	200

sion of this view. Fill in the missing data in this view, using the data from Figure 1.

Patient Name: Dolan, Mark

Patient Number: _____

Patient Address: _____

Item Code	Item Description	Amount
_____	_____	_____
_____	_____	_____
_____	_____	_____

4. Using the shorthand notation introduced in this chapter, draw a single diagram that represents the following relationships in the hospital environment.

• A HOSPITAL has on its staff one or more PHYSICIANs. A PHYSICIAN is on the staff of only one HOSPITAL.

• A PHYSICIAN may admit one or more PATIENTs. A PATIENT is admitted by only one PHYSICIAN.

• Each PATIENT may incur any number of CHARGEs. A particular CHARGE may be incurred by any number of PATIENTs.

• A HOSPITAL has one or more WARDs. Each WARD is located in exactly one HOSPITAL.

• A WARD has any number of EMPLOYEEs. An EMPLOYEE may work in one or more WARDs.

5. The goal of Mountain View Community Hospital is to provide high-quality health care for its surrounding community, while containing costs that have been rising in accordance with national trends in recent years. How would a well-managed database help the hospital achieve its mission? Give some examples of how the use of databases in the hospital might improve health care quality or contain costs.

Chapter **2**

The Database Development Process

LEARNING OBJECTIVES

After studying this chapter, you should be able to:

- Define the following key terms: **enterprise data modeling, information systems architecture (ISA), information engineering, top-down planning, business functions, functional decomposition, systems development life cycle (SDLC), prototyping, computer-aided software engineering (CASE), repository, project, incremental commitment, conceptual schema, physical schema,** and **client/server architecture.**

- Describe the life cycle of a systems development project, with emphasis on the purpose of database analysis, design, and implementation activities.

- Explain the prototyping approach to database and application development.

- Explain the roles of individuals who design, implement, use, and administer databases.

- Explain the differences between conceptual, external, and physical schemas and the reasons for a three-schema architecture for databases.

- Explain the three-tiered location architecture for databases and database processing.

- Explain the scope of a database design and development class project.

- Draw simple data models, which show the scope of a database.

INTRODUCTION

Chapter 1 introduced the database approach to information systems and the database application environment found in many organizations. An example organization, Pine Valley Furniture Company, was used to illustrate many of the principles and concepts of the database approach to information systems. You will again see Pine Valley Furniture in this, as well as subsequent chapters, as a continuing example of the application of database management.

Chapter 2 presents an overview of the general steps followed in the analysis, design, implementation, and administration of databases. Because a database is one part of an information system, you will see in this chapter how the database development process fits into the overall information systems development process. The chapter emphasizes the need to coordinate database development with all the other activities in the development of a complete information system. The chapter includes highlights from a hypothetical database development process in Pine Valley Furniture. In this example, the chapter introduces tools for developing databases on personal computers and the process of extracting data from enterprise databases for use in stand-alone applications.

There are several reasons for discussing database development at this point. First, although you may have used the basic capabilities of a database management system, such as Microsoft Access®, you may not yet have developed an understanding of how the database was developed. The primary goal of this text is to introduce you to the concepts and many of the skills you will use to design and build database applications. Using simple examples, this chapter briefly illustrates what you will be able to do after you complete a database course using this text. Thus, this chapter helps you to develop a vision and context for each topic developed in detail in subsequent chapters.

Second, many students learn best from a text full of concrete examples. Although all of the chapters in this text contain numerous examples, illustrations, and actual database designs and code, each chapter concentrates on a specific aspect of database management. We have designed this chapter to help you to understand how all of these individual aspects of database management are related. Although we keep the technical details to a minimum, we hope you will develop a thirst to learn the data modeling and development skills presented thoroughly in subsequent chapters.

Finally, many instructors want you to begin the initial steps of a database development group or individual course project early in your database course. Because of the logical progression of topics in this book, you will study many pages before you see your target for the project. This chapter gives you an idea of how to structure a database development project, sufficient to begin on a course exercise. Obviously, since this is only Chapter 2, many of the examples and notations we will use will be much simpler than those required for your project, for other course assignments, or in a real organization.

One note of caution: You will not learn how to design or develop databases just from this chapter. We have purposely kept the content of this chapter introductory and simplified. Many of the notations used in this chapter are not exactly like the ones you will learn in subsequent chapters. Our purpose in Chapter 2 is to give you a general understanding of the key steps and types of skills, not to teach you specific techniques. You will, however, develop an intuition and motivation for the skills and knowledge presented in later chapters.

DATABASE DEVELOPMENT WITHIN INFORMATION SYSTEMS DEVELOPMENT

In many organizations, database development begins with **enterprise data modeling**, which establishes the range and general contents of organizational databases. This step typically occurs during information systems planning for an organization. Its purpose is to create an overall picture or explanation of organizational data, not the design for a particular database. A particular database provides the data for one or more information systems, whereas an enterprise data model, which may encompass many databases, describes the scope of data maintained by the organization. In enterprise data modeling you review current systems, analyze the nature of the business areas to be supported, describe the data needed at a very high level of abstraction, and plan one or more database development projects. Figure 2-1, a duplicate of Figure 1-3, shows a segment of an enterprise data model for Pine Valley Furniture using a simplified version of the notation you will learn in Chapters 3 and 4.

Enterprise data modeling: The first step in database development, in which the scope and general contents of organizational databases are specified.

Figure 2-1
Segment from enterprise data model
(Pine Valley Furniture Company)

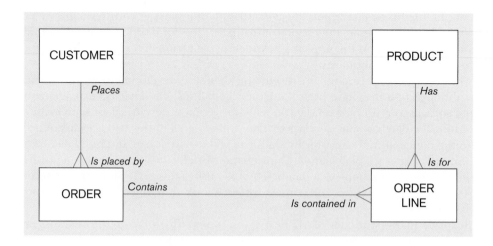

Information Systems Architecture

Information systems architecture (ISA): A conceptual blueprint or plan that expresses the desired future structure for the information systems in an organization.

A high-level data model, such as Figure 2-1, is only one part of an overall **information systems architecture (ISA)**, or blueprint, for information systems in an organization. You would develop an enterprise data model as part of developing the total information systems architecture during information systems planning. According to Zachman (1987) and Sowa and Zachman (1992), an information systems architecture consists of six key components:

1. *Data* (which can be represented as in Figure 2-1, but there are other representations, some of which are depicted in the next section on information systems planning)

2. *Processes* that manipulate data (these can be represented by data flow diagrams, object-models with methods, or other notations)

3. *Network,* which transports data around the organization and between the organization and its key business partners (which can be shown by a schematic of the network links and topology)

4. *People,* who perform processes and are the source and receiver of data and information (people can be shown on process models as senders and receivers of data)

5. *Events and points in time* when processes are performed (these can be shown by state-transition diagrams and other means)

6. *Reasons* for events and rules that govern the processing of data (often shown in textual form, but some diagramming tools exist for rules, such as decision tables)

Information Engineering

Information engineering: A formal, top-down methodology that uses a data orientation to create and maintain information systems.

Top-down planning: A generic information systems planning methodology that attempts to gain a broad understanding of the information system needs of the entire organization.

An information systems architecture is developed by information systems planners following a particular methodology for IS planning. One such formal and popular methodology is information engineering. **Information engineering** is a data-oriented methodology to create and maintain information systems. Because of its data orientation, a brief explanation of information engineering can be helpful as you begin to understand how databases are identified and defined. Information engineering follows a **top-down planning** approach in which specific information systems are deduced from a broad understanding of information needs (for example, we need data about our customers, products, suppliers, salespersons, work centers, etc.) rather than from consolidating many specific information requests (such as an order entry screen or sales summary by territory report). Top-down planning offers the advantages of a broad perspective, a way to look at integration of individual system components, an understanding of the relationship of information systems to business objectives, and an understanding of the impact of information systems across the whole organization.

Information engineering includes four steps: planning, analysis, design, and implementation. The planning phase of information engineering results in an information systems architecture, including an enterprise data model. We review the planning phase of information engineering in the next section. Although this book does not follow the information engineering methodology per se, the remaining chapters address activities that fall under the remaining three phases of information engineering.

Information Systems Planning

The goal of information systems planning is to align information technology with the business strategies of the organization. Such an alignment is important in order to achieve the maximum benefits from investments in information systems and technologies. As depicted in Table 2-1, the planning phase of the information engineering methodology includes three steps, which are discussed in the following three sections.

Identifying Strategic Planning Factors   The strategic planning factors are organization goals, critical success factors, and problem areas. The purpose of identifying these factors is to develop the planning context and to link information systems plans to the strategic business plans. Table 2-2 shows some possible strategic planning factors for Pine Valley Furniture. These factors help information system managers to set priorities to address requests for new information systems and, hence, the development of databases. For example, the problem area of inaccurate sales forecasts might cause information system managers to place additional historical sales data, new market research data, or data concerning results from test trials of new products in organizational databases.

Identifying Corporate Planning Objects   The corporate planning objects define the business scope. The scope limits subsequent systems analysis and where information system changes can occur. Five key planning objects are as follows (see Table 2-3 for examples of these for Pine Valley Furniture):

- *Organizational units*   The various departments of the organization
- *Organizational locations*   The places where business operations occur

Table 2-1 Information Engineering Planning Phase

Step	Explanation
1.	Identify strategic planning factors a. Goals b. Critical success factors c. Problem areas
2.	Identify corporate planning objects a. Organizational units b. Locations c. Business functions d. Entity types
3.	Develop an enterprise model a. Functional decomposition b. Entity-relationship diagram c. Planning matrixes

Table 2-2 Example Results of Information Engineering Planning Phase (Pine Valley Furniture Company)

Planning Factor	Examples
Goals	Maintain 10% per year growth rate Maintain 15% before-tax return on investment Avoid employee layoffs Be a responsible corporate citizen
Critical success factors	High-quality products On-time deliveries of finished products High productivity of employees
Problem areas	Inaccurate sales forecasts Increasing competition Stockouts of finished products

Table 2-3 Example Corporate Planning Objects (for Pine Valley Furniture Company)

Planning Object	Examples

Organizational units	Sales Department
	Orders Department
	Accounting Department
	Manufacturing
	   Fabrication Department
	   Assembly Department
	   Finishing Department
	Purchasing Department

Organizational locations	Corporate Headquarters Durango Plant Western Regional Sales Office Lumber Mill

Business functions	Business planning
	Product development
	Materials management
	Marketing and sales
	   Order fulfillment
	   Order shipment
	   Sales summarization
	Production operations
	Finance and accounting

Entity types	CUSTOMER PRODUCT RAW MATERIAL ORDER WORK CENTER INVOICE EQUIPMENT EMPLOYEE

Information systems	Transaction processing systems
	   Order tracking
	   Order processing
	   Plant scheduling
	   Payroll
	Management information systems
	   Sales management
	   Inventory control
	   Production scheduling

Business function: A related group of business processes that support some aspect of the mission of an enterprise.

- *Business functions* Related groups of business processes that support the mission of the organization. Note that business functions are different from organizational units; in fact, a function may be assigned to more than one organizational unit (for example, product development, a function, may be the joint responsibility of the Sales and Manufacturing departments).

- *Entity types* Major categories of data about the people, places, and things managed by the organization

- *Information systems* The application software and supporting procedures for handling sets of data

Developing an Enterprise Model A comprehensive enterprise model consists of a functional breakdown (or decomposition) model of each business function, an enterprise data model, and various planning matrixes. **Functional decomposition** is the process of breaking down the functions of an organization into progressively greater levels of detail. Functional decomposition is a classical process employed in systems analysis in order to simplify problems, isolate attention, and identify components. An example of decomposition of an order fulfillment function for Pine Valley

Functional decomposition: An iterative process of breaking down the description of a system into finer and finer detail in which one function is described in greater detail by a set of other, supporting functions.

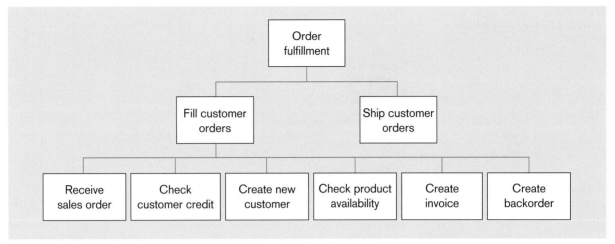

Figure 2-2

Example process decomposition of an order fulfillment function (Pine Valley Furniture Company)

Furniture appears in Figure 2-2. Often many databases are necessary to handle the full set of business functions and supporting functions (for example, all of the functions and subfunctions listed in Table 2-3), whereas a particular database may support only a subset of the supporting functions (for example, those in Figure 2-2). It is helpful, however, to have a total, high-level enterprise view in order to minimize redundancy of data and make the data purposeful.

An enterprise data model is described using a particular notation. Figure 2-1 uses a general notation that could be employed, although a popular format is entity-relationship diagramming, which is explained in Chapters 3 and 4. Besides such a graphical depiction of the entity types, a thorough enterprise data model would also include descriptions of each entity type and a compendium of various statements about how the business operates, called *business rules,* which govern the validity of data. Business rules are also defined and illustrated in Chapters 3 and 4.

An enterprise data model shows not only the entity types but also the relationships between data entities. Other relationships, between various planning objects, are also depicted during enterprise modeling. A common format for showing the interrelationships between planning objects is matrixes. The planning matrixes serve an important function because they provide an explicit approach for describing business requirements without requiring that the database be explicitly modeled. Often elicited from the business rules, planning matrixes aid in setting development priorities, sequencing of development activities, and scheduling of those activities from the top-down view sought by taking an enterprise-wide approach. A wide variety of planning matrixes can be used; several common ones are:

- *Location-to-function* Indicates which business functions are being performed at which business locations

- *Unit-to-function* Identifies which business functions are performed by or are the responsibility of which business units

- *Information system-to-data entity* Explains how each information system interacts with each data entity (e.g., whether each system creates, retrieves, updates, or deletes data in each entity)

- *Supporting function-to-data entity* Identifies which data are captured, used, updated, or deleted within each function

- *Information system-to-objective* Shows which information systems support each business objective

Data Entity Types / Business Functions	Customer	Product	Raw Material	Order	Work Center	Work Order	Invoice	Equipment	Employee
Business Planning	X	X						X	X
Product Development		X	X		X			X	
Materials Management		X	X	X	X	X		X	
Order Fulfillment	X	X	X	X	X	X	X	X	X
Order Shipment	X	X		X	X		X		X
Sales Summarization	X	X		X			X		X
Production Operations		X	X	X	X	X		X	X
Finance and Accounting	X	X	X	X	X		X	X	X

X = data entity (column) is used within business function (row)

Figure 2-3 illustrates a possible function-to-data entity matrix. Such a matrix could be used for various purposes, including the following three:

1. *Identify orphans*   Indicate which data entities are not used by any function, or which functions do not use any entities

2. *Spot missing entities*   Employees involved with each function who examine the matrix can identify any entities that may have been missed

3. *Prioritize development*   If a given function has a high priority for systems development (maybe because it is related to important organizational objectives), then the entities used by that area also have a high priority in database development

See Hoffer, George, and Valacich (2002) for a more thorough description of how to use planning matrixes for information engineering and systems planning.

DATABASE DEVELOPMENT PROCESS

Information systems planning, based on information engineering, is one source of database development projects. Such projects develop new databases often to meet strategic organizational needs, such as improved customer support, better production and inventory management, or more accurate sales forecasting. Many database development projects arise, however, more in a *bottom-up* fashion. In this case, projects are requested by information system users, who need certain information to do their job, or from other information systems professionals, who see a need to improve data management in the organization. Even in the bottom-up case, enterprise data modeling still must be done in order to understand whether existing databases can provide the desired data, and if not, what new databases, data entities, and attributes need to be added to the current organizational data resource.

Whether identified from strategic or operational information needs, each database development project usually focuses on one database. Some database projects concentrate only on defining, designing, and implementing a database as a foundation for subsequent information systems development. In most cases, however, a database and the associated information processing functions are developed together as part of a comprehensive information systems development project.

Systems Development Life Cycle

A traditional process for conducting an information systems development project is called the **systems development life cycle (SDLC)**. The SDLC is a complete set of steps that a team of information systems professionals, including database designers and programmers, follow in an organization to specify, develop, maintain, and replace information systems. This process is often viewed as a cascade of steps, as depicted in Figure 2-4 (Hoffer, George, and Valacich, 2002). The metaphor of a cascade or waterfall is used since each step flows into the next; that is, the total specification of the information system is developed in pieces, and the output from one piece is used as input to subsequent pieces. As depicted in the figure, however, the steps are not purely linear: Steps overlap in time (thus steps can be conducted in parallel), and it is possible to backtrack to previous steps when prior decisions need to be reconsidered (thus, the water can run back up the waterfall!).

Figure 2-4 is annotated with a brief explanation of the purpose and deliverables of each SDLC phase. Each phase of the SDLC includes activities related to database development, so database management issues are pervasive throughout the systems development process. We repeat these same seven SDLC steps in Figure 2-5, this time annotating the figure with an outline of the database development activities typically included in each phase. Note that there is not a one-to-one correspondence between SDLC phases and database development steps: *conceptual data modeling* occurs in two SDLC phases. We will briefly illustrate each of these database development steps later in this chapter for Pine Valley Furniture Company.

Systems development life cycle (SDLC): The traditional methodology used to develop, maintain, and replace information systems.

Figure 2-4
Systems development life cycle (SDLC)

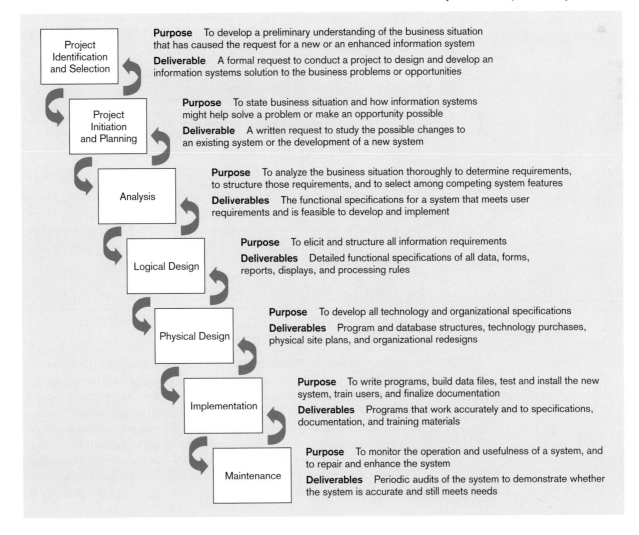

Project Identification and Selection

Purpose To develop a preliminary understanding of the business situation that has caused the request for a new or an enhanced information system

Deliverable A formal request to conduct a project to design and develop an information systems solution to the business problems or opportunities

Project Initiation and Planning

Purpose To state business situation and how information systems might help solve a problem or make an opportunity possible

Deliverable A written request to study the possible changes to an existing system or the development of a new system

Analysis

Purpose To analyze the business situation thoroughly to determine requirements, to structure those requirements, and to select among competing system features

Deliverables The functional specifications for a system that meets user requirements and is feasible to develop and implement

Logical Design

Purpose To elicit and structure all information requirements

Deliverables Detailed functional specifications of all data, forms, reports, displays, and processing rules

Physical Design

Purpose To develop all technology and organizational specifications

Deliverables Program and database structures, technology purchases, physical site plans, and organizational redesigns

Implementation

Purpose To write programs, build data files, test and install the new system, train users, and finalize documentation

Deliverables Programs that work accurately and to specifications, documentation, and training materials

Maintenance

Purpose To monitor the operation and usefulness of a system, and to repair and enhance the system

Deliverables Periodic audits of the system to demonstrate whether the system is accurate and still meets needs

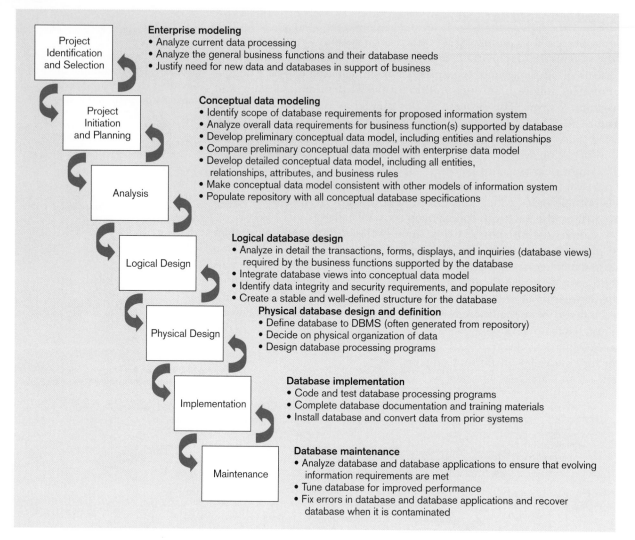

Figure 2-5
Database development activities during the systems development life cycle (SDLC)

Enterprise Modeling The database development process begins with enterprise modeling (part of Project Identification and Selection in the SDLC) to set the range and general contents of organizational databases. Recall that enterprise modeling occurs during information systems planning and other activities, where the need for information system changes and enhancements is identified and the scope of all organizational data is outlined. In this step, review current databases and information systems, analyze the nature of the business area that is the subject of the development project, and describe, in very general terms, the data needed for each information system under consideration for development. Only selected projects move into the next phase based on the projected value of each project to the organization.

Conceptual Data Modeling For an information system project that is initiated, in conceptual data modeling analyze the overall data requirements of the proposed information system. This is done in two stages. First, during the Project Initiation and Planning phase, develop a diagram similar to Figure 2-1 as well as other documentation to outline the scope of data involved in this particular development project without consideration of what databases already exist. Only high-level categories of data (entities) and major relationships are included at this point. Then during the Analysis phase of the SDLC, produce a detailed data model, which identifies all the organizational data that must be managed for this information system. Define every data attribute, list all categories of data, represent every business relationship between data entities, and specify every rule that dictates the integrity of data. It is also during the analysis phase that the conceptual data model (also called a *conceptual schema* later in this chapter) is checked for consistency with other types of models developed to explain other dimensions of the target information system, such as processing steps, rules for handling data, and the timing of events. However, even this detailed conceptual data model is preliminary, since subsequent SDLC activities may find missing elements or errors when designing specific transactions, reports, displays, and inquiries. Thus it is often said that conceptual data modeling is done in a top-down fashion, driven from a general understanding of the business area, not from specific information processing activities.

Logical Database Design Logical database design approaches database development from two perspectives. First, transform the conceptual data model into a standard notation called relations, based on relational database theory. You will learn how to conduct this important process in Chapter 5. Then, as each computer program in the information system is designed, including the program's input and output formats, perform a detailed review of the transactions, reports, displays, and inquiries supported by the database. During this so-called bottom-up analysis, verify exactly what data are to be maintained in the database and the nature of those data as needed for each transaction, report, and so forth.

The analysis of each individual report, transaction, and so on considers a particular, limited, but thorough, view of the database. It may be possible to change, as needed, the conceptual data model as each report, transaction, and so on is analyzed. Especially on larger projects, different teams of analysts and systems developers may work independently on different programs or sets of programs. The details of all of their work may not be revealed until well into the logical design phase. In this case, one must combine, or integrate, the original conceptual data model along with these individual *user views* into a comprehensive design during logical database design. It is also possible that additional information processing requirements will be identified during logical information systems design, in which case these new requirements must be integrated into the previously identified logical database design.

The final step in logical database design is to transform the combined and reconciled data specifications into basic, or atomic, elements following well-established rules for well-structured data specifications. For most databases today, these rules come from relational database theory and a process called *normalization*, which we will describe in detail in Chapter 5. The result is a complete picture of the database without any reference to a particular database management system for managing these data. With a final logical database design in place, begin to specify the logic of the particular computer programs and queries needed to maintain and report the database contents.

Physical Database Design and Definition In physical database design and definition, one decides on the organization of the database in computer storage (usually disk) and defines the physical structure of the database management system. Outline the programs to process transactions and to generate anticipated management information and decision-support reports. The goal is to design a database that will efficiently and securely handle all data processing against it. Thus, physical database design is done in close coordination with the design of all other aspects of the physical information system: programs, computer hardware, operating systems, and data communications networks.

Database Implementation In database implementation, one writes, tests, and installs the programs that process the database. One might program in standard programming languages (like COBOL, C, or Visual Basic), in special database processing languages (like SQL), or use special-purpose nonprocedural languages to produce stylized reports and displays, possibly including graphs. Also during implementation, finalize all database documentation, train users, and put procedures into place for the ongoing support of information system (and database) users. The last step is to load data from existing information sources (files and databases from legacy applications plus new data now needed). Loading is often done by first unloading data from existing files and databases into a neutral format (such as binary or text files) and then loading these data into the new database. Finally, put the database and its associated applications into production for data maintenance and retrieval by the actual users. During production, periodically back up the database and recover the database in case of contamination or destruction.

Database Maintenance The database evolves during database maintenance. In this step, one adds, deletes, or changes characteristics of the structure of a database in order to meet changing business conditions, to correct errors in database design, or to improve the processing speed of database applications. One might also need to rebuild a database if it becomes contaminated or destroyed due to a program or computer system malfunction. This is typically the longest step of database development, since it lasts throughout the life of the database and its associated applications. View each time the database evolves as an abbreviated database development process, in which conceptual data modeling, logical and physical database design, and database implementation occur to deal with proposed changes.

Alternative IS Development Approaches

The systems development life cycle or slight variations on it are often used to guide the development of information systems and databases. The SDLC is a methodical, highly structured approach, which includes many checks and balances to insure that each step produces accurate results and the new or replacement information system is consistent with existing systems with which it must communicate or for which there needs to be consistent data definitions. Consequently, the SDLC is often criticized for the length of time needed until a working system is produced, which occurs only at the end of the process. Increasingly, organizations use more rapid application development (RAD) methods, which follow an iterative process of rapidly repeating analysis, design, and implementation steps until you converge on the system the user wants. These RAD methods work best when most of the database needed already exists, and hence for systems that primarily retrieve data, rather than for those that populate and revise databases.

One of the most popular RAD methods is **prototyping**. Prototyping is an iterative process of systems development in which requirements are converted to a working system that is continually revised through close work between analysts and users. Figure 2-6 shows the prototyping process. We have included on this figure annotations to indicate roughly which database development activities occur in each prototyping phase. Typically one does only a very cursory attempt at conceptual data modeling when the information system problem is identified. During the development of the initial prototype, one simultaneously designs the displays and reports the user wants while understanding any new database requirements and defining a database to be used by the prototype. This is typically a new database, which is a copy of portions of existing databases, possibly with new content. If new contents are required, they will usually come from external data sources, such as market research data, general economic indicators, or industry standards.

Repeat database implementation and maintenance activities as new versions of the prototype are produced. Often security and integrity controls are minimal since the emphasis is on getting working prototype versions ready as quickly as possible. Also, documentation tends to be delayed until the end of the project, and user training occurs from hands-on use. Finally, once an accepted prototype is created, the

Prototyping: An iterative process of systems development in which requirements are converted to a working system that is continually revised through close work between analysts and users.

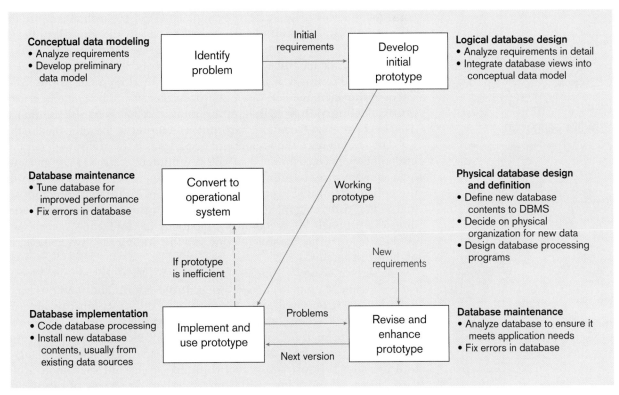

Figure 2-6
The prototyping methodology and database development process

developer and the user decide if the final prototype, and its database, can be put into production as is. If the system, including the database, is too inefficient, then the system and database will be reprogrammed and reorganized to meet performance expectations.

With the increasing popularity of visual programming tools (such as Visual Basic, Java, Visual C++, and fourth-generation languages) in which it is easy to modify the interface between user and system, prototyping is becoming the systems development methodology of choice. With prototyping it is relatively easy to change the contents and layout of user reports and displays. During this process, new database requirements may be identified, and hence existing databases used by the evolving application will need to change. It is even possible to use prototyping for a system that requires a new database. In this case, sample data are acquired to build and rebuild the database prototype as the system requirements evolve through the iterative development process.

The Role of CASE and a Repository

At several points in the preceding section we mentioned the role of CASE tools in information systems development. **Computer-aided software engineering (CASE)** tools are software that provides automated support for some portion of the systems development process. For our purposes in the study of database development, there are three relevant features of CASE tools. First is the ability to help us draw data models using entity-relationship and other notations (see Figure 2-1 for an example of a form of E-R notation). A CASE tool's drawing capabilities are "database intelligent" in that each symbol represents specific data modeling constructs, and these symbols can be used only in ways consistent with the properties of the associated constructs. Database drawing tools are used in enterprise modeling, conceptual data modeling, logical database design, and physical data modeling. CASE tools can help us insure

Computer-aided software engineering (CASE): Software tools that provide automated support for some portion of the systems development process.

consistency across diagrams. For example, a CASE tool will make sure that each use of the PRODUCT entity on any diagram has exactly the same meaning. CASE drawing tools enforce unique names for each data object and may be able to automatically redraw a data model when characteristics of data objects change.

Often, different drawing tools and associated methods are used for different stages of the database development process. For example, one tool is used for enterprise modeling to draw high-level diagrams and matrixes. Still another tool may be used in conceptual data modeling, and yet another in logical database design.

The second important feature of CASE tools is the ability to generate code. Most often, this code contains the database definition commands to be given to a database management system. During database implementation, the CASE tool will refer to all the conceptual, logical, and physical data specifications and compose SQL commands to create relational tables, define each attribute of each table, and define key indexes. Although less frequently a capability of CASE tools, some CASE tools can generate C or other language code for the rudiments of database retrieval and updating programs.

As with drawing tools, many organizations use separate tools ("best of breed") for code generation as well as drawing. If these tools and methods are to be effective, they must be integrated. In particular, the tools must be able to share the metadata that are developed during each stage of the process. Unfortunately, the ability to share such information among CASE tools has not been common, especially among tools from different vendors. A so-called *integrated-CASE* (or *I-CASE*) tool provides support across the whole life cycle, but such tools are rarely used since they tend to be strong in supporting certain phases and weak in supporting other phases of the systems development process. Tools that support the SDLC from the Project Identification and Selection phase through Physical Design are called *upper CASE tools*; tools that support the Implementation and Maintenance phases are called *lower CASE tools*.

Tool integration depends on a formal, detailed architecture for building and maintaining information systems. This architecture includes formal definitions of interfaces between tools, data model standards among tools, and common controls across the life cycle. This leads to the third feature of CASE tools important to our discussion of the database development process: an information repository (or *repository* for short). A **repository** is a knowledge base of information about the facts that an enterprise must be able to access and the processes it must perform to be successful (Moriarty, 1991). Thus, for example, all of the information that is collected during the six stages of database development is maintained in a repository. In a sense, a repository is a database itself, which contains information needed to generate all the diagrams, form and report definitions, and other system documentation. A repository helps systems and database analysts achieve a seamless integration of data from several CASE tools.

Repository: A knowledge base of information about the facts that an enterprise must be able to access and the processes it must perform to be successful.

MANAGING THE PEOPLE INVOLVED IN DATABASE DEVELOPMENT

Project: A planned undertaking of related activities to reach an objective that has a beginning and an end.

As implied in Figure 2-5, a database is developed as part of a project. A **project** is a planned undertaking of related activities to reach an objective that has a beginning and an end. A project begins with the first steps of the Project Initiation and Planning phase and ends with the last steps of the Implementation phase. A senior systems or database analyst will be assigned to be project leader. This person is responsible for creating detailed project plans as well as staffing and supervising the project team. A good project leader will possess skills in leadership, management, customer relations and communications, technical problem solving, conflict management, team building, and risk and change management.

A project is initiated and planned in the Project Initiation and Planning phase, executed during Analysis, Logical Design, Physical Design, and Implementation phases, and closed down at the end of implementation. During initiation the project team is formed. A systems or database development team can include one or more of each the following:

- *Systems analysts*   Analyze the business situation and identify the need for information and information services to meet the problems or opportunities of the business

- *Database analysts*   Concentrate on determining the requirements and design for the database component of the information system

- *Users*   Provide assessment of their information needs and monitor that the developed system meets their needs

- *Programmers*   Design and write computer programs that have embedded in them commands to maintain and access data in the database

- *Database and data administrators*   Have responsibility for existing and future databases and ensure consistency and integrity across databases, and as experts on database technology, provide consulting and training to other project team members

- *Other technical experts*   For example, networking, operating systems, testing, and documentation

It is the responsibility of the project leader to select and manage all of these people as an effective team. See Hoffer, George, and Valacich (2002) for details on how to manage a systems development project team.

Project closedown occurs when the project is naturally or unnaturally terminated. An unnatural termination occurs when the system no longer appears to have business value, when the performance of the system or the development team is unacceptable, or the project runs out of time, funding, or support. To determine whether a project is progressing on time and within budget, the project leader develops detailed schedules of project activities. Often these schedules are depicted in graphical form, such as shown in the sample charts in Figure 2-7. These charts show when project activities begin and end, who is responsible for doing each activity, how much effort is required to do each activity, and the precedence relationships between activities (that is, which activities depend on the output of other activities).

A characteristic of successful systems development projects is frequent review points, when project team members report the results of the project to date. Often these results are reported to people outside the project team, including other users, those who are providing the funding for the project, and senior information systems and possibly general management. The reasons for these review points are to

- Validate that the project is progressing in a satisfactory way.

- Step back from the details of daily activities and verify that all the parts of the project are coming together.

- Gain renewed commitment from all parties to the project (especially important for projects which last more than a few months).

Central to the third reason is the concept of incremental commitment. **Incremental commitment** is a strategy in systems development projects in which the project is reviewed after each phase and continuation of the project is rejustified in each of these reviews. Incremental commitment allows those interested in the project to commit only to the next phase (with limited time and cost) and then to reassess whether further commitment of resources (people and money) is warranted after some results are shown. Thus, significant resources are not wasted when the original concept for the system does not prove valuable. Incremental commitment also allows a project to be easily redirected or killed.

Incremental commitment: A strategy in systems development projects in which the project is reviewed after each phase and continuation of the project is rejustified in each of these reviews.

Figure 2-7
Graphical diagrams for depicting
project plans
(a) Gantt chart

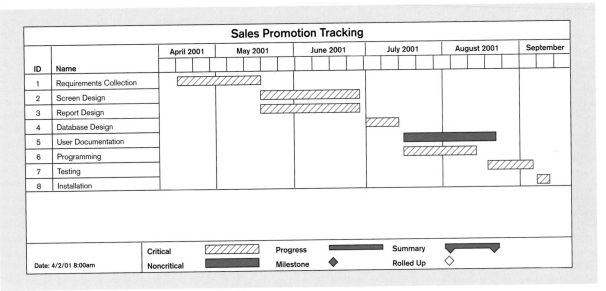

(b) PERT chart

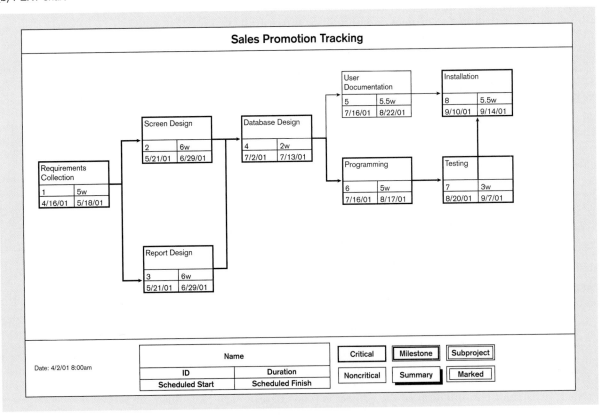

THREE-SCHEMA ARCHITECTURE FOR DATABASE DEVELOPMENT

The explanation earlier in this chapter of the database development process referred to several different, but related, views or models of databases developed on a systems development project:

- Conceptual schema (during the Analysis phase),
- External schema, or user view (during the Analysis and Logical Design phases), and
- Physical or internal schema (during the Physical Design phase)

Figure 2-8 depicts the relationship between these three views of a database. It is important to keep in mind that these are all views or models of the same organizational database; that is, each organizational database has one physical and one conceptual schema and one or more user views. Thus, the three-schema architecture defines one database, with multiple ways to look at this one set of data.

A **conceptual schema** is a detailed specification of the overall structure of organizational data that is independent of any database management technology. A conceptual schema defines the whole database without reference to how data are stored in a computer's secondary memory. Usually a conceptual schema is depicted in graphical format using entity-relationship (E-R) or object modeling notations; we have called this type of conceptual schema a *data model*. In addition, specifications for the conceptual schema are stored as metadata in a repository or data dictionary.

A *user view* was defined in Chapter 1 as a logical description of some portion of the database that is required by a user to perform some task. Thus, a user view (or external schema) is also independent of database technology but typically contains a subset of the associated conceptual schema, relevant to a particular user or group of users (for example, an inventory manager or accounts receivable department). A user view is also the version of the schema used in a particular program (for example, an order entry program), because a program is used by a particular user or group of

Conceptual schema: A detailed, technology independent specification of the overall structure of a database.

Figure 2-8
Three-schema database architecture

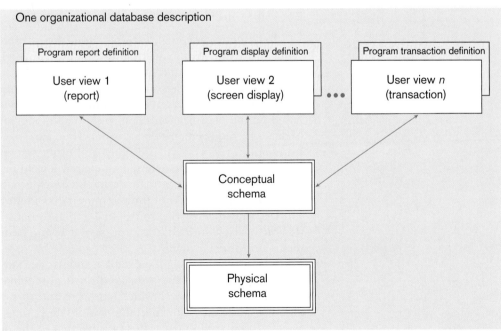

users. Thus, a user view is defined in both logical (technology-independent) terms as well as programming language terms (that is, consistent with the syntax of the program's language). Often the original depiction of a user view is a computer screen display, business transaction (such as a subscription renewal form), or a report since each of these often depicts all of the data needed by a program that processes that display, transaction, or report. A logical version of a user view can be represented as an E-R or object diagram or as relations. The process of translating an E-R diagram into relations and then merging relations (view integration) into one complete relational description of a database is described in Chapter 5.

Physical schema: Specifications for how data from a conceptual schema are stored in a computer's secondary memory.

A **physical schema** contains the specifications for how data from a conceptual schema are stored in a computer's secondary memory. Of importance to the database analyst and designer is the *definition* of the physical database (the physical schema), which provides all the specifications to the database technology to allocate and manage physical secondary memory space where data are to be stored and accessed.

Database development and database technologies are based on encouraging the distinction among these three views of databases. A role on a database development project may deal exclusively with tasks associated with only one of these three views. For example, early in a career, one may design external schemas used in one or more programs. Later, with experience, one will design physical schemas or conceptual schemas. Database design issues vary across the levels. For this reason, this text is organized to focus attention on the issues in the design of each of these three representations of databases:

- *Conceptual* Chapters 3 and 4 discuss entity-relationship modeling. Chapter 14 discusses object-oriented modeling. These are two different graphical notations for depicting conceptual schemas or data models.

- *External* Chapter 5 discusses relational databases, normalization, translating E-R diagrams into relations, and merging sets of relations; all of these topics assist in the development and analysis of external schemas.

- *Physical* Chapter 6 discusses the decisions you have to make in designing a physical database, and Chapters 7 and 8 review how to specify these decisions in one language used to define physical schemas and databases—SQL. Chapter 15 discusses design of object-oriented databases and Appendix D discusses hybrid, object-relational databases.

Together, conceptual, external, and physical schemas form the three-schema architecture for databases. Note that even though Figure 2-8 shows external schemas at the top, external schemas are not necessarily developed before the conceptual schema. In fact, you will typically develop conceptual and external schemas iteratively (see Figure 2-9). Often, a first cut at the conceptual schema is developed based on the organization's enterprise data model and the general understanding of database requirements on a project. Then external schemas (user views) for each transaction, report, screen display, and other system use are developed. In most cases, an analysis of the external schemas will yield new attributes and possibly entities and relationships not shown in the conceptual schema. So, the conceptual schema is augmented with these requirements identified from so-called bottom-up sources, thus making the conceptual and external schemas consistent. When new user views are identified, this process of evolving both the conceptual and external schemas repeats.

To begin developing the database and its associated application programs, write the specifications for the associated physical schema. Besides the conceptual and external schemas, also consider hardware and software characteristics and users' database performance expectations while designing the physical database with its associated physical schema. It is possible that in the design of the physical database

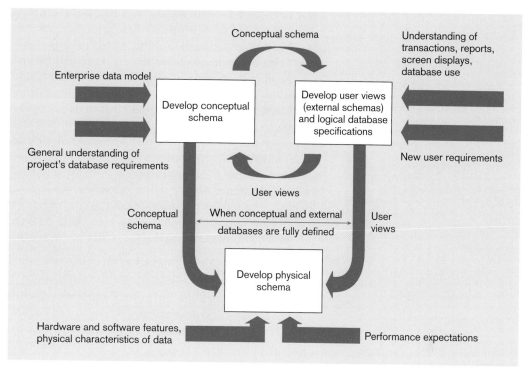

Figure 2-9
Process of developing three-schema architecture for a database project

inconsistencies or other issues with the conceptual schema or user views will be encountered, so it is possible to cycle back to these design steps (not shown on Figure 2-9). When additional user requirements are identified later, the process begins again. Usually new requirements are batched and considered together in a new cycle of external and conceptual schema design, so that the database is not constantly changing. Periodic revisions of the database occur during the Maintenance phase of systems development.

THREE-TIERED DATABASE LOCATION ARCHITECTURE

Apparently, all good (database) things come in threes!

When designing a database, you have choices about where to store the data. These choices are made during physical database design. We will consider a wide range of physical database design decisions in Chapter 6, but in this section we want to outline a major database architectural choice that can affect the database development process.

In Chapter 1 you learned that there are personal, workgroup, department, enterprise, and Internet databases. Personal databases are often designed and developed by end users themselves, with only training and consulting help from database professionals, if the database contains data of interest only to its end user. Sometimes a personal database is an extract from a workgroup or enterprise database, in which case database professionals often write the extracting routines to create the local database. Workgroup and department databases are often developed in combination by end users, systems professionals working in business units, and central database professionals. A combination of people is necessary since a wide variety of issues must be balanced in the design of shared databases: processing speed, ease of use, differences in data definitions, and the like. Enterprise and Internet databases, because of their organization-wide impact and extensive size, tend to be developed by highly trained database professionals, often in a centralized database development group.

This view of database location, which implies that a database is located strictly at one of these four levels, is somewhat simplified for many modern organizations. In fact, the data for a given information system may reside in multiple locations or tiers of computers, in order to balance various organizational and technical factors. Also, different types of processing of data from a database may occur at different locations, in order to take advantage of the processing speed, ease of use, or ease of programming on different computer platforms. Extensive use of browser-based interfaces with company databases has caused a growing market for application servers, which handle the business software and transactions between the Web browser and the back-end database. Most application server vendors, including Sun, IBM, and Oracle, have adopted Java 2 Enterprise Edition (J2EE) as their standard for application servers. Four tiers are possible—data on a client server, on an application server, on a Web server, and on a database server; three tiers are more commonly considered:

1. *Client tier* A desktop or laptop computer, which concentrates on managing the user-system interface and localized data—also called the presentation tier; Web scripting tasks may be executed on this tier

2. *Application/Web server tier* Processes HTTP protocol, scripting tasks, performs calculations, and provides access to data—also called the process services tier

3. *Enterprise server (minicomputer or mainframe) tier* Performs sophisticated calculations and manages the merging of data from multiple sources across the organization—also called the data services tier

This three-tiered architecture is depicted in Figure 2-10. A limited view of the client/server architecture considers only the client tier and a general server tier.

Figure 2-10
Three-tiered client/server database architecture

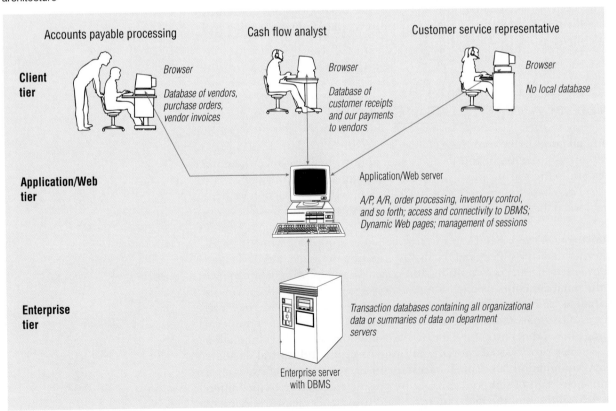

The tiered architecture for databases and information systems is related to the concept of a client/server architecture for distributed computing in an organization. In a **client/server architecture**, which is based on a local area network, database software on a server (called a *database server* or *database engine*) performs database commands sent to it from client workstations, and application programs on each client concentrate on user interface functions. In practice, the total conceptual database (as well as the application processing routines that access this database) can be distributed across the local PC workstation, an intermediate server (workgroup or department), and a centralized server (department or enterprise) as one distributed database or as separate but related physical databases. Hoffer, George, and Valacich (2002) and Thompson (1997) outline why this type of architecture is increasingly popular. Briefly, the reasons for the use of a client/server architecture are:

Client/server architecture: A local area network–based environment in which database software on a server (called a database server or database engine) performs database commands sent to it from client workstations and application programs on each client concentrate on user interface functions.

- It allows for simultaneous processing on multiple processors for the same application, thus improving application response time and data processing speed.

- It is possible to take advantage of the best data processing features of each computer platform (e.g., the advanced user interface capabilities of PCs versus the computational speed of minicomputers and mainframes).

- You can mix client technologies (personal computers with Intel or Motorola processors, network computers, information kiosks, etc.) and, yet, share common data; in addition, you can change technologies at any tier with limited impact on the system modules on other tiers.

- Processing can be performed close to the source of processed data, thereby improving response times and reducing network traffic.

- It allows for and encourages the acceptance of open system standards.

The most significant implication for database development from the use of a multiple-tiered client/server architecture is the ease of separating the development of the database and the modules that maintain the database from the information system modules that present the contents of the database to end users. Presentation routines can use languages like PowerBuilder, Java, and Visual Basic to provide easy-to-use, graphic user interfaces. Through middleware (see Chapter 9), the presentation routines can interact through the tiers to access the routines that access the required data and analyze these data to form the needed information. As a database developer and programmer, you might work at any of these tiers, developing the requisite software.

We will consider the client/server architecture in more detail in Chapter 9, which outlines how to decide where to distribute data across the multiple tiers of the computer network.

DEVELOPING A DATABASE APPLICATION FOR PINE VALLEY FURNITURE

Pine Valley Furniture Company was introduced in Chapter 1. The company has been using relational database management technology since 1990, with a variety of databases on personal computers, departmental minicomputers, and a corporate server (see Figure 1-6 for a general schematic of the computer network within Pine Valley Furniture).

Helen Jarvis, product manager for home office furniture at Pine Valley Furniture, knows that competition has become fierce in this growing product line. Thus, it is increasingly important to Pine Valley Furniture that Helen be able to more thoroughly analyze sales of her products. Often these analyses are ad hoc, driven by rapidly changing and unanticipated business conditions, comments from furniture store managers, trade industry gossip, or experience. Helen has requested that she be given direct access to sales data with an easy-to-use interface so that she can search for answers to the various marketing questions she will generate.

Chris Martin is a systems analyst in Pine Valley Furniture's information systems development area. Chris has worked at Pine Valley Furniture for five years, and has experience with information systems from several business areas within Pine Valley. From the various systems development projects Chris has worked on, his information systems education at Western Florida University, and the extensive training Pine Valley has given Chris, he has become one of Pine Valley's best systems developers. Chris is skilled in data modeling and is familiar with several relational database management systems used within the firm. Because of his experience, expertise, and availability, the head of information systems has assigned Chris to work with Helen on her request for a marketing support system.

Since Pine Valley Furniture has been careful in the development of their systems, especially since adopting the database approach, the company already has a fairly complete information systems architecture, including databases for all operational business functions. Thus, it is likely that Chris will be able to extract the data Helen needs from existing databases. Pine Valley's information system architecture calls for such systems as Helen is requesting to be built on stand-alone databases, so the unstructured and unpredictable use of data will not interfere with the access to the operational databases needed to support efficient transaction processing systems.

Further, since Helen's needs are for data analysis, not creation and maintenance, and are personal, not institutional, Chris decides to follow a combination of prototyping and life cycle approaches to developing the system Helen has requested. By a combination, Chris means that he will follow all the life cycle steps, but he will conduct very quickly and in a cursory way those steps not integral to prototyping. Thus, he will very quickly address project initiation and planning (including placing this project within the company's information system architecture), then use an iterative cycle of analysis, design, and implementation to work closely with Helen to develop a working prototype of the system she needs. Because the system will be personal and likely will require a database with limited scope, Chris hopes the prototype will end up being the actual system Helen will use. Chris has chosen to develop the system using Microsoft Access, Pine Valley's preferred technology for personal databases. However, in most cases, the SQL necessary to define the database structure will also be illustrated, because these commands can be used to define a database using any relational database management system.

Matching User Needs to the Information Systems Architecture

Chris begins the project to develop the database and associated marketing support system for the home office furniture area by interviewing Helen. Chris asks Helen about her business area, taking notes about business area objectives, business functions, data entity types, and other business objects with which she deals. At this point, Chris listens more than talks, so that he can concentrate on understanding Helen's business area; he interjects questions and makes sure that Helen does not try to jump ahead to talk about what she thinks she needs as computer screens and reports from the information system. Chris asks very general questions, using, as much as possible, business and marketing terminology. For example, Chris asks Helen what issues she faces managing the home office products; what people, places, and things are of interest to her in her job; how far back in time does she need data to do her analyses; and what events occur in the business that are of interest to her.

Table 2-4 summarizes what Chris learns from this initial interview. This table lists the various business objects Helen mentioned and indicates which of these are already in Pine Valley Furniture's information systems architecture. There are a few

Table 2-4 Business Objects for Product Line Marketing Support System

Planning Object	Objects for Home Office Product Line Tracking	Does Object Exist in Pine Valley Information Systems Architecture?
Objectives	Increase annual sales ($) of home office products by at least 16%	No
	Increase annual profit margin of home office product line by at least 10%	No
	Increase same customer repeat sales ($) of home office products by at least 5%	No
	Exceed sales goals for each product finish category of home office products	No
	Have home office products perform above average for all Pine Valley products	No
	Reduce time to fill office product orders by 5%	No
	Reduce time to receive final payment on office product invoices by 5%	No
Organizational units	Marketing Department	Yes
	Office Furniture Product Line Management	No
	Accounting Department	Yes
	Orders Department	Yes
Organizational locations	Regional Sales Offices	Yes
	Corporate Headquarters	Yes
Business functions	Payment receipt	Yes
	Product development	—
	Demographics analysis	No
	Target market analysis	Yes
	Marketing and sales	—
	Order fulfillment	Yes
	Sales summarization	Yes
	Order taking	Yes
Entity types	CUSTOMER	Yes
	PRODUCT	Yes
	PRODUCT LINE	Yes
	ORDER	Yes
	INVOICE	Yes
	PAYMENT	Yes
Information systems	Order processing	Yes
	Sales management	Yes

entries in the figure that are not in the information systems architecture. However, all of the major categories of data Helen mentioned are covered in the architecture and are managed in existing information systems. Thus, Chris is confident that most, if not all, of the data Helen might want already exist within company databases.

Chris does two quick analyses before talking with Helen again. First, he identifies all of the databases that contain data associated with the data entities Helen mentioned. From these databases, Chris makes a list of all of the data attributes from these data entities that he thinks might be of interest to Helen in her analyses of the home office furniture market. Chris's previous involvement in projects that developed Pine Valley's standard sales tracking and forecasting system and cost accounting system helps him extrapolate from the information in Table 2-4 to speculate about the kinds of data Helen might want. For example, the objective to exceed sales goals for each product finish category of office furniture suggests that Helen wants product annual sales goals in her system; also, the objective of achieving at least a 16 percent annual sales growth means that the prior year's orders for each product need to be included. He also concludes that Helen's database must include all products, not just those in the office furniture line, because she wants to compare her line to others. He is able to eliminate, however, many data attributes kept on each data entity. For example, Helen does not appear to need various customer data such as address, phone number, contact person, store size, and salesperson. He does, though, include a few attributes, customer type and zip code, which are not obvious from Table 2-4. He includes these because they were important attributes in the sales forecasting system.

Second, from this list, Chris draws a graphic data model that represents the data entities with the associated data attributes as well as the major relationships between these data entities. Chris's hope is that he can reduce the time for the analysis phase of the systems development process (and hence the time to do conceptual data modeling) by presenting this data model to Helen. A graphic of the data model for the preliminary database that Chris produces appears in Figure 2-11. Table 2-5 lists the data attributes about each entity Chris thinks Helen wants for the system. Chris lists in Table 2-5 only basic data attributes from existing databases, since Helen will likely want to combine these data in various ways for the analyses she will want to do.

Analyzing Database Requirements

Chris's initial meeting with Helen lasted only 45 minutes, but he feels that it resulted in a lot of ideas to share with Helen from the data he collected then and his subsequent work. He schedules a longer session, two hours, with Helen to go over these findings. Prior to the meeting, he sends Helen a rough project schedule outlining the steps he plans to follow and the estimated length of each step. Because prototyping is a user-driven process, in which the user says when to stop iterating on the new prototype versions, Chris can provide only rough estimates of the duration of certain project steps. For this reason, Chris's boss has decided that this project should be billed to Helen on a consulting time basis, not at a fixed cost.

Chris does more of the talking at this second meeting. He methodically walks through each data entity in Figure 2-11 explaining what it means, what each data attribute associated with it (in Table 2-5) means, and what business policies and procedures are represented by each line between entities. For example, Chris explains that each order is billed on one invoice and each invoice is a bill for exactly one order. An Order_Number uniquely identifies each order, and an order is placed by one customer. Other data about an order Chris thinks Helen might want to know include the date when the order was placed and the date when the order was filled

Figure 2-11
Preliminary data model for product line marketing support system

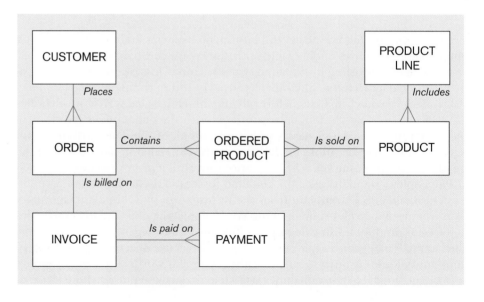

Table 2-5 Data Attributes for Entities in Preliminary Data Model

Entity Type	Attribute
CUSTOMER	Customer_Identifier
	Customer_Name
	Customer_Type
	Customer_ZIPCODE
PRODUCT	Product_Identifier
	Product_Finish
	Product_Price
	Product_Cost
	Product_Annual_Sales_Goal
	Product_Line_Name
PRODUCT LINE	Product_Line_Name
	Product_Line_Annual_Sales_Goal
ORDER	Order_Number
	Order_Placement_Date
	Order_Fulfillment_Date
	Customer_Identifier
ORDERED PRODUCT	Order_Number
	Product_Identifier
	Order_Quantity
INVOICE	Invoice_Number
	Order_Number
	Invoice_Date
PAYMENT	Invoice_Number
	Payment_Date
	Payment_Amount

(this would be the latest shipment date for the products on the order). Chris also explains that the Payment_Date attribute represents the most recent date when the customer made any payments, in full or partial, for the order.

During this discussion, Helen tells Chris about some additional data she wants (the number of years a customer has purchased products from Pine Valley Furniture and the number of shipments necessary to fill each order). Helen also notes that Chris has only one year of sales goals indicated for a product line. She reminds him that she wants these data for both the past and current years. As she reacts to the data model, Chris asks her how she intends to use the data she wants. Chris does not try to be thorough at this point, since he knows that Helen has not worked with an information set like the one being developed; thus, she may not yet be positive what data she wants or what she wants to do with the data. Rather, Chris's objective is to understand a few ways in which Helen intends to use the data so he can develop an initial prototype, including the database and several computer displays or reports. The final list of attributes that Helen agrees she needs appears in Table 2-6.

Designing the Database

Because Chris is following a prototyping methodology and because the first two sessions with Helen quickly identified the data Helen might need, Chris is able to begin immediately to build the prototype. First, Chris creates extracts from the corporate databases for the data entities and attributes Helen suggested. Chris is able to create all of these files using the SQL query language. Some of the data Helen wants are computed from raw, operational data (e.g., Customer_Years), but SQL makes it easy for Chris to specify these calculations. This extracting results in a single ASCII file for each data entity; each row in a file contains all of the data attributes associated with that data entity in the data model, and the rows are different instances of the entity. For example, each row of the ASCII file for the

Table 2-6 Data Attributes for Entities in Final Data Model

Entity Type	Attribute*
CUSTOMER	Customer_Identifier
	Customer_Name
	Customer_Type
	Customer_ZIPCODE
	Customer_Years
PRODUCT	Product_Identifier
	Product_Finish
	Product_Price
	Product_Cost
	Product_Prior_Year_Sales_Goal
	Product_Current_Year_Sales_Goal
	Product_Line_Name
PRODUCT LINE	Product_Line_Name
	Product_Line_Prior_Year_Sales_Goal
	Product_Line_Current_Year_Sales_Goal
ORDER	Order_Number
	Order_Placement_Date
	Order_Fulfillment_Date
	Order_Number_of_Shipments
	Customer_Identifier
ORDERED PRODUCT	Order_Number
	Product_Identifier
	Order_Quantity
INVOICE	Invoice_Number
	Order_Number
	Invoice_Date
PAYMENT	Invoice_Number
	Payment_Date
	Payment_Amount

*Changes from preliminary list of attributes appear in italics.

PRODUCT LINE data entity contains data for product line name and the annual sales goals for the past and current years.

Second, Chris translates the final data model from his discussion with Helen into a set of tables for which the columns are data attributes and the rows are different sets of values for those attributes. Tables are the basic building blocks of a relational database, which is the database style for Microsoft Access. The definitions of the PRODUCT LINE and PRODUCT tables Chris created, including associated data attributes, are shown in Figures 2-12 and 2-13 (we show both SQL and Access definitions in Figure 2-13). Chris did this translation so that each table had an attribute, called the table's *primary key*, which will be distinct for each row in the table. The other major properties of each table are that there is only one value for each attribute in each row, and if we know the value of the identifier, there can be only one value for each of the other attributes. For example, for any product line, there can be only one value for the current year's sales goal.

The design of the database includes specifying the format, or properties, for each attribute (Access calls attributes fields). These design decisions were easy in this case because most of the attributes were already specified in the corporate data dictionary. In Figure 2-13b the properties for one field, Product_ID, are

Figure 2-12
SQL definition of PRODUCT_LINE table

```
CREATE TABLE PRODUCT_LINE
        (PRODUCT_LINE_NAME          VARCHAR (40)    NOT NULL PRIMARY KEY,
        PL_PRIOR_YEAR_GOAL          DECIMAL,
        PL_CURRENT_YEAR_GOAL        DECIMAL);
```

```
CREATE TABLE PRODUCT
        (PRODUCT_ID                      INTEGER NOT NULL PRIMARY KEY,
        PRODUCT_FINISH                   VARCHAR (20),
        PRODUCT_PRICE                    DECIMAL,
        PRODUCT_COST                     DECIMAL,
        PR_PRIOR_YEAR_GOAL               DECIMAL,
        PR_CURRENT_YEAR_GOAL             DECIMAL,
        PRODUCT_LINE_NAME                VARCHAR (40),
FOREIGN KEY (PRODUCT_LINE_NAME) REFERENCES
    PRODUCT_LINE (PRODUCT_LINE_NAME));
```

Figure 2-13
Definition of PRODUCT table using SQL or ACCESS
(a) SQL definition of PRODUCT table

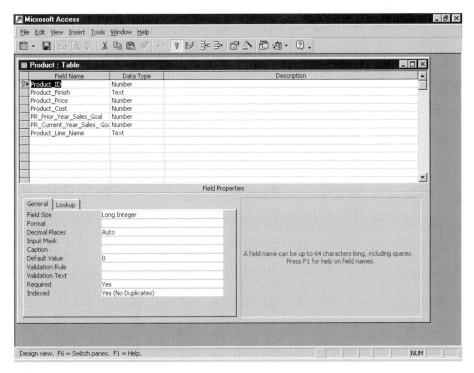

(b) ACCESS definition of PRODUCT table

shown, indicated by the arrow to the left of the field name. A few attributes, such as Order_Number_of_Shipments on the ORDER table, were computed from raw data in Pine Valley databases, so Chris had to create the specifications for such attributes.

The other major decision Chris has to make about database design is how to physically organize the database to respond the fastest to the queries Helen will write. Since the database will be used for decision support, neither Chris nor Helen can anticipate all of the queries that will arise; thus, Chris must make the physical design choices from experience rather than precise knowledge of the way the database will be used. The key physical database design decision that Microsoft Access and SQL allows a database designer to make is on which attributes to create indexes (an index is like a card catalog in the library, through which rows with common characteristics can be quickly located). All primary key attributes (like Order_ Number for the ORDER table), those with unique values across the rows of the table, are indexed. In addition to this, Chris uses a general rule of thumb: create an index for any attribute that has more than 10 different values and that Helen might use to segment the database. For example, Helen indicated that one of the ways she wanted to use the database is to look at sales by product finish. Thus, it might make sense to create an index on the PRODUCT table using the Product_Finish attribute.

Figure 2-14
Database definition for Home Office product line marketing support system—Access data model prototype

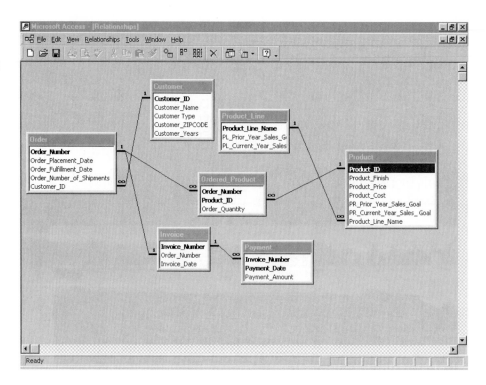

However, Pine Valley uses only six product finishes, or types of wood, so this is not a useful index candidate. On the other hand, Order_Placement_Date (called a secondary key since there may be more than one row in the ORDER table with the same value of this attribute), which Helen also wants to use to analyze sales in different type periods, is a good index candidate. Look in Figures 2-13a for the primary key clause and Figure 2-13b for an entry in the Indexed box near the bottom of the screen to see if the selected attribute is indexed and, if so, whether the index allows duplicates (a primary key may not have duplicates).

Figure 2-14 shows the prototype data model developed by Chris for the home office marketing database. Each box represents one table in the database; the attributes of a table are listed inside the associated box. Although the notation for relationships is slightly different from Figure 2-11, the meaning is the same. For example, the line from the CUSTOMER entity to the ORDER entity in Figure 2-14 shows a 1 near CUSTOMER and an infinity symbol next to ORDER, which has the same meaning as the Places relationship in Figure 2-11.

Using the Database

Helen will use the database Chris has built mainly for ad hoc questions, so Chris will train her on Microsoft Access, especially the database query features. Chris wants to wait to do this training after the system is better specified and Helen has learned about the database and Microsoft Access from the prototyping process. Helen has indicated, however, a few standard questions she expects to ask periodically. Microsoft Access provides capabilities for Chris to develop several types of prewritten routines that can make it easier for Helen to answer these standard questions (so she does not have to program these questions from scratch):

- *Form*   A set of attributes, in a predetermined format, all based on a single database record. Thus, a form might contain the data about a given customer, or might contain the data about a specific order and the customer attributes for the customer associated with the order.

- *Report*   A set of attributes, in a predetermined format, based on many unrelated records. A report usually contains the same attributes about each record. For example, a report might list the product identifier, current year sales, and current year sales goal for all the products for which sales are below goal. A report usually includes page numbers, titles on each page, the date the report was printed, and other descriptive information.

- *Query*   A question to be answered from the database as posed in a particular querying language, Query-by-Example. The result of a query is a table in which the columns are the attributes the user wants to see and the rows are different instances of those attributes that satisfy the qualification entered by the user.

During the prototyping development process Chris may develop many examples of each of these routines as Helen communicates more clearly what she wants the system to be able to do. At this early stage of development, however, Chris wants to develop one routine to create the first prototype. One of the standard sets of information Helen says she wants is a list of each of the products in the Home Office line showing each product's total sales to date compared to its current year sales goal. An Access query can produce this result. Helen may want the results of this query to be displayed in a more stylized fashion—an opportunity to use a report—but for now Chris will present this feature to Helen only as a query.

The query to produce this list of products appears in Figure 2-15, with sample output in Figure 2-16. The query in Figure 2-15 shows the relationship of the data model needed for this query at the top and the Query-by-Example code below. If a field is checked in the Show box, then that field is to be included in the result. Two fields, Product_Line_Name and Order_Placement_Date, are only used to select the Home Office furniture and orders in the current year, 2000. The Group By phase on the PR_Current_Year_Goal and also on the Product_ID field tells Access to sum the total sales for each product. Only limited data are included for this example, so the Total Sales results in Figure 2-16 are fairly small, but the format is the result of the query in Figure 2-15.

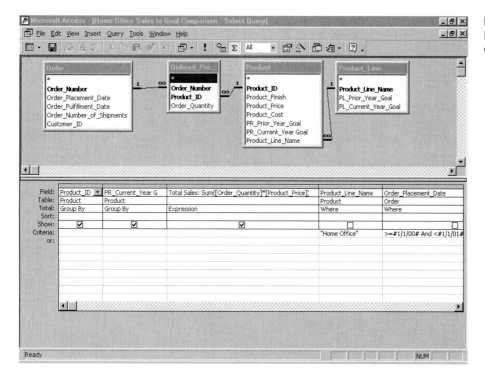

Figure 2-15
Home Office sales-to-goal comparison query

Figure 2-16
Home Office product line sales comparison

Product_ID	PR_Current_Year_Sales	Total Sales
3	$23,500.00	9375
5	$26,500.00	4550
7	$17,000.00	2250
10	$22,500.00	4400

Chris is now ready to meet with Helen again to see if the prototype is beginning to meet her needs. Chris shows Helen the system (by running Access and displaying screens like those in Figures 2-14 through 2-16). As Helen makes suggestions, Chris is able to make a few changes on-line, but many of Helen's observations will have to wait for more careful work at his desk.

Space does not permit us to review the whole project to develop the Home Office marketing support system. Chris and Helen ended up meeting about a dozen times before Helen was satisfied that all the attributes she needed were in the database; that the standard queries, forms, and reports Chris wrote were of use to her; and that she knew how to write queries for unanticipated questions. Chris will be available to Helen at any time to provide consulting support when she has trouble with the system, including writing more complex queries, forms, or reports. One final decision that Chris and Helen made was that the performance of the final prototype was efficient enough that the prototype did not have to be rewritten or redesigned. Helen was now ready to use the system.

Administering the Database

The administration of the Home Office marketing support system is fairly simple. Helen decided that she could live with weekly downloads of new data from Pine Valley's operational databases into her Access database. Chris wrote a C program with SQL commands embedded in it to perform the necessary extracts and wrote an Access program in Visual Basic to rebuild the Access tables from these extracts; he scheduled these jobs to run every Sunday evening. Chris also updated the corporate information systems architecture model to include the Home Office marketing support system. This step was important so that when changes occurred to formats for data included in Helen's system, the corporate CASE tool could alert Chris that changes might have to be made also in her system.

Summary

This chapter discussed the process of developing databases and the applications that used them. Database development begins with enterprise data modeling, where the range and general contents of organizational databases are established. Enterprise data modeling is part of an overall process that develops an information systems architecture (including data, processes, network, people, events, and reasons) for an organization. One popular methodology for developing an information systems architecture is information engineering, a top-down information systems planning approach.

Information systems planning must consider organization goals, critical success factors, and problem areas of the organization. During information systems planning, data entities need to be related to other organizational planning objects: organizational units, locations, business functions, and information systems. Business functions can be represented at various levels of detail by breaking them down through a process called functional decomposition. Relationships between data entities and the other organizational planning objects can be represented at a high level by planning matrixes, which can be manipulated to understand patterns of relationships.

Once the need for a database is identified either from information systems planning or from a specific request (such as the one from Helen Jarvis for a Home

Office products marketing support system), a project team is formed to develop all elements. The project team follows a systems development process, such as the systems development life cycle or prototyping. The systems development life cycle can be represented by seven methodical steps: (1) project identification and selection, (2) project initiation and planning, (3) analysis, (4) logical design, (5) physical design, (6) implementation, and (7) maintenance. Database development activities occur in each of these overlapping phases, and feedback may occur that causes a project to return to a prior phase. In prototyping, a database and its applications are iteratively refined through a close interaction of systems developers and users. Prototyping works best when the database application is small and stand-alone, and a small number of users exist.

Throughout the systems development process, CASE tools are used to develop data models and to maintain the metadata for the database and applications. A repository maintains all of the documentation. Various people might use the CASE tools and associated repository during a database development project: systems analysts, database analysts, users, programmers, database and data administrators, and other technical specialists. As a significant new portion of a project is completed and entries are made in the repository, a review point occurs so that those working on the project and funding the human and capital resources of the project can assess progress and renew commitment based on incremental achievements.

Those working on a database development project deal with three views, or schemas, for a database: (1) conceptual schema, which provides a complete, technology-independent picture of the database; (2) physical or internal schema, which specifies the complete database as it will be stored in computer secondary memory; and (3) external schemas, or user views, which describe a subset of the database relevant to a specific set of users.

A modern database and the applications that use it may be located on multiple computers. Although any number from one to many tiers may exist, three tiers of computers relate to the client/server architecture for database processing: (1) the client tier, where database contents are presented to the user; (2) the application/Web server tier, where analyses on database contents are made and user sessions are managed; and (3) the enterprise server tier, where the data from across the organization are merged into an organizational asset.

We closed the chapter with the review of a hypothetical database development project in Pine Valley Furniture Company. This system to support marketing a Home Office furniture product line illustrated the use of a personal database management system, Microsoft Access and SQL coding for developing a retrieval-only database. The database in this application contained data extracted from the enterprise databases and then stored in a separate database on the client tier. Prototyping was used to develop this database application because the user, Helen Jarvis, had rather unstructured needs that could best be discovered through an iterative process of developing and refining the system.

CHAPTER REVIEW

Key Terms

Business function	Functional decomposition	Project
Client/server architecture	Incremental commitment	Prototyping
Computer-aided software engineering (CASE)	Information engineering	Repository
Conceptual schema	Information systems architecture (ISA)	Systems development life cycle (SDLC)
Enterprise data modeling	Physical schema	Top-down planning

Review Questions

1. Define each of the following key terms:
   a. Information systems architecture (ISA)
   b. Systems development life cycle (SDLC)
   c. Client/server architecture
   d. Incremental commitment
   e. Enterprise data model
   f. Conceptual data modeling

2. Match the following terms and definitions:

_____ conceptual schema

_____ business function

_____ prototyping

_____ systems development life cycle

_____ functional decomposition

_____ top-down planning

_____ incremental commitment

_____ physical schemaa

a. repeatedly breaking a function into finer and finer detail

b. periodic review points in a systems development project

c. a rapid approach to systems development

d. a comprehensive description of business data

e. gains a broad understanding of information system needs

f. a related group of business processes

g. the structure of data stored in secondary memory

h. a structured, step-by-step approach to systems development

3. Contrast the following terms:
   a. physical schema; conceptual schema
   b. systems development life cycle; prototyping
   c. top-down planning; functional decomposition
   d. enterprise data modeling; information engineering
   e. repository; computer-aided software engineering

4. List and explain the four steps of information engineering.

5. Describe the three steps in the information engineering planning phase.

6. List and explain the three information engineering strategic planning factors.

7. List and define the five key corporate planning objects.

8. Explain the significance of functional decomposition in information systems and database development.

9. Explain the use of information system planning matrixes in information systems development.

10. Name the seven phases of the traditional systems development life cycle, and explain the purpose and deliverables of each phase.

11. In which of the seven phases of the SDLC do database development activities occur?

12. Define the steps in the prototyping systems development process. Which database development activities occur in each prototyping step?

13. Explain the differences between user views, a conceptual schema, and a physical schema as different views of the same database.

14. Are the design of external schemas and a conceptual schema done in a particular sequence? Why or why not?

15. Define a three-tiered database architecture.

16. In the three-tiered database architecture, is it possible for there to be no database on a particular tier? If not, why? If yes, give an example.

17. List the six key components of an information systems architecture (ISA). Which of these components relate to database design? Why?

18. What is the significance of the waterfall metaphor for the systems development life cycle (SDLC)?

19. When during the database development process might an entity-relationship diagram be drawn? How are these different diagrams of the same database different from one another?

20. What are the reasons for implementing a client/server database architecture?

Problems and Exercises

1. Is the waterfall metaphor a good representation of the systems development life cycle? Explain any problems you have with this metaphor.

2. Rearrange the rows and columns of Figure 2-3 into a more useful sequence. Why did you choose this new sequence of rows and columns? For what purpose can you now use the rearranged matrix?

3. List three additional entities that might appear in an enterprise data model for Pine Valley Furniture (Figure 2-1).

4. Consider your business school or other academic unit as a business enterprise.
   a. Define several functions and do a functional decomposition to at least three levels.
   b. Define several major data entity types, and draw a preliminary enterprise data model (similar in notation to Figure 2-1).
   c. Develop a planning matrix with the lowest level functions from part a of the exercise as rows and data entity types from part b as columns. Fill in the cells of this matrix similar to Figure 2-3.

   d. Define four critical success factors (CSFs) for the academic unit.
   e. Would your business school or academic unit benefit from a multiple-tiered architecture for data? Why or why not?

5. Consider a student club in which you are involved.
   a. Define several information systems (manual or automated) used by this club.
   b. Define several major data entity types, and draw a preliminary enterprise data model (similar in notation to Figure 2-1).
   c. Develop an Information System-to-Data Entity planning matrix. Fill in the cells to show how each information system interacts with each data entity (code the cell with a C for create new instances of that entity, R for retrieves data about that entity, U for updates values of data for that entity, and D for deletes instances of that entity.
   d. Reorganize the rows and columns of your answer to part c of this exercise to create, as best you can, a matrix with cells with entries along the main diagonal and empty cells off the main diagonal. What does this reorganized matrix tell you?

6. Imagine a planning matrix of Business Functions-to-Data Entities. Suppose that by studying this matrix you determine that three of the business functions provide the bulk of the use of five of the data entities. What implications might this have for identifying databases for development?

7. Consider Table 2-3. Develop a hypothetical Information System-to-Entity Type matrix from the information in this table. Make assumptions about which information systems create, retrieve, update, and delete data from each data entity. Code the cells to indicate create (C), retrieve (R), update (U), and delete (D). Since the information systems listed include both transaction processing and management information systems, what patterns of entity usage do you observe?

8. Consider Table 2-3. Develop a hypothetical functional decomposition of the Product development business function, similar to what is shown for the Order fulfillment function in Figure 2-2. Do any of the same subfunctions appear in both Figure 2-2 and your diagram? Why?

9. Explain the differences between an enterprise data model and a conceptual data model. How many databases does each represent? What scope of the organization does each address? What are other salient differences?

10. Is it possible that during the physical database design and creation step of database development you might want to return to the logical database design activity? Why or why not? If it is possible, give an example of what might arise during physical database design and creation that would cause you to want to reconsider the conceptual and external database designs from prior steps.

11. Contrast the top-down nature of database development during conceptual data modeling with the bottom-up nature of database development during logical database design. What major differences exist in the type of information considered in each of these two database development steps?

12. The objective of the prototyping systems development methodology is to rapidly build and rebuild an information system as the user and systems analyst learn from use of the prototype what features should be included in the evolving information system. Since the final prototype does not have to become the working system, where do you think would be an ideal location to develop a prototype: on a personal computer, workgroup computer, department computer, or enterprise server? Does your answer depend on any assumptions?

13. Consider an organization with which you frequently interact, such as a bank, credit card company, university, or insurance company, from which you receive several computer-generated messages, such as monthly statements, transaction slips, and so forth. Depict the data included in each message you receive from the organization as its own user view; use the notation of Figure 2-1 to represent these views. Now, combine all of these user views together into one conceptual data model, also using the notation of Figure 2-1. What did you observe about the process of combining the different user views? Were there inconsistencies across the user views? Once you have created

the conceptual data model, would you like to change anything about any of the user views?

14. Consider Figure 2-10, which depicts a hypothetical three-tiered database architecture. Identify potential duplications of data across all the databases listed on this figure. What problems might arise because of this duplication? Does this duplication violate the principles of the database approach outlined in Chapter 1? Why or why not?

15. Consider Figure 2-11. Explain the meaning of the line that connects ORDER to INVOICE and the line that connects INVOICE to PAYMENT. What does this say about how Pine Valley does business with its customers?

16. Answer the following questions concerning Figures 2-12 and 2-13:
    a. What will be the field size for the Product_Line_Name field in the PRODUCT table? Why?
    b. In Figure 2-13b, why is the Product_ID field in the PRODUCT table specified to be required?
    c. In Figure 2-13b, why does Product_ID have a key next to it for the PRODUCT table?
    d. What is the purpose of the last line of the SQL statement in Figure 2-13a?

17. Consider the Access query in Figure 2-15.
    a. Why is it necessary to include the Order_Placement_Date field in this query even though it is not displayed in the query result?
    b. How would the query have to change if Helen Jarvis wanted to see the results for all of the product lines, not just Home Office?

18. If you look ahead to Figure 3-22 in Chapter 3, you will see an entity-relationship diagram for part of the Pine Valley organization database. The entity PRODUCT LINE is diagrammed like this:

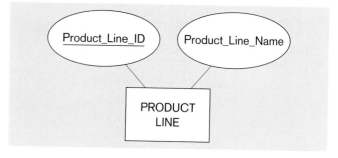

The draft prepared by Chris for Helen shows the following for PRODUCT LINE:

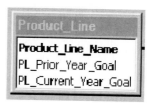

Explain the differences you note between the two definitions of PRODUCT LINE.

Field Exercises

1. Interview systems and database analysts at several organizations. Ask them to describe their systems development process. Does it resemble more the systems development life cycle or prototyping? Do they use methodologies similar to both? When do they use their different methodologies? Explore the methodology used for developing applications to be used through the Web. How have they adapted their methodology to fit this new systems development process?

2. Choose an organization with which you are familiar, possibly where you work, your university, or an organization where a friend works. For this organization, describe its information systems architecture (ISA). Does it have a formally prepared architecture, or did you have to create one? Interview information system managers in this organization to find out why they do or do not have a formally recognized information systems architecture.

3. Choose an organization with which you are familiar, possibly your employer, your university, or an organization where a friend works. Consider a major database in this organization, such as one supporting customer interactions, accounting, or manufacturing. What is the architecture for this database? Is the organization using some form of client/server architecture? Interview information system managers in this organization to find out why they chose the architecture for this database.

4. Choose an organization with which you are familiar, possibly your employer, your university, or an organization where a friend works. Interview a systems analyst or database analyst and ask questions about the typical composition of an information systems development team. Specifically, what role does a database analyst play in project teams? Is a database analyst used throughout the systems development process or is the database analyst used only at selected points?

5. Choose an organization with which you are familiar, possibly your employer, your university, or an organization where a friend works. Interview a systems analyst or database analyst and ask questions about how that organization uses CASE tools in the systems development process. Concentrate your questions on how CASE tools are used to support data modeling and database design and how the CASE tool's repository maintains the information collected about data, data characteristics, and data usage. If multiple CASE tools are used on one or many projects, ask how the organization attempts to integrate data models and data definitions. Finally, inquire how satisfied the systems and database analysts are with CASE tool support for data modeling and database design.

References

Hoffer, J. A., J. F. George, and J. S. Valacich. 2002. *Modern Systems Analysis and Design.* 3rd ed. Upper Saddle River, NJ: Prentice Hall.

Moriarty, T. 1991. "Framing Your System." *Database Programming & Design* 4 (June): 38–43.

Sowa, J. F., and J. A. Zachman. 1992. "Extending and Formalizing the Framework for Information Systems Architecture." *IBM Systems Journal* 31 (3): 590–616.

Thompson, C. 1997. "Committing to Three-Tier Architecture." *Database Programming & Design* 10 (August): 26–30, 32, 33.

Zachman, J. A. 1987. "A Framework for Information Systems Architecture." *IBM Systems Journal* 26 (March): 276–92.

Further Reading

Finkelstein, C. 1989. *An Introduction to Information Engineering.* Reading, MA: Addison-Wesley.

Shank, M. E., A. C. Boynton, and R. W. Zmud. 1985. "Critical Success Factor Analysis as a Methodology for IS Planning." *MIS Quarterly* 9 (June): 121–29.

Web Resources

http://netmation.com/docs/bb10.htm A short paper on Netmation that discusses enterprise-wide data modeling.

http://www.usdoj.gov/jmd/irm/lifecycle/table.htm The Department of Justice Systems Development Life Cycle Guidance Document. This is an example of a systems methodology that you may want to look over.

http://www-4.ibm.com/software/developer/library/cl-platform.html?dwzone=collaboration A short paper about "building a prototyping platform with open-source data stores," by Sean Gallagher.

http://www.qucis.queensu.ca/Software-Engineering/ The software engineering archives for USENET newsgroup comp.software-eng. This site contains many links that you may want to explore.

http://osiris.sunderland.ac.uk/sst/case2/welcome.html Computer-aided software engineering site at Sunderland University, U.K.

http://www.sei.cmu.edu/str/descriptions/clientserver_body.html Client/Server Software Architectures—An Overview. Carnegie Mellon Software Engineering Institute.

http://www.acinet.org/acinet/ America's Career InfoNet. Information about careers, outlook, requirements, and so forth.

MOUNTAIN VIEW COMMUNITY HOSPITAL

Project Case

PROJECT DESCRIPTION

You were introduced to Mountain View Community Hospital in Chapter 1. Figure 1 shows an organizational chart for Mountain View Community Hospital as of January 1, 2001. Like most general hospitals, Mountain View Community is divided into two primary organizational groups. The physicians, headed by Dr. Browne (chief of staff), are responsible for the quality of medical care provided to their patients. The group headed by Ms. Baker (administrator) provides the nursing, clinical, and administrative support the physicians need to serve their patients.

Goals and Critical Success Factors As stated in Chapter 1, Mountain View Community Hospital's basic goal is to provide high-quality health care for its surrounding community while containing costs that have been rising in accordance with national trends in recent years. Mountain View Community Hospital serves a com-

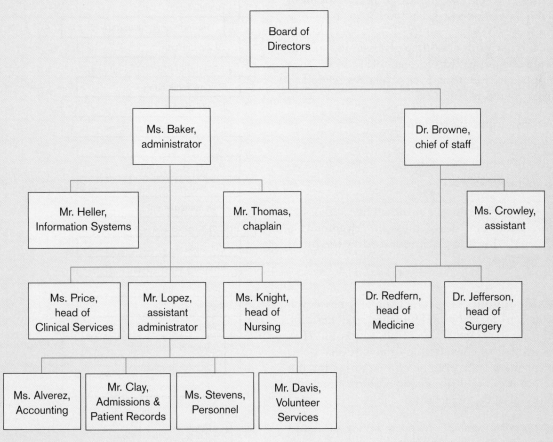

Figure 1
Organization chart, January 2001

munity of about 50,000 with an annual growth rate of 10 percent, a trend that is expected to continue since the surrounding area is attracting many retirees. Thus, Mountain View Community Hospital has a goal to expand its capacity (adding another 50 beds in five years) and opening a managed care retirement center with independent apartments and assisted living facilities. Adequate land exists for expansion adjacent to the current hospital facilities. Because of this expansion, Mountain View Community Hospital plans to increase the size of both administrative and medical staff, create a new department of Retirement Living under Ms. Baker, and create a new department of Geriatric Medicine under Dr. Browne.

In response to the steady growth and expansion plans at Mountain View Community Hospital, a special study team including Mr. Heller, Mr. Lopez, Dr. Jefferson, and a consultant has been developing a long-term business plan, including an information systems plan for the Hospital. Their work is not complete, but they have begun to identify many of the elements necessary to build the plan. In order to meet the goals of high-quality health care, cost containment, and expansion into new services, the team concluded that the Hospital has four critical success factors: quality of medical care, control of operating costs, control of capital costs, and recruitment and retention of skilled personnel (especially nurses). The development of improved information systems is an enabler in dealing with each of these CSFs.

The team is currently at work to generate two to four short- or long-term objectives for each CSF. So far they have developed the following four objectives related to the control of operating costs CSF:

1. Reduce costs for purchased items
2. More efficiently schedule staff
3. Lower cost of liability insurance
4. Expand volunteer services

The study team described each of these CSFs and objectives in more detail and stored these descriptions in a repository managed by the CASE tool used by the information systems department.

Enterprise Modeling   The study team also has developed a preliminary list of business functions that describe the administrative and medical activities within the Hospital. These functions consider the organizational goals and CSFs explained in the prior section. At this point, the study team has identified five major business functions that cut across all of the organizational units:

- *Patient care administration*   Manage the logistical and record-keeping aspects of patient care.
- *Clinical services*   Provide laboratory testing and procedures, and patient monitoring and screening.

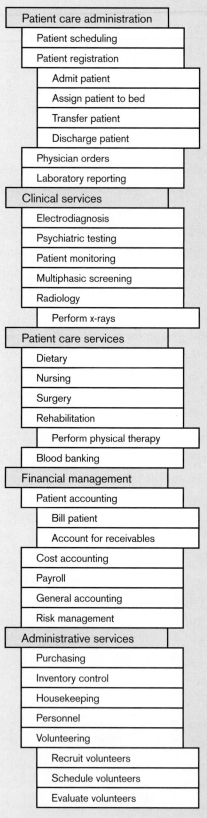

Figure 2
Business functions

- *Patient care services* Provide patients with medical care and support services.
- *Financial management* Manage the financial resources and operations of the hospital.
- *Administrative services* Provide general management and support services not directly related to patient care.

The study team has been able to break each of these high-level functions into lists of more detailed functions (see Figure 2), but the team knows that these lists are not complete nor well defined at this point.

The study team initially has a preliminary set of 10 entity types that describe the data required by the hospital for its operation and administration: FACILITY, PHYSICIAN, PATIENT, WARD, STAFF, LABORATORY, TEST, MEDICAL/SURGICAL ITEM, SUPPLY ITEM, and VENDOR. From discussions with hospital staff, reviewing hospital documents, and studying existing information systems, the study team developed a list of business rules describing the policies of the hospital and nature of the hospital's operation that govern the relationships between these entities. Some of these rules are:

1. A FACILITY maintains a number of LABORATORY(ies): radiology, electrodiagnosis, hematology, and so on.

2. A FACILITY contains a number of WARDs (obstetrics, emergency, rehabilitation, geriatrics, etc.).

3. Each WARD is assigned a certain number of STAFF members (nurses, secretaries, etc.); a STAFF member may be assigned to multiple WARDs.

4. A FACILITY staffs its medical team with a number of PHYSICIANs. A PHYSICIAN may be on the staff of more than one FACILITY.

5. A PHYSICIAN treats PATIENTs, and a PATIENT is treated by any number of PHYSICIANs.

6. A PHYSICIAN diagnoses PATIENTs, and a PATIENT is diagnosed by any number of PHYSICIANs.

7. A PATIENT may be assigned to a WARD (outpatients are not assigned to a WARD). The hospital cares only about the current WARD a patient is assigned to (if assigned at all).

8. A PATIENT uses MEDICAL/SURGICAL ITEMS, which are supplied by VENDORs. A VENDOR also provides SUPPLY ITEMs that are used for housekeeping and maintenance purposes.

9. A LABORATORY performs TESTs about PATIENTs.

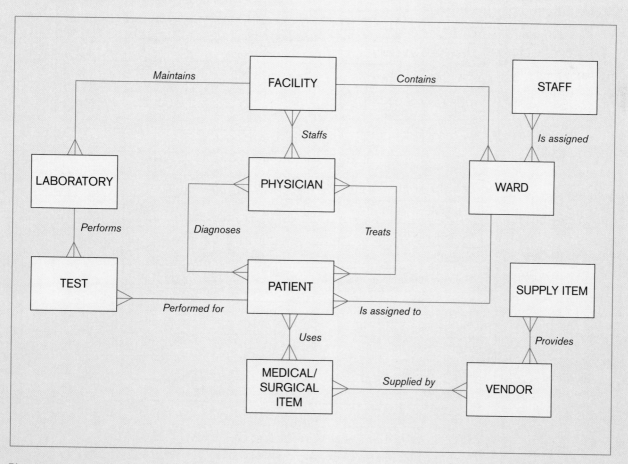

Figure 3
Preliminary enterprise data model

They recognized that certain business functions, such as risk management and volunteering, were not adequately represented in the set of data entities and business rules, but they decided to deal with these and other areas later. The study team stored descriptions of these data entities and the business rules in the CASE repository for later analysis. Using the identified entities and business rules, the study team developed a preliminary enterprise data model (see Figure 3). Again, this data model is preliminary since it does not follow all the conventions used in the information systems department for drawing data models, but the purpose of this enterprise model is to give only a general overview of organizational data.

Developing Planning Matrixes   The study team used the CASE tool to produce a first version of a function-to-entity type matrix (see Figure 4). This matrix maps the

Figure 4
Business function-to-data entity matrix

Business Functions	Facility	Physician	Patient	Ward	Staff	Laboratory	Test	Medical/ Surgical Item	Supply Item	Vendor
Patient Scheduling		R	R			R				
Patient Registration			M	R						
Physician Orders		R	R				R			
Laboratory Reporting			R			R	R			
Electrodiagnosis							M			
Psychiatric Testing							M			
Patient Monitoring			R							
Multiphasic Screening			R			R	M			
Radiology						R	M			
Dietary			R							
Nursing			R							
Surgery		R	R							
Rehabilitation			R							
Blood Banking			R			R				
Patient Accounting			R	R		R	R			
Cost Accounting	R		R	R			R			
Payroll		R		R	R					
General Accounting	M			M		M				
Risk Management	R	R	R				R			R
Purchasing								M	M	M
Inventory Control								R	R	
Housekeeping									R	
Personnel		M			M				R	
Volunteering	R		R	R		R				

M = data entity (column) is maintained by business function (row)

R = data entity (column) is used by business function (row)

business functions from Figure 2 with the 10 data entities. The cells of the matrix are coded as follows:

M = function maintains instances of entity (creates, updates, and deletes)

R = function uses data about entity

As an initial pass at this matrix, the study team decided not to separately code data creation, update, and deletion activities.

The study team also used the CASE tool to relate business functions to the four critical success factors (see Figure 5 for the result of their work). In this figure the cells indicate:

E = doing the function well is essential in achieving the CSF

D = doing the function well helps in achieving the CSF

The study team is looking for ways to combine the results shown in Figures 4 and 5 to help them set some priorities for information systems development.

PROJECT QUESTIONS

1. Which information system planning matrixes (among those shown in this case study or others not shown) might assist the study team at Mountain View Community Hospital to determine a tiered location plan for databases? Why?

2. In the project description above, objectives are listed for one of the four critical success factors, operating cost control. Write plausible objectives, given the structure and plans of the hospital, for the other three CSFs.

3. What additional activities might occur within the "volunteering" business function?

4. What activities might occur within the "risk management" business function?

5. What additional data entities, besides the 10 entities mentioned in this case, might the risk management business function need?

6. Do you think that the study team will be able to identify all the data entities by doing the kind of analysis they have been doing? If not, what other database development steps will need to be done and when?

7. Why do you think the people on the business planning study team were selected for this assignment? Would you have chosen different or additional people?

8. In the case description above, nine business rules are listed. The study team used these rules to develop Figure 3. What other business rules, besides these nine, are implied by or depicted in Figure 3?

Business Functions	Quality Care	Operating Cost Control	Capital Cost Control	Staff Recruitment and Retention
Patient Scheduling	D			
Patient Registration				
Physician Orders	D			
Laboratory Reporting	D			
Electrodiagnosis			D	
Psychiatric Testing	D			
Patient Monitoring	E			
Multiphasic Screening	E			
Radiology	D			
Dietary	E			
Nursing	E	E		E
Surgery	D	D	E	
Rehabilitation	E			
Blood Banking	D			
Patient Accounting	D	E		
Cost Accounting		E		
Payroll				D
General Accounting				
Risk Management		E		D
Purchasing		E		
Inventory Control		E		
Housekeeping		D		
Personnel				E
Volunteering		E		E

E = business function (row) is essential in achieving CSF (column)
D = business function (row) is desirable in achieving CSF (column)

Figure 5
Business function-to-CSF matrix

9. Even though capital cost control is a critical success factor, only two business functions in Figure 5 mention this CSF. Why? What would need to be done to enhance this figure so that more entries indicated a relationship between business functions and this CSF?

PROJECT EXERCISES

1. Rearrange the rows and columns of Figure 4 so that the entries form a block diagonal pattern. What conclusions do you reach from analyzing this pattern?

2. Redraw Figure 1 to reflect the structure of the hospital after its planned future expansion and growth. Given this expansion and growth, what else would need to change about Figures 2, 3, and 4?

3. Based on Figures 4 and 5, determine which data entities are essential for operating cost control. What implications does this result have for information systems development?

4. In Project Question 5 you listed additional data entities needed for the risk management business function. Modify Figure 3 to include these additional entities and the relevant relationships among all data entities.

5. One of the important outputs from the "bill patient" business function is the Patient Bill. Project Exercise 2 in Chapter 1 introduced a reduced version of this bill, which is repeated below. That exercise asked you to add missing data that would typically appear on a patient bill. Using your result from that exercise, verify that the enterprise data model in Figure 3 contains the data necessary to generate a patient bill. Explain what you have to do to perform this verification. What did you discover from your analysis?

```
Patient Name:   Dolan, Mark

Patient Number:  _____

Patient Address:  _____

Item Code      Item Description      Amount

_____      _____      _____

_____      _____      _____

_____      _____      _____
```

6. The study team activities described in this case study have related to very early stages of information system and database development. Outline the next steps that should be followed within the Information Systems unit to align current systems and databases to the future information systems needs of the hospital.

7. The manager of the risk management area is anxious to receive computerized support for his activities. The hospital is increasingly facing malpractice claims and litigation, and he does not believe he can wait for improved information services until the information systems and database plans are set. What this manager wants is a system that will track claims, legal suits, lawyers, judges, medical staff, disbursements against claims, and judgments. How would you proceed to deal with this request for improved information services? What methodology would you apply to design the systems and databases he needs? Why?

8. Consider again the request of the manager of risk management from Project Exercise 7. On what tier or tiers would you recommend the system and database he needs be developed? Why?

Part TWO

Database Analysis

An Overview of Part TWO

The first step in database development is database analysis, in which we determine user requirements for data and develop data models to represent those requirements. The two chapters in Part II describe in depth the de facto standard for conceptual data modeling—entity-relationship diagramming. A conceptual data model is one that represents data from the viewpoint of the user, independent of any technology that will be used to implement the model.

Chapter 3 (Modeling Data in the Organization) begins with an orientation towards data modeling by describing business rules, which are the policies and rules about the operation of a business that a data model represents. Characteristics of good business rules are described and the process of gathering business rules is discussed. General guidelines for naming and defining elements of a data model are presented within the context of business rules. Then the chapter presents the main features of the entity-relationship (or E-R) data model. This chapter introduces the notation and main constructs of this modeling technique including entities, relationships, and attributes; for each construct, we provide specific guidelines for naming and defining these elements of a data model. We distinguish between strong and weak entity types and the use of identifying relationships. We describe different types of attributes including simple versus composite attributes, single-valued versus multivalued attributes, derived attributes, and identifiers. We contrast relationship types and instances and introduce associative entities. We describe and illustrate relationships of various degrees including unary, binary, and ternary relationships. We also describe the various relationship cardinalities that arise in modeling situations. We discuss the common problem of how to model time-dependent data. Finally, we describe the situation where multiple relationships are defined between a given set of entities. The E-R modeling concepts are illustrated with an extended example for Pine Valley Furniture Company.

Chapter 4 (The Enhanced E-R Model and Business Rules) presents advanced concepts in entity-relationship modeling and introduces recently developed notation for capturing more complex business rules on E-R diagrams. These additional modeling features are often required to cope with the increasingly complex business environment encountered in organizations today.

The most important new modeling construct incorporated in the enhanced entity-relationship (or EER) diagram is supertype/subtype relationships. This facility allows us to model a general entity type (called a supertype) and then subdivide it into several specialized entity types called subtypes. For example, sports cars and sedans are subtypes of automobiles. We introduce a simple notation for representing supertype/subtype relationships. We also introduce generalization and specialization as two contrasting techniques for identifying supertype/subtype relationships. We introduce notation to further refine the basic supertype/subtype relationships. The comprehensiveness of a well-documented relationship can be overwhelming, so we introduce a technique called entity clustering for simplifying the presentation of an E-R diagram to meet the needs of a given audience.

Business rules are statements that define or constrain some aspect of the business. We develop a classification for the different types of business rules that are commonly encountered. We then describe and illustrate a declarative approach for expressing business rules, together with a notation for the rules that is superimposed on the EER diagram.

There is another, alternative notation for data modeling—the UML class diagrams for systems developed using object-oriented technologies. This technique is presented later, in Chapter 14 in Part V. It is possible to read Chapter 14 immediately after Chapter 4 if you want to compare these alternative, but conceptually similar, approaches.

The conceptual data modeling concepts presented in the two chapters in Part II provide the foundation for your career in database analysis and design. As a database analyst you will be expected to apply the E-R notation in modeling user requirements for data and information.

3

Modeling Data in the Organization

LEARNING OBJECTIVES

After studying this chapter, you should be able to:

- Concisely define each of the following key terms: **business rule, term, fact, entity-relationship model (E-R model), entity-relationship diagram (E-R diagram), entity, entity type, entity instance, strong entity type, weak entity type, identifying owner, identifying relationship, attribute, composite attribute, simple attribute, multivalued attribute, derived attribute, identifier, composite identifier, relationship type, relationship instance, associative entity, degree of a relationship, unary relationship, binary relationship, ternary relationship, cardinality constraint, minimum** and **maximum cardinality,** and **time stamp.**

- State reasons why many system developers believe that data modeling is the most important part of the system development process.

- Write good names and definitions for entities, relationships, and attributes.

- Distinguish unary, binary, and ternary relationships and give a common example of each.

- Model each of the following constructs in an E-R diagram: composite attribute, multivalued attribute, derived attribute, associative entity, identifying relationship, and minimum and maximum cardinality constraints.

- Draw an E-R diagram to represent common business situations.

- Convert a many-to-many relationship to an associative entity type.

- Model simple time-dependent data using time stamps in an E-R diagram.

INTRODUCTION

You have already been introduced to modeling data and the entity-relationship model through simplified examples in the first two chapters of this text. In this chapter we formalize data modeling based on the powerful concept of business rules and we describe the entity-relationship (E-R) data model in detail.

Business rules are derived from policies, procedures, events, functions, and other business objects, and state constraints on the organization. Business rules are important in data modeling because they govern how data are handled and stored. Basic business rules are data names and definitions. This chapter explains guidelines for the clear naming and definition of data objects in a business. In terms of conceptual data modeling, names and definitions must be provided for entity types, attributes, and relationships.

Other business rules may state constraints on these data objects. These constraints can be captured in a data model, such as an entity-relationship diagram, and associated documentation.

After some years of use, the E-R model remains the mainstream approach for conceptual data modeling. Its popularity stems from factors such as relative ease of use, widespread CASE tool support, and the belief that entities and relationships are natural modeling concepts in the real world.

The E-R model is most often used as a tool for communications between database designers and end users during the analysis phase of database development (described in Chapter 2). The E-R model is used to construct a *conceptual* data model, which is a representation of the structure and constraints of a database that is independent of the software (such as a database management system) and its associated data model that will be used to implement the database.

Some authors introduce terms and concepts peculiar to the relational data model when discussing E-R modeling. In particular, they recommend that the E-R model be completely normalized, with full resolution of primary and foreign keys. However, we believe that this forces a premature commitment to the relational data model. In today's database environment, the database may be implemented with object-oriented technology or with a mixture of object-oriented and relational technology. Therefore, we defer discussion of normalization concepts to Chapter 5.

The entity-relationship model was introduced in a key article by Chen (1976), in which he described the main constructs of the E-R model—entities and relationships—and their associated attributes. The model has subsequently been extended to include additional constructs by Chen and others; for example, see Teorey, Yang, and Fry (1986) and Storey (1991). The E-R model continues to evolve, but unfortunately there is not yet a standard notation for E-R modeling. Song, Evans, and Park (1995) present a side-by-side comparison of 10 different E-R modeling notations, explaining the major advantages and disadvantages of each approach.

Many systems developers believe that data modeling is the most important part of the systems development process. This belief is based on three important reasons (Hoffer, George, and Valacich, 2002):

1. The characteristics of data captured during data modeling are crucial in the design of databases, programs, and other system components. The facts and rules captured during the process of data modeling are essential in assuring data integrity in an information system.

2. Data rather than processes are the most complex aspects of many modern information systems and hence require a central role in structuring system requirements. Often the goal is to provide a rich data resource that might support any type of information inquiry, analysis, and summary.

3. Data tend to be more stable than the business processes that use that data. Thus an information system design that is based on a data orientation should have a longer useful life than one based on a process orientation.

In this chapter we present the main features of E-R modeling, using common notation and conventions. We begin by defining the basic constructs of the E-R model: entities, attributes, and relationships. We define three types of entities that are common in E-R modeling: strong entities, weak entities, and associative entities. We also define several important types of attributes, including single- and multivalued attributes, derived attributes, and composite attributes. We then introduce three important concepts associated with relationships: the degree of a relationship, the cardinality of a relationship, and participation constraints in a relationship. We conclude with an extended example of an E-R diagram for Pine Valley Furniture Company.

MODELING THE RULES OF THE ORGANIZATION

We will see in this and the next chapter how to use data models, in particular the entity-relationship notation, to document rules and policies of an organization. *In fact, documenting rules and policies of an organization that govern data is exactly what data modeling is all about.* Business rules and policies govern creating, updating, and removing data in an information processing and storage system, thus they must be described along with the data to which they are related. For example, a policy that "every student in the university must have a faculty adviser" forces data (in a database) about each student to be associated with data about some student adviser. Also, the statement that "a student is any person who has applied for admission or taken a course or training program from any credit or noncredit unit of the university" not only defines the concept of "student" but also states a policy of the university (e.g., implicitly, alumni are students, and a high school student who attended a college fair but has not applied is not a student, assuming the college fair is not a noncredit training program).

Business rules and policies are not universal; different universities may have different policies for student advising and may include different types of people as students. Also, the rules and policies of an organization may change (usually slowly) over time; a university may decide that a student does not have to be assigned a faculty adviser until the student chooses a major.

Your job as a database analyst is to

- Identify and understand those rules *that govern data*
- Represent those rules so that they can be unambiguously understood by information systems developers and users
- Implement those rules in database technology

Data modeling is an important tool in this process. Since the purpose of data modeling is to document business rules about data, we introduce the discussion of data modeling and the entity-relationship notation with an overview of business rules. Data models cannot represent all business rules (and do not need to, since not all business rules govern data); data models along with associated documentation and other types of information system models (for example, models that document the processing of data) represent all business rules that must be enforced through information systems.

Overview of Business Rules

A **business rule** is "a statement that defines or constrains some aspect of the business. It is intended to assert business structure or to control or influence the behavior of the business. . . . rules prevent, cause, or suggest things to happen" (GUIDE Business Rules Project, 1997). For example, the following two statements are common expressions of business rules that affect data processing and storage:

- "A student may register for a section of a course only if he or she has successfully completed the prerequisites for that course."
- "A preferred customer qualifies for a 10 percent discount, unless he has an overdue account balance."

Most organizations today (and their employees) are guided by thousands of combinations of such rules. In the aggregate these rules influence behavior and determine how the organization responds to its environment (Gottesdiener, 1997). Capturing and documenting business rules is an important, complex task. Thoroughly capturing and structuring business rules, then enforcing them through database technologies, help to insure that information systems work right and users of the information understand what they enter and see.

Business rule: A statement that defines or constrains some aspect of the business. It is intended to assert business structure or to control or influence the behavior of the business.

The Business Rules Paradigm The concept of business rules has been used in information systems for some time. However, it has been more common (especially in the database world) to use the related term "integrity constraint" when referring to such rules. The intent of this term is somewhat more limited in scope, usually referring to maintaining valid data values and relationships in the database.

Today the term "business rules" has a much broader scope, so that it includes all rules (such as the two examples quoted above) that have an impact on the databases in an organization. In fact, a business rules approach has been advocated by a number of authors as a new paradigm for specifying information systems requirements (von Halle, 1997). This approach is based on the following premises:

- Business rules are a core concept in an enterprise since they are an expression of business policy and guide individual and aggregate behavior. Well-structured business rules can be stated in natural language for end users and in a data model for systems developers.

- Business rules can be expressed in terms that are familiar to end users. Thus users can define and then maintain their own rules.

- Business rules are highly maintainable. They are stored in a central repository, and each rule is expressed only once, then shared throughout the organization.

- Enforcement of business rules can be automated through the use of software that can interpret the rules and enforce them using the integrity mechanisms of the database management system (Moriarity, 2000).

Although much progress has been made, the industry has not realized all of these objectives to date. Research and tools development is continuing (especially on automating business rules), and the business rules approach holds considerable promise for the future. Possibly the premise with greatest potential benefit is "Business rules are highly maintainable." The ability to specify and maintain the requirements for information systems as a set of rules has considerable power when coupled with an ability to automatically generate information systems from a repository of rules. Automatic generation and maintenance of systems not only will simplify the systems development process but also will improve the quality of systems.

Scope of Business Rules

In this and the next chapter we are concerned with business rules that impact only an organization's databases. Most organizations have a host of rules and/or policies that fall outside this definition. For example, the rule "Friday is business casual dress day" may be an important policy statement, but it has no immediate impact on databases. On the other hand, the rule "A student may register for a section of a course only if he or she has successfully completed the prerequisites for that course" is within our scope since it constrains the transactions that may be processed against the database. In particular, it causes any transaction to be rejected that attempts to register a student who does not have the necessary prerequisites. Some business rules cannot be represented in common data modeling notation; those rules which cannot be represented in a variation of an entity-relationship diagram are stated in natural language and some can be represented in the relational data model, which we describe in Chapter 5.

Good Business Rules Whether stated in natural language, a structured data model, or other information systems documentation, a business rule will have certain characteristics if it is to be consistent with the premises outlined above. These characteristics are summarized in Table 3-1. These characteristics will have a better chance of being satisfied if a business rule is defined, approved, and owned by business, not technical, people. Business people become stewards of the business rules.

Table 3-1   Characteristics of A Good Business Rule

Characteristic	Explanation
Declarative	A business rule is a statement of policy, not how policy is enforced or conducted; the rule does not describe a process or implementation, but rather describes what a process validates
Precise	With the related organization, the rule must have only one interpretation among all interested people, and its meaning must be clear
Atomic	A business rule marks one statement, not several; no part of the rule can stand on its own as a rule (that is, the rule is indivisibie, yet sufficient)
Consistent	A business rule must be internally consistent (that is, not contain conflicting statements) and must be consistent with (and not contradict) other rules
Expressible	A business rule must be able to be stated in natural language, but it will be stated in a structured natural language so that there is no misinterpretation
Distinct	Business rules are not redundant, but a business rule may refer to other rules (especialiy refer to definitions)
Business-oriented	A business rule is stated in terms business people can understand, and since it is a statement of business policy, only business people can modify or invalidate a rule; thus, a business rule is owned by the business

Adapted from Gottesdiener (1999) and Plotkin (1999).

You, as the database analyst, facilitate the surfacing of the rules and the transformation of ill-stated rules into ones that satisfy the desired characteristics.

Gathering Business Rules   Business rules appear in descriptions of business functions, events, policies, units, stakeholders, and other objects. These descriptions can be found in interview notes from individual and group information systems requirements collection sessions, organizational documents (e.g., personnel manuals, policies, contracts, marketing brochures, and technical instructions), and other sources. Rules are identified by asking questions about the who, what, when, where, why, and how of the organization. Usually, the data analyst has to be persistent in clarifying initial statements of rules because initial statements may be vague or imprecise (what some people have called *business ramblings*). Thus, precise rules are formulated from an iterative inquiry process. You should be prepared to ask such questions as "Is this always true," "Are there special circumstances when an alternative occurs," "Are there distinct kinds of that person," "Is there only one of those or are there many," and "Is there a need to keep a history of those, or is the current data all that is useful?" We will illustrate specific questions that can be useful for surfacing rules for each type of data modeling construct as we introduce that construct in this and the subsequent chapter.

Data Names and Definitions

Fundamental to understanding and modeling data are naming and defining data objects. Data objects must be named and defined before they can be used unambiguously in a model of organizational data. In the entity-relationship notation you will learn in this chapter, you have to give entities, relationships, and attributes clear and distinct names and definitions.

Data Names   We will say more about specifically naming entities, relationships, and attributes as we develop the entity-relationship data model, but there are some general guidelines about naming any data object. Data names should (Salin, 1990)

- *Relate to business, not technical (hardware or software) characteristics*; so, Customer is a good name, but File10, Bit7, and PayrollReportSortKey are not good names.

- *Be meaningful*, almost to the point of being self-documenting (that is, the definition will refine and explain the name without having to state the essence of the object's meaning); you should avoid using generic words such as "has," "is," "person," or "it."

- *Be unique* from the name used for every other distinct data object; words should be included in a data name if they distinguish the data object from other similar data objects (e.g., *Home*Address versus *Campus*Address).

- *Readable*, so that the name is structured as the concept would most naturally be said (e.g., GradePointAverage is a good name, whereas AverageGradeRelativeToA, although possibly accurate, is an awkward name).

- *Composed of words taken from an approved list*; each organization often chooses a vocabulary from which significant words in data names must be chosen (e.g., maximum is preferred, never upper limit, ceiling, or highest); alternative, or alias names, can also be included in the complete set of database documentation; words in the vocabulary may also have approved abbreviations (e.g., CUST for Customer) and you may be encouraged to use the abbreviations so that data names are short enough to meet maximum length limits of database technology.

- *Repeatable*, meaning that different people or the same person at different times should develop exactly or almost the same name; this often means that there is a standard hierarchy or pattern for names (e.g., the birth date of a student would be StudentBirthDate and the birth date of an employee would be EmployeeBirthDate).

Salin (1990) suggests that you develop data names by

1. Preparing a definition of the data (we talk about definitions next).
2. Removing insignificant or illegal words (words not on the approved list for names); note that the presence of AND and OR in the definition may imply that two or more data objects are combined, and you may want to separate the objects and assign different names.
3. Arranging the words in a meaningful, repeatable way.
4. Assigning a standard abbreviation for each word.
5. Determining if the name already exists, and if so, adding other qualifiers that make the name unique.

We will see examples of good data names as we develop a data modeling notation in this chapter.

Data Definitions A definition (sometimes called a structural assertion) is considered a type of business rule (GUIDE Business Rules Project, 1997). A definition is an explanation of a term or a fact. A **term** is a word or phrase that has a specific meaning for the business. Examples of terms are: course, section, rental car, flight, reservation, and passenger. Terms are often the key words used to form data names. Terms must be defined carefully and concisely. However, there is no need to define common terms such as "day," "month," "person," or "television" since these terms are understood without ambiguity by most persons.

A **fact** is an association between two or more terms. Examples of facts that are definitions are the following (the defined terms are underlined):

- "A <u>course</u> is a module of instruction in a particular subject area." This definition associates two terms: *module of instruction* and *subject area*. We assume that these are common terms that do not need to be further defined.

- "A <u>customer</u> may request a <u>model of car</u> from a <u>rental branch</u> on a particular <u>date</u>." This fact, which is a definition of *model rental request*, associates the four underlined terms (GUIDE Business Rules Project, 1997). Three of these terms

Term: A word or phrase that has a specific meaning for the business.

Fact: An association between two or more terms.

are business-specific terms that would need to be defined individually (date is a common term).

Good Data Definitions We will illustrate good definitions for entities, relationships, and attributes as we develop the entity-relationship notation in this and the next chapters. There are, however, some general guidelines to follow (Aranow, 1989).

- Definitions (and all types of business rules) are gathered from the same sources as all requirements for information systems. Thus, systems and data analysts should be looking for data objects and their definitions as these sources of information systems requirements are studied.

- Definitions will usually be accompanied by diagrams, such as entity-relationship diagrams. The definition does not need to repeat what is shown on the diagram, but rather supplement the diagram. A definition will state such characteristics of a data objects as

  - subtleties

  - special or exceptional conditions

  - examples

  - where, when, and how the data is created or calculated in the organization

  - whether the data is static or changes over time

  - whether the data is singular or plural in its atomic form

  - who determines the value for the data

  - who owns the data (that is, who controls the definition and usage)

  - whether the data is optional or an empty (what we will call null) value is allowed, and

  - whether this data can be broken down into more atomic parts or if it is often combined with other data into some more composite or aggregate form.

  If not included in a data definition, then these characteristics need to be documented elsewhere, where other metadata are stored.

- A data object should not be added to a data model, such as an entity-relationship diagram, until after it has been carefully defined (and named), and agreement has been obtained on this definition. But, expect that the definition may change once you place the object on the diagram because the process of developing a data model tests your understanding of the meaning of data (in other words, *modeling data is an iterative process*).

There is an unattributed phrase in data modeling that highlights the importance of good data definitions. This phrase is "He who controls the meaning of data controls the data." It might seem that obtaining concurrence in an organization on the definitions to be used for the various terms and facts should be relatively easy. However, this is usually far from the case. In fact, it is likely to be one of the most difficult challenges you will face in data modeling or, for that matter, in any other endeavor. It is not unusual for an organization to have multiple definitions (perhaps a dozen or more) for common terms such as "customer" or "order."

To illustrate the problems inherent in developing definitions, consider a data object of Student found in a typical university. A sample definition for Student is: "a person who has been admitted to the school and who has registered for at least one course during the past year." This definition is certain to be challenged, since it is probably too narrow. A person who is a student typically proceeds through several stages in relationship with the school, such as the following:

1. Prospect: some formal contact, indicating an interest in the school.

2. Applicant: applies for admission.

3. Admitted applicant: admitted to the school and perhaps to a degree program.

4. Matriculated student: registers for at least one course.

5. Continuing student: registers for courses on an ongoing basis (no substantial gaps).

6. Former student: fails to register for courses during some stipulated period (now may reapply).

7. Graduate: satisfactorily completes some degree program (now may apply for another program).

Imagine the difficulty of obtaining consensus on a single definition in this situation! It would seem you might consider three alternatives:

1. Use multiple definitions to cover the various situations. This is likely to be highly confusing if there is only one entity type, and is not recommended (multiple definitions are not good definitions). It might be possible to create multiple entity types, one for each student situation above. However, since there is likely considerable similarity across the entity types, the fine distinctions between the entity types may be confusing, and the data model will show many constructs.

2. Use a very general definition that will cover most situations. This approach may necessitate adding additional data about students to record a given student's actual status. For example, data for a student's status, with values of prospect, applicant, and so forth might be sufficient. On the other hand, if the same student could hold multiple statuses (e.g., prospect for one degree and matriculated for another degree), this may not work.

3. Consider using multiple, but related, data objects for Student. For example, we could create a general entity type for Student, and then other specific entity types for kinds of students with unique characteristics. We describe the conditions that suggest this approach in Chapter 4.

THE E-R MODEL

Entity-relationship model (E-R model): A logical representation of the data for an organization or for a business area.

Entity-relationship diagram (E-R diagram): A graphical representation of an entity-relationship model.

An **entity-relationship model** (or **E-R model**) is a detailed, logical representation of the data for an organization or for a business area. The E-R model is expressed in terms of entities in the business environment, the relationships (or associations) among those entities, and the attributes (or properties) of both the entities and their relationships. An E-R model is normally expressed as an **entity-relationship diagram** (or **E-R diagram**), which is a graphical representation of an E-R model.

Sample E-R Diagram

To jump-start your understanding of E-R diagrams, Figure 3-1 presents a simplified E-R diagram for a small furniture manufacturing company, Pine Valley Furniture. This company can purchase items from a number of different suppliers, who then ship the items to the manufacturer. The items are assembled into products that are sold to customers who order the products. Each customer order may include one or more lines corresponding to the products appearing on that order.

The diagram in Figure 3-1 shows the entities and relationships for this company (attributes are omitted to simplify the diagram for now). Entities are represented by the rectangle symbol, while relationships between entities are represented by the diamond symbol connected by lines to the related entities. The entities in Figure 3-1 are:

• CUSTOMER   A person or organization who has ordered or might order products. *Example*: L. L. Fish Furniture.

- PRODUCT   A type of furniture made by Pine Valley Furniture, which may be ordered by customers. Note that a product is not a specific bookcase since individual bookcases do not need to be tracked. *Example:* A 6-foot, 5-shelf, oak bookcase called O600.

- ORDER   The transaction associated with the sale of one or more products to a customer and identified by a transaction number from sales or accounting. *Example:* The event of L. L. Fish buying one product O600 and four products O623 on September 10, 2001.

- ITEM   A type of component that goes into making one or more products and can be supplied by one or more suppliers. *Example:* A 4-inch, ball-bearing caster called I-27–4375.

- SUPPLIER   Another company that may provide items to Pine Valley Furniture. *Example:* Sure Fasteners, Inc.

- SHIPMENT   The transaction associated with items received in the same package by Pine Valley Furniture from a supplier. All items in a shipment appear on one bill-of-lading document. *Example:* The receipt of 300 I-27-4375 and 200 I-27-4380 items from Sure Fasteners, Inc. on September 9, 2001.

Note that it is important to clearly define, as metadata, each entity. For example, it is important to know that the CUSTOMER entity includes persons or organizations that have not yet purchased products from Pine Valley Furniture. It is common that

Figure 3-1
Sample E-R diagram

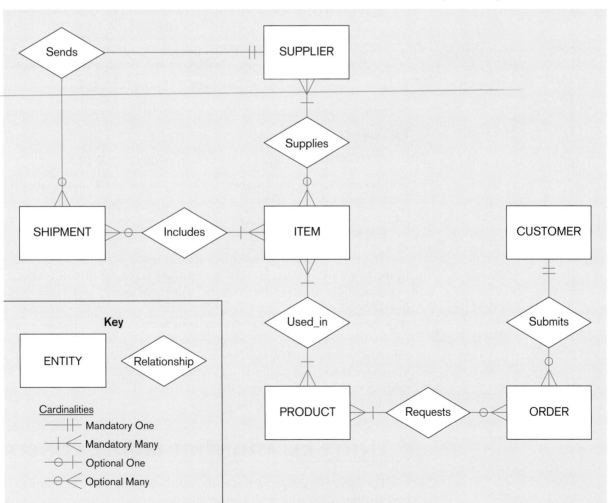

different departments in an organization have different meanings for the same term (homonyms). For example, Accounting may designate as customers only those persons or organizations who have ever made a purchase, thus excluding potential customers, whereas Marketing designates as customers anyone they have contacted or who has purchased from Pine Valley Furniture or any known competitor. An accurate and thorough E-R diagram without clear metadata may be interpreted in different ways by different people.

The symbols at the end of each line on an E-R diagram represent relationship cardinalities. On examining Figure 3-1, we can see that these cardinality symbols express the following business rules:

1. A SUPPLIER may supply many ITEMs (by "may supply" we mean the supplier may not supply any items). Each ITEM is supplied by any number of SUPPLIERs (by "is supplied" we mean must be supplied by at least one supplier).

2. Each ITEM must be used in the assembly of at least one PRODUCT, and may be used in many products. Conversely, each PRODUCT must use one or more ITEMs.

3. A SUPPLIER may send many SHIPMENTs. On the other hand, each shipment must be sent by exactly one SUPPLIER. Notice that sends and supplies are separate concepts. A SUPPLIER may be able to supply an item, but may not yet have sent any shipments of that item.

4. A SHIPMENT must include one (or more) ITEMs. An ITEM may be included on several SHIPMENTs.

5. A CUSTOMER may submit any number of ORDERs. However, each ORDER must be submitted by exactly one CUSTOMER.

6. An ORDER must request one (or more) PRODUCTs. A given PRODUCT may not be requested on any ORDER, or may be requested on one or more orders.

Note that each of these business rules roughly follows a certain grammar:

<entity> <minimum cardinality> <relationship> <maximum cardinality> <entity>

For example, rule 5 is:

<CUSTOMER> <may> <submit> <any number> <ORDER>

This grammar gives you a standard way to put each relationship into a natural English business rule statement.

E-R Model Notation

The basic notation we use for E-R diagrams is shown in Figure 3-2. As indicated in the previous section, there is no industry standard notation (in fact, you saw a slightly simpler notation in Chapters 1 and 2). However, we believe that the notation in Figure 3-2 combines most of the desirable features of the different notations that are commonly used, and also allows us to accurately model most situations that are encountered in practice. We introduce additional notation for enhanced entity-relationship models (including class-subclass relationships) in Chapter 4. Appendix A illustrates the E-R notation from several commonly used guidelines and diagramming tools. This appendix may help you to translate between the notation in the text and the notation you use in classes.

ENTITY-RELATIONSHIP MODEL CONSTRUCTS

The basic constructs of the entity-relationship model are entities, relationships, and attributes. As shown in Figure 3-2, the model allows numerous variations for each of these constructs. The richness of the E-R model allows designers to model

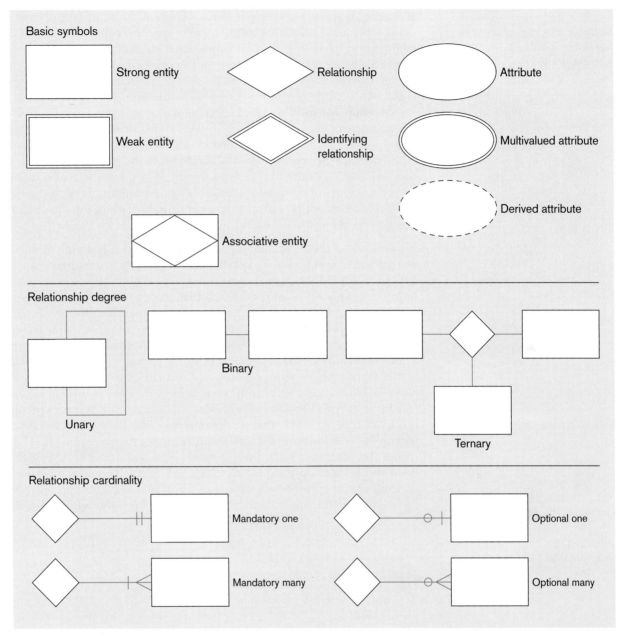

Figure 3-2
Basic E-R notation

real-world situations accurately and expressively, which helps account for the popularity of the model.

Entities

An **entity** is a person, place, object, event, or concept in the user environment about which the organization wishes to maintain data. Some examples of each of these *types* of entities follow:

Person: EMPLOYEE, STUDENT, PATIENT
Place: STORE, WAREHOUSE, STATE
Object: MACHINE, BUILDING, AUTOMOBILE
Event: SALE, REGISTRATION, RENEWAL
Concept: ACCOUNT, COURSE, WORK CENTER

Entity: A person, place, object, event, or concept in the user environment about which the organization wishes to maintain data.

Entity type: A collection of entities that share common properties or characteristics.

Entity instance: A single occurrence of an entity type.

Entity Type Versus Entity Instance There is an important distinction between entity types and entity instances. An **entity type** is a collection of entities that share common properties or characteristics. Each entity type in an E-R model is given a name. Since the name represents a collection (or set) of items, it is always singular. We use capital letters for names of entity type(s). In an E-R diagram the entity name is placed inside the box representing the entity type (see Figure 3-1).

An **entity instance** is a single occurrence of an entity type. Figure 3-3 illustrates the distinction between an entity type and two of its instances. An entity type is described just once (using metadata) in a database, while many instances of that entity type may be represented by data stored in the database. For example, there is one EMPLOYEE entity type in most organizations, but there may be hundreds (or even thousands) of instances of this entity type stored in the database. We often use the single term "entity" rather than entity instance, when the meaning is clear from the context of our discussion.

Entity Type Versus System Input, Output, or User A common mistake made when you are just learning to draw E-R diagrams, especially if you already are familiar with data process modeling (such as data flow diagramming), is to confuse data entities with other elements of an overall information systems model. A simple rule to avoid such confusion is that a true data entity will have many possible instances, each with a distinguishing characteristic, as well as one or more other descriptive pieces of data.

Consider Figure 3-4a, which might be drawn to represent a database needed for a college sorority's expense system. In this situation, the sorority treasurer manages accounts, receives expense reports, and records expense transactions against each account. However, do we need to keep track of data about the Treasurer (the TREASURER entity type) and her supervision of accounts (the Manages relationship) and receipt of reports (the Receives relationship)? The Treasurer is the person entering data about accounts and expenses and receiving expense reports. That is, she is a *user* of the database. Since there is only one Treasurer, TREASURER data do not need to be kept. Further, is the EXPENSE REPORT entity necessary? Since an expense report is computed from expense transactions and account balances, it is the result of extracting data from the database. Even though there will be multiple

Figure 3-3
Entity type (EMPLOYEE) with two instances

Entity type: EMPLOYEE

Attributes:
EMPLOYEE NUMBER	CHAR (10)
NAME	CHAR (25)
ADDRESS	CHAR (30)
CITY	CHAR (20)
STATE	CHAR (2)
ZIP	CHAR (9)
DATE HIRED	DATE
BIRTHDATE	DATE

Two Instances of EMPLOYEE:
642-17-8360	534-10-1971
Michelle Brady	David Johnson
100 Pacific Avenue	450 Redwood Drive
San Francisco	Redwood City
CA	CA
98173	97142
03-21-1992	08-16-1994
06-19-1968	09-04-1975

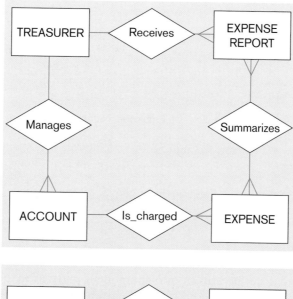

Figure 3-4
Example of inappropriate entities
(a) System user (Treasurer) and output
(Expense Report) shown as entities

(b) E-R model with only the necessary
entities

instances of expense reports given to the Treasurer over time, data needed to compute the report contents each time are already represented by the ACCOUNT and EXPENSE entity types.

Another key to understanding why the E-R diagram in Figure 3-4a might be in error is the nature of the *relationship names* Receives and Summarizes. These relationship names refer to business activities that transfer or translate data, not to simply the association of one kind of data with another kind of data. The simple E-R model in Figure 3-4b shows entities and a relationship that would be sufficient to handle the sorority expense system as described here.

Strong Versus Weak Entity Types Most of the basic entity types to identify in an organization are classified as strong entity types. A **strong entity type** is one that exists independently of other entity types. Examples include STUDENT, EMPLOYEE, AUTOMOBILE, and COURSE. Instances of a strong entity type always have a unique characteristic (called an *identifier*)—that is, an attribute or combination of attributes that uniquely distinguish each occurrence of that entity.

In contrast, a **weak entity type** is an entity type whose existence depends on some other entity type. A weak entity type has no business meaning in the E-R diagram without the entity on which it depends. The entity type on which the weak entity type depends is called the **identifying owner** (or simply **owner** for short). A weak entity type does not have its own identifier. Generally on an E-R diagram a weak entity type has an attribute that serves as a *partial* identifier. During a later design stage (described in Chapter 5), a full identifier will be formed for the weak entity by combining the partial identifier with the identifier of its owner.

An example of a weak entity type with an identifying relationship is shown in Figure 3-5. EMPLOYEE is a strong entity type with identifier Employee_ID (we note the identifier attribute by underlining it). DEPENDENT is a weak entity type, as indicated by the double-lined rectangle. The relationship between a weak entity type and its owner is called an **identifying relationship**. In Figure 3-5, "Has" is the identifying relationship (indicated by the double-lined diamond symbol). The attribute Dependent_Name serves as a *partial* identifier (Dependent_Name is a composite attribute

Strong entity type: An entity that exists independently of other entity types.

Weak entity type: An entity type whose existence depends on some other entity type.

Identifying owner: The entity type on which the weak entity type depends.

Identifying relationship: The relationship between a weak entity type and its owner.

Figure 3-5
Example of a weak entity and its
identifying relationship

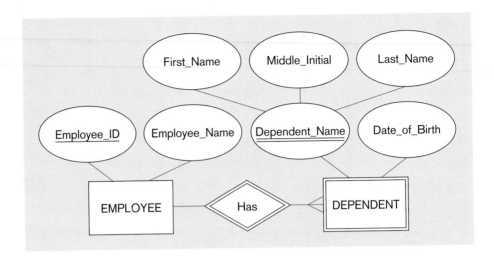

that can be broken into component parts, as we describe below); we use a double underline to indicate a partial identifier. During a later design stage, Dependent_Name will be combined with Employee_ID (the identifier of the owner) to form a full identifier for DEPENDENT.

Naming and Defining Entity Types In addition to the general guidelines for naming and defining data objects, there are a few special guidelines for naming entity types, which follow:

- An entity type name is a *singular noun* (such as CUSTOMER, STUDENT, or AUTOMOBILE); an entity is a person, place, object, event, or concept and the name is for the entity type, which represents *a set* of entity instances (i.e., STUDENT represents students Hank Finley, Jean Krebs, and so forth). It is common to also specify the plural form (possibly in a CASE tool repository accompanying the E-R diagram) because sometimes the E-R diagram is read best by using plurals. For example, in Figure 3-1, we would say that a SUPPLIER may supply ITEMs. Because plurals are not always formed by adding an "s" to the singular noun, it is best to document the exact plural form.

- An entity type name should be *specific to the organization*. Thus, one organization may use the entity type name CUSTOMER and another organization may use the term CLIENT. The name should be descriptive for the organization and distinct from all other entity type names within that organization. For example, a PURCHASE ORDER for orders placed with suppliers is distinct from CUSTOMER ORDER for orders placed with us by our customers. Both of these entity types cannot be named ORDER.

- An entity type name should be *concise*, using as few words as possible. For example, in a university database, an entity type REGISTRATION for the event of a student registering for a class is probably a sufficient name for this entity type; STUDENT REGISTRATION FOR CLASS, although precise, is probably too wordy since the reader will understand REGISTRATION from its use with other entity types.

- An *abbreviation or short name* should be specified for each entity type name, and the abbreviation may be sufficient to use in the E-R diagram; abbreviations must follow all of the same rules as do the full entity names.

- *Event entity types* should be named for the *result of the event*, not the activity or process of the event. For example, the event of a project manager assigning an employee to work on a project results in an ASSIGNMENT, and the event of a student contacting his or her faculty adviser seeking some information is a CONTACT.

- The *name* used for the same entity type *should be the same* on all E-R diagrams on which the entity type appears. Thus, as well as being specific to the organization, the name used for an entity type should be a standard, adopted by the organization for all references to the same kind of data. However, some entity types will have *aliases*, or alternative names, which are synonyms used in different parts of the organization. For example, the entity type ITEM may have aliases of MATERIAL (for production) and DRAWING (for engineering). Aliases are specified in documentation about the database, such as the repository of a CASE tool.

There are also some specific guidelines for defining entity types, which follow:

- An entity type definition usually *starts with* "An X is . . . ." This is the most direct and clear way to state the meaning of an entity type.

- An entity type definition should include a statement of *what the unique characteristic is for each instance* of the entity type. In many cases, stating the identifier for an entity type helps to convey the meaning of the entity. For example, for Figure 3-4b, "An expense is a payment of the purchase of some good or service. An expense is identified by a journal entry number."

- An entity type definition should make it clear *what entity instances are included and not included* in the entity type; often, it is necessary to list the kinds of entities that are excluded. For example, "A customer is a person or organization that has placed an order for a product from us or one that we have contacted to advertise or promote our products. A customer does not include persons or organizations that buy our products only through our customers, distributors, or agents."

- An entity type definition often includes a description of *when an instance of the entity type is created and deleted*. For example, in the previous bullet point, a customer instance is implicitly created when the person or organization places its first order; since this definition does not specify otherwise, implicitly a customer instance is never deleted or it is deleted based on general rules that are specified about the purging of data from the database. A statement about when to delete an entity instance is sometimes referred to as the retention of the entity type. A possible deletion statement for a customer entity type definition might be "A customer ceases to be a customer if it has not placed an order for more than three years."

- For some entity types, the definition must specify *when an instance might change into an instance of another entity type*. For example, consider the situation of a construction company for which bids accepted by potential customers become contracts. In this case, a bid might be defined by "A bid is a legal offer by our organization to do work for a customer. A bid is created when an officer of our company signs the bid document; a bid becomes an instance of contract when we receive a copy of the bid signed by an officer of the customer." This definition is also a good example to note how one definition can use other entity type names (in this case, the definition of bid uses the entity type name Customer).

- For some entity types, the definition must specify *what history is to be kept about instances of the entity type*. For example, the characteristics of an ITEM in Figure 3–1 may change over time, and we may need to keep a complete history of the individual values and when they were in effect. As we will see in some examples later, such statements about keeping history may have ramifications about how we represent the entity type on an E-R diagram and eventually how we store data for the entity instances.

Attributes

Attribute: A property or characteristic of an entity type that is of interest to the organization.

Each entity type has a set of attributes associated with it. An **attribute** is a property or characteristic of an entity type that is of interest to the organization. Following are some typical entity types and their associated attributes:

STUDENT   Student_ID, Student_Name, Home_Address, Phone_Number, Major

AUTOMOBILE Vehicle_ID, Color, Weight, Horsepower

EMPLOYEE   Employee_ID, Employee_Name, Payroll_Address, Skill

In naming attributes, we use an initial capital letter followed by lowercase letters. If an attribute name consists of two words, we use an underscore character to connect the words and we start each word with a capital letter; for example: Employee_Name. In E-R diagrams, we represent an attribute by placing its name in an ellipse with a line connecting it to its associated entity. Attributes may also be associated with relationships, as described below. Note that an attribute is associated with exactly one entity or relationship.

Notice in Figure 3-5 that all of the attributes of DEPENDENT are characteristics only of an employee's dependent, not characteristics of an employee. An entity type (not just weak entities but any entity) does not include attributes of entities to which it is related (what might be called foreign attributes). For example, DEPENDENT does not include any attribute that indicates to which employee this dependent is associated. This nonredundant feature of the E-R data model is consistent with the shared data property of databases. Because of relationships, which we discuss shortly, someone accessing data from a database will be able to associate attributes from related entities (e.g., show on a display screen a Dependent_Name and the associated Employee_Name).

Each entity (or instance of an entity type) has a value associated with each of the attributes of that entity type. For example, Figure 3-6 shows two entities with their respective attribute values. A database is, in essence, the collection of all of these attribute values for all of the entities. Thus, each entity has an identifying attribute plus one or more other attributes. If you try to create an entity that has only an identifier, then that entity is likely not legitimate. Such a data structure may simply hold a list of legal values for some attribute, which is better kept outside the database.

Figure 3-6
Two entity instances with attribute values

Entity 1

Student_ID = 638124289
Student_Name = Allison Smith
Home_Address = 482 Walnut St.
                          Denver CO 86391
Phone = 303-839-1479
Major = Psychology

Entity 2

Student_ID = 726153972
Student_Name = Cedric Thomas
Home_Address = 944 Maple St.
                          Houston, TX 51269
Phone = 631-347-9847
Major = English

Simple Versus Composite Attributes Some attributes can be broken down into meaningful component parts. The most common example is Address, which can usually be broken down into the following components: Street_Address, City, State, and Postal_Code. A **composite attribute** is an attribute (such as Address) that can be broken down into component parts. Figure 3-7 shows the notation that we use for composite attributes applied to this example. The component attributes may appear above or below the composite attribute on an E-R diagram.

Composite attributes provide considerable flexibility to users, who can either refer to the composite attribute as a single unit or else refer to individual components of that attribute. Thus, for example, a user can either refer to Address or refer to one of its components, such as Street_Address. The decision whether to subdivide an attribute into its component parts depends on whether users will need to refer to those individual components. Of course, the designer must always attempt to anticipate possible future usage patterns for the database.

A **simple** (or **atomic**) **attribute** is an attribute that cannot be broken down into smaller components. For example, all of the attributes associated with AUTOMOBILE are simple: Vehicle_ID, Color, Weight, and Horsepower.

Single-Valued Versus Multivalued Attributes Figure 3-6 shows two entities with their respective attribute values. For each entity instance, each of the attributes in the figure has one value. It frequently happens that there is an attribute that may have more than one value for a given instance. For example, the EMPLOYEE entity type in Figure 3-8 has an attribute named Skill, whose values record the skill (or skills) for that employee. Of course, some employees may have more than one skill (such as COBOL Programmer and C++ Programmer). A **multivalued attribute** is an attribute that may take on more than one value for a given entity instance. We indicate a multivalued attribute with an ellipse with double lines, as shown for the Skill attribute in the EMPLOYEE example in Figure 3-8.

Stored Versus Derived Attributes Some attribute values that are of interest to users can be calculated or derived from other related attribute values that are stored in the database. For example, suppose that for an organization, the EMPLOYEE entity type has a Date_Employed attribute. If users need to know how many years a person has been employed, that value can be calculated using Date_Employed and today's date. A **derived attribute** is an attribute whose values can be calculated from related attribute values (plus possibly data not in the database, such as today's date, the current time, or a security code provided by a system user). We indicate a derived attribute in an E-R diagram by using an ellipse with a dashed line, as shown in Figure 3-8.

Composite attribute: An attribute that can be broken down into component parts.

Simple attribute: An attribute that cannot be broken down into smaller components.

Multivalued attribute: An attribute that may take on more than one value for a given entity instance.

Derived attribute: An attribute whose values can be calculated from related attribute values.

Figure 3-7
A composite attribute

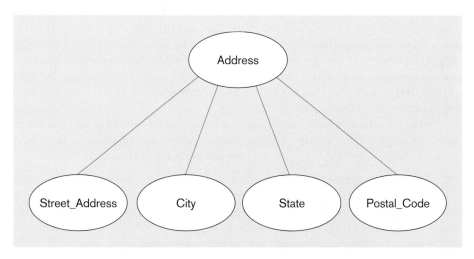

Figure 3-8
Entity with multivalued attribute (Skill)
and derived attribute (Years_Employed)

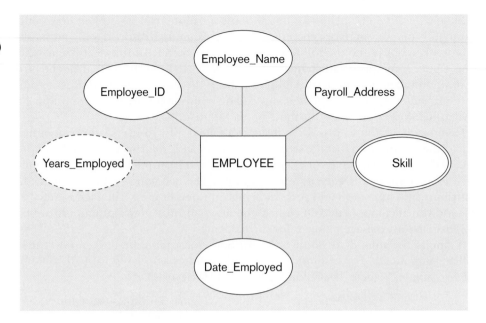

In some situations the value of an attribute can be derived from attributes in related entities. For example, consider the invoice created for each customer at Pine Valley Furniture Company (see Figure 1–6). Order_Total is an attribute of the INVOICE entity, which indicates the total dollar amount that is billed to the customer. The value of Order_Total can be computed by summing the Extended_Price values for the various line items that are billed on the invoice. Formulas for computing values such as this are one type of business rule.

Identifier: An attribute (or combination of attributes) that uniquely identifies individual instances of an entity type.

Identifier Attribute An **identifier** is an attribute (or combination of attributes) that uniquely identifies individual instances of an entity type. The identifier for the STUDENT entity type introduced earlier is Student_ID, while the identifier for AUTOMOBILE is Vehicle_ID. Notice that an attribute such as Student_Name is not a candidate identifier, since many students may potentially have the same name and students, like all people, can change their names. To be a candidate identifier, each entity instance must have a single value for the attribute and the attribute must be associated with the entity. We underline identifier names on the E-R diagram, as shown in the example in Figure 3-9a.

For some entity types, there is no single (or atomic) attribute that can serve as the identifier (that is, will ensure uniqueness). However, two (or more) attributes used in combination may serve as the identifier. A **composite identifier** is an identifier that consists of a composite attribute. Figure 3-9b shows the entity FLIGHT with the composite identifier Flight_ID. Flight_ID in turn has component attributes Flight_Number and Date. This combination is required to uniquely identify individual occurrences of FLIGHT. We use the convention that the composite attribute (Flight_ID) is underlined to indicate it is the identifier, while the component attributes are not underlined.

Composite identifier: An identifier that consists of a composite attribute.

Some entities may have more than one candidate identifier. If there is more than one candidate identifier, the designer must choose one of them as the identifier. Bruce (1992) suggests the following criteria for selecting identifiers:

1. Choose an identifier that will not change its value over the life of each instance of the entity type. For example, the combination of Employee_Name and Payroll_Address (even if unique) would be a poor choice as an identifier for EMPLOYEE because the values of Employee_Name and Payroll_Address could easily change during an employee's term of employment.

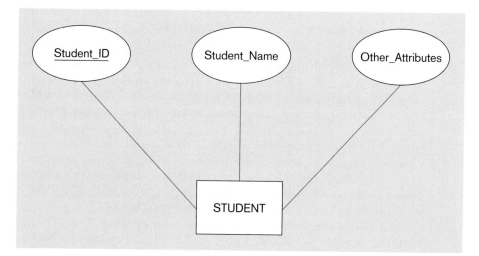

Figure 3-9
Simple and composite key attributes
(a) Simple key attribute

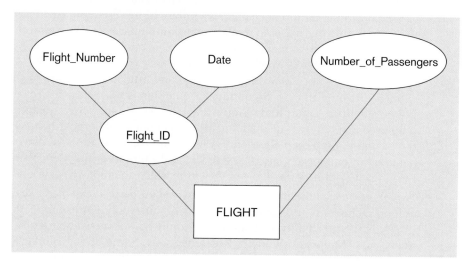

(b) Composite key attribute

2. Choose an identifier such that for each instance of the entity, the attribute is guaranteed to have valid values and not be null (or unknown). If the identifier is a composite attribute (such as Flight_ID in Figure 3-9), make sure that all parts of the identifier will have valid values.

3. Avoid the use of so-called intelligent identifiers (or keys), whose structure indicates classifications, locations, and so on. For example, the first two digits of an identifier may indicate the warehouse location. Such codes are often changed as conditions change, which renders the identifier values invalid.

4. Consider substituting single-attribute surrogate identifiers for large composite identifiers. For example, an attribute called Game_Number could be used for the entity type GAME instead of the combination of Home_Team and Visiting_Team.

Naming and Defining Attributes In addition to the general guidelines for naming data objects, there are a few special guidelines for naming attributes, which follow:

• An attribute name is a *noun* (such as Customer_ID, Age, Product_Minimum_Price, or Major). Attributes, which materialize as data values, are concepts or physical characteristics of entities. Concepts and physical characteristics are described by nouns.

- An attribute name should be *unique*. No two attributes of the same entity type may have the same name, and it is desirable, for clarity purposes, that no two attributes across all entity types have the same name.

- To make an attribute name unique and for clarity purposes, *each attribute name should follow a standard format*. For example, your university may establish Student_GPA, as opposed to GPA_of_Student, as an example of the standard format for attribute naming. The format to be used will be established by each organization. A common format is: [Entity type name{[_Qualifier]}_]Class, where [. . .] is an optional clause and {. . .} indicates that the clause may repeat. *Entity type name* is the name of the entity with which the attribute is associated. The entity type name may be used to make the attribute name explicit. It is almost always used for the identifier attribute (e.g., Customer_ID) of each entity type. *Class* is a phrase from a list of phrases defined by the organization that are the permissible characteristics of entities (or abbreviations of these characteristics). For example, permissible values (and associated approved abbreviations) for Class might be Name (Nm), Identifier (ID), Date (Dt), or Amount (Amt). Class is, obviously, required. *Qualifier* is a phrase from a list of phrases defined by the organization that are used to place constraints on classes. One or more qualifiers may be needed to make each attribute of an entity type unique. For example, a qualifier might be Maximum (Max), Hourly (Hrly), or State (St). A qualifier may not be necessary: Employee_Age and Student_Major are both fully explicit attribute names. Sometimes a qualifier is necessary. For example, Employee_Birth_Date and Employee_Hire_Date are two attributes of Employee that require one qualifier. More than one qualifier may be necessary. For example, Employee_Residence_City_Name (or Emp_Res_Cty_Nm) is the name of an employee's city of residence, and Employee_Tax_City_Name (or Emp_Tax_Cty_Nm) is the name of the city in which an employee pays city taxes.

- *Similar attributes* of different entity types *should use the same qualifiers and classes*, as long as those are the names used in the organization. For example, the city of residence for faculty and students should be, respectively, Faculty_Residence_City_Name and Student_Residence_City_Name. Using similar names makes it easier for users to understand that values for these attributes come from the same possible set of values, what we will call *domains*. Users may want to take advantage of common domains in queries (e.g., find students who live in the same city as their adviser), and it will be easier for users to recognize that such a matching may be possible if the same qualifier and class phrases are used.

There are also some specific guidelines for defining attributes, which follow:

- An attribute definition states *what the attribute is and possibly why it is important*. The definition will often parallel the attribute's name; for example, Student_Residence_City_Name could be defined as "The name of the city in which a student maintains his or her permanent residence."

- An attribute definition should make it clear *what is included and not included* in the attribute's value; for example, "Employee_Monthly_Salary_Amount is the amount of money paid each month in the currency of the country of residence of the employee exclusive of any benefits, bonuses, reimbursements, or special payments."

- Any *aliases*, or alternative names, for the attribute can be specified in the definition, or may be included elsewhere in documentation about the attribute, possibly stored in the repository of a CASE tool used to maintain data definitions.

- It may also be desirable to state in the definition *the source of values for the attribute*. Stating the source may make the meaning of the data clearer. For example, "Customer_Standard_Industrial_Code is an indication of the type of business for the customer. Values for this code come from a standard set of values provided by the Federal Trade Commission, and are found on a CD we purchase named SIC provided annually by the FTC."

- An attribute definition (or other specification in a CASE tool repository) also should indicate *if a value for the attribute is required or optional*. This business rule about an attribute is important for maintaining data integrity. The identifier attribute of an entity type is, by definition, required. If an attribute value is required, then to create an instance of the entity type, a value of this attribute must be provided. Required means that an entity instance must always have a value for this attribute, not just when an instance is created. Optional means that a value may not exist for an instance of an entity instance to be stored. Optional can be further qualified by stating whether once a value is entered, a value must always exist. For example, "Employee_Department_ID is the identifier of the department to which the employee is assigned. An employee may not be assigned to a department when hired (so this attribute is initially optional), but once an employee is assigned to a department, the employee must always be assigned to some department."

- An attribute definition (or other specification in a CASE tool repository) may also indicate *if a value for the attribute may change* once a value is provided and before the entity instance is deleted. This business rule also controls data integrity. Nonintelligent identifiers may not change values over time. To assign a new nonintelligent identifier to an entity instance, that instance must first be deleted and then re-created.

- For a multivalued attribute, the attribute definition should indicate *the maximum and minimum number of occurrences of an attribute value for an entity instance*. For example, "Employee_Skill_Name is the name of a skill an employee possesses. Each employee must possess at least one skill, and an employee can choose to list at most 10 skills." The reason for a multivalued attribute may be that a history of the attribute needs to be kept. For example, "Employee_Yearly_Absent_Days_Number is the number of days in a calendar year the employee has been absent from work. An employee is considered absent if he or she works less than 50 percent of the scheduled hours in the day. A value for this attribute should be kept for each year in which the employee works for our company."

- An attribute definition may also indicate any *relationships that attribute has with other attributes*. For example, "Employee_Vacation_Days_Number is the number of days of paid vacation for the employee. If the employee has a value of 'Exempt' for Employee_Type, then the maximum value for Employee_Vacation_Days_Number is determined by a formula involving the number of years of service for the employee."

RELATIONSHIPS

Relationships are the glue that holds together the various components of an E-R model. Intuitively, a *relationship* is an association among the instances of one or more entity types that is of interest to the organization. But to understand this definition more clearly we must distinguish between relationship types and relationship instances. To illustrate, consider the entity types EMPLOYEE and COURSE, where COURSE represents training courses that may be taken by employees. To track courses that have been completed by particular employees, we define a relationship called Completes between the two entity types (see Figure 3-10a). This is a many-to-many relationship, since each employee may complete any number of courses, while a given course may be completed by any number of employees. For example, in

Figure 3-10
Relationship type and instances
(a) Relationship type (Completes)

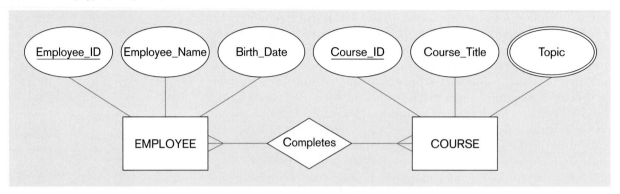

(b) Relationship instances

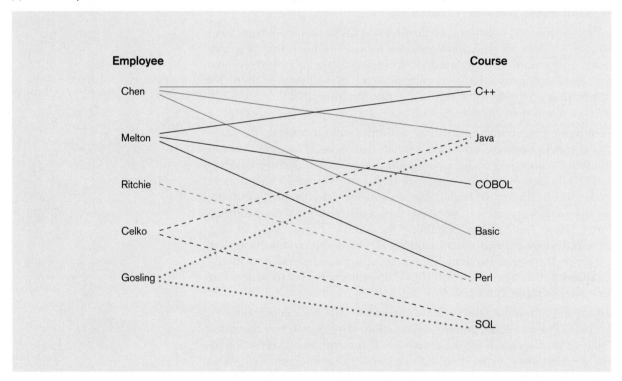

Figure 3-10b, the employee Melton has completed three courses (C++, COBOL, and Perl). The SQL course has been completed by two employees (Celko and Gosling).

In this example, there are two entity types (EMPLOYEE and COURSE) that participate in the relationship named Completes. In general, any number of entity types (from one to many) may participate in a relationship.

We use in this and subsequent chapters the convention of a diamond with a single verb phrase label to represent a relationship. Because relationships often occur because of an organizational event, entity instances are related because an action was taken; thus a verb phrase is appropriate for the label. This verb phrase should be in the present tense and descriptive. There are, however, many ways to represent a relationship. In Chapter 1 (e.g., Figure 1–3) we used another popular notation of just a line without a diamond, but with two relationship names, one for each direction of the relationship. Some data modelers prefer the format with two relationship names. These two notations have the same structural meaning, so you may use either format.

Basic Concepts and Definitions in Relationships

A **relationship type** is a meaningful association between (or among) entity types. The phrase "meaningful association" implies that the relationship allows us to answer questions that could not be answered given only the entity types. A relationship type is denoted by a diamond symbol containing the name of the relationship, as in the example shown in Figure 3-10a. We suggest you use a short, descriptive verb phrase that is meaningful to the user in naming the relationship (we say more about naming and defining relationships later in this section).

A **relationship instance** is an association between (or among) entity instances, where each relationship instance includes exactly one entity from each participating entity type (Elmasri and Navathe, 1994). For example, in Figure 3-10b, each line in the figure represents a relationship instance between one employee and one course, indicating that the employee has completed that course.

Attributes on Relationships Attributes may be associated with a many-to-many (or one-to-one) relationship, as well as with an entity. For example, suppose the organization wishes to record the date (month and year) when an employee completes each course. This attribute is named Date_Completed. For some sample data, see Table 3-2.

Where should the attribute Date_Completed be placed on the E-R diagram? Referring to Figure 3-10a, you will notice that Date_Completed has not been associated with either the EMPLOYEE or COURSE entity. That is because Date_Completed is a property of the *relationship* Completes, rather than a property of either entity. In other words, for each instance of the relationship Completes, there is a value for Date_Completed. One such instance (for example) shows that the employee named Melton completed the course titled C++ on 06/2000.

A revised version of the E-R diagram for this example is shown in Figure 3-11a. In this diagram the attribute Date_Completed is connected to the relationship symbol joining the two entities. Other attributes might be added to this relationship if appropriate, such as Course_Grade, Instructor, and Room_Location.

Associative Entities The presence of one or more attributes on a relationship suggests to the designer that the relationship should perhaps instead be represented as an entity type. An **associative entity** is an entity type that associates the instances of one or more entity types and contains attributes that are peculiar to the relationship between those entity instances. The associative entity CERTIFICATE is represented with the diamond relationship symbol enclosed within the entity box, as shown in Figure 3-11b. The purpose of this special symbol is to preserve the information that the entity was initially specified as a relationship on the E-R diagram. Associative entities are sometimes referred to as *gerunds*, since the relationship name (a verb) is usually converted to an entity name that is a noun (an -*ing* form of the verb). Note in Figure 3-11b

Relationship type: A meaningful association between (or among) entity types.

Relationship instance: An association between (or among) entity instances where each relationship instance includes exactly one entity from each participating entity type.

Associative entity: An entity type that associates the instances of one or more entity types and contains attributes that are peculiar to the relationship between those entity instances.

Table 3-2   Instances Showing Date_Completed

Employee_Name	Course_Title	Date_Completed
Chen	C++	06/2000
Chen	Java	09/2000
Chen	Basic	10/2000
Melton	C++	06/2000
Melton	COBOL	02/2001
Melton	SQL	03/2000
Ritchie	Perl	11/2000
Celko	Java	03/2000
Celko	SQL	03/2001
Gosling	Java	09/2000
Gosling	Perl	06/2000

Figure 3-11
An associative entity
(a) Attribute on a relationship

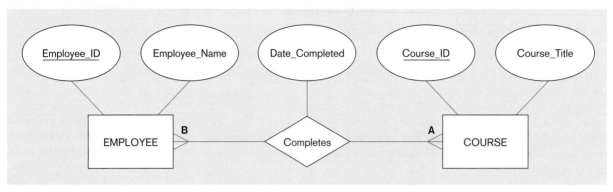

(b) An associative entity
(CERTIFICATE)

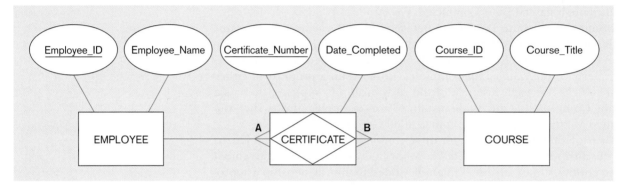

that there is no relationship diamond on the line between an associative entity and a strong entity. This is because the associative entity represents the relationship.

How do you know whether or not to convert a relationship to an associative entity type? Following are four conditions that should exist:

1. All of the relationships for the participating entity types are "many" relationships.
2. The resulting associative entity type has independent meaning to end users, and preferably can be identified with a single-attribute identifier.
3. The associative entity has one or more attributes, in addition to the identifier.
4. The associative entity participates in one or more relationships independent of the entities related in the associated relationship.

Figure 3-11b shows the relationship Completes converted to an associative entity type. In this case, the training department for the company has decided to award a certificate to each employee who completes a course. Thus the entity is named CERTIFICATE, which certainly has independent meaning to end users. Also, each certificate has a number (Certificate_Number) that serves as the identifier. The attribute Date_Completed is also included.

Notice that converting a relationship to an associative entity has caused the relationship notation to move. That is, the "many" cardinality now terminates at the associative entity, rather than at each participating entity type. In Figure 3-11, this shows that an employee, who may complete one or more courses (notation A in Figure 3-11a), may be awarded more than one certificate (notation A in Figure 3-11b); and that a course, which may have one or more employees complete it (notation B in Figure 3-11a), may have many certificates awarded (notation B in Figure 3-11b).

Degree of a Relationship

The **degree** of a relationship is the number of entity types that participate in that relationship. Thus, the relationship Completes is of degree 2, since there are two entity types: EMPLOYEE and COURSE. The three most common relationship degrees in E-R models are unary (degree 1), binary (degree 2), and ternary (degree 3). Higher-degree relationships are possible, but they are rarely encountered in practice, so we restrict our discussion to these three cases. Examples of unary, binary, and ternary relationships appear in Figure 3-12.

As you look at Figure 3-12, understand that any particular data model represents a specific situation, not a generalization. For example, consider the Manages relationship in Figure 3-12a. In some organizations, it may be possible for one employee

Degree: The number of entity types that participate in a relationship.

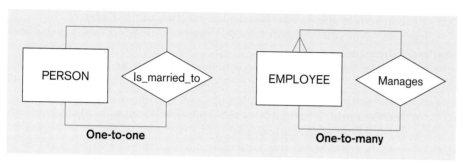

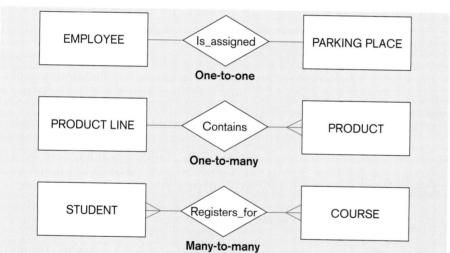

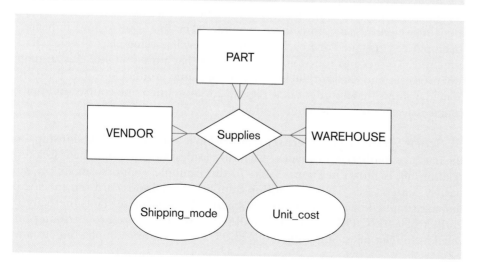

Figure 3-12
Examples of relationships of different degrees
(a) Unary relationships

(b) Binary relationships

(c) Ternary relationship

to be managed by many other employees (e.g., in a matrix organization). It is important when you develop an E-R model that you understand the business rules of the particular organization you are modeling.

Unary relationship: A relationship between the instances of a single entity type.

Unary Relationship A **unary relationship** is a relationship between the instances of a *single* entity type (unary relationships are also called *recursive* relationships). Two examples are shown in Figure 3-12a. In the first example, "Is_married_to" is shown as a one-to-one relationship between instances of the PERSON entity type. Because this is a one-to-one relationship, this notation indicates that only the current marriage, if one exists, needs to be kept about a person. In the second example, "Manages" is shown as a one-to-many relationship between instances of the EMPLOYEE entity type. Using this relationship, we could identify (for example) the employees who report to a particular manager. (*Note:* In these examples, we ignore whether these are mandatory- or optional-cardinality relationships, as shown in the notation of Figure 3-2; we will introduce these concepts in a later section of this chapter.)

Figure 3-13 shows an example of another unary relationship, called a *bill-of-materials structure*. Many manufactured products are made of assemblies, which in turn are composed of subassemblies and parts, and so on. As shown in Figure 3-13a, we can represent this structure as a many-to-many unary relationship. In this figure, the entity type ITEM is used to represent all types of components, and we use "Has_components" for the name of the relationship type that associates lower-level items with higher-level items.

Two occurrences of this bill-of-materials structure are shown in Figure 3-13b. Each of these diagrams shows the immediate components of each item as well as the quantities of that component. For example, item X consists of item U (quantity 3) and item V (quantity 2). You can easily verify that the associations are in fact many-to-many. Several of the items have more than one component type (for example, item A has three immediate component types: V, X, and Y). Also, some of the components are used in several higher-level assemblies. For example, item X is used in both item A and item B. The many-to-many relationship guarantees that, for example, the same subassembly structure of X is used each time item X goes into making some other item.

The presence of the attribute Quantity on the relationship suggests that the analyst consider converting the relationship "Has_components" to an associative entity. Figure 3-13c shows the entity type BOM_STRUCTURE, which forms an association between instances of the ITEM entity type. A second attribute (named Effective_Date) has been added to BOM_STRUCTURE to record the date when this component was first used in the related assembly. Effective dates are often needed when a history of valves is required.

Binary relationship: A relationship between the instances of two entity types.

Binary Relationship A **binary relationship** is a relationship between the instances of two entity types and is the most common type of relationship encountered in data modeling. Figure 3-12b shows three examples. The first (one-to-one) indicates that an employee is assigned one parking place, and each parking place is assigned to one employee. The second (one-to-many) indicates that a product line may contain several products, and each product belongs to only one product line. The third (many-to-many) shows that a student may register for more than one course, and that each course may have many student registrants.

Ternary relationship: A simultaneous relationship among the instances of three entity types.

Ternary Relationship A **ternary relationship** is a *simultaneous* relationship among the instances of three entity types. A typical business situation that leads to a ternary relationship is shown in Figure 3-12c. In this example, vendors can supply various parts to warehouses. The relationship Supplies is used to record the specific parts that are supplied by a given vendor to a particular warehouse. Thus there are three entity types: VENDOR, PART, and WAREHOUSE. There are two attributes on the relationship Supplies: Shipping_Mode and Unit_Cost. For example, one instance of

Figure 3-13
Representing a bill-of-materials
structure
(a) Many-to-many relationship

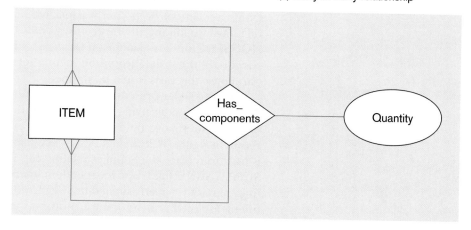

(b) Two instances

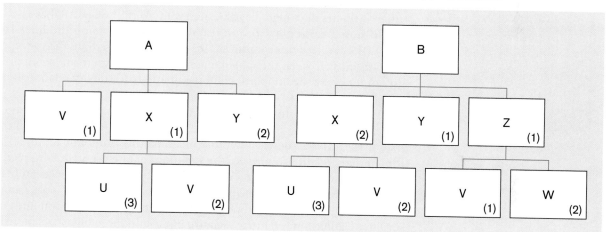

(c) Associative entity

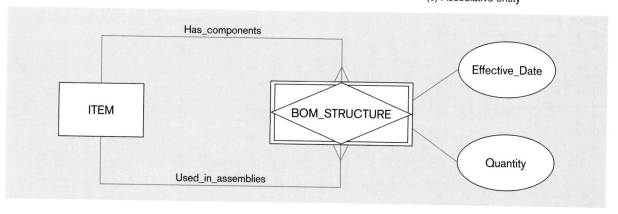

Supplies might record the fact that vendor X can ship part C to warehouse Y, that the shipping mode is next-day air, and that the cost is $5 per unit.

Note that a ternary relationship is not the same as three binary relationships. For example, Unit_Cost is an attribute of the Supplies relationship in Figure 3-12c. Unit_Cost cannot be properly associated with any one of the three possible binary relationships among the three entity types (such as that between PART and WAREHOUSE). Thus, for example, if we were told that vendor X can ship part C for a unit cost of $8, those data would be incomplete since they would not indicate to what warehouse the parts would be shipped.

As usual, the presence of an attribute on the relationship Supplies in Figure 3-12c suggests converting the relationship to an associative entity type. Figure 3-14 shows an alternative (and equally correct) representation of the ternary relationship shown in Figure 3-12c. In Figure 3-14, the (associative) entity type SUPPLY SCHEDULE is used to replace the Supplies relationship from Figure 3-12c. Clearly the entity type SUPPLY SCHEDULE is of independent interest to users. However, notice that an identifier has not yet been assigned to SUPPLY SCHEDULE. This is acceptable. If no identifier is assigned to an associative entity during E-R modeling, an identifier (or key) will be assigned during logical modeling (discussed in Chapter 6). This will be a composite identifier whose components will consist of the identifier for each of the participating entity types (in this example, PART, VENDOR, and WAREHOUSE). Can you think of other attributes that might be associated with SUPPLY SCHEDULE?

As noted earlier, we do not use diamond symbols on the lines from SUPPLY SCHEDULE to the three entities. This is because these lines do not represent binary relationships. To keep the same meaning as the ternary relationship of Figure 3-12c, we cannot break the Supplies relationship into three binary relationships, as we have already mentioned.

We strongly recommend that you convert all ternary (or higher) relationships to associative entities, as in this example. Song, Evans, and Park (1995) show that participation constraints (described in the next section) cannot be accurately represented for a ternary relationship, given the notation that we use in this chapter. However, by converting to an associative entity, the constraints can be accurately represented. Also, many E-R diagram drawing tools, including most CASE tools, cannot represent ternary relationships. So, although not semantically accurate, you must represent the ternary relationship with an associative entity and three binary relationships.

Figure 3-14
Ternary relationship as an associative entity

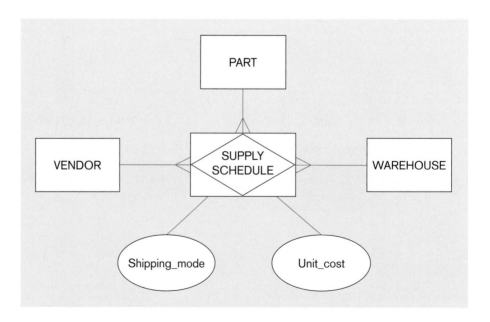

Attributes or Relationship?

Figure 3-15 includes three examples of situations when an attribute could be represented via a relationship. In Figure 3-15a, the prerequisites of a course are also courses (and a course may be a prerequisite for many other courses). Thus, prerequisite could be viewed as a unary relationship between courses, not a multivalued attribute of COURSE. Representing prerequisites via a unary relationship also means that finding the prerequisites of a course and finding the courses for which a course is prerequisite both deal with relationships between entity types. When prerequisites are a multivalued attribute of COURSE, finding the courses for which a course is prerequisite means looking for a specific value for prerequisite across all COURSE instances. In Figure 3-15b, employees have skills, but skill could be viewed instead as an entity type about which the organization wants to maintain data (the unique code to identify each skill, a descriptive title, and the type of skill [e.g., technical or managerial]). An employee has skills, but not as attributes but rather as instances of a related entity type. In the cases of Figures 3-15a and 15b, representing the data as a multivalued attribute rather than via a relationship with another entity type may, in the view of some people, simplify the diagram.

So, when *should* an attribute be linked to an entity type via a relationship? The answer is: when the attribute is the identifier or some other characteristic of an entity type in the data model and multiple entity instances need to share these same attributes. Figure 3-15c represents an example of this rule. In this example, EMPLOYEE has a composite attribute of Department. Since Department is a concept of the business, and multiple employees will share the same department data, department data could be represented (nonredundantly) in a DEPARTMENT entity type, with attributes for the data about departments all other related entity instances need to know. With this approach, not only can different employees share the storage of the same department data, but also projects (which are assigned to a department) and organizational units (which are composed of departments) can share the storage of this same department data.

Cardinality Constraints

Suppose there are two entity types, A and B, that are connected by a relationship. A **cardinality constraint** specifies the number of instances of entity B that can (or must) be associated with each instance of entity A. For example, consider a video store that rents videotapes of movies. Since the store may stock more than one videotape for each movie, this is intuitively a "one-to-many" relationship as shown in Figure 3-16a. Yet it is also true that the store may not have any tapes of a given movie in stock at a particular time (for example, all copies may be checked out). We need a more precise notation to indicate the *range* of cardinalities for a relationship. This notation was introduced in Figure 3-2, which you may want to review at this time.

Cardinality constraint: Specifies the number of instances of one entity that can (or must) be associated with each instance of another entity.

Minimum Cardinality
The **minimum cardinality** of a relationship is the minimum number of instances of entity B that may be associated with each instance of entity A. In our videotape example, the minimum number of videotapes for a movie is zero. When the minimum number of participants is zero, we say that entity type B is an *optional* participant in the relationship. In this example, VIDEOTAPE is an optional participant in the "Is_stocked_as" relationship. This fact is indicated by the symbol zero through the arrow near the VIDEOTAPE entity in Figure 3-16b.

Minimum cardinality: The minimum number of instances of one entity that may be associated with each instance of another entity.

Maximum Cardinality
The **maximum cardinality** of a relationship is the maximum number of instances of entity B that may be associated with each instance of entity A. In the video example, the maximum cardinality for the VIDEOTAPE entity type is "many"—that is, an unspecified number greater than one. This is indicated by the "crow's foot" symbol on the arrow next to the VIDEOTAPE entity symbol in Figure 3-16b.

Maximum cardinality: The maximum number of instances of one entity that may be associated with each instance of another entity.

Figure 3-15
Using relationships to link related attributes
(a) Multivalued attribute versus relationship

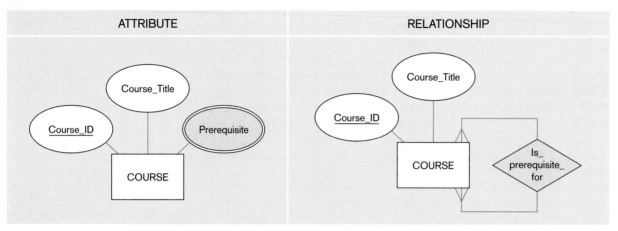

(b) Composite, multivalued attribute versus relationship

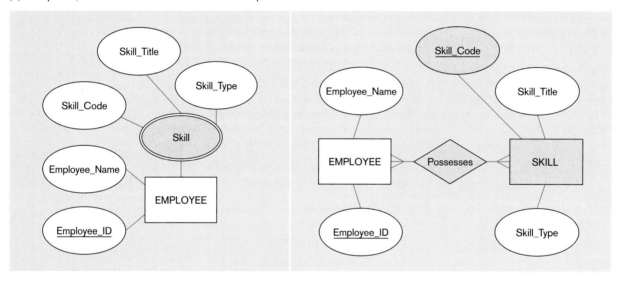

(c) Composite attribute of data shared with other entity types

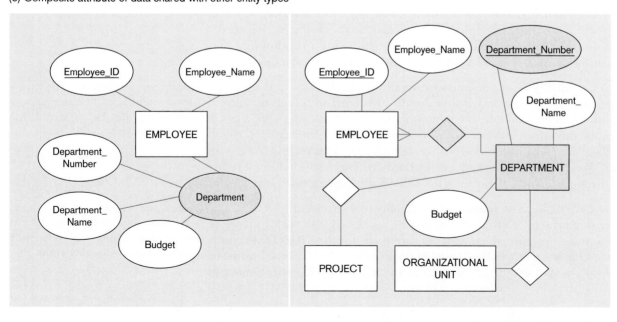

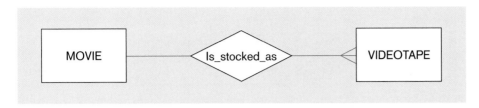

Figure 3-16
Introducing cardinality constraints
(a) Basic relationship

(b) Relationship with cardinality
constraints

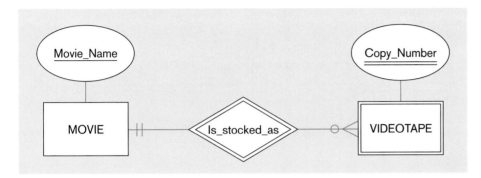

A relationship is, of course, bidirectional, so there is also cardinality notation next to the MOVIE entity. Notice that the minimum and maximum are both one (see Figure 3-16b). This is called a *mandatory one* cardinality. In other words, each videotape of a movie must be a copy of exactly one movie. In general, participation in a relationship may be optional or mandatory for the entities involved. If the minimum cardinality is zero, participation is optional; if the minimum cardinality is 1, participation is mandatory.

In Figure 3-16b, some attributes have been added to each of the entity types. Notice that VIDEOTAPE is represented as a weak entity. This is because a videotape cannot exist unless the owner movie also exists. The identifier of MOVIE is Movie_Name. VIDEOTAPE does not have a unique identifier. However, Copy_Number is a *partial* identifier, which, together with Movie_Name, would uniquely identify an instance of VIDEOTAPE.

Some Examples Examples of three relationships that show all possible combinations of minimum and maximum cardinalities appear in Figure 3-17. Each example states the business rule for each cardinality constraint, and shows the associated E-R notation. Each example also shows some relationship instances to clarify the nature of the relationship. You should study each of these examples carefully. Following are the business rules for each of the examples in Figure 3-17:

1. PATIENT Has PATIENT HISTORY (Figure 3-17a). Each patient has one or more patient histories (the initial patient visit is always recorded as an instance of PATIENT HISTORY). Each instance of PATIENT HISTORY "belongs to"' exactly one PATIENT.

2. EMPLOYEE Is_assigned_to PROJECT (Figure 3-17b). Each PROJECT has at least one EMPLOYEE assigned to it (some projects have more than one). Each EMPLOYEE may or (optionally) may not be assigned to any existing PROJ-ECT (e.g., employee "Pete"), or may be assigned to one or more PROJECTs.

3. PERSON Is_married_to PERSON (Figure 3-17c). This is an optional zero or one cardinality in both directions, since a person may or may not be married.

It is possible for the maximum cardinality to be a fixed number, not an arbitrary "many" value. For example, suppose corporate policy states that an employee may work on at most five projects at the same time. We could show this business rule by placing a 5 above or below the crow's foot next to the PROJECT entity in Figure 3-17b.

Figure 3-17
Examples of cardinality constraints
(a) Mandatory cardinalities

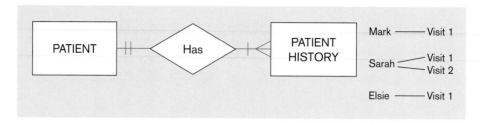

(b) One optional, one mandatory
cardinality

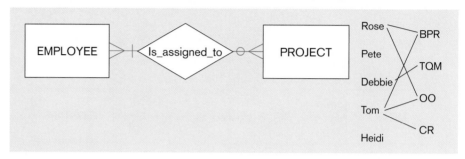

(c) Optional cardinalities

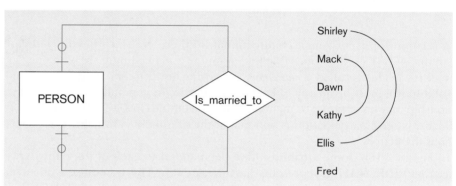

A Ternary Relationship We showed the ternary relationship with the associative entity type SUPPLY SCHEDULE in Figure 3-14. Now let's add cardinality constraints to this diagram, based on the business rules for this situation. The E-R diagram, with the relevant business rules, is shown in Figure 3-18. Notice that PART and WARE-HOUSE are mandatory participants in the relationship, while VENDOR is an optional participant. The cardinality at each of the participating entities is mandatory one, since each SUPPLY SCHEDULE instance must be related to exactly one instance of each of these participating entity types.

As noted earlier, a ternary relationship is not equivalent to three binary relationships. Unfortunately, you are not able to draw ternary relationships with many CASE tools; instead, you are forced to represent ternary relationships as three binaries. If you are forced to do this, then do not draw the binary relationships with diamonds, and be sure to make the cardinality next to the three strong entities mandatory one.

Modeling Time-Dependent Data

Database contents vary over time. For example, in a database that contains product information, the unit price for each product may be changed as material and labor costs and market conditions change. If only the current price is required, then Price can be modeled as a single-valued attribute. However for accounting, billing, and other purposes, we are likely to need to preserve a history of the prices and the time period over which each was in effect. As Figure 3-19 shows, we can conceptualize this requirement as a series of prices and the effective date for each price. This

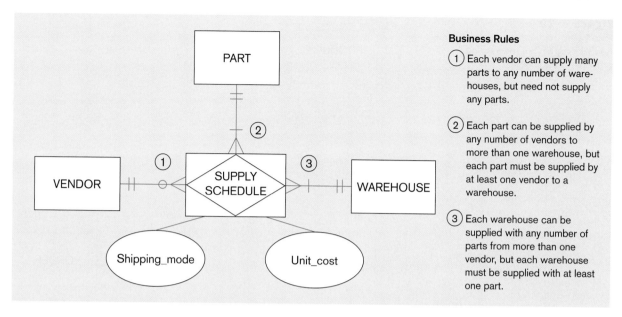

1. Each vendor can supply many parts to any number of warehouses, but need not supply any parts.

2. Each part can be supplied by any number of vendors to more than one warehouse, but each part must be supplied by at least one vendor to a warehouse.

3. Each warehouse can be supplied with any number of parts from more than one vendor, but each warehouse must be supplied with at least one part.

Figure 3-18
Cardinality constraints in a ternary relationship

results in the (composite) multivalued attribute named Price_History. The components of Price_History are Price and Effective_Date. An important characteristic of such a composite, multivalued attribute is that the component attributes go together. Thus, in Figure 3-19, each Price is paired with the corresponding Effective_Date.

In Figure 3-19, each value of the attribute Price is time stamped with its effective date. A **time stamp** is simply a time value (such as date and time) that is associated with a data value. A time stamp may be associated with any data value that changes over time when we need to maintain a history of those data values. Time stamps may be recorded to indicate the time the value was entered (transaction time), the time the value becomes valid or stops being valid, or the time when critical actions were performed (such as updates, corrections, or audits).

Time stamp: A time value that is associated with a data value.

The use of simple time stamping (as in the preceding example) is often adequate for modeling time-dependent data. However, time often introduces subtler complexities in data modeling. For example, Figure 3-20a represents a portion of an E-R diagram for Pine Valley Furniture Company. Each product is assigned to a product line (or related group of products). Customer orders are processed throughout the year, and monthly summaries are reported by product line and by product within product line.

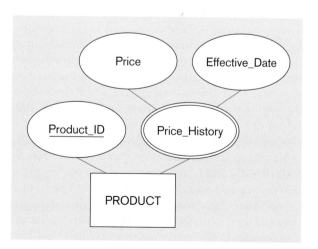

Figure 3-19
Simple example of time stamping

Figure 3-20
Pine Valley Furniture product database
(a) E-R diagram not recognizing
product reassignment

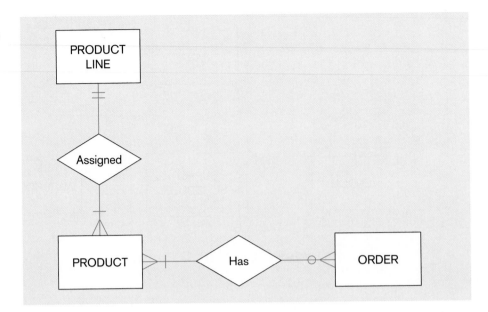

(b) E-R diagram recognizing product
reassignment

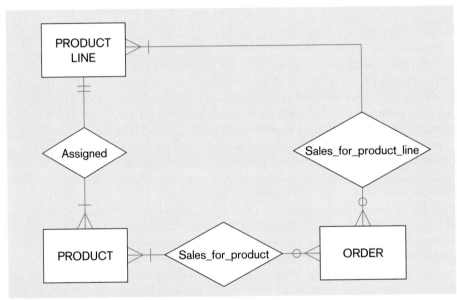

Suppose that in the middle of the year, due to a reorganization of the sales function, some products are reassigned to different product lines. The model shown in
Figure 3-20a is not designed to track the reassignment of a product to a new product
line. Thus, all sales reports will show cumulative sales for a product based on its *current* product line, rather than the one at the time of the sale. For example, a product
may have total year-to-date sales of $50,000 and be associated with product line B, yet
$40,000 of those sales may have occurred while the product was assigned to product
line A. This fact will be lost using the model of Figure 3-20a. The simple design
change shown in Figure 3-20b will correctly recognize product reassignments. A new
relationship (called Sales_for_product_line) has been added between ORDER and
PRODUCT LINE. As customer orders are processed, they are credited to both the
correct product and the correct product line as of the time of the sale.

We have discussed the problem of time-dependent data with managers in several
organizations who are considered leaders in the use of data modeling and database
management. These discussions revealed that current data models (and database
management systems based on those models) are generally inadequate in handing

time-dependent data, and that organizations often ignore this problem and hope that the resulting inaccuracies balance out. However, data warehousing applications are designed to remove many of these uncertainties by providing explicit designs for time-dependent data. You need to be alert to the complexities posed by time-dependent data as you develop data models in your organization.

Multiple Relationships

In some situations an organization may wish to model more than one relationship between the same entity types. Two examples are shown in Figure 3-21. Figure 3-21a shows two relationships between the entity types EMPLOYEE and DEPARTMENT. The relationship Works_in associates employees with the department in which they work. This relationship is one-to-many and is mandatory in both directions. That is, a department must have at least one employee who works there (perhaps the department manager), and each employee must be assigned to exactly one department. (*Note:* These are specific business rules we assume for this illustration. It is crucial when you develop an E-R diagram for a particular situation that you understand the business rules that apply for that setting. For example, if EMPLOYEE were to include retirees, then each employee may not be currently assigned to exactly one department; further, the E-R model in Figure 3-21a assumes that the organization needs to remember in which DEPARTMENT each EMPLOYEE currently works, rather than remembering the history of department assignments. Again, the structure of the data model reflects the information the organization needs to remember.)

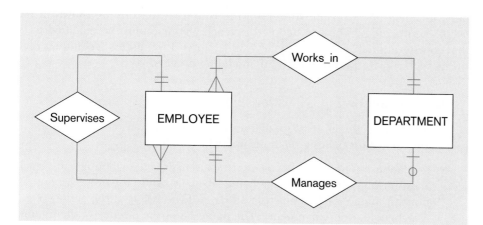

Figure 3-21
Examples of multiple relationships
(a) Employees and departments

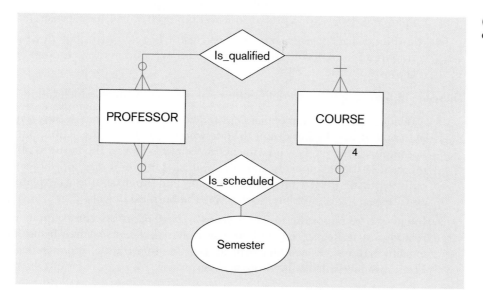

(b) Professors and courses (fixed upon constraint)

The second relationship between EMPLOYEE and DEPARTMENT (named "Manages") associates each department with the employee who manages that department. The relationship from DEPARTMENT to EMPLOYEE is mandatory one, indicating that a department must have exactly one manager. From EMPLOYEE to DEPARTMENT the relationship is optional one since a given employee either is or is not a department manager.

Figure 3-21a also shows the unary relationship Supervises that associates each employee with his or her supervisor, and vice versa. This relationship records the business rule that each employee must have exactly one supervisor. Conversely, each employee may supervise any number of employees, or may not be a supervisor.

The example in Figure 3-21b shows two relationships between the entity types PROFESSOR and COURSE. The relationship Is_qualified associates professors with the courses they are qualified to teach. A given course may have more than one qualified instructor, or (optionally) may not have any qualified instructors. This might happen (for example) if the course is new and has just been entered in the catalog. Conversely, each instructor must be qualified to teach at least one course (a reasonable expectation!).

The second relationship in this figure associates professors with the courses they are actually scheduled to teach during a given semester. Notice that the maximum cardinality for courses scheduled for an instructor during a semester is four. This is an example of how you can record a fixed constraint (upper or lower) on an E-R diagram. The attribute Semester (which could be a composite attribute with components Semester_Name and Year) is on the relationship Is_scheduled.

The E-R diagram in Figure 3-21b captures the basic cardinality constraints. Often, however, there are other business rules that cannot easily be captured on a basic E-R diagram. Consider the following rule for the example shown in Figure 3-21b: An instructor who is scheduled to teach a course must be qualified to teach that course (another reasonable rule!). In Chapter 4 we discuss techniques for capturing such rules as part of the overall modeling process.

Naming and Defining Relationships

In addition to the general guidelines for naming data objects, there are a few special guidelines for naming relationships, which follow:

- A relationship name is a *verb phrase* (such as Assigned_to, Supplies, or Teaches). Relationships represent actions being taken, usually in the present tense. A relationship name states the action taken, not the result of the action (e.g., use Assigned_to, not Assignment). The name states the essence of the interaction between the participating entity types, not the process involved (e.g., use an Employee is *Assigned_to* a project, not an Employee is *Assigning* a project).

- You should *avoid vague names*, such as Has or Is_related_to. Use descriptive verb phrases, often taken from the action verbs found in the definition of the relationship.

There are also some specific guidelines for defining relationships, which follow:

- A relationship definition explains *what action is being taken and possibly why it is important*. It may be important to state who or what does the action, but it is not important to explain how the action is taken. Stating the business objects involved in the relationship is natural, but since the E-R diagram shows what entity types are involved in the relationship and other definitions explain the entity types, you do not have to describe the business objects.

- It may also be important to *give examples to clarify the action*. For example, for a relationship of Registered_for between student and course, it may be useful to explain that this covers both on-site and on-line registration, and includes registrations made during the drop/add period.

- The definition should explain any *optional participation.* You should explain what conditions lead to zero associated instances, whether this can happen only when an entity instance is first created, or whether this can happen at any time. For example, "Registered_for links a course with the students who have signed up to take the course and the courses a student has signed up to take. A course will have no students registered for it before the registration period begins, and may never have any registered students. A student will not be registered for any courses before the registration period begins, and may not register for any classes (or may register for classes and then drop any or all classes)."

- A relationship definition should also *explain the reason for any explicit maximum cardinality* other than many. For example, "Assigned_to links an employee with the projects to which that employee is assigned and the employees assigned to a project. Due to our labor union agreement, an employee may not be assigned to more than four projects at a given time." This example, typical of many upper bound business rules, suggests that maximum cardinalities tend not to be permanent. In this example, the next labor union agreement could increase or decrease this limit. Thus, the implementation of maximum cardinalities must be done to allow changes.

- A relationship definition should *explain any mutually exclusive relationships.* Mutually exclusive relationships are ones for which an entity instance can participate in only one of several alternative relationships. We will show examples of this situation in Chapter 4. For now, consider the following example: "Plays_on links an intercollegiate sports team with its student players and indicates on which teams a student plays. Students who play on intercollegiate sports teams cannot also work in a campus job (that is, a student cannot be linked to both an intercollegiate sports team via Plays_on as well as a campus job via the Works_on relationship)." Another example of a mutually exclusive restriction is when an employee cannot both be Supervised_by and be Married_to the same employee.

- A relationship definition should *explain any restrictions on participation in the relationship.* Mutual exclusivity is one restriction, but there can be others. For example, "Supervised_by links an employee with the other employees he or she supervises and links an employee with the other employee who supervises him or her. An employee cannot supervise him- or herself, and an employee cannot supervise other employees if his or her job classification level is below 4."

- A relationship definition should *explain the extent of history that is kept in the relationship.* For example, "Assigned_to links a hospital bed with a patient. Only the current bed assignment is stored. When a patient is not admitted, that patient is not assigned to a bed, and a bed may be vacant at any given point in time." Another example of describing history for a relationship is "Places links a customer with the orders they have placed with our company and links an order with the associated customer. Only two years of orders are maintained in the database, so not all orders can participate in this relationship."

- A relationship definition should *explain whether an entity instance* involved in a relationship instance *can transfer participation to another relationship instance.* For example, "Places links a customer with the orders they have placed with our company and links an order with the associated customer. An order is not transferable to another customer." Another example is "Categorized_as links a product line with the products sold under that heading and links a product to its associated product line. Due to changes in organization structure and product design features, products may be recategorized to a different product line. Categorized_as keeps track of only the current product line to which a product is linked."

E-R MODELING EXAMPLE: PINE VALLEY FURNITURE COMPANY

Developing an entity-relationship diagram can proceed from one (or both) of two perspectives. With a top-down perspective, the designer proceeds from basic descriptions of the business, including its policies, processes, and environment. This approach is most appropriate for developing a high-level E-R diagram with only the major entities and relationships and with a limited set of attributes (such as just the entity identifiers). With a bottom-up approach, the designer proceeds from detailed discussions with users, and from a detailed study of documents, screens, and other data sources. This approach is necessary for developing a detailed, "fully attributed" E-R diagram.

In this section we develop a high-level E-R diagram for Pine Valley Furniture Company, based largely on the first of these approaches (see Figure 3-22). We reference the customer invoice (from Chapter 1) to add some detail and illustrate how the two approaches can be combined.

From a study of the business processes at Pine Valley Furniture Company, we have identified the following entity types. An identifier is also suggested for each entity, together with selected important attributes.

- The company sells a number of different furniture products. These products are grouped into several product lines. The identifier for a product is Product_ID, while the identifier for a product line is Product_Line_ID. Referring to the customer invoice (Figure 1-6), we identify the following additional attributes for product: Product_Description, Product_Finish, and Standard_Price.[1] Another attribute for product line is Product_Line_Name. A product line may group any number of products, but must group at least one product. Each product must belong to exactly one product line.

- Customers submit orders for products. The identifier for an order is Order_ID, and another attribute is Order_Date. A customer may submit any number of orders, but need not submit any orders. Each order is submitted by exactly one customer. The identifier for a customer is Customer_ID. Other attributes include Customer_Name, Customer_Address, and Postal_Code.

- A given customer order must request at least one product and only one product per order line item. Any product sold by Pine Valley Furniture may not appear on any order line item, or may appear on one or more order line items. An attribute associated with each order line item is Ordered_Quantity, which is the number of units requested.

- Pine Valley Furniture has established sales territories for its customers. Each customer does business in one or more of these sales territories. The identifier for a sales territory is Territory_ID and an attribute of a Territory_Name. A sales territory may have any number of customers, or may not have any customers doing business.

- Pine Valley Furniture Company has several salespersons. The identifier for a salesperson is Salesperson_ID. Other attributes include Salesperson_Name, Salesperson_Telephone, and Salesperson_Fax. A salesperson serves exactly one sales territory. Each sales territory is served by one or more salespersons.

---

[1] The invoice in Figure 1-6 displays the title unit price, but we chose the attribute name standard price. In the future actual unit price to a customer may be discounted, so we need to store the standard product price.

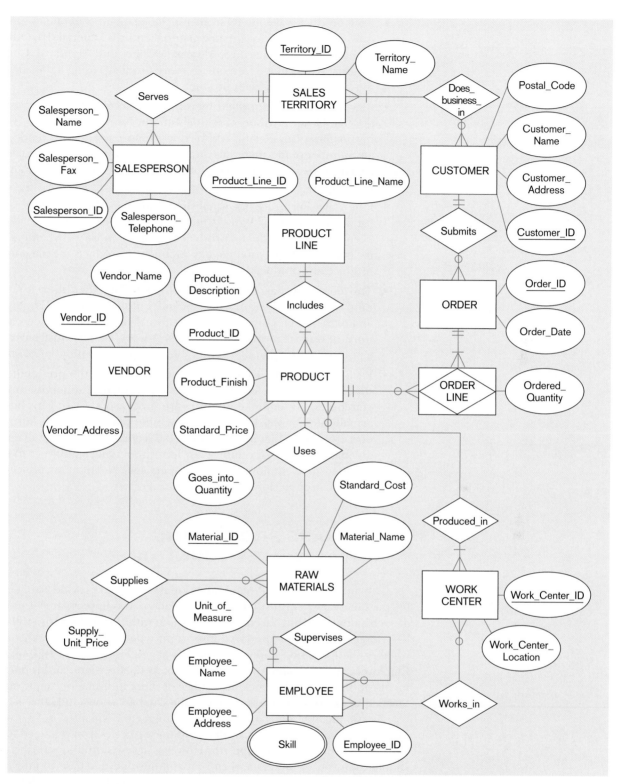

Figure 3-22
E-R diagram for Pine Valley Furniture
Company

- Each product is assembled from a specified quantity of one or more raw materials. The identifier for the raw material entity is Material_ID. Other attributes include Unit_of_Measure, Material_Name, and Standard_Cost. Each raw material is assembled into one or more products, using a specified quantity of the raw material for each product.

- Raw materials are supplied by vendors. The identifier for a vendor is Vendor_ID. Other attributes include Vendor_Name and Vendor_Address. Each raw material can be supplied by one or more vendors. A vendor may supply any number of raw materials, or may not supply any raw materials to Pine Valley Furniture. An attribute of the relationship between vendor and raw material is Supply_Unit_Price.

- Pine Valley Furniture has established a number of work centers. The identifier for a work center is Work_Center_ID. Another attribute is Work_Center_Location. Each product is produced in one or more work centers. A work center may be used to produce any number of products, or may not be used to produce any products.

- The company has over 100 employees. The identifier for employee is Employee_ID. Other attributes include Employee_Name, Employee_Address, and Skill. An employee may have more than one skill. Each employee may work in one or more work centers. A work center must have at least one employee working in that center, but may have any number of employees.

- Each employee has exactly one supervisor except the president, who has no supervisor. An employee who is a supervisor may supervise any number of employees, but not all employees are supervisors. (*Note:* This business rule is actually ambiguous, but the E-R diagram notation we have introduced so far obscures the ambiguity. We cannot tell from the rule or the diagram whether an employee may be a supervisor but without any employees to supervise, or whether some employees are not supervisors. Notation introduced in Chapter 4 can be used to clarify this distinction.)

DATABASE PROCESSING AT PINE VALLEY FURNITURE

The purpose of the E-R diagram in Figure 3-22 is to provide a conceptual design for the Pine Valley Furniture Company database. It is important to check the quality of such a design through frequent interaction with the persons who will use the database after it is implemented. An important type of quality check is to determine whether the E-R model can easily satisfy user requests for data and/or information. Employees at Pine Valley Furniture have many data retrieval and reporting requirements. In this section we show how a few of these information requirements can be satisfied by database processing against the database shown in Figure 3-22.

We use the SQL database processing language (explained in Chapters 7 and 8) to state these queries. To fully understand these queries, you will need to understand concepts introduced in Chapter 5. However, a few simple queries in this chapter should help you to understand the capabilities of a database to answer important organizational questions and give you a jump start toward understanding SQL queries in Chapter 5 as well as in later chapters.

Showing Product Information

Many different users have a need to see data about the products Pine Valley Furniture produces; for example, salespersons, inventory managers, and product managers. One specific need is for a salesperson who wants to respond to a request from a customer for a list of products of a certain type. An example of this query is:

List all details for the various computer desks that are stocked by the company.

The data for this query is maintained in the PRODUCT entity (see Figure 3-22). The query scans this entity and displays all the attributes for products that contain the description "Computer Desk."

The SQL code for this query is:

```
SELECT *
FROM PRODUCT
WHERE Product_Description LIKE "Computer Desk%";
```

Typical output for this query is:

Product_ID	Product_Description	Product_Finish	Standard_Price
3	Computer Desk 48"	Oak	375.00
8	Computer Desk 64"	Pine	450.00

SELECT * FROM PRODUCT says display all attributes of PRODUCT entities. The WHERE clause says to limit the display to only products whose description begins with the phrase "Computer Desk."

Showing Customer Information

Another common information need is to show data about Pine Valley Furniture customers. One specific type of person who needs this information is a territory sales manager. The following is a typical query from a territory sales manager:

List the details of customers in the Northwest sales territory.

The data for this query are maintained in the CUSTOMER entity. As we explain in Chapter 5, the attribute Territory_ID will be added to the CUSTOMER entity when the E-R diagram in Figure 3-22 is translated into a database that can be accessed via SQL. The query scans that entity and displays all attributes for customers who are in the selected territory.

The SQL code for this query is:

```
SELECT *
FROM CUSTOMER
WHERE Territory_ID = "Northwest";
```

Typical output for this query is:

Customer_ID	Customer_Name	Customer_Address	Territory_ID
5	Value Furniture	394 Rainbow Dr., Seattle, WA 97954	Northwest
9	Furniture Gallery	816 Peach Rd., Santa Clara, CA 96915	Northwest

The explanation of this SQL query is similar to the previous one.

Showing Customer Order Status

The previous two queries were relatively simple, involving data from only one table in each case. Often, data from multiple tables are needed in one information request. Although the query was simple, we did have to look through the whole database to find the entity and attributes needed to satisfy the request.

To simplify query writing and for other reasons many database management systems support creating restricted views of a database suitable for the information needs of a particular user. For queries related to customer order status, Pine Valley utilizes such a user view "orders for customers" shown in Figure 3-23a. This user view allows users to see only CUSTOMER and ORDER entities in the database, and only the attributes of these entities shown in the figure. As we explain in Chapter 5, the attribute Customer_ID will be added to the ORDER entity (as shown in Figure 3-23a). A typical order status query is:

How many orders have we received from "Value Furniture"?

We can write the SQL code for this query in several ways. The way we have chosen is to compose a query within a query, called a subquery. The query is performed in two steps. First, the subquery (or inner query) scans the CUSTOMER entity to determine the Customer_ID for the customer named "Value Furniture" (the ID for this customer is 5, as shown in the output for the previous query). Then the query (or outer query) scans the ORDER entity and counts the order instances for this customer.

Figure 3-23
Two user views for Pine Valley Furniture
(a) User View 1: Orders for customers

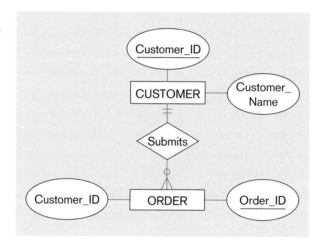

(b) User View 2: Orders for products

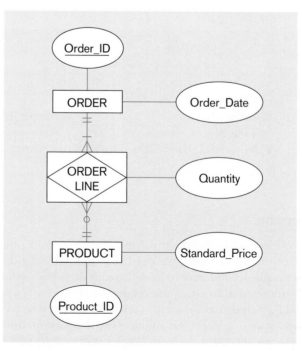

The SQL code for this query against the "orders for customer" user view is:

```
SELECT COUNT (Order_ID)
FROM ORDER
WHERE Customer_ID =
    (SELECT Customer_ID
    FROM CUSTOMER
    WHERE Customer_Name = "Value Furniture");
```

Typical output for this query is:

COUNT(Order_ID)
4

Showing Product Sales

Salespersons, territory managers, product managers, production managers, and others have a need to know the status of product sales. One kind of sales question is what products are having an exceptionally strong sales month. Typical of this question is the following query:

What products have had total sales exceeding $25,000 during the past month (June, 2001)?

This query can be written using the user view "orders for products" shown in Figure 3-23b. Data to respond to the query are obtained from the following sources:

- Order_Date from the ORDER entity (to find only orders in the desired month).

- Quantity for each product on each order from the associative entity ORDER LINE for an ORDER entity in the desired month.

- Standard_Price for the product ordered from the PRODUCT entity associated with the ORDER LINE entity.

For each item that has been ordered during the month of June 2001, the query needs to multiply Quantity times Standard_Price to get the dollar value of a sale. The total amount is then obtained for that item by summing over all orders. Data are displayed only if the total exceeds $25,000.

The SQL code for this query is beyond the scope of this chapter, since it requires techniques introduced in Chapter 5. We show this SQL query in that chapter. We introduce this query now only to suggest the power that a database such as shown in Figure 3-22 has to find information for management from detailed data. In many organizations today, users can use a Web browser to obtain information as described above. The programming code associated with a Web page then invokes the required SQL commands to obtain the requested information.

Summary

This chapter has described the fundamentals of modeling data in the organization. Business rules, derived from policies, procedures, events, functions, and other business objects, state constraints that govern the organization and, hence, how data are handled and stored. It was argued that business rules are a powerful way to describe the requirements for an information system, especially a database. The power of business rules results from business rules being core concepts of the business, being able to be expressed in terms familiar to end users, being highly maintainable, and being able to be enforced through automated means, many through a database. Good business rules are ones that are declarative, precise, atomic, consistent, expressible, distinct, and business-oriented.

Basic business rules are data names and definitions. This chapter explained guidelines for the clear naming and definition of data objects in a business. In terms of conceptual data modeling, names and definitions must be provided for entity types, attributes, and relationships. Other business rules may state constraints on these data objects. These constraints can be captured in a data model and associated documentation.

The data modeling notation most frequently used today is the entity-relationship data model. An E-R model is a detailed, logical representation of the data for an organization. An E-R model is usually expressed in the form of an E-R diagram, which is a graphical representation of an E-R model. The E-R model was introduced by Chen in 1976. However, at the present time there is no standard notation for E-R modeling.

The basic constructs of an E-R model are entity types, relationships, and related attributes. An entity is a person, place, object, event, or concept in the user environment about which the organization wishes to maintain data. An entity type is a collection of entities that share common properties, while an entity instance is a single occurrence of an entity type. A strong entity type is an entity that has its own identifier and can exist without other entities. A weak entity type is an entity whose existence depends on the existence of a strong entity type. Weak entities do not have their own identifier, although they normally have a partial identifier. Weak entities are identified through an identifying relationship with their owner entity type.

An attribute is a property or characteristic of an entity or relationship that is of interest to the organization. There are several types of attributes. A simple attribute is one that has no component parts. A composite attribute is an attribute that can be broken down into component parts. For example, Person_Name can be broken down into the parts First_Name, Middle_Initial, and Last_Name.

A multivalued attribute is one that can have multiple values for a single instance of an entity. For example, the attribute College_Degree might have multiple values for an individual. A derived attribute is one whose values can be calculated from other attribute values. For example, Average_Salary can be calculated from values of Salary for all employees.

An identifier is an attribute that uniquely identifies individual instances of an entity type. Identifiers should be chosen carefully to ensure stability and ease of use. Identifiers may be simple attributes, or they may be composite attributes with component parts.

A relationship type is a meaningful association between (or among) entity types. A relationship instance is an association between (or among) entity instances. The degree of a relationship is the number of entity types that participate in the relationship. The most common relationship types are unary (degree 1), binary (degree 2), and ternary (degree 3).

In developing E-R diagrams, we sometimes encounter many-to-many (and one-to-one) relationships that have one or more attributes associated with the relationship, rather than with one of the participating entity types. This suggests that we consider converting the relationship to an associative entity. This type of entity associates the instances of one or more entity types and contains attributes that are peculiar to the relationship. Associative entity types may have their own simple identifier, or they may be assigned a composite identifier during logical design.

A cardinality constraint is a constraint that specifies the number of instances of entity B that may (or must) be associated with each instance of entity A. Cardinality constraints normally specify the minimum and maximum number of instances. The possible constraints are mandatory one, mandatory many, optional one, optional many, and a specific number. The minimum cardinality constraint is also referred to as the participation constraint. A minimum cardinality of zero specifies optional participation, while a minimum cardinality of one specifies mandatory participation.

CHAPTER REVIEW

Key Terms

Associative entity	Composite attribute	Entity instance
Attribute	Composite identifier	Entity-relationship diagram
Binary relationship	Degree	(E-R diagram)
Business rule	Derived attribute	Entity-relationship model
Cardinality constraint	Entity	(E-R model)

Entity type
Fact
Identifier
Identifying owner
Identifying relationship
Maximum cardinality

Minimum cardinality
Multivalued attribute
Relationship instance
Relationship type
Simple attribute
Strong entity type

Term
Ternary relationship
Time stamp
Unary relationship
Weak entity type

Review Questions

1. Define each of the following terms:
   a. entity type
   b. entity-relationship model
   c. entity instance
   d. attribute
   e. relationship type
   f. identifier
   g. multivalued attribute
   h. associative entity
   i. cardinality constraint
   j. weak entity
   k. identifying relationship
   l. derived attribute
   m. multivalued attribute
   n. business rule

2. Match the following terms and definitions.

   _____ composite attribute
   _____ associative entity
   _____ unary relationship
   _____ weak entity
   _____ attribute
   _____ entity
   _____ relationship type
   _____ cardinality constraint
   _____ degree
   _____ identifier
   _____ entity type
   _____ ternary
   _____ bill-of-materials

   a. uniquely identifies entity instances
   b. relates instances of a single entity type
   c. specifies maximum and minimum number of instances
   d. relationship modeled as an entity type
   e. association between entity types
   f. collection of similar entities
   g. number of participating entity types in relationship
   h. property of an entity
   i. can be broken into component parts
   j. depends on the existence of another entity type
   k. relationship of degree three
   l. many-to-many unary relationship
   m. person, place, object, concept, event

3. Contrast the following terms:
   a. stored attribute; derived attribute
   b. entity type; entity instance
   c. simple attribute; composite attribitre
   d. entity type; relationship type
   e. strong entity type; weak entity type
   f. degree; cardinality

4. Give three reasons why many system designers believe that data modeling is the most important part of the system development process.

5. Give four reasons why a business rules approach is advocated as a new paradigm for specifying information systems requirements.

6. Explain where you can find business rules in an organization.

7. State six general guidelines for naming data objects in a data model.

8. State four criteria for selecting identifiers for entities.

9. State three conditions that suggest the designer should model a relationship as an associative entity type.

10. List the four types of cardinality constraints, and draw an example of each.

11. Give an example of a weak entity type, other than those described in this chapter. Why is it necessary to indicate an identifying relationship?

12. What is the degree of a relationship? List the three types of relationship degrees described in the chapter, and give an example of each.

13. Give an example (other than those described in this chapter) for each of the following:
    a. Derived attribute
    b. Multivalued attribute
    c. Composite attribute

14. Give an example of each of the following, other than those described in this chapter.
    a. Ternary relationship
    b. Unary relationship

15. Give an example of the use of effective dates as attributes of an entity.

16. State a rule that says when to extract an attribute from one entity type and place it in a linked entity type.

Problems and Exercises

1. Contrast the terms "term" and "fact" as they apply to business rules. Give an example of a business rule and indicate which are the terms and facts in that rule.

2. There is a bulleted list on pages 112 and 114 describing Figure 3-22. For each of the 10 points in the list, identify the subset of Figure 3-22 described by that point.

3. Draw an E-R diagram for each of the following situations (if you believe that you need to make additional assumptions, clearly state them for each situation):

   a. A company has a number of employees. The attributes of EMPLOYEE include Employee_ID (identifier), Name, Address, and Birthdate. The company also has several projects. Attributes of PROJECT include Project_ID (identifier), Project_Name, and Start_Date. Each employee may be assigned to one or more projects, or may not be assigned to a project. A project must have at least one employee assigned, and may have any number of employees assigned. An employee's billing rate may vary by project, and the company wishes to record the applicable billing rate (Billing_Rate) for each employee when assigned to a particular project. Do the attribute names in this description follow the guidelines for naming attributes? If not, suggest better names.

   b. A university has a large number of courses in its catalog. Attributes of COURSE include Course_Number (identifier), Course_Name, and Units. Each course may have one or more different courses as prerequisites, or may have no prerequisites. Similarly, a particular course may be a prerequisite for any number of courses, or may not be prerequisite for any other course. Provide a good definition of COURSE. Why is your definition a good one?

   c. A laboratory has several chemists who work on one or more projects. Chemists also may use certain kinds of equipment on each project. Attributes of CHEMIST include Employee_ID (identifier), Name, and Phone_No. Attributes of PROJECT include Project_ID (identi-

fier) and Start_Date. Attributes of EQUIPMENT include Serial_No and Cost. The organization wishes to record Assign_Date—that is, the date when a given equipment item was assigned to a particular chemist working on a specified project. A chemist must be assigned to at least one project and one equipment item. A given equipment item need not be assigned, and a given project need not be assigned either a chemist or an equipment item. Provide good definitions for all of the relationships in this situation.

   d. A college course may have one or more scheduled sections, or may not have a scheduled section. Attributes of COURSE include Course_ID, Course_Name, and Units. Attributes of SECTION include Section_Number and Semester_ID. Semester_ID is composed of two parts: Semester and Year. Section_Number is an integer (such as "1" or "2") that distinguishes one section from another for the same course but does not uniquely identify a section. How did you model SECTION? Why did you choose this way versus alternative ways to model SECTION?

   e. A hospital has a large number of registered physicians. Attributes of PHYSICIAN include Physician_ID (the identifier) and Specialty. Patients are admitted to the hospital by physicians. Attributes of PATIENT include Patient_ID (the identifier) and Patient_Name. Any patient who is admitted must have exactly one admitting physician. A physician may optionally admit any number of patients. Once admitted, a given patient must be treated by at least one physician. A particular physician may treat any number of patients, or may not treat any patients. Whenever a patient is treated by a physician, the hospital wishes to record the details of the treatment (Treatment_Detail). Components of Treatment_Detail include Date, Time, and Results. Did you draw more than one relationship between physician and patient? Why or why not?

4. Figure 3-24 shows a Grade Report that is mailed to students at the end of each semester. Prepare an E-R diagram reflect-

Figure 3-24
Grade Report

MILLENNIUM COLLEGE GRADE REPORT FALL SEMESTER 200X				
NAME: CAMPUS ADDRESS: MAJOR:	Emily Williams 208 Brooks Hall Information Systems	ID: 268300458		
COURSE ID	TITLE	INSTRUCTOR NAME	INSTRUCTOR LOCATION	GRADE
IS 350	Database Mgt.	Codd	B104	A
IS 465	System Analysis	Parsons	B317	B

ing the data contained in Grade Report. Assume that each course is taught by one instructor.

5. The entity type STUDENT has the following attributes: Student_Name, Address, Phone, Age, Activity, and No_of_Years. Activity represents some campus-based student activity, while No_of_Years represents the number of years the student has engaged in this activity. A given student may engage in more than one activity. Draw an E-R diagram for this situation.

6. Prepare an E-R diagram for a real estate firm that lists property for sale. Also prepare a definition for each entity type, attribute, and relationship on your diagram. The following describes this organization:
   - The firm has a number of sales offices in several states. Attributes of sales office include Office_Number (identifier) and Location.
   - Each sales office is assigned one or more employees. Attributes of employee include Employee_ID (identifier) and Employee_Name. An employee must be assigned to only one sales office.
   - For each sales office, there is always one employee assigned to manage that office. An employee may manage only the sales office to which she is assigned.
   - The firm lists property for sale. Attributes of property include Property_ID (identifier) and Location. Components of Location include Address, City, State, and Zip_Code.
   - Each unit of property must be listed with one (and only one) of the sales offices. A sales office may have any number of properties listed, or may have no properties listed.
   - Each unit of property has one or more owners. Attributes of owners are Owner_ID (identifier) and Owner_Name. An owner may own one or more units of property. An attribute of the relationship between property and owner is Percent_Owned.

7. Add minimum and maximum cardinality notation to each of the following figures, as appropriate:
   a. Figure 3-5.   d. Figure 3-12 (all parts).
   b. Figure 3-10a.   e. Figure 3-13c.
   c. Figure 3-11b.   f. Figure 3-14.

8. After completing a course in database management, you have been asked to develop a preliminary E-R diagram for a symphony orchestra. You discover the following entity types should be included:
   - CONCERT SEASON   The season during which a series of concerts will be performed. Identifier is Opening_Date, which includes Month, Day, and Year.
   - CONCERT   A given performance of one or more compositions. Identifier is Concert_Number. Another important attribute is Concert_Date, which consists of the following: Month, Day, Year, and Time. Each concert typically has more than one concert date.
   - COMPOSITION   Compositions to be performed at each concert. Identifier is Composition_ID, which consists of the following: Composer_Name and Composition_Name.

Another attribute is Movement_ID, which consists of two parts: Movement_Number and Movement_Name. Many, but not all, compositions have multiple movements.
   - CONDUCTOR   Person who will conduct the concert. Identifier is Conductor_ID. Another attribute is Conductor_Name.
   - SOLOIST   Solo artist who performs a given composition on a particular concert. Identifier is Soloist_ID. Another attribute is Soloist_Name.

During further discussions you discover the following:
   - A concert season schedules one or more concerts. A particular concert is scheduled for only one concert season.
   - A concert includes the performance of one or more compositions. A composition may be performed at one or more concerts, or may not be performed.
   - For each concert there is one conductor. A conductor may conduct any number of concerts, or may not conduct any concerts.
   - Each composition may require one or more soloists, or may not require a soloist. A soloist may perform one or more compositions at a given concert, or may not perform any composition. The symphony orchestra wishes to record the date when a soloist last performed a given composition (Date_Last_Performed).

Draw an E-R diagram to represent what you have discovered, as explained above. Identify a business rule in this description and explain how this business rule is modeled on the E-R diagram.

9. Obtain a common user view such as a credit card statement, phone bill, or some other common document. Prepare an E-R diagram for this document.

10. Draw an E-R diagram for some organization that you are familiar with—Boy Scouts/Girl Scouts, sports team, etc.

11. Draw an E-R diagram for the following situation (Batra, Hoffer, and Bostrom, 1988). Also, develop the list of words for qualifiers and classes that you use to form attribute names. Explain why you chose the words on your list.

   Projects, Inc., is an engineering firm with approximately 500 employees. A database is required to keep track of all employees, their skills, projects assigned, and departments worked in. Every employee has a unique number assigned by the firm, required to store his or her name and date of birth. If an employee is currently married to another employee of Projects, Inc., the date of marriage and who is married to whom must be stored; however, no record of marriage is required if an employee's spouse is not also an employee. Each employee is given a job title (for example, engineer, secretary, and so on). An employee does only one type of job at any given time, and we only need to retain information for an employee's current job.

   There are 11 different departments, each with a unique name. An employee can report to only one department. Each department has a phone number.

To procure various kinds of equipment, each department deals with many vendors. A vendor typically supplies equipment to many departments. We are required to store the name and address of each vendor and the date of the last meeting between a department and a vendor.

Many employees can work on a project. An employee can work on many projects (for example, Southwest Refinery, California Petrochemicals, and so on) but can only be assigned to at most one project in a given city. For each city, we are interested in its state and population. An employee can have many skills (preparing material requisitions, checking drawings, and so on), but she or he may use only a given set of skills on a particular project. (For example, an employee MURPHY may prepare requisitions for the Southwest Refinery project and prepare requisitions as well as check drawings for California Petrochemicals.) Employees use each skill that they possess in at least one project. Each skill is assigned a number, and we must store a short description of each skill. Projects are distinguished by project numbers, and we must store the estimated cost of each project.

12. Draw an E-R diagram for the following situation (state any assumptions you believe you have to make in order to develop a complete diagram): Stillwater Antiques buys and sells one-of-a-kind antiques of all kinds (for example, furniture, jewelry, china, and clothing). Each item is uniquely identified by an item number and is also characterized by a description, asking price, condition, and open-ended comments. Stillwater works with many different individuals, called clients, who sell items to and buy items from the store. Some clients only sell items to Stillwater, some only buy items, and some others both sell and buy. A client is identified by a client number and is also described by a client name and client address. When Stillwater sells an item in stock to a client, the owners want to record the commission paid, the actual selling price, sales tax (tax of zero indicates a tax exempt sale), and date sold. When Stillwater buys an item from a client, the owners want to record the purchase cost, date purchased, and condition at time of purchase.

13. Draw an E-R diagram for the following situation (state any assumptions you believe you have to make in order to develop a complete diagram): The H. I. Topi School of Business operates international business programs in 10 locations throughout Europe. The School had its first class of 9000 graduates in 1965. The School keeps track of each graduate's student number, name when a student, country of birth, current country of citizenship, current name, cur-

rent address, and the name of each major the student completed (each student has one or two majors). In order to maintain strong ties to its alumni, the School holds various events around the world. Events have a title, date, location, and type (for example, reception, dinner, or seminar). The School needs to keep track of which graduates have attended which events. For an attendance by a graduate at an event, a comment is recorded about information School officials learned from that graduate at that event. The School also keeps in contact with graduates by mail, e-mail, telephone, and fax interactions. As with events, the School records information learned from the graduate from each of these contacts. When a School official knows that he or she will be meeting or talking to a graduate, a report is produced showing the latest information about that graduate and the information learned during the past two years from that graduate from all contacts and events the graduate attended.

14. Assume that at Pine Valley Furniture each product (described by product number, description, and cost) comprises at least three components (described by component number, description, and unit of measure) and components are used to make one or many products. In addition, assume that components are used to make other components and that raw materials are also considered to be components. In both cases of components, we need to keep track of how many components go into making something else. Draw an E-R diagram for this situation, and place minimum and maximum cardinalities on the diagram.

15. Stock brokerages sell stocks and the prices are continually changing. Draw an E-R diagram that takes into account the changing nature of stock price.

16. Each semester, each student must be assigned an adviser who counsels students about degree requirements and helps students register for classes. Each student must register for classes with the help of an adviser, but if the student's assigned adviser is not available, the student may register with any adviser. We must keep track of students, the assigned adviser for each, and the name of the adviser with whom the student registered for the current term. Represent this situation of students and advisers with an E-R diagram.

17. In Figure 3-22, consider each many-to-many (M:N) relationship. For each, should it be represented as an associative entity instead. Explain. For those M:N relationships that should be associative entities, redraw that segment of the E-R diagram.

Field Exercises

1. Interview a database or systems analyst and document how he or she decides on names for data objects in data models. Does the organization in which this person works have nam-

ing guidelines? If so, describe the pattern used. If there are no guidelines, ask if your contact has ever had any problems because guidelines did not exist.

2. Visit two local small businesses, one in the service sector (such as a dry cleaner, auto repair shop, veterinarian, or bookstore) and one that manufactures tangible goods. Interview employees from these organizations to elicit from them the entities, attributes, and relationships that are commonly encountered in these organizations. Use this information to construct entity-relationship diagrams. What differences and similarities are there between the diagrams for the service- and the product-oriented companies? Does the entity-relationship diagramming technique handle both situations equally well? Why or why not?

3 Ask a database or systems analyst to give you examples of unary, binary, and ternary relationships that the analyst has dealt with personally at his or her company. Ask which is most common and why.

4. Ask a database or systems analyst in a local company to show you an E-R diagram for one of the organization's primary databases. Ask questions to be sure you understand what each entity, attribute, and relationship means. Does this organization use the same E-R notation used in this text? If not, what other or alternative symbols are used and what do these symbols mean? Does this organization model associative entities on the E-R diagram? If not, how are associative entities modeled?

5. For the same E-R diagram used in Field Exercise 4 or for a different database in the same or a different organization, identify any uses of time stamping or other means to model time-dependent data. Why are time-dependent data necessary for those who use this database? Would the E-R diagram be much simpler if it were not necessary to represent the history of attribute values?

References

Aranow, E. B. 1989. "Developing Good Data Definitions." *Database Programming & Design* 2 (8): 36–39.

Batra, D., J. A. Hoffer, and R. B. Bostrom. 1988. "A Comparison of User Performance Between the Relational and Extended Entity Relationship Model in the Discovery Phase of Database Design." *Proceedings of the Ninth International Conference on Information Systems*. Minneapolis, Nov. 30–Dec. 3: 295–306.

Bruce, T. A. 1992. *Designing Quality Databases with IDEF1X Information Models*. New York: Dorset House.

Chen, P. P.-S. 1976. "The Entity-Relationship Model—Toward a Unified View of Data." *ACM Transactions on Database Systems* 1 (March): 9–36.

Elmasri, R., and S. B. Navathe. 1994. *Fundamentals of Database Systems*. 2nd ed. Menlo Park, CA: Benjamin/Cummings.

Gottesdiener, E. 1977. "Business Rules Show Power, Promise." *Application Development Trends* 4 (3): 36–54.

Gottesdiener, E. 1999. "Turning Rules into Requirements." *Application Development Trends* 6 (7): 37–50.

GUIDE, "GUIDE Business Rules Project." Final Report, revision1.2. October, 1997.

Hoffer, J. A., J. F. George, and J. S. Valacich. 2002. *Modern Systems Analysis and Design*. 3rd ed.Upper Saddle River, NJ: Prentice Hall.

Moriarty, T. 2000. "The Right Tool for the Job." *Intelligent Enterprise* 3 (9): 68, 70–71.

Plotkin, D. 1999. "Business Rules Everywhere." *Intelligent Enterprise* 2 (4): 37–44.

Salin, T. "What's in a Name?" *Database Programming & Design* 3 (3): 55–58.

Song, I.-Y., M. Evans, and E. K. Park. 1995. "A Comparative Analysis of Entity-Relationship Diagrams." *Journal of Computer & Software Engineering* 3 (4): 427–59.

Storey, V. C. 1991. "Relational Database Design Based on the Entity-Relationship Model." *Data and Knowledge Engineering* 7 (1991): 47–83.

Teorey, T. J., D. Yang, and J. P. Fry. 1986. "A Logical Design Methodology for Relational Databases Using the Extended Entity-Relationship Model." *Computing Surveys* 18 (June): 197–221.

Von Halle, B. 1997. "Digging for Business Rules." *Database Programming & Design* 8 (11): 11–13.

Further Reading

Batini, C., S. Ceri, and S. B. Navathe. 1992. *Conceptual Database Design: An Entity-Relationship Approach*. Menlo Park, CA: Benjamin/Cummings.

Keuffel, W. 1996. "Battle of the Modeling Techniques." *DBMS* 9 (August): 83, 84, 86, 97.

Moody, D. 1996. "The Seven Habits of Highly Effective Data Modelers." *Database Programming & Design* 9 (October): 57, 58, 60–62, 64.

Teorey, T. 1999. *Database Modeling & Design*. 3rd ed. San Francisco, CA: Morgan Kaufman.

Tillman, G. 1994. "Should You Model Derived Data?" *DBMS* 7 (November): 88, 90.

Tillman, G. 1995. "Data Modeling Rules of Thumb." *DBMS* 8 (August): 70, 72, 74, 76, 80–82, 87.

Web Resources

www.adtmag.com *Application Development Trends* magazine, a leading publication on the practice of information systems development.

www.businessrulesgroup.org The Business Rules Group, formerly part of GUIDE International, formulates and supports standards about business rules.

www.guide.org SHARE is a volunteer organization that provides education, networking, and influence for the IT industry.

SHARE and GUIDE have combined; both were originally user groups for IBM Corporation customers.

www.intelligententerprise.com *Intelligent Enterprise* magazine, a leading publication on database management and related areas. This magazine is the result of combining two previous publications, *Database Programming & Design* and *DBMS*.

Project Case

PROJECT DESCRIPTION

After completing a course in database management, you have been hired as a summer intern by Mountain View Community Hospital. Your first assignment is to work as part of a team of three persons to develop a high-level E-R diagram for the hospital. You conduct interviews with a number of hospital administrators and staff to identify the key entity types for the hospital. After a short time your team has identified the following entity types:

- *Care center*—a treatment center within the hospital. Examples of care centers are maternity and emergency care. Each care center has a care center ID (identifier) and a care center name.

- *Patient*—a person who is either admitted to the hospital or is registered in an outpatient program. Each patient has a patient number (identifier) and name.

- *Physician*—a member of the hospital medical staff who may admit patients to the hospital and who may administer medical treatments. Each physician has a physician ID (identifier) and name.

- *Bed*—a hospital bed that may be assigned to a patient who is admitted to the hospital. Each bed has a bed number (identifier), a room number, and a care center ID.

- *Item*—any medical or surgical item that may be used in treating a patient. Each item has an item number (identifier), description, and unit cost.

- *Employee*—any person employed as part of the hospital staff. Each employee has an employee number and name.

- *Treatment*—any test or procedure performed by a physician on behalf of a patient. Each treatment has a treatment ID that consists of two parts: treatment number and treatment name.

The team next recorded the following information concerning relationships:

- Each hospital employee is assigned to work in one or more care centers. Each care center has at least one

employee, and may have any number of employees. The hospital records the number of hours per week that a given employee works in a particular care center.

- Each care center has exactly one employee who is designated nurse in charge for that care center.

- A given patient may or may not be assigned to a bed (since some patients are outpatients). A bed may or may not be assigned to a patient.

- A patient must be referred to the hospital by exactly one physician. A physician may refer any number of patients, or may not refer any patients.

- Physicians may perform any number of treatments on behalf of any number of patients, or may not perform any treatments. A patient may have treatments performed by any number of physicians. For each treatment performed on behalf of a given patient by a particular physician, the hospital records the following information: treatment date, treatment time, and results.

- A patient may optionally consume any number of items. A given item may be consumed by one or more patients, or may not be consumed. For each item consumed by a patient, the hospital records the following: date, time, quantity, and total cost (which can be computed by multiplying quantity times unit cost).

PROJECT QUESTIONS

1. Why would Mountain View Community Hospital want to use entity-relationship modeling to understand its data requirements? What other ways might the hospital want to model its information requirements?

2. Do there appear to be any weak entities in the description of the Mountain View Community Hospital data requirements? If so, what are they?

3. What is the significance in developing an E-R diagram for Mountain View Community Hospital to the third entry in the preceding list, which states that some

patients are assigned to a bed, but outpatients are not assigned to a bed?

4. Is Mountain View Community Hospital itself an entity type in a data model to represent its data requirements?

PROJECT EXERCISES

1. Study the project description very closely. What other questions would you like to ask in order to better understand the data requirements at Mountain View Community Hospital?

2. Develop an E-R diagram for Mountain View Community Hospital. State any assumptions you had to make in developing the diagram.

3. The project description describes an entity type called Item. Given your answer to Project Exercise 2, will this entity type also be able to represent in-room TVs as a billable item to patients? Why or why not?

4. Suppose the attribute bed number were a composite attribute, composed of care center ID, room number, and individual bed number. Redraw any parts of your answer to Project Exercise 2 that would have to change to handle this composite attribute.

5. Consider your new E-R diagram for Mountain View Community Hospital after changing your answer to Project Exercise 2 to handle the situation in Project Exercise 4. Now, additionally assume that a care center contains many rooms, and each room may contain items that are billed to patients assigned to that room. Redraw your E-R diagram to accommodate this new assumption.

6. Does your answer to Project Exercise 2 allow more than one physician to perform a treatment on a patient at the same time? If not, redraw your answer to Project Exercise 2 to accommodate this situation. Make any additional assumptions you consider necessary in order to represent this situation.

7. Does your answer to Project Exercise 2 allow the same treatment to be performed more than once on the same patient by the same physician? If not, redraw your answer to Project Exercise 2 to accommodate this situation. Make any additional assumptions you consider necessary in order to represent this situation.

Chapter 4

The Enhanced E-R Model and Business Rules

LEARNING OBJECTIVES

After studying this chapter, you should be able to:

- Concisely define each of the following key terms: **enhanced entity-relationship (EER) model, subtype, supertype, attribute inheritance, generalization, specialization, total specialization rule, partial specialization rule, disjoint rule, overlap rule, subtype discriminator, supertype/subtype hierarchy, entity cluster, structural assertion, action assertion** and **derived fact.**

- Recognize when to use subtype/supertype relationships in data modeling.

- Use both specialization and generalization as techniques for defining supertype/subtype relationships.

- Specify both completeness constraints and disjointness constraints in modeling supertype/subtype relationships.

- Develop a supertype/subtype hierarchy for a realistic business situation.

- Develop an entity cluster to simplify presentation of an E-R diagram.

- Name the various categories of business rules.

- Define a simple operational constraint using a graphical model or structured English statement.

INTRODUCTION

The basic E-R model described in Chapter 3 was first introduced during the mid-1970s. It has been suitable for modeling most common business problems and has enjoyed widespread use. However, the business environment has changed dramatically since that time. Business relationships are more complex and as a result, business data are much more complex as well. For example organizations must be prepared to segment their markets and to customize their products, which places much greater demands on organizational databases.

To better cope with these changes, researchers have continued to enhance the E-R model so that it can more accurately represent the complex data encountered in today's business environment. The term **enhanced entity-relationship (EER) model** is used to identify the model that has resulted from extending the original E-R model with these new modeling constructs.

Enhanced entity-relationship (EER) model: The model that has resulted from extending the original E-R model with new modeling constructs.

The most important new modeling construct incorporated in the EER model is supertype/subtype relationships. This facility allows us to model a general entity type (called the *supertype*) and then subdivide it into several specialized entity types (called *subtypes*). Thus, for example, the entity type CAR can be modeled as a supertype, with subtypes SEDAN, SPORTS CAR, COUPE, and so on. Each subtype inherits attributes from its supertype and in addition may have special attributes of its own. Adding new notation for modeling supertype/subtype relationships has greatly improved the flexibility of the basic E-R model.

E-R, and especially EER, diagrams can become large and complex, requiring multiple pages (or very small font) for display. Some commercial databases include hundreds of entities. Many users and managers specifying requirements for a database do not need to see all the entities, relationships, and attributes to understand the part of the database with which they are most interested. Entity clustering is a way to turn a part of an entity-relationship data model into a more macro-level view of the same data. Entity clustering is a hierarchical decomposition technique, which can make E-R diagrams easier to read. By grouping entities and relationships, you can lay out an E-R diagram to allow you to give attention to the details of the model that matter most in a given data modeling task.

Enhanced E-R diagrams are used to capture important business rules such as constraints in supertype/subtype relationships. However, most organizations use a multitude of business rules to guide behavior. Many of these rules cannot be expressed with basic E-R diagrams, or even with enhanced E-R diagrams. Promising research at present is directed at developing new ways of expressing business rules, which would allow end users with some training to define their own rules to the system. These rules then automatically become constraints that are enforced by the database management system and are used to maintain the database in a consistent or valid state. This business rules approach allows organizations to respond much more quickly to changing business conditions than previous approaches to systems development.

REPRESENTING SUPERTYPES AND SUBTYPES

Recall from Chapter 3 that an entity type is a collection of entities that share common properties or characteristics. While the entity instances that compose an entity type are similar, we do not expect them to be identical. One of the major challenges in data modeling is to recognize and clearly represent entities that are almost the same, that is, entity types that share common properties but also have one or more distinct properties that are of interest to the organization.

Subtype: A subgrouping of the entities in an entity type that is meaningful to the organization and that shares common attributes or relationships distinct from other subgroupings.

Supertype: A generic entity type that has a relationship with one or more subtypes.

For this reason, the E-R model has been extended to include supertype/subtype relationships. A **subtype** is a subgrouping of the entities in an entity type that is meaningful to the organization. For example, STUDENT is an entity type in a university. Two subtypes of STUDENT are GRADUATE STUDENT and UNDERGRADUATE STUDENT. In this example, we refer to STUDENT as the supertype. A **supertype** is a generic entity type that has a relationship with one or more subtypes.

In the E-R diagramming we have done so far, supertypes and subtypes have been hidden. For example, consider again Figure 3-22, which is the E-R diagram for Pine Valley Furniture Company. Notice that not all customers do business in a sales territory. Why is this? One possible reason is that there are two types of customers—national account customers and regular customers—and only regular customers are assigned to a sales territory. Thus, in Figure 3-22 the reason for the optional cardinality next to CUSTOMER on the Does-business-in relationship is obscured. Explicitly drawing a customer entity supertype and several entity subtypes will help us to make the E-R diagram more meaningful. Later in this chapter we will show a revised E-R diagram for Pine Valley Furniture, which will demonstrate several EER notations to make vague aspects of Figure 3-22 more explicit.

Basic Concepts and Notation

The basic notation that we use for supertype/subtype relationships is shown in Figure 4-1. The supertype is connected with a line to a circle, which in turn is connected by a line to each subtype that has been defined. The U-shaped symbol on each line connecting a subtype to the circle indicates that the subtype is a subset of the supertype. It also indicates the direction of the subtype/supertype relationship.

Attributes that are shared by all entities (including the identifier) are associated with the supertype. Attributes that are unique to a particular subtype are associated with that subtype. Other components will be added to this notation to provide additional meaning in supertype/subtype relationships as we proceed through the remainder of this chapter.

An Example Let us illustrate supertype/subtype relationships with a simple yet common example. Suppose that an organization has three basic types of employees: hourly employees, salaried employees, and contract consultants. Some of the important attributes for each of these types of employees are the following:

- *Hourly employees* Employee_Number, Employee_Name, Address, Date_Hired, Hourly_Rate
- *Salaried employees* Employee_Number, Employee_Name, Address, Date_Hired, Annual_Salary, Stock_Option

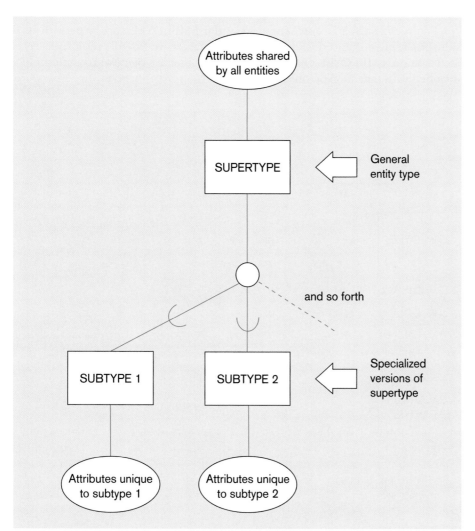

Figure 4-1
Basic notation for supertype/subtype relationships

- *Contract consultants*   Employee_Number, Employee_Name, Address, Date_Hired, Contract_Number, Billing_Rate

Notice that all of the employee types have several attributes in common: Employee_Number, Employee_Name, Address, and Date_Hired. In addition, each type has one or more attributes distinct from the attributes of other types (for example, Hourly_Rate is unique to hourly employees). If you were developing a conceptual data model in this situation, you might consider three choices:

1. Define a single entity type called EMPLOYEE. Although conceptually simple, this approach has the disadvantage that EMPLOYEE would have to contain all of the attributes for the three types of employees. For an instance of an hourly employee (for example), attributes such as Annual_Salary and Contract_Number would not apply and would be null or not used. When taken to a development environment, programs that use this entity type would necessarily be quite complex to deal with the many variations.

2. Define a separate entity type for each of the three entities. This approach would fail to exploit the common properties of employees, and users would have to be careful to select the correct entity type when using the system.

3. Define a supertype called EMPLOYEE, with subtypes for HOURLY EMPLOYEE, SALARIED EMPLOYEE, and CONSULTANT. This approach exploits the common properties of all employees, yet recognizes the distinct properties of each type.

Figure 4-2 shows a representation of the EMPLOYEE supertype with its three subtypes, using enhanced ER notation. Attributes shared by all employees are associated with the EMPLOYEE entity type. Attributes that are peculiar to each subtype are included with that subtype only.

Figure 4-2
Employee supertype with three subtypes

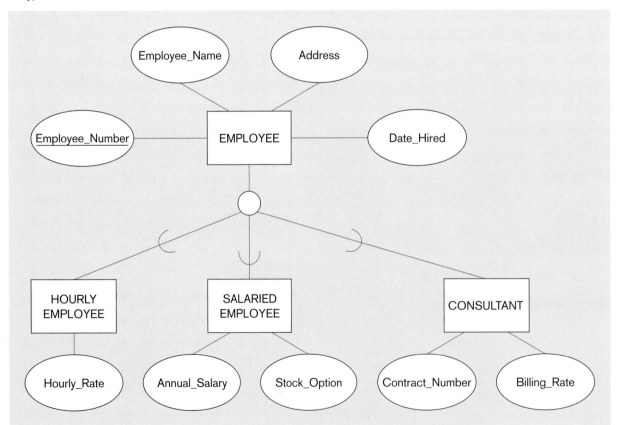

Attribute Inheritance A subtype is an entity type in its own right. An entity instance of a subtype represents the *same* entity instance of the supertype. For example, if 'Therese Jones' is an occurrence of the CONSULTANT subtype, then this same person is necessarily an occurrence of the EMPLOYEE supertype. As a consequence, an entity in a subtype must possess not only values for its own attributes, but also values for its attributes as a member of the supertype.

Attribute inheritance is the property by which subtype entities inherit values of all attributes of the supertype. This important property makes it unnecessary to include supertype attributes redundantly with the subtypes. For example, Employee_Name is an attribute of EMPLOYEE (Figure 4-2), but not of the subtypes of EMPLOYEE. Thus the fact that the employee's name is 'Therese Jones' is inherited from the EMPLOYEE supertype. However, the Billing_Rate for this same employee is an attribute of the subtype CONSULTANT.

We have established that a member of a subtype *must* be a member of the supertype. Is the converse also true—that is, is a member of the supertype also a member of one (or more) of the subtypes? This may or may not be true, depending on the business situation. We discuss the various possibilities later in this chapter.

When to Use Supertype/Subtype Relationships Whether to use supertype/subtype relationships or not is a decision that the data modeler must make in each situation. You should consider using subtypes when either (or both) of the following conditions are present:

1. There are attributes that apply to some (but not all) of the instances of an entity type. For example, see the EMPLOYEE entity type in Figure 4-2.

2. The instances of a subtype participate in a relationship unique to that subtype.

Figure 4-3 is an example of the use of subtype relationships that illustrates both of these situations. The hospital entity type PATIENT has two subtypes:

> **Attribute inheritance:** A property by which subtype entities inherit values of all attributes of the supertype.

Figure 4-3
Supertype/subtype relationships in a hospital

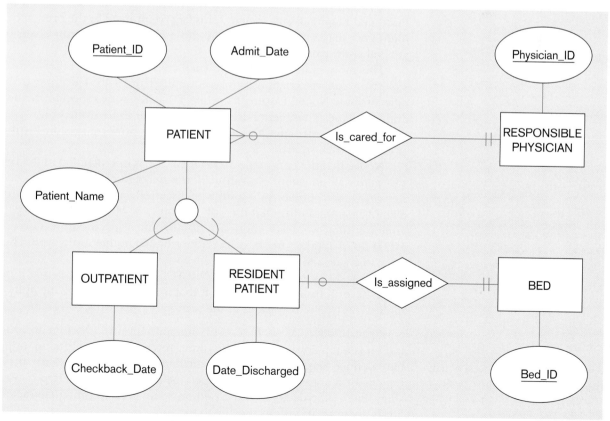

OUTPATIENT and RESIDENT PATIENT (the primary key is Patient_ID). All patients have an Admit_Date attribute, as well as a Patient_Name. Also, every patient is cared for by a RESPONSIBLE PHYSICIAN who develops a treatment plan for the patient.

Each subtype has an attribute that is unique to that subtype. Outpatients have a Checkback_Date, while resident patients have a Date_Discharged. Also, resident patients have a unique relationship that assigns each patient to a bed (notice that this is a mandatory relationship). Each bed may or may not be assigned to a patient.

Earlier we discussed the property of attribute inheritance. Thus each outpatient and each resident patient inherits the attributes of the parent supertype PATIENT: Patient_ID, Patient_Name, and Admit_Date. Figure 4-3 also illustrates the principle of relationship inheritance. OUTPATIENT and RESIDENT PATIENT are also instances of PATIENT; therefore, each Is_cared_for by a RESPONSIBLE PHYSICIAN.

Representing Specialization and Generalization

We have described and illustrated the basic principles of supertype/subtype relationships, including the characteristics of "good" subtypes. But in developing real-world data models, how can you recognize opportunities to exploit these relationships? There are two processes—specialization and generalization—that serve as mental models in developing supertype/subtype relationships.

Generalization A unique aspect of human intelligence is the ability and propensity to classify objects and experiences and to generalize their properties. In data modeling, **generalization** is the process of defining a more general entity type from a set of more specialized entity types. Thus generalization is a bottom-up process.

An example of generalization is shown in Figure 4-4. In Figure 4-4a, three entity types have been defined: CAR, TRUCK, and MOTORCYCLE. At this stage, the data modeler intends to represent these separately on an E-R diagram. However, on closer examination we see that the three entity types have a number of attributes in common: Vehicle_ID (identifier), Vehicle_Name (with components Make and Model), Price, and Engine_Displacement. This fact (reinforced by the presence of a common identifier) suggests that each of the three entity types is really a version of a more general entity type.

This more general entity type (named VEHICLE) together with the resulting supertype/subtype relationships is shown in Figure 4-4b. The entity CAR has the specific attribute No_of_Passengers, while TRUCK has two specific attributes: Capacity and Cab_Type. Thus, generalization has allowed us to group entity types along with their common attributes and at the same time preserve specific attributes that are peculiar to each subtype.

Notice that the entity type MOTORCYCLE is not included in the relationship. Is this simply an omission? No—instead, it is deliberately not included because it does not satisfy the conditions for a subtype discussed earlier. Comparing Figure 4-4 parts a and b, you will notice that the only attributes of MOTORCYCLE are those that are common to all vehicles; there are no attributes specific to motorcycles. Further, MOTORCYCLE does not have a relationship to another entity type. Thus there is no need to create a MOTORCYCLE subtype.

The fact that there is no MOTORCYCLE subtype suggests that it must be possible to have an instance of VEHICLE that is not a member of any of its subtypes. We discuss this type of constraint in the section on specifying constraints.

Specialization As we have seen, generalization is a bottom-up process. Specialization is a top-down process, the direct reverse of generalization. Suppose that we have defined an entity type with its attributes. **Specialization** is the process of defining one or more subtypes of the supertype and forming supertype/subtype relationships. Each subtype is formed based on some distinguishing characteristic such as attributes or relationships specific to the subtype.

Generalization: The process of defining a more general entity type from a set of more specialized entity types.

Specialization: The process of defining one or more subtypes of the supertype and forming supertype/subtype relationships.

Figure 4-4
Example of generalization
(a) Three entity types: CAR, TRUCK, and MOTORCYCLE

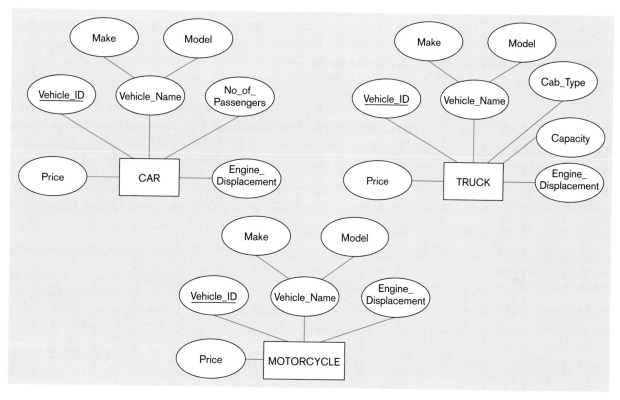

(b) Generalization to VEHICLE supertype

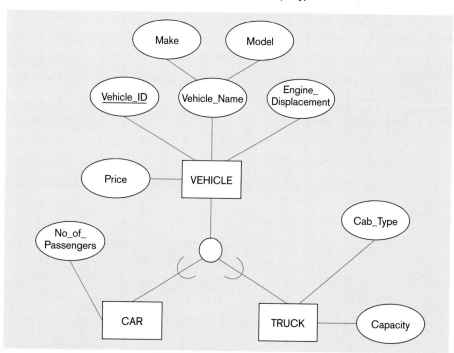

An example of specialization is shown in Figure 4-5. Figure 4-5a shows an entity type named PART, together with several of its attributes. The identifier is Part_No, and other attributes include Description, Unit_Price, Location, Qty_on_Hand, Routing_Number, and Supplier (the last attribute is multivalued since there may be more than one supplier with associated unit price for a part).

In discussions with users, we discover that there are two possible sources for parts: Some are manufactured internally, while others are purchased from outside suppliers. Further, we discover that some parts are obtained from both sources. In this case the choice depends on factors such as manufacturing capacity, unit price of the parts, and so on.

Some of the attributes in Figure 4-5a apply to all parts, regardless of source. However, others depend on the source. Thus Routing_Number applies only to manufactured parts, while Supplier_ID and Unit_Price apply only to purchased parts. These factors suggest that PART should be specialized by defining the subtypes MANUFACTURED PART and PURCHASED PART (see Figure 4-5b).

In Figure 4-5b, Routing_Number is associated with MANUFACTURED PART. The data modeler initially planned to associate Supplier_ID and Unit_Price with

Figure 4-5
Example of specialization
(a) Entity type PART

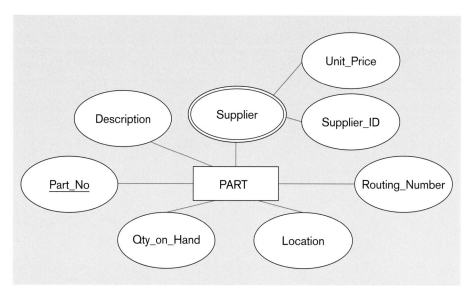

(b) Specialization to MANUFACTURED PART and PURCHASED PART

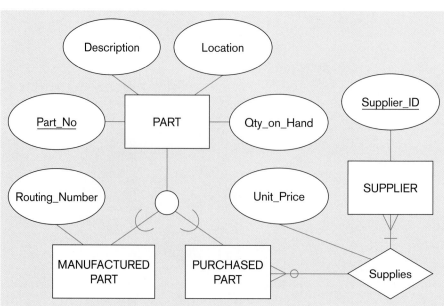

PURCHASED PART. However, in further discussions with users she suggested instead that they create a new relationship between PURCHASED PART and SUPPLIER. This relationship (named Supplies in Figure 4-5b) allows users to more easily associate purchased parts with their suppliers. Notice that the attribute Unit_Price is now associated with the relationship Supplies, so that the unit price for a part may vary from one supplier to another. In this example, specialization has permitted a preferred representation of the problem domain.

Combining Specialization and Generalization   Specialization and generalization are both valuable techniques for developing supertype/subtype relationships. Which technique you use at a particular time depends on several factors such as the nature of the problem domain, previous modeling efforts, and personal preference. You should be prepared to use both approaches and to alternate back and forth as dictated by the preceding factors.

SPECIFYING CONSTRAINTS IN SUPERTYPE/SUBTYPE RELATIONSHIPS

So far we have discussed the basic concepts of supertype/subtype relationships and introduced some basic notation to represent these concepts. We have also described the processes of generalization and specialization, which assist a data modeler to recognize opportunities for exploiting these relationships. In this section we introduce additional notation to represent constraints on supertype/subtype relationships. These constraints allow us to capture some of the important business rules that apply to these relationships. The two most important types of constraints that are described in this section are completeness and disjointness constraints (Elmasri and Navathe, 1994).

Specifying Completeness Constraints

A **completeness constraint** addresses the question whether an instance of a supertype must also be a member of at least one subtype. The completeness constraint has two possible rules: total specialization and partial specialization. The **total specialization rule** specifies that each entity instance of the supertype *must* be a member of some subtype in the relationship. The **partial specialization rule** specifies that an entity instance of the supertype is allowed not to belong to any subtype. We illustrate each of these rules with earlier examples from this chapter (see Figure 4-6).

Total Specialization Rule   Figure 4-6a repeats the example of PATIENT (Figure 4-3) and introduces the notation for total specialization. In this example, the business rule is the following: A patient must be either an outpatient or a resident patient (there are no other types of patient in this hospital). Total specialization is indicated by the *double* line extending from the PATIENT entity type to the circle.

In this example, every time a new instance of PATIENT is inserted into the supertype, a corresponding instance is inserted into either OUTPATIENT or RESIDENT PATIENT. If the instance is inserted into RESIDENT PATIENT, an instance of the relationship Is_assigned is created to assign the patient to a hospital bed.

Partial Specialization Rule   Figure 4-6b repeats the example of VEHICLE and its subtypes CAR and TRUCK from Figure 4-4. Recall that in this example motorcycle is a type of vehicle, but that it is not represented as a subtype in the data model. Thus if a vehicle is a car, it must appear as an instance of CAR, and if it is a truck, it must appear as an instance of TRUCK. However, if the vehicle is a motorcycle, it cannot appear as an instance of any subtype. This is an example of partial specialization, and it is specified by the *single* line from the VEHICLE supertype to the circle.

Completeness constraint: A type of constraint that addresses the question whether an instance of a supertype must also be a member of at least one subtype.

Total specialization rule: Specifies that each entity instance of the supertype *must* be a member of some subtype in the relationship.

Partial specialization rule: Specifies that an entity instance of the supertype is allowed not to belong to any subtype.

Figure 4-6
Examples of completeness constraints
(a) Total specialization rule

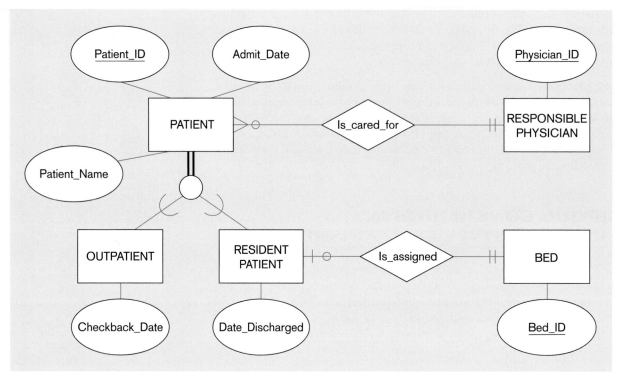

(b) Partial specialization rule

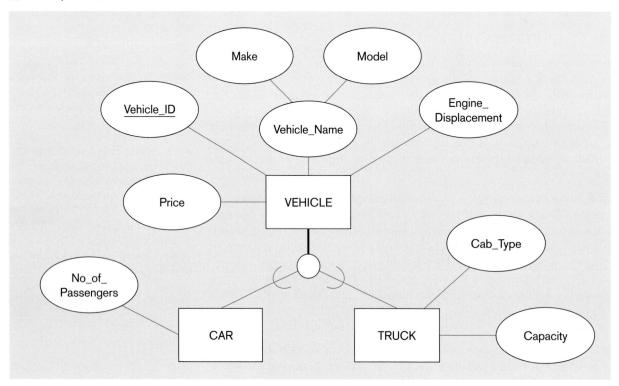

Specifying Disjointness Constraints

A **disjointness constraint** addresses the question whether an instance of a supertype may simultaneously be a member of two (or more) subtypes. The disjointness constraint has two possible rules: the disjoint rule and the overlap rule. The **disjoint rule** specifies that if an entity instance (of the supertype) is a member of one subtype, it cannot simultaneously be a member of any other subtype. The **overlap rule** specifies that an entity instance can simultaneously be a member of two (or more) subtypes. An example of each of these rules is shown in Figure 4-7.

Disjoint Rule Figure 4-7a shows the PATIENT example from Figure 4-6a. The business rule in this case is the following: *At any given time*, a patient must be either an outpatient or a resident patient but cannot be both. This is the disjoint rule, as specified by the letter '**d**' in the circle joining the supertype and its subtypes. Note in this figure, the subclass of a PATIENT may change over time, but at a given time, a PATIENT is of only one type.

Overlap Rule Figure 4-7b shows the entity type PART with its two subtypes, MANUFACTURED PART and PURCHASED PART (from Figure 4-5b). Recall from our discussion of this example that some parts are both manufactured and purchased. Some clarification of this statement is required. In this example an instance of PART is a particular part number (that is, a *type of part*), not an individual part (this is indicated by the identifier, which is Part_No). For example, consider part number 4000. At a given time the quantity on hand for this part might be 250, of which 100 are manufactured and the remaining 150 are purchased parts. In this case, it is not important to keep track of individual parts. When tracking individual parts is important, then each part is assigned a serial number identifier, and the quantity on hand is 1 or 0, depending on whether that individual part exists or not.

The overlap rule is specified by placing the letter '**o**' in the circle, as shown in Figure 4-7b. Notice in this figure that the total specialization rule is also specified, as indicated by the double line. Thus any part must be either a purchased part or a manufactured part, or it may simultaneously be both of these.

Defining Subtype Discriminators

Given a supertype/subtype relationship, consider the problem of inserting a new instance of the supertype. Into which of the subtypes (if any) should this instance be inserted? We have already discussed the various possible rules that apply to this situation. We need a simple mechanism to implement these rules, if one is available. Often this can be accomplished by using a subtype discriminator. A **subtype discriminator** is an attribute of the supertype whose values determine the target subtype or subtypes.

Disjoint Subtypes An example of the use of a subtype discriminator is shown in Figure 4-8. This example is for the EMPLOYEE supertype and its subtypes, introduced in Figure 4-2. Notice that the following constraints have been added to this figure: total specialization and disjoint subtypes. Thus each employee must be either hourly, salaried, or a consultant.

A new attribute (Employee_Type) has been added to the supertype, to serve as subtype discriminator. When a new employee is added to the supertype, this attribute is coded with one of three values, as follows: "H" (for Hourly), "S" (for Salaried), or "C" (for Consultant). Depending on this code, the instance is then assigned to the appropriate subtype.

The notation we use to specify the subtype discriminator is also shown in Figure 4-8. The expression "Employee_Type=" (which is the left-hand side of a condition statement) is placed next to the line leading from the supertype to the circle. The

Disjointness constraint: A constraint that addresses the question whether an instance of a supertype may simultaneously be a member of two (or more) subtypes.

Disjoint rule: Specifies that if an entity instance (of the supertype) is a member of one subtype, it cannot simultaneously be a member of any other subtype.

Overlap rule: Specifies that an entity instance can simultaneously be a member of two (or more) subtypes.

Subtype discriminator: An attribute of the supertype whose values determine the target subtype or subtypes.

Figure 4-7
Examples of disjointness constraints
(a) Disjoint rule

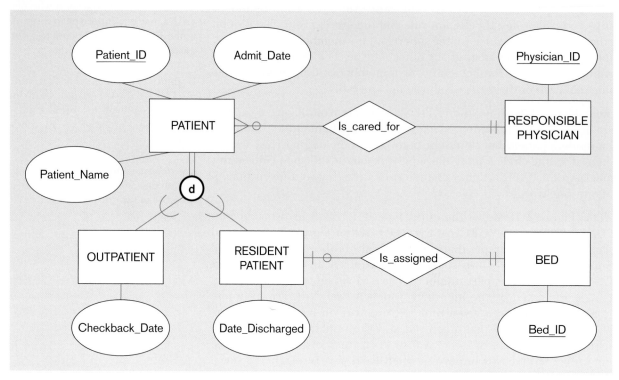

(b) Overlap rule

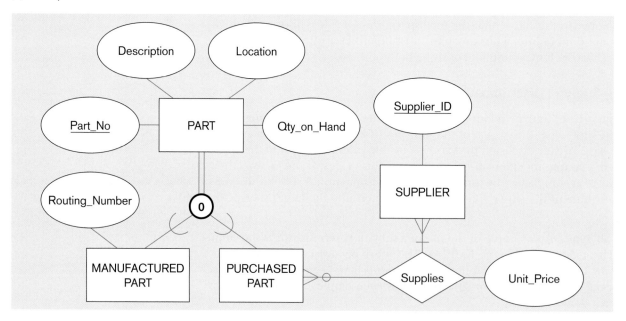

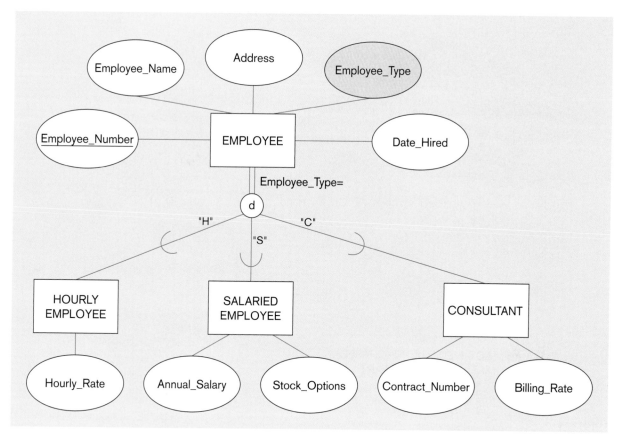

Figure 4-8
Introducing a subtype discriminator
(disjoint rule)

value of the attribute that selects the appropriate subtype (in this example, either "H," "S," or "C") is placed adjacent to the line leading to that subtype. Thus for example, the condition "Employee_Type= "S" causes an entity instance to be inserted into the SALARIED EMPLOYEE subtype.

Overlapping Subtypes   When subtypes overlap, a slightly modified approach must be applied for the subtype discriminator. The reason is that a given instance of the supertype may require that we create an instance in more than one subtype.

An example of this situation is shown in Figure 4-9 for PART and its overlapping subtypes. A new attribute named Part_Type has been added to PART. Part_Type is a composite attribute with components Manufactured? and Purchased? Each of these attributes is a Boolean variable (that is, it takes on only the values yes, "Y", and no, "N"). When a new instance is added to PART, these components are coded as follows:

Type of Part	Manufactured?	Purchased?
Manufactured only	"Y"	"N"
Purchased only	"N"	"Y"
Purchased and manufactured	"Y"	"Y"

The method for specifying the subtype discriminator for this example is shown in Figure 4-9. Notice that this approach can be used for any number of overlapping subtypes.

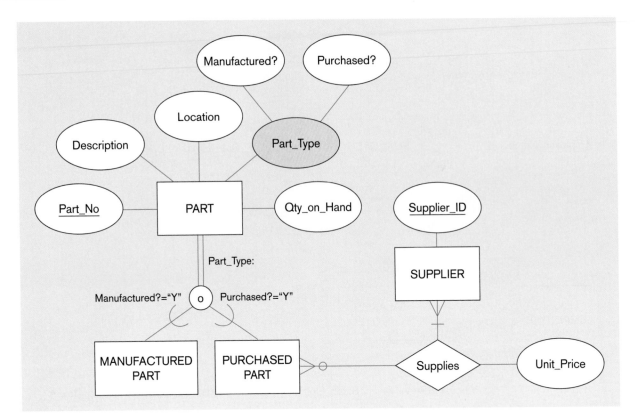

Figure 4-9
Subtype discriminator (overlap rule)

Defining Supertype/Subtype Hierarchies

We have considered a number of examples of supertype/subtype relationships in this chapter. It is possible for any of the subtypes in these examples to have other subtypes defined on it (in this case, the subtype becomes a supertype for the newly defined subtypes). A **supertype/subtype hierarchy** is a hierarchical arrangement of supertypes and subtypes, where each subtype has only one supertype (Elmasri and Navathe, 1994).

We present an example of a supertype/subtype hierarchy in this section (see Figure 4-10). This example includes most of the concepts and notation we have used in this chapter to this point. It also presents a methodology (based on specialization) that you can use in many data modeling situations.

An Example Suppose that you are asked to model the human resources in a university. Using specialization (top-down approach) you might proceed as follows. Starting at the top of a hierarchy, model the most general entity type first. In this case, the most general entity type is PERSON. List and associate all attributes of PERSON. The attributes shown in Figure 4-10 are: SSN (identifier), Name, Address, Gender, and Date_of_Birth. The entity type at the top of a hierarchy is sometimes called the *root*.

Next, define all major subtypes of the root. In this example, there are three subtypes of PERSON: EMPLOYEE (persons who work for the university), STUDENT (persons who attend classes), and ALUMNUS (persons who have graduated). Assuming there are no other types of persons of interest to the university the total specialization rule applies, as shown in the figure. A person might belong to more than one subtype (for example, ALUMNUS and EMPLOYEE), so the overlap rule is used. Note, overlap allows for any overlap (a PERSON may be simultaneous in any pair or in all three subtypes). If certain combinations are not allowed, then a more refined supertype/subtype hierarchy would have to be developed to eliminate the prohibited combinations.

Supertype/subtype hierarchy: A hierarchical arrangement of supertypes and subtypes, where each subtype has only one supertype.

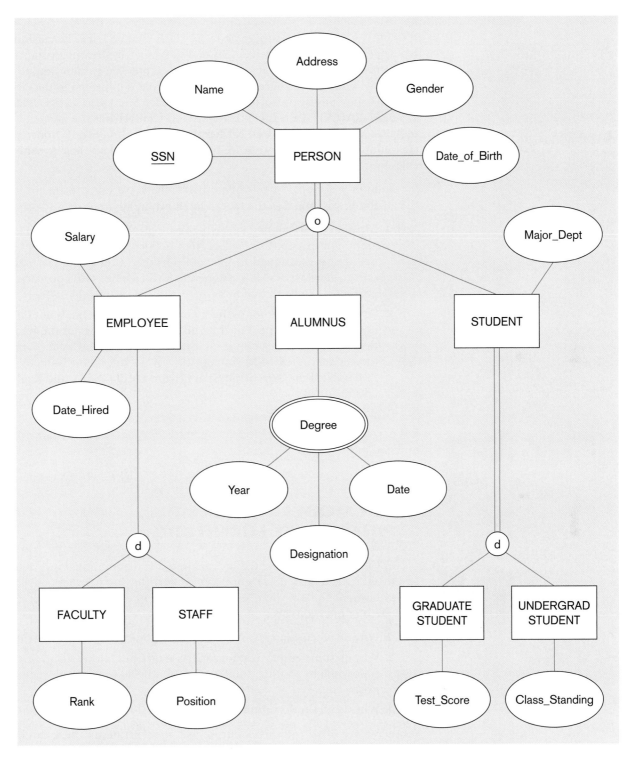

Figure 4-10
Example of supertype/subtype hierarchy

Attributes that apply specifically to each of these subtypes are shown in the figure. Thus each instance of EMPLOYEE has a value for Date_Hired and Salary. Major_Dept is an attribute of STUDENT, and Degree (with components Year, Designation, and Date) is an attribute of ALUMNUS.

The next step is to evaluate whether any of the subtypes already defined qualify for further specialization. In this example, EMPLOYEE is partitioned into two subtypes: FACULTY and STAFF. FACULTY has the specific attribute Rank, while STAFF has the specific attribute Position. Notice that in this example, the subtype EMPLOYEE becomes a supertype to FACULTY and STAFF. Because there may be types of employees other than faculty and staff (such as student assistants), the partial specialization rule is indicated. However, an employee cannot be both faculty and staff at the same time. Therefore, the disjoint rule is indicated in the circle.

Two subtypes are also defined for STUDENT: GRADUATE STUDENT and UNDERGRAD STUDENT. UNDERGRAD STUDENT has the attribute Class_Standing, while GRADUATE STUDENT has the attribute Test_Score. Notice that total specialization and the disjoint rule are specified; you should be able to state the business rules for these constraints.

Summary of Supertype/Subtype Hierarchies We note two features concerning the attributes contained in the hierarchy shown in Figure 4-10.

1. Attributes are assigned at the highest logical level that is possible in the hierarchy. For example, since SSN (that is, Social Security Number) applies to all persons, it is assigned to the root. On the other hand, Date_Hired applies only to employees so it is assigned to EMPLOYEE. This approach ensures that attributes can be shared by as many subtypes as possible.

2. Subtypes that are lower in the hierarchy inherit attributes not only from their immediate supertype, but from all supertypes higher in the hierarchy, up to the root. Thus for example, an instance of faculty has values for all of the following attributes: SSN, Name, Address, Gender, and Date_of_Birth (from PERSON), Date_Hired and Salary (from EMPLOYEE), and Rank (from FACULTY).

In the student case at the end of this chapter, we ask you to develop an enhanced E-R diagram for Mountain View Community Hospital using the same procedure we outlined in this section.

EER MODELING EXAMPLE: PINE VALLEY FURNITURE

In Chapter 3, we presented an example E-R diagram for Pine Valley Furniture (this diagram is repeated in Figure 4-11). After studying this diagram, you might use some questions to help you clarify the meaning of entities and relationships. Three such areas of questions are:

1. Why do all customers not do business in one or more sales territories?
2. Why do some employees not supervise other employees, and why are they not supervised by another employee? And, why do some employees not work in a work center?
3. Why do all vendors not supply raw materials to Pine Valley Furniture?

You may have other questions, but we will concentrate on these three to illustrate how supertype/subtype relationships can be used to convey a more specific (semantically rich) data model.

After some investigation into the above questions, we discover the following business rules that apply to how Pine Valley Furniture does business:

1. There are two types of customers—regular and national account. Only regular customers do business in sales territories. A sales territory exists only if it has at least one regular customer associated with it. A national account customer is associated with an account manager. It is possible for a customer to be both a regular and a national account customer.

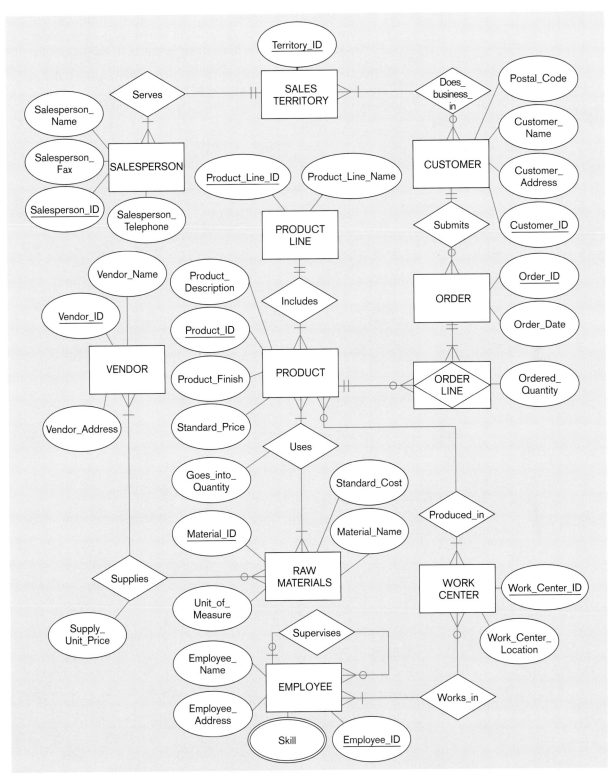

Figure 4-11
E-R diagram for Pine Valley Furniture
Company

2. Two special types of employees exist—management and union. Only union
employees work in work centers, and a management employee supervises
union employees. There are other kinds of employees besides management
and union. A union employee may be promoted into management, at which
time that employee stops being a union employee.

3. Pine Valley Furniture keeps track of many different vendors, not all of which have ever supplied raw materials to the company. A vendor is associated with a contract number once that vendor becomes an official supplier of raw materials.

The above business rules have been used to modify the E-R diagram in Figure 4-11 into the EER diagram in Figure 4-12 (we have left most attributes off of this diagram except for those that are essential to see the changes that have occurred). Rule

Figure 4-12
EER diagram for Pine Valley Furniture

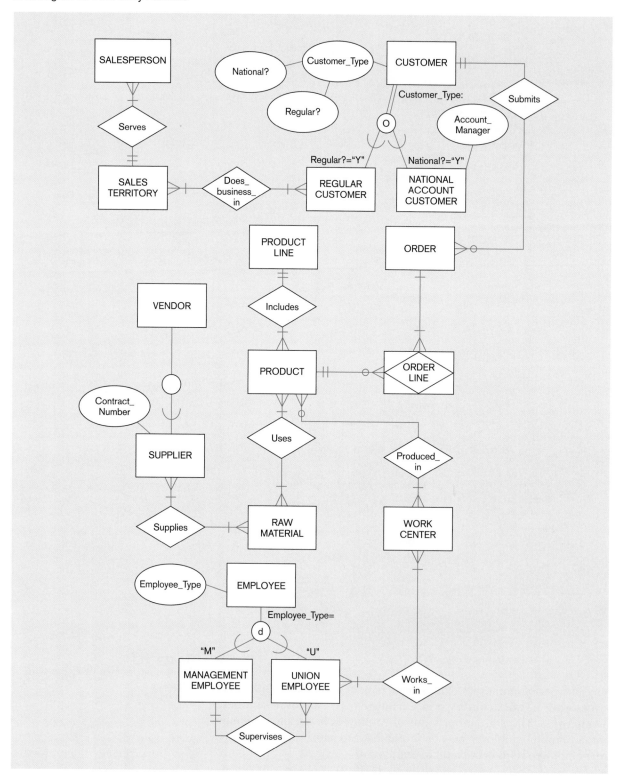

1 means that there is a total, overlapping specialization of CUSTOMER into REGU-LAR CUSTOMER and NATIONAL ACCOUNT CUSTOMER. A composite attribute of CUSTOMER, Customer_Type, is used to designate whether a customer instance is a regular customer, a national account, or both. Since only regular customers do business in sales territories, only regular customers are involved in the Does_business_in relationship, and the minimum cardinality next to regular customer is one, because a sales territory, to exist, must have at least one regular customer.

Rule 2 means that there is a partial, disjoint specialization of EMPLOYEE into MANAGEMENT EMPLOYEE and UNION EMPLOYEE. An attribute of EMPLOYEE, Employee_Type, discriminates between the two special types of employees. Specialization is partial because there are other kinds of employees besides these two types. Only union employees are involved in the Works_in relationship, but all union employees work in some work center, so the minimum cardinality of Works_in next to WORK CENTER is now mandatory. Because an employee cannot be both management and union, the specialization is disjoint.

Rule 3 means that there is a partial specialization of VENDOR into SUPPLIER because only some vendors become suppliers. A supplier, not a vendor, has a contract number. Because there is only one subtype of VENDOR, there is no reason to specify a disjoint or overlap rule. Because all suppliers supply some raw material, the minimum cardinality next to RAW MATERIAL in the Supplies relationship now is one.

The above examples show how an E-R diagram can be transformed into an EER diagram once generalization/specialization of entities is understood. Not only are supertype and subtype entities now in the data model, but also additional attributes, including discriminating attributes, are added, minimum cardinalities change (from optional to mandatory), and relationships move from the supertype to a subtype.

This is a good time to emphasize a point made earlier about data modeling. A data model is a conceptual picture of the data required by an organization. A data model does not map one-for-one to elements of an implemented database. For example, for those of you familiar with a database product like Microsoft Access, although SUPPLIER is an entity type and Supplies is a relationship, both will appear as tables in an Access database. Such details are not important now. The purpose now is to explain all the rules that govern data, not how data will be stored and accessed to achieve efficient, required information processing. We will address technology and efficiency issues in subsequent chapters when we cover database design and implementation.

Although the EER diagram in Figure 4-12 clarifies some questions and makes the data model in Figure 4-11 more explicit, it still can be difficult for some people to comprehend. Some people will not be interested in all types of data, and some may not need to see all the details in the EER diagram in order to understand what the database will cover. The next section addresses how we can simplify a complete and explicit data model for presentation to specific user groups and management.

ENTITY CLUSTERING

Some enterprise-wide information systems have over 1,000 entity types and relationships. How do we present such an unwieldy picture of organizational data to developers and users? One approach is to create multiple, E-R diagrams, each showing the details of different (possibly overlapping) segments or subsets of the data model (e.g., different segments that apply to different departments, information system applications, business processes, or corporate divisions). This works, but is really insufficient by itself since a total picture would not exist.

Entity clustering (Teorey, 1999) is a useful way to present a data model for a large and complex organization. An **entity cluster** is a set of one or more entity types and associated relationships grouped into a single abstract entity type. Because an entity cluster behaves like an entity type, entity clusters and entity types can be further

Entity cluster: A set of one or more entity types and associated relationships grouped into a single abstract entity type.

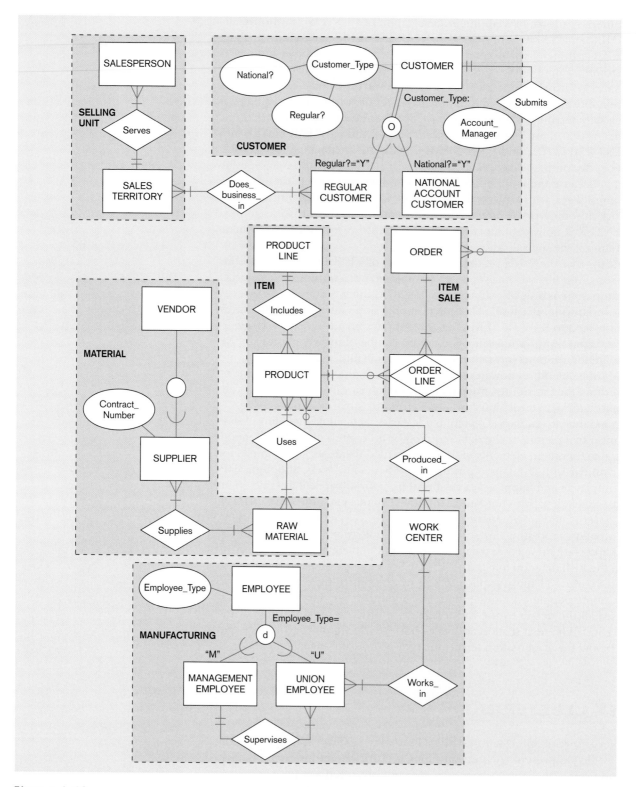

Figure 4-13
Entity clustering for Pine Valley
Furniture
(a) Possible entity clusters

grouped to form a higher-level entity cluster. Entity clustering is a hierarchical decomposition of a macro-level view of the data model into finer and finer views, eventually resulting in the full, detailed data model.

Figure 4-13 illustrates one possible result of entity clustering for the Pine Valley Furniture data model of Figure 4-12. Figure 4-13a shows the complete data model with dashed lines drawn around possible entity clusters; Figure 4-13b shows the final result

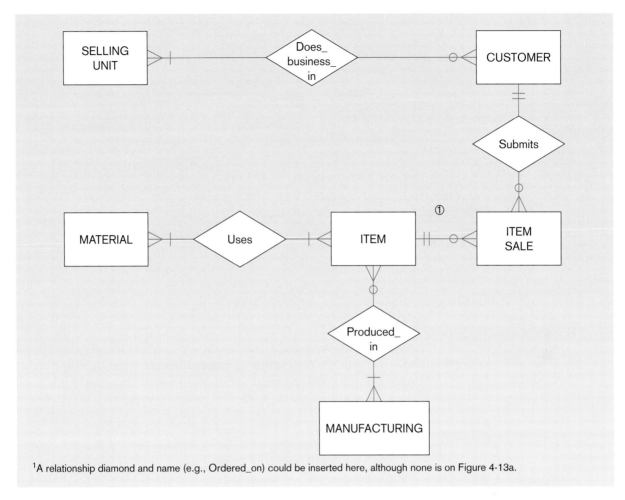

¹A relationship diamond and name (e.g., Ordered_on) could be inserted here, although none is on Figure 4-13a.

(b) EER diagram of entity clusters

of transforming the detailed EER diagram into an EER diagram of only entity clusters and relationships (an EER diagram may include both entity clusters and entity types, but this diagram includes only entity clusters). In this figure, the entity cluster

- *SELLING UNIT* represents the SALESPERSON and SALES TERRITORY entity types and the Serves relationship
- *CUSTOMER* represents the CUSTOMER entity supertype, its subtypes, and the relationship between supertype and subtypes
- *ITEM SALE* represents the ORDER entity type and ORDER LINE associative entity as well as the relationship between them
- *ITEM* represents the PRODUCT LINE and PRODUCT entity types and the Includes relationship
- *MANUFACTURING* represents the WORK CENTER and EMPLOYEE supertype entity and its subtypes as well as the Works-in and Supervises relationships and the relationship between the supertype and its subtypes (Figure 4-14 shows an explosion of the MANUFACTURING entity cluster into its components)
- *MATERIAL* represents the RAW MATERIAL and VENDOR entity types, the SUPPLIER subtype, the Supplies relationship, and the supertype/subtype relationship between VENDOR and SUPPLIER.

The E-R diagrams in Figures 4-13 and 4-14 can be used to explain details to people most concerned with assembly processes and the information needed to support

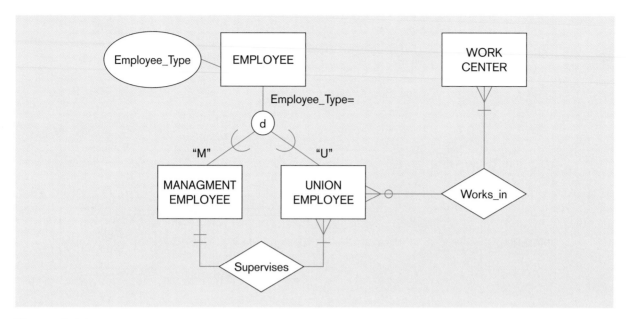

Figure 4-14
MANUFACTURING entity cluster

this part of the business. For example, an inventory control manager can see in Figure 4-13 that the data about manufacturing can be related to item data (the Produced_in relationship). Further Figure 4-14 shows what detail is kept about the production process involving work centers and employees. This person probably does not need to see the details about, for example, the selling structure, which is embedded in the SELLING UNIT entity cluster.

Entity clusters in Figure 4-13 were formed (1) by abstracting a supertype and its subtype (see the CUSTOMER entity cluster) and (2) by combining directly related entity types and their relationships (see the SELLING UNIT, ITEM, MATERIAL, and MANUFACTURING entity clusters). An entity cluster can also be formed by combining a strong entity and its associated weak entity types (not illustrated here). Because entity clustering is hierarchical, if it were desirable, we could draw another EER diagram in which we combine the SELLNG UNIT and CUSTOMER entity clusters with the Does_business_in relationship into one entity cluster, because these are directly related entity clusters.

An entity cluster should focus on an area of interest to some community of users, developers, or managers. Which entity types and relationships are grouped to form an entity cluster depends on your purpose. For example, the ORDER entity type could be grouped in with the CUSTOMER entity cluster and the ORDER LINE entity type could be grouped in with the ITEM entity cluster in the example of entity clustering for the Pine Valley Furniture data model. This regrouping would eliminate the ITEM SALE cluster, which might not be of interest to any group of people. Also, you can do several different entity clusterings of the full data model, each with a different focus.

BUSINESS RULES REVISITED

We have seen that E-R diagrams (and enhanced E-R diagrams) are a useful means for expressing certain types of business rules. Thus, for example, the participation and disjointness constraints associated with supertypes and subtypes discussed in this chapter are an expression of the business rules associated with those relationships. However, there are many other types of business rules in an organization that cannot be expressed with this notation. In this section we develop a general framework for business rules and show how to express some important types of rules that elude the standard E-R (and enhanced E-R) notation.

Classification of Business Rules

There are many different types of business rules. You have already seen examples in Chapter 3 and in this chapter of some of these, such as rules about relationships between entity types (e.g., cardinality values), supertype/subtype relationships, and facts about attributes and entity types (e.g., definitions). Figure 4-15, adapted from the GUIDE Business Rules Project, shows an E-R diagram that classifies business rules and the potential relationships between different types of rules.

There are three main types of business rules—derivation, structural assertion, and action assertion. A **derivation** is a statement derived from other knowledge in the business. Most commonly, a derivation is a mathematical or logical inference involving literals and facts. Since in data modeling we are concerned more with derived facts, which are derived by using derivations, we will address derivations only indirectly when we discuss derived facts in a subsequent section. A **structural assertion** is a statement that expresses some aspect of the static structure of the organization. E-R

Derivation: A statement derived from other knowledge in the business.

Structural assertion: A statement that expresses some aspect of the static structure of the organization.

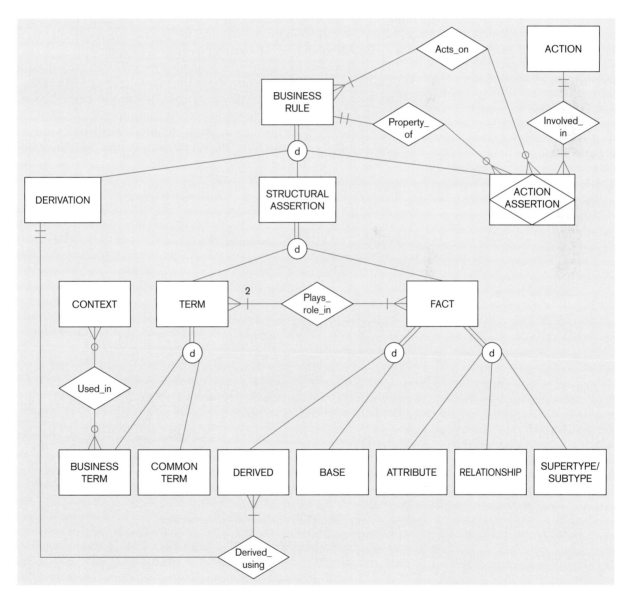

Figure 4-15
E-R diagram to describe business rules
(Adapted from GUIDE Business Rules Project, 1997)

Action assertion: A statement of a constraint or control on the actions of the organization.

diagrams are a common way to show structural assertions. As can be seen in Figure 4-15, a structural assertion is stated either as a term or a fact (term and fact were defined in Chapter 3), and terms play a role in the statement of a fact. A term is either a common term, one that is generally understood, or a business term, one that can be understood only within the context of a given setting. An **action assertion** is a statement of a constraint or control on the actions of the organization. An action assertion is the property of some business rule and states under what conditions a particular action can be performed on which business rules (remember, a business rule can be as simple as the definition of an entity type, relationship, or attribute). For example, an action assertion can state under what conditions a new customer can be created or a new purchase order written. Another common type of an action assertion states what values a particular attribute may hold (sometimes called a domain constraint).

In the following sections we describe various forms of structural assertions, which are commonly shown in E-R and EER diagrams and in associated database documentation. Then in the following section we explain action assertions, which can be implemented in a database as triggers and stored procedures, which we discuss later in the text. We use a simple data model for class scheduling to illustrate these assertions. The E-R model for this example is shown in Figure 4-16.

The E-R model in Figure 4-16 contains four entity types: FACULTY, COURSE, SECTION, and STUDENT. It also shows the relationships between these entity types. Notice that SECTION is a weak entity type, because it cannot exist without the COURSE entity type. The identifying relationship for SECTION is "Is_scheduled" and the partial identifier is Section_ID (a composite attribute). Only selected attributes are shown for the various entity types to simplify the diagram.

Figure 4-16
Data model segment for class scheduling

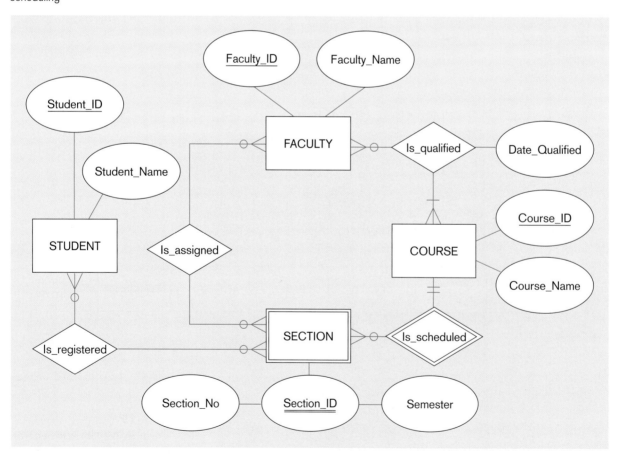

Stating a Structural Assertion

A structural assertion says that something of importance to the organization either exists or exists in relationship with other things of interest. A structural assertion can be as simple as the definition of a term, or a fact, which is a statement of a relationship between terms. Four examples of facts are:

- A course is a module of instruction in a particular subject area. This *definition of the term* course associates two terms: module of instruction and subject area. We assume these are common terms that do not need to be further defined or placed in a business context.
- Student name is an *attribute* of student. This fact is shown in Figure 4-16 by the Student_Name attribute oval.
- A student may register for many sections, and a section may be registered for by many students. This fact states the participation of entity types in a *relationship*. Both student and section are business terms that require definitions. This fact is shown in Figure 4-16 by the Is_registered relationship.
- A faculty is an employee of the university. Although not shown in Figure 4-16, this fact designates a *supertype/subtype* relationship between the subtype of faculty and its supertype of employee.

Derived Facts The type of facts described above are called *base* facts—that is, they are fundamental facts that cannot be derived from other terms or facts. Another type of fact (shown in Figure 4-15) is called a derived fact. A **derived fact** is a fact that is derived from business rules using an algorithm or inference. A derived fact may be treated just like a base fact (for example, since a derived fact is a type of business rule, an action assertion may be a property of a derived fact). A derived attribute, defined in Chapter 3, is an example of a derived fact. Following are two examples of derived facts:

> **Derived fact:** A fact that is derived from business rules using an algorithm or inference.

- Student_GPA = Quality_Points/Total_Hours_Taken
    where Quality_Points = sum [for all courses attempted]
    (Credit_Hours*Numerical_Grade)

  In this example, Student_GPA is derived from other base and derived facts. Quality_Points and Total_Hours are also derived facts. Student_GPA could be shown in Figure 4-16 in a dashed oval connected to STUDENT, Numerical_Grade as an attribute of Is_registered, and Credit_Hours as an attribute of COURSE.
- A student is taught by the faculty assigned to the sections for which the student is registered. You can see how this fact can be derived by following the Is_registered relationship from STUDENT or SECTION and then the Is_assigned relationship from SECTION to FACULTY in the E-R diagram in Figure 4-16.

Stating an Action Assertion

Whereas a structural assertion deals with the static structure of an organization, an action assertion deals with the dynamic aspects of the organization. Action assertions impose "must (must not)" and "should (should not)" constraints on handling data. An action assertion is the property of some business rule (called the **anchor object**); for a data handling **action** (e.g., create, update, delete, or read) it states how other business rules (called the **corresponding objects**) act on the anchor object. Some examples of action assertions are:

> **Anchor object:** A business rule (a fact) on which actions are limited.
>
> **Action:** An operation, such as create, delete, update, or read, which may be performed on data objects.
>
> **Corresponding object:** A business rule (a fact) that influences the ability to perform an action on another business rule.

- A course (anchor object) must have a course name (corresponding object). In this example, the action is updating the course name property of a course.

- A student (anchor object) must have a value of 2.0 or greater for Student_GPA (corresponding object) to graduate (action). In this example, the anchor object is a structural assertion, but it is possible for the anchor object to be another action assertion.
- A student cannot register for (the anchor object is the Is_registered relationship) a section of a course for which there is no qualified faculty (the corresponding object is the Is_qualified relationship).

Types of Action Assertions For simplicity, we do not show in Figure 4-15 the various types of action assertions that exist. There are three ways to classify action assertions:

1. Action assertions can be classified based on the type of result from the assertion. Looking at action assertions in this way yields three types of assertions:
   a. *Condition*, which states that if something is true, then another business rule will apply. The third example of an action assertion above could be stated as a condition in the form of "If a course has a qualified faculty, then students can register for a section of that course."
   b. *Integrity constraint*, which states something that must always be true. The first example of an action assertion above illustrates an integrity constraint. Another example would be "The date a faculty becomes qualified to teach a course cannot be after the semester in which the faculty is assigned to teach a section of that course."
   c. *Authorization*, which states a privilege; for example, only department chairs (a type of user) can qualify a faculty to teach a course.

2. Action assertions can be classified based on the form of the assertion. Looking at action assertions in this way yields three types of assertions:
   a. *Enabler*, which, if true, permits or leads to the existence of the corresponding object. An example of an enabler is "A faculty can be created once the faculty is qualified to teach at least one course."
   b. *Timer*, which enables (disables) or creates (deletes) an action. An example of a timer assertion is "When a student has a GPA above 2.0 and a total credit hours above 125, then student may graduate." Note, the action of graduating does not occur because of this timer assertion, but rather the timer enables the action to occur.
   c. *Executive*, which causes the execution of one or more actions. An executive action assertion can be thought of as a trigger for some action. An example of an executive assertion is "When a student has a GPA below 2.0, then the student goes on academic probation." This executive action might result in a status attribute of the student to be updated to the value of "probation."

3. Action assertions can be classified based on the rigor of the assertion. Looking at action assertions in this way yields two types of assertions:
   a. *Controlling*, which state that something must or must not be or happen. The examples we have used so far all fall in this category.
   b. *Influencing*, which are guidelines or items of interest for which a notification must occur. An example of an influencing action assertion is "When the number of students registered for a section exceeds 90 percent of the capacity of that section, notify the responsible department chair." In this situation, nothing is controlled (students may continue to register for the near-capacity section and no additional sections are created), but management wants to know that a particular condition has occurred.

Representing and Enforcing Business Rules

Most organizations have hundreds (or thousands) of such rules. Action assertions have traditionally been implemented in procedural logic buried deep within *individual* application programs—in a form that is virtually unrecognizable, unmanageable, and inconsistent. This approach places a heavy burden on the programmer, who must know all the constraints that an action may violate and must include checks for each of these constraints. An omission, misunderstanding, or error by the programmer will likely leave the database in an invalid state.

The more modern approach is to declare action assertions at a conceptual level without specifying how the rule will be implemented. Thus, there needs to be a specification language for business rules. We have seen that the EER notation works well for specifying many types of business rules. In fact, the EER notation was invented to allow more business rules to be shown in graphical form than the simpler E-R notation. An alternative to a graphical notation would be a structured grammar (such as a limited form of English). Whether graphical or grammatical, two desirable features for a business rule specification language would be:

1. It should be relatively simple so that end users not only can understand the rule statements, but also can define the rules themselves.

2. The language should be sufficiently structured to be automatically convertible to the computer code that enforces the specifications.

In the following section we illustrate both graphical and structured grammar approaches to specifying business rules. The graphical approach we used is adapted from Ross (1997), a leader in the development of business rule specifications.

Sample Business Rules In this section we augment the data model for class scheduling, Figure 4-16, with two new business rules. You will be asked to add additional rules in the problems and exercises at the end of the chapter.

Business Rule 1 For a faculty member to be assigned to teach a section of a course, the faculty member must be qualified to teach the course for which that section is scheduled.

This rule refers to three entity types in Figure 4-16: FACULTY, SECTION, and COURSE. The question is whether a faculty member can be assigned to teach a section (of a course). Thus the anchor object is the relationship Is_assigned. We are not constraining the faculty member, nor are we constraining the section. Rather, we are constraining the assignment of the faculty member to the section. Figure 4-17 shows the dashed line from Is_assigned to the action assertion symbol.

What are the corresponding objects in this rule? For a faculty member to be assigned to teach a section of a course, *two* conditions are necessary:

1. The faculty member must be qualified to teach the course (this information is recorded by the Is_qualified relationship), and

2. The section must be scheduled for the course (this information is recorded by the Is_scheduled relationship).

Thus in this case there are two corresponding objects. This fact is represented by the dashed lines from the action assertion symbol to each of the two relationships.

Business Rule 2 For a faculty member to be assigned to teach a section of a course, the faculty member must not be assigned to teach a total of more than three course sections.

This rule imposes a limitation on the *total* number of sections a faculty member may teach at a given time. Since the rule involves a total, it requires a modification of the previous notation.

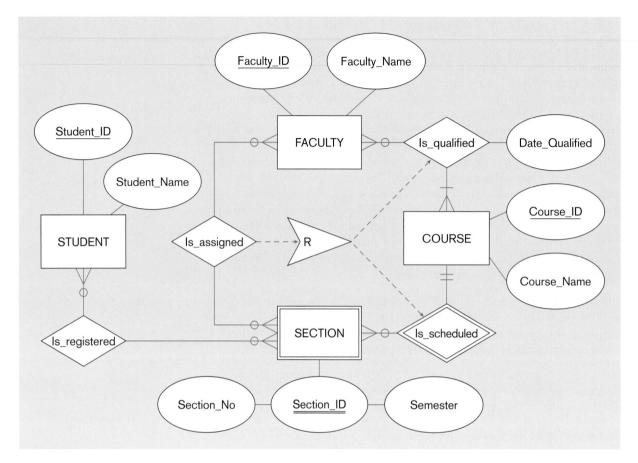

Figure 4-17
Business Rule 1: For a faculty member to be assigned to teach a section of a course, the faculty member must be qualified to teach the course for which that section is scheduled. (The letter "R" inside the symbol represents "Restricted," which is one of the many options for constraints.)

As shown in Figure 4-18, the anchor object is again the relationship Is_assigned. However, in this case, the corresponding object is also the relationship Is_assigned! In particular, it is a count of the total sections assigned to the faculty member. The letters "LIM" in the action assertion symbol stand for "limit." The arrow leaving this symbol then points to a circle with the letter "U", which stands for "upper." The second circle then contains the number 3, which is the upper limit. Thus the constraint is read as follows: "The corresponding object is a count of the number of sections assigned to the faculty member, which has an upper limit of three." If a faculty member is already assigned three sections, any transaction that attempts to add another section will be rejected.

You can implement business rules such as those above using the SQL language, and store the rules as part of the database definitions. One way to implement a rule with SQL is to use the **CREATE ASSERTION** statement, which is included in the most recent version of this language (SQL2). For example, consider Business Rule 2. The following statement creates an assertion named "Overload_Protect:"

```
CREATE ASSERTION Overload_Protect
CHECK (SELECT COUNT(*)
FROM ASSIGNED
WHERE Faculty_ID = '12345') <= 3;
```

This statement checks whether the total number of course sections assigned to a particular faculty member is less than or equal to the limit (three). The database management system is responsible for ensuring that this constraint is not violated.

Many other business rules, besides the few examples of this section, are possible. See Ross (1997) for a comprehensive list and associated notation.

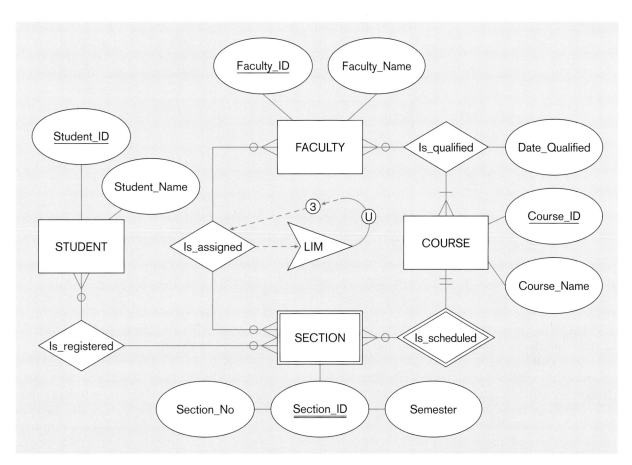

Figure 4-18
Business Rule 2: For a faculty member
to be assigned to teach a section of a
course, the faculty member must not be
assigned to teach a total of more than
three course sections.

Identifying and Testing Business Rules

You have seen in this chapter a wide variety of business rules and how they can be represented in structured grammar and EER diagrams and extensions. It is your job as a data analyst to document the specifications of business rules and then insure that the business rules are enforced as much as possible through database technologies. But, before business rules can be specified, they must be identified. Then, once specified, they should be tested before being implemented in technology.

An approach to identifying and testing business rules is scenarios (Moriarty, 1993). A scenario is a story or script that describes how a business reacts to a given situation. A scenario is similar to the concept of a use case, which is an important tool in object modeling (see Chapters 14 and 15). For example, a scenario related to the E-R diagram of Figure 4-16 would focus on the events related to a student. Events include being admitted, registering for (and dropping) classes, obtaining grades for a class, and graduating. A scenario would trace through these events for a given individual. The scenario is used to either identify elements (business rules) for the data model or to test that the data model handles all possible circumstances for these events (e.g., a student trying to register for a nonexisting class, a student on probation trying to register, or a graduated student trying to register).

A student scenario might read as follows: "Missi Davies logs on to the class registration system to sign up for classes next semester. Missi enters her student ID and password to gain authorization to sign up for classes. Missi is an MIS major in good academic standing. Missi wants to make sure she gets into the courses required in her major, so she searches among the list of MIS courses for the required database course. Missi discovers that there are two sections of this course offered in the next semester, but one is already closed. Thus, for the on-line registration system, Missi must register for the open section. Depending on her overall schedule, Missi may see the department chair to be signed into the closed section and drop registration in the open section." If a set of business rules had not already been identified, this and other scenarios could be used to identify terms, facts, and action assertions to be included in the data model. If a set of business rules already exist, then statements in scenarios can be used to validate that the business rules handle all possible circumstances.

Summary

This chapter has described how the basic E-R model has been extended to include supertype/subtype relationships. A *supertype* is a generic entity type that has a relationship with one or more subtypes. A *subtype* is a grouping of the entities in an entity type that is meaningful to the organization. For example, the entity type PERSON is frequently modeled as a supertype. Subtypes of PERSON may include EMPLOYEE, VOLUNTEER, and CLIENT. Subtypes inherit the attributes and relationships associated with their supertype.

Supertype/subtype relationships should normally be considered in data modeling with either (or both) of the following conditions present: First, there are attributes that apply to some (but not all) of the instances of an entity type. Second, the instances of a subtype participate in a relationship unique to that subtype.

The techniques of generalization and specialization are important guides in developing supertype/subtype relationships. Generalization is the bottom-up process of defining a generalized entity type from a set of more specialized entity types. Specialization is the top-down process of defining one or more subtypes of a supertype that has already been defined.

The EER notation allows us to capture the important business rules that apply to supertype/subtype relationships. The completeness constraint allows us to specify whether an instance of a supertype must also be a member of at least one subtype. There are two cases: With total specialization, an instance of the supertype *must* be a member of at least one subtype. With partial specialization, an instance of a supertype may or may not be a member of any subtype. The disjointness constraint allows us to specify whether an instance of a supertype may simultaneously be a member of two or more subtypes. Again, there are two cases. With the disjoint rule, an instance can be a member of only *one* subtype *at a given time*. With the overlap rule, an entity instance can simultaneously be a member of two (or more) subtypes.

A subtype discriminator is an attribute of a supertype whose values determine to which subtype (or subtypes) a supertype instance belongs. A supertype/subtype hierarchy is a hierarchical arrangement of supertypes and subtypes, where each subtype has only one supertype.

There are extensions to the E-R notation other than supertype/subtype relationships. One of the other more useful extensions is aggregation, which represents how some entities are part of other entities (e.g., a PC is composed of a disk drive, RAM, motherboard, etc.). For space limitations we have not discussed these extensions here. Most of these extensions, like aggregation, are also a part of object-oriented data modeling, which is explained in Chapters 14 and 15.

E-R diagrams can become large and complex, including hundreds of entities. Many users and managers do not need to see all the entities, relationships, and attributes to understand the part of the database with which they are most interested. Entity clustering is a way to turn a part of an entity-relationship data model into a more macro-level view of the same data. An entity cluster is a set of one or more entity types and associated relationships grouped into a single abstract entity type. Several entity clusters and associated relationships can be further grouped into even a higher entity cluster, so entity clustering is a hierarchical decomposition technique. By grouping entities and relationships, you can lay out an E-R diagram to allow you to give attention to the details of the model that matter most in a given data modeling task.

A business rule is a statement that defines or constrains some aspect of the business. It is intended to assert business structure or control or influence the behavior of the business. Rules can be divided into three major categories: derivations, structural assertions, and action assertions. Structural assertions define the static structure of the organization, while action assertions are rules that constrain the dynamic operations of the organization. A structural assertion is a term or a fact. A term is a definition of a concept about the business, and a fact is a statement involving the association of two or more terms. Facts can be base, or fundamental, facts or derivations from mathematical or logical manipulations of other facts; they can deal with an attribute, relationship, or supertype/subtype association between facts.

Action assertions state that the actions (such as create, delete, update, and read) on some business rule, called the anchor object, are constrained by other corresponding objects. Constraints can be if . . . then . . . else conditions, integrity rules, or authorization privileges. An action assertion can permit the existence of the corresponding object, enable or disable an action, or cause an action to be taken. Other types of action assertions are simply guidelines that trigger notification of special conditions.

CHAPTER REVIEW

Key Terms

Action	Disjoint rule	Specialization
Action assertion	Disjointness constraint	Structural assertion
Anchor object	Enhanced entity-relationship (EER)	Subtype
Attribute inheritance	model	Subtype discriminator
Completeness constraint	Entity cluster	Supertype
Corresponding object	Generalization	Supertype/subtype hierarchy
Derivation	Overlap rule	Total specialization rule
Derived fact	Partial specialization rule	

Review Questions

1. Define each of the following terms:
   a. supertype
   b. subtype
   c. specialization
   d. entity cluster
   e. structural assertion
   f. anchor object
   g. subtype discriminator
   h. total specialization rule
   i. generalization
   j. disjoint rule
   k. overlap rule
   l. action assertion

2. Match the following terms and definitions.

   _____ supertype
   _____ entity cluster
   _____ structural assertion
   _____ subtype
   _____ specialization
   _____ anchor object
   _____ action
   _____ subtype discriminator
   _____ attribute inheritance
   _____ overlap rule
   _____ corresponding object
   _____ derived fact

   a. subset of supertype
   b. entity belongs to two subtypes
   c. subtype gets supertype attributes
   d. rule on which actions are limited
   e. business rule that influences an action
   f. create, delete, update, or read
   g. calculated using an algorithm
   h. generalized entity type
   i. static structure of organization
   j. creating subtypes for an entity type
   k. a group of associated entity types and relationships
   l. locates target subtype for an entity

3. Contrast the following terms:
   a. supertype; subtype
   b. generalization; specialization
   c. anchor object; corresponding object
   d. disjoint rule; overlap rule
   e. structural assertion; action assertion
   f. total specialization rule; partial specialization rule

4. State two conditions that indicate when a designer should consider using supertype/subtype relationships.

5. State the reason for entity clustering.

6. Give an example (other than those discussed in the chapter) of a supertype/subtype relationship.

7. Give an example (other than those discussed in the chapter) of each of the following:
   a. structural assertion
   b. action assertion

8. What is attribute inheritance? Why is it important?

9. Give an example of each of the following:
   a. supertype/subtype relationship where the disjoint rule applies
   b. supertype/subtype relationship where the overlap rule applies

10. What types of business rules are normally captured in an EER diagram?

11. What is the purpose of a subtype discriminator?

Problems and Exercises

1. Examine the hierarchy for the university EER diagram (Figure 4-10). As a student, you are an instance of one of the subtypes: either UNDERGRAD STUDENT or GRADUATE STUDENT. List the names of all the attributes that apply to you, and then for each attribute record the data value that applies to you.

2. Add a subtype discriminator for each of the supertypes shown in Figure 4-10. Show the discriminator values that assign instances to each subtype. Use the following subtype discriminator names and values:

   a. PERSON: Person_Type (Employee?, Alumnus?, Student?)

   b. EMPLOYEE: Employee_Type (Faculty, Staff)

   c. STUDENT: Student_Type (Grad, Undergrad)

3. Draw an EER diagram for the following problem. A non-profit organization depends on a number of different types of persons for its successful operation. The organization is interested in the following attributes for all of these persons: SSN, Name, Address, City/State/Zip, and Telephone. Three types of persons are of greatest interest: employees, volunteers, and donors. Employees only have a Date_Hired attribute, and volunteers only have a Skill attribute. Donors only have a relationship (named Donates) with an Item entity type. A donor must have donated one or more items, and an item may have no donors, or one or more donors.

   There are persons other than employees, volunteers, and donors who are of interest to the organization, so that a person need not belong to any of these three groups. On the other hand, at a given time a person may belong to two or more of these groups (for example, employee and donor).

4. Add a subtype discriminator (named Person_Type) to the EER diagram you created in Problem and Exercise 3.

5. A rental car agency classifies the vehicles it rents into four categories: compact, mid-size, full-size, and sport utility. The agency wants to record the following data for all vehicles: Vehicle_ID, Make, Model, Year, and Color. There are no unique attributes for any of the four classes of vehicle. The entity type vehicle has a relationship (named Rents) with a customer entity type. None of the four vehicle classes has a unique relationship with an entity type. Would you consider creating a supertype/subtype relationship for this problem? Why or why not?

6. At a weekend retreat, the entity type PERSON has three subtypes: CAMPER, BIKER, and RUNNER. Draw a separate EER diagram segment for each of the following situations:

   a. At a given time, a person must be exactly one of these subtypes.

   b. A person may or may not be one of these subtypes. However, a person who is one of these subtypes cannot at the same time be one of the other subtypes.

   c. A person may or may not be one of these subtypes. On the other hand, a person may be any two (or even three) of these subtypes at the same time.

   d. At a given time, a person must be at least one of these subtypes.

7. A bank has three types of accounts: checking, savings, and loan. Following are the attributes for each type of account:

   CHECKING: Acct_No, Date_Opened, Balance, Service_Charge

   SAVINGS: Acct_No, Date_Opened, Balance, Interest_Rate

   LOAN: Acct_No, Date_Opened, Balance, Interest_Rate, Payment

   Assume that each bank account must be a member of exactly one of these subtypes. Using generalization, develop an EER model segment to represent this situation. Remember to include a subtype discriminator.

8. Refer to the employee EER diagram (Figure 4-2) to perform the following exercises. Make any assumptions that you believe are necessary.

   a. Develop a sample definition for each entity type, attribute, and relationship in the diagram.

   b. Develop sample integrity constraint action assertions for all of the attributes in the figure.

9. Refer to the data model for class scheduling (Figure 4-16). Add graphical notation to the figure to express each of the following business rules:

   a. For a section of a course to be scheduled, there must be a faculty member who is qualified to teach that course (*Hint*: See Figure 4-17.)

   b. For a student to register in a section of a course, that student may not be registered in a total of more than six course sections at a given time (*Hint*: See Figure 4-18.)

10. Refer to the EER diagram for hospital relationships (Figure 4-3). Add notation to express the following business rule: A resident patient can be assigned a bed only if that patient has been assigned a responsible physician. In this example, what is (are):

    a. the anchor object?

    b. the corresponding object(s)?

11. Consider the following "business" rule: "A student may attend a concert only if that student has completed his (her) homework."

    a. Draw an EER diagram segment to portray the entities and relationships implied in this rule.

    b. Add suitable notation to express the business rule.

    c. Identify each of the following: (i) anchor object; (ii) corresponding object(s).

12. Refer to the EER diagram for patients (Figure 4-3) and perform the following exercises. Make any assumptions you believe are necessary.

    a. Develop sample definitions for each entity type, attribute, and relationship in the diagram.

    b. Develop sample integrity constraint action insertions for each attribute in the diagram.

13. Figure 4-13 shows the development of entity clusters for the Pine Valley Furniture E-R diagram. In Figure 4-13b, explain the following:

    a. Why the minimum cardinality next to CUSTOMER for the Does_business_in relationship is 0.

    b. What the attributes of ITEM would be (refer to Figure 3-22).

    c. What the attributes of MATERIAL would be (refer to Figure 3-22).

14. Refer to your answer to Problem and Exercise 6 in Chapter 3. Develop entity clusters for this E-R diagram and redraw the diagram using the entity clusters. Explain why you chose the entity clusters you used.

15. Refer to your answer to Problem and Exercise 11 in Chapter 3. Develop entity clusters for this E-R diagram and redraw the diagram using the entity clusters. Explain why you chose the entity clusters you used.

Field Exercises

1. Interview a friend or family member to elicit common examples of the following things they may come in contact with at work.

   a. *Supertype/subtype relationships.* You will have to explain the meaning of this term to the person you are interviewing and provide a common example, such as: PROPERTY: RESIDENTIAL, COMMERCIAL; or BONDS: CORPORATE, MUNICIPAL. Use the information the person provides to construct an EER diagram segment and present it to the person. Revise if necessary until it seems appropriate to you and your friend or family member.

   b. *Business rules.* Give the person you are interviewing examples of business rules, using the ones provided in this chapter (Figures 4-17 and 4-18). When your informant gives you a rule from his or her environment, restructure it if necessary to conform to the syntax of this chapter.

2. Visit two local small businesses, one in the service sector and one in manufacturing. Interview employees from these organizations to obtain examples of both supertype/subtype relationships and business rules (such as "A customer can return merchandise only with a valid sales slip"). In which of these environments is it easier to find examples of these constructs? Why?

3. Ask a database administrator or database or systems analyst in a local company to show you an EER (or E-R) diagram for one of the organization's primary databases. Does this organization model supertype/subtype relationships? If so, what notation is used and does the CASE tool the company uses support these relationships? Also, what types of business rules are included during the EER modeling phase? How are business rules represented, and how and where are they stored?

4. Read the summary of business rules published by the GUIDE Business Rules Project (1997) and the article by Gottesdiener (1997). Search the Web for additional information on business rules. Then write a three-page executive summary of current directions in business rules and their potential impact on systems development and maintenance.

References

Elmasri, R., and S. B. Navathe. 1994. *Fundamentals of Database Systems.* Menlo Park, CA: Benjamin/Cummings.

Gottesdiener, E. 1997. "Business Rules Show Power, Promise." *Application Development Trends* 4 (3) (March): 36–54.

"GUIDE Business Rules Project." Final Report, revision, 1.2. October, 1997.

Moriarty, T. "Using Scenarios in Information Modeling: Bringing Business Rules to Life." *Database Programming & Design* 6 (8): 65–67.

Ross, R. G. 1997. *The Business Rule Book.* Version 4. Boston: Business Rule Solutions, Inc.

Teorey, T. 1999. *Database Modeling & Design.* San Francisco, CA: Morgan Kaufman Publishers.

Further Reading

Schmidt, B. 1997. "A Taxonomy of Domains." *Database Programming & Design* 10 (9) (September): 95, 96, 98, 99.

von Halle, B. 1996. "Object-Oriented Lessons." *Database Programming & Design* 9 (1) (January): 13–16.

von Halle, B., and R. Kaplan. 1997. "Is IT Falling Short?" *Database Programming & Design* 10 (6) (June): 15–17.

Web Resources

www.adtmag.com *Application Development Trends* magazine, a leading publication on the practice of information systems development.

www.brsolutions.com Business Rules Solutions is the consulting company of Ronald Ross, a leader in the development of a business rule methodology.

www.businessrulesgroup.org The Business Rules Group, formerly part of GUIDE International, formulates and supports standards about business rules.

www.guide.org SHARE is a volunteer organization that provides education, networking, and influence for the IT industry.

SHARE and GUIDE have combined; both were originally user groups for IBM Corporation customers.

www.Intelligententerprise.com *Intelligent Enterprise* magazine, a leading publication on database management and related areas. This magazine is the result of combining two previous publications, *Database Programming & Design* and *DBMS.*

www.kpiusa.com/BusinessRuleProducts.htm A Website maintained by Knowledge Partners, Inc., where vendors of business rule products can list information.

# MOUNTAIN VIEW COMMUNITY HOSPITAL

Project Case

PROJECT DESCRIPTION

As a large service organization, Mountain View Community Hospital depends on a large number of persons for its continued success. There are four groups of persons on whom the hospital is most dependent: employees, physicians, patients, and volunteers. Of course some common attributes are shared by all of these persons: Person_ID (identifier), Name, Address, City/State/Zip, Birth_Date, and Phone.

Each of the four groups of persons has at least one unique attribute of its own. Employees have a Date_Hired, Volunteers have a Skill, Physicians have a Specialty and a Pager# (pager number), and Patients have a Contact_Date (date of first contact with the hospital).

Some other persons in the hospital community do not belong to one of these four groups (their numbers are relatively small). However, a particular person may belong to two (or more) of these groups at a given time (for example, Patient and Volunteer).

Each patient has one (and only one) physician responsible for that patient. A given physician may not be responsible for a patient at a given time or may be responsible for one or more patients. Patients are divided into two groups: resident and outpatient. Each resident patient has a Date_Admitted attribute. Each outpatient is scheduled for zero or more visits. The entity visit has two attributes: Date (partial identifier) and Comments. Notice that an instance of visit cannot exist without an outpatient owner entity.

Employees are subdivided into three groups: nurse, staff, and technician. Only nurse has the attribute Certificate, which indicates the qualification (RN, LPN, etc.). Only staff has the attribute Job_Class, and only technician has the attribute Skill. Each nurse is assigned to one (and only one) care center. Examples of care centers are Maternity, Emergency, and Cardiology. Attributes of care center are Name (identifier) and Location. A care center may have one or more nurses assigned to it. Also for each care center, one of the nurses assigned to that care center is appointed nurse_in_charge. A nurse cannot be

appointed nurse_in_charge of a care center unless she or he has an RN certificate.

Each technician is assigned to one or more laboratories. Attributes of laboratory include Name (identifier) and Location. A laboratory must have at least one technician assigned to it and may have any number of technicians assigned.

There may be no beds assigned to a care center, or a care center may have one or more beds (up to any number) assigned to it. The only attribute of bed is Bed_ID (identifier). Bed_ID is a composite attribute, with components Bed# and Room#. Each resident patient must be assigned to a bed. A bed may or may not have a resident patient assigned to it at a given time.

PROJECT QUESTIONS

1. Is the ability to model supertype/subtype relationships likely to be important in a hospital environment such as Mountain View Community Hospital? Why or why not?
2. Can the business rules paradigm and the ability to easily define, implement, and maintain business rules be used as a competitive advantage in a hospital environment such as Mountain View Community Hospital? Why or why not?
3. Do there appear to be any weak entities in the description of the data requirements in this project segment? If so, what are they?
4. Can you think of any business rules (other than the one explicitly described in the case) that are likely to be used in a hospital environment?

PROJECT EXERCISES

1. Draw an EER diagram to accurately represent this set of requirements, carefully following the notation from this chapter.
2. Develop definitions for each of the following types of objects in your EER diagram from Project Exercise 1. Consult with some member of the hospital or health

care community if one is available; otherwise make reasonable assumptions based on your own knowledge and experience.

a. Entity types

b. Attributes

c. Relationships

3. You should recognize the statement "a nurse cannot be appointed nurse_in_charge of a care center unless she or he has an RN certificate" as a statement of a business rule. Answer the following questions:

a. What is the anchor object? Is it an entity, an attribute, a relationship, or some other object?

b. What is the corresponding object (or objects, if more than one)? Is it an entity, an attribute, a relationship, or some other object?

4. Compare the EER diagram that you developed in this chapter with the E-R diagram you developed in Chapter 3 in Project Exercise 2. What are the differences between these two diagrams? Why are there differences?

5. Merge the two diagrams from Project Exercise 4 above and from Project Exercise 2 in Chapter 3 into a single diagram. Explain decisions you make during the merging.

Part THREE

Database Design

- **Chapter 5**
Logical Database Design
and the Relational Model

- **Chapter 6**
Physical Database Design and Performance

An Overview of Part

By the end of the database analysis phase of database development, systems and database analysts have a fairly clear understanding of data storage and access requirements. However, the data model developed during analysis explicitly avoided any ties to database technologies. Before we can implement a database, the conceptual data model must be mapped into a data model that is compatible with the database management system to be used.

The activities of database design transform the requirements for data storage developed during database analysis into specifications to guide database implementation. There are two forms of specifications:

1. logical, which maps the conceptual requirements into the data model associated with a specific database management system, and

2. physical, which indicates all the parameters for data storage that are then input to database implementation, during which a database is actually defined using a data definition language.

In Chapter 5 (Logical Database Design and the Relational Model) we describe logical database design, with special emphasis on the relational data model. Logical database design is the process of transforming the conceptual data model (described in Chapters 3 and 4) into a logical data model. Most database management systems in use today use the relational data model, so this data model is the basis for our discussion of logical database design.

In this chapter, we first define the important terms and concepts for this model, including relation, primary key, foreign key, anomaly, normal form, normalization, functional dependency, partial functional dependency, and transitive dependency. We next describe and illustrate the process of transforming an E-R model to the relational model. Many CASE tools support this transformation; however, it is important that you understand the underlying principles and procedures. We then describe in detail the important concepts of normalization (the process of designing well-structured relations). Finally, we describe how to merge relations from separate logical design activities (e.g., different groups

within a large project team) while avoiding common pitfalls that may occur in this process.

The purpose of physical database design, the topic of Chapter 6 (Physical Database Design and Performance), is to translate the logical description of data into the technical specifications for storing and retrieving data. The goal is to create a design for storing data that will provide adequate performance and ensure database integrity, security, and recoverability. Physical database design produces the technical specifications that programmers and others involved in information systems construction will use during the implementation phase, which we discuss in Chapters 7 through 11.

In Chapter 6 you will learn key terms and concepts for physical database design, including data type, page, pointer, denormalization, partitioning, indexed file organization, and hashed file organization. You will study the basic steps to develop an efficient physical database design. You will learn about choices for storing attribute values and how to select among these choices. You will also learn why normalized tables do not always form the best physical data files, and how you can denormalize the data to achieve data retrieval speed improvements. You will learn about different file organizations and different types of indexes, which are important in speeding the retrieval of data. Chapter 6 also addresses how to use redundant data storage schemes (RAID) to provide improved performance and reliability to databases. In addition, you will learn the major differences between different architectures for databases. Finally, you will address some techniques of database design and query handling that improve the speed of data access.

You must carefully perform physical database design because decisions made during this stage have a major impact on data accessibility, response times, security, user friendliness, and similarly important information system design factors. Database administration (described in Chapter 12) plays a major role in physical database design, so we will return to some advanced design issues in that chapter, and Chapter 13 addresses distributed database design issues.

Chapter 5

Logical Database Design
and the Relational Model

LEARNING OBJECTIVES

After studying this chapter, you should be able to:

● Define the following key terms: **relation, primary key, composite key, foreign key, null, entity integrity rule, referential integrity constraint, well-structured relation, anomaly, recursive foreign key, normalization, normal form, functional dependency, determinant, candidate key, first normal form, second normal form, partial functional dependency, third normal form, transitive dependency, synonyms, alias, homonym,** and **enterprise key.**

● List five properties of relations.

● State two properties that are essential for a candidate key.

● Give a concise definition of each of the following: first normal form, second normal form, and third normal form.

● Briefly describe four problems that may arise when merging relations.

● Transform an E-R (or EER) diagram to a logically equivalent set of relations.

● Create relational tables that incorporate entity integrity and referential integrity constraints.

● Use normalization to decompose a relation with anomalies into well-structured relations.

INTRODUCTION

In this chapter we describe logical database design, with special emphasis on the relational data model. Logical database design is the process of transforming the conceptual data model (described in Chapters 3 and 4) into a logical data model. Although there are other data models, we have two reasons for emphasizing the relational data model in this chapter. First, the relational data model is most commonly used in con-temporary database applications. Second, some of the principles of logical database design for the relational model apply to the other logical models as well.

We have introduced the relational data model informally through simple examples in earlier chapters. In this chapter, we first define the important terms and concepts for this model. (We will often use the abbreviated term *relational model* when referring to the rela-

165

tional data model.) We next describe and illustrate the process of transforming an E-R model into the relational model. Many CASE tools support this transformation today; however, it is important that you understand the underlying principles and procedures. We then describe the concepts of normalization in detail. Normalization, which is the process of designing well-structured relations, is an important component of logical design for the relational model. Finally, we describe how to merge relations while avoiding common pitfalls that may occur in this process.

The objective of logical database design is to translate the conceptual design (which represents an organization's requirements for data) into a logical database design that can be implemented on a chosen database management system. The resulting databases must meet user needs for data sharing, flexibility, and ease of access. The concepts presented in this chapter are essential to your understanding of the database development process.

THE RELATIONAL DATA MODEL

The relational data model was first introduced in 1970 by E. F. Codd, then of IBM (Codd, 1970). Two early research projects were launched to prove the feasibility of the relational model and to develop prototype systems. The first of these, at IBM's San Jose Research Laboratory, led to the development of System R (a prototype relational DBMS–RDBMS) during the late 1970s. The second, at the University of California at Berkeley, led to the development of Ingres, an academically oriented RDBMS. Commercial RDBMS products from numerous vendors started to appear about 1980 (see the Website for this book for links to RDBMS and other DBMS vendors). Today RDBMSs have become the dominant technology for database management, and there are literally hundreds of RDBMS products for computers ranging from personal computers to mainframes.

Basic Definitions

The relational data model represents data in the form of tables. The relational model is based on mathematical theory and therefore has a solid theoretical foundation. However, we need only a few simple concepts to describe the relational model, and it is therefore easily understood and used by those unfamiliar with the underlying theory. The relational data model consists of the following three components (Fleming and von Halle, 1989):

1. *Data structure* Data are organized in the form of tables with rows and columns.

2. *Data manipulation* Powerful operations (using the SQL language) are used to manipulate data stored in the relations.

3. *Data integrity* Facilities are included to specify business rules that maintain the integrity of data when they are manipulated.

We discuss data structure and data integrity in this section. Data manipulation is discussed in Chapters 7, 8, and 10.

Relation: A named two-dimensional table of data.

Relational Data Structure A **relation** is a named, two-dimensional table of data. Each relation (or table) consists of a set of named columns and an arbitrary number of unnamed rows. An attribute, consistent with its definition in Chapter 3, is a named column of a relation. Each row of a relation corresponds to a record that contains data (attribute) values for a single entity. Figure 5-1 shows an example of a relation named EMPLOYEE1. This relation contains the following attributes describing employees: Emp_ID, Name, Dept_Name, and Salary. The five rows of the table correspond to five employees. It is important to understand that the sample data in Figure

EMPLOYEE1

Emp_ID	Name	Dept_Name	Salary
100	Margaret Simpson	Marketing	48,000
140	Allen Beeton	Accounting	52,000
110	Chris Lucero	Info Systems	43,000
190	Lorenzo Davis	Finance	55,000
150	Susan Martin	Marketing	42,000

Figure 5-1
EMPLOYEE1 relation with sample data

5-1 are intended to illustrate the structure of the EMPLOYEE1 relation; they are not part of the relation itself. Even if we add another row of data to the figure, it is still the same EMPLOYEE1 relation. Nor does deleting a row change the relation. In fact, we could delete *all* of the rows shown in Figure 5-1, and the EMPLOYEE1 relation would still exist. Stated differently, Figure 5-1 is an instance of the EMPLOYEE1 relation.

We can express the *structure* of a relation by a shorthand notation in which the name of the relation is followed (in parentheses) by the names of the attributes in that relation. For EMPLOYEE1 we would have:

EMPLOYEE1(Emp_ID,Name,Dept_Name,Salary).

Relational Keys We must be able to store and retrieve a row of data in a relation, based on the data values stored in that row. To achieve this goal, every relation must have a primary key. A **primary key** is an attribute (or combination of attributes) that uniquely identifies each row in a relation. We designate a primary key by underlining the attribute name. For example, the primary key for the relation EMPLOYEE1 is Emp_ID. Notice that this attribute is underlined in Figure 5-1. In shorthand notation we express this relation as follows:

EMPLOYEE1(Emp_ID,Name,Dept_Name,Salary)

Primary key: An attribute (or combination of attributes) that uniquely identifies each row in a relation.

The concept of a primary key is related to the term "identifier" defined in Chapter 3. The same attribute (or attributes) indicated as an entity's identifier in an E-R diagram may be the same attributes that compose the primary key for the relation representing that entity. There are exceptions; for example, associative entities do not have to have an identifier and the identifier of a weak entity forms only part of a weak entity's primary key. In addition, there may be several attributes of an entity that may serve as the associated relation's primary key. All of these situations will be illustrated later in this chapter.

A **composite key** is a primary key that consists of more than one attribute. For example, the primary key for a relation DEPENDENT would likely consist of the combination Emp_ID and Dependent_Name. We show several examples of composite keys later in this chapter.

Composite key: A primary key that consists of more than one attribute.

Often we must represent the relationship between two tables or relations. This is accomplished through the use of foreign keys. A **foreign key** is an attribute (possibly composite) in a relation of a database that serves as the primary key of another relation in the same database. For example, consider the relations EMPLOYEE1 and DEPARTMENT:

Foreign key: An attribute in a relation of a database that serves as the primary key of another relation in the same database.

EMPLOYEE1(Emp_ID,Name,Dept_Name,Salary)

DEPARTMENT(Dept_Name,Location, Fax)

The attribute Dept_Name is a foreign key in EMPLOYEE1. It allows a user to associate any employee with the department to which he or she is assigned. Some authors emphasize the fact that an attribute is a foreign key by using a dashed underline, such as

EMPLOYEE1(Emp_ID,Name,Dept_Name,Salary)

We provide numerous examples of foreign keys in the remainder of this chapter and discuss the properties of foreign keys under the heading Referential Integrity.

Properties of Relations We have defined relations as two-dimensional tables of data. However, not all tables are relations. Relations have several properties that distinguish them from nonrelational tables. We summarize these properties below.

1. Each relation (or table) in a database has a unique name.
2. An entry at the intersection of each row and column is atomic (or single-valued). There can be no multivalued attributes in a relation.
3. Each row is unique; no two rows in a relation are identical.
4. Each attribute (or column) within a table has a unique name.
5. The sequence of columns (left to right) is insignificant. The columns of a relation can be interchanged without changing the meaning or use of the relation.
6. The sequence of rows (top to bottom) is insignificant. As with columns, the rows of a relation may be interchanged or stored in any sequence.

Removing Multivalued Attributes from Tables The second property of relations above states that there can be no multivalued attributes in a relation. Thus a table that contains one or more multivalued attributes is not a relation. As an example, Figure 5-2a shows the employee data from the EMPLOYEE1 relation extended to include courses that may have been taken by those employees. Since a given employee may have taken more than one course, the attributes Course_Title and Date_Completed are multivalued attributes. For example, the employee with

Figure 5-2
Eliminating multivalued attributes
(a)Table with repeating groups

Emp_ID	Name	Dept_Name	Salary	Course_Title	Date_Completed
100	Margaret Simpson	Marketing	48,000	SPSS	6/19/200X
				Surveys	10/7/200X
140	Alan Beeton	Accounting	52,000	Tax Acc	12/8/200X
110	Chris Lucero	Info Systems	43,000	SPSS	1/12/200X
				C++	4/22/200X
190	Lorenzo Davis	Finance	55,000		
150	Susan Martin	Marketing	42,000	SPSS	6/16/200X
				Java	8/12/200X

(b) EMPLOYEE2 relation

EMPLOYEE2

Emp_ID	Name	Dept_Name	Salary	Course_Title	Date_Completed
100	Margaret Simpson	Marketing	48,000	SPSS	6/19/200X
100	Margaret Simpson	Marketing	48,000	Surveys	10/7/200X
140	Alan Beeton	Accounting	52,000	Tax Acc	12/8/200X
110	Chris Lucero	Info Systems	43,000	SPSS	1/12/200X
110	Chris Lucero	Info Systems	43,000	C++	4/22/200X
190	Lorenzo Davis	Finance	55,000		
150	Susan Martin	Marketing	42,000	SPSS	6/19/200X
150	Susan Martin	Marketing	42,000	Java	8/12/200X

Emp_ID 100 has taken two courses. If an employee has not taken any courses, the Course_Title and Date_Completed attribute values are null (see employee with Emp_ID 190 for an example).

We show how to eliminate the multivalued attributes in Figure 5-2b by filling the relevant data values into the previously vacant cells of Figure 5-2a. As a result, the table in Figure 5-2b has only single-valued attributes and now satisfies the atomic property of relations. The name EMPLOYEE2 is given to this relation to distinguish it from EMPLOYEE1. However, as you will see below, this new relation does have some undesirable properties.

Example Database

A relational database consists of any number of relations. The structure of the database is described through the use of a conceptual schema (defined in Chapter 2), which is a description of the overall logical structure of the database. There are two common methods for expressing a (conceptual) schema:

a. Short text statements, in which each relation is named and the names of its attributes follow in parentheses (see EMPLOYEE1 and DEPARTMENT relations defined earlier in this chapter).

b. A graphical representation, in which each relation is represented by a rectangle containing the attributes for the relation.

Text statements have the advantage of simplicity. On the other hand, a graphical representation provides a better means of expressing referential integrity constraints (as you will see shortly). In this section we use both techniques for expressing a schema so that you can compare them.

We developed an entity-relationship diagram for Pine Valley Furniture in Chapter 3 (see Figure 3-22). In Chapter 1 we showed the following four relations from this database (see Figure 1-4): CUSTOMER, ORDER, ORDER LINE, and PRODUCT. In this section we show a schema for these four relations. A graphical representation is shown in Figure 5-3.

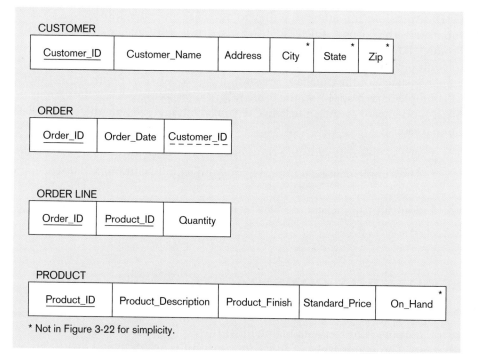

Figure 5-3
Schema for four relations (Pine Valley Furniture)

CUSTOMER

| Customer_ID | Customer_Name | Address | City* | State* | Zip* |

ORDER

| Order_ID | Order_Date | Customer_ID |

ORDER LINE

| Order_ID | Product_ID | Quantity |

PRODUCT

| Product_ID | Product_Description | Product_Finish | Standard_Price | On_Hand* |

* Not in Figure 3-22 for simplicity.

Figure 5-4
Instance of a relational schema

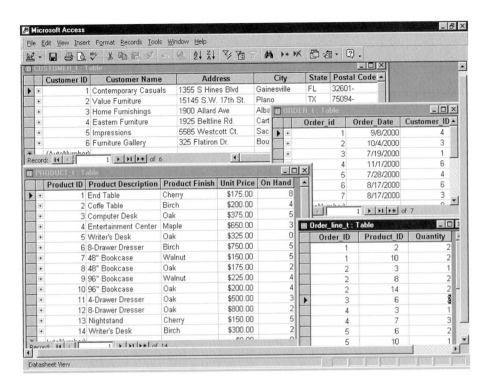

Following is a text description for the relations:

CUSTOMER(Customer_ID,Customer_Name,Address,City, State,Zip)

ORDER(Order_ID,Order_Date,Customer_ID)

ORDER LINE(Order_ID,Product_ID,Quantity)

PRODUCT(Product_ID,Product_Description,Product_Finish,Standard_Price, On_Hand)

Notice that the primary key for ORDER LINE is a composite key consisting of the attributes Order_ID and Product_ID. Also Customer_ID is a foreign key in the ORDER relation; this allows the user to associate an order with the customer who submitted the order. ORDER LINE has two foreign keys: Order_ID, and Product_ID. These keys allow the user to associate each line on an order with the relevant order and product.

An instance of this database is shown in Figure 5-4. This figure shows four tables with sample data. Notice how the foreign keys allow us to associate the various tables. It is a good idea to create an instance of your relational schema with sample data for three reasons:

1. The sample data provide a convenient way to check the accuracy of your design.

2. The sample data help improve communications with users in discussing your design.

3. You can use the sample data to develop prototype applications and to test queries.

INTEGRITY CONSTRAINTS

The relational data model includes several types of constraints, or business rules, whose purpose is to facilitate maintaining the accuracy and integrity of data in the database. The major types of integrity constraints are domain constraints, entity integrity, referential integrity, and action assertions.

Domain Constraints

All of the values that appear in a column of a relation must be taken from the same domain. A domain is the set of values that may be assigned to an attribute. A domain definition usually consists of the following components: domain name, meaning, data type, size (or length), and allowable values or allowable range (if applicable). Table 5-1 shows domain definitions for the domains associated with the attributes in Figure 5-3.

Entity Integrity

The entity integrity rule is designed to assure that every relation has a primary key, and that the data values for that primary key are all valid. In particular, it guarantees that every primary key attribute is non-null.

In some cases a particular attribute cannot be assigned a data value. There are two situations where this is likely to occur: Either there is no applicable data value, or the applicable data value is not known when values are assigned. Suppose for example that you fill out an employment form that has a space reserved for a fax number. If you have no fax number, you leave this space empty since it does not apply to you. Or suppose that you are asked to fill in the telephone number of your previous employer. If you do not recall this number, you may leave it empty since that information is not known.

The relational data model allows us to assign a null value to an attribute in the just described situations. A **null** is a value that may be assigned to an attribute when no other value applies or when the applicable value is unknown. In reality, a null is not a value but rather the absence of a value. For example, it is not the same as a numeric zero or a string of blanks. The inclusion of nulls in the relational model is somewhat controversial, since it sometimes leads to anomalous results (Date, 1995). On the other hand, Codd advocates the use of nulls for missing values (Codd, 1990).

Null: A value that may be assigned to an attribute when no other value applies or when the applicable value is unknown.

One thing on which everyone agrees is that primary key values must not be allowed to be null. Thus the **entity integrity rule** states the following: No primary key attribute (or component of a primary key attribute) may be null.

Entity integrity rule: No primary key attribute (or component of a primary key attribute) can be null.

Referential Integrity

In the relational data model, associations between tables are defined through the use of foreign keys. For example in Figure 5-4, the association between the CUSTOMER and ORDER tables is defined by including the Customer_ID attribute as a foreign key in ORDER. This of course implies that before we insert a new row in the ORDER table, the customer for that order must already exist in the CUSTOMER

Table 5-1 Domain Definitions for Selected Attributes

Attribute	Domain Name	Description	Domain
Customer_ID	Customer_IDs	Set of all possible customer IDs	character: size 5
Customer_Name	Customer_Names	Set of all possible customer names	character: size 25
Customer_Address	Customer_Addresses	Set of all possible customer addresses	character: size 30
Customer_City	Cities	Set of all possible cities	character: size 20
Customer_State	States	Set of all possible states	character: size 2
Customer_Zip	Zips	Set of all possible zip codes	character: size 10
Order_ID	Order_IDs	Set of all possible order IDs	character: size 5
Order_Date	Order_Dates	Set of all possible order dates	date format mm-dd-yy
Product_ID	Product_IDs	Set of all possible product IDs	character: size 5
Product_Description	Product_Descriptions	Set of all possible product descriptions	character size 25
Product_Finish	Product_Finishes	Set of all possible product finishes	character: size 12
Standard_Price	Unit_Prices	Set of all possible unit prices	monetary: 6 digits
On_Hand	On_Hands	Set of all possible on hands	integer: 3 digits

Referential integrity constraint: A rule that states that either each foreign key value must match a primary key value in another relation or the foreign key value must be null.

table. If you examine the rows in the ORDER table in Figure 5-4, you will find that every customer number for an order already appears in the CUSTOMER table.

A **referential integrity constraint** is a rule that maintains consistency among the rows of two relations. The rule states that if there is a foreign key in one relation, either each foreign key value must match a primary key value in another relation or the foreign key value must be null. You should examine the tables in Figure 5-4 to check whether the referential integrity rule has been enforced.

The graphical version of the relational schema provides a simple technique for identifying associations where referential integrity must be enforced. Figure 5-5 shows the schema for the relations introduced in Figure 5-3. An arrow has been drawn from each foreign key to the associated primary key. A referential integrity constraint must be defined for each of these arrows in the schema.

How do you know if a foreign key is allowed to be null? A simple answer can be seen in Figure 3-22, the E-R diagram associated with Figures 5-4 and 5-5. In Figure 3-22, because each order must have a customer (the minimum cardinality next to CUSTOMER on the Submits relationship is one), the foreign key of Customer_ID cannot be null on the ORDER relation. If the minimum cardinality had been zero, then the foreign key could be null. Whether a foreign key can be null must be specified as a property of the foreign key attribute when the database is defined.

Actually, whether a foreign key can be null is more complex to model on an E-R diagram and to determine than we have shown so far. For example, what happens to order data if we choose to delete a customer who has submitted orders? We may want to see sales even if we do not care about the customer any more. Three choices are possible:

1. Delete the associated orders (called a cascading delete), in which case we lose not only the customer but also all the sales history.

2. Prohibit deletion of the customer until all associated orders are first deleted (a safety check).

3. Place a null value in the foreign key (an exception that says although an order must have a Customer_ID value when the order is created, Customer_ID can become null later if the associated customer is deleted).

We will see how each of these choices is implemented when we describe the SQL database query language in Chapter 7.

Figure 5-5
Referential integrity constraints (Pine Valley Furniture)

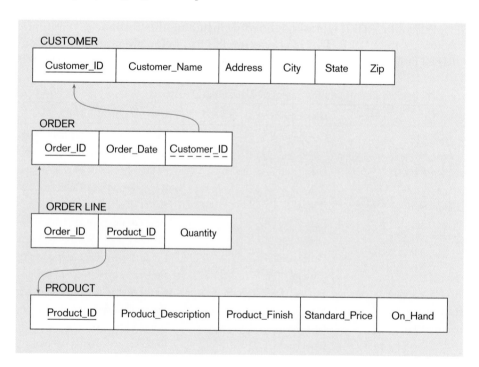

Action Assertions

In Chapter 4 we discussed business rules and introduced a new category of business rules we called action assertions. For example, a typical action assertion might state the following: "A person may purchase a ticket for the all-star game only if that person is a season-ticket holder." There are various techniques for defining and enforcing such rules. We discuss some of these techniques in later chapters.

Creating Relational Tables

In this section we create table definitions for the four tables shown in Figure 5-5. These definitions are created using **CREATE TABLE** statements from the SQL data definition language. In practice, these table definitions are actually created during the implementation phase later in the database development process. However, we show these sample tables in this chapter for continuity and especially to illustrate the way the integrity constraints described above are implemented in SQL.

The SQL table definitions are shown in Figure 5-6. One table is created for each of the four tables shown in the relational schema (Figure 5-5). Each attribute for a table is then defined. Notice that the data type and length for each attribute is taken from the domain definitions (Table 5-1). For example, the attribute Customer_Name in the CUSTOMER relation is defined as VARCHAR (variable character) data type with length 25. By specifying **NOT NULL**, each attribute can be constrained from being assigned a null value.

The primary key for each table is specified for each table using the **PRIMARY KEY** clause at the end of each table definition. The ORDER_LINE table illustrates how to specify a primary key when that key is a composite attribute. In this example,

```
CREATE TABLE CUSTOMER
        (CUSTOMER_ID             VARCHAR(5)      NOT NULL,
        CUSTOMER_NAME            VARCHAR(25)     NOT NULL,
        CUSTOMER ADDRESS         VARCHAR(30)     NOT NULL,
        CUSTOMER_CITY            VARCHAR(20)     NOT NULL,
        CUSTOMER_STATE           CHAR(2)         NOT NULL,
        CUSTOMER_ZIP             CHAR(10)        NOT NULL,
PRIMARY KEY (CUSTOMER_ID);

CREATE TABLE ORDER
        (ORDER_ID                CHAR(5)         NOT NULL,
        ORDER DATE               DATE            NOT NULL,
        CUSTOMER_ID              VARCHAR(5)      NOT NULL,
PRIMARY KEY (ORDER_ID),
FOREIGN KEY (CUSTOMER_ID) REFERENCES CUSTOMER (CUSTOMER_ID);

CREATE TABLE ORDER_LINE
        (ORDER_ID                CHAR(5)         NOT NULL,
        PRODUCT_ID               CHAR(5)         NOT NULL,
        QUANTITY                 INT             NOT NULL,
PRIMARY KEY (ORDER_ID, PRODUCT_ID),
FOREIGN KEY (ORDER_ID) REFERENCES ORDER (ORDER_ID),
FOREIGN KEY (PRODUCT_ID) REFERENCES PRODUCT (PRODUCT_ID);

CREATE TABLE PRODUCT
        (PRODUCT_ID              CHAR(5)         NOT NULL,
        PRODUCT_DESCRIPTION      VARCHAR(25),
        PRODUCT_FINISH           VARCHAR(12),
        STANDARD_PRICE           DECIMAL(8,2)    NOT NULL,
        ON_HAND                  INT             NOT NULL,
PRIMARY KEY (PRODUCT_ID);
```

Figure 5-6
SQL table definitions

the primary key of ORDER_LINE is the combination of Order_ID and Product_ID. Each primary key attribute in the four tables is constrained with **NOT NULL**. This enforces the entity integrity constraint described in the previous section. Notice that the **NOT NULL** constraint can also be used with non–primary key attributes.

Referential integrity constraints are easily defined, using the graphical schema shown in Figure 5-5. An arrow originates from each foreign key and "points to" the related primary key in the associated relation. In the SQL table definition, a **FOREIGN KEY REFERENCES** statement corresponds to each of these arrows. Thus for the table ORDER, the foreign key CUSTOMER_ID references the primary key of CUSTOMER, which is also CUSTOMER_ID. Although in this case the foreign key and primary keys have the same name, this need not be the case. For example, the foreign key attribute could be named CUST_NO instead of CUSTOMER_ID. However, the foreign and primary keys must be from the *same* domain.

The ORDER_LINE table provides an example of a table that has two foreign keys. Foreign keys in this table reference both the ORDER and PRODUCT tables.

Well-Structured Relations

Well-structured relation: A relation that contains minimal redundancy and allows users to insert, modify, and delete the rows in a table without errors or inconsistencies.

To prepare for our discussion of normalization, we need to address the following question: What constitutes a well-structured relation? Intuitively, a **well-structured relation** contains minimal redundancy and allows users to insert, modify, and delete the rows in a table without errors or inconsistencies. EMPLOYEE1 (Figure 5-1) is such a relation. Each row of the table contains data describing one employee, and any modification to an employee's data (such as a change in salary) is confined to one row of the table. In contrast, EMPLOYEE2 (Figure 5-2b) is not a well-structured relation. If you examine the sample data in the table, you will notice considerable redundancy. For example, values for Emp_ID, Name, Dept_Name, and Salary appear in two separate rows for employees 100, 110, and 150. Consequently, if the salary for employee 100 changes, we must record this fact in two rows (or more, for some employees).

Anomaly: An error or inconsistency that may result when a user attempts to update a table that contains redundant data. The three types of anomalies are insertion, deletion, and modification.

Redundancies in a table may result in errors or inconsistencies (called **anomalies**) when a user attempts to update the data in the table. Three types of anomalies are possible: insertion, deletion, and modification.

1. *Insertion anomaly* Suppose that we need to add a new employee to EMPLOYEE2. The primary key for this relation is the combination of Emp_ID and Course_Title (as noted earlier). Therefore, to insert a new row, the user must supply values for both Emp_ID and Course_Title (since primary key values cannot be null or nonexistent). This is an anomaly, since the user should be able to enter employee data without supplying course data.

2. *Deletion anomaly* Suppose that the data for employee number 140 are deleted from the table. This will result in losing the information that this employee completed a course (Tax Acc) on 12/8/200X. In fact, it results in losing the information that this course had an offering that completed on that date.

3. *Modification anomaly* Suppose that employee number 100 gets a salary increase. We must record the increase in each of the rows for that employee (two occurrences in Figure 5-2); otherwise the data will be inconsistent.

These anomalies indicate that EMPLOYEE2 is not a well-structured relation. The problem with this relation is that it contains data about two entities: EMPLOYEE and COURSE. We will use normalization theory (described below) to divide EMPLOYEE2 into two relations. One of the resulting relations is EMPLOYEE1 (Figure 5-1). The other we will call EMP_COURSE, which appears with sample data in Figure 5-7. The primary key of this relation is the combination of Emp_ID and

Emp_ID	Course_Title	Date_Completed
100	SPSS	6/19/200X
100	Surveys	10/7/200X
140	Tax Acc	12/8/200X
110	SPSS	1/12/200X
110	C++	4/22/200X
150	SPSS	6/19/200X
150	Java	8/12/200X

Figure 5-7
EMP_COURSE

Course_Title, and we underline these attribute names in Figure 5-7 to highlight this fact. Examine Figure 5-7 to verify that EMP_COURSE is free of the types of anomalies described above and is therefore well-structured.

TRANSFORMING EER DIAGRAMS INTO RELATIONS

During logical design you transform the E-R (and EER) diagrams that were developed during conceptual design into relational database schemas. The inputs to this process are the entity-relationship (and enhanced E-R) diagrams that you studied in Chapters 3 and 4. The outputs are the relational schemas described in the first two sections of this chapter.

Transforming (or mapping) E-R diagrams to relations is a relatively straightforward process with a well-defined set of rules. In fact, many CASE tools can automatically perform many of the conversion steps. However, it is important that you understand the steps in this process for three reasons:

1. CASE tools often cannot model more complex data relationships such as ternary relationships and supertype/subtype relationships. For these situations you may have to perform the steps manually.

2. There are sometimes legitimate alternatives where you will need to choose a particular solution.

3. You must be prepared to perform a quality check on the results obtained with a CASE tool.

In the following discussion we illustrate the steps in the transformation with examples taken from Chapters 3 and 4. It will help for you to recall that we discussed three types of entities in those chapters:

1. *Regular entities* are entities that have an independent existence and generally represent real-world objects such as persons and products. Regular entity types are represented by rectangles with a single line.

2. *Weak entities* are entities that cannot exist except with an identifying relationship with an owner (regular) entity type. Weak entities are identified by a rectangle with a double line.

3. *Associative entities* (also called gerunds) are formed from many-to-many relationships between other entity types. Associative entities are represented by a rectangle with a single line that encloses the diamond relationship symbol.

Step 1: Map Regular Entities

Each regular entity type in an ER diagram is transformed into a relation. The name given to the relation is generally the same as the entity type. Each simple attribute of the entity type becomes an attribute of the relation. The identifier of the entity type becomes the primary key of the corresponding relation. You should check to make sure that this primary key satisfies the desirable properties of identifiers outlined in Chapter 3.

Figure 5-8a shows a representation of the CUSTOMER entity type for Pine Valley Furniture Company from Chapter 3 (see Figure 3-22). The corresponding CUSTOMER relation is shown in graphical form in Figure 5-8b. In this figure and those that follow in this section we show only a few key attributes for each relation to simplify the figures.

Composite Attributes When a regular entity type has a composite attribute, only the simple component attributes of the composite attribute are included in the new relation. Figure 5-9 shows a variation on the example of Figure 5-8, where Customer_Address is represented as a composite attribute with components Street, City, State, and Zip (see Figure 5-9a). This entity is mapped to the CUSTOMER relation, which contains the simple address attributes, as shown in Figure 5-9b.

Multivalued Attributes When the regular entity type contains a multivalued attribute, two new relations (rather than one) are created. The first relation contains all of the attributes of the entity type except the multivalued attribute. The second relation contains two attributes that form the primary key of the second relation. The first of these attributes is the primary key from the first relation, which becomes a foreign key in the second relation. The second is the multivalued attribute. The name of the second relation should capture the meaning of the multivalued attribute.

An example of this procedure is shown in Figure 5-10. This is the EMPLOYEE entity type for Pine Valley Furniture Company (Figure 3-22). As shown in Figure 5-10a, EMPLOYEE has Skill as a multivalued attribute. Figure 5-10b shows the two relations that are created. The first (called EMPLOYEE) has the primary key Employee_ID. The second relation (called EMPLOYEE_SKILL) has the two attributes Employee_ID and Skill, which form the primary key. The relationship between foreign and primary keys is indicated by the arrow in the figure.

The relation EMPLOYEE_SKILL contains no nonkey attributes (also called *descriptors*). Each row simply records the fact that a particular employee possesses a particular skill. This provides an opportunity for you to suggest to users that new attributes can be added to this relation. For example, the attributes Years_Experience and/or Certification_Date might be appropriate new values to add to this relation.

Figure 5-8
Mapping the regular entity
CUSTOMER
(a) CUSTOMER entity type

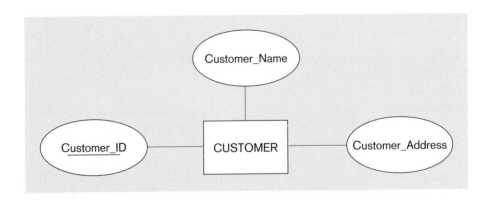

(b) CUSTOMER relation

Figure 5-9
Mapping a composite attribute
(a) CUSTOMER entity type with
composite attribute

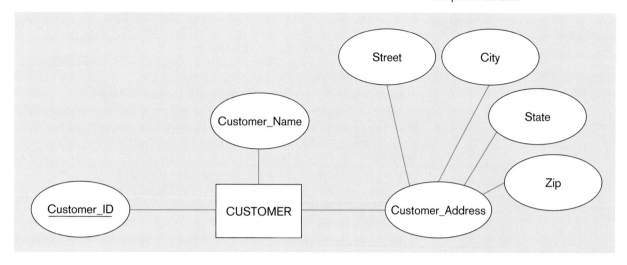

(b) CUSTOMER relation with address
detail

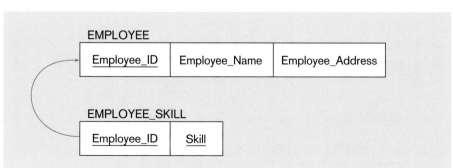

Figure 5-10
Mapping an entity with a multivalued
attribute
(a) Employee entity type with
multivalued attribute

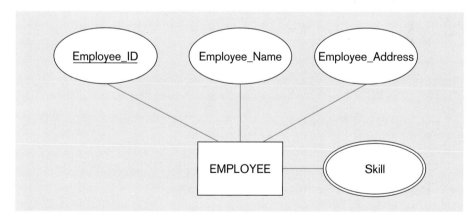

(b) Mapping a multivalued attribute

Step 2: Map Weak Entities

Recall that a weak entity type does not have an independent existence, but exists only through an identifying relationship with another entity type called the owner. A weak entity type does not have a complete identifier, but must have an attribute called a partial identifier that permits distinguishing the various occurrences of the weak entity for each owner entity instance.

The following procedure assumes that you have already created a relation corresponding to the identifying entity type during Step 1. If you have not, you should create that relation now using the process described in Step 1.

For each weak entity type, create a new relation and include all of the simple attributes (or simple components of composite attributes) as attributes of this relation. Then include the primary key of the *identifying* relation as a foreign key attribute in this new relation. The primary key of the new relation is the combination of this primary key of the identifying and the partial identifier of the weak entity type.

An example of this process is shown in Figure 5-11. Figure 5-11a shows the weak entity type DEPENDENT and its identifying entity type EMPLOYEE, linked by the identifying relationship Has (see Figure 3–5). Notice that the attribute Dependent_Name, which is the partial identifier for this relation, is a composite attribute with components First_Name, Middle_Initial, and Last_Name. Thus we assume that, *for a given employee*, these items will uniquely identify a dependent (a notable exception being the case of prizefighter George Foreman, who has named all his sons after himself!).

Figure 5-11b shows the two relations that result from mapping this E-R segment. The primary key of DEPENDENT consists of four attributes: Employee_ID, First_Name, Middle_Initial, and Last_Name. Date_of_Birth and Gender are the nonkey attributes. The foreign key relationship with its primary key is indicated by the arrow in the figure.

Figure 5-11
Example of mapping a weak entity
(a) Weak entity DEPENDENT

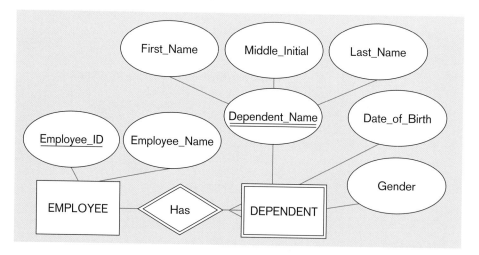

(b) Relations resulting from weak entity

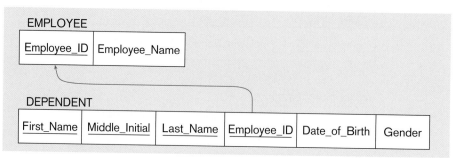

Step 3: Map Binary Relationships

The procedure for representing relationships depends on both the degree of the relationships (unary, binary, ternary) and the cardinalities of the relationships. We describe and illustrate the important cases in the following discussion.

Map Binary One-to-Many Relationships For each binary 1:M relationship, first create a relation for each of the two entity types participating in the relationship, using the procedure described in Step 1. Next, include the primary key attribute (or attributes) of the entity on the one-side of the relationship as a foreign key in the relation that is on the many-side of the relationship (a mnemonic you can use to remember this rule is this: The primary key <u>migrates</u> to the <u>many</u> side).

To illustrate this simple process, we use the Submits relationship between customers and orders for Pine Valley Furniture Company (see Figure 3-22). This 1:M relationship is illustrated in Figure 5-12a. Figure 5-12b shows the result of applying the above rule to map the entity types with the 1:M relationship. The primary key Customer_ID of CUSTOMER (the one-side) is included as a foreign key in ORDER (the many-side). The foreign key relationship is indicated with an arrow.

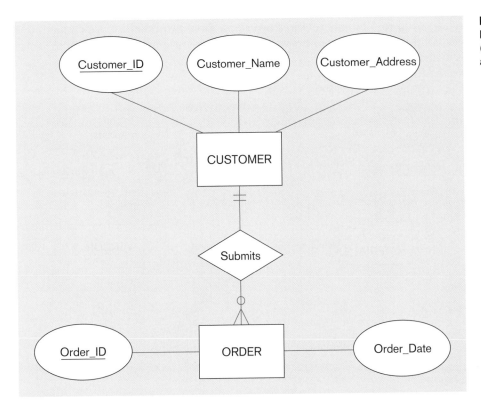

Figure 5-12
Example of mapping a 1:M relationship
(a) Relationship between customers and orders

(b) Mapping the relationship

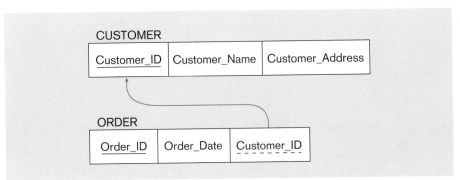

Map Binary Many-to-Many Relationships Suppose that there is a binary many-to-many (M:N) relationship between two entity types A and B. For such a relationship, we create a new relation C. Include as foreign key attributes in C the primary key for each of the two participating entity types. These attributes become the primary key of C. Any nonkey attributes that are associated with the M:N relationship are included with the relation C.

Figure 5-13 shows an example of applying this rule. Figure 5-13a shows the Supplies relationship between the entity types VENDOR and RAW MATERIALS for Pine Valley Furniture Company (introduced in Figure 3-22). Figure 5-13b shows the three relations (VENDOR, RAW MATERIALS, and QUOTE) that are formed from the entity types and the Supplies relationship. First, a relation is created for each of the two regular entity types VENDOR and RAW MATERIALS. Then a relation (named QUOTE in Figure 5-13b) is created for the Supplies relationship. The primary key of QUOTE is the combination of Vendor_ID and Material_ID, which are the respective primary keys of VENDOR and RAW MATERIALS. As indicated in the diagram, these attributes are foreign keys that "point to" the respective primary keys. The nonkey attribute Unit_Price also appears in QUOTE.

Map Binary One-to-One Relationships Binary one-to-one relationships can be viewed as a special case of one-to-many relationships. The process of mapping such a relationship to relations requires two steps. First, two relations are created, one for each of the participating entity types. Second, the primary key of one of the relations is included as a foreign key in the other relation.

Figure 5-13
Example of mapping an M:N relationship
(a) Requests relationship (M:N)

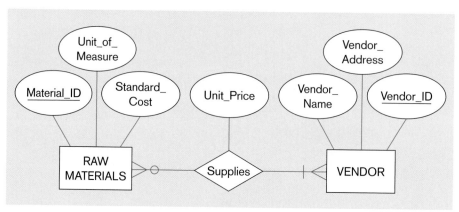

(b) Three resulting relations

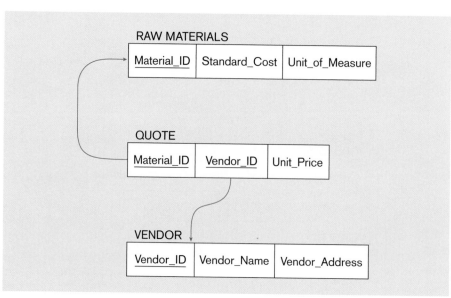

In a 1:1 relationship, the association in one direction is nearly always optional one, while the association in the other direction is mandatory one (you can review the notation for these terms in Figure 3–1). You should include in the relation on the optional side of the relationship the foreign key of the entity type that has the mandatory participation in the 1:1 relationship. This approach will avoid the need to store null values in the foreign key attribute. Any attributes associated with the relationship itself are also included in the same relation as the foreign key.

An example of applying this procedure is shown in Figure 5-14. Figure 5-14a shows a binary 1:1 relationship between the entity types NURSE and CARE CENTER. Each care center must have a nurse who is in charge of that center. Thus the association from CARE CENTER to NURSE is a mandatory one, while the association from NURSE to CARE CENTER is an optional one (since any nurse may or may not be in charge of a care center). The attribute Date_Assigned is attached to the In_charge relationship.

The result of mapping this relationship to a set of relations is shown in Figure 5-14b. The two relations NURSE and CARE CENTER are created from the two entity types. Since CARE CENTER is the optional participant, the foreign key is placed in this relation. In this case the foreign key is called Nurse_in_Charge. It has the same domain as Nurse_ID, and the relationship with the primary key is shown in the figure. The attribute Date_Assigned is also located in CARE CENTER and would not be allowed to be null.

Figure 5-14
Mapping a binary 1:1 relationship
(a) Binary 1:1 relationship

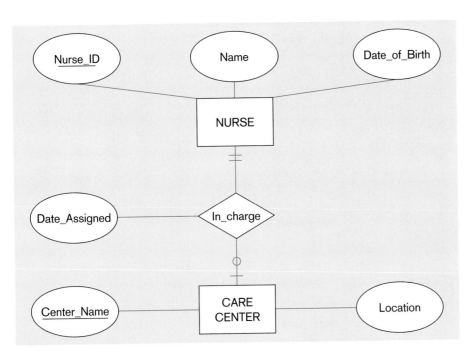

(b) Resulting relations

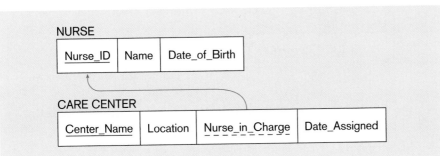

Step 4: Map Associative Entities

As explained in Chapter 3, when the data modeler encounters a many-to-many relationship, he or she may choose to model that relationship as an associative entity in the E-R diagram. This approach is most appropriate when the end user can best visualize the relationship as an entity type rather than as an M:N relationship. Mapping the associative entity involves essentially the same steps as mapping an M:N relationship, as described in Step 3.

The first step is to create three relations: one for each of the two participating entity types, and the third for the associative entity. We refer to the relation formed from the associative entity as the *associative relation.* The second step then depends on whether on the E-R diagram an identifier was assigned to the associative entity.

Identifier Not Assigned If an identifier was not assigned, the default primary key for the associative relation consists of the two primary key attributes from the other two relations. These attributes are then foreign keys that reference the other two relations.

Figure 5-15
Mapping an associative entity
(a) An associative entity

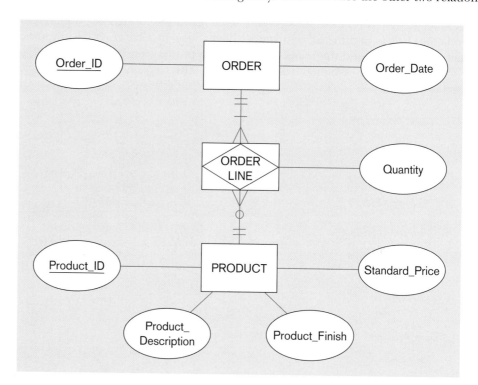

(b) Three resulting relations

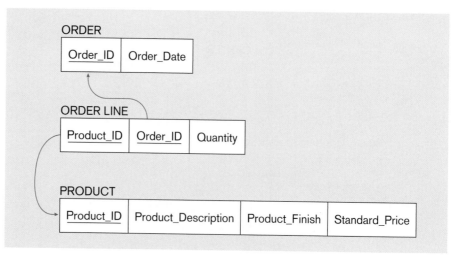

An example of this case is shown in Figure 5-15. Figure 5-15a shows the associative entity ORDER LINE that links the ORDER and PRODUCT entity types at Pine Valley Furniture Company (see Figure 3-22). Figure 5-15b shows the three relations that result from this mapping. Note the similarity of this example to that of an M:N relationship shown in Figure 5-13.

Identifier Assigned Sometimes the data modeler will assign an identifier (called a *surrogate* identifier or key) to the associative entity type on the E-R diagram. There are two reasons that may motivate this approach:

1. The associative entity type has a natural identifier that is familiar to end users.

2. The default identifier (consisting of the identifiers for each of the participating entity types) may not uniquely identify instances of the associative entity.

The process for mapping the associative entity in this case is now modified as follows. As before, a new (associative) relation is created to represent the associative entity. However, the primary key for this relation is the identifier assigned on the E-R diagram (rather than the default key). The primary keys for the two participating entity types are then included as foreign keys in the associative relation.

An example of this process is shown in Figure 5-16. Figure 5-16a shows the associative entity type SHIPMENT that links the CUSTOMER and VENDOR entity types. Shipment_No has been chosen as the identifier for SHIPMENT for two reasons:

1. Shipment_No is a natural identifier for this entity that is very familiar to end users.

2. The default identifier consisting of the combination of Customer_ID and Vendor_ID does not uniquely identify the instances of SHIPMENT. In fact, a

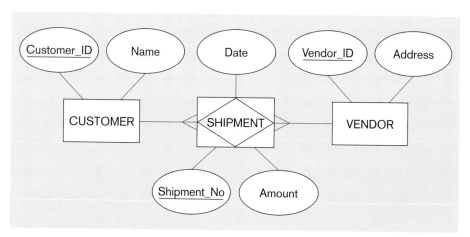

Figure 5-16
Mapping an associative entity with an identifier
(a) Associative entity (SHIPMENT)

(b) Three relations

given vendor will make many shipments to a given customer. Even including the attribute Date does not guarantee uniqueness, since there may be more than one shipment by a particular vendor on a given date, but the surrogate key Shipment_No will uniquely identify each shipment.

Two nonkey attributes associated with SHIPMENT are Date and Amount.

The result of mapping this entity to a set of relations is shown in Figure 5-16b. The new associative relation is named SHIPMENT. The primary key is Shipment_No. Customer_ID and Vendor_ID are included as foreign keys in this relation, and Date and Amount are nonkey attributes.

Step 5: Map Unary Relationships

In Chapter 3 we defined a unary relationship as a relationship between the instances of a single entity type. Unary relationships are also called recursive relationships. The two most important cases of unary relationships are one-to-many and many-to-many. We discuss these two cases separately since the approach to mapping is somewhat different for the two types.

Unary One-to-Many Relationships The entity type in the unary relationship is mapped to a relation using the procedure described in Step 1. Then a foreign key attribute is added *within* the same relation that references the primary key values (this foreign key must have the same domain as the primary key). A **recursive foreign key** is a foreign key in a relation that references the primary key values of that same relation.

Figure 5-17a shows a unary one-to-many relationship named Manages that associates each employee of an organization with another employee who is his or her manager. Each employee has exactly one manager; a given employee may manage zero to many employees.

Recursive foreign key: A foreign key in a relation that references the primary key values of that same relation.

Figure 5-17
Mapping a unary 1:N relationship
(a) EMPLOYEE entity with Manages relationship

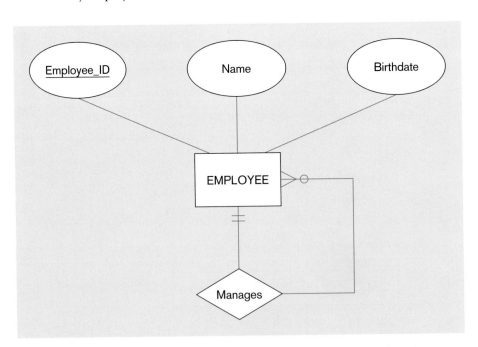

(b) EMPLOYEE relation with recursive foreign key

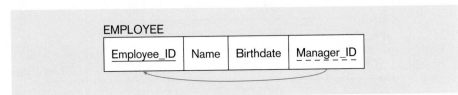

The EMPLOYEE relation that results from mapping this entity and relationship is shown in Figure 5-17b. The (recursive) foreign key in the relation is named Manager_ID. This attribute has the same domain as the primary key Employee_ID. Each row of this relation stores the following data for a given employee: Employee_ID, Name, Birthdate, and Manager_ID (that is, the Employee_ID for this employee's manager). Notice that since it is a foreign key, Manager_ID references Employee_ID.

Unary Many-to-Many Relationships With this type of relationship, two relations are created: one to represent the entity type in the relationship and the other an associative relation to represent the M:N relationship itself. The primary key of the associative relation consists of two attributes. These attributes (which need not have the same name) both take their values from the primary key of the other relation. Any nonkey attribute of the relationship is included in the associative relation.

An example of mapping a unary M:N relationship is shown in Figure 5-18. Figure 5-18a shows a bill-of-materials relationship among items that are assembled from other items or components (this structure was described in Chapter 3 and an example appears in Figure 3–13). The relationship (called Contains) is M:N since a given item can contain numerous component items, and conversely an item can be used as a component in numerous other items.

The relations that result from mapping this entity and its relationship are shown in Figure 5-18b. The ITEM relation is mapped directly from the same entity type. COMPONENT is an associative relation whose primary key consists of two attributes that are arbitrarily named Item_No and Component_No. The attribute Quantity is a nonkey attribute of this relation that for a given item, records the quantity of a particular component item used in that item. Notice that both Item_No and Component_No reference the primary key (Item_No) of the ITEM relation.

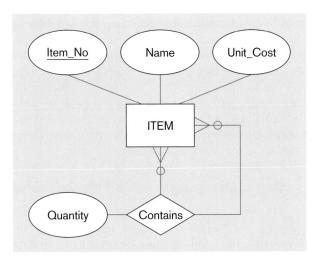

Figure 5-18
Mapping a unary M:N relationship
(a) Bill-of-materials relationships (M:N)

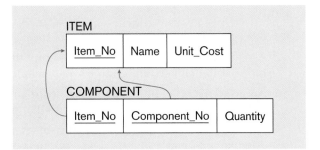

(b) ITEM and COMPONENT relations

We can easily query the above relations to determine (for example) the components of a given item. The following SQL query will list the immediate components (and their quantity) for item number 100:

```
SELECT Component_No, Quantity
FROM COMPONENT
WHERE Item_No = 100;
```

Step 6: Map Ternary (and *n*-ary) Relationships

Recall from Chapter 3 that a ternary relationship is a relationship among three entity types. In that chapter we recommended that you convert a ternary relationship to an associative entity in order to represent participation constraints more accurately.

To map an associative entity type that links three regular entity types, we create a new associative relation. The default primary key of this relation consists of the three primary key attributes for the participating entity types (in some cases, additional attributes are required to form a unique primary key). These attributes then act in the role of foreign keys that reference the individual primary keys of the participating entity types. Any attributes of the associative entity type become attributes of the new relation.

An example of mapping a ternary relationship (represented as an associative entity type) is shown in Figure 5-19. Figure 5-19a is an E-R segment (or view) that represents a *patient* receiving a *treatment* from a *physician*. The associative entity type PATIENT TREATMENT has the attributes Date, Time, and Results; values are recorded for these attributes for each instance of PATIENT TREATMENT.

The result of mapping this view is shown in Figure 5-19b. The primary key attributes Patient_ID, Physician_ID, and Treatment_Code become foreign keys in PATIENT TREATMENT. These attributes are components of the primary key of PATIENT TREATMENT. However, they do not uniquely identify a given treatment, since a patient may receive the same treatment from the same physician on more than one occasion. Does including the attribute Date as part of the primary key (along with the other three attributes) result in a primary key? This would be so if a given patient receives only one treatment from a particular physician on a given date. However, this is not likely to be the case. For example, a patient may receive a treatment in the morning, then the same treatment in the afternoon. To resolve this issue, we include Time as part of the primary key. Therefore, the primary key of PATIENT TREATMENT consists of the five attributes shown in Figure 5-19b: Patient_ID, Physician_ID, Treatment_Code, Date, and Time. The only nonkey attribute in the relation is Results.

Step 7: Map Supertype/Subtype Relationships

The relational data model does not yet directly support supertype/subtype relationships. Fortunately, there are various strategies that database designers can use to represent these relationships with the relational data model (Chouinard, 1989). For our purposes we use the following strategy, which is the one most commonly employed:

1. Create a separate relation for the supertype and for each of its subtypes.
2. Assign to the relation created for the supertype the attributes that are common to all members of the supertype, including the primary key.
3. Assign to the relation for each subtype the primary key of the supertype, and only those attributes that are unique to that subtype.
4. Assign one (or more) attributes of the supertype to function as the subtype discriminator (the role of the subtype discriminator was discussed in Chapter 4).

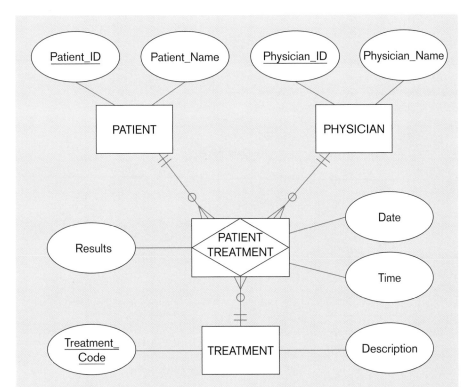

Figure 5-19
Mapping a ternary relationship
(a) Ternary relationship with associative entity

(b) Mapping the ternary relationship

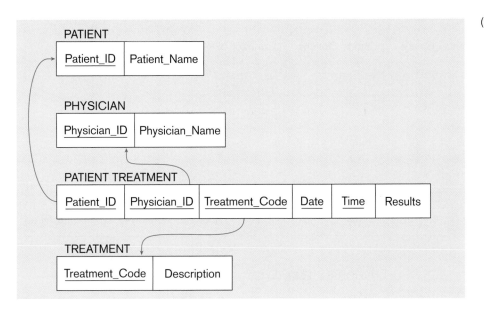

An example of applying this procedure is shown in Figures 5-20 and 5-21. Figure 5-20 shows the supertype EMPLOYEE with subtypes HOURLY EMPLOYEE, SALARIED EMPLOYEE, and CONSULTANT (this example is described in Chapter 4, and Figure 5-20 is a repeat of Figure 4–8). The primary key of EMPLOYEE is Employee_Number, and the attribute Employee_Type is the subtype discriminator.

The result of mapping this diagram to relations using the above rules is shown in Figure 5-21. There is one relation for the supertype (EMPLOYEE) and one for each of the three subtypes. The primary key for each of the four relations is Employee_Number. A prefix is used to distinguish the name of the primary key for each subtype. For example, S_Employee_Number is the name for the primary key of

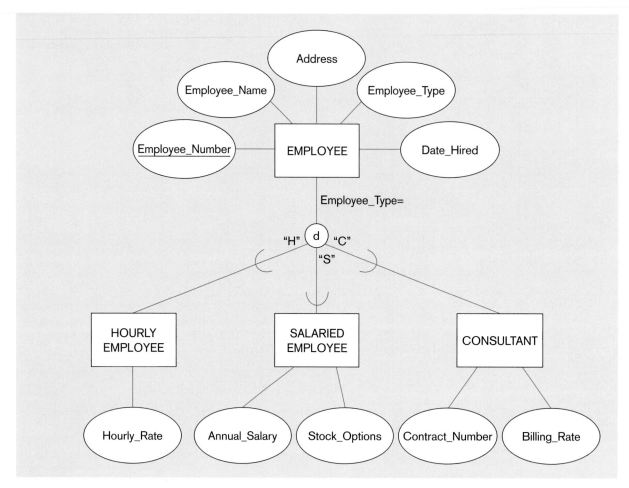

Figure 5-20
Supertype/subtype relationships

Figure 5-21
Mapping supertype/subtype
relationships to relations

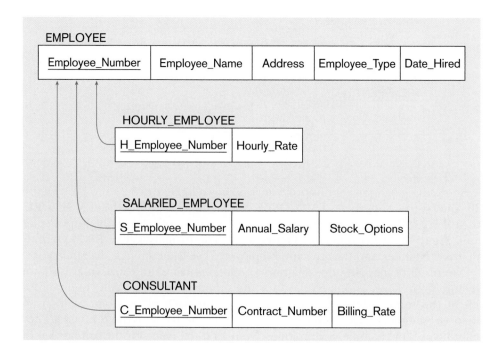

the relation SALARIED_EMPLOYEE. Each of these attributes is a foreign key that references the supertype primary key, as indicated by the arrows in the diagram. Each subtype relation contains only those attributes peculiar to the subtype.

For each subtype, a relation can be produced that contains *all* of the attributes of that subtype (both specific and inherited) by using an SQL command that joins the subtype with its supertype. For example, suppose that we want to display a table that contains all of the attributes for SALARIED_EMPLOYEE. The following command is used:

SELECT *
FROM EMPLOYEE, SALARIED_EMPLOYEE
WHERE Employee_Number = S_Employee_Number;

Although you have not yet formally studied such commands, you can intuitively see that this command will join the two tables and produce a larger table that contains all of the attributes from both tables.

INTRODUCTION TO NORMALIZATION

Normalization is a formal process for deciding which attributes should be grouped together in a relation. In Chapters 3 and 4 you used common sense to group attributes into entity types during conceptual data modeling. In the previous section of this chapter you learned how to map E-R diagrams to relations. Before proceeding with physical design, we need a method to validate the logical design to this point. Normalization is primarily a tool to validate and improve a logical design, so that it satisfies certain constraints that avoid unnecessary duplication of data.

We have presented an intuitive discussion of well-structured relations; however, we need formal definitions of such relations, together with a process for designing them. **Normalization** is the process of decomposing relations with anomalies to produce smaller, well-structured relations. For example, we used the principles of normalization to convert the EMPLOYEE2 table (with its redundancy) to EMPLOYEE1 (Figure 5-1) and EMP_COURSE (Figure 5-7).

> **Normalization:** The process of decomposing relations with anomalies to produce smaller, well-structured relations.

Steps in Normalization

Normalization can be accomplished and understood in stages, each of which corresponds to a normal form (see Figure 5-22). A **normal form** is a state of a relation that results from applying simple rules regarding functional dependencies (or relationships between attributes) to that relation. We describe these rules briefly in this section and illustrate them in detail in the following sections.

> **Normal form:** A state of a relation that results from applying simple rules regarding functional dependencies (or relationships between attributes) to that relation.

1. *First normal form* Any multivalued attributes (also called repeating groups) have been removed, so there is a single value (possibly null) at the intersection of each row and column of the table (as in Figure 5-2b).

2. *Second normal form* Any partial functional dependencies have been removed.

3. *Third normal form* Any transitive dependencies have been removed.

4. *Boyce/Codd normal form* Any remaining anomalies that result from functional dependencies have been removed.

5. *Fourth normal form* Any multivalued dependencies have been removed.

6. *Fifth normal form* Any remaining anomalies have been removed.

We describe and illustrate first through third normal forms in this chapter. The remaining normal forms are described in Appendix B.

Figure 5-22
Steps in normalization

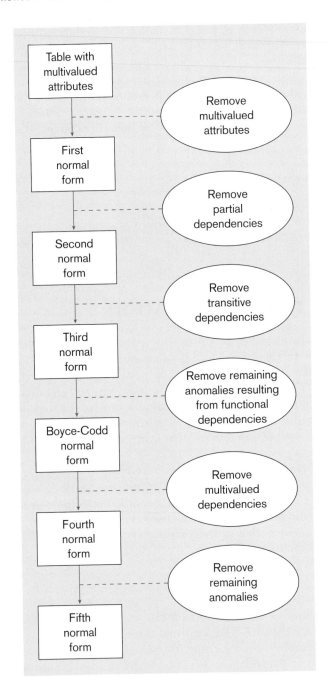

Functional Dependencies and Keys

Functional dependency: A constraint between two attributes or two sets of attributes.

Normalization is based on the analysis of functional dependencies. A **functional dependency** is a constraint between two attributes or two sets of attributes. For any relation R, attribute B is functionally dependent on attribute A if, for every valid instance of A, that value of A uniquely determines the value of B (Dutka and Hanson, 1989). The functional dependency of B on A is represented by an arrow, as follows: A → B. An attribute may be functionally dependent on two (or more) attributes, rather than on a single attribute. For example, consider the relation EMP_COURSE (Emp_ID,Course_Title,Date_Completed) shown in Figure 5-7. We represent the functional dependency in this relation as follows:

Emp_ID,Course_Title → Date_Completed.

The functional dependency in this statement implies that the date a course is completed is completely determined by the identity of the employee and the title of the course. Common examples of functional dependencies are the following:

1. SSN → Name, Address, Birthdate   A person's name, address, and birthdate are functionally dependent on that person's Social Security number.

2. VIN → Make, Model, Color   The make, model, and color of a vehicle are functionally dependent on the vehicle identification number.

3. ISBN → Title, First_Author_Name   The title of a book and the name of the first author are functionally dependent on the book's International Standard Book Number (ISBN).

Determinants   The attribute on the left-hand side of the arrow in a functional dependency is called a **determinant**. SSN, VIN, and ISBN are determinants (respectively) in the preceding three examples. In the EMP_COURSE relation (Figure 5-7) the combination of Emp_ID and Course_Title is a determinant.

Determinant: The attribute on the left-hand side of the arrow in a functional dependency.

Candidate Keys   A **candidate key** is an attribute, or combination of attributes, that uniquely identifies a row in a relation. A candidate key must satisfy the following properties (Dutka and Hanson, 1989), which are a subset of the six properties of a primary key previously listed:

Candidate key: An attribute, or combination of attributes, that uniquely identifies a row in a relation.

1. *Unique identification*   For every row, the value of the key must uniquely identify that row. *This property implies that each nonkey attribute is functionally dependent on that key.*

2. *Nonredundancy*   No attribute in the key can be deleted without destroying the property of unique identification.

Let's apply the preceding definition to identify candidate keys in two of the relations described in this chapter. The EMPLOYEE1 relation (Figure 5-1) has the following schema: EMPLOYEE1(Emp_ID,Name,Dept_Name,Salary). Emp_ID is the only determinant in this relation. All of the other attributes are functionally dependent on Emp_ID. Therefore Emp_ID is a candidate key and (since there are no other candidate keys) also is the primary key.

We represent the functional dependencies for a relation using the notation shown in Figure 5-23. Figure 5-23a shows the representation for EMPLOYEE1. The horizontal line in the figure portrays the functional dependencies. A vertical line drops from the primary key (Emp_ID) and connects to this line. Vertical arrows then point to each of the nonkey attributes that are functionally dependent on the primary key.

For the relation EMPLOYEE2 (Figure 5-2b), notice that (unlike EMPLOYEE1), Emp_ID does not uniquely identify a row in the relation. For example, there are two rows in the table for Emp_ID number 100. There are two functional dependencies in this relation:

1. Emp_ID → Name, Dept_Name, Salary

2. Emp_ID, Course_Title → Date_Completed

The functional dependencies indicate that the combination of Emp_ID and Course_Title is the only candidate key (and therefore the primary key) for EMPLOYEE2. In other words, the primary key of EMPLOYEE2 is a composite key. Neither Emp_ID nor Course_Title uniquely identifies a row in this relation, and therefore property 1 cannot by itself be a candidate key. Examine the data in Figure 5-2b to verify that the combination of Emp_ID and Course_Title does uniquely identify each row of EMPLOYEE2. We represent the functional dependencies in this relation in Figure 5-23b. Notice that Date_Completed is the only attribute that is functionally dependent on the full primary key consisting of the attributes Emp_ID and Course_Title.

Figure 5-23
Representing functional dependencies
(a) Functional dependencies in
EMPLOYEE1

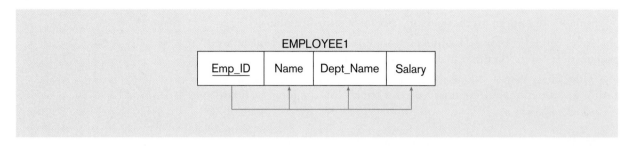

(b) Functional dependencies in
EMPLOYEE2

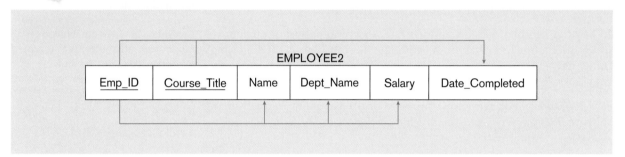

We can summarize the relationship between determinants and candidate keys as follows. A candidate key is always a determinant, while a determinant may or may not be a candidate key. For example, in EMPLOYEE2, Emp_ID is a determinant but not a candidate key. A candidate key is a determinant that uniquely identifies the remaining (nonkey) attributes in a relation. A determinant may be a candidate key (such as Emp_ID in EMPLOYEE1), part of a composite candidate key (such as Emp_ID in EMPLOYEE2), or a nonkey attribute. We will describe examples of this shortly.

THE BASIC NORMAL FORMS

Now that we have examined functional dependencies and keys, we are ready to describe and illustrate first through third normal forms. We also describe the normalization of summary data that appear in information bases.

First Normal Form

First normal form: A relation that contains no multivalued attributes.

A relation is in **first normal form** (1NF) if it contains no multivalued attributes. Recall that the first property of a relation is that the value at the intersection of each row and column must be atomic. Thus a table that contains multivalued attributes or repeating groups is not a relation.

In the previous section, in describing how to map E-R diagrams to relations, we described a procedure for removing multivalued attributes from entity types on the E-R diagram. Thus if you developed a logical design by transforming E-R diagrams to relations, there should not be any multivalued attributes remaining. However, many older legacy systems written in languages such as COBOL supported multivalued attributes. Since you may participate in efforts to convert these older systems to relational databases, it is important that you understand how to eliminate multivalued attributes.

We illustrated a table with repeating groups in Figure 5-2a and then converted it to the relation EMPLOYEE2 in Figure 5-2b by removing the multivalued attributes. Thus EMPLOYEE2 is a relation in first normal form. A table with multivalued attributes is converted to a relation in first normal form by extending the data in each column to fill cells that are empty because of the multivalued attributes.

Second Normal Form

A relation is in **second normal form** (2NF) if it is in first normal form and every nonkey attribute is fully functionally dependent on the primary key. Thus no nonkey attribute is functionally dependent on part (but not all) of the primary key. A relation that is in first normal form will be in second normal form if any one of the following conditions applies:

1. The primary key consists of only one attribute (such as the attribute Emp_ID in EMPLOYEE1).

2. No nonkey attributes exist in the relation (thus all of the attributes in the relation are components of the primary key).

3. Every nonkey attribute is functionally dependent on the full set of primary key attributes.

EMPLOYEE2 (Figure 5-2b) is an example of a relation that is not in second normal form. The primary key for this relation is the composite key Emp_ID, Course_Title. Therefore the nonkey attributes Name, Dept_Name, and Salary are functionally dependent on part of the primary key (Emp_ID) but not on Course_Title. These dependencies are shown graphically in Figure 5-23b.

A **partial functional dependency** is a functional dependency in which one or more nonkey attributes (such as Name) are functionally dependent on part (but not all) of the primary key. The partial functional dependency in EMPLOYEE2 creates redundancy in that relation, which results in anomalies when the table is updated as we noted in a previous section.

To convert a relation to second normal form, we decompose the relation into new relations that satisfy one (or more) of the conditions described above. EMPLOYEE2 is decomposed into the following two relations:

1. EMPLOYEE1(Emp_ID,Name,Dept_Name, Salary) This relation satisfies condition 1 above and is in second normal form (sample data are shown in Figure 5-1).

2. EMP_COURSE(Emp_ID,Course_Title,Date_Completed)   This relation satisfies property 3 above and is also in second normal form (sample data appear in Figure 5-7).

You should examine these new relations to verify that they are free of the anomalies associated with EMPLOYEE2.

Third Normal Form

A relation is in **third normal form** (3NF) if it is in second normal form and no transitive dependencies exist. A **transitive dependency** in a relation is a functional dependency between two (or more) nonkey attributes. For example, consider the relation

SALES(Cust_ID,Name,Salesperson,Region)

(Sample data for this relation appear in Figure 5-24a.)

Second normal form: A relation in first normal form in which every nonkey attribute is fully functionally dependent on the primary key.

Partial functional dependency: A functional dependency in which one or more nonkey attributes are functionally dependent on part (but not all) of the primary key.

Third normal form: A relation that is in second normal form and has no transitive dependencies present.

Transitive dependency: A functional dependency between two (or more) nonkey attributes.

Figure 5-24
Relation with transitive dependency
(a) SALES relation with sample data

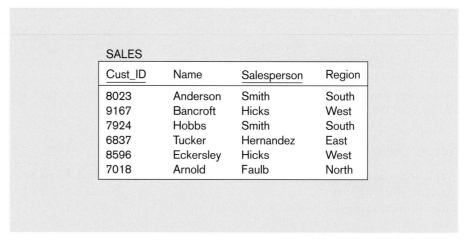

(b) Transitive dependency in SALES relation

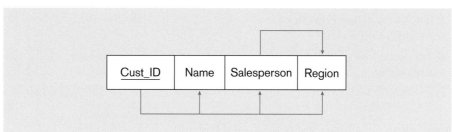

The functional dependencies in the SALES relation are shown graphically in Figure 5-24b. Cust_ID is the primary key, so that all of the remaining attributes are functionally dependent on this attribute. However, there is a transitive dependency (Region is functionally dependent on Salesperson and Salesperson is functionally dependent on Cust_ID). As a result, there are update anomalies in SALES.

1. *Insertion anomaly*   A new salesperson (Robinson) assigned to the North region cannot be entered until a customer has been assigned to that salesperson (since a value for Cust_ID must be provided to insert a row in the table).

2. *Deletion anomaly*   If customer number 6837 is deleted from the table, we lose the information that salesperson Hernandez is assigned to the East region.

3. *Modification anomaly*   If salesperson Smith is reassigned to the East region, several rows must be changed to reflect that fact (two rows are shown in Figure 5-24a).

These anomalies arise as a result of the transitive dependency. The transitive dependency can be removed by decomposing SALES into two relations, as shown in Figure 5-25a. Note that Salesperson, which is the determinant in the transitive dependency in SALES, becomes the primary key in SPERSON. Salesperson[1] becomes a foreign key in SALES1. Often the normalized relations of Figure 5-25 will also use less storage space when implemented than will a database based on the relation in Figure 5-24a because the dependent data (Region and any other salesperson data) do not have to repeat for each customer. Thus, normalization, besides solving anomalies, also often reduces redundant data storage.

---

[1]Because Salesperson is an intelligent business key, it is a poor choice for a primary key. This was briefly explained in Chapter 3, and we elaborate on this issue later in this chapter.

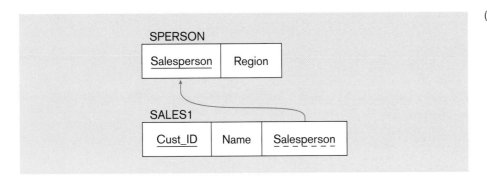

Figure 5-25
Removing a transitive dependency
(a) Decomposing the SALES relation

(b} Relations in 3NF

As shown in Figure 5-25b, the new relations are now in third normal form, since no transitive dependencies exist. You should verify that the anomalies that exist in SALES are not present in SALES1 and SPERSON.

Transitive dependencies may also occur between sets of attributes in a relation. For example, the relation SHIPMENT (Snum,Origin,Destination,Distance) could be used to record shipments according to origin, destination, and distance (Dutka and Hanson, 1989). Sample data for this relation appear in Figure 5-26a. The functional dependencies in the SHIPMENT relation are shown in Figure 5-26b. The primary key of the SHIPMENT relation is the attribute Snum (for Shipment Number). As a result, we know that the relation is in second normal form (why?). However, there is a transitive dependency in this relation: The Distance attribute is functionally dependent on the *pair* of nonkey attributes Origin and Destination. As a result there are anomalies in SHIPMENT (as an exercise, you should examine Figure 5-26a and identify insertion, deletion, and modification anomalies). We can remove the transitive dependency in SHIPMENT by decomposing it into two relations (both in 3NF):

SHIPTO(Snum,Origin,Destination)

DISTANCES(Origin,Destination,Distance)

The first of these relations provides the origin and destination for any given shipment, while the second provides the distance between an origin and destination pair. Sample data for these relations appear in Figure 5-26c.

Normalizing Summary Data

Databases to support managerial decision making in an organization often contain subsets and summaries of data from operational databases. These "data warehouses" used to support higher levels of management are often normalized (at least to a certain extent) to avoid the same anomalies that arise in operational databases. We describe the issues associated with normalizing data in data warehouses in Chapter 11.

Figure 5-26
Another example of transitive dependencies
(a) SHIPMENT relation with sample data

SHIPMENT

Snum	Origin	Destination	Distance
409	Seattle	Denver	1,537
618	Chicago	Dallas	1,058
723	Boston	Atlanta	1,214
824	Denver	Los Angeles	1,150
629	Minneapolis	St. Louis	587

(b) Functional dependencies in SHIPMENT

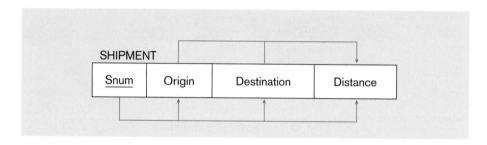

(c) Relations in 3NF

SHIPTO

Snum	Origin	Destination
409	Seattle	Denver
618	Chicago	Dallas
723	Boston	Atlanta
824	Denver	Los Angeles
629	Minneapolis	St. Louis

DISTANCES

Origin	Destination	Distance
Seattle	Denver	1,537
Chicago	Dallas	1,058
Boston	Atlanta	1,214
Denver	Los Angeles	1,150
Minneapolis	St. Louis	587

MERGING RELATIONS

In a previous section, we described how to transform E-R diagrams to relations. We then described how to check the resulting relations to determine whether they are in third normal form, and perform normalization steps if necessary.

As part of the logical design process, normalized relations may have been created from a number of separate E-R diagrams and (possibly) other user views. Some of the relations may be redundant; that is, they may refer to the same entities. If so, we should merge those relations to remove the redundancy. This section describes merging relations (also called *view integration*). An understanding of how to merge relations is important for three reasons:

1. On large projects, the work of several subteams comes together during logical design, so there is a need to merge relations.

2. Integrating existing databases with new information requirements often leads to the need to integrate different views.

3. New data requirements may arise during the life cycle, so there is a need to merge any new relations with what has already been developed.

An Example

Suppose that modeling a user view results in the following 3NF relation:

EMPLOYEE1(Employee_ID,Name,Address,Phone)

Modeling a second user view might result in the following relation:

EMPLOYEE2(Employee_ID,Name,Address,Jobcode,No_Years)

Since these two relations have the same primary key (Employee_ID), they likely describe the same entity and may be merged into one relation. The result of merging the relations is the following relation:

EMPLOYEE(Employee_ID,Name,Address,Phone,Jobcode,No_Years).

Notice that an attribute that appears in both relations (such as Name in this example) appears only once in the merged relation.

View Integration Problems

When integrating relations as in the preceding example, the database analyst must understand the meaning of the data and must be prepared to resolve any problems that may arise in that process. In this section we describe and briefly illustrate four problems that arise in view integration: *synonyms, homonyms, transitive dependencies,* and *supertype/subtype relationships.*

Synonyms In some situations, two (or more) attributes may have different names but the same meaning, as when they describe the same characteristic of an entity. Such attributes are called **synonyms**. For example, Employee_ID and Employee_No may be synonyms. When merging the relations that contain synonyms, you should obtain agreement (if possible) from users on a single, standardized name for the attribute and eliminate any other synonyms. (Another alternative is to choose a third name to replace the synonyms.) For example, consider the following relations:

> **Synonyms:** Two (or more) attributes having different names but the same meaning, as when they describe the same characteristic of an entity.

STUDENT1(Student_ID,Name)

STUDENT2(Matriculation_No,Name,Address)

In this case, the analyst recognizes that both the Student_ID and Matriculation_No are synonyms for a person's Social Security number and are identical attributes. (Another possibility is that these are both candidate keys, and only one of them should be selected as the primary keys.) One possible resolution would be to standardize on one of the two attribute names, such as Student_ID. Another option is to use a new attribute name, such as SSN, to replace both synonyms. Assuming the latter approach, merging the two relations would produce the following result:

STUDENT(SSN,Name,Address)

Often when there are synonyms, there is a need to allow some database users to refer to the same data by different names. Users may need to use familiar names that are consistent with terminology in their part of the organization. An **alias** is an alternative name used for an attribute. Many database management systems allow the definition of an alias that may be used interchangeably with the primary attribute label.

> **Alias:** An alternative name used for an attribute.

Homonyms An attribute that may have more than one meaning is called a **homonym**. For example, the term "account" might refer to a bank's checking account, savings account, loan account, or other type of account (therefore, "account" refers to different data, depending on how it is used).

> **Homonym:** An attribute that may have more than one meaning.

You should be on the lookout for homonyms when merging relations. Consider the following example:

STUDENT1 (Student_ID,Name,Address)

STUDENT2 (Student_ID,Name,Phone_No,Address)

In discussions with users, the analyst may discover that the attribute Address in STUDENT1 refers to a student's campus address, while in STUDENT2 the same attribute refers to a student's permanent (or home) address. To resolve this conflict, we would probably need to create new attribute names, so that the merged relation would become

STUDENT (Student_ID,Name,Phone_No,Campus_Address,Permanent_Address).

Transitive Dependencies When two 3NF relations are merged to form a single relation, transitive dependencies (described earlier in this chapter) may result. For example, consider the following two relations:

STUDENT1 (Student_ID,Major)

STUDENT2 (Student_ID,Advisor)

Since STUDENT1 and STUDENT2 have the same primary key, the two relations may be merged:

STUDENT (Student_ID,Major,Advisor)

However, suppose that each major has exactly one advisor. In this case, Advisor is functionally dependent on Major:

Major → Advisor

If the preceding functional dependency exists, then STUDENT is in 2NF but not in 3NF, since it contains a transitive dependency. The analyst can create 3NF relations by removing the transitive dependency (Major becomes a foreign key in STUDENT):

STUDENT (Student_ID,Major)

MAJOR ADVISOR (Major,Advisor)

Supertype/Subtype Relationships These relationships may be hidden in user views or relations. Suppose that we have the following two hospital relations:

PATIENT1 (Patient_ID,Name,Address)

PATIENT2 (Patient_ID,Room_No)

Initially, it appears that these two relations can be merged into a single PATIENT relation. However, the analyst correctly suspects that there are two different types of patients: resident patients and outpatients. PATIENT1 actually contains attributes common to *all* patients. PATIENT2 contains an attribute (Room_No) that is a characteristic only of resident patients. In this situation, the analyst should create supertype/subtype relationships for these entities:

PATIENT (Patient_ID,Name,Address)

RESIDENT PATIENT (Patient_ID,Room_No)

OUTPATIENT (Patient_ID,Date_Treated)

For an extended discussion of view integration in database design, see Navathe, Elmasri, and Larson (1986).

A FINAL STEP FOR DEFINING RELATIONAL KEYS

In Chapter 3 we provided some criteria for selecting *identifiers*: does not change value over time, must be unique and known, nonintelligent, and use a single attribute surrogate for composite identifier. Actually, none of these criteria must apply until the database is implemented (that is, when the identifier becomes a primary key and is defined as a field in the physical database). Before the relations are defined as tables, the primary keys of relations should, if necessary, be changed to conform to these criteria.

Recently database experts (Johnston, 2000) have strengthened the criteria for primary key specification. Experts now also recommend that a primary key be unique across *the whole database* (a so-called **enterprise key**), not just unique within the relational table to which it applies. This criterion makes a primary key more like what in object-oriented databases is called an *object identifier* (see Chapters 14 and 15). With this recommendation, the primary key of a relation becomes a value internal to the database system and has no business meaning.

Enterprise key: A primary key whose value is unique across all relations.

A candidate primary key, such as Emp_ID in the EMPLOYEE1 relation of Figure 5-1 or Salesperson in the SPERSON relation of Figure 5-25, if ever used in the organization, is called a "business key" and would be included in the relation as a nonkey attribute. The EMPLOYEE1 and SPERSON relations (and every other relation in the database) then have a new enterprise key attribute (called, say, Object_ID), which has no business meaning.

Why create this extra attribute? One of the main motivations for an enterprise key is database evolvability—merging new relations into a database once the database is created. For example, consider the following two relations:

EMPLOYEE(Emp_ID,Emp_Name,Dept_Name,Salary)

CUSTOMER(Cust_ID,Cust_Name,Address)

In this example without an enterprise key, Emp_ID and Cust_ID may or may not have the same format, length, and datatype, whether they are intelligent or nonintelligent. Suppose the organization evolves its information processing needs and recognizes that employees can also be customers, so employee and customer are simply two subtypes of the same PERSON supertype. Thus, the organization would then like to have three relations:

PERSON(Person_ID,Person_Name)

EMPLOYEE(Person_ID,Dept_Name,Salary)

CUSTOMER(Person_ID,Address)

In this case Person_ID is supposed to be the same value for the same person throughout. But if values for Emp_ID and Cust_ID were selected before relation PERSON was created, the values for Emp_ID and Cust_ID probably will not match. Moreover, if we change the values of Emp_ID and Cust_ID to match the new Person_ID, then how do we ensure all Emp_IDs and Cust_IDs are unique should another employee or customer already have the associated Person_ID value? Even worse, if there are other tables that relate to, say, EMPLOYEE, then foreign keys in these other tables have to change, creating a ripple effect of foreign key changes. The only way to guarantee that each primary key of a relation is unique across the database is to create an enterprise key from the very beginning so primary keys never have to change.

In our example, the original database (without PERSON) with an enterprise key is shown in Figures 5-27a (the relations) and 5-27b (sample data). In this figure, Emp_ID and Cust_ID are now business keys and OBJECT is the supertype of all other relations. OBJECT can have attributes such as the name of the type of object (included in this example as attribute Object_Type), date created, date last changed, or any other internal system attributes for an object instance. Then when PERSON is needed, the database evolves to the design shown in Figures 5-27c (the relations) and 5-27d (sample data). Evolution to the database with PERSON still requires some alterations to existing tables, but not to primary key values—the name attribute is moved to PERSON since it is common to both subtypes and a foreign key is added to EMPLOYEE and CUSTOMER to point to the common person instance. As you will see in Chapter 7, it is easy to add and delete nonkey columns, even foreign keys, to table definitions. In contrast, changing the primary key of a relation is not allowed by most database management systems because of the extensive cost of the foreign key ripple effect.

Figure 5-27
Enterprise key
(a) Relations with enterprise key

OBJECT (<u>OID</u>, Object_Type)
EMPLOYEE (<u>OID</u>, Emp_ID, Emp_Name, Dept_Name, Salary)
CUSTOMER (<u>OID</u>, Cust_ID, Cust_Name, Address)

(b) Sample data with enterprise key

OBJECT

OID	Object_Type
1	EMPLOYEE
2	CUSTOMER
3	CUSTOMER
4	EMPLOYEE
5	EMPLOYEE
6	CUSTOMER
7	CUSTOMER

EMPLOYEE

OID	Emp_ID	Emp_Name	Dept_Name	Salary
1	100	Jennings, Fred	Marketing	50000
4	101	Hopkins, Dan	Purchasing	45000
5	102	Huber, Ike	Accounting	45000

CUSTOMER

OID	Cust_ID	Cust_Name	Address
2	100	Fred's Warehouse	Greensboro, NC
3	101	Bargain Bonanza	Moscow, ID
6	102	Jasper's	Tallahassee, FL
7	103	Desks 'R Us	Kettering, OH

(c) Relations after adding PERSON relation

OBJECT (<u>OID</u>, Object_Type)
EMPLOYEE (<u>OID</u>, Emp_ID, Dept_Name, Salary, Person_ID)
CUSTOMER (<u>OID</u>, Cust_ID, Address, Person_ID)
PERSON (<u>OID</u>, Name)

OBJECT

OID	Object_Type
1	EMPLOYEE
2	CUSTOMER
3	CUSTOMER
4	EMPLOYEE
5	EMPLOYEE
6	CUSTOMER
7	CUSTOMER
8	PERSON
9	PERSON
10	PERSON
11	PERSON
12	PERSON
13	PERSON
14	PERSON

PERSON

OID	Name
8	Jennings, Fred
9	Fred's Warehouse
10	Bargain Bonanza
11	Hopkins, Dan
12	Huber, Ike
13	Jasper's
14	Desks 'R Us

Figure 5-27
(continued)
(d) Sample data after adding PERSON relation

EMPLOYEE

OID	Emp_ID	Dept_Name	Salary	Person_ID
1	100	Marketing	50000	8
4	101	Purchasing	45000	11
5	102	Accounting	45000	12

CUSTOMER

OID	Cust_ID	Address	Person_ID
2	100	Greensboro, NC	9
3	101	Moscow, ID	10
6	102	Tallahassee, FL	13
7	103	Kettering, OH	14

Summary

Logical database design is the process of transforming the conceptual data model into a logical data model. The emphasis in this chapter has been on the relational data model, because of its importance in contemporary database systems. The relational data model represents data in the form of tables called relations. A relation is a named, two-dimensional table of data. A key property of relations is that they cannot contain multivalued attributes.

In this chapter, we described the major steps in the logical database design process. This process is based on transforming E-R diagrams to normalized relations. The three steps in this process are the following: Transform E-R (and EER) diagrams to relations, normalize the relations, and merge the relations. The result of this process is a set of rela-

tions in third normal form that can be implemented using any contemporary relational database management system.

Each entity type in the E-R diagram is transformed to a relation that has the same primary key as the entity type. A one-to-many relationship is represented by adding a foreign key to the relation that represents the entity on the many-side of the relationship. (This foreign key is the primary key of the entity on the one-side of the relationship.) A many-to-many relationship is represented by creating a separate relation. The primary key of this relation is a composite key, consisting of the primary key of each of the entities that participate in the relationship.

The relational model does not directly support supertype/subtype relationships, but we can model these relationships by creating a separate table (or relation) for the supertype and for each subtype. The primary key of each subtype is the same (or at least from the same domain) as for the supertype. The supertype must have an attribute called the subtype discriminator that indicates to which subtype (or subtypes) each instance of the supertype belongs. The purpose of normalization is to derive well-structured relations that are free of anomalies (inconsistencies or errors) that would otherwise result when the relations are updated or modified. Normalization is based on the analysis of functional dependencies, which are constraints between two attributes (or two sets of attributes). It may be accomplished in several stages. Relations in first normal form (1NF) contain no multivalued attributes or repeating groups. Relations in 2NF contain no partial dependencies, and relations in 3NF contain no transitive dependencies. We can use diagrams that show the functional dependencies in a relation to help decompose that relation (if necessary) to obtain relations in third normal form. Higher normal forms (beyond 3NF) have also been defined; we discuss these normal forms in Appendix B.

We must be careful when combining relations to deal with problems such as synonyms, homonyms, transitive dependencies, and supertype/subtype relationships. In addition, before relations are defined to the database management system, all primary keys should be described as single attribute nonintelligent keys, and preferably, as enterprise keys.

CHAPTER REVIEW

Key Terms

Alias
Anomaly
Candidate key
Composite key
Determinant
Enterprise key
Entity integrity rule
First normal form

Foreign key
Functional dependency
Homonym
Normal form
Normalization
Null
Partial functional dependency
Primary key

Recursive foreign key
Referential integrity constraint
Relation
Second normal form
Synonyms
Third normal form
Transitive dependency
Well-structured relation

Review Questions

1. Define each of the following terms:
   a. determinant
   b. functional dependency
   c. transitive dependency
   d. recursive foreign key
   e. normalization
   f. composite key
   g. relation
   h. normal form
   i. partial functional dependency
   j. enterprise key

2. Match the following terms to the appropriate definitions:

   _____ well-structured relation
   _____ anomaly
   _____ functional dependency
   _____ determinant
   _____ composite key
   _____ 1NF
   _____ 2NF
   _____ 3NF

   a. constraint between two attributes
   b. functional dependency between nonkey attributes
   c. references primary key in same relation
   d. multivalued attributes removed
   e. inconsistency or error
   f. contains little redundancy
   g. contains two (or more) attributes
   h. contains no partial functional dependencies

   _____ recursive foreign key
   _____ relation
   _____ transitive dependency

   i. transitive dependencies eliminated
   j. attribute on left-hand side of functional dependency
   k. named two-dimensional table of data

3. Contrast the following terms:
   a. normal form; normalization
   b. candidate key; primary key
   c. functional dependency; transitive dependency
   d. composite key; recursive foreign key
   e. determinant; candidate key
   f. foreign key; primary key

4. Summarize six important properties of relations.

5. Describe two properties that must be satisfied by candidate keys.

6. Describe three types of anomalies that can arise in a table.

7. Fill in the blanks in each of the following statements:
   a. A relation that has no partial functional dependencies is in _____ normal form.
   b. A relation that has no multivalued attributes is in _____ normal form.
   c. A relation that has no transitive dependencies is in _____ normal form.

8. What is a well-structured relation? Why are well-structured relations important in logical database design?

9. Describe how the following components of an E-R diagram are transformed to relations:
   a. regular entity type
   b. relationship (1:M)
   c. relationship (M:N)
   d. relationship (supertype/subtype)
   e. multivalued attribute
   f. weak entity
   g. composite attribute

10. Briefly describe four typical problems that often arise in merging relations, and common techniques for addressing those problems.

11. List three conditions that you can apply to determine whether a relation that is in first normal form is also in second normal form.

12. Explain how each of the following types of integrity constraints are enforced in the SQL CREATE TABLE commands:
   a. Entity integrity
   b. Referential integrity

13. How are relationships between entities represented in the relational data model?

14. How do you represent a 1:M unary relationship in a relational data model?

15. How do you represent an M:N ternary relationship in a relational data model?

16. What is the relationship between the primary key of a relation and the functional dependencies among all attributes within that relation?

17. Under what conditions must a foreign key not be null?

18. Explain what can be done with primary keys to eliminate key ripple effects as a database evolves.

Problems and Exercises

1. For each of the following E-R diagrams from Chapter 3:
   I. Transform the diagram to a relational schema that shows referential integrity constraints (see Figure 5-5 for an example of such a schema).
   II. For each relation, diagram the functional dependencies (see Figure 5-23 for an example).
   III. If any of the relations are not in 3NF, transform those relations to 3NF.
      a. Figure 3-8
      b. Figure 3-9b
      c. Figure 3-11a
      d. Figure 3-11b
      e. Figure 3-15a (relationship version)
      f. Figure 3-16
      g. Figure 3-19

2. For each of the following EER diagrams from Chapter 4:
   I. Transform the diagram to a relational schema that shows referential integrity constraints (see Figure 5-5 for an example of such a schema).
   II. For each relation, diagram the functional dependencies (see Figure 5-23 for an example).

   III. If any of the relations are not in 3NF, transform those relations to 3NF.
      a. Figure 4-6b   c. Figure 4-9   e. Figure 4-18
      b. Figure 4-7a   d. Figure 4-10

3. For each of the following relations, indicate the normal form for that relation. If the relation is not in third normal form, decompose it into 3NF relations. Functional dependencies (other than those implied by the primary key) are shown where appropriate.
   a. CLASS(Course_No,Section_No)
   b. CLASS(Course_No,Section_No,Room)
   c. CLASS(Course_No,Section_No,Room,Capacity)Room → Capacity
   d. CLASS(Course_No,Section_No,Course_Name,Room, Capacity)
      Course_No → Course_Name   Room → Capacity

4. Figure 5-28 shows a class list for Millennium College. Convert this user view to a set of 3NF relations using an enterprise key. Assume the following:
   • An instructor has a unique location.
   • A student has a unique major.
   • A course has a unique title.

```
MILLENNIUM COLLEGE
CLASS LIST
FALL SEMESTER 200X

COURSE NO.:   IS 460
COURSE TITLE:   DATABASE
INSTRUCTOR NAME:   NORMA L. FORM
INSTRUCTOR LOCATION:   B 104

STUDENT NO.    STUDENT NAME    MAJOR    GRADE

   38214         Bright           IS        A
   40875         Cortez           CS        B
   51893         Edwards          IS        A
```

Figure 5-28
Class list (Millennium College)

5. Figure 5-29 shows an E-R diagram for a simplified credit card environment. There are two types of card accounts: debit cards and credit cards. Credit card accounts accumulate charges with merchants. Each charge is identified by the date and amount of the charge.
   a. Develop a relational schema (similar to Figure 5-5).
   b. Show the functional dependencies (similar to Figure 5-23).
   c. Develop a set of 3NF relations using an enterprise key.

6. Table 5-2 contains sample data for parts and for vendors who supply those parts. In discussing these data with users, we find that part numbers (but not descriptions) uniquely identify parts, and that vendor names uniquely identify vendors.
   a. Convert this table to a relation (named PART SUPPLIER) in first normal form. Illustrate the relation with the sample data in the table.

Figure 5-29
E-R diagram for bank cards

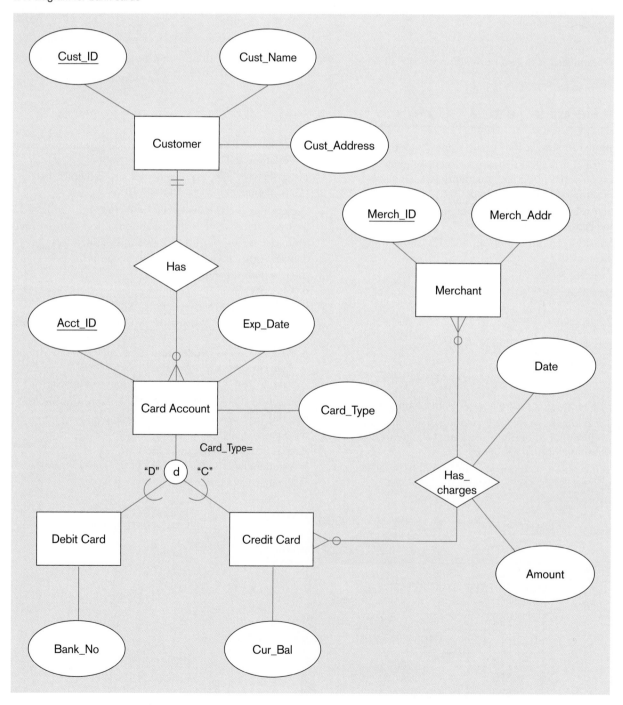

Table 5-2 Sample Data for Parts and Vendors

Part_No.	Description	Vendor_Name	Address	Unit_Cost
1234	Logic chip	Fast Chips	Cupertino	10.00
		Smart Chips	Phoenix	8.00
5678	Memory chip	Fast Chips	Cupertino	3.00
		Quality Chips	Austin	2.00
		Smart Chips	Phoenix	5.00

b. List the functional dependencies in PART SUPPLIER and identify a candidate key.

c. For the relation PART SUPPLIER, identify each of the following: an insert anomaly, a delete anomaly, and a modification anomaly.

d. Draw a relational schema for PART SUPPLIER (similar to Figure 5-23) and show the functional dependencies.

e. In what normal form is this relation?

f. Develop a set of 3NF relations from PART SUPPLIER.

7. Table 5-3 shows a relation called GRADE REPORT for a university. Following is a description of the functional dependencies in GRADE REPORT:

- Student_ID → Student_Name,Campus_Address,Major
- Course_ID → Course_Title,Instructor_Name, Instructor_Location
- Student_ID,Course_ID → Grade
- Instructor_Name → Instructor_Location

Following is your assignment:

a. Draw a relational schema (similar to Figure 5-23) and diagram the functional dependencies in the relation.

b. In what normal form is this relation?

c. Decompose GRADE REPORT into a set of 3NF relations.

d. Draw a relational schema for your 3NF relations (similar to Figure 5-5) and show the referential integrity constraints.

8. Transform Figure 3-15b, attribute version, to 3NF relations. Transform Figure 3-15b, relationship version, to 3NF relations. Compare these two sets of 3NF relations to those in Figure 5-10. What observations and conclusions do you reach by comparing these different sets of 3NF relations?

Field Exercises

1. Interview systems and database designers at several organizations. Ask them to describe the process they use for logical design. How do they transform their conceptual data models (e.g., E-R diagrams) to relational schema? What is the role of CASE tools in this process? Do they use normalization? If so, to what level?

2. Obtain a common document such as a sales slip, customer invoice from an auto repair shop, credit card statement, etc. Then do the following:

a. List the attribute names on the document.

b. List the functional dependencies among the attributes (make any assumptions you find necessary).

c. Draw a schema for the relation (similar to Figure 5-23) and diagram the functional dependencies.

d. Decompose the relation into a set of 3NF relations, and draw the relational schema (similar to Figure 5-5).

3. Obtain documentation for three popular PC-based CASE tools and compare the notation they use for representing relational schemas. You may use the following Internet

Table 5-3 GRADE REPORT Relation

GRADE REPORT

Student_ID	Student_Name	Campus_Address	Major	Course_ID	Course_Title	Instructor_Name	Instructor_Location	Grade
168300458	Williams	208 Brooks	IS	IS 350	Database Mgt	Codd	B 104	A
268300458	Williams	208 Brooks	IS	IS 465	Systems Analysis	Parsons	B 317	B
543291073	Baker	104 Phillips	Acctg	IS 350	Database Mgt	Codd	B 104	C
543291073	Baker	104 Phillips	Acctg	Acct 201	Fund Acctg	Miller	H 310	B
543291073	Baker	104 Phillips	Acctg	Mktg 300	Intro Mktg	Bennett	B 212	A

addresses to obtain on-line information for the following three tools:

a. Microsoft Access: www.microsoft.com/Visual Tools/

b. Erwin: www.logicworks.com

c. EasyER: www.esti.com

4. Find a form or report from a business organization, possibly a statement, bill, or document you have received. Draw an EER diagram of the data in this form or report. Transform the diagram into a set of 3NF relations.

References

Chouinard, P. 1989. "Supertypes, Subtypes, and DB2." *Database Programming & Design* 2 (October): 50–57.

Codd, E. F. 1970. "A Relational Model of Data for Large Relational Databases." *Communications of the ACM* 13 (June): 77–87.

Codd, E. F. 1990. *The Relational Model for Database Management Version 2.* Reading, MA: Addison-Wesley.

Date, C. J. 1995. *An Introduction to Database Systems.* 6th ed. Reading, MA: Addison-Wesley.

Dutka, A. F., and H. H. Hanson. 1989. *Fundamentals of Data Normalization.* Reading, MA: Addison-Wesley.

Fleming, C. C., and B. von Halle. 1989. *Handbook of Relational Database Design.* Reading, MA: Addison-Wesley.

Johnston, T. 2000. "Primary Key Reengineering Projects: The Problem" and "Primary Key Reengineering Projects: The Solution" available from www.dmreview.com.

Navathe, S., R. Elmasri, and J. Larson. 1986. "Integrating User Views in Database Design." *Computer* (January): 50–62.

Further Reading

Elmasri, R., and Navathe, S. 1994. *Fundamentals of Database Systems.* 2nd ed. Menlo Park, CA: Benjamin Cummings.

Hoffer, J. A., J. F. George, and J. S. Valacich. 1999. *Modern Systems Analysis and Design.* 2nd ed. Reading, MA: Addison-Wesley.

Storey, V. C. 1991. "Relational Database Design Based on the Entity-Relationship Model." *Data and Knowledge Engineering* 7: 47–83.

Web Resources

http://databases.about.com/compute/databases/msub0045.htm This is a page on the About Network. This page explains the concepts of normalization.

http://oracle.com/tools/designer Oracle Corp. is a leading vendor of database products, including the Designer CASE tool. Designer, among other capabilities, can help a database analyst draw an E-R diagram, and then Designer will automatically transform an E-R diagram into 3NF relations. You might want to search for other CASE tool vendors.

www.troubleshooters.com/littslip/ltnorm.html This is a page on Steve Litt's site that contains various troubleshooting tips for avoiding programming and systems development problems.

MOUNTAIN VIEW COMMUNITY HOSPITAL

Project Case

You have been introduced to the Mountain View Community Hospital case in the preceding chapters. This chapter continues the case with special emphasis on logical design for the relational data model. Although the hospital will continue to evaluate newer object-oriented and object-relational technology, it is expected that relational technology will continue to dominate its systems development over the next few years.

PROJECT QUESTIONS

1. Why will Mountain View Community Hospital continue to use relational technology for systems development, despite the continuing emergence of newer technology?

2. Should Mountain View Community Hospital use normalization in designing its relational databases? Why or why not?

3. Why are entity integrity and referential integrity constraints of importance to the hospital?

4. Who in the hospital should be involved in data normalization?

PROJECT EXERCISES

Your assignment is to perform a logical design for the databases at Mountain View Community Hospital. In Chapters 3 and 4 you developed conceptual data models

for the hospital. Specifically, in those chapters you prepared the following:

- E-R diagram for the major entities and relationships in the hospital (see Project Exercise 2 in Chapter 3).
- EER diagram emphasizing the human resources in the hospital (see Project Exercise 1 in Chapter 4).

Your assignment in this chapter is to develop a logical design for one or both of these conceptual designs. For each logical design, you are to perform the following tasks:

1. Map the E-R (and/or EER) diagram to a relational schema, using the techniques described in this chapter. Be sure to underline all primary keys, include all necessary foreign keys, and indicate referential integrity constraints.

2. Diagram the functional dependencies in each relation.

3. If any relation is not in 3NF, decompose that relation into 3NF relations and revise the relational schema.

4. Create enterprise keys for all relations and redefine all relations.

5. Write CREATE TABLE commands for each relation for your answer to Project Exercise 4. Make reasonable assumptions concerning the data type for each attribute in each of the relations.

6. If you develop a logical design for the E-R diagram for both chapters, merge the relations into a single set of 3NF relations.

Physical Database Design and Performance

After studying this chapter, you should be able to:

- Define the following key terms: **field, data type, physical record, page, blocking factor, denormalization, horizontal partitioning, vertical partitioning, physical file, tablespace, extent, pointer, file organization, sequential file organization, indexed file organization, index, secondary key, bitmap index, join index, hashed file organization, hashing algorithm, hash index table, Redundant Array of Inexpensive Disks (RAID), and stripe.**

- Describe the physical database design process, its objectives, and deliverables.

- Choose storage formats for attributes from a logical data model.

- Select an appropriate file organization by balancing various important design factors.

- Describe three important types of file organization.

- Describe the purpose of indexes and the important considerations in selecting attributes to be indexed.

- Translate a relational data model into efficient database structures, including knowing when and how to denormalize the logical data model.

INTRODUCTION

In Chapters 3 through 5 you learned how to describe and model organizational data during the conceptual data modeling and logical database design phases of the database development process. You learned how to use EER notation, and the relational data model and normalization to develop abstractions of organizational data that capture the meaning of data; however, these notations do not explain *how* data will be processed or stored. The purpose of physical database design is to translate the logical description of data into the technical specifications for storing and retrieving data. The goal is to create a design for storing data that will provide adequate performance and insure database integrity, security, and recoverability.

Physical database design does not include implementing files and databases (i.e., creating them and loading data into them). Physical database design produces the technical specifications that programmers and others involved in information systems construction will use during the implementation phase, which we discuss in Chapters 7 through 11.

In this chapter you will study the basic steps required to develop an efficient physical database design. We concentrate in this chapter on the design of a single, centralized database. Later in Chapter 13 you will learn about the design of databases that are stored at multiple, distributed sites. In Chapter 6 you will learn how to estimate the amount of data that users will require in the database, and how data are likely to be used. You will learn about choices for storing attribute values and how to select among these choices. You will also learn why normalized tables do not always form the best physical data files, and how you can denormalize the data to improve the speed of data retrieval. You will learn about different file organizations and about the use of indexes, which are important in speeding up the retrieval of data. And you will learn the major differences between different architectures for databases.

You must carefully perform physical database design, since the decisions made during this stage have a major impact on data accessibility, response times, security, user friendliness, and similarly important information system design factors. Database administration (described in Chapter 12) plays a major role in physical database design, so we will return to some advanced design issues in that chapter.

PHYSICAL DATABASE DESIGN PROCESS

In most situations, many physical database design decisions are implicit or eliminated when you choose the database management technologies to use with the information system you are designing. Since many organizations have standards for operating systems, database management systems, and data access languages, you must deal only with those choices not implicit in the given technologies. Thus, we will cover only those decisions you will make most frequently, as well as other selected decisions that may be critical for some types of applications, such an on-line data capture and retrieval.

The primary goal of physical database design is data processing efficiency. Today, with ever-decreasing costs for computer technology per unit of measure (both speed and space measures), it is typically very important for you to design the physical database to minimize the time required by users to interact with the information system. Thus, we concentrate on how to make processing of physical files and databases efficient, with less attention on efficient use of space.

Designing physical files and databases requires certain information that should have been collected and produced during prior system development phases. The information needed for physical file and database design includes these requirements:

- Normalized relations, including volume estimates
- Definitions of each attribute
- Descriptions of where and when data are used: entered, retrieved, deleted, and updated (including frequencies)
- Expectations or requirements for response time and data security, backup, recovery, retention, and integrity
- Descriptions of the technologies (database management systems) used for implementing the database

Physical database design requires several critical decisions that will affect the integrity and performance of the application system. These key decisions include the following:

1. Choosing the storage format (called *data type*) for each attribute from the logical data model. The format is chosen to minimize storage space and to maximize data integrity.

2. Grouping attributes from the logical data model into *physical records*. You will discover that although the columns of a relational table are a natural definition for the contents of a physical record, this is not always the most desirable grouping of attributes.

3. Arranging similarly structured records in secondary memory (primarily hard disks) so that individual and groups of records (called *file organizations*) can be stored, retrieved, and updated rapidly. Consideration must be given also to protecting data and recovering data after errors are found.

4. Selecting structures (called *indexes* and *database architectures*) for storing and connecting files to make retrieving related data more efficient.

5. Preparing strategies for handling queries against the database that will optimize performance and take advantage of the file organizations and indexes that you have specified. Efficient database structures will be of benefit only if queries and the database management systems that handle those queries are tuned to intelligently use those structures.

Data Volume and Usage Analysis

As mentioned above, data-volume and frequency-of-use statistics are critical inputs to the physical database design process. Thus, either the final step you need to take in logical database design or the first step you need to take in physical database design is to estimate the size and usage patterns of the database.

An easy way to show the statistics about data volumes and usage is by adding notation to the EER diagram that represents the final set of normalized relations from logical database design. Figure 6-1 shows the EER diagram (without attributes) for a simple inventory database in Pine Valley Furniture Company. This EER diagram represents the normalized relations constructed during logical database design for the original conceptual data model of this situation depicted in Figure 4–7b. The Supplies many-to-many relationship from Figure 4–7b is shown in Figure 6-1 as an associative entity, QUOTATION, corresponding to the relation created from this relationship.

Figure 6-1
Composite usage map (Pine Valley Furniture Company)

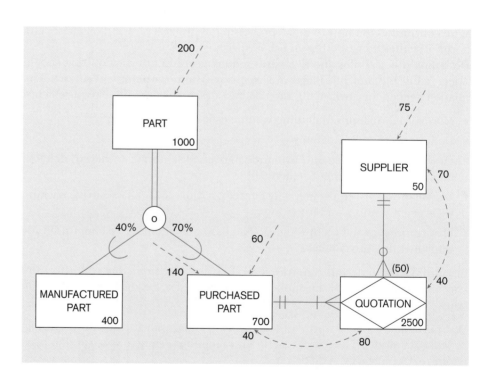

Both data volume and access frequencies are shown in Figure 6-1. For example, there are 1000 PARTs in this database. The supertype PART has two subtypes, MANUFACTURED (40 percent of all PARTs are manufactured) and PURCHASED (70 percent are purchased—since some PARTs are of both subtypes, the percentages sum to more than 100 percent). The analysts at Pine Valley estimate that there are typically 50 SUPPLIERs, and Pine Valley receives on average 50 QUOTATIONs from each SUPPLIER, yielding a total of 2500 QUOTATIONs. The dashed arrows represent access frequencies. So, for example, across all applications that use this database, there are on average 200 accesses per hour of PART data, and these then yield, based on subtype percentages, 140 accesses per hour to PURCHASED PART data. There are an additional 60 direct accesses to PURCHASED PART data. Of this total of 200 accesses to PURCHASED PART, 80 accesses then also require QUOTATION data and of these 80 accesses to QUOTATION, there are 70 subsequent accesses to SUPPLIER data. For on-line and Web-based applications, usage maps should show the accesses per second. Several usage maps may be needed to show vastly different usage patterns for different times of day. Performance will also be affected by network specifications.

The volume and frequency statistics are generated during the systems analysis phase of the systems development process when systems analysts are studying current and proposed data processing and business activities. The data-volume statistics represent the size of the business, and should be calculated assuming business growth over at least a several-year period. The access frequencies are estimated from the timing of events, transaction volumes, the number of concurrent users, and reporting and querying activities. Since many databases support ad hoc accesses, and such accesses may change significantly over time, and known database access can peak and valley over a day, week, or month, the access frequencies tend to be less certain and even than the volume statistics. Fortunately, precise numbers are not necessary. What is crucial is the relative size of the numbers, which will suggest where the greatest attention needs to be given in order to achieve the best possible performance. For example, in Figure 6-1 notice that for each of the 40 times per hour that QUOTATION is accessed, so is then PURCHASED PART. Thus, the diagram would suggest possibly combining these two entities into are database table (or file). This act of combining normalized tables is an example of denormalization, which we discuss later in this chapter.

It can be helpful for subsequent physical database design steps if you can also explain the nature of the access for the access paths shown by the dashed lines. For example, it can be helpful to know that of the 200 accesses to PART data, 150 ask for a part or a set of parts based on the primary key, Part_No (e.g., access a part with a particular number); the other 50 accesses qualify part data for access by the value of Qty_on_Hand (these specifics are not shown in Figure 6-1). This more precise description can help in selecting indexes, one of the major topics we discuss later in this chapter. It might also be helpful to know if an access results in data creation, retrieval, update, or deletion. Such a refined description of access frequencies can be handled by additional notation on a diagram such as in Figure 6-1 or by text and tables kept in other documentation.

DESIGNING FIELDS

A **field** is the smallest unit of application data recognized by system software, such as a programming language or database management system. A field corresponds to a simple attribute from the logical data model, so a field represents each component of a composite attribute.

The basic decisions you must make in specifying each field concern the type of data (or storage type) used to represent values of this field, data integrity controls built into the database, and how the DBMS should handle missing values for the

Field: The smallest unit of named application data recognized by system software.

field. There are other field specifications, such as display format, which must be made as part of the total specification of the information system, but we will not be concerned here with those specifications typically handled by programs rather than the DBMS.

Choosing Data Types

Data type: A detailed coding scheme recognized by system software, such as a DBMS, for representing organizational data.

A **data type** is a detailed coding scheme recognized by system software, such as a DBMS, for representing organizational data. The bit pattern of the coding scheme is usually transparent to you, but the space to store data and the speed required to access data are of consequence in physical database design. The specific DBMS you will use will dictate which choices are available to you. For example, Table 6-1 lists the data types available in the Oracle 8*i* DBMS, a typical DBMS that uses the SQL data definition and manipulation language. Additional data types might be available for currency, voice, image, and user defined for some DBMSs.

Selecting a data type involves four objectives that will have different relative importances for different applications:

1. Minimize storage space.
2. Represent all possible values.
3. Improve data integrity.
4. Support all data manipulations.

The correct data type to choose for a field can, in minimal space, represent every possible value (but eliminate illegal values) for the associated attribute and can support the required data manipulation (e.g., numeric data types for arithmetic and character data types for string manipulation). Any attribute domain constraints from the conceptual data model are helpful in selecting a good data type for that attribute. Achieving these four objectives can be subtle. For example, consider a DBMS for which a data type has a maximum width of 2 bytes. Suppose this data type is sufficient to represent a quantity sold field. When quantity sold fields are summed, the sum may require a number larger than 2 bytes. If the DBMS uses the field's data type for results of any mathematics on that field, the 2-byte length will not work. Some data

Table 6-1 Data Types in Oracle 8*i*

Data Type	Description
VARCHAR2	Variable-length character data with a maximum length of 4000 characters; you must enter a maximum field length (e.g., VARCHAR2(30) for a field with a maximum length of 30 characters). A value less than 30 characters will consume only the required space.
CHAR	Fixed-length character data with a maximum length of 2000 characters; default length is 1 character (e.g. CHAR(5) for a field with a fixed length of 5 characters, capable of holding a value from 0 to 5 characters long).
LONG	Capable of storing up to 4 gigabytes of one variable-length character data field (e.g., to hold a medical instruction or a customer comment).
NUMBER	Positive and negative numbers in the range 10^{-130} to 10^{126}; can specify the precision (total number of digits to the left and right of the decimal point) and the scale (the number of digits to the right of the decimal point) (e.g., NUMBER(5) specifies an integer field with a maximum of 5 digits and NUMBER(5,2) specifies a field with no more than 5 digits and exactly 2 digits to the right of the decimal point).
DATE	Any date from January 1, 4712 B.C. to December 31, 4712 A.D.; date stores the century, year, month, day, hour, minute, and second.
BLOB	Binary large object, capable of storing up to 4 gigabytes of binary data (e.g., a photograph or sound clip).

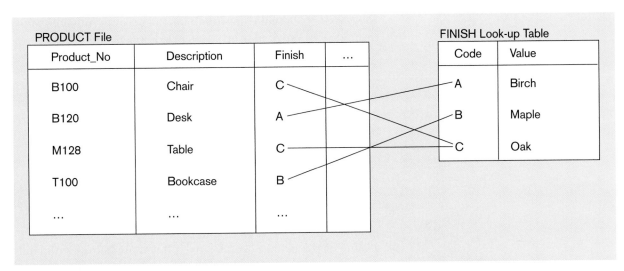

Figure 6-2
Example code look-up table (Pine Valley Furniture)

types have special manipulation capabilities; for example, only the DATE data type allows true date arithmetic.

Coding and Compression Techniques Some attributes have a sparse set of values or are so large that given data volumes, considerable storage space will be consumed (large data fields mean that data are farther apart, which yields slower data processing). A field with a limited number of possible values can be translated into a code that requires less space. Consider the example of the product Finish field illustrated in Figure 6-2. Products at Pine Valley Furniture come in only a limited number of woods: Birch, Maple, and Oak. By creating a code or translation table, each Finish field value can be replaced by a code, a cross-reference to the look-up table, similar to a foreign key. This will decrease the amount of space for the Finish field, and hence for the PRODUCT file. There will be additional space for the FINISH look-up table, and when the Finish field value is needed, an extra access to this look-up table will be required. If the Finish field is infrequently used or the number of distinct Finish values very large, the relative advantages of coding may outweigh the costs. Note that the code table would not appear in the conceptual or logical model. The code table is a physical construct to achieve data processing performance improvements, not a set of data with business value.

A form of a code table is used by data compression techniques, such as file zip routines. A data compression technique looks for patterns in data and then codes frequently appearing patterns with fewer bits. Although such routines are typically used to compress a whole file, such a routine could be used with some DBMSs to compress specific fields. Related to data compression techniques are encryption techniques, which translate a field into a secure format. In both cases, for a user to see the actual field value, software must know the reverse translation process.

Controlling Data Integrity

For many DBMSs, data integrity controls (i.e., controls on the possible value a field can assume) can be built into the physical structure of the fields and controls enforced by the DBMS on those fields. The data type enforces one form of data integrity control since it may limit the type of data (numeric or character) and length of a field value. Some other typical integrity controls that a DMBS may support are the following:

- *Default value* A default value is the value a field will assume unless a user enters an explicit value for an instance of that field. Assigning a default value to a field can reduce data entry time since entry of a value can be skipped and it can also help to reduce data entry errors for the most common value.

- *Range control* A range control limits the set of permissible values a field may assume. The range may be a numeric lower to upper bound or a set of specific values. Range controls must be used with caution since the limits of the range may change over time. A combination of range controls and coding led to the Year 2000 problem faced by many organizations, in which a field for year is represented by only the numbers 00 to 99. It is better to implement any range controls through a DBMS since range controls in programs may be inconsistently enforced and it is more difficult to find and change them.

- *Null value control* A null value was defined in Chapter 5 as an empty value. Each primary key must have an integrity control that prohibits a null value. Any other required field may also have a null value control placed on it if that is the policy of the organization. For example, a university may prohibit adding a course to its database unless that course has a title as well as a value of the primary key, Course _ID. Many fields legitimately may have a null value, so this control should be used only when truly required by business rules.

- *Referential integrity* The term "referential integrity" was defined in Chapter 5. Referential integrity on a field is a form of range control in which the value of that field must exist as the value in some field in another row of the same or different table. That is, the range of legitimate values comes from the dynamic contents of a field in a database table, not from some prespecified set of values. Note that referential integrity guarantees that only some existing cross-referencing value is used, not that it is the correct one.

Handling Missing Data When a field may be null, simply entering no value may be sufficient. For example, suppose a customer zip code field is null and a report summarizes total sales by month and zip code. How should sales to customers with unknown zip codes be handled? Two options for handling or preventing missing data have already been mentioned: using a default value and not permitting missing (null) values. Missing data are inevitable. According to Babad and Hoffer (1984), other possible methods for handling missing data are the following:

1. Substitute an estimate of the missing value. For example, for a missing sales value when computing monthly product sales, use a formula involving the mean of the existing monthly sales values for that product indexed by total sales for that month across all products. Such estimates must be marked so that users know that these are not actual values.

2. Track missing data so that special reports and other system elements cause people to quickly resolve unknown values. This can be done by setting up a trigger in the database definition. A trigger is a routine that will automatically execute when some event occurs or time period passes. One trigger could log the missing entry to a file when a null or other missing value is stored, and another trigger runs periodically to create a report of the contents of this log file.

3. Perform sensitivity testing so that missing data are ignored unless knowing a value might significantly change results; if, for example, total monthly sales for a particular salesperson are almost over a threshold that would make a difference in that person's compensation. This is the most complex of the methods mentioned and hence requires the most sophisticated programming. Such routines for handling missing data may be written in application programs. Many modern DBMSs now have more sophisticated programming capabilities, such as case expressions, user defined funtions, and triggers, so that such logic can be available in the database for all users without application-specific programming.

DESIGNING PHYSICAL RECORDS AND DENORMALIZATION

In a logical data model you group into a relation those attributes that are determined by the same primary key. In contrast, a **physical record** is a group of fields stored in adjacent memory locations and retrieved and written together as a unit by a DBMS. The design of a physical record involves choosing the sequencing of fields into adjacent storage locations to achieve two goals: efficient use of secondary storage and data processing speed.

The efficient use of secondary storage is influenced by both the size of the physical record and the structure of secondary storage. Computer operating systems read data from hard disks in units called pages, not physical records. A **page** is the amount of data read or written by an operating system in one secondary memory input or output operation. The page size is fixed by system programmers and is selected to most efficiently use RAM across all applications. Depending on the computer system, a physical record may or may not be allowed to span two pages. Thus, if page length is not an integer multiple of the physical record length, wasted space may occur at the end of a page. The number of physical records per page is called the **blocking factor**. If storage space is scarce and physical records cannot span pages, creating multiple physical records from one logical relation will minimize wasted storage space. Some DBMSs will also block multiple physical records into a data block; in this case, the DBMS manages a data block, whereas the operating system manages a page.

> **Physical record:** A group of fields stored in adjacent memory locations and retrieved and written together as a unit by a DBMS.

> **Page:** The amount of data read or written by an operating system in one secondary memory (disk) input or output operation. For I/O with a magnetic tape, the equivalent term is record block.

> **Blocking factor:** The number of physical records per page.

Denormalization

The preceding discussion of physical record design concentrated on efficient use of storage space. In most cases the second goal of physical record design—efficient data processing—dominates the design process. Efficient processing of data, just like efficient accessing of books in a library, depends on how close together related data (or books) are. Often all the attributes that appear within a relation are not used together, and data from different relations are needed together to answer a query or produce a report. Thus, although normalized relations solve data maintenance anomalies and minimize redundancies, normalized relations, if implemented one for one as physical records, may not yield efficient data processing.

The processing performance difference between totally normalized and partially normalized databases can be dramatic. Inmon (1988) reports of a study to quantify fully and partially normalized databases. A fully normalized database contained eight tables with about 50,000 rows each, another partially normalized one had four tables with roughly 25,000 rows each, and yet another partially normalized database had two tables. The result showed that the less than fully normalized databases could be as much as an order of magnitude faster than the fully normalized one. Although such results depend greatly on the database and the type of processing against it, these results suggest that you should carefully consider whether the physical records should exactly match the normalized relations for a database.

Denormalization is the process of transforming normalized relations into unnormalized physical record specifications. We will review various forms and reasons for denormalization in this section. In general, denormalization may partition a relation into several physical records, may combine attributes from several relations together into one physical record, or may do a combination of both. As Finkelstein (1988) points out, denormalization can increase the chance of errors and inconsistencies and can force reprogramming systems if business rules change. Further, denormalization optimizes certain data processing at the expense of others, so if the frequencies of different processing activities change, the benefits of denormalization may no

> **Denormalization:** The process of transforming normalized relations into unnormalized physical record specifications.

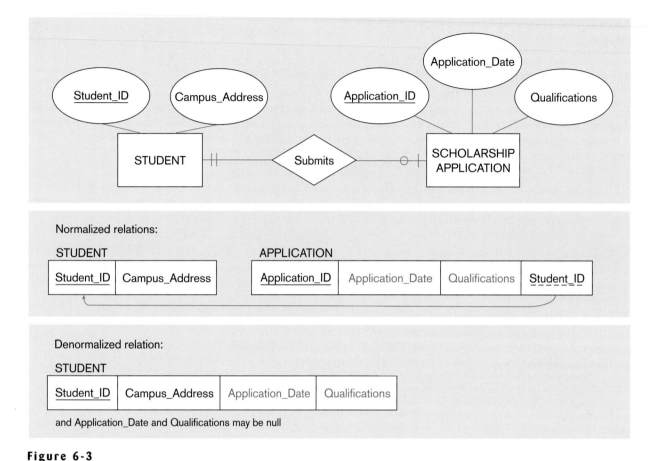

Figure 6-3
A possible denormalization situation: two entities with one-to-one relationship (*Note*: We assume Application_ID is not necessary when all fields are stored in one record, but this field can be included if it is required application data.)

longer exist. Further, denormalization almost always leads to more storage space for raw data and maybe more space for database overhead (e.g., indexes). Thus, denormalization should be an explicit act to gain significant processing speed when other physical design actions are not sufficient to achieve processing expectations.

Rogers (1989) introduces several common denormalization opportunities (Figures 6-3 through 6-5 show examples of normalized and denormalized relations for each of these three situations):

1. *Two entities with a one-to-one relationship* Even if one of the entities is an optional participant, if the matching entity exists most of the time, then it may be wise to combine these two relations into one record definition (especially if the access frequency between these two entity types is high). Figure 6-3 shows student data with optional data from a standard scholarship application a student may complete. In this case, one record could be formed with four fields from the STUDENT and SCHOLARSHIP APPLICATION normalized relations (assuming Application_ID is no longer needed). (*Note:* In this case, fields from the optional entity must have null values allowed.)

2. *A many-to-many relationship (associative entity) with nonkey attributes* Rather than joining three files to extract data from the two basic entities in the relationship, it may be advisable to combine attributes from one of the entities into the record representing the many-to-many relationship, thus avoiding one join operation in many data access modules. Again, this would be most advantageous if this joining occurs frequently. Figure 6-4 shows price quotes for different items from different vendors. In this case, fields from ITEM and PRICE QUOTE relations might be combined into one record to avoid having to join all three files together. (*Note:* This may create considerable duplication of

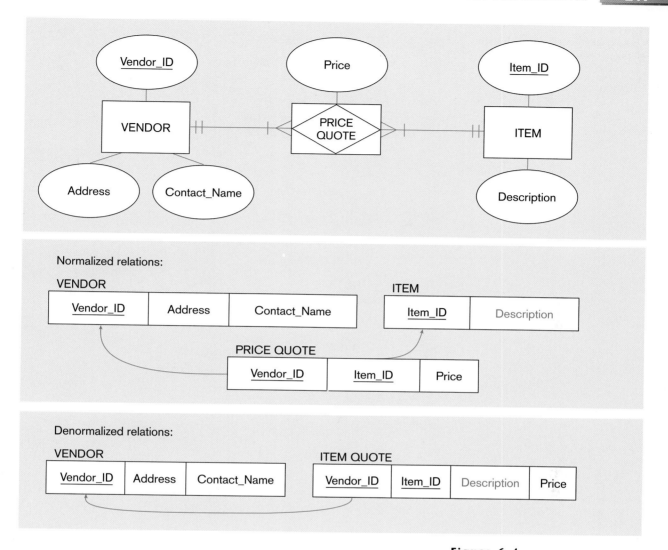

Figure 6-4
A possible denormalization situation: a many-to-many relationship with nonkey attributes

data—in the example, the ITEM fields, such as Description, would repeat for each price quote. This would necessitate excessive updating if duplicated data change.)

3. *Reference data*   Reference data exist in an entity on the one-side of a one-to-many relationship, and this entity participates in no other database relationships. You should seriously consider merging the two entities in this situation into one record definition when there are few instances of the entity on the many-side for each entity instance on the one-side. See Figure 6-5 in which several ITEMs have the same STORAGE INSTRUCTIONS and STORAGE INSTRUCTIONS only relate to ITEMs. In this case, the storage instruction data could be stored in the ITEM record creating, of course, redundancy and potential for extra data maintenance. (Instr_ID is no longer needed.)

The opportunities just listed all deal with combining tables to avoid doing joins. In contrast, denormalization can also be used to create more tables by partitioning a relation into multiple tables. Both horizontal and vertical partitioning, or a combination, are possible. **Horizontal partitioning** breaks a relation into multiple record specifications by placing different rows into different records based upon common column values. In a library setting, horizontal partitioning is similar to placing the business journals in a business library, the science books in a science library, and so

Horizontal partitioning: Distributing the rows of a table into several separate files.

Figure 6-5
A possible denormalization situation:
reference data

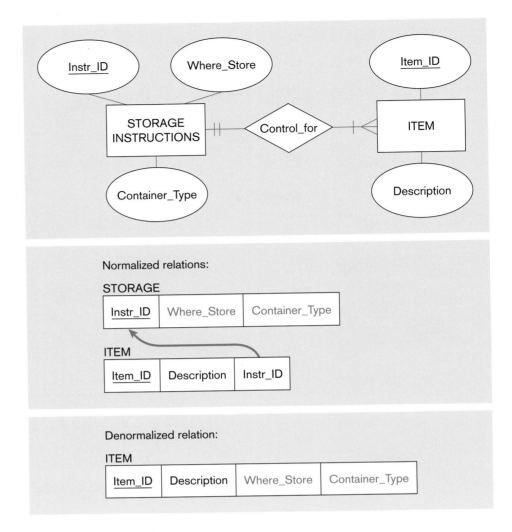

on. Each file created from the partitioning has the same record layout. For example, a customer relation could be broken into four regional customer files based on the value of a field Region.

Horizontal partitioning makes sense when different categories of rows of a table are processed separately; for example, for the customer table just mentioned, if a high percentage of the data processing needs to work with only one region at a time. Horizontal partitioning can also be more secure since file level security can be used to prohibit users from seeing certain rows of data. Also, each partitioned table can be organized differently, appropriate for how it is individually used. It is likely also faster to recover one of the partitioned files than one file with all the rows. In addition, taking one of the partitioned files out of service because it was damaged or so it can be recovered still allows processing against the other partitioned files to continue. Finally, each of the partitioned files can be placed on a separate disk drive to reduce contention for the same drive and hence improve performance across the database. These advantages of horizontal partitioning (actually all forms of partitioning), along with the disadvantages, are summarized in Table 6-2.

Note that horizontal partitioning is very similar to creating a supertype/subtype relationship because different types of the entity (where the subtype discriminator is the field used for segregating rows) are involved in different relationships, hence different processing. In fact, when you have a supertype/subtype relationship, you need to decide if you will create separate tables for each subtype or combine them in vari-

Table 6-2 Advantages and Disadvantages of Data Partitioning

Advantages of Partitioning

1. *Efficiency*:   Data used together are stored close to one another and separate from data not used together.

2. *Local optimization*:   Each partition of data can be stored to optimize performance for its own use.

3. *Security:*   Data not relevant to one group of users can be segregated from data they are allowed to use.

4. *Recovery and uptime*:   Smaller files will take less time to recover, and other files are still accessible if one file is damaged, so the effects of damage are isolated.

5. *Load balancing*:   Files can be allocated to different storage areas (disks or other media), which minimizes contention for access to the same storage area or even allows for parallel access to the different areas.

Disadvantages of Partitioning

1. *Inconsistent access speed*:   Different partitions may yield different access speeds, thus confusing users. Also, when data must be combined across partitions, users may have to deal with significantly slower response times than in a nonpartitioned approach.

2. *Complexity*:   Partitioning is usually not transparent to programmers, who will have to write more complex programs when combining data across partitions.

3. *Extra space and update time*:   Data may be duplicated across the partitions, taking extra storage space compared to storing all the data in normalized files. Updates which affect data in multiple partitions can take more time than if one file were used.

ous combinations. Combining makes sense when all subtypes are used about the same way, whereas partitioning the supertype entity into multiple files makes sense when the subtypes are handled differently in transactions, queries, and reports. When a relation is partitioned horizontally, the whole set of rows can be reconstructed by the SQL UNION operator (described in Chapter 7). Thus, for example, all customer data can be viewed together when desired.

The Oracle database management system supports several forms of horizontal partitioning, designed in particular to deal with very large tables (Brobst et al, 1999). A table is partitioned when it is defined to the DBMS using the SQL data definition language (you will learn about the CREATE TABLE command in Chapter 7); that is, in Oracle, there is one table with several partitions, not separate tables per se. Oracle 8*i* has three horizontal partitioning methods:

1. *Key range partitioning*, in which each partition is defined by a range of values (lower and upper key value limits) for one or more columns of the normalized table. A table row is inserted in the proper partition based on its initial values for the range fields. Because partition key values may follow patterns, each partition may hold quite a different number of rows. A partition key may be generated by the database designer to create a more balanced distribution of rows. A row may be restricted from moving between partitions when key values are updated.

2. *Hash partitioning*, in which data are evenly spread across partitions independent of any partition key value. Hash partitioning overcomes the uneven distribution of rows that is possible with key range partitioning.

3. *Composite partitioning*, which combines aspects of both key range and hash partitioning. Partitions can be transparent to the database user (you need to refer to a partition only if you want to force the query processor to look at one or more partitions). The part of the DBMS that optimizes the processing of a query will look at the definition of partitions for a table involved in a query and will automatically decide if certain partitions can be eliminated when retrieving the data needed to form the query results, which can drastically improve query processing performance.

For example, suppose a transaction date is used to define partitions in key range partitioning. A query asking for only recent transactions can be more quickly processed by looking at only the one or few partitions with the most recent transactions rather than scanning the database or even using indexes to find rows in the desired range from a nonpartitioned table. A partition on date also isolates insertions of new rows to one partition, which may reduce the overhead of database maintenance, and dropping "old" transactions will require simply dropping a partition. Indexes can still be used with a partitioned table, and can improve performance even more than partitioning alone. See Brobst et al. (1999) for more details on the pros and cons of using dates for key range partitioning.

In hash partitioning, rows are more evenly spread across the partitions. If partitions are placed in different storage areas that can be processed in parallel, then query performance will improve noticeably compared to when all the data have to be accessed sequentially in one storage area for the whole table. As with key range partitioning, the existence of partitions can be transparent to a programmer of a query. With composite partitioning, partitions are defined by key ranges, and then subpartitions are defined by key hashing. Composite partitioning combines the advantages of range separation with the parallel processing of key hashing.

Vertical partitioning: Distributing the columns of a table into several separate physical records.

Vertical partitioning distributes the columns of a relation into separate physical records, repeating the primary key in each of the records. An example of vertical partitioning would be breaking apart a part relation by placing the part number along with accounting-related part data into one record specification, the part number along with engineering-related part data into another record specification, and the part number along with sales-related part data into yet another record specification. The advantages and disadvantages of vertical partitioning are similar to those for horizontal partitioning. When, for example, accounting-, engineering-, and sales-related part data need to be used together, these tables can be joined. Thus, neither horizontal nor vertical partitioning prohibits the ability to treat the original relation as a whole.

Combinations of horizontal and vertical partitioning are also possible. This form of denormalization—record partitioning—is especially common for a database whose files are distributed across multiple computers. Thus, you will study this topic again in Chapter 13.

A single physical table can be logically partitioned or several tables logically combined by using a concept of a user view, which will be defined in Chapter 7. With a user view, users can be given the impression that the database contains tables other than what are physically defined; you can create these logical tables by horizontal or vertical partitioning or other forms of denormalization. However, the purpose of any form of user view, including logical partitioning via views, is to simplify query writing and to create a more secure database, not to improve query performance. One form of a user view available in Oracle is called a Partition View. With a Partition View, physically separate tables with similar structures can be logically combined into one table using the SQL UNION operator. There are limitations to this form of partitioning. First, since there are actually multiple separate physical tables, there cannot be any global index on all the combined rows. Second, each physical table must be separately managed, so data maintenance is more complex (e.g., a new row must be inserted into a specific table). Third, the query optimizer has fewer options with a Partition View than with partitions of a single table for creating the most efficient query processing plan.

The final form of denormalization we introduce is data replication. In data replication, the same data are purposely stored in multiple places in the database. For example, consider again Figure 6-1. You learned earlier in this section that relations can be denormalized by combining data from an associative entity with data from one of the simple entities with which it is associated. So, in Figure 6-1, QUOTATION data might be stored with PURCHASED PART data in one expanded PURCHASED

PART physical record specification. With data duplication, the same QUOTATION data might also be stored with its associated SUPPLIER data in another expanded SUPPLIER physical record specification. With this data duplication, once either a SUPPLIER or PURCHASED PART record is retrieved, the related QUOTATION data will also be available without any further access to secondary memory. This improved speed is worthwhile only if QUOTATION data are frequently accessed with SUPPLIER and with PURCHASED PART data and if the costs for extra secondary storage and data maintenance are not great.

DESIGNING PHYSICAL FILES

A **physical file** is a named portion of secondary memory (such as a magnetic tape or hard disk) allocated for the purpose of storing physical records. Some computer operating systems allow a physical file to be split into separate pieces, sometimes called extents. In subsequent sections, we will assume that a physical file is not split and each record in a file has the same structure. That is, subsequent sections address how to store and link relational table rows from a single database in physical storage space. In order to optimize the performance of the database processing, the person who administers a database, the database administrator, often needs to know extensive details about how the database management system manages physical storage space. This knowledge is very DBMS specific, but the principles described in subsequent sections are the foundation for the physical data structures used by most relational DBMSs.

Most database management systems store many different kinds of data in one operating system file. By an operating system file we mean a named file that would appear on a disk directory listing (such as a listing of the files in a folder on the C: drive of your personal computer). For example, an important structure for physical storage space in Oracle is a tablespace. A **tablespace** is a named set of disk storage elements in which data from one or more database tables may be stored. An instance of Oracle will include many tablespaces, for example, one for system data (data dictionary or data about data), one for temporary work space, one for database recovery, and several to hold user business data. One or more tablespaces are contained in a physical operating system file. Thus, Oracle has responsibility for managing the storage of data inside a tablespace, whereas the operating system has many responsibilities for managing a tablespace as a whole as it would any operating system file (e.g., handling file level security, allocating space, and responding to disk read and write errors).

Because an instance of Oracle usually supports many databases for many users, the database administrator usually will create many user tablespaces, which helps to achieve database security by giving each user selected rights to access each tablespace. As noted above, as an operating system file, a tablespace may be spread over several **extents**, where an extent is a contiguous section of disk storage space. When a tablespace needs to enlarge to hold more data, it is assigned another extent. Each database table is assigned to one or more tablespaces (each table row is in one and only one tablespace, but different rows from the same table may be in different tablespaces); a tablespace may contain data from one or more tables. Managing tablespaces, or physical database files, is a significant job of a database administrator in an Oracle environment. For example, locating different tablespaces on different devices or channels and spreading tables across tablespaces, a database administrator can minimize disk drive contention across concurrent database users. Because this is not a text on Oracle, we do not cover specific details on managing tablespaces; however, the general principles of physical database design apply to the design and management of Oracle tablespaces as they do to whatever the physical storage unit is for any database management system. Figure 6-6 is an EER model to show the relationships

Physical file: A named portion of secondary memory (a magnetic tape or hard disk) allocated for the purpose of storing physical records.

Tablespace: A named set of disk storage elements in which physical files for database tables may be stored.

Extent: A contiguous section of disk storage space.

Figure 6-6
Physical file terminology in an Oracle environment

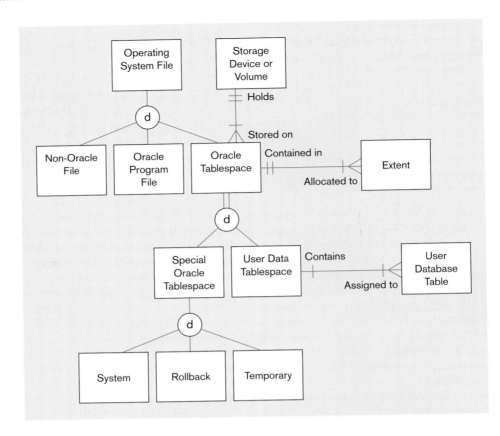

between various physical and logical database terms related to physical database design in an Oracle environment.

Pointer

Pointer: A field of data that can be used to locate a related field or record of data.

All files are organized by using two basic constructs to link one piece of data with another piece of data: sequential storage and pointers. With sequential storage one field or record is stored right after another field or record. Although simple to implement and use, sometimes sequential storage is not the most efficient way to organize data. A **pointer** is a field of data that can be used to locate a related field or record of data. In most cases, a pointer contains the address, or location, of the associated data. Pointers are used in a wide variety of data storage structures; however, we will see only a few of their uses in this chapter. The interested reader can read Appendix C for a broader coverage of the use of pointers. We define pointer here only because knowing what a pointer is is necessary for understanding file organizations. You will likely never work directly with pointers because the DBMS will handle all pointer use and maintenance automatically.

File Organizations

File organization: A technique for physically arranging the records of a file on secondary storage devices.

A **file organization** is a technique for physically arranging the records of a file on secondary storage devices. With modern relational DBMSs, you do not have to design file organizations, but you may be allowed to select an organization and its parameters for a table or physical file. In choosing a file organization for a particular file in a database, you should consider seven important factors:

1. Fast data retrieval
2. High throughput for processing data input and maintenance transactions

3. Efficient use of storage space
4. Protection from failures or data loss
5. Minimizing need for reorganization
6. Accommodating growth
7. Security from unauthorized use

Often these objectives conflict, and you must select a file organization that provides a reasonable balance among the criteria within resources available.

In this chapter we consider the following families of basic file organizations: sequential, indexed, and hashed. Figure 6-7 illustrates each of these organizations with the nicknames of some university sport teams.

Sequential File Organizations In a **sequential file organization**, the records in the file are stored in sequence according to a primary key value (see Figure 6-7a). To locate a particular record, a program must normally scan the file from the beginning until the desired record is located. A common example of a sequential file is the alphabetical list of persons in the white pages of a telephone directory (ignoring any index that may be included with the directory). A comparison of the capabilities of sequential files with the other two types of files appears later in Table 6-3. Because of their inflexibility, sequential files are not used in a database, but may be used for files that backup data from a database.

> **Sequential file organization:** The storage of records in a file in sequence according to a primary key value.

Indexed File Organizations In an **indexed file organization**, the records are stored either sequentially or nonsequentially and an index is created that allows the application software to locate individual records (see Figure 6-7b). Like a card catalog in a library, an **index** is a table that is used to determine the location of rows in a file that satisfy some condition. Each index entry matches a key value with one or more records. An index can point to unique records (a primary key index, such as on the Product_ID field of a product record) or to potentially more than one record. An index that allows each entry to point to more than one record is called a **secondary key** index. Secondary key indexes are important for supporting many reporting requirements and for providing rapid ad hoc data retrieval. An example would be an index on the Finish field of a product record.

> **Indexed file organization:** The storage of records either sequentially or nonsequentially with an index that allows software to locate individual records.

> **Index:** A table or other data structure used to determine the location of rows in a file that satisfy some condition.

Some index structures influence where table rows are stored, and other index structures are independent of where rows are located. Because the actual structure of an index does not influence database design and is not important in writing database queries, we will not address the actual physical structure of indexes in this chapter. Thus, Figure 6-7b should be considered a logical view of how an index is used, not a physical view of how data are stored in an index structure. Some relational DBMSs use the term primary index (that is different from a primary *key* index) to designate an index that determines the physical location of data, whereas a secondary index (again, distinct from secondary *key* index) is an index that plays no role in determining the storage location of data. For these systems, a table will have one primary index and may have many secondary indexes. The primary index may use the primary key of the table or may not; and a secondary index may use a field that is unique or is not unique across the rows of the table. When the terms primary and secondary index are used, there are four types of indexes:

> **Secondary key:** One field or a combination of fields for which more than one record may have the same combination of values. Also called a nonunique key.

- Unique primary index (UPI), which is an index on a unique field, possibly the primary key of the table, and which not only is used to find table rows based on this field value but also is used by the DBMS to determine where to store a row based on the primary index field value.

- Nonunique primary index (NUPI), which is an index on a nonunique field and which not only is used to find table rows based on this field value but also is used by the DBMS to determine where to store a row based on the primary index field value.

Figure 6-7
Comparison of file organizations
(a) Sequential

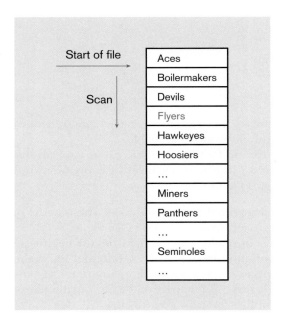

(b) Indexed

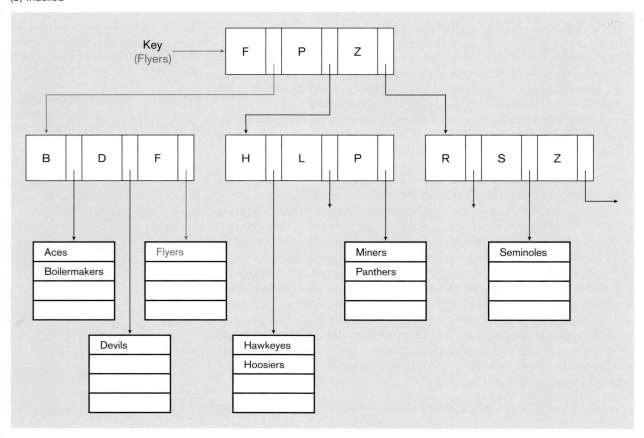

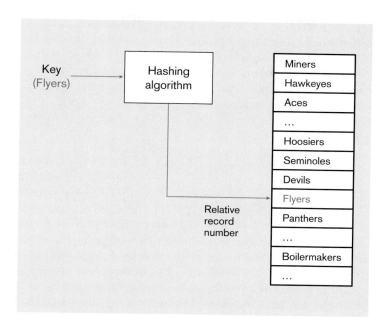

Figure 6-7
(continued)
(c) Hashed

- Unique secondary index (USI), which is an index on a unique field and which is used only to find table rows based on this field value.
- Nonunique secondary index (NUSI), which is an index on a nonunique field and which is used only to find table rows based on this field value.

The example in Figure 6-7b illustrates that indexes can be built on top of indexes, creating a hierarchical set of indexes. This may be desirable since an index itself is a file and, if it is very large, it too can be organized by indexing the index. Each index entry in Figure 6-7b has a key value and a pointer to another index or to a data record. For example, to find the record with key 'Flyers', the file organization would start at the top index and take the pointer after the entry F, which points to another index for all keys that begin with the letters A through F in the alphabet. Then the software would follow the pointer after the F in this index, which represents all those records with keys that begin with the letters E through F. Eventually, the search through the indexes either locates the desired record or indicates that no such record exists.

One of the most powerful capabilities of indexed file organizations is the ability to create multiple indexes. Multiple indexes exist in a library, where there are indexes on title, author, and subject pointing to the same set of books and journals. Thus, we can virtually create another file by simply creating another index on the same set of data records, so the voluminous data are not replicated. Multiple indexes can be manipulated. For example, if we use the Finish index to find the addresses for the set of product records with the Birch finish and the Cost index to find the set of product records that cost under $500 to make, we can intersect these two sets to find the addresses of those products, and only those products, that are Birch and cost under $500. This ability to use multiple indexes in one query is important in processing queries against a relational database. Logical AND, OR, and NOT operations can be handled by simply manipulating results from an index scan, thus avoiding the more costly access to data records that do not meet all the qualifications of the query.

The general structure of a hierarchical index like that in Figure 6-7b is called a tree (with the root node at the top and leaf nodes at the bottom—yes, the tree is upside down!). The performance of a tree of index entries is greatly influenced by the properties of the tree structure used. A common type of tree used by database management systems to store indexes is a balanced tree, or B-tree, and the most popular form of a B-tree is a B+-tree. In a B-tree, all the leaves (which typically contain the data records or pointers to each record) are stored at the same distance from the root, as in Figure 6-7b in which all the data records are stored two levels from the root. Because the operating system and DBMS manage whatever index tree structure is used, and usually you have little choice on how the index is structured, the management of the tree is transparent to you as database designer or programmer. Appendix C includes a review of tree data structures and the parameters of a tree design over which you might have some control.

Bitmap index: A table of bits in which each row represents the distinct values of a key and each column is a bit, which when on indicates that the record for that bit column position has the associated field value.

Of increasing popularity today is a type of index called a bitmap index. A **bitmap index** (see Figure 6-8) assigns a bitmap for each key value. Suppose a Product table has 10 rows and the Price attribute has 4 different values in these 10 rows (this example is small for illustration purposes). A bitmap index on the Price field would have 4 entries with 10 bits per entry. Each bit in each bitmap entry matches a row in the Product table. If, for example, bit 8 is on for the entry for Price of $400, it indicates that row 8 of the Product table has Price $400 (each bit column will have only one bit on). A bitmap is ideal for attributes that have even a few possible values, which is not true for conventional tree indexes. A bitmap also often requires less storage space (possibly as little as 25 percent) than a conventional tree index (Schumacher, 1997), but for an attribute with many distinct values, a bitmap index can exceed the storage space of a conventional tree index. In the proper situation, because bit manipulation and searching is so fast, the speed of query processing with a bitmap can be 10 times faster than a conventional tree index.

An interesting feature of a bitmap index is that one bitmap can be used for multiple keys. For example, we could add another set of rows to the bottom of Figure 6-8 for all the values of the Room attribute. Then, each bit column would have two bits on, one for the associated Product row's price and one for room. A query looking for $100 products for the dining room can intersect the bit pattern for the $100 price row with the dining room row to find only those products that satisfy both conditions. Bit manipulation of this nature can be very efficient.

Transaction processing applications require rapid response to queries that involve one or a few related table rows. For example, to enter a new customer order, an order entry application needs to rapidly find the specific customer table row, a few product table rows for the items being purchased, possibly a few other product table rows based on the characteristics of the products the customer wants (e.g., product finish), and then one customer order and one customer shipment row need to be added by the application to the respective tables. The types of indexes discussed so far work very well in such applications where the application is searching for a few, specific table rows.

Another increasingly popular type of index, especially in data warehousing and other decision support applications (see Chapter 11), is a join index. In decision

Figure 6-8
Bitmap index on Product Price attribute

Price	\multicolumn{10}{c}{Product Table Row Numbers}
	1	2	3	4	5	6	7	8	9	10
100	0	0	1	0	1	0	0	0	0	0
200	1	0	0	0	0	0	0	0	0	0
300	0	1	0	0	0	0	1	0	0	1
400	0	0	0	1	0	1	0	1	1	0

Products 3 and 5 have Price $100
Product 1 has Price $200
Products 2, 7, and 10 have Price $300
Products 4, 6, 8, and 9 have Price $400

support applications, the data accessing tends to want all rows from very large tables that are related to one another (e.g., all the customers who have bought items from the same store). A **join index** is an index on columns from two or more tables that come from the same domain of values. For example, consider Figure 6-9a, which shows two tables, Store and Customer. Each of these tables has a column, City. The join index of the City column indicates the row identifiers for rows in the two tables that have the same City value. Because of how many data warehouses are designed, there is a high frequency for queries to find data (facts) in common to a store and a customer in the same city (or similar intersections of facts across multiple dimensions). Figure 6-9b shows another possible application for a join index. In this case, the join index precomputes the matching of a foreign key in the Order table with the associated customer in the Customer table. A join index precomputes the result of a relational join operator, which will be discussed in Chapter 7. Simply stated, a join says find rows in the same or different tables that have values that match some criterion.

> **Join index:** An index on columns from two or more tables that come from the same domain of values.

Customer

RowID	Cust#	CustName	City	State
10001	C2027	Hadley	Dayton	Ohio
10002	C1026	Baines	Columbus	Ohio
10003	C0042	Ruskin	Columbus	Ohio
10004	C3861	Davies	Toledo	Ohio
. . .				

Store

RowID	Store#	City	Size	Manager
20001	S4266	Dayton	K2	E2166
20002	S2654	Columbus	K3	E0245
20003	S3789	Dayton	K4	E3330
20004	S1941	Toledo	K1	E0874
. . .				

Join Index

CustRowID	StoreRowID	Common Value*
10001	20001	Dayton
10001	20003	Dayton
10002	20002	Columbus
10003	20002	Columbus
10004	20004	Toledo
. . .		

*This column may or may not be included, as needed. Join index could be sorted on any of the three columns. Sometimes two join indexes are created, one as above and one with the two rowID columns reversed.

Figure 6-9
Join indexes
(a) Join index for common nonkey columns

Figure 6-9
(continued)
(b) Join index for matching a foreign key
(FK) and a primary key (PK)

Order

RowID	Order#	Order Date	Cust#(FK)
30001	O5532	10/01/2001	C3861
30002	O3478	10/01/2001	C1062
30003	O8734	10/02/2001	C1062
30004	O9845	10/02/2001	C2027
. . .			

Customer

RowID	Cust#(PK)	CustName	City	State
10001	C2027	Hadley	Dayton	Ohio
10002	C1026	Baines	Columbus	Ohio
10003	C0042	Ruskin	Columbus	Ohio
10004	C3861	Davies	Toledo	Ohio
. . .				

Join Index

CustRowID	OrderRowID	Cust#
10001	30004	C2027
10002	30002	C1062
10002	30003	C1062
10004	30001	C3861
. . .		

A join index is created as rows are loaded into a database, so the index, like all other indexes previously discussed, is always up-to-date. Without a join index in the database of Figure 6-9a, any query that wants to find stores and customers in the same city would have to compute the equivalent of the join index each time the query is run. For very large tables, joining all the rows of one table with matching rows in another possibly large table can be very time consuming and can significantly delay responding to an on-line query. In Figure 6-9b the join index provides one place for the DBMS to find information about related table rows. A join index, similar to any index, saves query processing time by finding data meeting a prespecified qualification at the expense of the extra storage space and maintenance of the index. Bontempo and Saracco (1996) discuss how to combine join indexing with bitmap indexing to speed up processing of certain types of join indexes.

Ballinger (1998) suggests an extension to a join index that may eliminate the need to access the actual data tables. For example, in Figure 6-9b, besides Cust#, other columns from either or both tables could be included as additional columns in the join index. Then, if the query using the join index requires only columns included in the join index, the base tables are not needed to process the query. When would it make sense to implement this extension? The answer is when the database is rather static, so that the join index, once created, has a fairly long life. This condition is true in many data warehousing environments, in which existing rows are not updated, and new rows are added and obsolete rows are deleted only periodically, for example, monthly. In this case when there are infrequent changes to the database but frequent and complex queries against very large data tables, an extended join index can be a very productive structure for improving query performance.

The use of databases for new applications, such as in data warehousing and on-line decision support, is generating the development of new types of indexes. We encourage you to investigate the indexing capabilities of the database management system you are using to fully understand when to apply each type of index and how to tune the performance of the index structures.

Hashed File Organizations

In a **hashed file organization**, the address of each record is determined using a hashing algorithm (see Figure 6–7c). A **hashing algorithm** is a routine that converts a primary key value into a record address. Although there are several variations of hashed files, in most cases the records are located non-sequentially as dictated by the hashing algorithm. Thus, sequential data processing is impractical.

A typical hashing algorithm uses the technique of dividing each primary key value by a suitable prime number and then using the remainder of the division as the relative storage location. For example, suppose that an organization has a set of approximately 1,000 employee records to be stored on magnetic disk. A suitable prime number would be 997, since it is close to 1,000. Now consider the record for employee 12396. When we divide this number by 997, the remainder is 432. Thus, this record is stored at location 432 in the file. Another technique (not discussed here) must be used to resolve duplicates (or overflow) that can occur with the division/remainder method when two or more keys hash to the same address (known as a "hash clash").

One of the severe limitations of hashing is that because data table row locations are dictated by the hashing algorithm, only one key can be used for hashing-based (storage and) retrieval. Hashing and indexing can be combined into what is called a hash index table to overcome this limitation. A **hash index table** uses hashing to map a key into a location *in an index* (sometimes called a scatter index table), where there is a pointer to the actual data record matching the hash key. The index is the target of the hashing algorithm, but the actual data are stored separately from the addresses generated by hashing. Because the hashing results in a position in an index, the table rows can be stored independently of the hash address, using whatever file organization for the data table makes sense (e.g., sequential or first available space). Thus, as with other indexing schemes but unlike most pure hashing schemes, there can be several primary and secondary keys, each with its own hashing algorithm and index table, sharing one data table. Also, because an index table is much smaller than a data table, the index can be more easily designed to reduce the likelihood of key collisions, or overflows, than can the more space-consuming data table. Again, the extra storage space for the index adds flexibility and speed for data retrieval, along with the added expense of storing and maintaining the index space. Another use of a hash index table is found in some data warehousing database technologies that use parallel processing. In this situation, the DBMS can evenly distribute data table rows across all storage devices to fairly distribute work across the parallel processors, yet use hashing and indexing to rapidly find on which processor desired data are stored.

One common caveat with all indexing techniques is the difficulty or cost for moving data once a table row is stored. If a row needs to move, then the pointer to it, in every index on the table, must be updated. This can be a significant overhead if the data must be frequently reorganized (sometimes this is caused by excessive deletion of rows and the creation of wasted space, or holes, in the middle of physical file reserved for data table rows). On the other hand, pure hashing will not permit the moving of data except as part of handling hashing overflows. Thus, a hash index table scheme provides the advantages of very rapid retrieval of data based on multiple

---

Hashed file organization: A storage system in which the address for each record is determined using a hashing algorithm.

Hashing algorithm: A routine that converts a primary key value into a relative record number (or relative file address).

Hash index table: A file organization that uses hashing to map a key into a location *in an index*, where there is a pointer to the actual data record matching the hash key.

key values and the ability to move data, with the disadvantage of an overhead expense to update indexes, if reorganization of the data space becomes important.

As stated earlier, the DBMS will handle the management of any hashing file organization. You do not have to be concerned with handling overflows, accessing indexes, or the hashing algorithm. What is important for you, as a database designer, is to understand the properties of different file organizations so that you can choose the most appropriate one for the type of database processing required in the database and application you are designing. Also, understanding the properties of the file organizations used by the DBMS can help query programmers to write a query in a way to take advantage of the file organization properties. As you will see in Chapters 7 and 8, many queries can be written in multiple ways in SQL; different query structures, however, can result in vastly different steps by the DBMS to answer the query. If you know how the DBMS thinks about using a file organization (e.g., what indexes it uses when and how and when it uses a hashing algorithm), you can design better databases and more efficient queries.

Summary of File Organizations

The three families of file organizations cover most of the file organizations you will have at your disposal as you design physical files and databases. Although more complex structures can be built using the data structures outlined in Appendix C, you are unlikely to be able to use these with a database management system.

Table 6-3 summarizes the comparative features of sequential, indexed, and hashed file organizations. You should review this table and study Figure 6-7 to see why each comparative feature is true.

Clustering Files

Some database management systems allow adjacent secondary memory space to contain rows from several tables. In this case, a physical file does not contain records with identical structures. For example, in Oracle, rows from one, two, or more related tables that are often joined together can be stored in the same disk area. A cluster is defined by the tables and the column or columns by which the tables are

Table 6-3 Comparative Features of Different File Organizations

	File Organization		
Factor	**Sequential**	**Indexed**	**Hashed**
Storage Space	No wasted space	No wasted space for data, but extra space for index	Extra space may be needed to allow for addition and deletion of records after initial set of records is loaded
Sequential Retrieval on Primary Key	Very fast	Moderately fast	Impractical, unless use hash index
Random Retrieval on Primary Key	Impractical	Moderately fast	Very fast
Multiple Key Retrieval	Possible, but requires scanning whole file	Very fast with multiple indexes	Not possible, unless use hash index
Deleting Records	Can create wasted space or require reorganizing	If space can be dynamically allocated, this is easy, but requires maintenance of indexes	Very easy
Adding New Records	Requires rewriting file	If space can be dynamically allocated, this is easy, but requires maintenance of indexes	Very easy, except multiple keys with same address require extra work
Updating Records	Usually requires rewriting file	Easy, but requires maintenance of indexes	Very easy

usually joined. For example, a Customer table and a Customer_Order table would be joined by the common value of Customer_ID, or the rows of a Price_Quote table (which contains prices on items purchased from vendors) might be clustered by common values of Item_ID). Clustering reduces the time to access related records compared to the normal allocation of different files to different areas of a disk. Time is reduced since related records will be closer to each other than if the records are stored in separate files in separate areas of the disk. Defining a table to be in only one cluster reduces retrieval performance for only those tables stored in the same cluster.

The following Oracle database definition commands show how a cluster is defined and tables assigned to the cluster. First, the cluster (adjacent disk space) is specified, as in the following example:

```
CREATE CLUSTER ORDERING (CLUSTERKEY CHAR(25));
```

The term ORDERING names the cluster space; the term CLUSTERKEY is required but not used again.

Then tables are assigned to the cluster when the tables are created, such as:

```
CREATE TABLE CUSTOMER (
    CUSTOMER_ID          VARCHAR2(25)   NOT NULL,
    CUSTOMER_ADDRESS     VARCHAR2(15)
    )
    CLUSTER ORDERING (CUSTOMER_ID);

CREATE TABLE ORDER (
    ORDER_ID             VARCHAR2(20)   NOT NULL,
    CUSTOMER_ID          VARCHAR2(25)   NOT NULL,
    ORDER_DATE           DATE
    )
    CLUSTER ORDERING (CUSTOMER_ID);
```

Access to records in a cluster can be specified in Oracle to be via an index on the cluster key or via a hashing function on the cluster key. Reasons for choosing an indexed versus a hashed cluster are similar to those for choosing between indexed and hashed files (see Table 6-3). Clustering records is best used when the records are fairly static; when records are frequently added, deleted, and changed, wasted space can arise and it may be difficult to locate related records close to one another after the initial loading of records, which defines the clusters. Clustering is, however, one option a file designer has to improve the performance of tables that are frequently used together in the same queries and reports.

Designing Controls for Files

One additional aspect of a database file about which you may have design options are the types of controls you can use to protect the file from destruction or contamination or to reconstruct the file if it is damaged. Because a database file is stored in a proprietary format by the DBMS, there is a basic level of access control. You may require additional security controls on fields, files, or databases. We address these options in detail in Chapters 8 and 12. Briefly, files will be damaged, so the key is the ability to rapidly restore a damaged file. Backup procedures provide a copy of a file and of the transactions that have changed the file. When a file is damaged, the file copy or current file along with the log of transactions are used to recover the file to an uncontaminated state. In terms of security, the most effective method is to encrypt the contents of the file so that only programs with access to the decryption routine will be able to see the file contents. Again, these important topics will be covered later when you study the relational data manipulation language SQL in Chapter 8 and the activities of data and database administration in Chapter 12.

USING AND SELECTING INDEXES

Most database manipulations require locating a row (or collection of rows) that satisfy some condition. For example, we may want to retrieve all customers in a given zip code or all students with a particular major. Scanning every row in a table looking for the desired rows may be unacceptably slow, particularly when tables are large, as they often are in real-world applications. Using indexes, as described above, can greatly speed up this process, and defining indexes is an important part of physical database design.

As described in the section on indexes above, indexes on a file can be created for either a primary or a secondary key or both. It is typical that an index would be created for the primary key of each table. The index is itself a table with two columns: the key and the address of the record or records that contain that key value. For a primary key, there will be only one entry in the index for each key value.

Creating a Unique Key Index

The Customer table defined in the section on clustering has a primary key of Customer_ID. A unique key index would be created on this field using the following SQL command:

CREATE UNIQUE INDEX CUSTINDEX ON CUSTOMER(CUSTOMER_ID);

In this command, CUSTINDEX is the name of the index file created to store the index entries. The ON clause specifies which table is being indexed and the column (or columns) that form the index key. When this command is executed, any existing records in the Customer table would be indexed. If there are duplicate values of Customer_ID, the CREATE INDEX command will fail. Once the index is created, the DBMS will reject any insertion or update of data in the CUSTOMER table that would violate the uniqueness constraint on Customer_IDs.

When a composite unique key exists, you simply list all the elements of the unique key in the ON clause. For example, a table of line items on a customer order might have a composite unique key of Order_ID and Product_ID. The SQL command to create this index for the Order_Line table would be as follows:

CREATE UNIQUE INDEX LINEINDEX ON ORDER_LINE(ORDER_ID,PRODUCT_ID);

Creating a Secondary (Nonunique) Key Index

Database users often want to retrieve rows of a relation based on values for various attributes other than the primary key. For example, in a Product table, users might want to retrieve records that satisfy any combination of the following conditions:

- All table products (Description = 'Table')
- All oak furniture (Finish = 'Oak')
- All dining room furniture (Room = 'DR')
- All furniture priced below $500 (Price<500)

To speed up such retrievals, we can define an index on each attribute that we use to qualify a retrieval. For example, we could create a nonunique index on the Description field of the Product table with the following SQL command:

CREATE INDEX DESCINDX ON PRODUCT(DESCRIPTION);

Notice that the term UNIQUE should not be used with secondary (nonunique) key attributes, since each value of the attribute may be repeated. As with unique keys, a secondary key index can be created on a combination of attributes.

To create a bitmap index, you follow a similar command structure. If we wanted a bitmap index for the Description field, the command would be:

```
CREATE BITMAP INDEX DESCBITINDX ON PRODUCT(DESCRIPTION);
```

When to Use Indexes

During physical database design, you must choose which attributes to use to create indexes. There is a trade-off between improved performance for retrievals through the use of indexes, and degraded performance for inserting, deleting, and updating the records in a file. Thus, indexes should be used generously for databases intended primarily to support data retrievals, such as for decision support and data warehouse applications. Indexes should be used judiciously for databases that support transaction processing and other applications with heavy updating requirements, since the indexes impose additional overhead.

Following are some rules of thumb for choosing indexes for relational databases.

1. Indexes are most useful on larger tables.

2. Specify a unique index for the primary key of each table.

3. Indexes are most useful for columns that frequently appear in WHERE clauses of SQL commands either to qualify the rows to select (e.g., WHERE FINISH = "Oak", for which an index on Finish would speed retrieval) or for linking (joining) tables (e.g., WHERE PRODUCT.PRODUCT_ID = ORDER_LINE.PRODUCT_ID, for which a secondary key index on Product_ID in the Order_Line table and a primary key index on Product_ID in the Product table would improve retrieval performance). In the latter case, the index is on a foreign key in the Order_Line table that is used in joining tables.

4. Use an index for attributes referenced in ORDER BY (sorting) and GROUP BY (categorizing) clauses. You do have to be careful, though, about these clauses. Be sure that the DBMS will, in fact, use indexes on attributes listed in these clauses (e.g., Oracle uses indexes on attributes in ORDER BY clauses but not GROUP BY clauses).

5. Use an index when there is significant variety in the values of an attribute. Oracle suggests that an index is not useful when there are fewer than 30 different values for an attribute, and an index is clearly useful when there are 100 or more different values for an attribute. Similarly, an index will be helpful only if the results of a query which uses that index do not exceed roughly 20 percent of the total number of records in the file (Schumacher, 1997).

6. Check your DBMS for the limit, if any, on the number of indexes allowable per table. Many systems permit no more than 16 indexes, and may limit the size of an index key value (e.g., no more than 2000 bytes for each composite value). If there is such a limit in your system, you will have to choose those secondary keys that will most likely lead to improved performance.

7. Be careful indexing attributes that have null values. For many DBMSs, rows with a null value will not be referenced in the index (so they cannot be found from an *index search* of ATTRIBUTE = NULL). Such a search will have to be done by scanning the file.

Selecting indexes is arguably the most important physical database design decision, but it is not the only way you can improve the performance of a database. Other ways address such issues as reducing the costs to relocate records, optimizing the use of extra or so-called free space in files, and optimizing query processing algorithms (see Viehman, 1994, for a discussion of these additional ways to enhance physical database design and efficiency). We briefly discuss the topic of query optimization in a later section of this chapter since such optimization can be used to overrule how the DBMS would use certain database design options included because of their expected improvement in data processing performance in most instances.

RAID: IMPROVING FILE ACCESS PERFORMANCE BY PARALLEL PROCESSING

In previous sections of this chapter you learned about denormalization and clustering, two schemes for placing data used together close to one another in disk storage. Denormalization and clustering work well to minimize data access time if data used together in a program can be located within one physical data page. For small records, this is certainly possible. However, data used together or immediately after one another may have to be stored in separate pages; in this case, multiple, sequential disk input/output operations will be required for reading and writing these data. Thus, denormalization and clustering may not be sufficient schemes for significantly improving data read and write performance.

Two of the inevitable trends in computer technology are the constant reduction in cost and size of computer technologies. These two trends make redundancy of computer components, and thus fault tolerance, both economically and physically feasible. The feasibility of using multiple, small computer components also allows parallel processing of data. The result of parallel processing of data is that, for example, four input/output operations, when done in parallel, take as long as only one such operation. These features can be critical for the success of a very large database for an on-line application, such as e-commerce.

Redundant Array of Inexpensive Disks (RAID): A set, or array, of physical disk drives that appear to the database user (and programs) as if they form one large logical storage unit.

Parallel database processing and fault tolerance can be accomplished by a database designer using hardware or software technology called **Redundant Array of Inexpensive Disks (RAID)**. RAID storage uses a set, or array, of physical disk drives that appear to the database user (and programs) as if they form one large logical storage unit. Thus, RAID does not change the logical or physical structure of application programs or database queries.

In order to maximize input/output performance of RAID, all the disk drives need to be kept busy. Striping accomplishes the balancing of the workload across the disk drives. Segments of data, called **stripes**, cut across all of the disk drives, as illustrated in Figure 6-10. Logically sequential pages of data (for example, multiple pages for one record, a cluster of records, or several logically sequential records from one file) are stored in round-robin fashion across the physical disk drives. Thus, for the hypothetical RAID storage illustrated in Figure 6-10, it would be possible to read four *logically sequential* pages of data in parallel, in the elapsed time it takes to read just one page. A very long data record (containing possibly an audio or video field), which is stored in several physical pages, can be read in a fraction of the time it would take without RAID. Or multiple related records (a cluster) that span several pages can be read all at the same time.

Stripe: The set of pages on all disks in a RAID that are the same relative distance from the beginning of the disk drive.

Most multiuser operating systems today, including Microsoft NT, UNIX, and Novell NetWare, support some forms of RAID. Such operating systems initiate the parallel read operations and concatenate the results together into one logical record for the requesting program. These operating systems also permit multithreading, in which parallel input/output operations come from different user programs or tasks. RAID can also be implemented in hardware using special adapters, thus offloading from the host computer the work to break down input and output operations into parallel steps.

RAID has one important risk: the increased likelihood of a disk drive failure across the whole database. If the mean time between failures of an individual disk drive is, say, 1.2 million operations, then the mean time between failures of a RAID with, say, four disk drives will be 1.2 million divided by 4, or every 300,000 parallel disk operations. To cope with this risk and to make disk storage fault tolerant, many types of RAID technologies redundantly store data so that at least one copy of the

Figure 6-10
RAID with four disks and striping

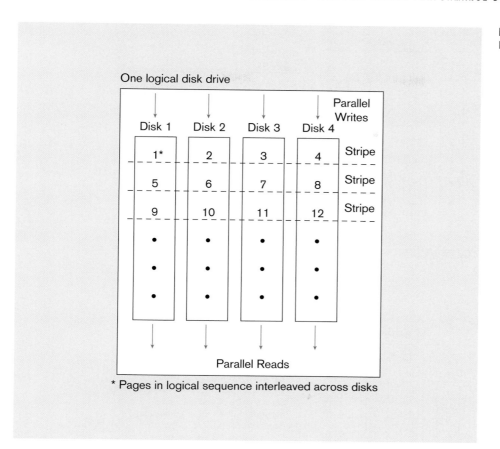

One logical disk drive

Parallel Writes

Disk 1   Disk 2   Disk 3   Disk 4

1*	2	3	4	Stripe
5	6	7	8	Stripe
9	10	11	12	Stripe

Parallel Reads

* Pages in logical sequence interleaved across disks

data is accessible when demanded, or store extra error correction codes so that damaged or lost data can be rebuilt.

Choosing Among RAID Levels

As a file and database designer, you likely will have six or more types of redundant or error-correcting RAID architectures, from which to choose. RAID-0, which uses no redundant storage, is also used since it has the fastest performance by utilizing the highest degree of parallelism. Figure 6-11 compares six forms of RAID and lists a few key features of each form. Specific disk drives and operating systems may provide additional alternatives.

RAID-0 The fastest read/write time and most efficient data storage of any disk array type is achieved with RAID-0 (see Figure 6-11a). In RAID-0 (often called disk striping), every disk in the array is used in parallel to read and write application data. RAID-0 is typically used when the database application accesses very large records (thus requiring most of one or even several stripes) or a group of related records or is extremely input/output intensive. Since RAID-0 does not utilize any form of data redundancy or stripe error correction codes, a failure in any of the disk drives can corrupt the database. Also, RAID-0 allows only one I/O command to be processed at one time (i.e., no multithreaded I/O). The bottleneck in RAID-0 is the disk controller, which can be saturated by many parallel I/O operations. Ideally, multiple controllers can be used across the disks.

RAID-1 One way to improve fault tolerance is to store application data redundantly. A fully redundant storage, or disk mirror, is accomplished in RAID-1 (see Figure 6-11b), in which each page is redundantly written. Although the total disk array

Figure 6-11
Six levels of RAID (*Note*: Numbers are sequential data block numbers. Letters indicate segments of a data block.)
(a) RAID-0 (striping)

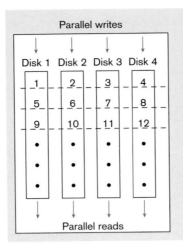

- Uses all disks for data storage.
- Greatest parallel access, so fast access time.
- No redundancy or error correction.
- Only single-threaded I/O.
- Useful for very large records or many related records and for applications requiring extensive I/O activity (for example, temporary storage areas and index space).

(b) RAID-1 with two pairs of mirrored disks

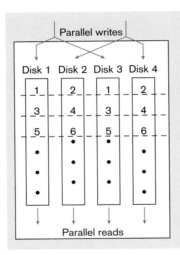

- Disk data storage space is cut in half, but the advantage is fault tolerance.
- Each write operation is redundant, and writes can be done in parallel across pairs of disks (it is best if redundant disks are on different disk controllers).
- Read operations can be done in parallel across all disks.
- Useful for very large records and for applications requiring extensive I/O activity (for example, recovery log files or data files with a mixture of random and sequential reads and writes).

(c) RAID-2 with half the drives used for data

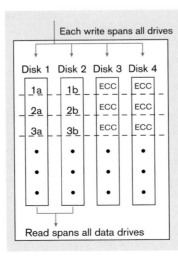

- Each data record spans all data disks.
- Some disks are used exclusively for error correction codes (ECCs).
- Each write operation uses all drives in parallel.
- Each read operation uses all drives in parallel.

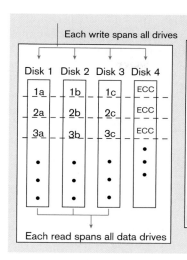

Figure 6-11
(continued)
(d) RAID-3

Each write spans all drives

Disk 1 Disk 2 Disk 3 Disk 4

1a   1b   1c   ECC
2a   2b   2c   ECC
3a   3b   3c   ECC

Each read spans all data drives

- Each data record may span all data disks or separate records may be in a stripe.
- **One** disk is used exclusively for error correction codes (ECCs) (so more data space than in RAID-2).
- ECC is used to recover damaged data or drive in stripe.
- Each write operation uses all drives in parallel (can be slow).
- Each read operation uses all drives in parallel (can make read very fast).
- Only one program accesses array at a time.

(e) RAID-4

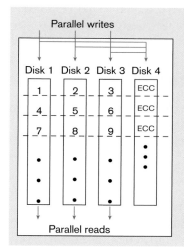

Parallel writes

Disk 1 Disk 2 Disk 3 Disk 4

1   2   3   ECC
4   5   6   ECC
7   8   9   ECC

Parallel reads

- Potentially many records in one stripe.
- **One** disk is used exclusively for error correction codes (ECCs) (so more data space than in RAID-2), but this drive is very busy if frequent write operations.
- ECC is used to recover damaged data or drive in stripe.
- Write operations done in parallel.
- Read operations done in parallel.
- Accesses from several programs can be processed in parallel in the array.

(f) RAID-5

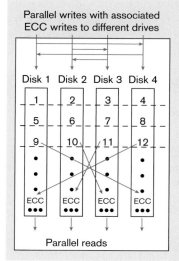

Parallel writes with associated ECC writes to different drives

Disk 1 Disk 2 Disk 3 Disk 4

1   2   3   4
5   6   7   8
9   10   11   12

ECC ECC ECC ECC

Parallel reads

- Potentially many records in one stripe.
- **All** disks are used for data and error correction codes (ECCs), so no bottleneck to write ECCs.
- ECC is used to recover damaged data or drive in stripe.
- Write operations are done in parallel.
- Read operations are done in parallel.
- Accesses from several programs can be processed in parallel in the array.

storage space is effectively cut in half, the database has a high degree of fault tolerance since it is unlikely that exactly the same page will be damaged in both copies. A single RAID-1 array of two disk drives does not use striping, but it is possible to append several dual disk RAID-1 arrays together to form a larger array with striping (see RAID 0+1 below). In RAID-1, each page write operation is done in parallel to a pair of disk drives, so no performance improvement is achieved. However, two read operations, even if generated from separate database queries in different user programs (multithreaded), can be done in parallel *for each dual array.* Thus, RAID-1 has both excellent performance and fault tolerance for single-user and multiple-user environments. Falling disk strong prices have made RAID-1 arguably the most common form of RAID in use today.

RAID 0+1 As we have seen, RAID-0 emphasizes high performance via parallel reads and writes whereas RAID-1 emphasizes fault tolerance via redundant storage. By building a RAID-0 configuration and then mirroring it, you get the best of both RAID-0 and RAID-1. This configuration is called RAID 0+1 or RAID-10 (Compaq) or RAID-6 (Hewlett Packard) (RAID 0+1 not shown in Figure 6-11). RAID 0+1 provides very large volume data storage, high reliability, and protection from drive failures (Musciano, 1999). It is, however, very expensive, and thus is used in environments that require extremely high uptime percentages with very rapid response, such as for real-time applications for military command and control, air traffic control, utility process control, and some electronic commerce situations (for example, on-line investing).

RAID-2 In RAID-2 (see Figure 6-11c), some disks are used with data striping for parallel data processing (without redundant storage) and other disks are dedicated to storing error correction codes. The error correction codes are used to detect errors in the stripes and to reconstruct data when pages within the data stripes are damaged. Thus, whereas RAID-1 uses redundancy to allow recovery from damaged data, RAID-2 (and subsequent levels) uses more efficient error correction, or parity, codes. However, since most disk drives in computers today already store page-level error correction codes, or parity information, within each physical page, RAID-2 is less desirable than RAID-3.

RAID-3 As with RAID-2, RAID-3 stripes data across drives, but only one drive stores stripe-level error correction codes (see Figure 6-11d). Error correction codes embedded within each page are used to detect page errors, and the ECC page is used to recover a damaged page. Assume that drive 3 in Figure 6-11d crashes. Then page 3 in each stripe can be recovered from the other data pages and the error correction page in its stripe by an exclusive OR calculation within the stripe. To be able to do this, an update on any page in a stripe requires reading all pages in the stripe so the ECC page can be recomputed and rewritten. RAID-3 is usually used when very long records exist, such that one record requires one or more stripes. Thus, each logical input/output operation uses, or spans, all the drives in the array. Consequently, since each logical input/output operation utilizes the whole array, it is not possible to process in parallel requests from multiple users or programs. So, RAID-3 works best in single-user and uniprogramming environments with high volume of read and a low volume of write activity. The overhead space for RAID-3 decreases as the number of disks in a strip increases. The ECC drive becomes a bottleneck.

RAID-4 In RAID-4, stripe-level error correction codes are stored on only one drive as in RAID-3, but multiple records are stored in a stripe (see Figure 6-11e). Thus, read operations to different records from the same or different programs can be done in parallel across the drives. The bottleneck is the parity drive, since it must be accessed to have an error correction page updated when any data record is rewritten. For databases with frequent record updates, such as for on-line transaction processing, this can create considerable contention (and hence delay) for the parity drive, reducing the advantages of parallel processing. This bottleneck can be avoided by using RAID-5. *Note.* Some authors do not distinguish RAID-3 and RAID-4.

RAID-5 Also called *Rotating Parity Array*, RAID-5 (see Figure 6-11f) does not use a dedicated parity drive. Each drive contains both data and parity pages. Read operations can be done in parallel on all drives. A write operation will access its one or more drives to write the new record plus the parity drive *for that record*. Different records store their error correction codes, for recovery purposes, on different drives. Thus, write operations can also be done in parallel with less likelihood of delay compared to RAID-4 since random record updates will generate random error correction page updates randomly distributed across the drives.

RAID Performance

As noted in the prior sections, RAID-1, RAID-3, and RAID-5 dominate the other forms of fault-tolerant RAID. Since RAID-3 is designed for single-user or data-intensive situations, this form of RAID has specialized applicability. For most database applications, this means that you will most likely choose between RAID-1, RAID 0+1, or RAID-5.

One RAID manufacturer, Adaptec (http://www.dpt.com), has compared the performance of RAID-1 and RAID-5 for both read and write operations with various numbers of disk drives in the array and for disk drives with different transfer rates. As you might expect, RAID-5 more efficiently uses storage space since it does not store data redundantly. RAID-5 outperforms RAID-1 in read operations since greater parallelism is possible with the same number of disk drives in the array. However, write times with RAID-5 can be anywhere from 1.67 to 3 times greater than those for RAID-1 (depending on the benchmark application and array configuration). Thus, RAID-5 is less desirable than RAID-1 for highly volatile files. Adaptec has also estimated that in order to make write operations twice as fast as on one drive, RAID-1 requires an array of four disk drives whereas RAID-5 requires from seven to twelve disk drives.

So, what form of RAID is best? RAID-1 is best for fault-tolerant, database maintenance applications (those requiring a high percentage of uptime) or when only two disk drive controllers are affordable. RAID-1 can be costly, but is best for a variety of workloads. RAID-5 is best for read-intensive applications against very large data sets and at least three (and more typically five) disk drives are affordable. RAID-5 becomes less desirable as disk drives become larger.

Storage devices continue to be an area of rapid change. New technologies of storage area networks (SAN) and network-attached storage (NAS) are emerging for large enterprise storage environments (Shah, 1999).

DESIGNING DATABASES

Most modern information systems utilize database technologies, either database management systems or data warehouse systems, for data storage and retrieval. Recall that a database is a collection of logically related data, designed to meet the information needs of multiple users in an organization. The relationship between files in a database is due to relationships identified in the conceptual and logical data models. The relationships imply access paths between data. Each type of database technology allows different types of access paths. So, the process of choosing the appropriate type of DBMS or data warehousing technology is one of matching the needed access paths with the capabilities of the database technology.

Choosing Database Architectures

There are different styles of database management and data warehousing systems, each characterized by the way data are defined and structured, called database architectures. Deciding which database architecture best suits your database is fundamental

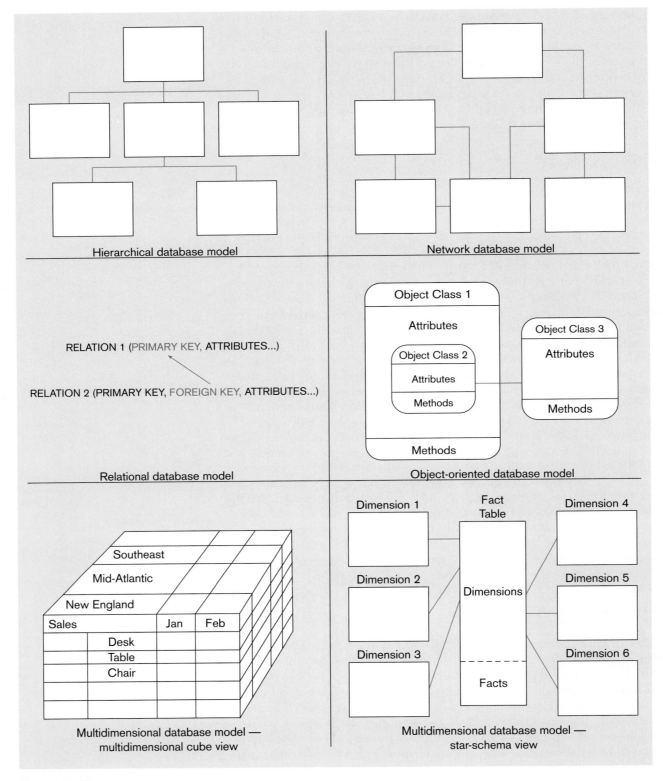

Figure 6-12
Database architectures

to database design. A particular database management or warehousing system supports one of five different architectures. Figure 6-12 compares these five architectures:

1. *Hierarchical database model*   In this model, files are arranged in a top-down structure that resembles a tree or genealogy chart. Data are related in a nested, one-to-many set of relationships. The top file is called the root, the bottom files are called leaves, and intermediate files have one parent, or owner, file and one or several children files. Among the oldest of the database architectures, many hierarchical databases exist in larger organizations today. This technology is best applied when the conceptual data model also resembles a tree and when most data access begins with the same (root) file. Hierarchical database technology is used for high-volume transaction processing and MIS applications. Few new databases are developed with hierarchical DBMSs since newer applications tend to have broader needs than simply transaction processing or summarization of transaction data.

2. *Network database model*   In this model, each file may be associated with an arbitrary number of files. Although very flexible because any relationships can be implemented (a hierarchy is a special case of a network), the form of implementation, usually using pointers between related records in different files, creates significant overhead in storage space and maintenance time. Typically, network model systems support only one-to-many relationships along each arc in the network, but some support many-to-many relationships. Network model systems are still popular on powerful mainframes and for high-volume transaction processing applications. Since the database designer has such detailed control over data organizations, it is possible to design highly optimized databases with network systems. For example, each record type (a record type is shown by each box in the network) can be organized using hashing algorithms or located near another related record type—an early form of clustering. Network systems support a wider variety of processing requirements than do hierarchical database systems, but network systems still require significant programming and database design knowledge and time, and hence are used primarily in those organizations with significant expertise with such technologies.

3. *Relational database model*   The most common database model for new systems defines simple tables for each relation and many-to-many relationships. Cross-reference keys link the tables together, representing the relationships between entities. Primary and secondary key indexes provide rapid access to data based upon qualifications. Most new applications are built using relational DBMSs, and many relational DBMS products exist. See Chapter 5 for a thorough review of the features of the relational database model and Chapter 9 for an introduction to query-by-example, one style of relational query language and Chapters 7 and 8 for coverage of the SQL relational data manipulation language, the most widely used relational language.

4. *Object-oriented database model*   In this model, attributes and methods that operate on those attributes are encapsulated in structures called object classes. Relationships between object classes are shown, in part, by nesting or encapsulating one object class within another. New object classes are defined from more general object classes. A major advantage of this data model is that complex data types like graphics, video, and sound are supported easily as simpler data types. This is the newest DBMS technology and larger organizations are gaining experience with it by selectively using it when complex data or event-driven programming is appropriate for the application. Chapters 14 and 15 provide extensive coverage of the use of the data model for conceptual data modeling and database implementation.

5. *Multidimensional database model*   This database model is used in data warehousing applications. Two ways of viewing this model exist. The first views data as a multidimensional cube in which each cell contains one or more simple attributes and the dimensions are ways to categorize the raw data. These categories, or dimensions, are the factors on which users want to summarize or segment the data, such as time periods, geography, lines of business, or people. A cell contains data relevant to the intersection of all of its dimension values. For example, a cell might hold the number-of-units-sold attribute for a given time period, location, line of business, and salesperson. The second (equivalent) view is called a star schema. At the center is a fact table, equivalent to the cell in the multidimensional view. This table contains all the raw attributes and a composite key made up of the primary keys of all the surrounding dimension tables. The surrounding dimension tables define each of the ways to categorize data, such as all the description data about each salesperson. The key design issue with the multidimensional database model is identifying in advance the lowest common denominator of data, and hence all the dimensions or categories by which users wish to summarize the raw facts. Although the multidimensional database model is a special case of both the relational and network data models, special DBMSs have been developed that optimize dimensional data processing. Chapter 11 deals with data warehousing and the multidimensional data model.

We have chosen to cover in greater detail in this textbook only the three newest of these database models: relational, object-oriented, and multidimensional. If you want to know more about hierarchical and network database models, refer to some of the sources listed in Further Reading at the end of this chapter.

OPTIMIZING FOR QUERY PERFORMANCE

The primary purpose today for physical database design is to optimize the performance of database processing. Database processing includes adding, deleting, and modifying a database, as well as a variety of data retrieval activities. For databases that have greater retrieval traffic than maintenance traffic, optimizing the database for query performance (producing on-line or off-line anticipated and ad hoc screens and reports for end users) is the primary goal. This chapter has already covered most of the decisions you can make to tune the database design to meet the need of database queries (clustering, indexes, file organizations, etc.). In this final section of this chapter we introduce a few additional advanced database design and processing options now available in many DBMSs.

The amount of work a database designer needs to put into optimizing query performance depends greatly on the DBMS. Because of the high cost of expert database developers, the less database and query design work developers have to do, the less costly will be the development and use of a database. Some DBMS give very little control to the database designer or query writer on how a query is processed or on the physical location of data for optimizing data reads and writes. Other systems give the application developers considerable control, and often demand extensive work to tune the database design and the structure of queries to obtain acceptable performance. Sometimes, the workload varies so much and the design options are so subtle, good performance is all that can be achieved. When the workload is fairly focused, say for data warehousing where there are a few batch updates and very complex queries requiring large segments of the database, performance can be well tuned either by smart query optimizers in the DBMS or by intelligent database and query design or a combination of both. For example, the NCR

Teradata DBMS is highly tuned for parallel processing in a data warehousing environment. In this case, rarely can a database designer or query writer improve on the capabilities of the DBMS to store and process data. Since this situation is rare, it is important as a database designer to consider options for improving database processing performance.

Parallel Query Processing

One of the major computer architectural changes over the last few years is the increased use of multiple processors in database servers. Database servers frequently use symmetric multiprocessor (SMP) technology (Schumacher, 1997). To take advantage of this parallel processing capability, some of the more sophisticated DBMSs include strategies for breaking apart a query into modules that can be processed in parallel by each of the related processors. The most common approach is to replicate the query so that each copy works against a portion of the database, usually a horizontal partition (sets of rows). The partitions need to be defined in advance by the database designer. The same query is run against each portion in parallel on separate processors, and the intermediate results from each processor are combined to create the final query result as if the query were run against the whole database.

Suppose you have an Order table with several million rows for which query performance has been slow. To ensure that subsequent scans of this table are performed in parallel using at least three processors, you would alter the structure of the table with the SQL command:

```
ALTER TABLE ORDER PARALLEL 3
```

You need to tune each table to the best degree of parallelism, so it is not uncommon to alter a table several times until the right degree is found.

Parallel query processing speed can be impressive. Schumacher (1997) reports of a test in which the time to perform a query was cut in half with parallel processing compared to a normal table scan. Since an index is a table, indexes can also be given the parallel structure, so that scans of an index are also faster. Again, Schumacher (1997) shows an example where the cost, in time, to create an index by parallel processing was reduced from approximately seven minutes to five seconds!

Besides table scans, other elements of a query can be processed in parallel, such as certain types of joining of related tables, grouping query results into categories, combining several parts of a query result together (called union), sorting rows, and computing aggregate values. Row update, delete, and insert operations can also be processed in parallel. In addition, the performance of some database creation commands can be improved by parallel processing; these include creating and rebuilding an index and creating a table from data in the database. The Oracle environment must be preconfigured with a specification for the number of virtual parallel database servers to exist. Once this is done, the query processor will decide what it thinks is the best use of parallel processing for any command.

Overriding Automatic Query Optimization

Sometimes, the query writer knows (or can learn) key information about the query that may be overlooked or unknown to the query optimizer module of the DBMS. With such key information in hand, a query writer may have an idea for a better way to process a query. But before you as the query writer can know you have a better way, you have to know how the query optimizer (which usually picks a query processing plan that will minimize expected query processing time, or cost) will process the query. This is especially true for a query you have not submitted before. Fortunately, with most relational DBMSs you can learn the optimizer's plan for processing the query before running the query. A command such as EXPLAIN or EXPLAIN PLAN (the exact command varies by DBMS) will display how the query optimizer intends to access indexes, use parallel servers, and join tables to prepare the query result. If you preface the actual relational command with the explain clause, the query processor displays the logical steps to process the query, and stops processing before actually accessing the database. The query optimizer chooses the best plan based on statistics about each table, such as average row length and number of rows. It may be necessary to force the DBMS to calculate up-to-date statistics about the database (e.g., the Analyze command in Oracle) to get an accurate estimate of query costs. You may submit several explain commands with your query written in different ways to see if the optimizer predicts different performance. Then, you can submit the form of the query for actual processing that had the best predicted processing time, or you may decide not to submit the query because it will be too costly to run.

You may even see a way to improve query processing performance. With some DBMSs, you can force the DBMS to do the steps differently or to use the capabilities of the DBMS, such as parallel servers, differently than the optimizer thinks is the best plan.

For example, suppose we wanted to count the number of orders processed by a particular sales representative, Smith. In Oracle, parallel table processing works only when a table is scanned, not when it is accessed via an index. So, in Oracle, we may want to force both a full table scan as well as scanning in parallel. The SQL command for this query would be as follows:

```
SELECT /*+ FULL(ORDER) PARALLEL(ORDER,3) */ COUNT(*)
    FROM ORDER
    WHERE SALESPERSON = "SMITH";
```

The clause inside the /* */ delimiters is the hint to Oracle. This hint overrides whatever query plan Oracle would naturally create for this query. Thus, a hint is specific to each query, but the use of such hints must be anticipated by altering the structure of tables to be handled with parallel processing.

Picking Data Block Size

As mentioned earlier in the chapter, data are transferred between RAM and disk memory in blocks, or pages. The size of a data block can significantly affect the performance of queries. Too small a size may result in many physical I/O operations per table row being accessed or in accessing many rows. Too large a block size may result in extra data being transferred, with wasted time. Usually the minimum block size is 2K bytes; the upper limit is determined by the computer operating system, but a typical limit is 32K bytes or more. Once the block size is established for a database, it can be changed only by unloading the data, redefining the database, and reloading the data.

You make trade-offs among five performance factors as you switch from small to large block sizes. These factors are (Yuhanna, 2000):

- *Block contention*: This is a measure of the need for concurrently accessing the same data block by several I/O commands. Smaller blocks create less contention. Contention matters the most in environments with many concurrent jobs running against the same database, such as when there are many on-line users.

- *Random row access speed*: This is how fast one row from a table can be accessed. Again, smaller blocks are best. Random row accessing is common in on-line transaction processing applications.

- *Sequential row access speed*: This is how fast a table is scanned. In this case, larger block sizes are better. Large block sizes allow many rows to be cached in RAM in one I/O operation so that fewer physical I/O operations are required to retrieve all the table rows needed for the query. A large block size fits well with clustering (discussed earlier in this chapter) because a whole cluster may be cached in one I/O operation. Sequential scans can occur in decision support and data warehousing applications and in applications that produce transaction summary reports.

- *Row size*:   This is the length of all the fields in a table row. It is usually best to try to match the block size with the physical table row size or a multiple of the row size.

- *Overhead*:   This is the cost, in time, for the DBMS to manage all the I/O operations needed to produce the result for a query or other database operation. Small block sizes produce more overhead than do large block sizes.

Rarely will all these factors point to one block size. In general, smaller block sizes are used for on-line transaction processing applications and larger block sizes are used for databases with a decision support or data warehousing system. Environments with a mixed workload can be very difficult to tune in terms of data block size.

Balancing I/O Across Disk Controllers

A disk controller manages the I/O operations for the disk drives attached to that controller. More controllers are better than a few (as before, more parallelism means better performance), but cost will limit the number of controllers you can have. The benefits of multiple controllers come when they can all be kept busy. Thus, you want to allocate database and DBMS system files to drives so that there is roughly the same workload on each controller, and better yet, each disk.

Tables can usually be easily moved from one disk to another after the tables contain data. So, the initial assignment of files to disks can be changed. To improve query processing performance:

- understand what files are on which drives and which drives are attached to which controllers

- understand the predefined programs and the nature of the ad hoc queries run against the database (you may need to concentrate on the most important programs or the most troublesome days or times)

- collect statistics on disk and controller utilization and on table (or partition) accessing

- rebalance the workload by moving tables between drives and controllers

In general, when it is not possible to have data required together in a query (or across concurrently running queries) stored in the same data block, then it is best to have those data on different disks on different controllers so that the data can be accessed in parallel. Again, it is difficult, if not impossible, to optimize this when there is a highly varied workload pattern. You may need to concentrate on a few of the most important applications (or the applications running with unacceptable performance today), do the analysis above for those applications, and balance file assignments to create the best possible performance for those applications without serious degradation for other applications.

Guidelines for Better Query Design

The prior sections of this chapter have provided many techniques and approaches for database and query design that result in fast query processing. Various database experts have developed additional guidelines that do not relate directly to the topics already covered. See DeLoach (1987), Holmes (1996), and Kurka

(1999) for suggestions for improving query processing in a variety of settings. We summarize below some of their suggestions that apply to many situations.

- *Understand how indexes are used in query processing.* Many DBMS will use only one index per table in a query. Learn how the DBMS selects which index to use and monitor accesses to indexes, then drop indexes that are infrequently used. This will improve the performance of database update operations. In general, queries that have equality criteria for selecting table rows (e.g., WHERE Finish = "Birch" OR "Walnut") will result in faster processing than queries involving more complex qualifications (e.g., WHERE Finish NOT = "Walnut") because equality criteria can be evaluated via indexes. Again, learn how the DBMS treats different types of clauses in queries.

- *Use compatible data types for fields and literals in queries.* Compatible data types likely will mean that the DBMS can avoid having to convert data during query processing.

- *Write simple queries.* Usually the simplest form of a query will be the easiest for the DBMS to process. For example, since relational DBMSs are based on set theory, write queries that manipulate sets of rows and literals.

- *Break complex queries into multiple, simple parts.* Because the DBMS may use only one index per query, it is often good to break a complex query into multiple, simpler parts (which each use an index) and then combine the results of the smaller queries together. For example, since a relational DBMS works with sets, it is very easy for the DBMS to UNION two sets of rows that are the result of two simple, independent queries.

- *Don't nest one query inside another query.* As you will see in Chapters 7 and 8, the SQL database language allows you to write one query inside another query (the query inside is called a subquery). Usually, such queries are less efficient than a query that avoids subqueries to produce the same result.

- *Don't combine a table with itself.* Avoid, if possible, using the same table in two (or more) different roles in the same query (this is called a self-join, and will be illustrated in Chapter 7). It is usually better (more efficient for processing the query) to make a temporary copy of the table and then relate the original table with the temporary one.

- *Create temporary tables for groups of queries.* When possible, reuse data used in a sequence of queries. For example, if a series of queries all refer to the same subset of data from the database, it may be more efficient to first store this subset in one or more temporary tables and then refer to those temporary tables in the series of queries. This will avoid repeatedly combining the same data together or repeatedly scanning the database to find the same database segment for each query. The trade-off is that the temporary tables will not change if the original tables are updated when the queries are running.

- *Combine update operations.* When possible, combine multiple update commands into one. This will reduce query processing overhead and allow the DMBS to seek ways to process the updates in parallel.

- *Retrieve only the data you need.* This will reduce the data blocks accessed and transferred. This may seem obvious, but there are some shortcuts for query writing that violate this guideline. For example, in SQL the command SELECT * from EMP will retrieve all the fields from all the rows of the EMP table. But, if the user needs to see only some of the columns of the table, transferring the extra columns increases the query processing time.

- *Don't have the DBMS sort without an index.* If data are to be displayed in sorted order and an index does not exist on the sort key field, then sort the data outside the DMBS after the unsorted results are retrieved. Usually a sort utility will be faster than a sort without the aid of an index by the DBMS.

- *Learn!* Track query processing times, review query plans with the EXPLAIN command, and improve your understanding of the way the DBMS determines how to process queries. Attend specialized training by your DBMS vendor on writing efficient queries, which will better inform you about the query optimizer.

- *Finally, consider the total query processing time for ad hoc queries.* The total time includes the time it takes the programmer (or end user) to write the query as well as the time to process the query. Many times, for ad hoc queries, it is better to have the DBMS do extra work to allow the user to more quickly write a query. And isn't that what technology is supposed to accomplish—allow people to be more productive. So, don't spend too much time, especially for ad hoc queries, trying to write the most efficient query. Write a query that is logically correct (produces the desired results), and let the DBMS do the work (of course, do an EXPLAIN first to be sure you haven't written "the query from hell" so that all other users will see a serious delay in query processing time). This suggests a corollary: When possible, run your query when there is a light load on the database, since the total query processing time includes delays induced by other load on the DBMS and database.

This concludes our discussion of advanced options for tuning the performance of a database. All options are not available with every DBMS, and each DBMS often has unique options due to its underlying design. You should refer to reference manuals for your DBMS to know what specific tuning options are available to you.

Summary

During physical database design, you the designer translate the logical description of data into the technical specifications for storing and retrieving data. The goal is to create a design for storing data that will provide adequate performance and insure database integrity, security, and recoverability. In physical database design you consider normalized relations and data volume estimates, data definitions, data processing requirements and their frequencies, user expectations, and database technology characteristics to establish field specifications, record designs, file organizations, and a database architecture.

A field is the smallest unit of application data, corresponding to an attribute in the logical data model. You must determine the data type, integrity controls, and how to handle missing values for each field, among other factors. A data type is a detailed coding scheme for representing organizational data. Data may be coded or compressed to reduce storage space. Field integrity control includes specifying a default value, range of permissible values, null value permission, and referential integrity.

A physical record is a group of fields stored in adjacent memory locations and retrieved together as a unit. Physical records are usually stored in a page (or data block), which is the amount of data read or written in one secondary memory input or output operation. The number of records in a page is called the blocking factor. For efficiency reasons, the attributes of one relation may not be stored in one physical record and attributes from sev-

eral relations may be stored in one physical record. A process of denormalization transforms normalized relations into unnormalized physical record specifications. Denormalization is done to place in one physical record those attributes frequently needed together in an I/O operation. Denormalization includes horizontal partitioning, which breaks a relation into multiple record specifications by placing different rows into different records based upon common column values. Denormalization also includes vertical partitioning, which distributes the columns of a relation into separate files, repeating the primary key in each of the files.

A physical file is a named portion of secondary memory allocated for the purpose of storing physical records. Data within a physical file are organized through a combination of sequential storage and pointers. A pointer is a field of data that can be used to locate a related field or record of data.

A file organization arranges the records of a file on a secondary storage device. The three major categories of file organizations are: (1) sequential, which stores records in sequence according to a primary key value; (2) indexed, in which records are stored sequentially or nonsequentially and an index is used to keep track of where the records are stored; (3) hashed, in which the address of each record is determined using an algorithm that converts a primary key value into a record address. Physical records of several types can be clustered together into one physical file in order to place records frequently used together close to one another in secondary memory.

The indexed file organization is one of the most popular in use today. An index may be based on a unique key or a secondary (nonunique) key, which allows more than one record to be associated with the same key value. The new form of an index, a bitmap index, creates a table of bits in which an on bit means that the related record has the related key value. A join index indicates rows from two or more tables that have common values for related fields. A hash index table makes the placement of data independent of the hashing algorithm and permits the same data to be accessed via several hashing functions on different fields. Indexes are important in speeding up data retrieval, especially when multiple conditions are used for selecting, sorting, or relating data. Indexes are useful in a wide variety of situations, including for large tables, for columns that are frequently used to qualify the data to be retrieved, when a field has a large number of distinct values, and when data processing is dominated by data retrieval rather than data maintenance.

File access efficiency and file reliability can be enhanced by the use of a Redundant Array of Inexpensive Disks (RAID), which allows blocks of data from one or several programs to be read and written in parallel to different disks, thus reducing the input/output delays with traditional sequential I/O operations on a single disk drive. Various levels of RAID allow a file and database designer to choose the combination of access efficiency, space utilization, and fault tolerance best suited for the database applications.

Database architectures in use today are hierarchical, network, relational, object-oriented, and multidimensional. Hierarchical and network architectures primarily appear in legacy applications, whereas relational, object-oriented, and multidimensional architectures are used for new systems development.

The introduction of multiprocessor database servers has made possible new capabilities in database management systems. One major new feature is the ability to break a query apart and to process the query in parallel against segments of a table. Such parallel query processing can greatly improve the speed of query processing. Also, database programmers can improve database processing performance by providing the DBMS with hints about the sequence in which to perform table operations. These hints override the cost-based optimizer of the DBMS. Both the DBMS and programmers can look at statistics about the database to determine how to process a query. A wide variety of guidelines for good query design were included in the chapter.

This chapter concludes the section of this book on database design. Having developed complete physical data specifications, you are now ready to begin implementing the database with database technology. Implementation means defining the database and programming client and server routines to handle the queries, reports, and transactions against the database. These are primary topics of the next five chapters, which cover relational database implementation on client platforms, server platforms, client/ server environments, and data warehouse technologies.

CHAPTER REVIEW

Key Terms

Bitmap index
Blocking factor
Data type
Denormalization
Extent
Field
File organization
Hash index table
Hashed file organization

Hashing algorithm
Horizontal partitioning
Index
Indexed file organization
Join index
Page
Physical file
Physical record

Pointer
Redundant Array of Inexpensive Disks (RAID)
Secondary key
Sequential file organization
Stripe
Tablespace
Vertical partitioning

Review Questions

1. Define each of the following terms:
   a. file organization
   b. sequential file organization
   c. indexed file organization
   d. hashing file organization
   e. denormalization
   f. index
   g. secondary key
   h. data type
   i. bitmap index
   j. RAID
   k. join index
   l. stripe

2. Match the following terms to the appropriate definitions:

_____ bitmap index

_____ hashing algorithm

_____ page

_____ physical record

_____ pointer

_____ blocking factor

_____ physical file

a. data read in one I/O operation

b. the number of records in a page

c. a named area of secondary memory

d. a table of zeros and ones

e. a field not containing business data

f. converts a key value into an address

g. adjacent fields

3. Contrast the following terms:
   a. horizontal partitioning; vertical partitioning
   b. physical file; tablespace
   c. physical record; physical file
   d. page; physical record
   e. secondary key; primary key

4. What are the major inputs to physical database design?

5. What are the key decisions in physical database design?

6. What information is shown on a composite usage map?

7. What decisions have to be made to develop a field specification?

8. What are the objectives of selecting a data type for a field?

9. Why are field values coded or compressed?

10. What options are available for controlling field integrity?

11. Describe three ways to handle missing field values.

12. Explain why normalized relations may not be efficient physical records.

13. List three common situations that suggest denormalizing relations to form physical records.

14. What are the advantages and disadvantages of horizontal and vertical partitioning?

15. List seven important criteria in selecting a file organization.

16. Under what circumstances is a bitmap index desirable?

17. What are the benefits of a hash index table?

18. What is the purpose of clustering of data in a file?

19. State seven rules of thumb for choosing indexes.

20. Contrast the two ways of viewing multidimensional databases.

21. How can use of the EXPLAIN command help in writing a more efficient query?

22. Explain four options for optimizing query performance.

23. Which level of RAID is best? Why?

Problems and Exercises

1. Consider the following two relations for Millennium College:

   STUDENT (Student_ID, Student _Name, Campus _Address, GPA)

   REGISTRATION (Student _ID, Course _ID, Grade)

   Following is a typical query against these relations:

   SELECT STUDENT.STUDENT_ID, STUDENT_NAME, COURSE_ID, GRADE
       FROM STUDENT, REGISTRATION
           WHERE   STUDENT.STUDENT_ID =
                    REGISTRATION.STUDENT_ID
           AND   GPA > 3.0
       ORDER BY STUDENT_NAME;

   a. On what attributes should indexes be defined to speed up the above query? Give the reasons for each attribute selected.
   b. Write SQL commands to create indexes for each attribute you identified in (a).

2. Consider the composite usage map in Figure 6-1. After a period of time, the assumptions for this usage map have changed as follows:

   a. There is an average of 40 quotations (rather than 50) for each supplier.
   b. Manufactured parts represent only 30 percent of all parts, and purchased parts represent 75 percent.
   c. The number of direct access to purchased parts increases to 75 per hour (rather than 60).

   Draw a new composite usage map reflecting this new information to replace Figure 6-1.

3. Choose Oracle data types for the attributes in the normalized relations in Figure 6-4.

4. Suppose you were designing a default value for the age field in a student record at your university. What possible values would you consider and why? How might the default vary by other characteristics about the student, such as school within the university or degree sought?

5. When a student has not chosen a major at a university, the university often enters a value of "Undecided" for the major field. Is "Undecided" a default value or a way to represent the null value?

6. Consider the following normalized relations from a database in a large retail chain:

STORE (Store_ID, Region, Manager_ID, Square _Feet)
EMPLOYEE (Employee_ID, Where_Work, Employee_Name, Employee_Address)
DEPARTMENT (Department_ID, Manager_ID, Sales_Goal)
SCHEDULE (Department_ID, Employee_ID, Date)

What opportunities might exist for denormalizing these relations when defining the physical records for this database? Under what circumstances would you consider creating such denormalized records?

7. Assume that you have a hard disk file designated to accommodate a maximum of 1,000 records of 240 bytes each. Assume that a page is 4,000 bytes in length and that records may not span pages. How many bytes will be needed for this file?

8. What problems might arise from vertically partitioning a relation? Given these potential problems, what general conditions influence when to partition a relation vertically?

9. Is it possible with a sequential file organization to permit sequential scanning of the data based on several sorted orders? If not, why not? If it is possible, how?

10. Suppose each record in a file were connected to its prior and next record in key sequence using pointers. Thus, each record might have the following format:

Primary key, other attributes, pointer to prior record, pointer to next record.
a. What would be the advantages of this file organization compared to a sequential file organization?
b. In contrast to a sequential file organization, would it be possible to keep the records in multiple sequences? Why or why not?

11. Assume a student file in a university database had an index on Student_ID (the primary key) and indexes on Major, Age, Marital_Status, and Home_Zipcode (all secondary keys). Further, assume that the university wanted a list of students majoring in MIS or Computer Science, over the age of 25, and married OR students majoring in Computer Engineering, single, and from the 45462 zipcode. How could indexes be used so that only records that satisfy this qualification are accessed?

12. Consider again the student file described in Problem and Exercise 11. For which of the indexes would it make sense to use a bitmap index? What conditions have to hold for a bitmap index to make sense? Choose one of the keys that is a likely candidate for a bitmap index and draw a figure similar to Figure 6-8 showing the structure of that index.

13. Create a join index on the Customer_ID fields of the customer and order tables in Figure 5-4.

14. Consider Figure 6-7c. Assuming that the empty rows in the leaves of this index show space where new records can be stored, explain where the record for 'Sooners' would be stored. Where would the record for 'Flashes' be stored? What might happen when one of the leaves is full and a new record needs to be added to that leaf?

15. Consider Figure 6-12, which compares the general characteristics of the most popular database architectures. Write relations equivalent to the multidimensional table view database model.

16. Can clustering of files occur after the files are populated with records? Why or why not?

17. Parallel query processing, as described in this chapter, means that the same query is run on multiple processors and each processor accesses in parallel a different subset of the database. Another form of parallel query processing, not discussed in this chapter, would partition the query so that each part of the query runs on a different processor but that part accesses whatever part of the database it needs. Most queries involve a qualification clause that selects the records of interest in the query. In general, this qualification clause is of the form:

(condition OR condition OR . . .) AND (condition OR condition OR . . .) AND . . .

Given this general form, how might a query be broken apart so that each parallel processor handles a subset of the query and then combines the subsets together after each part is processed?

18. In Figure 6-11f, suppose records 2, 3, 7, and 9 are being updated simultaneously by four different users. Which of these records could be updated in parallel? Design the scheduling of these updates to maximize parallel processing.

Field Exercises

1. Find out what database management systems are available at your university for student use. Investigate which data types these DBMSs support. Compare these DBMSs based upon data types supported and suggest which types of applications each DBMS is best suited for based on this comparison.

2. Using the Website for this text and other Internet resources, investigate the parallel processing capabilities of several leading DBMSs. How do their capabilities differ?

3. Using the Website for this text and other Internet resources, investigate the capabilities of object-oriented database products. How much do these DBMSs cost? For what types of applications do the vendors suggest using their products?

4. Contact a database designer or administrator in an organization with which you are familiar. Ask what file organizations are available in the various DBMSs used in that organization. Interview this person to learn what factors he or she considers when selecting an organization for database files.

For indexed files, ask how he or she decides what indexes to create. Are indexes ever deleted? Why?

5. Contact a database designer or administrator in an organization with which you are familiar. Ask if the person uses RAID technology with the organization's databases. Why or why not? If the person is using RAID, what level(s) are employed? Why?

References

Babad, Y. M., and J. A. Hoffer. 1984. "Even No Data Has a Value." *Communications of the ACM* 27 (August): 748–56.

Ballinger, C. 1998. "Introducing the Join Index." *Teradata Review* 1 (Fall): 18–23. Also found at www.teradatareview.com/Fall98/Ballinger.html.

Bontempo, C. J., and C. M. Saracco. 1996. "Accelerating Indexed Searching." *Database Programming & Design* 9 (July): 37–43.

Brobst, S, S. Gant, and F. Thompson. 1999. "Partitioning Very Large Database Tables with Oracle8." *Oracle Magazine* (March/April): 123–26.

DeLoach, A. 1987. "The Path to Writing Efficient Queries in SQL/DS." *Database Programming & Design* 1 (January): 26–32.

Finkelstein, R. 1988. "Breaking the Rules Has a Price." *Database Programming & Design* 1 (June): 11–14.

Holmes, J. "More Paths to Better Performance." *Database Programming & Design* 9 (February): 47–48.

Inmon, W. H. 1988. "What Price Normalization." *ComputerWorld* (October 17): 27, 31.

Kurka, A. "Rules for Better SELECTS." *SAP Technical Journal* 1(2): 75–79. Also available at www.saptechjournal.com.

Musciano, C. 1999. "0, 1, 0+1 . . . RAID Basics, Part 1." In *UnixInsider*, accessed via Web at www.unixinsider.com/unixinsideronline/swol-06–1999/swol-06–1999-raid1_p.html (address verified December 25, 2000).

Rogers, U. 1989. "Denormalization: Why, What, and How?" *Database Programming & Design* 2 (December): 46–53.

Schumacher, R. 1997. "Oracle Performance Strategies." *DBMS* 10 (May): 89–93.

Shah, R. 1999. "Storage Beyond RAID." In *UnixInsider*, accessed via Web at www.unixinsider.com/unixinsideronline/swol-07–1999/swol-07-connectivity_p.html (address verified December 25, 2000).

Viehman, P. 1994. "24 Ways to Improve Database Peformance." *Database Programming & Design* 7 (February): 32–41.

Yuhanna, N. 2000. *Oracle8i Database Administration.* Greenwich, CT: Manning Publications.

Further Reading

Elmasri, R. and S. Navathe. 1994. *Fundamentals of Database Systems,* 2nd ed. Menlo Park, CA: Benjamin/Cummings.

Loney, K., E. Aronoff, and N. Sonawalla. 1996. "Big Tips for Big Tables." *Database Programming & Design* 9 (November): 58–62.

Roti, S. 1996. "Indexing and Access Mechanisms." *DBMS* 9 (May): 65–70.

Web Resources

www.networkcomputing.com/605/605buyers.html *RAID Storage Solutions: Which is Right for You?*, by J. Milne (address verified December 25, 2000).

www.raid-advisory.com The RAID Advisory Board.

www.teradatareview.com A journal for the NCR Teradata data warehousing products, including articles on database design.

www.unixinsider.com/unixinsideronline/swol-07–1999/swol-07–1999-raid2_p.html *RAID Basics, Part 2: Moving on to RAID 3 and RAID 5,* by C. Musciano (address verified December 25, 2000).

www.win2000mag.com/Articles/Index.cfm?ArticleID=218 RAID Levels, an article with brief descriptions of common types of RAID (address verified December 25, 2000).

MOUNTAIN VIEW COMMUNITY HOSPITAL

Project Case

You have been developing a database for Mountain View Community Hospital throughout the preceding chapters. In this project case you will make some physical database design decisions based on the conceptual and relational database you developed in Chapters 3, 4, and 5.

PROJECT DESCRIPTION

Mountain View Community Hospital has decided to use a relational database management system (DBMS), Oracle, for this database. Thus, the design of the physical data-

base must conform to the capabilities of this DBMS. (If you are not familiar with Oracle, you can alternatively assume that Mountain View Community Hospital chose another DBMS with which you are familiar, and then answer the following questions accordingly.)

PROJECT QUESTIONS

1. What additional kinds of information, besides the 3NF relations you developed in the Project Case in Chapter 5 for the conceptual database of Chapter 3,

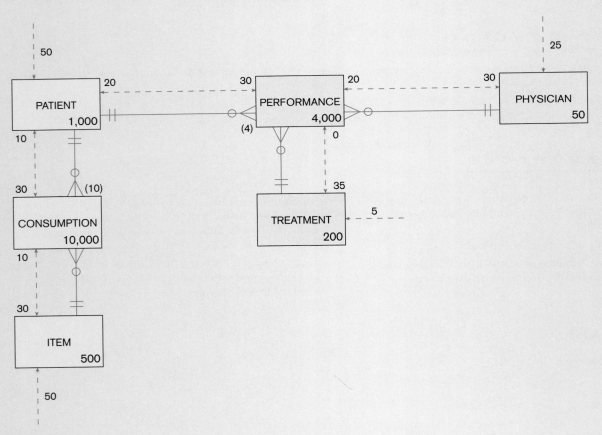

Figure 1
Composite usage map for a portion of the Mountain View Community Hospital database

do you need to do physical database design for this database?

2. Are there opportunities for horizontal or vertical partitioning of this database? If you are not sure, what other information would you need to answer this question with greater certainty?

3. Case Figure 1 shows an initial composite usage map for a portion of the Mountain View Community Hospital database. Since the usage map was developed, a few assumptions about the use of the data have changed:

- There is an average of 12 (rather than 10) item consumptions per patient.

- There is an average of 40 (rather than 30) times per hour that performance data are accessed for patients, and each time, the corresponding treatment data are also accessed.

Draw a new version of Figure 1 reflecting this new information.

PROJECT EXERCISES

1. In Project Exercise 5 from Chapter 5, you wrote CREATE TABLE commands for each relation in the logical database for the Mountain View Community Hospital conceptual database of Chapter 3. However, you did so not fully understanding the physical database design choices you might have available to you in Oracle (or whatever DBMS you are using for this project). Reconsider your previous CREATE TABLE commands in answering the following questions:

a. Would you choose different data types for any fields? Why?

b. Are any fields candidates for coding? If so, what coding scheme would you use for each of these fields?

c. Which fields may take on a null value?

d. Suppose the dates of performing a treatment were not entered. What procedures would you use for handling these missing data? Can you and should you use a default value for this field? Why or why not?

2. In Project Question 2, you were asked to identify opportunities for data partitioning. Besides partitioning, do you see other opportunities for denormalization of the relations for this database? If not, why not? If yes, where and how might you denormalize?

3. In Project Question 3, you updated Figure 1, a composite usage map, for part of the Mountain View Community Hospital database. Referring to this updated version of Figure 1, do you see any opportunities for clustering rows from two or more tables? Why or why not?

4. Write CREATE INDEX commands for the primary key indexes of each table in the Mountain View Community Hospital database.

5. Consider the following query against the Mountain View Community Hospital database: For each treatment performance in the past two weeks, list in order by treatment ID and for each ID by date in reverse chronological order, the physicians performing each treatment (grouped by treatment) and the number of times this physician performed that treatment that day. Create secondary key indexes to optimize the performance of this query. Make any assumptions you need to answer this question.

Part FOUR

Implementation

An Overview of Part FOUR

Part IV considers topics associated with implementing relational systems, including Web-enabled Internet applications and data warehouses. Database implementation, as indicated in Chapter 2, includes coding and testing database processing programs, completing database documentation and training materials, and installing databases and converting data, as necessary, from prior systems. Here, at last, is the point in the systems development life cycle for which we have been preparing. Our prior activities, enterprise modeling, conceptual data modeling, and logical and physical database design, are necessary previous stages. At the end of implementation, we expect a functioning system that meets users' information requirements. After that, the system will be put into production use, and database maintenance will be necessary for the life of the system. The chapters in Part IV help develop an initial understanding of the complexities and challenges of implementing a database system.

Chapter 7 describes SQL (Structured Query Language), which has become a standard language (especially on database servers) for creating and processing relational databases. In addition to a brief history of SQL that includes a thorough introduction to SQL-92, currently used by most DBMSs, along with discussion of the SQL-99 standard that is presently being implemented, the syntax of SQL is explored. Data definition language (DDL) commands used to create a database are included, as are single-table data manipulation language (DML) commands used to query the database. Dynamic and materialized views, which constrain a user's environment to relevant tables necessary to complete the user's work, are also covered.

Chapter 8 continues the explanation of more advanced SQL syntax and constructs. Multiple-table queries, along with subqueries and correlated subqueries, are demonstrated. These capabilities provide SQL with much of its power. Transaction integrity issues and an explanation of data dictionary construction place SQL within a wider context. Additional programming capabilities, including triggers and stored procedures, and embedding SQL in other programming language programs further demonstrate the capabilities of SQL. On-line analytical processing (OLAP) features of SQL-99, necessary for accessing data warehouses, are also covered.

Chapter 9 provides a discussion of the client/server architecture, applications, middleware, and client database access in contemporary database environments. It is important to understand this chapter because it lays the groundwork for understanding the Internet topics that are coming in Chapter 10. Multitiered architectures, including application and database servers, database processing alternatives for distribution among the tiers and browser (thin) clients are covered. Web-enabled database security and ODBC and JDBC connectivity material establish this chapter's connectivity to the Internet topics to come.

Chapter 10 describes the connectivity to databases from Web-based applications. Internet terminology is included for those who are less familiar with the Web. The use of scripting languages and embedding SQL in scripts are covered. A simple shopping cart application, implemented in both ASP and ColdFusion, is included in the chapter. The entire code and documentation for installing and running the shopping carts is included on the text's Website. Try to explore the code in detail, in order to see firsthand how to establish a Web-enabled database application. The role of Web servers and server-side extensions for database connectivity is addressed, as are Web security issues.

Chapter 11 describes the basic concepts of data warehousing, the reasons data warehousing is regarded as critical to competitive advantage in many organizations, and the database design activities and structures unique to data warehousing. Topics include alternative data warehouse architectures, techniques for data transformation and reconciliation, and the dimensional data model (star schema) for data warehouses. Database design for data marts, including surrogate keys, fact table grain, modeling dates and time, conformed dimensions, factless fact tables, and helper/hierarchy/reference tables, is explained and illustrated.

As indicated by the brief synopses of the chapters, Part IV provides both a conceptual understanding of the issues involved in implementing database applications and a practical initial understanding of the procedures necessary to construct a database prototype. The introduction of recent strategies, such as client/server, Web-enabled, and data warehousing, equip the reader to understand expected future developments in databases.

Chapter 7

SQL

LEARNING OBJECTIVES

After studying this chapter, you should be able to:

- Define the following key terms: **relational DBMS (RDBMS)**, **catalog**, **schema**, **data definition language**, **data manipulation language**, **data control language**, **base table**, **dynamic view**, **materialized view**, **referential integrity**, **scalar aggregate**, and **vector aggregate**.

- Interpret the history and role of SQL in database development.

- Define a database using the SQL data definition language.

- Write single table queries using SQL commands.

- Establish referential integrity using SQL.

- Discuss the SQL-92 and SQL-99 standards.

INTRODUCTION

Pronounced "S-Q-L" by some and "sequel" by others, SQL has become the de facto standard language used for creating and querying relational databases. The primary purpose of this chapter is to review SQL in depth. SQL is the most common language for relational systems. It has been accepted as an American standard by the American National Standards Institute (ANSI) and is a Federal Information Processing Standard (FIPS). It is also an international standard recognized by the International Organization for Standardization (ISO).

The ANSI SQL standards were first published in 1986 and updated in 1989, 1992 (SQL-92), and 1999 (SQL-99). SQL-99 is a significant extension beyond SQL-92, which was structured into three levels—Entry, Intermediate, and Full. SQL-99 establishes Core-level conformance, which must be met before any other level of conformance can be achieved. Eight additional types of enhanced conformance have been specified so far, including Active Database, Enhanced Integrity Management, and Basic Object Support. At the time of this writing, most database management systems are Entry-level

SQL-92 compliant and working to become Core SQL-99 compliant. For example, Oracle 8*i* supports Entry SQL-92 and is mostly Core SQL-99 compatible. Except where noted as Oracle SQL or Microsoft Access SQL, the examples in this chapter conform to the SQL standard.

SQL has been implemented in both mainframe and personal computer systems, so this chapter is relevant to both computing environments. While many of the PC-database packages use a query-by-example (QBE) interface, they also include SQL as an option. In Microsoft Access, for example, it is possible to switch back and forth between the two interfaces; a query that has been built using a QBE interface can be viewed in SQL by clicking a button. This feature may aid the reader in learning SQL syntax. In client/server architectures, SQL commands are executed on the server, and the results are returned to the client workstation.

The first commercial DBMS that supported SQL was Oracle in 1979. Oracle is now available in mainframe, client-server, and PC-based platforms for many operating systems, including OS/390 (MVS), various UNIX operating systems, Linux, Microsoft Windows and Windows NT, VAX/VMS, and VM/CMS. IBM's DB2, Informix, and Sybase are available for this range of operating systems also. Microsoft SQL Server 2000 runs on Windows NT and Windows 2000; the personal edition runs on Windows 98, Windows NT, Windows 2000, and Windows Me.

Core SQL-99 contains Entry SQL-92 and some additional capabilities, so vendors are moving from Entry SQL-92 to Core SQL-99 compliance. The standard has been published in several documents. They specify the enhanced levels that may be implemented in addition to Core SQL-99, and would eventually enable SQL to be used with persistent, complex objects in object databases, in addition to the relational databases that are currently supported. In this chapter we use Oracle 8*i* SQL*Plus, which is Entry SQL-92 compliant and is being moved toward Core SQL-99. At the time of this writing, it is not Core SQL-99 compliant but Oracle has announced that it is intended to be soon.

HISTORY OF THE SQL STANDARD

The concepts of relational database technology were first articulated in 1970 in a classic paper written by E. F. Codd entitled "A Relational Model of Data for Large Shared Data Banks." Workers at the IBM Research Laboratory in San Jose, California, undertook development of System R, a project whose purpose was to demonstrate the feasibility of implementing the relational model in a database management system. They used a language called Sequel, also developed at the San Jose IBM Research Laboratory. Sequel was renamed SQL during the project, which took place from 1974 to 1979. The knowledge gained was applied in the development of SQL/DS, the first relational database management system available commercially from IBM. SQL/DS was first available in 1981, running on the DOS/VSE operating system. A VM version followed in 1982, and the MVS version, DB2, was announced in 1983.

Because System R was well received at the user sites where it was installed, other vendors began developing relational products that used SQL. One product, Oracle, from Relational Software, was actually on the market before SQL/DS (1979). Other products included INGRES from Relational Technology (1981), IDM from Britton-Lee (1982), DG/SQL from Data General Corporation (1984), and Sybase from Sybase Inc. (1986). To provide some directions for the development of RDBMSs, the ANSI and the ISO approved a standard for the SQL relational query language (functions and syntax) proposed originally by the X3H2 Technical Committee on Database (Technical Committee X3H2—Database, 1986; ISO, 1987), often referred to as SQL/86. The 1986 standards have been extended to include an optional Integrity Enhancement Feature (IEF), often referred to as SQL/89. A related standard, Database Language Embedded SQL, was also adopted in the United States in 1989. The ISO and ANSI committees created SQL-92 (Technical Committee X3H2—Database, 1989; ISO, 1989, 1991), which was a more extensive expansion of SQL/86. This standard was ratified in late 1992 and is known as International Standard ISO/IEC 9075:1992, *Database Language SQL*. It was amended in 1994 and 1996. SQL-99 was ratified in July, 1999.

There are now many products available that support SQL, and they run on all machine sizes, from small personal computers to large mainframes. The database market is maturing and the rate of significant changes in products may slow, but they will continue to be SQL-based. In 1999, Oracle, IBM, and Microsoft together garnered over 73 percent of the overall database market (Gartner Dataquest press release, May 3, 1999), with Oracle and IBM each controlling about 30 percent of the market. Recent growth in e-commerce applications and customer relationship management (CRM) systems have fueled the growth of the major database vendors, but according to Gartner Dataquest, opportunities exist for smaller vendors to prosper through industry-specific systems or niche applications. Upcoming product releases may change the relative strengths of the database management systems by the time you read this book. But all of them will continue to use SQL, and they will follow, to a certain extent, the standards described below.

THE ROLE OF SQL IN A DATABASE ARCHITECTURE

With today's relational DBMSs and application generators, the importance of SQL within the database architecture is not usually apparent to the application users. Many users access database applications with no knowledge of SQL at all. For example, sites on the Web allow users to browse the catalog of the site being visited (see, for example, http://www.llbean.com). The information about an item that is presented, such as size, color, description, or availability, is stored in a database. The information has been retrieved using an SQL query, but the user has not issued an SQL command.

An SQL-based relational database application involves a user interface, a set of tables in the database, and a relational database management system (RDBMS) with an SQL capability. Within the RDBMS, SQL will be used to create the tables, translate user requests, maintain the data dictionary and system catalog, update and maintain the tables, establish security, and carry out backup and recovery procedures. A **relational DBMS (RDBMS)** is a data management system that implements a relational data model, one where data are stored in a collection of tables, and the data relationships are represented by common values, not links. This view of data was illustrated in Chapter 3 for the Pine Valley Furniture database system, and will be used throughout this chapter's SQL example queries.

The original purposes of the SQL standard follow:

1. To specify the syntax and semantics of SQL data definition and manipulation languages

2. To define the data structures and basic operations for designing, accessing, maintaining, controlling, and protecting an SQL database

3. To provide a vehicle for portability of database definition and application modules between conforming DBMSs

4. To specify both minimal (Level 1) and complete (Level 2) standards, which permit different degrees of adoption in products

5. To provide an initial standard, although incomplete, that will be enhanced later to include specifications for handling such topics as referential integrity,

Relational DBMS (RDBMS): A database management system that manages data as a collection of tables in which all data relationships are represented by common values in related tables.

transaction management, user-defined functions, join operators beyond the equi-join, and national character sets (among others)

The SQL-92 standard has been widely accepted, and most new products are SQL-92 compliant and moving toward Core SQL-99 compliance. However, each vendor's version of SQL also includes enhancements, features, and capabilities that extend their version beyond the baseline standards of SQL-92. For example, Oracle includes a DESCRIBE command, which lists all attributes, their datatypes, and constraints for a table. This is a very useful feature, especially for students who are becoming familiar with a demonstration database, but it is a command that they will not find if they use another vendor's SQL, such as MS-Access. Thus, the SQL standards have always served as a minimum set of capabilities rather than as a completely specified set of capabilities. What are the advantages and disadvantages of having an SQL standard?

The benefits of such a standardized relational language include the following:

- *Reduced training costs*   Training in an organization can concentrate on one language. A large labor pool of IS professionals trained in a common language reduces retraining when hiring new employees.

- *Productivity*   IS professionals can learn SQL thoroughly and become proficient with it from continued use. The organization can afford to invest in tools to help IS professionals become more productive. And since they are familiar with the language in which programs are written, programmers can more quickly maintain existing programs.

- *Application portability*   Applications can be moved from machine to machine when each machine uses SQL. Further, it is economical for the computer software industry to develop off-the-shelf application software when there is a standard language.

- *Application longevity*   A standard language tends to remain so for a long time; hence there will be little pressure to rewrite old applications. Rather, applications will simply be updated as the standard language is enhanced or new versions of DBMSs are introduced.

- *Reduced dependence on a single vendor*   When a nonproprietary language is used, it is easier to use different vendors for the DBMS, training and educational services, application software, and consulting assistance; further, the market for such vendors will be more competitive, which may lower prices and improve service.

- *Cross-system communication*   Different DBMSs and application programs can more easily communicate and cooperate in managing data and processing user programs.

On the other hand, a standard can stifle creativity and innovation; one standard is never enough to meet all needs, and an industry standard can be far from ideal since it may be the offspring of compromises among many parties. A standard may be difficult to change (because so many vendors have a vested interest in it), so fixing deficiencies may take considerable effort. Another disadvantage of standards is that using special features added to SQL by a particular vendor may result in the loss of some advantages, such as application portability.

The original SQL standard has been widely criticized, especially for its lack of referential integrity rules and certain relational operators. Date and Darwen (1997) express concern that SQL seems to have been designed without adhering to established principles of language design, and "As a result, the language is filled with numerous restrictions, *ad hoc* constructs, and annoying special rules" (p. 8). They feel that the standard is not explicit enough and that the problem of standard SQL implementations will continue to exist. Some of these limitations will be noticeable in this chapter.

THE SQL ENVIRONMENT

Figure 7-1 is a simplified schematic of an SQL environment, consistent with SQL-92 standards. As depicted, an SQL environment includes an instance of an SQL database management system along with the databases accessible by that DBMS and the users and programs that may use that DBMS to access the databases. Each database is contained in a **catalog**, which describes any object that is a part of the database, regardless of which user created that object. Figure 7-1 shows two catalogs: DEV_C and PROD_C. Most companies keep at least two versions of any database they are using. The production version, PROD_C here, is the live version, which captures real business data and thus must be very tightly controlled and monitored. The development version, DEV_C here, is used when the database is being built and continues to serve as a development tool where enhancements and maintenance efforts can be thoroughly tested before being applied to the production database. Typically this database is not as tightly controlled or monitored, because it does not contain live business data. Each database will have named schema(s) associated with a catalog. The **schema** is a collection of related objects, including but not limited to, base tables and views, domains, constraints, character sets, triggers, roles, and so forth.

Catalog: A set of schemas that, when put together, constitute a description of a database.

If more than one user has created objects in the database, combining information about all users' schemas will yield information for the entire database. Each catalog must also contain an information schema, which contains descriptions of all schemas in the catalog, tables, views, attributes, privileges, constraints, and domains, along with other information relevant to the database. The information contained in the catalog is maintained by the DBMS as a result of the SQL commands issued by the users and does not require conscious action by the user to build it. It is part of the power of the SQL language that the issuance of syntactically simple SQL commands may result in complex data management activities being carried out by the DBMS software. Users can browse the catalog contents by using SQL select statements.

Schema: That structure which contains descriptions of objects created by a user, such as base tables, views, and constraints, as part of a database.

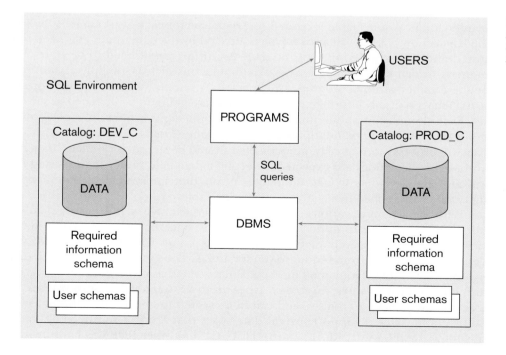

Figure 7-1
A simplified schematic of a typical SQL environment, as described by the SQL-92 standard

Figure 7-2
General syntax of the SELECT statement used in data manipulation language

```
SELECT [ALL DISTINCT] column_list
FROM table_list
[WHERE conditional expression]
[GROUP BY group_by_column_list]
[HAVING conditional expression]
[ORDER BY order_by_column_list]
```

Data definition language (DDL): Those commands used to define a database, including creating, altering, and dropping tables and establishing constraints.

Data manipulation language (DML): Those commands used to maintain and query a database, including updating, inserting, modifying, and querying data.

Data control language (DCL): Commands used to control a database, including administering privileges and the committing (saving) of data.

SQL commands can be classified into three types. First, there are **data definition language (DDL)** commands. These commands are used to create, alter, and drop tables, and will be covered first in this chapter. In a production database, the ability to use DDL commands will generally be restricted to one or more database administrators in order to protect the database structure from unexpected changes. In development or student databases, DDL privileges will be granted to more users.

Next, there are **data manipulation language (DML)** commands. Many consider the DML commands to be the core commands of SQL. These commands are used for updating, inserting, modifying, and querying the data in the database. They may be issued interactively, so that a result is returned immediately following the execution of the statement, or they may be included within programs written in a 3GL, such as C or COBOL. Embedding SQL commands may provide the programmer with more control over timing of report generation, interface appearance, error handling, and database security. Most of this chapter is devoted to covering basic DML commands, in interactive format. The general syntax of the SQL SELECT command used in DML is shown in Figure 7-2.

Last are **data control language (DCL)** commands. These commands help the DBA to control the database; they include commands to grant or revoke privileges to access the database or particular objects within the database and to store or remove transactions that would affect the database.

Each DBMS has a defined list of data types that it can handle. All contain numeric, string, and date/time-type variables. Some also contain graphic data types, spatial data types, or image data types, which greatly increase the flexibility of data manipulation. When a table is created, the data type for each attribute must be specified. Selection of a particular data type is affected by the data values that need to be stored and the expected uses of the data. A unit price will need to be stored in a numeric format because mathematical manipulations such as multiplying unit price by the number of units ordered are expected. A phone number may be stored as string data, especially if foreign phone numbers are going to be included in the data set. Even though the phone number contains only digits, no mathematical operations, such as adding or multiplying phone numbers, make sense. Since character data will process more quickly, numeric data should be stored as character data if no arithmetic calculations are expected. Selecting a date field rather than a string field will allow the developer to take advantage of date/time interval calculation functions that cannot be applied to a character field. See Table 7-1.

With the advent of various graphic and image data types, it is necessary to consider the business needs in deciding how to store data. For example, color may be stored as a descriptive character field, such as 'sand drift' or 'beige.' But such descriptions will vary from vendor to vendor and do not contain the amount of information that could be contained in a spatial data type that includes exact red, green, and blue intensity values. Such data types are now available in universal servers, which handle data warehouses, and can be expected to appear in RDBMSs as well. SQL-92 and SQL-99 support several data types that are not shown in Table 7-1, including TIMESTAMP, REAL, and INTERVAL, and other RDBMSs have included

Table 7-1 Sample Oracle8 Data Types

String	CHAR(*n*)	Fixed-length character data, *n* characters long. Maximum length is 2000.
	VARCHAR2(*n*)	Variable-length character data. Maximum size 4000 bytes.
	LONG	Variable-length character data. Maximum size 4 GB. Maximum one per table.
Numeric	NUMBER(*p, q*)	Signed decimal number with *p* digits and assumed decimal point *q* digits from right.
	INTEGER(*p*)	Signed integer, decimal or binary, *p* digits wide.
	FLOAT(*p*)	Floating-point number in scientific notation of *p* binary digits precision.
Date/time	DATE	Fixed-length date and time data in *dd-mm-yy* form.

data types such as CURRENCY and LOGICAL. It will be necessary to familiarize yourself with the available data types for each RDBMS with which you work, in order to achieve maximum advantage from its capabilities.

We are almost ready to illustrate sample SQL commands. The sample data that we will be using are shown in Figure 7-3. Each table name follows a naming standard that places an underscore and the letter *t* at the end of each table name, such

Customer_t

	Customer_ID	Customer_Name	Customer_Address	City	State	Postal_Code
	1	Contemporary Casuals	1355 S Hines Blvd	Gainesville	FL	32601-
	2	Value Furniture	15145 S.W. 17th St.	Plano	TX	75094-
	3	Home Furnishings	1900 Allard Ave.	Albany	NY	12209-
	4	Eastern Furniture	1925 Beltline Rd.	Carteret	NJ	07008-
	5	Impressions	5585 Westcott Ct.	Sacramento	CA	94206-
	6	Furniture Gallery	325 Flatiron Dr.	Boulder	CO	80514-
	7	Period Furniture	394 Rainbow Dr.	Seattle	WA	97954-
	8	Calfornia Classics	816 Peach Rd.	Santa Clara	CA	96915-
	9	M & H Casual Furniture	3709 First Street	Clearwater	FL	34620-
	10	Seminole Interiors	2400 Rocky Point Dr.	Seminole	FL	34646-
	11	American Euro Lifestyles	2424 Missouri Ave N.	Prospect Park	NJ	07508-
	12	Battle Creek Furniture	345 Capitol Ave. SW	Battle Creek	MI	49015-
	13	Heritage Furnishings	66789 College Ave.	Carlisle	PA	17013-
	14	Kaneohe Homes	112 Kiowai St.	Kaneohe	HI	96744-
	15	Mountain Scenes	4132 Main Street	Ogden	UT	84403-
*	(AutoNumber)					

Order_Line_t

Order_Id	Product_Id	Ordered_Quan
1001	1	2
1001	2	2
1001	4	1
1002	3	5
1003	3	3
1004	6	2
1004	8	2
1005	4	4
1006	4	1
1006	5	2
1006	7	2
1007	1	3
1007	2	2
1008	3	3
1008	8	3
1009	4	2
1009	7	3
1010	8	10
0	0	0

	Order_Id	Order_Date	Customer_ID
	1001	10/21/2000	1
	1002	10/21/2000	8
	1003	10/22/2000	15
	1004	10/22/2000	5
	1005	10/24/2000	3
	1006	10/24/2000	2
	1007	10/27/2000	11
	1008	10/30/2000	12
	1009	11/5/2000	4
	1010	11/5/2000	1
*	0		0

Order_t

Product_t

	Product_ID	Product_Description	Product_Finish	Standard_Price	Product_Line_Id
	1	End Table	Cherry	$175.00	10001
	2	Coffee Table	Natural Ash	$200.00	20001
	3	Computer Desk	Natural Ash	$375.00	20001
	4	Entertainment Center	Natural Maple	$650.00	30001
	5	Writer's Desk	Cherry	$325.00	10001
	6	8-Drawer Dresser	White Ash	$750.00	20001
	7	Dining Table	Natural Ash	$800.00	20001
	8	Computer Desk	Walnut	$250.00	30001
*	(AutoNumber)			$0.00	

Figure 7-3
Sample Pine Valley Furniture company data

as Order_t or Product_t. While looking at those tables, please take notice of the following:

1. Each order must have a valid customer number included in the Order_t table.

2. Each item in an order must have both a valid product number and a valid order number associated with it in the Order_Line_t table.

3. These four tables represent a simplified version of one of the most common sets of relations in business database systems—that of the customer order for products. SQL commands necessary to create the Customer table and the Order table were included in Chapter 3, and are expanded here.

The remainder of the chapter will illustrate DDL, DML, and DCL commands. Figure 7-4 gives an overview of where the various types of commands are used throughout the database development process. We will use the following notation in the illustrative SQL commands:

1. Capitalized words denote the command syntax. Type them exactly as shown, though capitalization may not be required by the RDBMS.

2. Lowercase words denote values that must be supplied by the user.

3. Brackets enclose optional syntax.

4. Ellipses (. . .) indicate that the accompanying syntactic clause may be repeated as necessary.

5. Each SQL command ends with a semicolon (;). In interactive mode, when the user pushes the RETURN key, the SQL command will execute. Be alert for alternative conventions, such as typing GO, or having to include a continuation symbol such as a hyphen at the end of each line used in the command. The spacing and indentations shown here are included for readability and are not a required part of standard SQL syntax.

Figure 7-4
DDL, DML, DCL, and the database development process

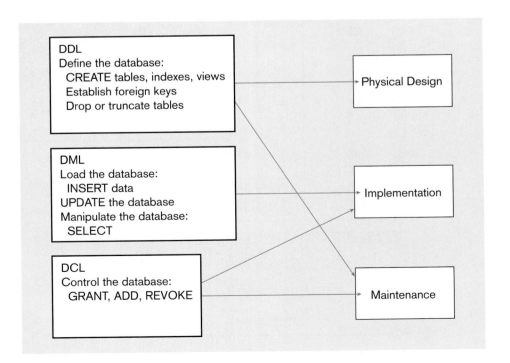

DEFINING A DATABASE IN SQL

Most systems allocate storage space to contain base tables, views, constraints, indexes, and other database objects when a database is created. Because of this, the privilege of creating databases may be reserved for the database administrator, and you may need to ask to have a database created. Students at a university may be assigned an account that gives access to an existing database, or they may be allowed to create their own database. In any case, the basic syntax to create a database is CREATE SCHEMA *database_name;* AUTHORIZATION *owner_user id.* The database will be owned by the authorized user, although it is possible for other specified users to work with the database or even to transfer ownership of the database. Physical storage of the database is dependent on both the hardware and software environment, and is usually the concern of the system administrator. The amount of control over physical storage that a database administrator is able to exert depends upon the RDBMS being used. There is little control possible when using MS Access 2000, but an Oracle 8*i* database administrator may exert considerable control over the placement of data, control files, index files, and so forth, thus improving the ability to tune the database to perform more efficiently.

Generating SQL Database Definitions

Three SQL DDL CREATE commands are included in Entry-Level SQL-92:

CREATE SCHEMA   Used to define that portion of a database that a particular user owns. Schemas are dependent on a catalog and contain schema objects, including base tables and views, domains, constraints, assertions, character sets, collations, and so forth.

CREATE TABLE   Defines a new table and its columns. The table may be a base table or a derived table. Tables are dependent on a schema. Derived tables are created by executing a query that uses one or more tables or views.

CREATE VIEW   Defines a logical table from one or more tables or views. Views may not be indexed. There are limitations on updating data through a view. Where views can be updated, those changes can be transferred to the underlying base tables originally referenced to create the view.

Each of these CREATE commands may be reversed by using a DROP command. Thus, DROP TABLE will destroy a table, including its definition, contents, and any constraints, views, or indexes associated with it. Usually only the table creator may delete the table. DROP SCHEMA and DROP VIEW will also destroy the named schema or view. ALTER TABLE may be used to change the definition of an existing base table by adding, dropping, or changing a column or by dropping a constraint.

There are also five other CREATE commands included in the SQL-92 standard. None of these are required to meet Entry Level or Intermediate Level SQL-92 standards:

CREATE CHARACTER SET   Allows the user to define a character set for text strings, and aids in the globalization of SQL by enabling the use of languages other than English. Each character set contains a set of characters, a way to represent each character internally, a data format used for this representation, and a collation, or way of sorting the character set.

CREATE COLLATION   A named schema object that specifies the order that a character set will assume. Existing collations may be manipulated to create a new collation.

CREATE TRANSLATION	A named set of rules that maps characters from a source character set to a destination character set for translation or conversion purposes.
CREATE ASSERTION	A schema object that establishes a CHECK constraint that is violated if the constraint is false.
CREATE DOMAIN	A schema object that establishes a domain, or set of valid values, for an attribute. Datatype will be specified, and a default value, collation, or other constraint may also be specified if desired.

Creating Tables

Once the data model is designed and normalized, the columns needed for each table can be defined using the SQL CREATE TABLE command. The general syntax for CREATE TABLE is shown in Figure 7-5. Here is a series of steps to follow when preparing to create a table:

1. Identify the appropriate datatype, including length, precision, and scale if required, for each attribute.

2. Identify those columns that should accept null values, as discussed in Chapter 6. Column controls that indicate a column cannot be null are established when a table is created and are enforced for every update of the table when data are entered.

3. Identify those columns that need to be unique. When a column control of UNIQUE is established for a column, then the data in that column must have a different value (that is, no duplicate values) for each row of data within that table. Where a column or set of columns is designated as UNIQUE, that column or set of columns is a candidate key, as discussed in Chapter 5. While each base table may have multiple candidate keys, only one candidate key may be designated as a PRIMARY KEY. When a column(s) is specified as the PRIMARY KEY, that column(s) is also assumed to be NOT NULL, even if NOT NULL is not explicitly stated. UNIQUE and PRIMARY KEY are both column constraints.

4. Identify all primary key–foreign key mates, as presented in Chapter 5. Foreign keys can be established immediately, as a table is created, or later by altering the table. The parent table in such a parent-child relationship should be created first, so that the child table will reference an existing parent table when it is created. The column constraint REFERENCES can be used to enforce referential integrity.

Figure 7-5
General syntax of the CREATE TABLE statement used in data definition language

```
CREATE TABLE tablename
( {column definition   [table constraint] } . , . .
[ON COMMIT {DELETE | PRESERVE} ROWS] );

where column definition ::=
column_name
       {domain name | datatype [(size)] }
       [column_constraint_clause . . .]
       [default value]
       [collate clause]

and table constraint ::=
       [CONSTRAINT constraint_name]
       Constraint_type [constraint_attributes]
```

5. Determine values to be inserted in any columns for which a default value is desired. DEFAULT, in SQL-92, can be used to define a value that is automatically inserted when no value is inserted during data entry. In Figure 7-6, the command that creates the ORDER_T table has defined a default value of SYSDATE (Oracle's name for the current date) for the DATE attribute.

6. Identify any columns for which domain specifications may be stated that are more constrained than those established by data type. Using CHECK as a column constraint in SQL-92 it may be possible to establish validation rules for values to be inserted into the database. In Figure 7-6, creation of the PRODUCT_T table includes a check constraint, which lists the possible values for PRODUCT_FINISH. Thus, even though an entry of 'White Maple' would meet the varchar datatype constraints, it would be rejected because 'White Maple' is not in the checklist.

7. Create the table and any desired indexes using the CREATE TABLE and CREATE INDEX statements. (CREATE INDEX is not a part of the SQL-92 standard because indexing is used to address performance issues, but is available in most RDBMSs.)

In Chapters 3 and 5, SQL database definition commands to create the Customer and Order tables for Pine Valley Furniture were shown that included establishing column constraints within the CREATE TABLE commands. In Figure 7-6, database definition commands using Oracle 8*i* are shown that include additional column constraints, and primary and foreign keys are given names. For example, the Customer

Figure 7-6
SQL database definition commands for Pine Valley Furniture Company (Oracle 8*i*)

```
CREATE TABLE CUSTOMER_T
          (CUSTOMER_ID              NUMBER(11, 0) NOT NULL,
          CUSTOMER_NAME             VARCHAR2(25) NOT NULL,
          CUSTOMER_ADDRESS          VARCHAR2(30),
          CITY                      VARCHAR2(20),
          STATE                     VARCHAR2(2),
          POSTAL_CODE               VARCHAR2(9),
CONSTRAINT CUSTOMER_PK PRIMARY KEY (CUSTOMER_ID));

CREATE TABLE ORDER_T
          (ORDER_ID                 NUMBER(11, 0) NOT NULL,
          ORDER_DATE                DATE          DEFAULT SYSDATE,
          CUSTOMER_ID               NUMBER(11, 0),
CONSTRAINT ORDER_PK PRIMARY KEY (ORDER_ID),
CONSTRAINT ORDER_FK FOREIGN KEY (CUSTOMER_ID) REFERENCES CUSTOMER_T(CUSTOMER_ID));

CREATE TABLE PRODUCT_T
          (PRODUCT_ID               INTEGER       NOT NULL,
          PRODUCT_DESCRIPTION       VARCHAR2(50),
          PRODUCT_FINISH            VARCHAR2(20)
                    CHECK (PRODUCT_FINISH IN ('Cherry', 'Natural Ash', 'White Ash',
                              'Red Oak', 'Natural Oak', 'Walnut')),
          STANDARD_PRICE            DECIMAL(6,2),
          PRODUCT_LINE_ID           INTEGER,
CONSTRAINT PRODUCT_PK PRIMARY KEY (PRODUCT_ID));

CREATE TABLE ORDER_LINE_T
          (ORDER_ID                 NUMBER(11,0)  NOT NULL,
          PRODUCT_ID                NUMBER(11,0)  NOT NULL,
          ORDERED_QUANTITY          NUMBER(11,0),
CONSTRAINT ORDER_LINE_PK PRIMARY KEY (ORDER_ID, PRODUCT_ID),
CONSTRAINT ORDER_LINE_FK1 FOREIGN KEY(ORDER_ID) REFERENCES ORDER_T(ORDER_ID),
CONSTRAINT ORDER_LINE_FK2 FOREIGN KEY (PRODUCT_ID) REFERENCES PRODUCT_T(PRODUCT_ID));
```

table's primary key is CUSTOMER_ID. The primary key constraint is named CUS-TOMER_PK. Now, in Oracle for example, when looking at the DBA_CONSTRAINTS table a database administrator will find it easy to identify the primary key constraint on the customer table because its name, CUSTOMER_PK, will be the value of the constraint_name column. Without the constraint name, a system identifier would be assigned automatically and the identifier would be difficult to read.

Using and Defining Views

Base table: A table in the relational data model containing the inserted raw data. Base tables correspond to the relations that are identified in the database's conceptual schema.

Dynamic view: A virtual table that is created dynamically upon request by a user. A dynamic view is not a temporary table. Rather, its definition is stored in the system catalog and the contents of the view are materialized as a result of an SQL query that uses the view. Distinguish from a materialized view, which may be stored on a disk and refreshed at intervals or when used, depending on the RDBMS.

Materialized view: Copies or replicas of data based on SQL queries created in the same manner as dynamic views. However, a materialized view exists as a table and thus care must be taken to keep it synchronized with its associated base tables.

The SQL syntax shown in Figure 7-6 demonstrates the creation of four **base tables** in a database schema. These tables, which are used to physically store data in the database, correspond to entities in the conceptual schema. Using SQL queries, it is possible to create virtual tables, or **dynamic views**, whose contents materialize when referenced. These views may often be manipulated in the same way as a base table can be manipulated, through SQL SELECT queries. Or, **materialized views**, which are stored physically on a disk and refreshed at appropriate intervals or events, may also be used.

The often-stated purpose of a view is to simplify query commands, but a view may also provide valuable data security and significantly enhance programming productivity for a database. To highlight the convenience of a view, consider the Pine Valley Invoice of Figure 1-6. Construction of this invoice requires access to the four tables from the Pine Valley database of Figure 7-3: CUSTOMER_T, ORDER_T, ORDER_LINE_T, and PRODUCT_T. A novice database user may make mistakes or be unproductive in properly formulating queries involving so many tables. A view allows us to predefine this association into a single virtual table as part of the database. With this view, a user who wants only customer invoice data does not have to reconstruct the joining of tables to produce the report or any subset of it. Table 7-2 summarizes the pros and cons of using views.

A view, INVOICE_V, is defined by specifying an SQL query (SELECT . . . FROM . . . WHERE) that has the view as its result.

Query: What are the data elements necessary to create an invoice for a customer? Save this query as a view named INVOICE_V.

```
CREATE VIEW INVOICE_V AS
    SELECT CUSTOMER_T.CUSTOMER_ID, CUSTOMER_ADDRESS,
    ORDER_T.ORDER_ID, PRODUCT_T.PRODUCT_ID, ORDERED_QUANTITY,
        and other columns as required
    FROM CUSTOMER_T, ORDER_T, ORDER_LINE_T, PRODUCT_T
    WHERE CUSTOMER_T.CUSTOMER_ID = ORDER_T.CUSTOMER_ID
        AND ORDER_T.ORDER_ID = ORDER_LINE_T.ORDER_ID
        AND PRODUCT_T.PRODUCT_ID = ORDER_LINE_T.PRODUCT_ID;
```

Table 7-2 Pros and Cons of Using Dynamic Views

Positive Aspects	Negative Aspects
Simplify query commands	Use processing time re-creating view each time it is referenced
Help provide data security and confidentiality	
Improve programmer productivity	May or may not be directly updateable
Contain most current base table data	
Use little storage space	
Provide a customized view for a user	
Establish physical data independence	

The SELECT clause specifies, or projects, what data elements (columns) are to be included in the view table. The FROM clause lists the tables and views involved in the view development. The WHERE clause specifies the names of the common columns used to join CUSTOMER_T to ORDER_T to ORDER_LINE_T to PRODUCT_T. Because a view is a table, and one of the relational properties of tables is that the order of rows is immaterial, the rows in a view may not be sorted. But queries that refer to this view may display their results in any desired sequence.

We can see the power of such a view when building a query to generate an invoice for order number 1004. Rather than having to specify the joining of four tables, the query can include all relevant data elements from the view table, INVOICE_V.

Query: What are the data elements necessary to create an invoice for order number 1004?

```
SELECT CUSTOMER_ID, CUSTOMER_ADDRESS, PRODUCT_ID, QUANTITY, and
other columns as required
    FROM INVOICE_V
        WHERE ORDER_ID = 1004;
```

A dynamic view is a virtual table; it is constructed automatically as needed by the DBMS, and is not maintained as real data. Any SQL SELECT statement may be used to create a view. The real data are stored in base tables, those that have been defined by CREATE TABLE commands. A dynamic view always contains the most current derived values and is thus superior in terms of data currency to constructing a temporary real table from several base tables. Also, in comparison to a temporary real table, a view consumes very little storage space. A view is costly, however, since its contents must be calculated each time that they are requested. Materialized views are now available and may address this drawback.

A view may join multiple tables or views together and may contain derived (or virtual) columns. For example, if a user of the Pine Valley Furniture database only wants to know the total value of orders placed for each furniture product, a view for this can be created from INVOICE_V in Oracle SQL*Plus.

Query: What is the total value of orders placed for each furniture product?

```
CREATE VIEW ORDER_TOTALS_V AS
SELECT PRODUCT_ID PRODUCT, SUM (UNIT_PRICE*QUANTITY) TOTAL
    FROM INVOICE_V
        GROUP BY PRODUCT_ID;
```

We can assign a different name (an alias) to a view column than the associated base table or expression column name. Here, PRODUCT is a renaming of PRODUCT_ID, local to only this view. TOTAL is the column name given the expression for total sales of each product. The expression can now be referenced via this view in subsequent queries as if it were a column, rather than a derived expression. Defining views based on other views can cause problems. For example, if we redefine INVOICE_V so that UNIT_PRICE is not included, then ORDER_TOTALS_V will no longer work because it won't be able to locate unit prices.

Views can also help to establish security. Tables and columns that are not included will not be obvious to the user of the view. Restricting access to a view with GRANT and REVOKE statements adds another layer of security. For example, granting some users access rights to aggregated data, such as averages, in a view but denying them access to base table, detailed data will not allow them to display the base table data. SQL security commands are explained further in Chapter 12.

Privacy and confidentiality of data can be achieved by creating views that restrict users to working with only the data they need to perform their assigned duties. If a clerical worker needs to work with employees' addresses but should not be able to access their compensation rates, they may be given access to a view that does not contain compensation information.

Some people advocate the creation of a view for every single base table, even if that view is identical to the base table. They suggest this approach because views can contribute to greater programming productivity as databases evolve. Consider a situation where 50 programs all use the CUSTOMER_T table. Suppose that the Pine Valley Furniture Company database evolves to support new functions that require the CUSTOMER_T table to be renormalized into two tables. If these 50 programs refer directly to the CUSTOMER_T base table, they will all have to be modified to refer to one of the two new tables or to joined tables. But if these programs all use the view on this base table, then only the view has to be re-created, saving considerable reprogramming effort. However, dynamic views require considerable run-time computer processing since the virtual table of a view is re-created each time the view is referenced. Therefore, referencing a base table through a view rather than directly can add considerable time to query processing. This additional operational cost must be balanced against the potential reprogramming savings from a view.

For the rest of this chapter, we will create and use dynamic views that replicate the Pine Valley Furniture tables that will be used to demonstrate SQL syntax. The following SQL statements set up the base table views:

```
CREATE VIEW CUSTOMER_V AS SELECT * FROM CUSTOMER_T;
CREATE VIEW ORDER_V AS SELECT * FROM ORDER_T;
CREATE VIEW ORDER_LINE_V AS SELECT * FROM ORDER_LINE_T;
CREATE VIEW PRODUCT_V AS SELECT * FROM PRODUCT_T;
```

Updating data directly from a view rather than from base tables is possible under certain limitations. In general, update operations to data in a view are permitted as long as the update is unambiguous in terms of data modification in the base table. But when the CREATE VIEW statement contains any of the following situations, that view may not be updated directly.

1. The SELECT clause includes the keyword DISTINCT. (SELECT clauses are covered in detail later in this chapter in the section titled Processing Single Tables.)

2. The SELECT clause contains expressions, including derived columns, aggregates, statistical functions, etc.

3. The FROM clause, or a subquery, or a UNION clause references more than one table.

4. The FROM clause or a subquery references another view that is not updateable.

5. The CREATE VIEW command contains a GROUP BY or HAVING clause.

It could happen that an update to an instance would result in the instance disappearing from the view. Let's create a view named EXPENSIVE_STUFF_V, which lists all furniture products that have a UNIT_PRICE over $300. That view will include PRODUCT_ID 5, a writer's desk, which has a unit price of $325. If we update data using EXPENSIVE_STUFF_V and reduce the unit price of the writer's desk to $295, then the writer's desk will no longer appear in the EXPENSIVE_STUFF_V virtual table because its unit price is now less than $300. If it is desired to track all merchandise with an original price over $300, include a WITH CHECK OPTION clause after the SELECT clause in the CREATE VIEW command. The WITH CHECK OPTION will cause UPDATE or INSERT statements to be rejected when those statements would cause updated or inserted rows to be removed from the view. This option can only be used with updateable views.

Here is the CREATE VIEW statement for EXPENSIVE_STUFF_V.

Query: List all furniture products that have ever had a UNIT_PRICE over $300.

```
CREATE VIEW EXPENSIVE_STUFF_V
    AS
    SELECT PRODUCT_ID, PRODUCT_NAME, UNIT_PRICE
        FROM PRODUCT_T
            WHERE UNIT_PRICE > 300
                WITH CHECK OPTION;
```

When attempting to update the unit price of the writer's desk to $295, using this Oracle SQL*Plus syntax:

```
UPDATE EXPENSIVE_STUFF_V
    SET UNIT_PRICE = 295
        WHERE PRODUCT_ID = 5;
```

Oracle will give the error message shown:

```
ERROR at line 1:
ORA-01402: view WITH CHECK OPTION where-clause violation
```

A price increase on the writer's desk to $350 will take effect with no error message because the view is updateable and the conditions specified in the view are not violated.

Information about views will be stored in the systems tables of the DBMS. In Oracle8, for example, the text of all views is stored in DBA_VIEWS. Users with system privileges can find this information.

Query: What information is available about the view named EXPENSIVE_STUFF?

```
SELECT * FROM DBA_VIEWS WHERE VIEW_NAME = 'EXPENSIVE_STUFF_V';
```

Result:

OWNER	VIEW_NAME	TEXT_LENGTH	TEXT
MPRESCOTT	EXPENSIVE_STUFF_V	103	

```
SELECT PRODUCT_ID,   PRODUCT_NAME,   UNIT_PRICE
        FROM PRODUCT_T
        WHERE UNIT_PRICE > 300
```

Materialized Views   Like dynamic views, materialized views can be constructed in different ways for various purposes. Tables may be replicated in whole or in part, and refreshed on a predetermined time interval or triggered when the table needs to be accessed. Materialized views can be based on queries from one or more tables. In Oracle 8*i*, it is possible to create summary tables based on aggregations of data. Copies of remote data that use distributed data may be stored locally as materialized views. Maintenance overhead will be incurred to keep the local view synchronized with the remote base tables or data warehouse, but the use of materialized views may improve the performance of distributed queries, especially if the data in the materialized view is relatively static and does not have to be refreshed very often.

Creating Data Integrity Controls

We have seen the syntax that establishes foreign keys in Figure 7-6. In order to establish **referential integrity** between two tables with a 1:M relationship in the relational data model, the primary key of the table on the one side will be referenced by a

Referential integrity: An integrity constraint specifying that the value (or existence) of an attribute in one relation depends on the value (or existence) of a primary key in the same or another relation.

column in the table on the many side of the relationship. Referential integrity means that a value in the matching column on the many side must correspond to a value in the primary key for some row in the table on the one side, or be NULL. The SQL REFERENCES clause prevents a foreign key value from being added if it is not already a valid value in the referenced primary key column, but there are other integrity issues.

If a CUSTOMER_ID value is changed, the connection between that customer and orders placed by that customer will be ruined. The REFERENCES clause prevents making such a change in the foreign key value, but not in the primary key value. This problem could be handled by asserting that primary key values cannot be changed once they are established. In this case, updates to the customer table will be handled in most systems by including an ON UPDATE RESTRICT clause. Then, any updates that would delete or change a primary key value will be rejected unless no foreign key references that value in any child table. See Figure 7-7 for the syntax associated with updates.

Another solution is to pass the change through to the child table(s) by using the ON UPDATE CASCADE option. Then, if a customer ID number is changed, that change will flow through (cascade) to the child table, ORDER_T, and the customer's ID will also be updated in the ORDER_T table.

A third solution is to allow the update on CUSTOMER_T but to change the involved CUSTOMER_ID value in the ORDER_T table to NULL by using the ON UPDATE SET NULL option. In this case, using the SET NULL option would result in losing the connection between the order and the customer, not a desired effect. The most flexible option to use would be the CASCADE option. Were a customer record to be deleted, ON DELETE RESTRICT, CASCADE, or SET NULL are also available. With DELETE RESTRICT, the customer record could not be deleted unless there were no orders from that customer in the ORDER_T table.

Figure 7-7
Ensuring data integrity through updates

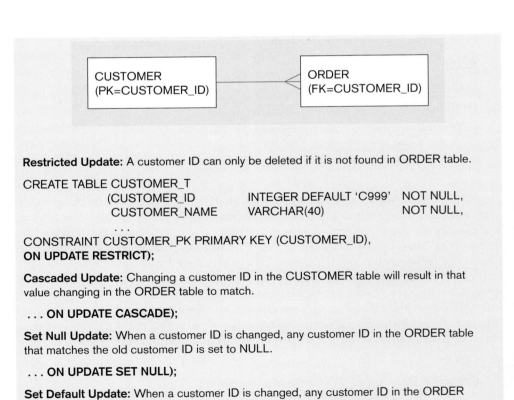

Restricted Update: A customer ID can only be deleted if it is not found in ORDER table.

```
CREATE TABLE CUSTOMER_T
            (CUSTOMER_ID        INTEGER DEFAULT 'C999'  NOT NULL,
             CUSTOMER_NAME      VARCHAR(40)             NOT NULL,
      . . .
CONSTRAINT CUSTOMER_PK PRIMARY KEY (CUSTOMER_ID),
ON UPDATE RESTRICT);
```

Cascaded Update: Changing a customer ID in the CUSTOMER table will result in that value changing in the ORDER table to match.

```
. . . ON UPDATE CASCADE);
```

Set Null Update: When a customer ID is changed, any customer ID in the ORDER table that matches the old customer ID is set to NULL.

```
. . . ON UPDATE SET NULL);
```

Set Default Update: When a customer ID is changed, any customer ID in the ORDER tables that matches the old customer ID is set to a predefined default value.

```
. . . ON UPDATE SET DEFAULT);
```

With DELETE CASCADE, removing the customer would remove all associated order records from ORDER_T. With DELETE SET NULL, the order records for that customer would be set to null before the customer's record is deleted. With DELETE SET DEFAULT, the order records for that customer would be set to a default value before the customer's record is deleted. DELETE RESTRICT would probably make the most sense. Not all SQL RDBMSs provide for primary key referential integrity. In that case, update and delete permissions on the primary key column may be revoked.

Changing Table Definitions

Table definitions may be changed by ALTERing column specifications. The ALTER TABLE command may be used to add new columns to an existing table. For example, a customer type column may be added to the CUSTOMER table.

Command: To add a customer type column to the CUSTOMER table.

```
ALTER TABLE CUSTOMER_T
   ADD (TYPE VARCHAR (2));
```

The ALTER TABLE command may include keywords such as ADD, DROP, or ALTER and allow changing the column's names, datatype, length, and constraints. Usually when adding a new column, its null status will be NULL, in order to deal with data that have already been entered in the table. When the new column is created, it is added to all of the instances in the table and a value of NULL would be the most reasonable. The ALTER command is invaluable for adapting the database to inevitable modifications due to changing requirements, prototyping, evolutionary development, and mistakes. This command cannot be used to change a view.

Removing Tables

To remove a table from a database, the owner of the table may use the DROP TABLE command. Views are dropped by using the similar DROP VIEW command.

Command: To drop a table from a database schema.

```
DROP TABLE CUSTOMER_T;
```

This command will drop the table and save any pending changes to the database. To drop a table, one must either own the table or have been granted the DROP ANY TABLE system privilege. Dropping a table will also cause associated indexes and privileges granted to be dropped. The DROP TABLE command can be qualified by the keywords RESTRICT or CASCADE. If RESTRICT is specified, the command will fail and the table will not be dropped if there are any dependent objects, such as views or constraints, that currently reference the table. If CASCADE is specified, all dependent objects will also be dropped as the table is dropped. Oracle allows one to retain the table's structure but remove all of the data that have been entered in the table, with its TRUNCATE TABLE command.

INSERTING, UPDATING, AND DELETING DATA

Once tables and views have been created, it is necessary to populate them with data and maintain those data before queries can be written. The SQL command that is used to populate tables is the INSERT command. If entering a value for every column in the table one could use a command like the following, which was used to add the first row of data to the CUSTOMER_T table. Notice that the data values must be ordered in the same order as the columns in the table.

Command: To insert a row of data into a table where a value will be inserted for every attribute.

INSERT INTO CUSTOMER_T VALUES
(001, 'Contemporary Casuals', '1355 S. Himes Blvd.', 'Gainesville', 'FL', 32601);

When data will not be entered into every column in the table, either enter the value NULL for the empty fields or specify those columns to which data are to be added. Here, too, the data values must be in the same order as the columns have been specified in the INSERT command. For example, the following statement was used to insert one row of data into the PRODUCT_T table, since there was no product description for the end table.

Command: To insert a row of data into a table where some attributes will be left null.

INSERT INTO PRODUCT_T (PRODUCT_ID, PRODUCT_DESCRIPTION,
PRODUCT_FINISH, STANDARD_PRICE, PRODUCT_ON_HAND)
    VALUES (1, 'End Table', 'Cherry', 175, 8);

In general, the INSERT command places a new row in a table based on values supplied in the statement, copies one or more rows derived from other database data into a table, or extracts data from one table and inserts them into another. When wanting to populate a table, CA_CUSTOMER_T, that has the same structure as CUSTOMER_T, with only Pine Valley's California customers, one could use the following INSERT command.

Command: Populating a table by using a subset of another table with the same structure.

INSERT INTO CA_CUSTOMER_T
    SELECT * FROM CUSTOMER_T
        WHERE STATE = 'CA';

The table identified in the INSERT command may be a view. However, the view must be updateable, so that data inserted through the view is also inserted into the base table on which the view is based. If the view definition included the WITH CHECK OPTION, attempts to insert data through the view will be rejected when the data values do not meet the specifications of the WITH CHECK OPTION.

Batch Input

The INSERT command is used to enter one row of data at a time or to add multiple rows as the result of a query. Some versions of SQL have a special command or utility for entering multiple rows of data as a batch: the INPUT command. Oracle includes a program, SQL*Loader, which runs from the command line, and can be used to load data from a file into the database. This popular program is tricky to use and is not included in the scope of this text.

Deleting Database Contents

Rows can be deleted individually or in groups. Suppose Pine Valley Furniture decides that it will no longer deal with customers located in Hawaii. CUSTOMER_T rows for customers with addresses in Hawaii could all be eliminated by the next command.

Command: Deleting rows that meet a certain criterion from the CUSTOMER table.

DELETE FROM CUSTOMER_T
    WHERE STATE = 'HI';

The simplest form of DELETE eliminates all rows of a table.

Command: Deleting all rows from the CUSTOMER table.

DELETE FROM CUSTOMER_T;

This form of the command should be used very carefully!

Deletion must also be done with care when rows from several relations are involved. For example, if we delete a CUSTOMER_T row before deleting associated ORDER_T rows, we will have a referential integrity violation. (*Note:* Including the ON DELETE clause with a field definition can mitigate such a problem. Refer back to the Creating Data Integrity Controls section of this chapter if you've forgotten about ON DELETE.) SQL will actually eliminate the records selected by a DELETE command. Therefore, always execute a SELECT command first to display the records that would be deleted and visually verify that only the desired rows are included.

Changing Database Contents

To update data in SQL we must inform the DBMS what relation, columns, and rows are involved. If an incorrect price is entered for the dining table in the PRODUCT_T table, the following SQL UPDATE statement would establish the correction.

Command: To modify unit price of product 7 in the PRODUCT table to 775.

```
UPDATE PRODUCT_T
   SET UNIT   PRICE = 775
         WHERE PRODUCT_ID = 7;
```

The SET command can also change a value to NULL; the syntax is SET *columname* = NULL. As with DELETE, the WHERE clause in an UPDATE command may contain a subquery, but the table being updated may not be referenced in the subquery. Subqueries are discussed in Chapter 8.

INTERNAL SCHEMA DEFINITION IN RDBMSs

The internal schema of a relational database can be controlled for processing and storage efficiency. Some techniques used to tune the operational performance of the relational database internal data model include:

1. Choosing to index primary and/or secondary keys to increase the speed of row selection, table joining, and row ordering. Dropping indexes to increase speed of table updating. You may want to review the section in Chapter 6 on selecting indexes.

2. Selecting file organizations for base tables that match the type of processing activity on those tables (for example, keeping a table physically sorted by a frequently used reporting sort key).

3. Selecting file organizations for indexes, which are also tables, appropriate to the way the indexes are used, and allocating extra space for an index file, so that an index can grow without having to be reorganized.

4. Clustering data, so that related rows of frequently joined tables are stored close together in secondary storage to minimize retrieval time.

5. Maintaining statistics about tables and their indexes, so that the DBMS can find the most efficient ways to perform various database operations.

Not all of these techniques are available in all SQL systems. Indexing and clustering are typically available, however, so we discuss these in the following sections.

Creating Indexes

Indexes are created in most RDBMSs to provide rapid random and sequential access to base-table data. Since the ISO SQL standards do not generally address performance issues, no standard syntax for creating indexes is included. The examples given here use Oracle syntax and give a feel for how indexes are handled in most RDBMSs. Note that although users do not directly refer to indexes when writing any SQL command, the DBMS recognizes which existing indexes would improve query performance. Indexes can usually be created for both primary and secondary keys and both single and concatenated (multiple-column) keys. In some systems, one can choose between ascending or descending sequences for the keys in an index.

For example, an alphabetical index on CUSTOMER_NAME in the CUSTOMER_T column in Oracle is created here.

Command: To create an alphabetical index on customer name in the CUSTOMER table.

CREATE INDEX NAME_IDX ON CUSTOMER_T (CUSTOMER_NAME);

Indexes may be created or dropped at any time. If data already exist in the key column(s), index population will automatically occur for the existing data. If an index is defined as UNIQUE (using the syntax CREATE UNIQUE INDEX . . .) and the existing data violate this condition, the index creation will fail. Once an index is created, it will be updated as data are entered, updated, or deleted.

When we no longer need tables, views, or indexes, we use the associated DROP statements. For example, the NAME_IDX index above is dropped here.

Command: To remove the index on the customer name in the CUSTOMER table.

DROP INDEX NAME_IDX;

Although it is possible to index every column in a table, use caution when deciding to create a new index. Each index consumes extra storage space and also requires overhead maintenance time whenever indexed data change value. Together, these costs may noticeably slow retrieval response times and cause annoying delays for on-line users. A system may use only one index even if several are available for keys in a complex qualification. The database designer must know exactly how indexes are used by the particular RDBMS to make wise choices on indexing. Oracle includes an *explain plan* tool that can be used to look at the order in which an SQL statement will be processed and the indexes that will be used. The output also includes a cost estimate that can be compared with estimates from running the statement with different indexes in order to determine which is most efficient.

PROCESSING SINGLE TABLES

Four data manipulation language commands are used in SQL. We have talked briefly about three of them (UPDATE, INSERT, and DELETE) and seen several examples of the fourth, SELECT. While the UPDATE, INSERT, and DELETE commands allow modification of the data in the tables, it is the SELECT command, with its various clauses, that allows one to query the data contained in the tables and ask many different questions, or ad hoc queries. The basic construction of an SQL command is fairly simple and easy to learn. Don't let that fool you; SQL is a powerful tool that enables one to specify complex data analysis processes. However, because the basic syntax is relatively easy to learn, it is also easy to write SELECT queries that are syntactically correct but do not answer the exact question that is intended. Before running queries against a large production database, always test queries carefully on a small test set of data to be sure that they are returning the correct results. In addition to checking the query results manually, it is often possible to parse queries into smaller parts, examine the results of these simpler queries, and then recombine them. This will ensure that they act together in the expected way. We begin by exploring SQL queries that affect only a single table. In Chapter 8, we join tables and use queries that require more than one table.

Clauses of the SELECT Statement

Most SQL data retrieval statements include the following three clauses:

SELECT Lists the columns (including expressions involving columns) from base tables or views to be projected into the table that will be the result of the command.

FROM Identifies the tables or views from which columns will be chosen to appear in the result table, and includes the tables or views needed to join tables to process the query.

WHERE Includes the conditions for row selection within a single table or view, and the conditions between tables or views for joining.

The first two are required, and the third is necessary when only certain table rows are to be retrieved, or multiple tables are to be joined. Our examples for this section are drawn from the data shown in Figure 7-3. As an example, we can display product name and quantity on hand from the PRODUCT view for all products that have a standard price of less than $275.

Query: Which products have a standard price of less than $275?

```
SELECT PRODUCT_NAME, STANDARD_PRICE
    FROM PRODUCT_V
        WHERE STANDARD_PRICE <275;
```

Result:

PRODUCT_NAME	STANDARD_PRICE
End Table	175
Computer Desk	250
Coffee Table	200

Every SELECT statement returns a result table when it executes. Two special keywords can be used along with the list of columns to display: DISTINCT and *. If the user does not wish to see duplicate rows in the result, SELECT DISTINCT may be used. In the preceding example, if the *other* computer desk carried by Pine Valley Furniture had also cost less than $275, the results of the query would have duplicate rows. SELECT DISTINCT PRODUCT_NAME would display a result table without the duplicate rows. SELECT *, where * is used as a wildcard to indicate all columns, displays all columns from all the tables or views in the FROM clause.

Also, note that the clauses of a SELECT statement must be kept in order, or syntax error messages will occur and the query will not execute. It may also be necessary to qualify the names of the database objects, according to the SQL version being used. If there is any ambiguity in an SQL command, one must indicate exactly from which table or view the requested data is to come. For example, in Figure 7-3 CUSTOMER_ID is a column in both CUSTOMER_T and ORDER_T. When one owns the database being used (that is, the user created the tables) and one wants the CUSTOMER_ID to come from CUSTOMER_T, specify it by asking for CUSTOMER_T.CUSTOMER_ID. If one wants CUSTOMER_ID to come from ORDER_T, then ask for ORDER_T.CUSTOMER_ID. Even if one doesn't care which table CUSTOMER_ID comes from, it must be specified because SQL can't resolve the ambiguity without user direction. When using data created by someone else, one must also specify the owner of the table by adding the owner's user ID. Now a request to SELECT the CUSTOMER_ID from CUSTOMER_T may look like *OWNER_ID*.CUSTOMER_T.CUSTOMER_ID. The examples in this book will assume that the reader owns the tables or views being used, as the SELECT statements will be easier to read without the qualifiers. Qualifiers will be included where necessary and may always be included in statements if desired. Problems may occur from leaving out qualifiers, but no problems will occur from including them.

If typing the qualifiers and column names is wearisome, or if the column names will not be meaningful to those who are reading the reports, establish aliases for columns, tables, or views that will then be used for the rest of the query.

Query: What is the address of the customer named Home Furnishings? Use an alias, NAME, for customer name.

```
SELECT CUST.CUSTOMER_NAME AS NAME, CUST.CUSTOMER_ADDRESS
    FROM ownerid.CUSTOMER_V CUST
        WHERE NAME = 'Home Furnishings';
```

This retrieval statement will give the result below in many versions of SQL. In Oracle's SQL*Plus, the alias for the column cannot be used in the rest of the SELECT statement, except in a HAVING clause, so CUSTOMER_NAME would have to be used in the last line rather than NAME in order to run. Notice that the column header prints as NAME rather than CUSTOMER_NAME, and that the view alias may be used in the SELECT clause even though it is not defined until the FROM clause.

Result:

NAME	CUSTOMER_ADDRESS
Home Furnishings	1900 Allard Ave.

When using the SELECT clause to pick out the columns for a result table, the columns can be rearranged so that they will be ordered differently in the result table than they were in the original table. In fact, they will be displayed in the same order as they are included in the SELECT statement. Look back at PRODUCT_T in Figure 7-3 to see the different ordering of the base table from the result table for this query:

Query: List the unit price, product name, and product ID for all products in the PRODUCT table.

```
SELECT STANDARD_PRICE, PRODUCT_DESCRIPTION, PRODUCT_ID
    FROM PRODUCT_T;
```

Result:

STANDARD_PRICE	PRODUCT_DESCRIPTION	PRODUCT_ID
175	End Table	1
200	Coffee Table	2
375	Computer Desk	3
650	Entertainment Center	4
325	Writer's Desk	5
750	8-Drawer Desk	6
800	Dining Table	7
250	Computer Desk	8

8 rows selected.

Using Expressions

Several other things can be done with the basic SELECT . . . FROM . . . WHERE clauses with a single table. One may create *expressions*, which are mathematical manipulations of the data in the table, or one may take advantage of stored functions, such as SUM or AVG, to manipulate the chosen rows of data from the table. Perhaps one would like to know the average standard price of each inventory item. To get the average value, use the AVG stored function. Name the resulting expression AVERAGE. Using SQL*Plus, here are the query and the results.

Query: What is the average standard price for each product in inventory?

```
SELECT AVG  (STANDARD_PRICE, AS AVERAGE
        FROM PRODUCT_V;
```

Mathematical manipulations can be constructed by using the ' +' for addition, ' –' for subtraction, '*' for multiplication, and '/' for division. These operators can be used with any numeric columns. Some systems also have an operand called *modulo*, usually indicated by '%'. A modulo is the integer remainder that results from dividing two integers. For example, 14 % 4 is 2 because 14/4 is 3 with a remainder of 2. The standard supports year–month and day–time intervals, which make it possible to perform date and time arithmetic. Notice that the result from the above query now shows the expressions, AVERAGE.

Result:

AVERAGE
440.625

The precedence rules for the order in which complex expressions are evaluated are the same as those used in other programming languages and in algebra. Expressions in parentheses will be calculated first. Where parentheses do not establish order, multiplication and division will be completed first, from left to right, followed by addition and subtraction, also left to right. To avoid confusion, use parentheses to establish order. Where parentheses are nested, the innermost calculations will be completed first.

Using Functions

Functions such as COUNT, MIN, MAX, SUM, and AVG of specified columns in the column list of a SELECT command may be used to specify that the resulting answer table is to contain aggregated data instead of row-level data. Using any of these aggregate functions will give a one-row answer.

Query: How many different items were ordered on order number 1004?

```
SELECT COUNT (*)
  FROM ORDER_LINE_V
        WHERE ORDER_ID = 1004;
```

Result:

COUNT (*)
2

It seems that it would be simple enough to list the order # 1004 by changing the above query.

Query: How many different items were ordered on order number 1004, and what are they?

```
SELECT PRODUCT_ID, COUNT (*)
  FROM ORDER_LINE_V
        WHERE ORDER_ID = 1004;
```

But in Oracle, here is the result.

Result:

```
ERROR at line 1:
ORA-00937: not a single-group group function
```

The problem is that PRODUCT_ID returns two values, 6 and 8, for the two rows selected, while COUNT returns one aggregate value, 2, for the set of rows with ID = 1004. In most implementations, SQL cannot return a row value and a set value; one must run two separate queries, one that returns row information and one that returns set information.

Also, it is easy to confuse the functions COUNT (*) and COUNT. The function COUNT (*), used above, counts all rows selected by a query regardless of whether any of the rows contain null values. COUNT tallies only those rows that contain a value; it ignores all null values.

SUM and AVG can only be used with numeric columns. COUNT, COUNT (*), MIN, and MAX can be used with any data type. Using MIN on a text column, for example, will find the lowest value in the column, the one whose first column is closest to the beginning of the alphabet. SQL implementations interpret the order of the alphabet differently. For example, some systems may start with A–Z, then a–z, then 0–9 and special characters. Others treat upper and lowercase letters as being equivalent. Yet others start with some special characters, then proceed to numbers, letters, and other special characters. In Oracle, the language character set is determined when the database is created and cannot be changed without re-creating the database. When a client terminal uses a different character set, Oracle automatically converts the character sets in both directions, changing the database set to that of the client terminal and vice versa. When a direct conversion between sets is not possible, replacement characters are used. Here is the query to ask for the first PRODUCT_NAME in PRODUCT_T alphabetically, which was done using the AMERICAN character set in Oracle 8*i*.

Query: Alphabetically, what is the first product name in the PRODUCT table?

```
SELECT MIN (PRODUCT_DESCRIPTION)
   FROM PRODUCT_V;
```

It gives the result shown below, which demonstrates that numbers are sorted before letters in this character set.

Result:

MIN(PRODUCT_DESCRIPTION)
8-Drawer Desk

Using Wildcards

The use of the asterisk (*) as a wildcard in a SELECT statement has been previously shown. Wildcards may also be used in the WHERE clause where an exact match is not possible. Here, the keyword LIKE is paired with wildcard characters and usually a string containing the characters that are known to be desired matches. The wildcard character, %, is used to represent any collection of characters. Thus, using LIKE '%Desk' when searching PRODUCT_DESCRIPTION will find all different types of desks carried by Pine Valley Furniture. The underscore ,_, is used as a wildcard character to represent exactly one character, rather than any collection of characters. Thus, using LIKE ' _-drawer' when searching PRODUCT_NAME will find any products with specified drawers, such as 3-drawer, 5-drawer, or 8-drawer dressers.

Comparison Operators

With the exception of the very first SQL example in this section, we have used the equality comparison operator in our WHERE clauses. The first example used the greater (less) than operator. The most common comparison operators for SQL implementations are listed in Table 7-3. You are used to thinking about using comparison operators with numeric data, but you can also use them with character data and dates in SQL. The query shown here asks for all orders placed after 10/24/2000.

Query: Which orders have been placed since 10/24/2000?

```
SELECT ORDER_ID, ORDER_DATE
    FROM ORDER_V
        WHERE ORDER_DATE > '24-OCT-2000';
```

Notice that the date is enclosed in single quotes and that the format of the date is different from that shown in Figure 7-3, which was taken from MS-Access. The query was run in SQL*Plus.

Result:

ORDER_ID	ORDER_DATE
1007	27-NOV-00
1008	30-OCT-00
1009	05-NOV-00
1010	05-NOV-00

Query: What furniture does Pine Valley carry that isn't made of cherry?

```
SELECT PRODUCT_DESCRIPTION, PRODUCT_FINISH
    FROM PRODUCT_V
        WHERE PRODUCT_FINISH != 'Cherry';
```

Result:

PRODUCT	PRODUCT_FINISH
Coffee Table	Natural Ash
Computer Desk	Natural Ash
Entertainment Center	Natural Maple
8-Drawer Desk	White Ash
Dining Table	Natural Ash
Computer Desk	Walnut

6 rows selected.

Table 7-3 Comparison Operators in SQL

Operator	Meaning
=	Equal to
>	Greater than
> =	Greater than or equal to
<	Less than
< =	Less than or equal to
<>	Not equal to
! =	Not equal to

Using Boolean Operators

More complex questions can be answered by adjusting the WHERE clause further. The Boolean or logical operators AND, OR, and NOT can be used to good purpose.

AND joins two or more conditions and returns results only when all conditions are true.

OR joins two or more conditions and returns results when any conditions are true.

NOT negates an expression.

If multiple Boolean operators are used in an SQL statement, NOT is evaluated first, then AND, then OR. For example, consider the following query.

Query: List product name, finish, and unit price for all desks and all tables that cost more than $300 in the PRODUCT view.

```
SELECT PRODUCT_DESCRIPTION, PRODUCT_FINISH, STANDARD_PRICE
    FROM PRODUCT_V
        WHERE PRODUCT_DESCRIPTION LIKE '%Desk'
            OR PRODUCT_DESCRIPTION LIKE '%Table'
            AND UNIT_PRICE > 300;
```

All of the desks are listed, even the computer desk that costs less than $300. Only one table is listed; the less expensive ones that cost less than $300 are not included. Looking at the query, the AND will be processed first, returning all tables with a unit price greater than $300. Then the OR is processed, returning all desks, regardless of cost, and all tables costing more than $300.

Result:

PRODUCT_DESCRIPTION	PRODUCT_FINISH	STANDARD_PRICE
Computer Desk	Natural Ash	375
Writer's Desk	Cherry	325
8-Drawer Desk	White Ash	750
Dining Table	Natural Ash	800
Computer Desk	Walnut	250

If we had wanted to return only desks and tables costing more than $300, we should have put parentheses after the WHERE and before the AND.

Query: List product name, finish, and unit price for all desks and tables in the PRODUCT view that cost more than $300.

```
SELECT PRODUCT_DESCRIPTION, PRODUCT_FINISH, UNIT_PRICE
   FROM PRODUCT_V
         WHERE (PRODUCT_NAME LIKE '%Desk'
              OR PRODUCT_NAME LIKE '%Table')
         AND UNIT_PRICE > 300;
```

Now the results returned are shown below. Only products with unit price greater than $300 are included.

Result:

PRODUCT_DESCRIPTION	PRODUCT_FINISH	STANDARD_PRICE
Computer Desk	Natural Ash	375
Writer's Desk	Cherry	325
8-Drawer Desk	White Ash	750
Dining Table	Natural Ash	800

Ranges

The comparison operators < and > are used to establish a range of values. The keywords BETWEEN or NOT BETWEEN can also be used. For example, to find those products with a standard price between $200 and $300, the following query could be used.

Query: Which products in the PRODUCT view have a standard price between $200 and $300?

```
SELECT PRODUCT_DESCRIPTION, STANDARD_PRICE
   FROM PRODUCT_V
      WHERE STANDARD_PRICE > 199 AND STANDARD_PRICE < 301;
```

Result:

PRODUCT_NAME	STANDARD_PRICE
Coffee Table	200
Computer Desk	250

The same result will be returned by this query.

Query: Which products in the PRODUCT view have a standard price between $200 and $300?

```
SELECT PRODUCT_DESCRIPTION, STANDARD_PRICE
   FROM PRODUCT_V
      WHERE STANDARD_PRICE BETWEEN 200 AND 300;
```

Result: Same as previous query.

Adding NOT before BETWEEN in this query will return all the other products in PRODUCT_V because their prices are less than $200 or more than $300.

Distinct

Sometimes when returning rows that don't include the primary key, duplicate rows will be returned. For example, look at this query and the results it returns.

Query: What are the order numbers included in the ORDER_LINE table?

```
SELECT ORDER_ID
   FROM ORDER_LINE_T;
```

Eighteen rows are returned, and many of them are duplicates since many orders were for multiple items.

Result:

ORDER_ID
```
    1001
    1001
    1001
    1002
    1003
    1004
    1004
    1005
    1006
    1006
    1006
    1007
    1007
    1008
    1008
    1009
    1009
    1010
```
18 rows selected.

If, however, we add the keyword DISTINCT, then only one occurrence of each ORDER_ID will be returned, one for each of the ten orders represented in the table.

Query: What are the order numbers included in the ORDER_LINE table?

```
SELECT DISTINCT ORDER_ID
   FROM ORDER_LINE_V;
```

Result:

ORDER_ID

1001
1002
1003
1004
1005
1006
1007
1008
1009
1010

10 rows selected.

DISTINCT and its counterpart, ALL, can only be used once in a SELECT statement. It comes after SELECT and before any columns or expressions are listed. If a SELECT statement projects more than one column, only rows that are identical for every column will be eliminated. Thus, if the statement above also includes QUANTITY, 14 rows are returned because there are now only four duplicate rows rather than eight. For example, both items ordered on ORDER_ID 1004 were for two items, so the second pairing of 1004 and 2 will be eliminated.

Query: What are the unique combinations of order number and order quantity included in the ORDER_LINE table?

SELECT DISTINCT ORDER_ID, ORDERED_QUANTITY
  FROM ORDER_LINE_V;

Result:

ORDER_ID	QUANTITY
1001	1
1001	2
1002	5
1003	3
1004	2
1005	4
1006	1
1006	2
1007	2
1007	3
1008	3
1009	2
1009	3
1010	10

14 rows selected.

IN and NOT IN Lists

To match a list of values, consider using IN.

Query: List all customers who live in warmer states.

SELECT CUSTOMER_NAME, CITY, STATE
  FROM CUSTOMER_V
    WHERE STATE IN ('FL', 'TX', 'CA', 'HI');

Results:

CUSTOMER_NAME	CITY	ST
Contemporary Casuals	Gainesville	FL
Value Furniture	Plano	TX
Impressions	Sacramento	CA
California Classics	Santa Clara	CA
M and H Casual Furniture	Clearwater	FL
Seminole Interiors	Seminole	FL
Kaneohe Homes	Kaneohe	HI

7 rows selected.

IN is particularly useful in SQL statements that use subqueries, which will be covered in Chapter 8.

Sorting Results: The ORDER BY Clause

Looking at the preceding results, it may seem that it would make more sense to list the California customers, followed by the Floridians, Hawaiians, and Texans. That brings us to the other three basic parts of the SQL statement:

ORDER BY   sorts the final results rows in ascending or descending order

GROUP BY   groups rows in an intermediate results table where the values in those rows are the same for one or more columns.

HAVING   can only be used following a GROUP BY and acts as a secondary WHERE clause, returning only those groups which meet a specified condition.

So, we can order the customers by adding an ORDER BY clause.

Query: List customer, city, and state for all customers in the CUSTOMER view whose address is Florida, Texas, California, or Hawaii. List the customers alphabetically by state, and alphabetically by customer within each state.

```
SELECT CUSTOMER_NAME, CITY, STATE
  FROM CUSTOMER_V
     WHERE STATE IN ('FL', 'TX', 'CA', 'HI')
        ORDER BY STATE, CUSTOMER_NAME;
```

Now the results are easier to read.

Result:

CUSTOMER_NAME	CITY	ST
California Classics	Santa Clara	CA
Impressions	Sacramento	CA
Contemporary Casuals	Gainesville	FL
M and H Casual Furniture	Clearwater	FL
Seminole Interiors	Seminole	FL
Kaneohe Homes	Kaneohe	HI
Value Furniture	Plano	TX

7 rows selected.

Notice that all customers from each state are listed together, and within each state, customer names are alphabetized. The sorting order is determined by the order in which the columns are listed in the ORDER BY clause; in this case, states were alphabetized first, then customer names. If sorting from high to low, use DESC as a keyword placed after the column used to sort.

How are NULLS sorted? SQL-92 stipulates that null values should be placed first or last, before or after columns that have values. Where the NULLS will be placed will depend upon the SQL implementation. SQL*Plus sorts NULLS last.

Categorizing Results: The GROUP BY Clause

GROUP BY is particularly useful when paired with aggregate functions, such as SUM or COUNT. GROUP BY divides a table into subsets (by groups); then an aggregate function can be used to provide summary information for that group. The single value returned by the previous aggregate function examples is called a **scalar aggregate**. When aggregate functions are used in a GROUP BY clause and several values are returned, they are called **vector aggregates**.

Scalar aggregate: A single value returned from an SQL query that includes an aggregate function.

Vector aggregate: Multiple values returned from an SQL query that includes an aggregate function.

Query: Count the number of customers with addresses in each state to which we ship.

```
SELECT STATE, COUNT (STATE)
   FROM CUSTOMER_V
      GROUP BY STATE;
```

Result:

ST	COUNT(STATE)
CA	2
CO	1
FL	3
HI	1
MI	1
NJ	2
NY	1
PA	1
TX	1
UT	1
WA	1

11 rows selected.

It is also possible to nest groups within groups; the same logic is used as when sorting multiple items.

Query: Count the number of customers with addresses in each city to which we ship. List the cities by state.

```
SELECT STATE, CITY, COUNT (CITY)
   FROM CUSTOMER_V
      GROUP BY STATE, CITY;
```

While the GROUP BY clause seems straightforward, it can produce unexpected results if the logic of the clause is forgotten. When a GROUP BY is included, the columns allowed to be specified in the SELECT clause are limited. Only those columns with a single value for each group can be included. In the previous query, each group consists of a city and its state. The SELECT statement includes both the 'city' and 'state' columns. This works because each combination of city and state is one value. But, if the SELECT clause of the first query in this section had also included 'city', that statement would fail because the GROUP BY is only by state. Since states can have more than one city, the requisite that each value in the SELECT clause have only one value in the GROUP BY group is not met, and SQL will not be able to present the city information so that it makes sense. In general, each column referenced in the SELECT statement must be referenced in the GROUP BY clause, unless the column is an argument for an aggregate function included in the SELECT clause.

Qualifying Results by Categories: The HAVING Clause

The HAVING clause acts like a WHERE clause, but it identifies groups that meet a criterion, rather than rows. Therefore, one usually sees a HAVING clause following a GROUP BY clause.

Query: Find only states with more than one customer.

```
SELECT STATE, COUNT (STATE)
   FROM CUSTOMER_V
         GROUP BY STATE
               HAVING COUNT (STATE) > 1;
```

This query returns a result that has removed all those states with one customer as seen above. Remember that using WHERE here would not work because WHERE doesn't allow aggregates; further, WHERE qualifies rows, whereas HAVING qualifies groups.

Result:

ST	COUNT(STATE)
CA	2
FL	3
NJ	2

To include more than one condition in the HAVING clause, use AND, OR, and NOT just as in the WHERE clause. In summary, here is one last command that includes all of the six clauses; remember that they must be used in this order.

Query: List the product finish and average standard price for each finish for selected finishes where the average standard price is less than 750.

```
SELECT PRODUCT_FINISH, AVG (STANDARD_PRICE)
   FROM PRODUCT_V
      WHERE PRODUCT_FINISH IN ('Cherry', 'Natural Ash', 'Natural Maple', 'White Ash')
            GROUP BY PRODUCT_FINISH
                  HAVING AVG (STANDARD_PRICE) < 750
                        ORDER BY PRODUCT_FINISH;
```

Result:

PRODUCT_FINISH	AVG(UNIT_PRICE)
Cherry	250
Natural Ash	458.333333
Natural Maple	650

Figure 7-8 shows the order in which SQL processes the clauses of a statement. Arrows indicate the paths that may or may not be followed. Remember, only the SELECT and FROM clauses are mandatory. Notice that the processing order is different from the order of the syntax used to create the statement. As each clause is processed an intermediate results table is produced that will be used for the next clause. Users do not see the intermediate results tables; they only see the final results. A query can be debugged by remembering the order shown in Figure 7-8. Take out the optional clauses, then add them back in one at a time in the order that they will be processed. In this way, intermediate results can be seen and, often, problems can be spotted.

Figure 7-8
SQL statement processing order
(adapted from van der Lans, p. 100)

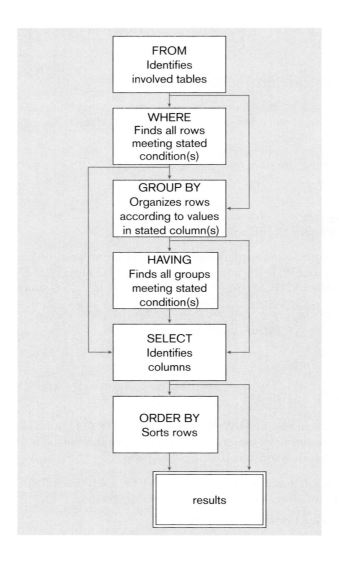

Summary

This chapter has introduced the SQL language for relational database definition (DDL), manipulation (DML), and control (DCL), commonly used to define and query relational database management systems (RDBMS). This standard has been criticized for many flaws, and in reaction to these, and to increase the power of the language, extensions are constantly under review by the ANSI X3H2 committee and ISO/IEC JTC1/SC 21/WG3 DBL. The current standard is known as SQL-99.

The establishment of SQL standards and conformance certification tests has contributed to relational systems being the current dominant form of new database development. Benefits of the SQL standards include reduced training costs, improved productivity, application portability and longevity, reduced dependence on single vendors, and improved cross-system communication.

The SQL environment includes an instance of an SQL DBMS along with accessible databases and associated users and programs. Each database is included in a catalog and has a schema that describes the database objects. Information contained in the catalog is maintained by the DBMS itself, rather than by the users of the DBMS.

The data definition language (DDL) commands of SQL are used to define a database, including its creation and the creation of its tables, indexes, and views. Referential integrity is also established through DDL commands. The data manipulation (DML) commands of SQL are used to load, update, and query the database through use of the SELECT command. Data control language (DCL) commands are used to establish user access to the database.

SQL commands may directly affect the base tables, which contain the raw data, or they may affect a database view which has been created. Changes and updates made to views may or may not be passed on to the base tables. The basic syntax of an SQL SELECT statement contains the following keywords: SELECT, FROM, WHERE, ORDER BY, GROUP BY, and HAVING. SELECT determines which attributes will be displayed in the query results table. FROM determines which tables or views will be used in the query. WHERE sets the criteria of the query, including any joins of multiple tables which are necessary. ORDER BY determines the order in which the results will be displayed. GROUP BY is used to categorize results and may return either scalar aggregates or vector aggregates. HAVING qualifies results by categories.

Understanding the basic SQL syntax presented in this chapter should enable the reader to start using SQL effectively, and to build a deeper understanding of the possibilities for more complex querying with continued practice. Advanced SQL topics are covered in Chapter 8.

CHAPTER REVIEW

Key Terms

Base table	Data manipulation language (DML)	Relational DBMS (RDBMS)
Catalog	Dynamic View	Scalar aggregate
Data control language (DCL)	Materialized view	Schema
Data definition language (DDL)	Referential integrity	Vector aggregate

Review Questions

1. Define each of the following terms:
   a. base table
   b. data definition language
   c. data manipulation language
   d. dynamic view
   e. materialized view
   f. referential integrity
   g. relational DBMS (RDBMS)
   h. schema

2. Match the following terms to the appropriate definitions.

   _____ view
   _____ referential integrity
   _____ dynamic view
   _____ materialized view
   _____ SQL-99
   _____ null value
   _____ scalar aggregate
   _____ vector aggregate
   _____ catalog
   _____ schema
   _____ host language

   a. list of values
   b. description of a database
   c. view materialized as result of SQL query that uses the view
   d. logical table
   e. missing or nonexistent value
   f. descriptions of database objects for a database
   g. third-generation programming language in which SQL commands are embedded
   h. established in relational data models by use by foreign keys
   i. view that exists as a table
   j. standard relational query and definition language
   k. single value

3. Contrast the following terms:
   a. base table; view
   b. dynamic view; materialized view
   c. catalog; schema

4. What are SQL-92 and SQL-99? Briefly describe how SQL-99 differs from SQL-92.

5. Describe a relational DBMS (RDBMS), its underlying data model, data storage structures, and manner of establishing data relationships.

6. List six potential benefits of achieving an SQL standard that is widely accepted.

7. Describe the components and structure of a typical SQL environment.

8. Distinguish among data definition commands, data manipulation commands, and data control commands.

9. Explain how referential integrity is established in databases that are SQL-92 compliant. Explain how the ON UPDATE RESTRICT, ON UPDATE CASCADE, and ON UPDATE SET NULL clauses differ. What happens if the ON DELETE CASCADE clause is set?

10. Explain some possible purposes of creating a view using SQL. In particular, explain how a view can be used to reinforce data security.

11. Explain why it is necessary to limit the kinds of updates performed on data when referencing data through a view.

12. Describe a set of circumstances for which using a view can save reprogramming effort.

13. Drawing on material covered in prior chapters, explain the factors to be considered in deciding whether to create a key index for a table in SQL.

14. Explain and provide at least one example of how one qualifies the ownership of a table in SQL.

15. How is the order in which attributes appear in a result table changed? How are the column heading labels changed?

16. What is the difference between COUNT, COUNT DISTINCT, and COUNT(*) in SQL? When will these three commands generate the same and different results?

17. What is the evaluation order for the Boolean operators (AND, OR, NOT) in an SQL command? How can one be sure that the operators will work in the desired order rather than in this prescribed order?

18. If an SQL statement includes a GROUP BY clause, the attributes that can be requested in the SELECT statement will be limited. Explain that limitation.

Problems and Exercises

Problems and Exercises 1 through 9 are based on the class schedule ERD depicted in Figure 4-16 in Chapter 4. The 3NF relations along with some sample data are repeated in Figure 7-9. For questions 4–9, draw an instance diagram and mark it to show the data you expect your query to return in the results.

1. Write a database description for each of the relations shown, using SQL DDL (shorten, abbreviate, or change any data names as needed for your SQL version). Assume the following attribute data types:

STUDENT_ID (integer, primary key)
STUDENT_NAME (25 characters)
FACULTY_ID (integer, primary key)
FACULTY_NAME (25 characters)
COURSE_ID (8 characters, primary key)
COURSE_NAME (15 characters)
DATE_QUALIFIED (date)
SECTION_ID (integer, primary key)
SEMESTER (7 characters)

2. Use SQL to define the following view:

STUDENT_ID	STUDENT_NAME
38214	Letersky
54907	Altvater
54907	Altvater
66324	Aiken
. . .	

3. Before any row can be entered in the SECTION table, the COURSE_ID to be entered must already exist in the COURSE table (referential integrity). Write an SQL assertion that will enforce this constraint.

4. Write SQL definition commands for each of the following queries:

a. How would you add an attribute, CLASS, to the STUDENT table?

b. How would you remove the IS_REGISTERED table?

c. How would you change the field for FACULTY_NAME from 25 characters to 40 characters?

5. a. Create two different forms of the INSERT command to add a student with a student ID of *65798* and last name *Lopez* to the STUDENT table.

b. Now write a command that will remove Lopez from the STUDENT table.

c. Create an SQL command that will modify the name of course ISM 4212 from 'Database' to 'Introduction to Relational Databases.'

6. Write SQL queries to answer the following questions:

a. Which students have an ID number that is less than 50000?

b. What is the name of the faculty member whose ID is 4756?

c. What is the smallest section number used in the first semester of 2001?

7. Write SQL queries to answer the following questions:

a. How many students are enrolled in Section 2714 in the first semester of 2001?

b. Which faculty members have qualified to teach a course since 1993? List the faculty ID, course, and date of qualification.

8. Write SQL queries to answer the following questions:

a. Which students are enrolled in Database and Networking? (*Hint*: Use the SECTION_ID for each class so you can determine the answer from the IS_REGISTERED table by itself.)

b. Which instructors cannot teach both Syst Analysis and Syst Design?

9. Write SQL queries to answer the following questions:

a. What are the courses included in the SECTION table? List each course only once.

b. List all students in alphabetical order by STUDENT_NAME.

c. List the students who are enrolled in each course in Semester I, 2001. Group the students by the sections in which they are enrolled.

d. List the courses available. Group them by course prefix. (ISM is the only prefix shown but there are many others throughout the university.)

STUDENT (STUDENT_ID, STUDENT_NAME)

STUDENT_ID	STUDENT_NAME
38214	Letersky
54907	Altvater
66324	Aiken
70542	Marra
...	

IS_QUALIFIED (FACULTY_ID, COURSE_ID, DATE_QUALIFIED)

FACULTY_ID	COURSE_ID	DATE_QUALIFIED
2143	ISM 3112	9/1988
2143	ISM 3113	9/1988
3467	ISM 4212	9/1995
3467	ISM 4930	9/1996
4756	ISM 3113	9/1991
4756	ISM 3112	9/1991
...		

FACULTY (FACULTY_ID, FACULTY_NAME)

FACULTY_ID	FACULTY_NAME
2143	Birkin
3487	Berndt
4756	Collins
...	

SECTION (SECTION_ID, COURSE_ID)

SECTION_ID	COURSE_ID
2712	ISM 3113
2713	ISM 3113
2714	ISM 4212
2715	ISM 4930
...	

COURSE (COURSE_ID, COURSE_NAME)

COURSE_ID	COURSE_NAME
ISM 3113	Syst Analysis
ISM 3112	Syst Design
ISM 4212	Database
ISM 4930	Networking
...	

IS_REGISTERED (STUDENT_ID, SECTION_ID, SEMESTER)

STUDENT_ID	SECTION_ID	SEMESTER
38214	2714	I-2001
54907	2714	I-2001
54907	2715	I-2001
66324	2713	I-2001
...		

Figure 7-9
Class scheduling relations (missing IS_ASSIGNED)

Problems and Exercises 10 through 19 are based on the entire Pine Valley Furniture database.

10. Modify the PRODUCT_t table by adding an attribute QTY_ON_HAND that can be used to track the finished goods inventory. The field should be an integer field of five characters and should accept only positive numbers.

11. Enter sample data of your own choosing into QTY_ON HAND in the PRODUCT_t table. Test the modification you made in Problem and Exercise 10 by attempting to update a product by changing the inventory to 10,000 units. Now test

it again by changing the inventory for the product to –10 units. If you do not receive error messages and are successful in making these changes, then you did not establish appropriate constraints in Problem and Exercise 10.

12. Add an order to the ORDER_t table and include a sample value for every attribute.

   a. First, look at the data in the CUSTOMER_t table and enter an order from any one of those customers.

   b. Now, enter an order from a new customer. Unless you have also inserted information about the new customer in the CUSTOMER_t table, your entry of the order data should be rejected. Referential integrity constraints should prevent you from entering an order if there is no information about the customer.

13. a. How many work centers does Pine Valley have?

b. Where are they located?

14. What products have some sort of oak finish?

15. List the customers who live in California or Washington. Order them by zip code, from high to low.

16. Determine the average standard price of each product line.

17. List the employees whose last name begins with an 'L.'

18. Which employees were hired during 1999?

19. For every product that has been ordered, determine the total quantity that has been ordered. List the most popular product first and the least popular, last.

Field Exercises

1. Arrange an interview with a database administrator in an organization in your area. When you interview the database administrator, familiarize yourself with one application that is actively used in the organization. Focus your interview questions toward determining end users' involvement with the application and understanding the extent to which end users must be familiar with SQL. For example, if end users are using SQL, what training do they receive? Do they use an interactive form of SQL for their work or do they use embedded SQL?

2. Arrange another interview with a database administrator in your area. Focus the interview toward understanding the environment within which SQL is used in the organization. Inquire about the version of SQL that is used, and deter-

mine if the same version is used at all locations. If different versions are used, explore any difficulties that the DBA has had in administering the database. Also inquire about any proprietary languages, such as Oracle's PL*SQL, which are being used. Again, learn about possible differences in versions used at different locations and explore any difficulties that occur if different versions are installed.

3. Talk with a database developer at a local organization. Explore the developer's use of SQL in her work. Does the developer use any code-generation facilities or does she write all SQL code herself? Is there a CASE tool, such as Designer 2000, that the developer has at her disposal? If possible, get the database developer to demonstrate any CASE tool that is being used.

References

Codd, E. F. 1970. "A Relational Model of Data for Large Relational Databases." *Communications of the ACM* 13 (June): 77—87.

Date, C. J., and H. Darwen. 1997. *A Guide to the SQL Standard*. Reading, MA: Addison-Wesley.

Gruber, M. 2000. *Mastering SQL*. Alameda, CA: SYBEX.

Gulutzan, P., and T. Petzer. 1999. *SQL-99 Complete, Really*. Lawrence, KS: R&D Books.

Melton, J. 1997. "A Case for SQL Conformance Testing." *Database Programming & Design* 10 (7): 66–69.

Van der Lans, R. F. 1993. *Introduction to SQL*, 2nd ed. Workingham, England: Addison-Wesley.

Further Reading

American National Standards Institute. http://www.ansi.org, 1997–2000. [Information on the ANSI federation and latest national and international standards.]

Bowman, J. S., S. L. Emerson, and M. Darnovsky. 1996. *The Practical SQL Handbook*, 3rd ed. Reading, MA: Addison-Wesley.

Celko, J. 1997. *Joe Celko's SQL Puzzles & Answers*. San Francisco: Morgan Kaufmann.

IEEE Standards Systems/Network Staff. *IEEE Standards Home Page*, http://standards.ieee.org, 2000. [IEEE Standards Association information.]

ODMG Home Page, http://www.odmg.org/, 1993–2000. [Consortium of object-oriented database management system (ODBMS) vendors and interested parties.]

OMG Home Page, http://www.omg.org/, 1997–2000. [Object Management Group: information about CORBA.]

SW Consulting, SA, *IEC—International Electrotechnical Commission—Home Page (English)*, http://www.iec.ch, 2000. [International standards and conformity assessment body for all fields of electrotechnology.]

Tibbs, A. *Welcome to NCITS*, http://www.ncits.org/, Undated. (Accessed December 28, 2000.) [National Committee for Information Technology Standards—used to be Accredited Standard Committee X3.]

Welcome to ISO Online, http://www.iso.ch, December 11, 2000. [Information about the International Organization for Standardization.]

Web Resources

Cramsessions for Oracle certifications, http://www.cramsession.com/cramsession/Oracle/. December 28, 2000. (Study help for Oracle OCP exams. Non-Oracle site.)

Cumming, A. *A Gentle Introduction to SQL,* http://www.dcs.napier.ac.uk/~andrew/sql. December 28, 2000. (An on-line SQL engine is included and examples are mostly from real data.)

Farland, D. *Exam Facts: Introduction to Oracle:SQL and PL/SQL,* http://www.oraclenotes.com/exam1.htm. 2000. (Information about Oracle Certified Profession exams, outlines, references, discussion groups. Non-Oracle site.)

Hoffman, J. *Introduction to Structured Query Language,* http://w3.one.net/~jhoffman/sqltut.htm. December 28, 2000. (Comprehensive ANSI SQL tutorial.)

Hot Oracle!, http://www.hot-oracle.com. December 28, 2000. (Oracle-related site that includes tutorials for SQL*Plus, PL/SQL, Java and Javscript.)

Oracle University. *Self Test Software,* http://education.oracle.com/certification/sts.html. December 28, 2000. (Information about Oracle Certified Professional exams and free sample test questions available. Oracle site.)

SQL Interpreter and Tutorial, http://www.sqlcourse.com/. December 28, 2000. (Subset of ANSI SQL with practice database.)

MOUNTAIN VIEW COMMUNITY HOSPITAL

Project Case

Use the SQL data model constructed for Mountain View Community Hospital in Chapter 4 to complete the project questions and project exercises.

PROJECT QUESTIONS

1. What version of SQL will you use to do the project exercises?

2. Which CASE tools are available to be used to do the project exercises?

PROJECT EXERCISES

1. Create in SQL the Mountain View Community Hospital database for the conceptual data model you have constructed in the previous chapters. Use the information provided in the Project Case sections at the end of Chapters 3, 4, 5, and 6 to help you choose column data types, lengths, indexes, etc.

2. If you did not remember to establish primary and foreign keys in the preceding question, create the SQL assertions necessary to accomplish that.

3. Select at least a portion of your database and populate it with sample data. For example, you may wish to work with the staff, care-center, patient part of your database. Or you may be interested in working with the vendor, medical/surgical items, tests, and patients part of your database. Be prepared to defend the sample test data that you insert into your database. How do the actual values you are using help you to test the functionality of your database?

4. Now write and test some queries that will work using your sample data. Write queries that:

   a. select information from only one of the tables

   b. aggregate information from one attribute in a table

   c. try out the various functions such as MIN, MAX, and AVG

Chapter **8**

Advanced SQL

LEARNING OBJECTIVES

After studying this chapter, you should be able to:

- Define the following key terms: **join, equi-join, natural join, outer join, correlated subquery, user-defined datatype, Persistent Stored Modules (SQL/PSM), trigger, function, procedure, embedded SQL,** and **dynamic SQL**.
- Write single and multiple table queries using SQL commands.
- Define three types of join commands and use SQL to write these commands.
- Write noncorrelated and correlated subqueries and know when to write each.
- Establish referential integrity using SQL.
- Understand common uses of database triggers and stored procedures.
- Discuss the SQL-99 standard and explain its enchancements and extensions to SQL-92.

INTRODUCTION

The previous chapter introduced SQL and explored its capabilities for querying one table. The real power of the relational model derives from its storage of data in many related entities. Taking advantage of this approach to data storage requires establishing the relationships and constructing queries that use data from multiple tables. This chapter demonstrates multiple-table queries in some detail. Different approaches to getting results from more than one table are demonstrated, including the use of subqueries, inner and outer joins, and union joins.

Once understanding of basic SQL syntax is gained, it is important to understand how SQL is used in the creation of applications. Triggers, small modules of code that include SQL, execute automatically when a particular condition, defined in the trigger, exists. Procedures are similar modules of code, but must be called before they execute. SQL commands are often embedded within modules written in a host language, such as C or Java. Dynamic SQL creates SQL statements on the fly, inserting parameter values as needed, and is essential to Web applications. Brief introductions and examples of each of these methods is included in this chapter. Some of the enhancements and extensions to SQL included in SQL-99 are also covered.

Completion of this chapter gives the student an overview of SQL and some of the ways in which it may be used. There are many additional features, often referred to as "obscure" in more detailed SQL texts, that will be needed in particular situations. Practice with the syntax included in this chapter will give the student a good start toward mastery of SQL.

PROCESSING MULTIPLE TABLES

Now that we have explored some of the possibilities for working with a single table, we will work with multiple tables simultaneously. The power of the RDBMS is realized when working with multiple tables. When relationships exist between tables they can be linked together in queries. Remember from Chapter 5 that these relationships are established by including a common column(s) in each table where a relationship is needed. Often this is accomplished by setting up a primary key–foreign key relationship, where the foreign key in one table references the primary key in another and the values in both come from a common domain. We can use these columns to establish the link between two tables by finding common values in the columns. For example in Figure 7-3, Customer_ID in Order_t matches Customer_ID in Customer_t. When we compare them, we learn that Contemporary Casuals placed orders # 1001 and 1010 because Contemporary Casuals' Customer_ID is 1, and Order_t shows that Order_ID 1001 and 1010 were placed by customer # 1. In a relational system, data from related tables are combined into one result table or view and then displayed or used as input to a form or report definition.

The linking of related tables varies among different types of relational systems. In SQL, the WHERE clause of the SELECT command is also used for multiple table operations. In fact, SELECT can include references to two, three, or more tables in the same command. As illustrated below, SQL has two ways to use SELECT for combining data from related tables.

Join: A relational operation that causes two tables with a common domain to be combined into a single table or view.

The most frequently used relational operation, which brings together data from two or more related tables into one resultant table, is called a **join**. SQL specifies a join implicitly by referring in a WHERE clause to the matching of common columns over which tables are joined. Two tables may be joined when each contains a column that shares a common domain with the other. The result of a join operation is a single table. Selected columns from all the tables are included. Each row returned contains data from rows in the different input tables where values for the common columns match.

An important rule of thumb in forming join conditions is the following: There should be one condition within the WHERE clause for each pair of tables being joined. Thus, if two tables are to be combined, one condition would be necessary, but if three tables (A, B, and C) are to be combined, then two conditions would be necessary because there are two pairs of tables (A-B and B-C), and so forth.

There are several possible types of joins in relational database queries, although each SQL implementation may support only some of these types. Four types of joins are described in this chapter: equi-joins, natural joins, outer joins, and union join.

Equi-join

Equi-join: A join in which the joining condition is based on equality between values in the common columns. Common columns appear (redundantly) in the result table.

With an **equi-join**, the joining condition is based on *equality* between values in the common columns. For example, if we want to know the names of customers who have placed orders, that information is kept in two tables, CUSTOMER_T and ORDER_T. (Note, we will use all capital letters for table and attribute names to emphasize the use of Oracle database elements.) It is necessary to match customers with their orders and then collect the information about name and order number in one table in order to answer our question.

Query: What are the names of all customers who have placed orders?

```
SELECT CUSTOMER_T.CUSTOMER_ID, ORDER_T.CUSTOMER_ID,
CUSTOMER_NAME, ORDER_ID
  FROM CUSTOMER_T, ORDER_T
        WHERE CUSTOMER_T.CUSTOMER_ID = ORDER_T.CUSTOMER_ID;
```

Result:

CUSTOMER_ID	CUSTOMER_ID	CUSTOMER_NAME	ORDER_ID
1	1	Contemporary Casuals	1001
8	8	California Classics	1002
15	15	Mountain Scenes	1003
5	5	Impressions	1004
3	3	Home Furnishings	1005
2	2	Value Furniture	1006
11	11	American Euro Lifestyles	1007
12	12	Battle Creek Furniture	1008
4	4	Eastern Furniture	1009
1	1	Contemporary Casuals	1010

10 rows selected.

The redundant CUSTOMER_ID columns, one from each table, demonstrate that the customer IDs have been matched, and that matching gives one row for each order placed. The importance of achieving the match between tables can be seen if the WHERE clause is omitted. That query will return all combinations of customers and orders, or 150 rows, which is not a useful or meaningful result. The number of rows is equal to the number of rows in each table, multiplied together (10 orders × 15 customers = 150 rows). This is called a Cartesian join.

Also, to demonstrate a difference between Oracle SQL and Access SQL, the syntax for this query as generated by Access is shown here.

Query: What are the names of all customers who have placed orders?

```
SELECT Customer_t.Customer_ID, Order_t.Customer_ID,
Customer_t.Customer_name, Order_t.Order_ID
FROM Customer_t INNER JOIN Order_t ON Customer_t.Customer_ID =
Order_t.Customer_ID;
```

Result: Same as previous query.

The join is denoted as an *inner join* between Customer_t and Order_t. The WHERE clause is represented by the clause ON Customer_t.Customer_ID = Order_t.Customer_ID. The INNER JOIN . . . ON is SQL-92 syntax and is expected to become more common over time. Notice that the join syntax has been moved to the FROM clause, leaving the WHERE clause to function only as a filter.

Natural Join

A **natural join** is the same as an equi-join, except that it is performed over matching columns that have been defined with the same name and one of the duplicate columns is eliminated. The natural join is the most commonly used form of join operation. The SQL command to find customer names and order numbers leaves out one CUSTOMER_ID. Notice that CUSTOMER_ID must still be qualified because there is still ambiguity; CUSTOMER_ID exists in both CUSTOMER_T and

Natural join: Same as equi-join except one of the duplicate columns is eliminated in the result table.

ORDER_T, and therefore it must be specified from which table SQL*Plus should pick CUSTOMER_ID.

> **Query:** For each customer who has placed an order, what is the customer's name and order number?

```
SELECT CUSTOMER_T.CUSTOMER_ID, CUSTOMER_NAME, ORDER_ID
  FROM CUSTOMER_T, ORDER_T
      WHERE CUSTOMER_T.CUSTOMER_ID = ORDER_T.CUSTOMER_ID;
```

Note that the order of table names in the FROM clause is immaterial. The query optimizer of the DBMS will decide in which sequence to process each table. Whether indexes exist on common columns will influence the sequence in which tables are processed, as will which table is on the 1 and which is on the M side of 1:M relationships. If a query takes significantly different amounts of time depending on the order in which tables are listed in the FROM clause, the DBMS does not have a very good query optimizer.

Outer Join

Often in joining two tables, we find that a row in one table does not have a matching row in the other table. For example, several CUSTOMER_ID numbers do not appear in the ORDER_T table (see Figure 7-3). We can assume this is because those customers have not placed orders since 10/21/2000, or their orders are not included in our very short sample ORDER_T table. As a result, the equi-join and natural join shown above do not include all of the customers shown in CUSTOMER_T.

Outer join: A join in which rows that do not have matching values in common columns are nevertheless included in the result table.

Of course the organization may be very interested in identifying those customers who have not placed orders. They may want to contact them to encourage new orders, or they may be interested in analyzing these customers in order to discern why they are not ordering. Using an **outer join** produces this information: rows that do not have matching values in common columns are also included in the result table. Null values appear in columns where there is not a match between tables.

Outer joins can be handled by the major RDBMS vendors, but the syntax used to accomplish an outer join still varies across vendors. The example given here uses ANSI standard syntax. Where an outer join is not available explicitly, use UNION and NOT EXISTS (discussed later in this chapter) to carry out an outer join. Here is an outer join.

> **Query:** List customer name, identification number, and order number for all customers listed in the CUSTOMER table. Include the customer identification number and name even if there is no order available for that customer.

```
SELECT CUSTOMER_T.CUSTOMER_ID, CUSTOMER_NAME, ORDER_ID
  FROM CUSTOMER_T LEFT OUTER JOIN ORDER_T
      WHERE CUSTOMER_T.CUSTOMER_ID = ORDER_T.CUSTOMER_ID;
```

The syntax LEFT OUTER JOIN was selected because the CUSTOMER_T table was named first, and it is the table from which we wish all rows returned, regardless of whether there is a matching order in the ORDER-T table. Had we reversed the order in which the tables were listed, the same results would be obtained by requesting a RIGHT OUTER JOIN. It is also possible to request a FULL OUTER JOIN. In that case, all rows would be matched and returned, including any rows that do not have a match in the other table. INNER JOINs are much more common than OUTER JOINs, as outer joins are only necessary when one expects that one may be missing necessary information by using an inner join.

It should also be noted that the OUTER JOIN syntax does not apply easily to a join condition of more than two tables. The results returned will vary according to the vendor, so be sure to test any outer join syntax that involves more than two tables until you understand how it will be interpreted by the DBMS being used.

Also, the results table from an outer join may indicate NULL as the values for columns in the second table where no match was achieved. If those columns could have NULL as a data value, one cannot know whether the row returned is a matched row or an unmatched row unless one runs another query that checks for null values in the base table or view. And, a column that is defined as NOT NULL may be assigned a NULL value in the results table of an OUTER JOIN.

Result:

CUSTOMER_ID	CUSTOMER_NAME	ORDER_ID
1	Contemporary Casuals	1001
1	Contemporary Casuals	1010
2	Value Furniture	1006
3	Home Furnishings	1005
4	Eastern Furniture	1009
5	Impressions	1004
6	Furniture Gallery	
7	Period Furnishings	
8	California Classics	1002
9	M & H Casual Furniture	
10	Seminole Interiors	
11	American Euro Lifestyles	1007
12	Battle Creek Furniture	1008
13	Heritage Furnishings	
14	Kaneohe Homes	
15	Mountain Scenes	1003

16 rows selected.

The advantage of the outer join is that information is not lost. Here, all customer names were returned whether or not they had placed an order. Requesting a RIGHT OUTER join would return all orders. (Since referential integrity requires that every order be associated with a valid customer ID, that right outer join would only assure that referential integrity is being enforced.)

Query: List customer name, identification number, and order number for all orders listed in the ORDER table. Include the order number even if there is no customer name and identification number available.

```
SELECT CUSTOMER_T.CUSTOMER_ID, CUSTOMER_NAME, ORDER_ID
   FROM CUSTOMER_T RIGHT OUTER JOIN ORDER_T ON
        CUSTOMER_T.CUSTOMER_ID = ORDER_T.CUSTOMER_ID;
```

Union Join

SQL-99 also allows for a UNION JOIN, which is not implemented in all DBMS products yet. The results of a UNION JOIN will be a table that includes all of the data from each table that is joined. The results table will contain all of the columns from each table and will contain an instance for each row of data included from each table. Thus, a UNION JOIN of the CUSTOMER_T table (15 customers and 6 attributes) and the ORDER_T table (10 orders and 3 attributes) will return a results table of 25 rows and 9 columns. Assuming that each original table contained no nulls, each customer row in the results table will contain 3 attributes with assigned null values and each order row will contain 6 attributes with assigned null values. Do not confuse this command with the UNION command that joins multiple SELECT statements and is covered later in this chapter.

CUSTOMER_ID	CUSTOMER_NAME	CUSTOMER_ADDRESS	CITY	ST	POSTAL_CODE	
2	Value Furniture	15145 S.W. 17th St.	Plano	TX	75094	
2	Value Furniture	15145 S.W. 17th St.	Plano	TX	75094	
2	Value Furniture	15145 S.W. 17th St.	Plano	TX	75094	

ORDER_ID	ORDER-DAT	QUANTITY	PRODUCT_NAME	UNIT_PRICE	(QUANTITY*UNIT_PRICE)
1006	24-OCT-00	1	Entertainment Center	650	650
1006	24-OCT-00	2	Writer's Desk	325	650
1006	24-OCT-00	2	Dining Table	800	1600

Figure 8-1
Results from a four-table join (edited for readability)

Sample Multiple Join Involving Four Tables

Much of the power of the relational model comes from its ability to work with the relations among the objects in the database. Designing a database so that data about each object is kept in separate tables simplifies maintenance and data integrity. The capability to relate the objects to each other by joining the tables provides critical business information and reports to employees. While the examples provided in Chapters 7 and 8 are simple, constructed to provide a basic understanding of SQL, it is important to realize that these commands can be built into much more complex queries that provide exactly the information needed for a report or process.

Here is a sample join query that involves a four-table join. This query produces a result table that includes the information needed to create an invoice for order #1006. We want the customer information, the order and order line information, and the product information, so we will need to join four tables.

Query: Assemble all information necessary to create an invoice for order number 1006.

```
SELECT CUSTOMER_T.CUSTOMER_ID, CUSTOMER_NAME,
CUSTOMER_ADDRESS, CITY, STATE, POSTAL_CODE, ORDER_T.ORDER_ID,
ORDER_DATE, QUANTITY, PRODUCT_NAME, UNIT_PRICE, (QUANTITY *
UNIT_PRICE)
    FROM CUSTOMER_T, ORDER_T, ORDER_LINE_T, PRODUCT_T
        WHERE CUSTOMER_T.CUSTOMER_ID = ORDER_T.CUSTOMER_ID
            AND ORDER_T.ORDER_ID = ORDER_LINE_T.ORDER_ID
            AND ORDER_LINE_T.PRODUCT_ID = PRODUCT_T.PRODUCT_ID
            AND ORDER_T.ORDER_ID = 1006;
```

The results of the query are shown in Figure 8-1. Remember, since the join involves four tables, there will be three column join conditions.

Subqueries

The preceding SQL examples illustrate one of the two basic approaches for joining two tables: the joining technique. SQL also provides the subquery technique, which involves placing an inner query (SELECT, FROM, WHERE) within a WHERE or HAVING clause of another (outer) query. The inner query provides values for the search condition of the outer query. Such queries are referred to as subqueries or nested subqueries, and may be nested multiple times.

Sometimes either the joining or the subquery technique may be used to accomplish the same result, and different people will have different preferences about which technique to use. Other times, only a join or a subquery will work. *The joining technique is useful when data from several relations are to be retrieved and displayed, and the relationships are not necessarily nested.* Let's compare two queries that return the same result. Both answer the question, What is the name and address of the customer who placed order #1008? First, we'll use a join query.

Query: What is the name and address of the customer who placed order number 1008?

```
SELECT CUSTOMER_NAME, CUSTOMER_ADDRESS, CITY, STATE, POSTAL_CODE
    FROM CUSTOMER_T, ORDER_T
        WHERE CUSTOMER_T.CUSTOMER_ID = ORDER_T.CUSTOMER_ID AND
            ORDER_ID = 1008;
```

Now, look at the equivalent query using the subquery technique.

Query: What is the name and address of the customer who placed order number 1008?

```
SELECT CUSTOMER_NAME, CUSTOMER_ADDRESS, CITY, STATE, POSTAL_CODE
    FROM CUSTOMER_T
        WHERE CUSTOMER_T.CUSTOMER_ID =
            (SELECT ORDER_T.CUSTOMER_ID
                FROM ORDER_T
                    WHERE ORDER_ID = 1008);
```

Notice that the subquery, enclosed in parentheses, follows the form learned for constructing SQL queries and this one could stand on its own as an independent query. *The subquery approach may be used for this query because we only need to display data from the table in the outer query.* The value for ORDER_ID does not appear in the query result—it is used as the selection criterion in the outer query. To include data from the subquery in the result, use the join technique since data from a subquery cannot be included in the final results.

We know in advance that the preceding subquery will return at most one value, the CUSTOMER_ID associated with ORDER_ID #1008. The result will be empty if an order with that ID does not exist. A subquery can also return a list of values (with zero, one, or many entries) by using the keyword IN. For example, which customers have placed orders? Here is a query that will answer that question.

Query: Which customers have placed orders?

```
SELECT CUSTOMER_NAME
    FROM CUSTOMER_T
        WHERE CUSTOMER_ID IN
            (SELECT DISTINCT CUSTOMER_ID
                FROM ORDER_T);
```

This query produces the result below. DISTINCT is used in the subquery since we do not care how many orders a customer has placed as long as they have placed an order. For each customer identified in the ORDER_T table, that customer's name has been returned from CUSTOMER_T. (You will study this query again in Figure 8-2a.)

Result:

CUSTOMER_NAME
Contemporary Casuals
Value Furniture
Home Furnishings
Eastern Furniture
Impressions
California Classics
American Euro Lifestyles
Battle Creek Furniture
Mountain Scenes

9 rows selected.

The qualifiers NOT, ANY, and ALL may be used in front of IN or with logical operators such as =, >, and <. Since IN works with zero, one, or many values from the inner query, many programmers simply use IN instead of = for all queries, even if the equal sign would work. The next example shows the use of NOT and it also demonstrates that a join can be used in an inner query.

Query: Which customers have not placed any orders for computer desks?

```
SELECT CUSTOMER_NAME
   FROM CUSTOMER_T
         WHERE CUSTOMER_ID NOT IN
               (SELECT CUSTOMER_ID
                     FROM ORDER_T, ORDER_LINE_T, PRODUCT_T
                           WHERE ORDER_T.ORDER_ID =
                                 ORDER_LINE_T.ORDER_ID AND
                                 ORDER_LINE_T.PRODUCT_ID =
                                 PRODUCT_T.PRODUCT_ID
                                 AND PRODUCT_NAME = 'Computer Desk');
```

Result:

CUSTOMER_NAME
Value Furniture
Home Furnishings
Eastern Furniture
Furniture Gallery
Period Funiture
M H Casual Furniture
Seminole Interiors
American Euro Lifestyles
Heritage Furnishings
Kaneohe Homes

10 rows selected.

The result shows that 10 of our customers have not yet ordered computer desks. The inner query returned a list of all customers who had ordered computer desks. The outer query listed the names of those customers who were not in the list returned by the inner query.

Two other conditions associated with using subqueries are EXISTS and NOT EXISTS. These keywords are included in an SQL query at the same location where IN would be, just prior to the beginning of the subquery. EXISTS will take a value of *true* if the subquery returns an intermediate results table which contains one or more rows, and *false* if no rows are returned. NOT EXISTS will take a value of *true* if no rows are returned, and *false* if one or more rows are returned. Consider the following SQL statement, which includes EXISTS.

Query: What are the order numbers for all orders that have included furniture finished in natural ash?

```
SELECT DISTINCT ORDER_ID FROM ORDER_LINE_T
WHERE EXISTS
   (SELECT *
         FROM PRODUCT_T
               WHERE PRODUCT_ID = ORDER_LINE_T.PRODUCT_ID
                     AND PRODUCT_FINISH = 'Natural Ash');
```

The subquery checks to see if the finish for the product on an order line is natural ash. The main query picks out the order numbers for all orders that have included furniture finished in natural ash. There have been seven such orders, as the result shows. (We discuss this query further in Figure 8.2b.)

Result:

ORDER_ID
1001
1002
1003
1006
1007
1008
1009

7 rows selected.

When EXISTS or NOT EXISTS is used in a subquery, the select list of the subquery will usually just select all columns (SELECT *) as a placeholder because it doesn't matter which columns are returned. The purpose of the subquery is testing to see if any rows fit the conditions, not to return values from particular columns. The columns that will be displayed are determined by the outer query. An EXISTS subquery is almost always a correlated subquery, as described next. Queries containing the keyword NOT EXISTS will return a results table when no rows are found that satisfy the subquery.

In summary, use the subquery approach when qualifications are nested or when qualifications are easily understood in a nested way. While SQL*Plus allows a subquery to return more than one column, most systems allow pairwise joining of *one and only one column* in an inner query with *one* column in an outer query. An exception to this is when a subquery is used with the EXISTS keyword. Data can be displayed only from the table(s) referenced in the outer query. Up to 16 levels of nesting are typically supported. Queries are processed inside out, although another type of subquery, a correlated subquery, is processed outside in.

Correlated Subqueries

In the first subquery example, it was necessary to examine the inner query before considering the outer query. That is, the result of the inner query was used to limit the processing of the outer query. In contrast, **correlated subqueries** use the result of the outer query to determine the processing of the inner query. That is, the inner query is somewhat different for each row referenced in the outer query. In this case, the inner query must be computed for *each* outer row, whereas in the earlier examples, the inner query was computed *only once* for all rows processed in the outer query. Figures 8-2a and 8-2b depict the different processing order that occurs for each of the examples from the previous section on subqueries.

Look at this query, which lists the details of the product that has a higher unit price than any other product in PRODUCT_T.

Correlated subquery: In SQL, a subquery in which processing the inner query depends on data from the outer query.

Query: List the details about the product with the highest unit price.

```
SELECT PRODUCT_NAME, PRODUCT_FINISH, UNIT_PRICE
  FROM PRODUCT_T PA
        WHERE UNIT_PRICE > ALL
            (SELECT UNIT_PRICE FROM PRODUCT_T PB
                WHERE PB.PRODUCT_ID != PA.PRODUCT_ID);
```

Here is the result—the dining table has a higher unit price than any other product.

Result

PRODUCT_NAME	PRODUCT_FINISH	UNIT_PRICE
Dining Table	Natural Ash	800

The logic of this SQL statement is that the subquery will be executed once for each product to be sure that no other product has a higher unit price. Notice that we are comparing a table to itself and that we are able to do this by giving the table two aliases, PA and PB. First, PRODUCT_ID 1, the end table, will be considered. When the subquery is executed, it will return the prices of every product except the one being considered in the outer query. Then, the outer query will check to see if the unit price for the product being considered is greater than all of the unit prices returned by the subquery. If it is, it will be returned as the result of the query. If not, the next value in the outer query will be considered, and the inner query will return a list of all the unit prices for the other products. The list returned by the inner query changes as each product in the outer query changes; that makes it a correlated subquery. Can you identify a special set of unit prices for which this query will not yield the desired result?

Figure 8-2
Subquery processing
(a) Processing a noncorrelated
subquery

```
SELECT CUSTOMER_NAME
            FROM CUSTOMER_T
                    WHERE CUSTOMER_ID IN

                        (SELECT DISTINCT CUSTOMER_ID
                            FROM ORDER_T);
```

1. The subquery (shown in the box) is processed first and an intermediate results table created:

CUSTOMER_ID
1
8
15
5
3
2
11
12
4

9 rows selected.

2. The outer query returns the requested customer information for each customer included in the intermediate results table:

CUSTOMER_NAME

Contemporary Casuals
Value Furniture
Home Furnishings
Eastern Furniture
Impressions
California Classics
American Euro Lifestyles
Battle Creek Furniture
Mountain Scenes
9 rows selected.

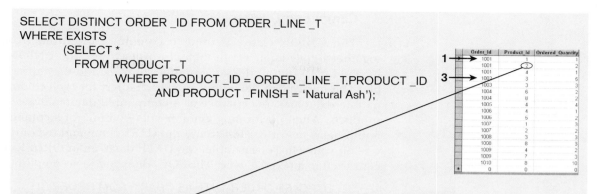

```
SELECT DISTINCT ORDER _ID FROM ORDER _LINE _T
WHERE EXISTS
        (SELECT *
            FROM PRODUCT _T
                WHERE PRODUCT _ID = ORDER _LINE _T.PRODUCT _ID
                    AND PRODUCT _FINISH = 'Natural Ash');
```

		Product_ID	Product_Description	Product_Finish	Standard_Price	Product_Line_Id
▶	+	1	End Table	Cherry	$175.00	10001
	+	2	Coffee Table	Natural Ash	$200.00	20001
	+	3	Computer Desk	Natural Ash	$375.00	20001
	+	4	Entertainment Center	Natural Maple	$650.00	30001
	+	5	Writer's Desk	Cherry	$325.00	10001
	+	6	8-Drawer Dresser	White Ash	$750.00	20001
	+	7	Dining Table	Natural Ash	$800.00	20001
	+	8	Computer Desk	Walnut	$250.00	30001
*		(AutoNumber)			$0.00	

1. The first order ID is selected from ORDER _LINE _T: ORDER _ID =1001.

2. The subquery is evaluated to see if any product in that order has a natural ash finish. Product 2 does, and is part of the order. EXISTS is valued as *true* and the order ID is added to the result table.

3. The next order ID is selected from ORDER _LINE _T: ORDER _ID =1002.

4. The subquery is evaluated to see if the product ordered has a natural ash finish. It does. EXISTS is valued as true and the order ID is added to the result table.

5. Processing continues through each order ID. Orders 1004, 1005, and 1010 are not included in the result table because they do not include any furniture with a natural ash finish. The final result table is shown in the text on page 303.

Figure 8-2
(continued)
(b) Processing a correlated subquery

Using Derived Tables

Subqueries are not limited to inclusion in the WHERE clause. They may also be used in the FROM clause, creating a temporary derived table that is used in the query. Creating a derived table that has an aggregate value in it, such as MAX, AVG, or MIN allows the aggregate to be used in the WHERE clause. Here, pieces of furniture that exceed the average standard price are listed.

Query: Which products have a standard price that is higher than the average standard price?

```
SELECT PRODUCT_DESCRIPTION, STANDARD_PRICE, AVGPRICE
    FROM
            (SELECT AVG(STANDARD_PRICE) AVGPRICE FROM PRODUCT_T),
            PRODUCT_T
                WHERE STANDARD_PRICE > AVGPRICE;
```

Result:

PRODUCT_DESCRIPTION	STANDARD_PRICE	AVGPRICE
Entertainment Center	650	440.625
8-Drawer Dresser	750	440.625
Dining Table	800	440.625

Combining Queries

The UNION clause is used to combine the output from multiple queries together into a single result table. In order to use the UNION clause, each query involved must output the same number of rows, and they must be UNION-compatible. This means that the output from each query for each column should be of compatible datatypes. Acceptance as a compatible datatype varies among the DBMS products. When performing a union where output for a column will merge two different datatypes, it is safest to use the CAST command to control the datatype conversion yourself. For example, the DATE datatype in ORDER_T might need to be converted to a text datatype. The SQL command to accomplish this would be:

SELECT CAST(ORDER_DATE AS CHAR) FROM ORDER_T;

The example query below determines the customer(s) who has purchased the largest quantity of any Pine Valley product, and the customer(s) who has purchased the smallest quantity, and returns the results in one table.

Query:

```
SELECT C1.CUSTOMER_ID,CUSTOMER_NAME,ORDERED_QUANTITY, 'LARGEST
QUANTITY' QUANTITY
    FROM CUSTOMER_T C1,ORDER_T O1, ORDER_LINE_T Q1
        WHERE C1.CUSTOMER_ID =O1.CUSTOMER_ID
        AND O1.ORDER_ID =Q1.ORDER_ID
        AND ORDERED_QUANTITY =
            (SELECT MAX(ORDERED_QUANTITY)
            FROM ORDER_LINE_T)
UNION
SELECT C1.CUSTOMER_ID,CUSTOMER_NAME,ORDERED_QUANTITY, 'SMALLEST
QUANTITY'
    FROM CUSTOMER_T C1,ORDER_T O1, ORDER_LINE_T Q1
        WHERE C1.CUSTOMER_ID =O1.CUSTOMER_ID
        AND O1.ORDER_ID =Q1.ORDER_ID
        AND ORDERED_QUANTITY =
            (SELECT MIN(ORDERED_QUANTITY)
            FROM ORDER_LINE_T)
ORDER BY ORDERED_QUANTITY
```

Notice that an expression QUANTITY has been created in which the strings 'Smallest Quantity' and 'Largest Quantity' have been inserted for readability. The ORDER BY clause has been used to organize the order in which the rows of output are listed:

Result:

CUSTOMER_ID	CUSTOMER_NAME	ORDERED_QUANTITY	QUANTITY
1	Contemporary Casuals	1	Smallest Quantity
2	Value Furniture	1	Smallest Quantity
1	Contemporary Casuals	10	Largest Quantity

Conditional Expressions

Establishing IF-THEN-ELSE logical processing within an SQL statement can now be accomplished by using the CASE keyword in a statement. Figure 8–3 gives the CASE syntax, which actually has four forms. The CASE form can be constructed using either an expression that equates to a value or a predicate. The predicate form is based on three-value logic, (true, false, don't know) but allows for more complex operations. The value expression form requires a match to the value expression.

Figure 8-3
CASE conditional syntax

```
{CASE expression
{WHEN expression
THEN {expression | NULL}} . . .
 | {WHEN predicate
THEN {expression | NULL}} . . .
[ELSE {expression   NULL}]
END }
 | ( NULLIF (expression, expression) }
 | ( COALESCE (expression . . .) }
```

NULLIF and COALESCE are the keywords associated with the other two forms of the CASE expression.

ENSURING TRANSACTION INTEGRITY

Relational DBMSs are no different from other types of database managers in that one of their primary responsibilities is to ensure that data maintenance is properly and completely handled. Data maintenance is defined in units of work called transactions, which involve one or more data manipulation commands. A transaction is the complete set of closely related update commands that must all be done, or none of them done, for the database to remain valid. Consider Figure 8-4. For example, when an order is entered into the Pine Valley database, all of the items ordered should be entered at the same time. Thus, either all ORDER_LINE_T rows from this form are to be entered, along with all the information in ORDER_T, or none of them should be entered. Here, the business transaction is the complete order, not the individual items that are ordered. What we need are commands to define the boundaries of a transaction, to commit the work of a transaction as a permanent change to the database, and to purposely and properly abort a transaction, if necessary. In addition, we need data recovery services to clean up after abnormal termination of database processing in the middle of a transaction. Perhaps the order form is accurate, but in

Figure 8-4
An SQL transaction sequence (in pseudocode)

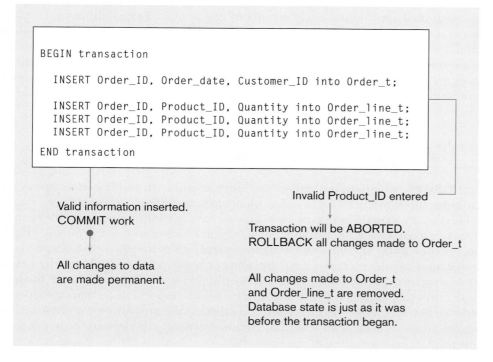

the middle of entering the order, the computer system malfunctions or loses power. In this case, we do not want some of the changes made and not others. It's all or nothing at all, if we want a valid database.

When a single SQL command constitutes a transaction, some RDBMSs will automatically commit or rollback after the command is run. With a user-defined transaction, however, where multiple SQL commands need to be run and either entirely committed or entirely rolled back, explicit commands to manage the transaction are needed. Many systems will have BEGIN TRANSACTION and END TRANSACTION commands, which are used to mark the boundaries of a logical unit of work. BEGIN TRANSACTION creates a log file and starts recording all changes (insertions, deletions, and updates) to the database in this file. END TRANSACTION or COMMIT WORK takes the contents of the log file and applies them to the database (thus making the changes permanent) and then empties the log file. ROLLBACK WORK asks SQL to empty the log file. There is also an AUTOCOMMIT (ON/OFF) command in some RDBMSs which specifies whether changes are made permanent after each data modification command (ON) or only when work is explicitly made permanent (OFF) by the COMMIT WORK command.

User-defined transactions can improve system performance because transactions will be processed as sets rather than as individual transactions, thus reducing system overhead. When AUTOCOMMIT is set to OFF, changes will not be made automatically until the end of a transaction is indicated. When AUTOCOMMIT is set to ON, changes will be made automatically at the end of each SQL statement; this would not allow for user-defined transactions to be committed or rolled back only as a whole.

SET AUTOCOMMIT is an interactive command, so a given user session can be dynamically controlled for appropriate integrity measures. Each SQL INSERT, UPDATE, and DELETE command typically works on only one table at a time. Some data maintenance requires updating of multiple tables for the work to be complete. Therefore, these transaction integrity commands are important in clearly defining whole units of database changes that must be completed in full for the database to retain integrity.

Further, some SQL systems have concurrency controls that handle the updating of a shared database by concurrent users. These can journalize database changes, so that a database can be recovered after abnormal terminations in the middle of a transaction. They can also undo erroneous transactions. For example, in a banking application, the update of a bank account balance by two concurrent users should be cumulative. Such controls are transparent to the user in SQL; no user programming is needed to ensure proper control of concurrent access to data. To ensure the integrity of a particular database, be sensitive to transaction integrity and recovery issues and make sure that application programmers are appropriately informed of when these commands are to be used.

DATA DICTIONARY FACILITIES

RDBMSs store database definition information in system-created tables; we can consider these system tables as a data dictionary. Becoming familiar with the systems tables for any RDBMS being used will provide valuable information, whether you are a user or a database administrator. Since the information is stored in tables, it can be accessed by using SQL SELECT statements that can generate reports about system usage, user privileges, constraints, etc. Further, a user who understands the systems table structure can extend existing tables or build other tables to enhance the built-in features (for example, to include data on who is responsible for data integrity). A user is, however, often restricted from modifying the structure or contents of the system tables directly, since the DBMS maintains them and depends on them for its interpretation and parsing of queries.

Each RDBMS keeps various internal tables for these definitions. In Oracle8*i*, there are 98 data dictionary views for database administrators to use. Many of these views, or subsets of the DBA view (that information relevant to an individual user), are also available to users who do not possess DBA privileges. Those tables' names begin with USER or ALL rather than DBA. Here is a list of those tables (accessible to DBAs) that keep information about tables, clusters, columns, and security. There are also tables related to storage, objects, indexes, locks, auditing, exports, and distributed environments.

DBA_TABLES	Describes all tables in the database.
DBA_TAB_COMMENTS	Comments on all tables in the database.
DBA_CLUSTERS	Describes all clusters in the database.
DBA_TAB_COLUMNS	Describes columns of all tables, views, and clusters.
DBA_COL_PRIVS	Includes all grants on columns in the database.
DBA_COL_COMMENTS	Comments on all columns in tables and views.
DBA_CONSTRAINTS	Constraint definitions on all tables in the database.
DBA_CLU_COLUMNS	Maps table columns to cluster columns.
DBA_CONS_COLUMNS	Information about all columns in constraint definitions.
DBA_USERS	Information about all users of the database.
DBA_SYS_PRIVS	Describes system privileges granted to users and to roles.
DBA_ROLES	Describes all roles that exist in the database.
DBA_PROFILES	Includes resources limits assigned to each profile.
DBA_ROLE_PRIVS	Describes roles granted to users and to other roles.
DBA_TAB_PRIVS	Describes all grants on objects in the database.

To give an idea of the type of information found in the system tables, consider DBA_USERS. DBA_USERS contains information about the valid users of the database, including user names, user IDs, encrypted passwords, default tablespace, temporary tablespace, date created, and profile assigned. DBA_TAB_COLUMNS has 15 attributes, including owner of each table, table name, column name, data type, data length, precision, and scale, among others. An SQL query against DBA_TABLES to find out who owns PRODUCT_T is shown below.

Query: Who is the owner of the PRODUCT table?

```
SELECT OWNER, TABLE_NAME
  FROM DBA_TABLES
     WHERE TABLE_NAME = 'PRODUCT_T';
```

Result:

OWNER	TABLE_NAME
MPRESCOTT	PRODUCT_T

SQL-99 ENHANCEMENTS
AND EXTENSIONS TO SQL

The previous sections of Chapters 7 and 8 have demonstrated the power and simplicity of SQL. However, readers with a strong interest in business analysis may well have wondered about the limited set of statistical functions available. Programmers familiar with other languages may have wondered how variables will be defined, flow control established, or **user-defined datatypes (UDTs)** created. And, as programming becomes more object-oriented, how is SQL going to adjust? SQL-99 has extended

User-defined datatype (UDT): SQL-99 allows users to define their own datatype by making it a subclass of a standard type or creating a type that behaves as an object. UDTs may also have defined functions and methods.

SQL by providing more programming capabilities. An amendment has been proposed that will standardize additional statistical functions. And, one begins to understand how the SQL standard will be modified to encompass object-oriented concepts.

Proposed Analytical Functions

A proposed amendment to SQL-99, Amendment 1, would add a set of analytical functions, referred to as OLAP (on-line analytical processing) functions, as SQL language extensions. Most of the functions have been implemented in Oracle8*i* R2, DB2 6.2, and Teradata V2R4 already. As the standard has not been finally established by early 2001, the implementations of these functions do not necessarily follow the proposed standard exactly. The amendment is an important development because it addresses the needs for analytical capabilities within the database engine. Linear regressions, correlations, and moving averages may now be calculated without moving the data outside the database. Over time, once the amendment is official, vendor implementations will adhere strictly to the standard and become more similar.

Thirty-two new functions are proposed. Table 8-1 lists the proposed functions. Both statistical and numeric functions are included. Functions such as ROW_NUMBER and RANK will allow the developer to work much more flexibly with an ordered result. For database marketing or customer relationship management applications, the ability to consider only the top *n* rows, or to subdivide the result into groupings by percentile is a welcome addition. Users can expect to achieve more efficient processing, too, as the functions are brought into the database engine and optimized. Once they are standardized, application vendors can depend on them, including their use in their applications and avoiding the need to create their own functions outside of the database.

If the amendment is accepted as proposed, the SQL statement will acquire an additional clause, the WINDOW clause. This clause consists of a list of window definitions, each of which defines a name and specification for the window. Specifications include partitioning, ordering, and aggregation grouping.

Here is a sample query from the paper that proposed the amendment (Zemke, et al., 1999, p.4):

```
SELECT SH.TERRITORY, SH.MONTH, SH.SALES,
    AVG (SH.SALES) OVER W1 AS MOVING_AVERAGE
FROM SALES_HISTORY AS SH
WINDOW W1 AS (PARTITION BY (SH.TERRITORY)
            ORDER BY (SH.MONTH ASC)
            ROWS 2 PRECEDING);
```

Table 8-1 OLAP Functions Proposed for Addition to SQL-99

CEILING	PERCENTILE_CONT	REGR_SLOPE
CORR	PERCENT_RANK	REGR_SXX
COVAR_POP	POWER	REGR_SXY
COVAR_SAMP	RANK	REGR_SYY
CUME_DIST	RANGE	ROW_NUMBER
DENSE_RANK	REGR_AVG	SQRT
EXP	REGR_AVGX	STDDEV_POP
FLOOR	REGR_AVGY	STDDEV_SAMP
LN	REGR_COUNT	VAR_POP
MOVING_AVG	REGR_INTERCEPT	VAR_SAMP
MOVING_SUM	REGR_R2	

From "The Extra Mile," by R. Winter, 2000, *Intelligent Enterprise* 3(10), p.63.

The window name is W1 and defined in the WINDOW clause that follows the FROM clause. The PARTITION clause partitions the rows in SALES_HISTORY by TERRITORY. Within each territory partition, the rows will be ordered in ascending order by month. Last, an aggregation group is defined as the current row and the two preceding rows of the partition, following the order imposed by the ORDER BY clause. Thus, a moving average of the sales for each territory will be returned as MOVING_AVERAGE.

Programming Extensions

The SQL-92 and earlier standards developed the capabilities of SQL as a data retrieval and manipulation language, and not as an application language. As a result, SQL has been used in conjunction with computationally complete languages such as C or Java in order to create business application programs, procedures, or functions. SQL-99, however, extends SQL by adding programmatic capabilities in Core SQL, SQL/PSM, and SQL/OLB.

The extensions that make SQL computationally complete include flow control capabilities, such as IF-THEN, FOR, WHILE statements, and loops, which are contained in a package of extensions to the essential SQL specifications. This package called **Persistent Stored Modules (SQL/PSM)** is so named because the capabilities to create and drop program modules are stored in it. *Persistent* means that a module of code will be stored until dropped, thus making it available for execution across user sessions, just as the base tables are retained until explicitly dropped. Each module is stored in a schema as a schema object. A schema does not have to have any program modules, or it may have multiple modules.

Each module must have a name, an authorization ID, association with a particular schema, indication of the character set to be used, and any temporary table declarations that will be needed when the module executes. Every module must contain one or more SQL procedures, named programs that each execute one SQL statement when called. Each procedure must also include an SQLSTATE declaration that acts as a status parameter and indicates whether or not an SQL statement has been successfully executed.

SQL/PSM can be used to create applications, or to incorporate procedures and functions, using SQL datatypes directly. Using SQL/PSM introduces procedurality to SQL, as statements are processed sequentially. Remember that SQL by itself is a nonprocedural language and no statement execution sequence is implied. SQL/PSM includes several SQL-control statements, including:

Persistent Stored Modules (SQL/PSM): Extensions defined in SQL-99 that include the capability to create and drop modules of code stored in the database schema across user sessions.

CASE	A statement that executes different sets of SQL sequences, according to a comparison of values or the value of a WHEN clause, using either search conditions or value expressions. The logic is similar to an SQL CASE expression, but ends with END CASE rather than END and has no equivalent to the ELSE NULL clause.
IF	If a predicate is TRUE, an SQL statement will be executed. The statement ends with an ENDIF, and contains ELSE and ELSEIF statements to manage flow control for different conditions.
LOOP	Causes a statement to be executed repeatedly until a condition exists that results in an exit.
LEAVE	Statement used to set a condition that results in exiting from a loop.
FOR	Statement that will execute once for each row of a results set.
WHILE	A statement that will be executed as long as a particular condition exists. Incorporates logic that functions as a LEAVE statement.

REPEAT   Similar to the WHILE statement, but the condition is tested after execution of the SQL statement.

ITERATE Statement used to restart a loop.

SQL/PSM brings the promise of addressing several widely noted deficiencies of essential SQL. It is still too soon to know if programmers are going to embrace SQL/PSM or continue to use host languages, invoking SQL through embedded SQL or via CLI. But, the new standard makes it possible to:

- Create procedures and functions within SQL, thus making it possible to accept input and also output parameters, or return a value directly.

- Detect and handle errors within SQL, rather than having to handle errors through another language.

- Create variables using the DECLARE statement that stay in scope throughout the procedure, method, or function in which they are contained.

- Pass groups of SQL statements rather than individual statements, thus improving performance.

- Handle the impedance mismatch problem, where SQL processes sets of data, while procedural languages process single rows of data, within modules.

SQL/PSM has not yet been widely implemented, and therefore we have not included extensive syntax examples in this chapter. Oracle's PL/SQL bears some resemblance to the new standard with its modules of code, BEGIN . . . END, LOOP, and WHILE statements. While SQL/PSM is not yet widely popular, this situation could change quickly.

TRIGGERS AND ROUTINES

Prior to the issuance of SQL-99, no support for user-defined functions or procedures was included in the SQL standards. Commercial products, recognizing the need for such capabilities, have provided them for some time, and we expect to see their syntax change over time to be in line with the SQL-99 requirements, just as we expect to see inclusion of SQL/PSM standards occur.

Triggers and routines are very powerful database objects because they are stored in the database and controlled by the DBMS. Thus, the code required to create them is stored in only one location and is administered centrally. This promotes stronger data integrity and consistency of use within the database. Since they are stored once, code maintenance is also simplified (Mullins, 1995).

Both triggers and routines consist of blocks of procedural code. Trigger code is stored in the database and runs automatically whenever the triggering event, such as an UPDATE, occurs. In contrast, routines do not run automatically. Routines are stored blocks of code that have to be called in order to operate (see Figure 8-5).

Trigger: A named set of SQL statements that are considered (triggered) when a data modification (INSERT, UPDATE, DELETE) occurs. If a condition stated within the trigger is met, then a prescribed action is taken.

Triggers

Since triggers are stored and executed in the database, they execute against all applications that access the database. Triggers can also cascade, causing other triggers to fire. Thus, a single request from a client can result in a series of integrity or logic checks being performed on the server without causing extensive network traffic between client and server. Triggers can be used to ensure referential integrity, enforce business rules, create audit trails, replicate tables, or activate a procedure (Rennhackkamp, 1996).

Constraints can be thought of as a special case of triggers. They also are applied (triggered) automatically as a result of data modification commands, but

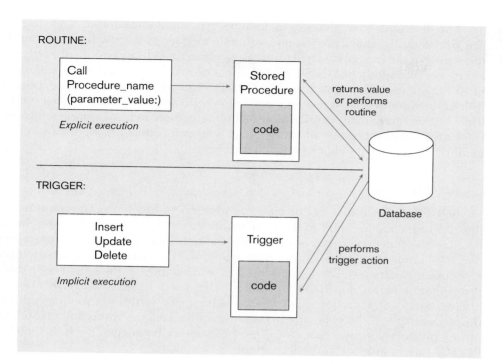

their precise syntax is determined by the DBMS and does not have the flexibility of a trigger.

Triggers have three parts, the *event*, the *condition*, and the *action*, and these parts are reflected in the coding structure for triggers. (See Figure 8-6 for sample trigger syntax). A simple example of a trigger written in PL/SQL is shown here:

```
CREATE TRIGGER ORDER_ID_BIR
   BEFORE INSERT ON ORDER_T
   FOR EACH ROW
BEGIN
   SELECT ID_SEQUENCE.NEXTVAL
   INTO :NEW.ORDER_ID
   FROM DUAL;
END ORDER_ID_BIR;
```

This trigger will automatically insert the order number whenever a new order is added. BIR is part of a trigger naming convention and stands for *Before Insert Row.* Triggers may occur either *before* or *after* the statement that aroused the trigger is executed. They may occur on INSERT, UPDATE, or DELETE commands. And they may fire each time a *row* is affected, or they may fire only once per *statement*, regardless of the number of rows affected. In the case illustrated above, the trigger should insert the order number before each order is added. A trigger that checks for inventory level after inventory is updated would be assigned an AUR naming label. The trigger above also requires that a sequence named ID_SEQUENCE has been previously defined, as the next value in this sequence will be used as the next order number.

```
CREATE [OR REPLACE] TRIGGER trigger_name
   {BEFORE AFTER} {INSERT | DELETE | UPDATE} ON table_name
   [FOR EACH ROW [WHEN (trigger_condition)]]
   trigger_body_here;
```

Figure 8-6
Simplified Oracle PL/SQL trigger syntax

The developer who wishes to include triggers should be careful. Since triggers fire automatically, unless the trigger includes a message to the user, the user will be unaware that the trigger has fired. Also, triggers can cascade and cause other triggers to fire. For example, a BEFORE UPDATE trigger could require that a row be inserted in another table. If that table has a BEFORE INSERT trigger, it will also fire, possibly with unintended results. It is even possible to create an endless loop of triggers! So, while triggers have many possibilities, including enforcement of complex business rules, creation of sophisticated auditing logs, and enforcement of elaborate security authorizations, they should be included with care.

Routines

SQL-invoked routines can be either procedures or functions. The terms procedure and function are used in the same manner as they are in other programming languages. A **function** returns one value and has only input parameters. A **procedure** may have input parameters, output parameters, and parameters that are both input and output parameters. You may declare and name a unit of procedural code using proprietary code of the RDBMS product being used, or invoke a host-language library routine. SQL products had developed their own versions of routines prior to the issuance of SQL-99, so be sure to become familiar with the syntax and capabilities of any product you use. Some of these proprietary languages, such as Oracle's PL/SQL, are in wide use and will continue to be available.

The advantages of SQL-invoked routines include:

- *Flexibility.* Routines may be used in more situations than constraints or triggers, which are limited to data modification circumstances. Just as triggers have more code options than constraints, routines have more code options than triggers.

- *Efficiency.* Routines can be carefully crafted and optimized to run more quickly than slower, generic SQL statements.

- *Sharability.* Routines may be cached on the server and made available to all users, so that they do not have to be rewritten.

- *Applicability.* Routines may apply to the entire database rather than being kept with one application. This advantage is a corollary to *sharability.*

The SQL-99 syntax for procedure and function creation is shown in Figure 8-7. As you can see, the syntax is complicated, and we will not go into the details about each clause here. However, a simple procedure follows, which will give you an idea of how the code works.

A procedure is a collection of procedural and SQL statements that are assigned a unique name within the schema and stored in the database. When it is desired to run the procedure, it is called by its name. When called, all of the statements in the

Function: A stored subroutine that returns one value and has only input parameters.

Procedure: A collection of procedural and SQL statements that are assigned a unique name within the schema and stored in the database.

Figure 8-7
Create routine syntax, SQL-99

```
{CREATE PROCEDURE | CREATE FUNCTION} routine_name
([parameter [{,parameter} . . .]])
[RETURNS data_type result_cast]    /* for functions only */
[LANGUAGE {ADA | C | COBOL | FORTRAN | MUMPS | PASCAL | PLI | SQL}]
[PARAMETER STYLE {SQL | GENERAL}]
[SPECIFIC specific_name]
[DETERMINISTIC | NOT DETERMINISTIC]
[NO SQL | CONTAINS SQL | READS SQL DATA | MODIFIES SQL DATA]
[RETURN NULL ON NULL INPUT | CALL ON NULL INPUT]
[DYNAMIC RESULT SETS unsigned_integer]      /* for procedures only */
[STATIC DISPATCH]                           /* for functions only */
routine_body
```

procedure will be executed. This characteristic of procedures helps to reduce network traffic, as all of the statements are transmitted at one time, rather than being sent individually.

In order to build a simple procedure that will set a sale price, the existing PRODUCT-T table is altered by adding a new column, SALE_PRICE, that will hold the sale price for the products:

```
ALTER TABLE PRODUCT_T
   ADD (SALE_PRICE DECIMAL (6,2));
```

Table altered.

Our simple procedure will execute two SQL statements. Products with a STANDARD_PRICE of $400 or higher are discounted 10 percent, and products with a STANDARD_PRICE of less than $400 are discounted 15 percent. Here is the Oracle code module that will create and store the procedure named PRODUCT_LINE_SALE:

```
CREATE OR REPLACE PROCEDURE PRODUCT_LINE_SALE
   AS BEGIN
     UPDATE PRODUCT_T
       SET SALE_PRICE = .90 * STANDARD_PRICE
       WHERE STANDARD_PRICE >= 400;
     UPDATE PRODUCT_T
       SET SALE_PRICE = .85 * STANDARD_PRICE
       WHERE STANDARD_PRICE < 400;
   END;
```

Oracle returns a comment, Procedure created, if the syntax has been accepted.
To run the procedure in Oracle, use this command:

```
SQL> EXEC PRODUCT_LINE_SALE
```

and Oracle gives this response:

PL/SQL procedure successfully completed. Now PRODUCT_T contains:

PRODUCT_LINE	PRODUCT_ID	PRODUCT_DESCRIPTION	PRODUCT_FINISH	STANDARD_PRICE	SALE_PRICE
10001	1	End Table	Cherry	175	148.75
20001	2	Coffee Table	Natural Ash	200	170
20001	3	Computer Desk	Natural Ash	375	318.75
30001	4	Entertainment Center	Natural Maple	650	585
10001	5	Writers Desk	Cherry	325	276.25
20001	6	8-Drawer Dresser	White Ash	750	675
20001	7	Dining Table	Natural Ash	800	720
30001	8	Computer Desk	Walnut	250	212.5

EMBEDDED SQL AND DYNAMIC SQL

The functionality of SQL/PSM introduced in SQL-99 provides for the types of programmatic extensions that had been previously developed using embedded SQL or dynamic SQL. Both approaches were developed prior to SQL-99 to enable the development of database applications. SQL was originally created to handle database access alone, and did not have flow control or the other structures necessary to create an application. **Embedded SQL** refers to the process of including hard-coded SQL statements in a program written in another language, such as C, Cobol, Ada, or Java. Dynamic SQL derives the precise SQL statement at runtime. Programmers write to an API (application programming interface) to achieve the interface between languages.

As this text is written, the Open Database Connectivity (ODBC) standard is the most commonly used API. SQL-99 standard includes the SQL Call Level Interface

Embedded SQL: The process of including hard-coded SQL statements in a program written in another language, such as C or Java.

(SQL/CLI). Both are written in C and both are based on the same earlier standard. Java Database Connectivity (JDBC) is an industry standard used for connecting from Java. It is not yet an ISO standard.

To embed SQL, place the SQL statements within the source code of the host program, preceded with the phrase EXEC SQL. A precompiler will convert the SQL statements that the host language can interpret, generating a database request module (DBRM). Once the host file is compiled into object code, a linker program links the DBMS calls in the host language to a DBMS library. A program usually named BIND processes the SQL statements in the access module, parsing and validating each statement and deriving an access plan that attempts to optimize the statements' execution. With some DBMSs, the access plan is not determined at execution time, taking into consideration the current state of the database. The access plan plus any necessary additional information is stored either in the database or in an external code module, an executable image. The image can be accessed and used by any database instance while storage in the database limits access to that database. Using embedded SQL in either way results in more efficient processing than interactive SQL because it takes advantage of the information stored in the library. Once written, access plans, procedure calls, and so forth will be transparent to the developer.

Dynamic SQL: The process of making an application capable of generating specific SQL code on the fly, as the application is processing.

Dynamic SQL is used to generate appropriate SQL code on the fly, as an application is processing. Most programmers write to an API, such as ODBC, which can then be passed through to any ODBC-compliant database. Dynamic SQL is central to most Internet applications and will be covered in more detail in Chapter 10. The developer is able to create a more flexible application because the exact SQL query is determined at runtime, including the number of parameters to be passed, which tables will be accessed, and so forth. Dynamic SQL is very useful where an SQL statement shell will be used repeatedly, with different parameter values being inserted each time it executes.

As SQL-99 is implemented more completely, the use of embedded and dynamic SQL will become more standardized, since the standard creates a computationally complete SQL language for the first time. Because most vendors have gone ahead and created these capabilities independently, though, the next few years will be a period in which SQL-99 compliant products exist side-by-side with older but entrenched versions. The user will need to be aware of these possibilities and deal with them.

Summary

This chapter continues from Chapter 7, which introduced the SQL language. Equi-joins, natural joins, outer joins, and union joins have been considered. Equi-joins are based on equal values in the common columns of the tables which are being joined and will return all requested results including the values of the common columns from each table included in the join. Natural joins return all requested results, but values of the common columns are included only once. Outer joins return all the values in one of the tables included in the join, regardless of whether a match exists in the other table or not. Union joins return a table that includes all data from each table that was joined.

Nested subqueries, where multiple SELECT statements are nested within a single query, are useful for more complex query situations. A special form of the subquery, a correlated subquery, requires that a value be known from the outer query before the inner query can be processed. Other subqueries process the inner query, return a result to the next outer query, and then that outer query is processed.

Other advanced SQL topics include the use of embedded SQL and the use of triggers and routines. SQL can be included within the context of many third-generation languages including COBOL, C, Fortran, and Ada. The use of embedded SQL allows for the development of more flexible interfaces, improved performance, and improved database security. User-defined functions that run automatically when records are inserted, updated, or deleted are called triggers. Procedures are user-defined code modules, which can be called in order to execute.

An amendment to SQL-99 that adds a set of analytical functions has been proposed. Extensions already included now make SQL computationally complete, and include flow control capabilities in a set of SQL specifications known as Persistent Stored Modules (SQL/PSM). SQL/PSM can be used to create applications, or to incorporate procedures and functions, using SQL datatypes directly. SQL-invoked routines, including triggers, functions, and procedures, are also included in SQL-99. Users must realize that these capabilities have been included as vendor-specific extensions previously, and will continue to exist for some time.

Dynamic SQL is an integral part of Web-enabling databases and will be demonstrated in more detail in Chapter 10. Chapter 8 presents some of the more complex capabilities of SQL, and creates awareness of the extended and complex capabilities of SQL that must be mastered in order to build database application programs.

CHAPTER REVIEW

Key Terms

Correlated subquery
Dynamic SQL
Embedded SQL
Equi-join

Function
Join
Natural join
Outer join

Persistent stored modules (SQL/PSM)
Procedure
Trigger
User-defined datatype (UDT)

Review Questions

1. Define each of the following terms:
   a. dynamic SQL
   b. correlated subquery
   c. embedded SQL
   d. procedure
   e. join
   f. equi-join
   g. natural join
   h. outer join
   i. function
   j. Persistent Stored Modules (SQL/PSM)

2. Match the following terms to the appropriate definitions.

   _____ equi-join
   _____ natural join
   _____ outer join
   _____ trigger
   _____ procedure
   _____ embedded SQL
   _____ UDT
   _____ COMMIT
   _____ SQL/PSM
   _____ Dynamic SQL
   _____ ROLLBACK

   a. changes to a table are undone
   b. user-defined datatype
   c. SQL-99 extension
   d. returns all records of designated table
   e. redundant columns are kept
   f. changes to a table are made permanent
   g. process that includes SQL statements within a host language
   h. process of making an application capable of generating specific SQL code on the fly
   i. redundant columns are not kept
   j. set of SQL statements that execute under stated conditions
   k. stored, named collection of procedural and SQL statements

3. When is an outer join used instead of a natural join?

4. Explain the processing order of a correlated subquery.

5. Explain the following statement regarding SQL: Any query that can be written using the subquery approach can also be written using the joining approach, but not vice-versa.

6. What is the purpose of the COMMIT command in SQL? How does commit relate to the notion of a business transaction (such as entry of a customer order or issuing a customer invoice)?

7. Care must be exercised when writing triggers for a database. What are some of the problems that could be encountered?

8. Explain the structure of a module of code that defines a trigger.

9. Under what conditions can a UNION clause be used?

10. Discuss the proposed Amendment 1 to SQL-99.

11. Explain the purpose of SQL/PSM.

12. List four advantages of SQL-invoked routines.

13. When would you consider using embedded SQL and when dynamic SQL?

Problems and Exercises

Problems and Exercises 1 through 5 are based on the class schedule ERD depicted in Figure 4-6 in Chapter 4. The 3NF relations along with some sample data are repeated in Figure 8-8. For questions 1–5, draw an instance diagram and mark it to show the data you expect your query to return in the results.

1. Write SQL retrieval commands for each of the following queries:
   a. Display the course ID and course name for all courses with an ISM prefix.

   b. Display all courses for which Professor Berndt has been qualified.
   c. Display the class roster, including student name, for all students enrolled in section 2714 of ISM 4212.

2. Write an SQL query to answer the following question: Which instructors are qualified to teach ISM 3113?

3. Write an SQL query to answer the following question: Is any instructor qualified to teach ISM 3113 and not qualified to teach ISM 4930?

STUDENT (STUDENT_ID, STUDENT_NAME)

STUDENT_ID	STUDENT_NAME
38214	Letersky
54907	Altvater
66324	Aiken
70542	Marra
. . .	

IS_QUALIFIED (FACULTY_ID, COURSE_ID, DATE_QUALIFIED)

FACULTY_ID	COURSE_ID	DATE_QUALIFIED
2143	ISM 3112	9/1988
2143	ISM 3113	9/1988
3467	ISM 4212	9/1995
3467	ISM 4930	9/1996
4756	ISM 3113	9/1991
4756	ISM 3112	9/1991
. . .		

FACULTY (FACULTY_ID, FACULTY_NAME)

FACULTY_ID	FACULTY_NAME
2143	Birkin
3487	Berndt
4756	Collins
. . .	

SECTION (SECTION_ID, COURSE_ID)

SECTION_ID	COURSE_ID
2712	ISM 3113
2713	ISM 3113
2714	ISM 4212
2715	ISM 4930
. . .	

COURSE (COURSE_ID, COURSE_NAME)

COURSE_ID	COURSE_NAME
ISM 3113	Syst Analysis
ISM 3112	Syst Design
ISM 4212	Database
ISM 4930	Networking
. . .	

IS_REGISTERED (STUDENT_ID, SECTION_ID, SEMESTER)

STUDENT_ID	SECTION_ID	SEMESTER
38214	2714	I-2001
54907	2714	I-2001
54907	2715	I-2001
66324	2713	I-2001
. . .		

Figure 8-8
Class scheduling relations (missing IS_ASSIGNED)

4. Write SQL queries to answer the following questions: How many students are enrolled in section 2714 during semester I-2001? How many students are enrolled in ISM 3113 during semester I-2001?

5. Write an SQL query to answer the following question: Which students were not enrolled in any courses during semester I-2001?

Problems and Exercises 6 through 12 are based on the entire Pine Valley Furniture database.

6. Write an SQL command to display the order number, customer number, order date, and items ordered for Order #1001.

7. Write an SQL command to display each item ordered for Order #1001, its standard price, and the total price for each item ordered.

8. Write an SQL command to total the cost of Order #1001.

9. Write an SQL command that will find any customers who have not placed orders.

10. Write an SQL query to produce a list of all the products and the number of times each product has been ordered.

11. Write an SQL query to display customer number, name, and order number for all customers and their orders.

12. Write an SQL query to list the order number and order quantity for all customer orders for which the order quantity is greater than the average order quantity of that product. *Hint:* This involves a correlated subquery.

Field Exercises

1. Conduct a search of the Web to locate as many links as possible that discuss SQL standards.

2. Compare two versions of SQL to which you have access, such as Microsoft Access and Oracle SQL*Plus. Identify at least five similarities in the SQL code used and three dissimilarities. Do the dissimilarities cause any different results?

References

Codd, E. F. 1970. "A Relational Model of Data for Large Relational Databases." *Communications of the ACM* 13 (June): 77–87.

Date, C. J., and H. Darwen. 1997. *A Guide to the SQL Standard.* Reading, MA: Addison-Wesley.

Melton, J. 1997. "A Case for SQL Conformance Testing." *Database Programming & Design* 10 (7): 66–69.

Mullins, C. S. 1995. "The Procedural DBA." *Database Programming & Design* 8 (12): 40–45.

Rennhackkamp, M. 1996. "Trigger Happy." *DBMS* 9 (5): 89–91, 95.

Van der Lans, R. F. 1993. *Introduction to SQL,* 2nd ed. Workingham, England: Addison-Wesley.

Winter, R. 2000. "SQL-99's New OLAP Functions." *Intelligent Enterprise* 3(2) (Jan. 20): 62, 64–65.

Winter, R. 2000. "The Extra Mile." *Intelligent Enterprise* 3(10) (June 26): 62–64.

Zemke, F., K. Kulkarni, A. Witkowski, and B. Lyle. 1999. "Introduction to OLAP Functions" ISO/IEC JTC1/SC32 WG3: YGS. nnn ANSI NCITS H2-99-154.

Further Reading

American National Standards Institute. http://www.ansi.org, 1996. [Information on the ANSI federation and latest national and international standards.]

ANSI Standards Action, Vol 31, # 11, 6/2/2000. p. 20 American National Standards Institute, NY. Also see Chapter 7 list of Further Reading.

Welcome to ISO Online, http://www.iso.ch, 1997. [Information about the International Organization for Standardization.]

Web Resources

SQL Archive, Jerry, ece, umassd.edu, University of Massachusetts, Dartmouth. ftp://jerry.ece.umassd.edu. (In particular, try catalog #99–154 to access the Zemke article.) See also sites listed in Chapter 7.

MOUNTAIN VIEW COMMUNITY HOSPITAL

Project Case

Use the SQL database design implemented in Chapter 7 for Mountain View Community Hospital to complete the project questions and project exercises.

PROJECT QUESTIONS

1. What version of SQL will you use to do the project exercises?
2. Does your SQL-based DBMS support dynamic SQL, functions, stored produres, and UDTs?

PROJECT EXERCISES

1. Now write and test some queries that will work using your sample data. Write queries that illustrate the more complex queries covered in Chapter 8:

   a. select information from two or more tables.

   b. use subquery syntax.

   c. return a result table that could be used to produce a hospital report, such as nursing staff assigned to each care center.

   d. use a UNION statement.

2. Write queries to determine the following (display columns of interest to you):

   a. For a given physician, which treatments has that physician performed on each patient referred by that physician to the hospital?

   b. For the query in a., also include physicians who have not referred patients to the hospital.

   c. For each patient, what is the average number of treatments performed on him or her by each physician who has treated that patient?

   d. For each nurse-in-charge, what is the total number of hours worked by all employees who work in the care center that nurse supervises?

Chapter 9

The Client/Server Database Environment

LEARNING OBJECTIVES

After studying this chapter, you should be able to:

- Define the following key terms: **client/server systems, file server, fat client, database server, stored procedure, three-tier architecture, thin client, application partitioning, symmetric multiprocessing (SMP), massively parallel processing (MPP)/shared nothing architecture, middleware, application program interface (API), Query-by-Example (QBE), open database connectivity (ODBC) standard, Visual Basic for Applications (VBA),** and **event-driven**.

- List several major advantages of the client/server architecture, compared to other computing approaches.

- Explain the three components of application logic: data presentation services, processing services, and storage services.

- Suggest the range of possibilities for partitioning these services in various client/server architectures.

- Distinguish among a file server, a database server, a three-tiered, and an *n*-tiered architecture.

- Describe middleware and explain how middleware facilitates client/server architectures.

- Explain the capabilities of a Query-by-Example (QBE) interface, its relationship to Microsoft Access 2000 and its advantages and disadvantages compared to SQL.

- Explain how to link external data tables to an application in a client/server environment using ODBC or JDBC.

- Explain how VBA is used with Access 2000 to build client applications.

INTRODUCTION

Client/server systems operate in networked environments, splitting the processing of an application between a front-end client and a back-end processor. Generally, the client process requires some resource, which the server provides to the client. Clients and servers can reside in the same computer, or they can be on different computers that are networked together. Both clients and servers are intelligent and programmable, so that the computing power of both can be used to devise effective and efficient applications.

It is difficult to overestimate the impact that client/server applications have had in the last 10 years. Advances in personal computer technology and the rapid evolution of graphical user interfaces (GUIs), networking, and communications have changed the way businesses use computing systems to meet ever more demanding business needs. Electronic commerce

Client/server systems: A networked computing model that distributes processes between clients and servers, which supply the requested services. In a database system, the database generally resides on a server that processes the DBMS. The clients may process the application systems or request services from another server that holds the application programs.

requires that client browsers be able to access dynamic Web pages attached to databases that provide real-time information. Personal computers linked through networks that support work-group computing are the norm. Mainframe applications have been rewritten to run in client/server environments and take advantage of the greater cost effectiveness of networks of personal computers and workstations. The need for strategies that fit specific business environments is being filled by client/server solutions because they offer flexibility, scalability (the ability to upgrade a system without having to redesign it), and extensibility (the ability to define new data types and operations). As businesses become more global in their operations, they must devise distributed systems (these will be covered in Chapter 13); their plans often include client/server architectures.

In this chapter we review developments in multiuser database management environments that have led to the development of various client/server strategies for data processing. These include LAN-based DBMSs, client/server DBMSs (including three-tiered architectures), parallel computing architectures, Internet and Intranet DBMSs, and middleware.

Driving the trend toward these database technologies are a variety of new opportunities and competitive pressures. In one sense the network has become the computer as users share data through network drives and turn to the Internet to access the information and data they require. Corporate restructurings, such as mergers, acquisitions, and consolidations, make it necessary to connect, integrate, or replace existing stand-alone applications. One consequence of corporate downsizing is that individual managers have broader control, necessitating access to a wider range of data. Applications are being downsized from expensive mainframes to networked microcomputers and workstations that are much more user friendly and sometimes more cost effective. Handling network traffic, which may become excessive with some architectures, is a key issue in developing successful client/server applications, especially as organizations place mission-critical applications in distributed environments. Establishing a good balance between centralized and decentralized systems is a matter of much current discussion, as organizations strive to gain maximum benefits from both client/server and mainframe-based DBMSs.

CLIENT/SERVER ARCHITECTURES

Client/server environments use a local area network to support a network of personal computers, each with its own storage, that are also able to share common devices (such as a hard disk or printer) and software (such as a DBMS) attached to the LAN. Each PC and workstation on a LAN is typically within 100 feet of the others, with a total network cable length of under 1 mile. At least one PC is designated as a file server, where the shared database is stored. The LAN modules of a DBMS add concurrent access controls, possibly extra security features, and query- or translation-queuing management to support concurrent access from multiple users of a shared database.

The several client/server architectures that have evolved can be distinguished by the distribution of application logic components across clients and servers. There are three components of application logic (see Figure 9-1). The first is the input/output (I/O) or presentation logic component. This component is responsible for formatting and presenting data on the user's screen or other output device, and for managing user input from a keyboard or other input device. The second component is the processing component. It handles data processing logic, business rules logic, and data management logic. Data processing logic includes such activities as data validation and identification of processing errors. Business rules that have not been coded at the DBMS level may be coded in the processing component. Data management logic identifies the data necessary for processing the transaction or query. The third

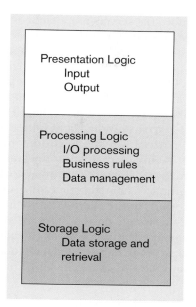

Figure 9-1
Application logic components

component is storage, the component responsible for data storage and retrieval from the physical storage devices associated with the application. Activities of a DBMS occur in the storage component logic.

File Server Architectures

The first client/server architectures developed were file servers. In a basic file server environment (see Figure 9-2), all data manipulation occurs at the workstations where data are requested. The client handles the presentation logic, processing logic, and much of the storage logic (that part associated with a DBMS). One or

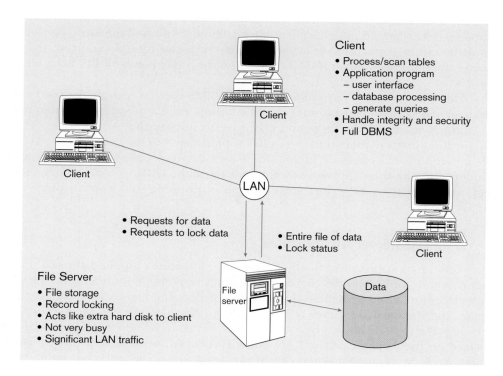

Figure 9-2
File server model

File server: A device that manages file operations and is shared by each of the client PCs attached to the LAN.

more file servers are attached to the LAN. A **file server** is a device that manages file operations and is shared by each of the client PCs attached to the LAN. Each of these file servers acts as an additional hard disk for each of the client PCs. For example, your PC might recognize a logical F: drive, which is actually a disk volume stored on a file server on the LAN. Programs on your PC refer to files on this drive by the typical path specification, involving this drive and any directories, as well as the filename. With a file server, each client PC may be called a **fat client**, one where most processing occurs on the client rather than on a server.

Fat client: A client PC that is responsible for processing presentation logic, extensive application and business rules logic, and many DBMS functions.

In a file server environment, each client PC is authorized to use the DBMS when a database application program runs on that PC. Thus, there is one database but many concurrently running copies of the DBMS, one on each of the active PCs. The primary characteristic of file server architecture is that all data manipulation is performed at the client PCs, not at the file server. The file server acts simply as a shared data storage device. Software at the file server queues access requests, but it is up to the application program at each client PC, working with the copy of the DBMS on that PC, to handle all data management functions. For example, data security checks and file and record locking are initiated at the client PCs in this environment.

Limitations of File Servers

There are three limitations when using file servers on local area networks. First, considerable data movement is generated across the network. For example, when an application program running on a client PC in Pine Valley Furniture wants to access the oak products, the whole Product table is transferred to the client PC and then scanned at the client to find the few desired records. Thus, the server does very little work, the client is busy with extensive data manipulation, and the network is transferring large blocks of data. Consequently, a client-based LAN places considerable burden on the client PC to do functions that have to be performed on all clients, and creates a high network traffic load.

Second, each client workstation must devote memory to a full version of the DBMS. This means that there is less room in memory for application programs on the client PC. Also, increasing RAM on the PC will improve performance by increasing the total amount of data that can reside on the PC while a transaction is being processed. Further, because the client workstation does most of the work, each client must be rather powerful to provide a suitable response time. In contrast, the file server does not need much RAM and need not be a very powerful PC, since it does little work.

Third, and possibly most important, the DBMS copy in each workstation must manage the shared database integrity. In addition, each application program must recognize, for example, locks and take care to initiate the proper locks. Thus, application programmers must be rather sophisticated to understand various subtle conditions that can arise in a multiple-user database environment. They must understand how their application will interact with the DBMS's concurrency, recovery, and security controls, and sometimes must program such controls into their applications.

Database Server Architectures

Database server: A computer that is responsible for database storage, access, and processing in a client/server environment. Some people also use this term to describe a two-tier client/server environment.

Two-tiered approaches to client/server architectures followed the file server approach. In this system the client workstation is responsible for managing the user interface, including presentation logic, data processing logic, and business rules logic, and the **database server** is responsible for database storage, access, and processing. Figure 9-3 shows a typical database server architecture. With the DBMS placed on the database server, LAN traffic is reduced, because only those records that match the requested criteria are transmitted to the client station, rather than

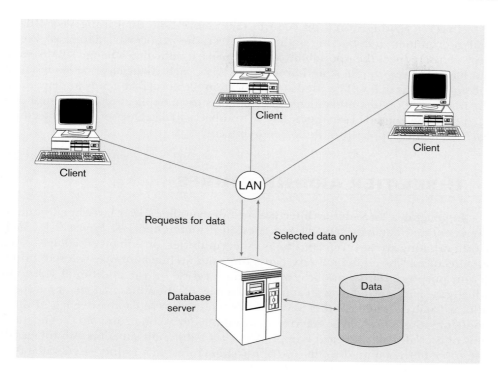

Figure 9-3
Database server architecture (two-tier architecture)

entire data files. Some people refer to the central DBMS functions as the *back-end functions,* whereas they call the application programs on the client PCs *front-end programs.*

Moving the DBMS to the database server has several advantages. With this architecture, only the database server requires processing power adequate to handle the database, and the database is stored on the server, not on the clients. Therefore, the database server can be tuned to optimize database-processing performance. Since less data are sent across the LAN, the communication load is reduced. User authorization, integrity checking, data dictionary maintenance, and query and update processing are all performed in one location, on the database server.

Client/server projects that use file server and database server architectures tend to be departmental applications, supporting a relatively small number of users. Such applications are not mission critical and have been most successful where transaction volumes are low, immediate availability is not critical, and security is not of the highest concern. As companies have sought to gain expected benefits from client/server projects, such as scalability, flexibility, and lowered costs, they have had to develop new approaches to client/server architectures.

The use of **stored procedures**, modules of code that implement application logic, which are included on the database server, pushed the database server architecture toward being able to handle more critical business applications (Quinlan, 1995). As pointed out by Quinlan, stored procedures have the following advantages:

- Performance improves for compiled SQL statements.
- Network traffic decreases as processing moves from the client to the server.
- Security improves if the stored procedure is accessed rather than the data and code is moved to the server, away from direct end-user access.
- Data integrity improves as multiple applications access the same stored procedure.
- Stored procedures result in a thinner client and a fatter database server.

Stored procedure: A module of code, usually written in a proprietary language such as Oracle's PL/SQL or Sybase's Transact-SQL, that implements application logic or a business rule and is stored on the server, where it runs when it is called.

However, writing stored procedures takes more time than using Visual Basic or Powerbuilder to create an application. Also, the proprietary nature of stored procedures reduces their portability and may make it difficult to change DBMSs without having to rewrite the stored procedures. Also, each client must be loaded with the applications that will be used at that location. Performance tends to degrade as the number of on-line users increases. Upgrades to an application will require that each client be upgraded separately. These drawbacks to database server architectures have led to the popularity of three-tier architecture.

THREE-TIER ARCHITECTURES

Three-tier architecture: A client/server configuration that includes three layers: a client layer and two server layers. While the nature of the server layers differs, a common configuration contains an application server.

In general, a **three-tier architecture** includes another server layer in addition to the client and database server layers previously mentioned (see Figure 9-4). Such configurations are also referred to as *n*-tier, multitier, or enhanced client/server architectures. The additional server in a three-tier architecture may be used for different purposes. Often application programs reside on the additional server, in which case it is referred to as an application server. Or the additional server may hold a local database while another server holds the enterprise database. Each of these configurations is likely to be referred to as a three-tier architecture, but the functionality of each differs, and each is appropriate for a different situation. Advantages of the three-tier compared to the two-tier architecture, such as increased scalability, flexibility, performance, and reusability, have made three-layer architectures a popular choice for Internet applications and Net-centric information systems. These advantages are discussed in more detail below.

In some three-tier architectures, most application code is stored on the application server. This case realizes the same benefits as come from putting stored procedures on the database server in a two-tier architecture. Using an application server can also improve performance by the use of true machine code, easier portability of the application code to other platforms, and less reliance on proprietary languages

Figure 9-4
Three-tier architecture

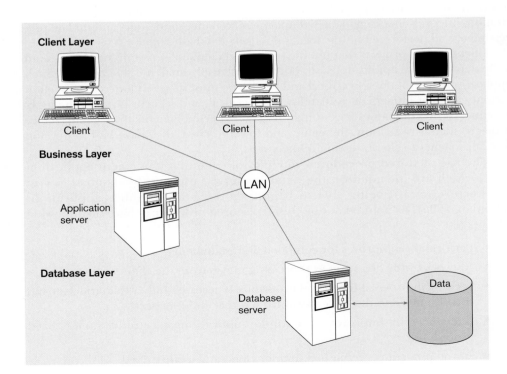

such as SQL/PLUS (Quinlan, 1995). In many situations, most business processing occurs on the application server rather than on the client workstation or database server, resulting in a **thin client**. The use of Internet browsers on clients for accessing the Web provides a contemporary example of a thin client architecture. Applications that reside on a server and execute on that server without downloading to the client are becoming more common. Thus, upgrading application programs requires loading the new version only on the application server, rather than on client workstations.

Thin client: A PC configured for handling user interfaces and some application processing, usually with no or limited local data storage.

Three-tier architectures can provide several benefits (Thompson, 1997):

- *Scalability* Three-tier architectures are more scalable than two-tier architectures. For example, the middle tier can be used to reduce the load on a database server by using a transaction processing (TP) monitor to reduce the number of connections to a server, and additional application servers can be added to distribute application processing. A TP monitor is a program that controls data transfer between clients and servers in order to provide a consistent environment for on-line transaction processing (OLTP).

- *Technological flexibility* It is easier to change DBMS engines, though triggers and stored procedures will need to be rewritten, with a three-tier architecture. The middle tier can even be moved to a different platform. Simplified presentation services make it easier to implement various desired interfaces such as Web browsers or kiosks.

- *Lower long-term costs* Use of off-the-shelf components or services in the middle tier can reduce costs, as can substitution of modules within an application rather than an entire application.

- *Better match of systems to business needs* New modules can be built to support specific business needs rather than building more general, complete applications.

- *Improved customer service* Multiple interfaces on different clients can access the same business processes.

- *Competitive advantage* The ability to react to business changes quickly by changing small modules of code rather than entire applications can be used to gain a competitive advantage.

- *Reduced risk* Again, the ability to implement small modules of code quickly and combine them with code purchased from vendors limits the risk assumed with a large-scale development project.

Three-tier and *n*-tier architectures are the most recent developments in client/server approaches. Challenges associated with moving to a three-tier or more complicated environment include (Thompson, 1997):

- *High short-term costs* Implementing a three-tier architecture requires that the presentation component be split from the process component. Accomplishing this split requires more programming in a 3GL language such as C than is required in implementing a two-tier architecture.

- *Tools and training* Because three-tier architectures are relatively new, tools for implementing them are not yet well developed. Also, because training programs are not yet widely available, companies must develop skills for their implementation in-house.

- *Experience* Similarly, few people have as yet had experience building three-tier systems.

- *Incompatible standards* Few standards have as yet been proposed for transaction processing monitors. It is not yet clear which of the several competing standards proposed for distributed objects will prevail.

- *Lack of end-user tools that work with middle-tier services* Widely available generic tools such as end-user spreadsheets and reporting tools do not yet operate through middle-tier services. This problem will be explained in more detail later in this chapter, in the middleware section.

PARTITIONING AN APPLICATION

Clearly there is no one optimal client/server architecture that is the best solution for all business problems. Rather, the flexibility inherent in client/server architectures offers organizations the possibility of tailoring their configurations to fit their particular processing needs. Figure 9–1 depicted the computing logics that must be distributed across the client and server(s). Presentation logic resides on the client, where the user interfaces with the system. Processing logic may be divided across client and servers, as was indicated in the previous discussion of file server, two-tier and three-tier client/server architectures. Storage logic usually resides on the database server, close to the physical location of the data. Data integrity control activities, such as constraint checking, are typically placed there. Triggers, which will always fire when appropriate conditions are met, are associated with insert, modify, update, and delete commands. As these commands affect the data directly, triggers are also usually stored on the database server. Stored procedures that use the data directly are usually stored on the database server. Those that work with a query result may be stored on an application server or on the client. Depending on the nature of the business problem being addressed, these general rules may not be followed, in order to achieve optimum throughput and performance.

Application partitioning: The process of assigning portions of application code to client or server partitions after it is written, in order to achieve better performance and interoperability (ability of a component to function on different platforms).

Application partitioning helps in this tailoring. It gives developers the opportunity to write application code they can later place either on a client workstation or on a server, depending which location will give the best performance. It is not necessary to include the code that will place the process being partitioned or to write the code that will establish the connections to the process. Those activities are handled by application partitioning tools.

The objects created by using object-oriented programming are very appropriate for application partitioning. Programmers have tremendous control over each object's content and it is easier to separate user interface code, business rules, and data. This separation supports today's rapidly developing *n*-tier systems. The strong business push toward Internet and e-commerce business solutions is causing application partitioning to develop more rapidly and in new ways. Web applications must be multitiered and partitioned. They require components that can be assembled on the fly, as they are requested by the browser, and they need to be compatible with different operating systems, user interfaces, and databases. Effective application partitioning is necessary in the Web environment in order to achieve desired performance along with acceptable maintainability, data integrity, and security in an unpredictable distributed environment.

The application code can be developed and tested on a client workstation and decisions about partitioning that code and placing it can be made later. This capability is likely to increase developers' productivity. Application modules can be placed on a client or server late in the design phase. However, the developer must understand how and where each process will need to run in order to synchronize each process or transaction correctly across databases and platforms. Decisions about placing code on the application or database server will depend partly on the DBMS capabilities. For example, a DBMS that supports static SQL (completely prewritten SQL code) through stored procedures and triggers that are located on the database server may give a performance decrement if dynamic SQL code (SQL code created at run time) is located on the application server. Each dynamic SQL statement will generate a dynamic bind (or linkage to database objects) at the database server as it is processed. The performance impact will depend on how intensively dynamic SQL statements are used. Whether to concentrate processing on the application server or the database server is a decision that must be made by the developer, who understands the hardware environment available, the interactions of the hardware and DBMS software, and the demands of the application.

It is also possible to add transaction processing monitors to client/server systems in order to improve performance. Where multiple application servers and database servers are available, TP monitors can balance the workload, directing transactions to servers that are not busy. TP monitors are also useful in distributed environments, where distributed transactions from a single unit of work can be managed across a heterogeneous environment.

ROLE OF THE MAINFRAME

The role of the mainframe has been uncertain over the last decade as distributed, client/server, and PC computing capabilities have developed. As mentioned above, mission-critical systems, which were resident on mainframe systems a decade ago, have tended to remain on mainframe systems. Less mission-critical, frequently workgroup-level, systems have been developed using client/server architectures. The popularity of client/server architectures and businesses' strong desire to achieve more effective computing in more distributed environments as their perspectives became broader and more global led to their expectation that mission-critical systems would be moved away from mainframes and onto client/server architectures.

But moving mission-critical systems from traditional mainframe legacy systems to client/server systems has been challenging. Successful distributed computing depends on workable software distribution, effective performance management and tuning of production systems, established troubleshooting procedures, and proactive code management (Hurwitz, 1996). Organizations have found that managing these mission-critical applications is much more complicated when they are converted to distributed systems. Among the software distribution problems that exist in a distributed processing environment are the following:

- Determining which code must be placed on which workstations and which will be available through a server
- Identifying potential conflicts with code from other applications
- Assuring that sufficient resources are available at all locations to handle the anticipated load

Unless developers anticipate scalability issues and address them as they develop code, moving mission-critical applications to client/server distributed environments is likely to cause serious problems in the transition from pilot phase to production. This has slowed the development of mission-critical client/server systems. Now, Internet applications are causing an upsurge in the need for applications to be interoperable. Troubleshooting such interactions is difficult, and many organizations may not be prepared to undertake such troubleshooting. Increasing use of component libraries (files of shared application modules) increases the need to manage interdependencies that will inevitably develop as these component libraries are shared across applications.

Supporting distributed environments is a very complex undertaking. Understanding the dynamics of different locations' environments and creating a distributed computing network can be very complex. The difficulties of managing distributed computing environments have caused IT managers to rethink their push to move mission-critical systems to client/server solutions. Powerful parallel processing equipment (discussed in the next section) is becoming more readily available, thus making it more attractive to remain centralized on an application or database server.

The difficulties of moving complex, mission-critical applications to a distributed environment using client/server architectures have discouraged many IT managers, and some have withdrawn completely from client/server initiatives, returning to a mainframe environment. However, we expect that each organization will need to achieve a balance between mainframe and client/server platforms, between centralized and distributed solutions, that is closely tailored to the nature of their data and location of business users of the data. As Hurwitz (1996) suggests, data that do not need to be moved often can be centralized on a mainframe. Data to which users need frequent access, complex graphics, and the user interface should be kept close to the users' workstations.

Enterprise resource planning (ERP) systems have faced many challenges. During the 1990s, ERP systems such as those of SAP, Baan, Oracle, and J.D. Edwards convinced many companies dealing with large amounts of data that buying integrated financial, human resources, manufacturing, and procurement systems would be more efficient and cost effective. Moving to a Y2K compliant suite of applications was more appealing than rewriting millions of lines of code in existing applications. However, the ERP systems were developed as strictly controlled, closed systems. Incorporating legacy systems, where the organization's historical data resides, often on a mainframe, has been one of the challenges. Now in the 2000s, attention has turned to achieving efficient supply chain management, customer relationship management (CRM), and business-to-business (B2B) procurement through e-commerce solutions. ERP systems establish an integrated infrastructure for companies' internal management needs, but they must also have e-commerce capabilities. Classic ERP systems are being rearchitected and positioned to compete in an ever more distributed and flexible environment. At this time it is not possible to predict how the ERP systems will fare.

USING PARALLEL COMPUTER ARCHITECTURES

Organizations' attempts to move mission-critical applications to client/server architectures involve building systems that can handle much larger databases than the original client/server projects. Projects that involve very large databases (VLDB) have benefited from the use of parallel computer architectures. Indeed, some projects are possible only because parallel processing of the database gives an acceptably fast response time. Data warehouses have used parallelism to achieve more efficient data extraction, transformation, and loading by running on multiple inexpensive servers in a multithreaded environment.

The ability to handle high transaction volumes, complex queries, and new data types has proven problematic in many uniprocessor environments (DeWitt and Gray, 1992). But, RDBMSs and the SQL language lend themselves to effecting a parallel environment in two ways (Ferguson, 1994):

1. In most queries, SQL acts as a nonprocedural set processing language. Therefore, queries can be divided into parts, each of which can then be run on a different parallel processor simultaneously.

2. Multiple queries can be run in parallel on parallel processors (see Figure 9-5).

Effective use of parallel computer architectures involves developing an awareness of the processing possibilities that can be exploited in a parallel server environment, not just changing serial algorithms into parallel algorithms. We will introduce two of several multiprocessor hardware architectures that are available; each is optimal for a certain kind of processing.

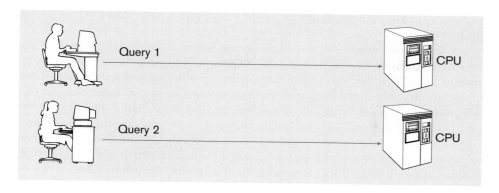

Figure 9-5
Parallel transactions and queries
(adapted from Ferguson, 1994)
(a) Parallel transactions

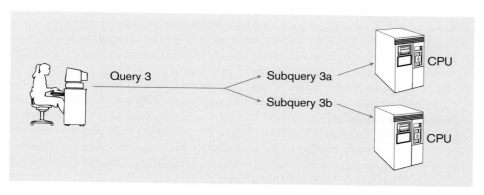

(b) Parallel query

Multiprocessor Hardware Architectures

Tightly coupled multiprocessor systems have a common shared memory among all processors (Figure 9-6). This architecture is often called **symmetric multiprocessing (SMP)** and has some advantages (Ferguson, 1994). First, a single copy of the operating system resides in the shared memory and is thus shared across all of the processors. The operating system must be written to operate in such a shared environment so that it can run parts of itself in parallel on any of the processors

Symmetric multiprocessing (SMP): A parallel processing architecture where the processors share a common shared memory.

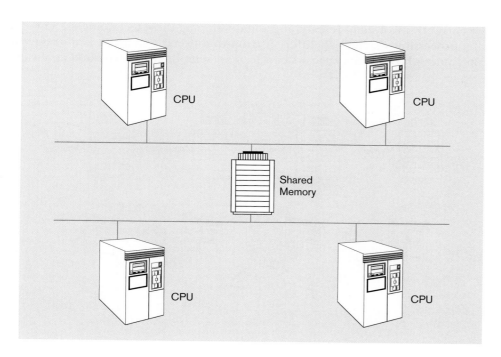

Figure 9-6
Tightly coupled multiprocessor
architecture (adapted from Ferguson,
1994)

without developing a tendency to use one processor more heavily than any of the others.

A second advantage is that bottlenecks are lessened compared to uniprocessor systems because all processors in symmetric multiprocessing share all the tasks. Even SMP systems may still develop I/O bottlenecks when memory request traffic going to shared memory is heavy, however. Equipping each processor with its own cache memory reduces this problem. Then, it is possible to reduce the volume of shared memory requests by reactivating waiting transactions to run on the processor where their processing was begun. This allows the transaction to reactivate more quickly, with fewer shared memory requests, and possibly to make use of variable information related to the transaction that is still available in the specific processor's memory cache (Ferguson, 1994).

Third, SMP architectures are useful for situations where data must remain in memory during processing to achieve the desired performance level. Problems to be addressed include the possibility of contention for the shared memory, the wide bandwidth required in order to retrieve data into shared memory, and the location of all memory at a single point of failure. I/O contention problems are likely as processors are added in a shared memory environment.

Massively parallel processing (MPP)/ shared nothing architecture: Massively parallel processing systems where each CPU has its own dedicated memory.

In contrast to SMP architectures, loosely coupled architectures (see Figure 9-7), also referred to as **massively parallel processing (MPP) architectures** or **shared nothing architectures**, set up each CPU with its own dedicated memory. Each node can be a uniprocessor or a multiprocessor. MPP systems thus require a complete copy of the operating system to be resident in each dedicated memory. Because there is little resource sharing among the processors, the problems of memory contention that occur in SMP systems are unlikely, and it is possible to add nodes (another processor and dedicated memory) in single units. This linear upgradability allows organizations to achieve parallel processing at lower costs, adding processing capability in small increments, as needed. This scalability creates a more manageable system in the dynamic business environment, where data warehouses are growing rapidly and exponentially. By passing messages across processors to achieve parallelism, these systems can divide up large tasks and spread them over several processors. In fact, it is applications that have large tasks that can benefit from being divided up and worked on simultaneously that are best suited to MPP architectures, rather than applications that can benefit from the use of shared memory. There is a lot of activity in developing MPP technology, and IBM, NCR, Intel, Oracle, DEC (division of Compaq), HP, Encore, Silicon Graphics, and others are currently involved in researching and developing these technologies. Since parallel processing systems are different from traditional systems, it is necessary for companies who consider such systems to reevaluate their database and application

Figure 9-7
Loosely coupled multiprocessor architecture (adapted from Ferguson, 1994)

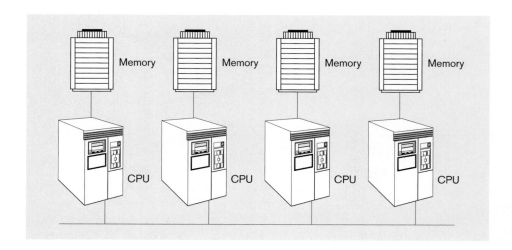

design, capacity planning, performance management, operational, and scheduling procedures.

Business-Related Uses of SMP and MPP Architectures

Organizations have vast stores of historical operational data of which they are anxious to take advantage, especially valuable information about many aspects of their business, including customers, products, inventories, and sales. Until recently, companies did not have enough computing power at their disposal to be able to take advantage of these stored data (Rudin, 1995). Now, however, parallel processing is enabling organizations to begin to analyze these massive amounts of historical data through the development of data warehouses and data marts. The emergence of parallel processing capabilities underlies the development of data warehousing, which is discussed in detail in Chapter 11. Retail organizations, with large amounts of sales data to analyze, have embraced parallel processing systems.

There are several considerations which organizations should take into account before moving into SMP or MPP systems (Rudin, 1995).

- *Data analysis requirements*   Parallel systems are going to be most effective at solving problems that involve handling large amounts of data (250 GB or larger), executing complex queries, or processing data that are used by large numbers of concurrent users. The problems should be addressed only if they are of strategic significance to the organization, or else the significant hardware costs, software development costs, and retraining costs will not be worth it to the organization. For example, retailing applications provide strategic value to retailers. An example is Catalina Marketing's market basket analysis system, which tracks not only what products are purchased but what assortments of products tend to be purchased at the same time. Retailers can use the results of such applications to plan coordinated promotions for related products, to allocate shelf space and placements, and to make pricing decisions.

- *Cost justification*   Remember that parallel systems tend to complement rather than replace existing operational systems. Businesses use them to increase revenues rather than to reduce costs. Therefore, traditional cost justification procedures may not be appropriate. Since many of the applications are intended to improve an organization's marketing strategies, treating the parallel system as an investment in marketing capabilities is appropriate.

- *Traditional technologies*   If the proposed application can be accomplished using traditional, existing technology within the organization, it probably makes sense to continue to rely on that technology. MPP systems are far from mature, and their implementation is sure to challenge any organization. Therefore, even when you are sure that parallel processing would make sense for the problem that the organization wants to address, a feasibility analysis of more mature technologies should be undertaken. It may be feasible to implement a solution for a problem that is expected to benefit from parallel processing in a uniprocessor environment, but traditional technologies should be ruled out before proceeding with a parallel processing solution.

The data warehousing and data mining applications discussed process queries that access large amounts of data and metadata, using join and aggregation operations. These queries involve many I/O operations and are likely to generate sizable intermediate results sets (Frazer, 1998). At present, there are no object/relational (O/R) databases large enough to qualify as VLDB systems. (See Appendix D to learn about O/R databases.) However, as O/R technology becomes more mature, it will be expected to handle databases at least the size of the current relational implementations, in part because O/R databases handle new data types that are much bulkier to store. O/R databases will deal with complex relationships among instances of the new data types, relationships that go beyond the simple row-and-column structure of the relational model. Parallel processing methods can be expected to enable these coming developments.

USING MIDDLEWARE

Middleware: Software that allows an application to interoperate with other software without requiring the user to understand and code the low-level operations necessary to achieve interoperability.

Middleware is often referred to as the glue that holds together client/server applications. It is a term that is commonly used to describe any software component between the PC-client and the relational database in *n*-tier architectures. Simply put, **middleware** is any of several classes of software that allow an application to interoperate with other software without requiring the user to understand and code the low-level operations required to achieve interoperability (Hurwitz, 1998). Middleware has existed for decades—examples are IBM's transaction-processing middleware, CICS, or BEA Systems' Tuxedo for UNIX machines. But the advent of client/server technologies and now Web-oriented development has stimulated new development of commercially available middleware. Universal middleware, one magical software package that could integrate and connect every type of system, would be ideal, of course. At this time, however, such a middleware package is not available. Most organizations use several different middleware packages, sometimes even within one application.

Another consideration is whether the communication involved is synchronous or asynchronous. With synchronous systems, the requesting system waits for a response to the request in real time. An on-line banking system where the teller checks an account balance before cashing a check is an example of a synchronous system. Asynchronous systems send a request but do not wait for a response in real time. Rather, the response is accepted whenever it is received. Electronic mail is an example of an asynchronous system with which you are probably familiar.

Hurwitz (1998) has provided a helpful classification system containing six categories that organize the many types of middleware that are currently available. Her classifications are based on scalability and recoverability:

- *Asynchronous remote procedure call (RPC)* The client requests services but does not wait for a response. It will typically establish a point-to-point connection with the server and perform other processing while it waits for the response. If the connection is lost, the client must reestablish the connection and send the request again. This type of middleware has high scalability but low recoverability, and has been largely replaced by synchronous RPC since 1998.

- *Synchronous RPC* A distributed program using synchronous RPC may call services available on different computers. This middleware makes it possible to establish this facility without undertaking the detailed coding usually necessary to write an RPC. Examples would include Microsoft Transaction Server and IBM's CICS. The Java equivalent of an RPC is a Remote Method Invocation (RMI).

- *Publish/subscribe* This type of middleware monitors activity and pushes information to subscribers. It is asynchronous—the clients, or subscribers, perform other activities between notifications from the server. The subscribers notify the publisher of information that they wish to receive, and when an event occurs that contains such information, it is sent to the subscriber, who can then elect to receive the information or not. For example, you can supply electronic bookstores with keywords of topics that interest you. Whenever the bookstore adds a book title that is keyword coded with one of your keywords, information about that title will be automatically forwarded to you for consideration. This type of middleware is very useful for monitoring situations where actions need to be taken when particular events occur.

- *Message-oriented middleware (MOM)*   MOM is also asynchronous software, sending messages that are collected and stored until they are acted upon, while the client continues with other processing. Workflow applications such as insurance policy applications, which often involve several processing steps, can benefit from MOM. The queue where the requests are stored can be journalized, thus providing some recoverability.

- *Object request broker (ORB)*   This type of middleware makes it possible for applications to send objects and request services in an object-oriented system. The ORB tracks the location of each object and routes requests to each object. Current ORBs are synchronous, but asynchronous ORBs are being developed.

- *SQL-oriented data access*   Connecting applications to databases over networks is achieved by using SQL-oriented data access middleware. This middleware also has the capability to translate generic SQL into the SQL specific to the database. Database vendors and companies that have developed multidatabase access middleware dominate this middleware segment.

While the preceding classifications provide an elementary understanding of the functional variations in middleware, many hybrid products combine these capabilities. For example, SQL-oriented and RPC middleware add awareness of objects and ORBs are adding transaction, queuing, and messaging services. Object transaction monitors should be available soon and promise to combine the functionality of distributed objects, currently handled by CORBA or DCOM, and transaction monitors, which provide transaction management for applications, helping to reduce I/O bottlenecks.

In client/server systems, database-oriented middleware provides some sort of **application program interface (API)** access to a database. APIs are sets of routines that an application program uses to direct the performance of procedures by the computer's operating system. For example, in achieving access to a database, an API calls library routines that transparently route SQL commands from the front-end client application to the database server. An API might work with existing front-end software, like a third-generation language or custom report generator, and it might include its own facilities for building applications. When APIs exist for several program development tools, then you have considerable independence to develop client applications in the most convenient front-end programming environment yet still draw data from a common server database. Such middleware makes it possible for developers to link an application easily to popular databases.

Open database connectivity (ODBC) is similar to API, but for Windows-based client/server applications. It is most useful for accessing relational data, and not well suited for accessing other types of data, such as ISAM files (LaRue, 1997). Even though ODBC is difficult to program and implement, it has been well accepted because it allows programmers to make connections to almost any vendor's database without learning proprietary code specific to that database. For a more detailed discussion of ODBC and establishing Internet database connectivity, see Chapter 10. Microsoft's OLE-DB adds value to the ODBC standard by providing a single point of access to multiple databases (Linthicum, 1997). Microsoft is planning to make OLE-DB a universal data access standard and has added OLE-DB for data mining applications and OLE-DB for OLAP. Access to legacy data while moving to client/server systems can be achieved by products such as EDA/SQL, which attempt to support many different operating systems, networks, and databases.

Java Database Connectivity (JDBC) classes can be used to help an applet access any number of databases without understanding the native features of each database. JDBC defines a call-level interface (CLI) for Java development and borrows from ODBC conventions. Establishing a common language to define interfaces between components and a mechanism to mediate will facilitate developing universal middleware (Keuffel, 1997). The Object Management Group (OMG), established in 1989, is an industry coalition that has produced the **Common Object Request Broker**

Application program interface (API): Sets of routines that an application program uses to direct the performance of procedures by the computer's operating system.

Architecture (CORBA), which sets the specification of object-oriented universal middleware. Microsoft has developed a competing model, Distributed Component Object Model (DCOM), but CORBA is a more robust specification because it has been developed to handle many different platforms. Interoperability between the two standards is slowly emerging. Such standards are particularly important on the World Wide Web because of the diversity of the platforms that are connecting.

ESTABLISHING CLIENT/SERVER SECURITY

Client/server database computing implies the existence of a network that connects the client/server components together. In this distributed environment, establishing database security is more complex than in a centralized environment. (See Chapter 12 for a more detailed discussion of database security.) Networks are susceptible to breaches of security through eavesdropping, unauthorized connections, or unauthorized retrieval of packets of information that are traversing the network. Thus, client/server architectures are more susceptible to security threats than centralized systems.

Security measures that should be taken in a client/server environment include measures that are common to securing all systems, but should also include measures taken to secure the more distributed environment of client/server architectures (Bobrowski, 1994):

- *System-level password security*   User names and passwords are typically used to identify and authorize users when they wish to connect to a multiuser client/server system. Security standards should include guidelines for password lengths, password naming conventions, frequency of password changes, and so on. Password management utilities should be included as part of the network and operating systems.

- *Database level password security*   Most client/server DBMSs have database level password security that is similar to system-level password security. It is also possible to pass through authentication information from the operating system authentication capability. Administration that takes advantage of the pass-through capabilities is easier, but external attempts to gain access will also be easier because using the pass-through capabilities reduces the number of password security layers from two to one. Reliance on operating system authentication should not be encouraged.

- *Secure client/server communication*   Encryption, transforming readable data (plain text) into unreadable (ciphertext) can help to ensure secure client/server communication. Most clients send database users' plain text passwords to database servers. The larger RDBMSs such as Oracle, Sybase, and Inform, have secure network password transmission capabilities. Encryption of all data that are passed across the network is obviously desired, but the costs are high for encryption software. Encryption also affects performance negatively because of the time required to encrypt and decrypt the data.

Client/Server Security Issues for Web-Enabled Databases

The explosion of Websites that make current data accessible to viewers through their Internet connections raises new issues that go beyond the traditional client/server security issues addressed in the previous section. The dynamic creation of a Web page from a database requires access to the database, and if the database is not properly protected, it is vulnerable to inappropriate access by any user. This is a new point of vulnerability that was previously avoided by strict database access authorization schemes or specialized client access software.

If an organization wishes only to make static HTML pages available, protection must be established for the HTML files stored on a Web server. Creation of a static Web page uses traditional client/server tools such as Visual Basic or Power-Builder, and thus their creation can be controlled by using standard methods of database access control. If some of the HTML files loaded on the Web server are sensitive, they can be placed in directories that are protected using operating system security, or they may be readable but not published in the directory. Thus, the user must know the exact file name in order to access the sensitive HTML page. It is also common to segregate the Web server and limit its contents to publicly browsable Web pages. Sensitive files may be kept on another server accessible through an organization's Intranet. Again, security measures such as those described above will be needed if some users should not have access to all of the files stored for the Intranet. User-authentication security can be used to control access to sensitive files.

Security measures for dynamic Web page generation are different. Dynamic Web pages are stored as a template into which the appropriate and current data is inserted from the database once the query(ies) associated with the page is run. This means that the Web server must be able to access the database. In order to function appropriately, the connection usually requires full access to the database. Thus, establishing adequate server security is critical to protecting the data. The server that owns the database connection should be physically secure, and execution of programs and common gateway interface (CGI) scripts should be controlled.

Access to data can also be controlled through another layer of security, user-authentication security. Use of an HTML login form will allow the DBA to define each user's privileges. Each session may be tracked by storing a piece of data, or "cookie," on the client machine. This information can be returned to the server and provide information about the login session. CGI scripts or other means must be established to perform the necessary authentication routines.

Session security must also be established to ensure that private data is not compromised during a session, since information is broadcast across a network for reception by a particular machine, and is thus susceptible to being intercepted. TCP/IP is not a very secure protocol, and encryption systems such as the ones discussed in the previous section on client/server security are essential. Many Internet systems use a combination of public-key and secret-key encryption. Both the server and the client may encrypt a secret key with their private keys. The encrypted data is sent along with their public key, or possibly their public key may be kept by a Certificate Saver that provides it. A standard encryption method, Secure Sockets Layer (SSL), is also used by many developers to encrypt all data travelling between client and server during a session. URLs that begin with https:// use SSL for transmission.

Other related security measures, such as digital signatures, Kerberos security servers, and vendor-specific security measures, are discussed in Chapter 12.

CLIENT/SERVER ISSUES

There is no question that the establishment of client/server architectures has affected the database computing environment. But, too often one hears of client/server implementation failures and disillusioned users. In order to succeed, client/server projects should address a specific business problem with well-defined technology and cost parameters. Certain areas should be carefully addressed in order to improve the chances for building a successful client/server application (Linthicum, 1996):

- *Accurate business problem analysis* Just as is the case with other computing architectures, it is critical to develop a sound application design and architecture for a new client/server system. Developers' tendencies to pick the technology and then fit the application to it seem to be more pronounced in the strong push toward client/server environments that has occurred in the last decade. It is more appropriate to accurately define the scope of the problem and determine requirements, and then use that information to select the technology.

- *Detailed architecture analysis* It is also important to specify the details of the client/server architecture. Building a client/server solution involves connecting many components, which may not work together easily. One of the often touted advantages of client/server computing, the ability to accept an open systems approach, can be very detrimental if the heterogeneous components chosen are difficult to connect. Besides specifying the client workstations, server(s), network, and DBMS, analysts also should specify network infrastructure, the middleware layer, and the application development tools to be used. At each juncture, analysts should take steps to assure that the tools will connect with the middleware, database, network, and so forth.

- *Avoiding tool-driven architectures* As above, determine project requirements *before* choosing software tools, and not the reverse. Choosing a tool first and then applying it to the problem risks having a poor fit between problem and tool. Tools selected this way are likely to have been chosen based on an emotional appeal rather than on the appropriate functionality of the tool.

- *Achieving appropriate scalability* A multitier solution allows client/server systems to scale to any number of users and handle diverse processing loads. But multitiered solutions are significantly more expensive and difficult to build. The tools to develop a multitier environment are still limited, too. Architects should avoid moving to a multitier solution when it's not really needed. Usually, multitier makes sense in environments of more than 100 concurrent users, high-volume transaction processing systems, or for real-time processing. Smaller, less intense environments can frequently run more efficiently on traditional two-tier systems, especially if triggers and procedures are used to manage the processing.

- *Appropriate placement of services* Again, a careful analysis of the business problem being addressed is important when making decisions about the placement of processing services. The move toward thin clients and fat servers is not always the appropriate solution. Moving the application logic to a server, thus creating a fat server, can affect capacity, as end users all attempt to use the application now located on the server. Sometimes it is possible to achieve better scaling by moving application processing to the client. Fat servers do tend to reduce network load because the processing takes place close to the data, and fat servers do lessen the need for powerful clients. Understanding the business problem intimately should help the architect to distribute the logic appropriately.

- *Network analysis* The most common bottleneck in distributed systems is still the network. Therefore, architects ignore at their peril the bandwidth capabilities of the network that the system must use. If the network is insufficient to handle the amount of information that must pass between client and server, response time will suffer badly, and the system is likely to fail.

- *Be aware of hidden costs* Client/server implementation problems go beyond the analysis, development, and architecture problems listed above (Atre, 1995). For example, systems that are intended to use existing hardware, networks, operating systems, and DBMSs are often stymied by the complexities of integrating these heterogeneous components to build the client/server system. Training is a significant and recurring expense that is often overlooked. The complexities of working in a multivendor environment can be very costly.

If these issues are addressed appropriately, there are benefits to be won from moving to client/server architectures (Atre, 1995):

- Functionality can be delivered in stages to the end users. Thus, it arrives more quickly as the first pieces of the project are deployed.
- The graphic user interfaces common in client/server environments encourage users to utilize the applications' functionality.
- The flexibility and scalability of client/server solutions facilitate business process re-engineering.
- More processing can be performed close to the source of data being processed, thereby improving response times and reducing network traffic.
- Client/server architectures allow the development of Web-enabled applications, facilitating the ability of organizations to communicate effectively internally and to conduct external business over the Internet.

DATABASE ACCESS FROM CLIENT APPLICATIONS

Earlier in this chapter, Figure 9-1 depicted the components of program logic that must be distributed across a two- or three-tier client/server application environment. Partitioning the environment to create a two-, three-, or n-tier architecture means that decisions must be made about the placement of the processing logic. In each case, storage logic (the database engine) is handled by the server, and presentation logic is handled by the client.

Figure 9-8a depicts some possible two-tier systems, placing the processing logic on the client (creating a fat client), on the server (creating a thin client), or partitioned across both the server and the client (a distributed environment). It is the placement of the processing logic that is emphasized in the three scenarios. In the fat client, the application processing occurs entirely on the client, while in the thin client, this processing occurs on the server. In the distributed example, application processing is partitioned between the client and the server.

Figure 9-8b presents a typical three-tier architecture and an n-tier architecture. Again, some processing logic could be placed on the client, if desired. But, a typical client in a Web-enabled client/server environment will be a thin client, using a browser for its presentation logic. The middle tiers are typically coded in a portable language such as C or Java. The flexibility and easier manageability of the n-tier approaches account for its increasing popularity, in spite of the increased complexity of managing communication among the tiers. The fast-paced, distributed, and heterogeneous environment of the Internet and e-commerce initiatives have also led to the development of many n-tier architectures.

The client, then, is responsible for the presentation logic. Users interface with the rest of the system through their browser, an application, or a programming interface. These interfaces have come to be predominantly graphical user interfaces (GUI). Interfaces for accessing databases are no different. Although SQL syntax is still used to communicate directly with databases, the Query-by-Example (QBE) approach to querying databases has proved to be a popular interface, too. The ease of use and inclusion of programming capabilities in desktop database products such as Microsoft Access have led many organizations to use such packages as a front-end attached to a more powerful back-end database such as Oracle or Informix. For example, by using pass-through queries, formulated in Access but run

Figure 9-8
Common logic distributions
(a) Two-tier client server environments

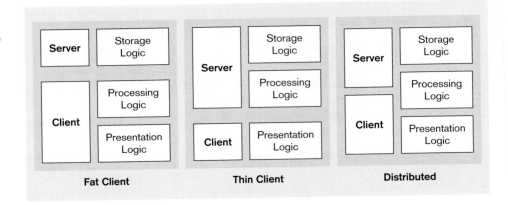

(b) *n*-tier client/server environments
(There are many possibilities; these are just samples.)

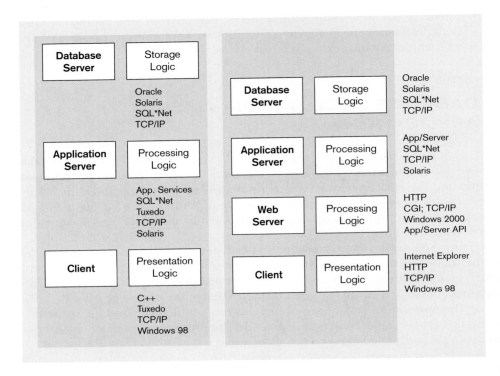

against the back-end Oracle database, organizations achieve faster development times but utilize the more robust and powerful RDBMSs for their mission-critical applications.

USING QUERY-BY-EXAMPLE

Query-by-Example (QBE): A direct manipulation database language that uses a graphical approach to query construction.

Query-by-Example (QBE) is the most widely available direct-manipulation database query language. Although not an international standard like SQL, QBE has been widely available, especially in the PC-RDBMS market, for many years. As a direct-manipulation query language, it is easy to learn for a wide variety of people wanting to make inquiries against a database. Also, its simplicity makes it a popular language for developing prototypes. Since some database systems, such as Microsoft Access, translate QBE queries into SQL, QBE can be used as at least a first pass at creating SQL code. QBE-based systems that generate SQL code can then be used to build presentation or client layer modules that access server databases. In this section, you will learn about the history of QBE and many of the querying capabilities of this important database manipulation language.

The History and Importance of QBE

Although QBE (like SQL) was originally developed for mainframe database processing, it has become prevalent in client/server and personal computer database systems as well. Query-by-Example was originally developed by Zloof (1977) and was first available for use with SQL/DS and DB2 database systems on IBM mainframes. The success of the first personal computer relational DBMS (PC-RDBMS) that was completely based on QBE, Paradox, encouraged other products to adopt a QBE interface as an option. Most current systems include a variation on QBE.

Coverage of QBE is essential for the understanding of modern database systems. This is true because QBE is considered a highly productive language in which to program. Visual versions of programming languages, such as Visual Basic, Visual C, and Visual Java have transformed the way programs are written. Research studies (for example, Greenblatt and Waxman, 1978; Thomas and Gould, 1975) have shown that even with relatively little training, student subjects find QBE easier to use than SQL or a relational algebra language. Although these studies are more than two decades old, no new database query language has been developed that beats QBE's usability.

QBE is especially useful for end-user database programming. The visual programming environment gives the nonprogramming user a single view of data no matter what database task is performed. As we will see (and as was shown in Chapter 2), queries are developed interactively on a CRT screen in a format that resembles the desired output. In most programs, both queries and results are shown in the same format, usually a spreadsheet-type format.

Complete database applications can be written in QBE, but it is more common to use QBE for interactive querying or updating of a database. That is, QBE is particularly useful for ad hoc database processing. Rather than developing a complete application in QBE, it is more common to use QBE to prototype an application, saving the queries that are developed. These saved queries can then be enhanced by using the application generator tools, such as screen, form, and report generators, and by adding modules of code using the database language associated with the PC-RDBMS to provide custom behaviors.

QBE: The Basics

There is no official standard for QBE as has been defined for SQL (see Chapter 8 for a discussion of the SQL standardization efforts). For this reason, there is no minimal set of capabilities that a query interface must meet to be considered a QBE implementation. However, because QBE has evolved from research on database query languages, because the Windows visual interface has been standardized, and because it is a visual language, all vendors have adopted similar approaches to QBE.

Both data retrieval and data modification can be done via entering keywords, constants, and example data into the cells of a table layout. Because data definitions are stored in internal tables, even data definition is done through a similar table layout interface. In MS Access 2000 (used along with Oracle 8*i* in this chapter for examples) clicking on an SQL button will reveal the Access SQL code that has been generated as the QBE-based query has been constructed.

Figure 9-9 depicts the original Microsoft Access usability hierarchy. The pyramid conveys that Access will be usable at all levels of programming ability and complexity. At the lowest level of the pyramid are the objects, which allow the creation of tables, queries, forms, and reports without any specific programming knowledge. The use of expressions, or functions, to perform simple processes such as multiplication of fields, validation of data, or enforcement of a specific business rule is possible at the

Figure 9-9
The Access usability hierarchy (adapted from Prague & Irwin, 1997)

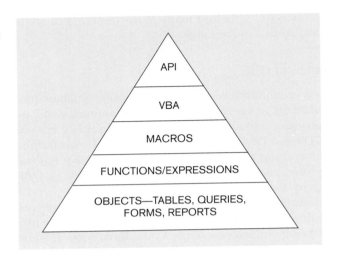

next pyramid level. At the next level, macros, users can take advantage of stored modules of Visual Basic for Applications (VBA) code to automate their application, again without explicit knowledge of VBA. At the next level, users can program their own modules of VBA code to custom tailor their own applications. At the top level, Windows API calls to functions or DLLs written in languages such as C, Java, or Visual Basic that can be used to write interfaces to other programs and sources of data.

QBE provides a simple, visual method for specifying qualified queries. Data for display may be limited to certain columns and records with desired values, just as was shown in Chapter 8 when using SQL. In fact, the Access SQL that conveys a query constructed in the QBE pane can always be viewed by clicking on the SQL icon.

In Access 2000, the QBE pane (see Figure 9-10) has an upper workspace where data model representations of the tables or queries involved in a query are placed. Previously established relationships will also show automatically. Occasionally, another relationship is needed for a single query, and that relationship can also be established in the QBE pane. The lower part of the QBE pane, called the query design pane or QBE grid, displays a spreadsheet-type form in which the fields needed for the query are placed, along with any sorting and limiting criteria needed for the query. Each column in the QBE grid contains information about a single field from a table or query in the upper pane. Figure 9-10 shows a QBE pane for a select query involving the product and order line tables that asks for information about orders on which each product has been ordered. Note that the result displayed in Figure 9-11 is called a *dynaset*. Although the result looks just like a table, it is not a base table like the raw materials table on which it was based. Rather, it is a *dynamic* or *virtual* set of records and is not stored in the database. Figure 9-12 shows the Access SQL view of this query.

The benefits of a dynaset are that the storage device being used requires less storage space, and that whenever the query is run, it will use the current copy of the database, which will include any records that have been added or updated since the query was last run. Thus, queries behave just like relational views, discussed in Chapter 8. If you need to save the results of the query into a new table, use a make-table query.

A quick review of multiple-table queries in SQL (in Chapter 8) will remind you of the need to specify which tables are needed in the query (in the FROM clause) and to set the equalities between each table that is needed in the query (in the WHERE clause). These links can be time consuming to code in SQL if one is not an excellent keyboarder. In MS Access 2000 QBE, these links were established when the relationships were made explicit in the Relationships screen, and putting the tables needed in the QBE pane brings those links in automatically, thus eliminating the need to type in each link. This can be a great saving in time and accuracy as a query is developed. Look at Figure 9-10, in which the two tables to be used in the query

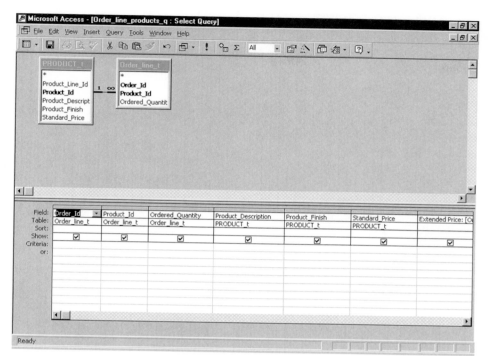

Figure 9-10
MS Access 2000 multiple-table query in design mode (Pine Valley Furniture)

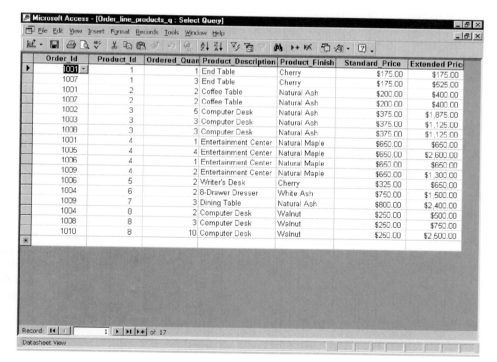

Figure 9-11
MS Access 2000 dynaset (query result from Figure 9-10) (Pine Valley Furniture)

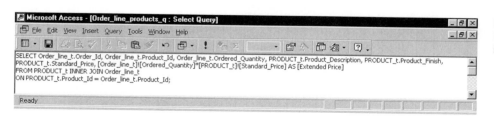

Figure 9-12
MS Access 2000 multiple-table query in SQL view (Pine Valley Furniture)

Figure 9-13
Query to select orders placed for three or more units of a particular product (Pine Valley Furniture)

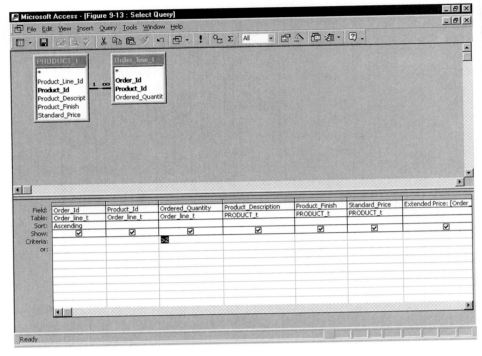

have been added to the QBE pane and the fields required for the query result have been selected and dragged to the QBE grid. Figure 9-12 shows you how much of the SQL has already been established just by the simple clicking and dragging that has occurred. Notice that even though the QBE grid does not contain the primary key column from the PRODUCT_t table (Product_ID) that has been used to establish the links among the two tables, the correct linkages have been made explicit in the SQL. Notice also how Access SQL varies from the Oracle SQL*Plus used in Chapter 8 (you may want to write the Oracle SQL equivalent to the code in Figure 9-12). The differences make it quite clear that each vendor has its own flavor of SQL.

Selecting Qualified Records

What if you are only interested in certain records? Figure 9-13 shows the basic approach to entering qualifications for which records to display from a table. Placing conditions under the associated column does this. The dynaset returned is shown in Figure 9-14. The condition can be an inequality, as in Figure 9-13, or it could involve a range or equality. For example, you could enter "Between 350 and 700" under the Standard_Price column in Figure 9-13 to learn which products are mid-range priced.

Operators, functions, and expressions can also be used when constructing criteria in queries. Mathematical operators, such as multiplication and division, operate with numeric fields. The relational operators, such as equal, not equal, and less than,

Figure 9-14
Dynaset from Figure 9-13 query (Pine Valley Furniture)

Order_Id	Product_Id	Ordered_Quan	Product_Description	Product_Finish	Standard_Price	Extended Pric
1002	3	5	Computer Desk	Natural Ash	$375.00	$1,875.00
1003	3	3	Computer Desk	Natural Ash	$375.00	$1,125.00
1005	4	4	Entertainment Center	Natural Maple	$650.00	$2,600.00
1007	1	3	End Table	Cherry	$175.00	$525.00
1008	8	3	Computer Desk	Walnut	$250.00	$750.00
1008	3	3	Computer Desk	Natural Ash	$375.00	$1,125.00
1009	7	3	Dining Table	Natural Ash	$800.00	$2,400.00
1010	8	10	Computer Desk	Walnut	$250.00	$2,500.00

Record: 1 of 8

can be used with numeric fields, date fields, and text fields. Boolean or logical operators are used for setting conditions in expressions.

Functions are modules of code that always return a value based on a calculation or comparison performed by the function. String, logic, or number values can be returned, depending on the nature of the function. Microsoft Access has many common functions already stored for use, such as *sum* or *average,* or specialized functions may be written in VBA. Expressions are a term or series of terms controlled by operators. Access will try to help with expression syntax by inserting needed characters, such as quotes, if they are left off.

Self-Join

Some queries are much easier to construct using a QBE interface because its visual representation is clearer than a complex syntax for most people. An example is the situation where a query requires a table to be joined with itself. This type of query is called a *self-join* or a *recursive join.* For example, suppose you want to know what orders have been placed that include any of the same products that were ordered on order number 1004. Such a query might arise because of, say, a packaging problem with this order, and you need it to find if any other orders have had the same problem. An Access 2000 QBE query to answer this question appears in Figure 9-15a. A

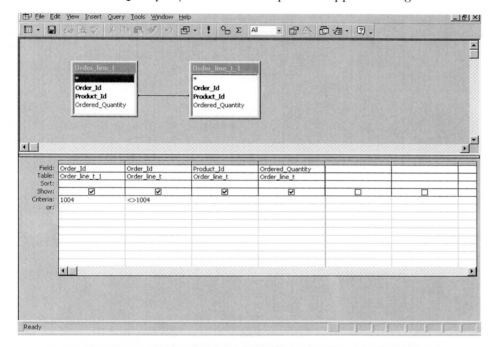

Figure 9-15
Example recursive join: What orders have the same products as order 1004?
(a) MS Access 2000 recursive join from Pine Valley Furniture

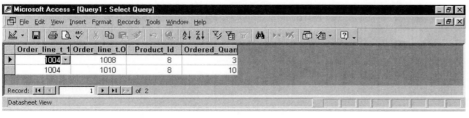

(b) MS Access 2000 dynaset from recursive join in (a)

(c) MS Access 2000 recursive join query in SQL View (Pine Valley Furniture)

self-join is done by putting two copies of the Order_Line_t table in the QBE pane, setting a relationship between product IDs (see the relationship line connecting the Product_ID fields in the two tables), and setting a criterion of 1004 in one table and a criterion of NOT 1004 in the other table that will return product ID and quantity values. It can be seen in Figure 9-15b that only product number 8 has been ordered on other orders. Three were ordered on order number 1008 and ten were ordered on order number 1010. The SQL (which could be run against a local or server database) is shown in Figure 9-15c.

Basing a Query on Another Query

It can be difficult even in QBE to answer a question in a single query. One way to deal with such difficult queries is to break a query into multiple steps, save the query generated to answer a particular step, and then base the next query on the saved query rather than the base tables. Such an approach is sometimes similar to using subqueries in SQL. So, basing a query on another query will allow you to compute values for SUM, COUNT, and so on using the dynaset generated by the saved query, thus solving some of the difficulties inherent in using functions with groups of records discussed in Chapter 8.

Suppose you want to find those customers who did not buy anything from Pine Valley Furniture during October 2000. That is, you want to know what customer numbers from records in the Customer_t table are not listed in the records of the Order_t table for October 2000. Figures 9-16a through 9-16d show you how you would answer this question by building one query and then building a second query that uses the first query. The first query (QBE in Figure 9-16a and dynaset result in Figure 9-16b) returns the customers who placed orders in October. The QBE for this query was saved in a query named First Query. The second query (QBE in Figure 9-16c and dynaset result in Figure 9-16d) then uses an outer join to compare the list of all customers (table Customer_t) with those who placed orders (the virtual table defined by First Query) and returns a dynaset with only those customers who are not found in the dynaset from the first query (see the Is Null qualification in Figure 9-16c).

Figure 9-16
Query based on another query
(a) MS Access 2000 base query to be used for next query in Figure 9-16c.

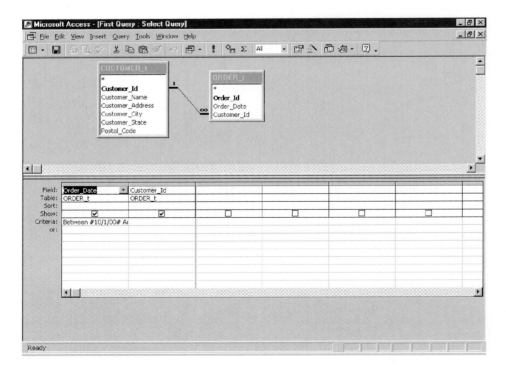

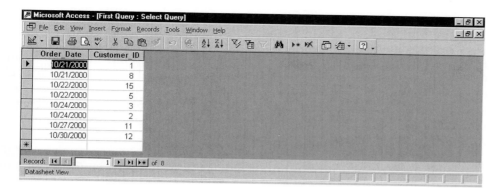

Figure 9-16
(continued)
(b) MS Access 2000 dynaset returned
by Figure 9-16a query

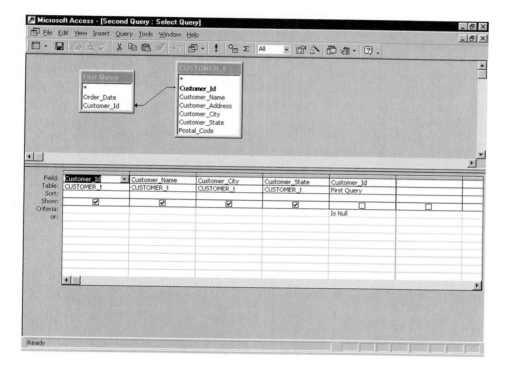

(c) MS Access 2000 query based on
Figure 9-16a

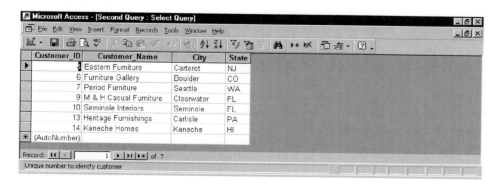

(d) MS Access 2000 dynaset returned
by Figure 9-16c query

Using SQL Pass-Through Queries

One reason that MS Access has been popular as a client interface for client/server applications is the ease with which one can send commands to any ODBC (open database connectivity) database server directly. Using a pass-through query, which is written in the SQL dialect of the ODBC database server rather than MS Access SQL, you work directly with the tables on the server instead of linking to them. This bypasses the MS Access Jet database engine and gives faster performance. All syntax checking, interpretation, and translation of the SQL queries will take place on the server database. Network traffic will be reduced because only the initial SQL query and the records that are returned have to be passed between the server and the client.

MS Access pass-through queries can be used to retrieve records, change data, or execute stored procedures or triggers located on the database server. One can even create new tables in the server database. Be careful, however, not to perform an operation that affects the state of the connection, as unexpected results may occur.

This method does not allow you to link the tables of the ODBC database to MS Access. (Linking tables is covered later in this chapter.) This means that you can't create an updateable record set based on these tables. The user must be familiar with the SQL dialect used by the ODBC database. So, while performance gains can be considerable and it is possible to take advantage of the power of the large database server, the user must be knowledgeable about the SQL dialect to be used and must be prepared to undertake more manual operations to achieve complete functionality.

Creation of an MS Access pass-through query requires that a connection string be specified, either as a property of the pass-through query or at the time that the query runs. Figure 9-17 shows the Oracle SQL syntax and the properties window of an MS Access 2000 pass-through query containing an Oracle SQL statement.

It is important to note that each RDBMS, such as Oracle, Informix, or SQL Server, will have its own syntax for the ODBC connect string that must be inserted into the properties window or entered at the time that the query is run. For example, the syntax of the Oracle connect string used here is:

ODBC;DSN =*ODBC Connection Name*;UID =*User*;PWD =*Password*;SERVER
=*Connection Alias from TnSNames.ora*;

Figure 9-17
MS Access 2000 SQL pass-through query with query properties window

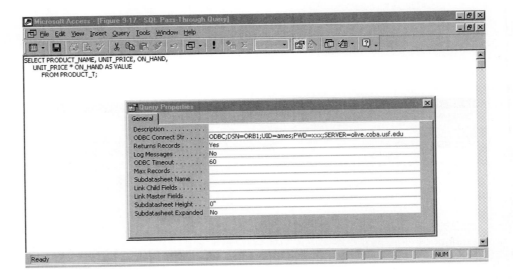

USING ODBC TO LINK EXTERNAL TABLES STORED ON A DATABASE SERVER

The **open database connectivity (ODBC) standard** was developed in the early 1990s by the X/Open and SQL Access Group committees. It proposed several levels of standards that RDBMSs could attain, thus enabling any application program to access them using a common application programming interface (API) for accessing and processing. Such RDBMSs are said to be ODBC-compliant. The standard has gained wide acceptance, originally propelled by Microsoft's implementation of ODBC for their products. ODBC is also important for Internet applications because it allows for the development of applications that access different database products. In order to achieve this capability, ODBC uses the ANSI standard generic SQL statements presented in Chapter 8, but it is unable to take advantage of the extensions and special features that each vendor has given its engine.

The ODBC specification allows drivers to conform to various levels of the specification, and that affects the level of functionality of the drivers. Differences in how the drivers themselves are written may affect performance achieved. Each vendor desiring to have an ODBC-compliant database provides an ODBC driver that can be installed on Windows machines. Thus, each Windows application can communicate, through the appropriate driver, with the desired version of the database server. For example, an MS Access application can be connected to operate with an Oracle database server. The database tables are linked to the MS Access application through the ODBC link and remain in the Oracle database. They are not brought into the MS Access database.

You may hear the Oracle database server referred to as the database server, but it may also be called the remote server, the back-end server, or the SQL server. As Microsoft's back-end server is called SQL Server, a reference to SQL server may be a reference to a type of server or to a particular vendor database server. This can be confusing.

Five parameters must be defined in order to establish an ODBC connection:

- Specific ODBC *driver* needed
- Back-end *server* name to connect to
- *Database* name to connect to
- *User id* to be granted access to database
- *Password* of user id

Additional information may be provided, if desired:

- Data source name (DSN)
- Windows client computer name
- Client application program's executable name

These parameters may be defined from different locations. They may be included in the program, or through the DSN, or by the user when prompted. Including all of the parameters in the program will make it possible for the program to connect directly to the database with no further communication. Of course, the program would have to be modified and new parameter values inserted in order to port the program to another server or RDBMS. Including the DSN, which includes some of the parameter values, in the program will allow local administrators to place the database and select an RDBMS. The user can provide the user ID and password when he logs on to use the application.

Figure 9-18 is a schematic of the typical ODBC architecture. The client application requests that a connection be established with a data source. The request is handled by Microsoft's driver manager, which identifies the appropriate ODBC driver to use. Remember that these drivers are supplied by the vendors, so there may be an SQL Server driver, an Oracle driver, an Informix driver, and so forth. Initialization

Open database connectivity (ODBC) standard: An application programming interface that provides a common language for application programs to access and process SQL databases independent of the particular RDBMS that is accessed.

Figure 9-18
Open database connectivity (ODBC)
architecture

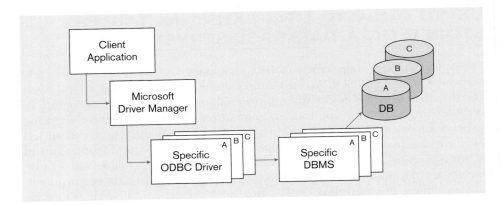

requests, format validation, and ODBC request management are also handled by the driver manager. The driver selected will process the request received from the client and submit queries to the selected RDBMS couched in that particular RDBMS's SQL syntax. The amount of processing required to create that query depends upon the capability of the RDBMS being accessed.

Also, the ODBC conformance level will be determined by the capabilities of the driver that has been supplied by the vendor. There are three defined levels of conformance: Core API, Level-1 API, and Level-2 API. These levels have been defined by the standards committees mentioned earlier in this section. Most drivers provide both Core API and Level-1 API functionalities, which include:

- Ability to connect to data sources with driver-specific information
- Prepare and execute SQL statements
- Retrieve data from a result set
- Commit or rollback transactions
- Retrieve error and catalog information
- Send and receive partial results
- Retrieve information about drivers

Distinguishing characteristics of Level-2 API capabilities include:

- Ability to browse potential data sources and connections
- Retrieve native (back-end dialect) SQL
- Call a translation library
- Process and display a scrollable cursor

Applications determine the level of API support available when they call the driver. If Level-2 API is needed and the application is only Level-1 API, then the execution sequence can be terminated in a controlled fashion, so that no corruption of the data occurs. Some applications are written to function at either Level 1 or Level 2, depending on the capabilities of the driver for the particular RDBMS being used.

USING JDBC TO LINK EXTERNAL TABLES STORED ON A DATABASE SERVER

The Java Database Connectivity (JDBC) API enables Java programs to execute SQL statements and connect to database servers. JDBC is similar to ODBC, but it is designed specifically for Java applications. ODBC is language independent. Java is a good language to use for client/server computing because it is network-oriented, strong in security, and portable. Oracle has embraced Java and it appears that Oracle's proprietary language, PL/SQL, will be replaced by Java to provide the additional programming functionality needed beyond SQL to build database applications.

The JDBC standard is similar in concept to Microsoft's ODBC. Based on the X/Open SQL Call Level Interface, JDBC consists of two main layers. One layer, the JDBC API, supports communications from a Java application to the JDBC driver manager. The other layer, JDBC Driver API, supports communications from the JDBC driver manager directly to JDBC drivers, and to network drivers and ODBC-based drivers.

Figure 9-19 includes a simple example of the code necessary to use JDBC to access a JDBC-compliant database. Note that the code has been marked in four boxes to emphasize the different tasks that are being performed.

```
//package.com.iteamsolutions.eis.tools.sql.sample;    Predefined Java packages
importjava.sql.CallableStatement;
importjava.sql.Connection;
importjava.sql.Driver;
importjava.sql.DriverManager;
importjava.sql.PreparedStatement;
importjava.sql.ResultSet;
importjava.sql.Statement;
importjava.sql.SQLException;
importjava.sql.Types;

/**
*This class is intended as a simple demonstration of how to use JDBC
*to access a JDBC compliant Database.

Oracle table structure and primary key sequence and trigger

*The database structure listed below will be used for all examples: ⟨br ⟩
* ⟨pre ⟩
*
TABLE temp_demo
*Name Null?   Type
*
*ID       NOT NULL NUMBER
*NAME          VARCHAR2(20)
*
*Sequence used to populate the primary key
*SEQUENCE temp_demo_seq
*
*—Trigger used to populate the primary key
*
*CREATE OR REPLACE TRIGGER temp_demo_trig
*BEFORE INSERT ON temp_demo
*FOR EACH ROW
*BEGIN
*—This will allow the key to be autopopulated
*—could be retrieved using the RETURNING
*—clause of the INSERT statement
*—IF(:NEW.id IS NULL)
*THEN
*   SELECT temp_demo_seq.nextval
*   INTO :NEW.id
*   FROM dual;
*END IF;

*END;
* ⟨/pre ⟩
* ⟨br ⟩
```

Figure 9-19
Using JDBC to access a JDBC-compliant database

Figure 9-19
(continued)

Initialization

```
public class OracleSqlTest
{
    /**constant used for retrieving the id column of the temp_demo table*/
    public static final String ID = "id";

    /**constant used for retrieving the name column of the temp_demo table*/
    public static final String NAME = "name";

    /**name of the database account*/
    private String NAME = "username";

    /**the password for the user*/
    private String m_password = "userpassword";

    /**the Driver class to use for connecting to the database*/
    private String m_driver = "oracle.jdbc.driver.OracleDriver";

    /**the type of driver to use*/
    private String m_drivertype = "jdbc:oracle:thin:@";

    /**the database to connect to */
    private String m_database = "servername:1521:databasename";

    /**insert a new record into the temp_demo*/
    private String m_insert = "INSERT INTO temp_demo (id, name) values (?,?)";

    /**insert a new record into the temp_demo*/
    private String m_insertReturning = "BEGIN\n" +
                        "INSERT INTO temp_demo (name) values (?)\n" +
                        "RETURNING id INTO ?; \n" +
                        "END;";

    /**the connection being used by this class to do all work */
    private Connection m_conn = null;

    /**
    Default constructor - could be modified to supply the above values
    * or to pull them from a properties file.
    *
    * @throws Exception - any failure is a terminal condition
    */
    public OracleSqlTest()
        throws Exception
    {
        m_conn = buildConnection();
    }

    /**
    *inserts the passed values into the temp_demo table
    *
    * @param id - number to be used as the primary key in the record
    * @param name - Name to be stored in the name column
    */
    public void insert(int id, String name)
        throws SQLException
    {
        PreparedStatement stmt = null;

        try
        {
            //build a preparedStatement - this will allow values to
            //be substituted for the "?" in the String passed
            stmt =m_conn.prepareStatement(m_insert);
```

Figure 9-19
(continued)

```
      //bind the value to the argument (?)
      //the first argument is the position of the ? to replace.
      //The position count begins from 1
      stmt.setInt(1, id);
      stmt.setString(2, name);

      //exec the statement
      stmt.execute();
   }
   catch (SQLException e)
   {
      throw e;
   }
   finally
   {
      //make sure that all resources are released
      //if this is not done then eventually an exception
      //will be thrown by the database because too many
      //cursors are open
      if(stmt! = null)
         stmt,close();
   }
}
```

```
                 Build connection object for Oracle db access
/**
*takes care of building the connection object for access to the Oracle database;
*/
private Connection buildConnection()
   throws SQLException
{
   //need to make sure the driver for the database is loaded
   //any exception thrown is caught and a SQLException is thrown to
   //caught by the client.
   try
   {
      DriverManager.registerDriver
                    ((Driver) Class.forName(m_driver).newInstance());
   }
         catch (InstantiationException e)
   {
      throw new SQLException("Unable to instantiate the Oracle Driver");
   }
         catch (IllegalAccessException e)
   {
      throw new SQLException("IllegalAccessException thrown when attempting to
      load the Oracle Driver class");
   }
   catch (ClassNotFoundException e)
   {
      throw new SQLException("Oracle Driver class not found");
   }

   //if all went well the driver has been registered, so now return a Connection
            return (DriverManager.getConnection (m_drivertype + m_database,
                             m_username,
                             m_password));
}
```

First, nine predefined Java packages are imported. Each driver provides class implementations for the virtual classes, such as java.sql.Connection, java.sql.Statement, java.sql.PreparedStatement, and java.sql.CallableStatement. These virtual classes describe the API, but must be specific to each database product being connected.

The example in Figure 9-19 is connecting to an Oracle database, so the next box of code includes information about the very simple structure of the table used for the example and the primary key sequence and trigger that can be used to insert the next primary key value. It is not essential that you understand the trigger code at this point, but is included for those who are interested.

Next, initialization occurs and values such as the user id, password, driver class, type of driver, database connection string, and so forth are specified. The largest box includes the code that shows how to establish the connection to the database (using buildConnection()) and insert the passed values into the temp_demo table.

The last box includes the code necessary to build the Connection object in order to gain access to the Oracle database, including the error messages that will be displayed if the connection is not established, for one reason or another. A more complete example of this JDBC example is also included on the textbook Website. It includes another method for inserting the primary key value and includes code not only for creating a new record, but also for modifying, updating, or deleting records.

USING VISUAL BASIC FOR APPLICATIONS (VBA) IN CLIENT APPLICATIONS

Visual Basic for Applications (VBA): The programming language that accompanies Access 2000.

Access 2000 allows the novice user to create a prototype of an application, including the database design, menus, forms, and reports. However, there is a limit to what can be accomplished by using the Access macros and the developer is going to be stymied when attempting to include all desired capabilities. While some capabilities require macros, and cannot be accomplished through **Visual Basic for Applications (VBA)**, many more capabilities can be accomplished or enhanced by using VBA in conjunction with Access 2000. Here are some of the reasons that the Access 2000 user will want to learn VBA once basic familiarity with Access 2000 has been achieved (Smith and Sussman, 1997):

- *Complex functionality* can only be accomplished by using VBA. Displaying your own error messages, graying out buttons when they shouldn't be clicked, and so on require VBA coding.

- *Error handling* can only be accomplished by using VBA. Relying on macros in a finished application is dangerous because there is no way for the user to recover if a macro crashes.

- *Faster execution* will be achieved when the application uses VBA modules rather than macros. Code executes faster than macros; this benefit will be more noticeable the larger and more complex the application becomes.

- *Maintenance* is easier because VBA modules are stored with the forms and reports. Macros are stored separately from their related forms and reports. Moving the application to another database will be easier because the VBA modules will move with their forms and reports, since they are stored with them.

- *OLE automation* can be used more completely.

- *More programmatic control* can be achieved by using VBA. Macros cannot pass variables as parameters for another variable and cannot easily control action sequencing.

- *Reading* VBA code is easier than reading macro arguments because you can see the entire module in the Full Module View, which has color-coded text.

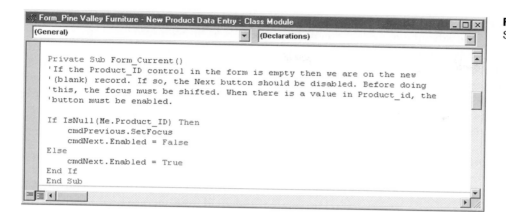

Figure 9-20
Sample VBA module

An autoexec macro must be created to open a database and macros must also be used to trap certain keystrokes in applications. Beyond that, converting a prototype from macros to VBA modules for a production version of the application will result in a more robust application with more capabilities.

The Windows operating system and Windows applications are **event-driven**. Everything that happens in an Access 2000 application is a response to an event, such as a mouse click, that Access 2000 has detected. An event occurs, it is detected, and a response to the event is generated. Thus, Access 2000 is not procedural—the next event can come from anywhere on the interface screen or from any key on the keyboard. Programming in an event-driven environment consists of creating objects and modifying their properties so they will behave as the programmer wishes for each event that affects the object.

Figure 9-20 shows VBA code that makes the NEXT button on the Product Entry Form disable itself (turn gray) when a new record is displayed. The records for the form come from the Product_t table. Product_ID is the primary key of that table. The value of the current record's Product_ID is determined using Me.Product_ID. If there is no primary key value for the current record, it must be a new record, and the NEXT button should be disabled. Because disabling the button that has the focus will cause a run-time error, the focus must first be shifted elsewhere. The focus is shifted to the PREVIOUS button and then the NEXT button is disabled. If the current record is not a new record, the NEXT button remains enabled.

Event-driven: Nonprocedural programming that detects an event when it occurs and generates an appropriate response to that event.

Summary

Client/server architectures have offered businesses opportunities to better fit their computer systems to their business needs. Establishing the appropriate balance between client/server and mainframe DBMSs is a matter of much current discussion. Client/server architectures are prominent in providing Internet applications, including dynamic data access. Several client/server architectures are discussed in this chapter, including file server architectures, where the file server manages file operations and is shared by each client PC that is attached to its LAN. File servers create a heavy network load, require a full version of the DBMS on each client, and require complex programming in order to manage shared database integrity.

Another approach, the database server architecture, makes the client manage the user interface while the database server manages database storage and access. This architecture reduces network traffic, reduces the power required for each client, and centralizes user authorization, integrity checking, data dictionary maintenance, and query and update processing on the database server.

Three-tier architectures, which include another server in addition to the client and database server layers, allow application code to be stored on the additional server. This approach allows business processing to be performed on the additional server, resulting in a thin client. Advantages of the three-tier architecture can include scalability, technological flexibility, lower long-term costs, better matching of systems to business needs, improved customer service, competitive advantage, and reduced risk. But, higher short-term costs, advanced tools and training, shortages of experienced personnel, incompatible standards, and lack of end-user tools are currently problems with using three-tier or *n*-tier architectures.

Application partitioning assigns portions of application code to client or server partitions after it is written, in order to achieve better performance and interoperability. Application developer productivity is expected to increase as a result of using application partitioning, but the developer must understand each process intimately in order to place it correctly.

While the hype associated with the widespread adoption of client/server architectures has led some to predict the demise of the mainframe, mission-critical applications have tended to remain on the mainframe. Converting these complex applications to distributed client/server environments has not been easy. The availability of parallel processing solutions is making it more attractive to remain centralized on an application or database server.

Because SQL is a nonprocedural set processing language, it has proven amenable to use in parallel processing environments. Two types of parallel processing have been discussed. Symmetric multiprocessing (SMP) is a tightly coupled multiprocessor system with a common shared memory among all processors. SMP systems are subject to develop I/O bottleneck problems when there is heavy memory request traffic going to shared memory.

Loosely coupled architectures (MPP) set up each CPU with its own dedicated memory. This type of architecture is commonly referred to as a *shared nothing* architecture. Because there is little resource sharing among the MPP processors, the problems of memory contention which occur in SMP systems are unlikely, and it is possible to add nodes in single units, making MPP architectures very scalable.

Middleware is any of several classes of software which allow an application to interoperate with other software without requiring the user to understand and code the low-level operations required to achieve interoperability. Six categories of middleware, based on scalability and recoverability, are discussed. These middleware types are asynchronous remote procedure call (RPC), publish/subscribe, message-oriented middleware (MOM), object-request broker (ORB), SQL-oriented data access middleware, and synchronous RPC. Recent developments in database-oriented middleware include open database connectivity (ODBC), Java Database Connectivity (JDBC), and Microsoft's OLE-DB.

Connecting databases to the Web so that browsers may interact with Web sites by placing orders, accessing updated pricing information, and so forth, has also received recent attention. The Web is changing the distri-

bution patterns of data, moving application logic to more centralized servers as browser interfaces are used.

Security is more complex in a client/server environment than in a centralized environment because networks must be secured in addition to the client workstations and the servers. Security measures to be included in a client/server environment include system-level password security, database-level password security, and secure client/server communications.

Client/server issues that should be addressed in order to improve the chances for building a successful client/server application include: accurate business problem analysis, detailed architecture analysis, avoidance of tool-driven architectures, achieving appropriate scalability, appropriate placement of services, adequate network analysis, and awareness of potential hidden costs.

Benefits that may be gained by moving to a client/server environment include deliverance of functionality in stages, flexibility, scalability, less network traffic, and development of Web-enabled applications.

The presentation services in most client/server architectures use Query-by-Example (QBE) interfaces. QBE provides a visual programming environment commonly used for the development of queries. There is no standard for QBE, so the interfaces differ among the products, but most utilize a data model approach combined with a spreadsheet layout for the result. The Microsoft Access 2000 QBE interface uses this spreadsheet layout extensively, including for table and query definition and for establishing data relationships.

The less robust relational database packages have gained popularity because of their GUI and QBE interfaces. For example, MS Access 2000 uses pass through queries to send commands to any open database connectivity (ODBC) compliant database server directly. Or database tables may be linked to an MS Access 2000 application interface if the database is ODBC compliant or Java Database Connectivity (JDBC) compliant. Several parameters must be defined in order to establish either an ODBC or JDBC connection. These include the specific ODBC or JDBC driver needed, the name of the back-end database server, the name of the database, and the id and password of the database user. There are different levels of conformance with the ODBC standard, which allow most application programs to achieve at least some connection to the desired database.

The programming language associated with Access 2000 is Visual Basic for Applications (VBA). Using Access 2000's macros, which are stored modules of VBA code, works well for prototyping, but building a robust application requires converting these macros to VBA modules. VBA can also be used to accomplish more complex functionality, handle errors, achieve faster execution, easier maintenance, more OLE automation, and more programmatic control.

CHAPTER REVIEW

Key Terms

Application partitioning
Application program interface (API)
Client/server architecture
Database server
Event-driven
Fat client

File server
Massively parallel processing (MPP)
Middleware
Open database connectivity (ODBC)
 standard
Query-by-Example (QBE)

Stored procedure
Symmetric multiprocessing (SMP)
Thin client
Three-tier architecture
Visual Basic for Applications (VBA)

Review Questions

1. Define each of the following terms:
   a. application partitioning
   b. application program interface (API)
   c. client/server architecture
   d. fat client
   e. file server
   f. middleware
   g. stored procedure
   h. three-tier architecture
   i. event-driven
   j. QBE
   k. VBA
   l. JDBC

2. Match each of the following terms with the most appropriate definition:

   _____ client/server architecture

   _____ application program interface (API)

   _____ fat client

   _____ database server

   _____ file server

   _____ middleware

   _____ three-tiered architecture

   _____ symmetric multi-processing (SMP)

   _____ massively parallel processing (MPP)

   _____ thin client

   _____ event-driven

   _____ pass-though query

   _____ QBE

   a. a client that is responsible for processing including application logic and presentation logic
   b. a PC configured for handling the presentation layer and some business logic processing for an application
   c. software that facilitates interoperability, reducing programmer coding effort
   d. detect and generate responses to events
   e. architecture where processors share common memory
   f. responsible for database storage and access
   g. systems where the application logic components are distributed
   h. a programming language that involves direct manipulation and is visually oriented
   i. responsible for managing file operations; shared by all attached clients
   j. shared nothing architecture
   k. software that facilitates communication between front-end programs and back-end database servers
   l. a query that uses the syntax of a back-end RDBMS
   m. three-layer client/server configuration

3. List several major advantages of the client/server architecture, compared to other computing approaches.

4. Contrast the following terms:
   a. symmetric multiprocessing (SMP); shared nothing architecture (MPP)
   b. file server; database server; three-tier architecture
   c. client/server computing; mainframe computing
   d. fat client; thin client
   e. Query-by-Example; line-mode interface

5. Describe the limitations of file servers.

6. Describe the advantages and disadvantages of database servers.

7. Describe the advantages and disadvantages of three-tier or n-tier architectures.

8. How can application partitioning help developers to tailor an application to a particular business situation?

9. Describe six categories of middleware.

10. How is the Web changing distribution patterns of data?

11. Explain the advantages and disadvantages of QBE compared to SQL.

12. What is the purpose of the ODBC specification?

13. What security issues are raised when building a Web-enabled database application?

14. Explain the relationship between Access 2000 and VBA.

Problems and Exercises

1. You have been asked to prepare a report that evaluates possible client/server solutions to handle a new customer application system for all branch offices. What business characteristics would you evaluate and what technology characteristics would you evaluate? Why?

2. What managerial issues do you feel are going to be important when introducing a new client/server architecture?

3. Discuss the different levels of security that should be established in a client/server database system.

4. How is the Web affecting client/server database systems?

5. Why is ODBC important? What other connectivity standards are being developed?

6. Historically, what types of applications have moved quickly to client/server database systems? What types have moved more slowly and why? What do you think will happen in the future to the balance of client/server database systems and mainframe database systems?

7. What are the advantages and drawbacks of middleware that is used in connection with database systems?

Problems and Exercises 8-12 are based on the Pine Valley Furniture database. They are intended for practice with a QBE interface.

8. Display the order number, customer number, product number, order date, and order quantity for orders of more than four units of products 3 or 8.

9. Display the customer number, name, and order numbers of all customer orders, and include in this list any customer who has no orders in the database.

10. Write a query that shows each product and the total quantity ordered for each product, including products that have never been ordered.

11. Display a list of all the products and the number of times each product has been ordered.

12. Display the order number, product number, and order quantity for all customer orders for which the order quantity is greater than the average order quantity of that product. *Hint:* This may require more than one query.

Field Exercises

1. Investigate the computing architecture of your university. Trace the history of computing at your university and determine what path the university followed to get to its present configurations. Some universities started early with mainframe environments—others started when PCs were available. Can you tell how your university's initial computing environment has affected today's computing environment?

2. On a lesser scale, investigate the computing architecture of one department within your university. Try to find out how well the current system is meeting the department's information processing needs.

3. Interview a systems professional at an organization in your location that you know has offices in other locations. Determine the computing architecture of that organization and find out how well the current system is meeting the department's information processing needs.

4. Locate three sites on the Web that have interactive database systems attached to the site. Evaluate the functionality of the site and discuss how the interactive database system is likely to affect that functionality. If you're not sure where to start, try http://www.amazon.com.

5. Locate two similar small businesses in your area that use different computer systems for keeping their records. Compare the functionality and the ease of use of the two systems.

6. Contract a database analyst or systems developer in an organization with which you are familiar. Investigate the use of personal computer and server database systems. What factors are considered in choosing the platform for a database? Does the organization use a mixed platform, in which client-based application modules are written in one language (e.g., QBE) and server application modules are written in another (e.g., SQL)? Why or why not?

References

Anderson, G., and B. Armstrong. 1995. "Client/Server: Where Are We Really?" *Health Management Technology* 16:6 (May): 34, 36, 38, 40, 44.

Atre, S. 1995. "The Hidden Costs of Client/Server." *DBMS* 8:7 (June): 71, 72, 74.

Bobrowski, S. 1994. "Database Security in a Client/Server World." *DBMS* 7:10 (October): 48–50, 54, 58.

DeWitt, D., and J. Gray. 1992. "Parallel Database Systems: The Future of High Performance Database Systems." *Communications of the ACM* 35:6 (June): 85–98.

Ferguson, M. 1994. "Parallel Database the Shape of Things to Come." *Database Programming & Design* 7:10 (October): 32–44.

Frazer, W. D. 1998. "Object/Relational Grows Up." *Database Programming & Design* 11:1 (January): 22–28.

Hurwitz, J. 1996. "Managing Complexity." *DBMS* 9:5 (May): 12, 80.

Hurwitz, J. 1998. "Sorting Out Middleware." *DBMS* 11:1 (January): 10–12.

Keuffel, W. 1997. "CORBA Masterminds Object Management." *DBMS* 10:3 (March): 42–50, 71.

Greenblatt, D., and J. Waxman. 1978. "A Study of Three Database Query Languages." In *Database: Improving Usability and Responsiveness,* ed. B. Schneiderman. New York: Academic Press.

LaRue, M. 1997. "Database Doorways." *Database Programming & Design* 10:12 (December): 62–67.

Linthicum, D. S. 1996. "Client/Server Collapse." *DBMS* 9:13 (December): 24, 26, 28.

Linthicum, D. S. 1997. "Next-Generation Middleware." *DBMS* 10:10 (October): 69–78.

Prague, C. and Irwin, M. 1997. *Access 97 Bible.* Foster City, CA: IDG Books.

Quinlan, T. 1995. "The Second Generation of Client/Server." *Database Programming & Design* 8:5 (May): 31–39.

Rudin, K. 1995. "The Practical Side of Going Parallel." *Database Programming & Design* 8:12 (December): 26–33.

Schneiderman, B. 1983. "Direct Manipulation: A Step Beyond Programming Languages." *IEEE Computer* 16:57–69.

Smith, R. and Sussman, D. 1997. *Beginning Access 97 VBA Programming.* Birmingham, UK: Wrox Press.

Thomas, J.C., and J.D. Gould. 1975. "A Psychological Study of Query by Example." *Proceedings of National Computer Conference.* New York: AFIPS Press.

Thompson, C. 1997. "Committing to Three-Tier Architecture." *Database Programming & Design* 10:8 (August): 26–33.

Zloof, M. M. 1977. "Query-by-Example: A Data Base Language." *IBM Systems Journal* 16(4): 324–43.

Web Resources

http://www.orafaq.com/faqodbc.htm Oracle ODBC Connectivity FAQ. by Frank Naudé, part of the Oracle Underground FAQ (http://www.ibi.co.za/frank/faq.htm

http://www.javaworld.com/javaworld/jw-05-1996/jw-05-shah.html Integrating Databases with Java via JDBC, by Rawn Shah, *Internet Systems,* April 1997.

http://www.javacoffeebreak.com/articles/jdbc Getting Started with JDBC, by David Reilly. 1996, ITWorld.com, Inc.

http://mindprod.com/jdbc.html An extensive list of JDBC interface packages by Roedy Green. Last updated February 22, 2001. Canadian Mind Products.

http://www.melbpc.org.au/pcupdate/9908/9908article8.htm Database Security: Systems and Methodologies for Identifying and Protecting Weak Spots in Your Web-Enabled Database—Before Someone Else Does, by Dan Rahmel, *Internet Systems,* April 1997.

http://www.microsoft.com/technet/ecommerce/MSF3Sec.asp Three-Tier Security in an E-Commerce Environment, by Craig Clayton. Last update July 28, 2000.

http://www.dbmsmag.com/9805d14.html The Middleware Muddle, by David Ritter. *DBMS,* May 1998.

Project Case

PROJECT DESCRIPTION

At the end of Chapter 2, you learned of the Mountain View Community Hospital special study team that is developing a long-term business plan. The planning team of Mr. Heller, Mr. Lopez, Dr. Jefferson, and a consultant have been considering the future technology needs of Mountain View. Currently, patients must negotiate a maze of health plans, administrators, physicians, and clinics, much like the maze shown in Figure 1. They would like to devise a system for Mountain View that integrates all of these data—data from health plans, physicians, and hospital systems—so that accurate real-time information will be available.

The team has heard that many hospitals are just beginning to move their mission-critical, enterprise-level systems off their legacy mainframe systems and onto new client/server systems. They have heard that such systems provide increased flexibility, integration, and functionality. They are wondering if they can integrate Mountain View's present patient accounting, care

management, and insurance systems to improve efficiency and support improved hospital systems. The consultant has drafted a potential client/server distributed architecture for the hospital, which is shown in Figure 2. To accomplish the move to client/server, the team has considered three different strategies described in the following paragraphs.

One possibility is to acquire existing client/server application packages and adapt them to fit Mountain View Community Hospital. Taking this approach will allow the existing MIS staff at Mountain View to become familiar with crucial portions of the client/server environment, such as network management, PC configuration management, and distributed-systems management, without having to manage a full-blown, large-scale systems development project in addition to their current work. Most of the packages they have examined, however, require the use of proprietary middleware to achieve client/server connections. The hospital expects to have to continue connection to the

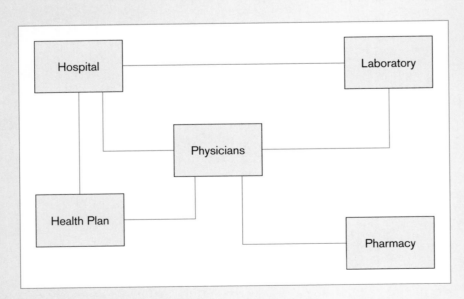

Figure 1
Mountain View Community Hospital's current technology base (adapted from Anderson and Armstrong, 1995)

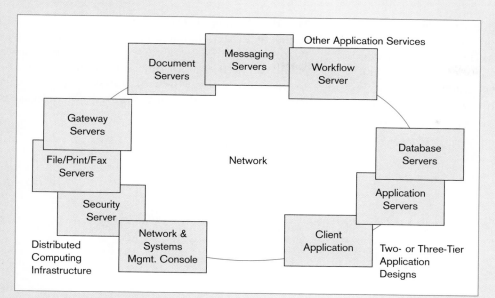

Figure 2
Potential client/server distributed architecture (adapted from Anderson and Armstrong, 1995)

legacy systems through the proposed servers and they are not sure how many programs are available that would let them move toward the environment they envision.

Another possibility the planning team is considering is custom development. Some large hospitals have undertaken custom development of their new client/server systems. Considerable risk attends such an undertaking, but the larger hospitals have assumed this risk in order to get the data and information when they need it. The Mountain View team is concerned about the risk of undertaking such a project and the need for increasing MIS staff that it would entail.

The last possibility being considered would be to layer the client/server applications on top of existing systems. Workflow applications could be used to facilitate the establishment of the front end interface. The need to connect to a data warehouse is also becoming apparent as the team works on the long-range plan, and the team wants to plan the infrastructure now so that the establishment of a data warehouse will be as easy as possible.

Of course, Mountain View Community Hospital could also adopt a Web-enabled system. Health care alliances are extending their member and patient services beyond their organizational boundaries, to the workplace, schools, and homes. Health plan members can check their claim status, send messages to service representatives, and review coverage. Patients can even make their own appointments by accessing appointment schedules. The members of the team are unsure of what the impact of these new services will be in their area, but they expect that some of the other hospitals will be quick to adopt and implement such features. They are currently

evaluating their other options, but will consider this newest option after completing further research, at the end of Chapter 10.

PROJECT QUESTIONS

1. Why do you think the Mountain View team feels that building its own custom client/server applications would be risky?

2. What are some of the possibilities for processing and providing information that could arise if Mountain View were to move to a client/server environment?

3. What activities would have to be planned if Mountain View were to decide to adopt and implement off-the-shelf client/server applications? Select one activity, such as the patient billing system, and think about what is likely to be involved in selecting, installing, and using such a system.

4. What advantages and disadvantages can you see from the third approach, layering the client/server applications on top of existing systems?

5. What advantages and disadvantages can you see from Mountain View remaining with their current systems for the next two years?

PROJECT EXERCISES

1. Outline what you see as the pros and cons of each of the four approaches to moving to a client/server environment: customizing off-the-shelf systems (COTS), custom system development, surrounding and layering, and doing nothing for a while.

2. Now, using the lists developed in the first project exercise, indicate which solution you feel Mountain View Community Hospital should try. Defend your answer. Indicate what additional information you would like to have to help you with your recommendation.

3. Try to get some material about off-the-shelf client/server hospital systems, such as Symphonia by Orion, Meridia Managed Care Information System, or Facets by Erisco Managed Care Technologies. Investigate the capabilities of each system, the number of installations, the client operating system used, and so on. Determine which of the systems you have found and learned about might be of interest to Mountain View.

Chapter 10

The Internet Database Environment

LEARNING OBJECTIVES

After studying this chapter, you should be able to:

- Concisely define each of the following key terms: **World Wide Web, electronic commerce, browser, electronic business, B2C, B2B, firewall, proxy server, World Wide Web Consortium, Hypertext Markup Language, Standard Generalized Markup Language, Extensible Markup Language, XHTML, Java, JavaScript, VBScript, Cascading Style Sheets, server-side extension, Common Gateway Interface, Java servlet, DNS balancing, software and hardware load balancing, reverse proxy, plug-ins, ActiveX, cookie, ColdFusion Markup Language, router, intrusion detection system, DCS-1000**.

- Explain the importance of attaching a database to a Web page.

- Describe the basic environment that must be set up to enable Internet and intranet database-enabled connectivity.

- Use Internet-related terminology appropriately.

- Explain the purpose and accomplishments of the World Wide Web Consortium.

- Explain the purpose of server-side extensions.

- Compare and contrast Web server interfaces, including CGI, API, and Java servlets.

- Describe three methods for balancing Web server loads.

- Explain plug-ins.

- Be able to explain how a simple shopping cart application would be put together in ColdFusion or ASP.

- Discuss Web security issues.

- Discuss Web privacy issues.

INTRODUCTION

As usage of the **World Wide Web (WWW)** has escalated, the importance of databases to this growth has become ever more evident. **Electronic commerce (e-commerce)**, business conducted over the Internet, has been a significant cause of the escalation. It seems that every business from AT&T to Rose's Flower Shoppe has stepped up to the challenge of adapting business to take advantage of the global network that we call the Internet. The use of Internet technology within companies to build Intranets has also been widely adopted.

The public Internet and private intranets can be thought of as vast client/server architectures with very

World Wide Web (WWW): The total set of interlinked hypertext documents residing on special servers, called Web servers or HTTP servers, worldwide. The Web servers are configured to make the information they hold easily accessible to each other and to allow files to be accessed, transferred, and downloaded. Also referred to as W3 or the Web.

Electronic commerce (e-commerce): Internet-based business transactions, including such activities as order processing and fulfillment, customer relationship management interactions, electronic data interchange (EDI), and bill payments.

Browser: Software that displays HTML documents and allows users to access files and software related to the HTML documents. Browsers are based on the use of hyperlinks, which allow the user to jump to other documents by clicking on an object. Most also allow a user to download and transfer files, access news groups, play audio and video files, and execute small modules of code, such as Java applets or ActiveX controls.

thin clients (browsers) and fat servers. The servers store information in databases to be sent to the browsers on request. It is necessary to access databases for current information, such as inventory availability, and to record information, such as the data items associated with an order, in these applications. However, attaching a database to a Web application may open up access to that database in unintended ways if the developer is not data security conscious. Problems with a new on-line shopping site will be evident to customers throughout the world very quickly. Database professionals must know how to prudently establish, operate, and administer Web interfaces to databases.

In this chapter, we will build an understanding of the fit of databases with Internet applications, cover various Internet database architectures, illustrate the use of ASP and ColdFusion to Web-enable databases, and discuss management issues associated with these topics.

The Internet and Database Connection

Several characteristics of the Web environment have supported the rapid adoption and implementation of Internet and intranet business applications. First, the simplicity and functional similarities of the browser interfaces have significantly reduced traditional barriers to adoption, such as complexity. Just as use of Microsoft Windows conventions has made it easier for people to learn new Windows-based applications, the most popular **browser** interfaces have similarities in functionality that make it easy for users to switch among browsers and among businesses' Websites. Toolbars with functionality similar to Windows toolbars are often displayed at the top of the screen and can be used to print or to copy and paste information from the pages displayed. Most browsers support e-mail, instant messaging, bookmarking of Websites, and Website addressing and searching. Use of HTML, DHTML, XML, and JavaScript (all explained later) result in a uniformity of presentation and function that make it easy to switch from site to site.

Second, the hardware and software independence of the browsers has eased the sharing of information across platforms and has resolved many previously thorny cross-platform issues of access. In particular, wide access to database information has become possible. Through the Internet network, location independence has been achieved. Companies can access their data both locally and remotely, making some information publicly available while protecting critical information from public access by placing it behind a firewall or on a different server. The movement of data files and updates to databases through the Internet is now commonplace.

Last, development costs and time have been reduced. Inexpensive or even free development and deployment tools are available, making the barriers to entry very low. Newborn babies have their own Websites managed by proud parents. One expects any business to have a Website, and although the functionality and timeliness of that Website still varies widely, it is rare not to be able to find a Website for any particular business you seek. At the same time, functionality and processing speed of each site may vary widely, and the bandwidth available on the Internet plays a part in how quickly Web pages display and load. Transactions abort with alarming frequency and displays freeze at the most inconvenient times. The navigation logic used at each site differs and is not always apparent.

Many sites do not have a database attached to them. They provide static information that is coded using HTML, JavaScript, CGI, or other scripting languages. Common to many of the sites, however, is the need to either extract or deposit information into a database that is attached to the site. Some sites are simply repositories of information that can be queried by the site visitor. The user can request information and read it, but not change it in any manner. In Hillsborough County, Florida, for example, anyone can find out who owns land in the county, details about the property such as valuation for taxation, and past purchase prices. The information is stored in a database that the site visitor can query. Information can be accessed by property record designation, street address, or owner's name. Other sites contain product inventory information, again stored in a database. These sites are able to provide information about particular products or classes of products because of the site visitor's query. Any set of data that lends itself to storage in a relational database can be attached to a site, and casual exploration of Websites will convince the reader that the possibilities are almost endless. Data stored in numeric, character, or graphic formats are all widely used.

Other sites provide more interactivity between the user and the database, in that the user can send back information to a database that is attached to a site. This capability has supported the explosive growth of electronic commerce, as orders may be placed on-line by customers. The customer is frequently able to determine prior to placing an order whether a desired product is in stock or not, and how long it should take to receive it. Applications that enable electronic commerce include the capability to both display and load databases attached to a site.

As previously existing and start-up businesses have rushed to utilize this technology, the term **electronic business (e-business)** has been introduced. E-business describes a technology-enabled business that is using Internet-related technology to facilitate the development of more integrated relationships with customers and suppliers. E-commerce is a more restricted concept than e-business, because it refers more to the transactions that occur as e-business is conducted.

Electronic business (e-business): A technology-enabled business that is using Internet-related technology to facilitate the development of more integrated relationships with customers and suppliers.

Potential advantages of e-business that organizations foresee are better supply chain management, improved customer service, faster time to market, lower costs, and increased sales. Companies have been able to achieve some of these goals more easily than other goals. Problems with supply chain management when sites have been swamped with orders have received much negative press. Improved customer service has proved costly to implement, and probably most readers of this book have sent requests for information or support to companies that have gone unanswered. Profitability has been elusive.

As companies have struggled to achieve seamless integration with their customers and suppliers, two broad categories of e-business that are commonly distinguished from each other have developed. They are referred to as **Business to Consumer (B2C)** and **Business to Business (B2B)**, or retail and business e-commerce undertakings. The B2B interface is simpler in some respects, often establishing previous existing trading relationships electronically. Companies have demonstrated significant savings by establishing on-line trading with their business partners. Retail e-businesses have had to work hard to get retail customers to place orders on-line, because many are concerned about security issues, do not have ready access to the Internet, or prefer shopping experiences where they can see and touch the product they are considering. Realized and anticipated increased profitability as a result of taking advantage of the Internet to improve business efficiencies and customer relationships mean that this area of database understanding will only continue to grow in importance.

Business to Consumer (B2C): Phrase used to describe electronic businesses that conduct retail sales businesses to consumers.

Business to Business (B2B): Phrase used to describe electronic businesses that conduct e-commerce transactions with other businesses, including their suppliers and vendors.

The Internet Environment

Common Internet architectures will be covered in more detail later; this section establishes a basic understanding of the Internet environment. Figure 10-1 depicts the basic environment needed to set up both Intranet and Internet database-enabled connectivity. In the box on the right-hand side of the diagram is a depiction of an Intranet. The client/server nature of the architecture is evident from the labeling. The network that connects the client workstations, Web server, and database server follows TCP/IP protocols. TCP stands for Transmission Control Protocol; IP stands for Internet Protocol. Both protocols are required for Internet transmission to occur, whether it is needed to send e-mail, browse the Web, or act as a Web server. TCP breaks long messages into packets, which are smaller pieces of data that can be routed independently over the Web, reassembled, and displayed upon arrival at the

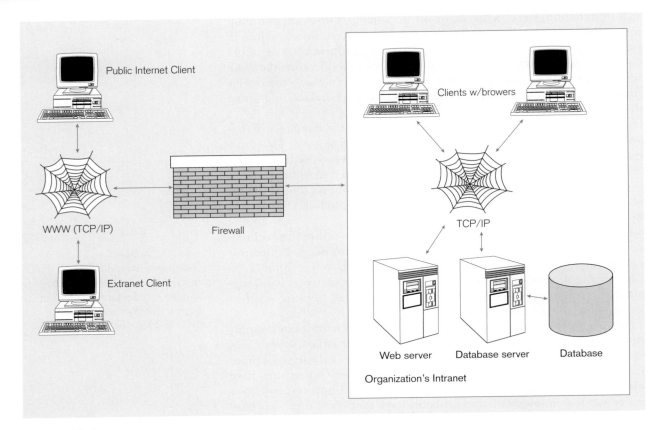

Figure 10-1
Database-enabled intranet/Internet environment

Firewall: A hardware/software security component that limits external access to company data.

Proxy server: A firewall component that manages Internet traffic to and from a local area network. It can also handle access control and document caching.

destination browser. Every computer that is connected to an intranet or extranet must have a distinct IP address. If Web connectivity is not required, intranet IP addresses can be specified that might not be distinct if opened up to the Internet communication network. Multitier intranet structures, as described in Chapter 9, are also permissible. Figure 10-1, however, depicts a simpler architecture, where a request from a client browser will be sent through the network to the Web server, which stores pages scripted in HTML to be returned and displayed through the client browser. If the request requires that data be obtained from the database, the Web server constructs a query and sends it to the database server, which processes the query and returns the results set when the query is run against the database. Similarly, data entered at the client station can be passed through and stored in the database by sending it to the Web server, which passes it on to the database server, which commits the data to the database.

The processing flow described above is similar when attaching to an extranet. This is so whether the connection is available only to a particular customer or supplier, or to any workstation connected to the Web. However, opening up the Web server to the outside world requires that additional data security measures be in place. Internally, access to data is typically controlled by the database management system, with the database administrator setting the permissions that determine employee access to data. **Firewalls** are used to limit external access to the company's data and to limit the movement of company data outside the company's boundaries. All communication is routed through a **proxy server** outside of the organization's network. The proxy server controls the passage of messages or files through to the organization's network. It can also improve a site's performance by caching frequently requested pages that can then be displayed without having to attach to the Web server.

Most intranets provide the following services:

- **Web server.** Used to process client requests and return HTML pages to the client.

- **Database-enabled services.** Database access through the Web server and database server are provided. Web-to-host access can provide access to legacy data stored on a mainframe computer.

- **Directory, security, and authentication services.** Used to prevent unauthorized access from within the corporate network and to provide accountability.

- **Electronic mail.** Provides the capability of transferring messages between computers in the intranet, extranet, or Internet.

- **File Transfer Protocol (FTP).** Provides the capability to copy files between computers in the intranet, extranet, or Internet. The user needs an FTP client and the remote system needs an FTP server.

- **Firewalls and proxy servers.** Used to provide security against unauthorized incursion from outside of the organization's intranet.

- **News or discussion groups.** Provides the capability to post information on shared bulletin boards for public access. Threaded discussions related to a subject indicated in the original posting's subject line help to organize the content of the bulletin boards.

- **Document search.** Provides the capability to search Website content.

- **Load balancing and caching.** Distribution of heavy traffic flows to improve operating performance.

Terminology

Each development stage in information technology has generated a set of new terms and acronyms. The introduction of networking and the Internet has been no exception to this custom. In addition to the terms covered in the previous Introduction and the Internet environment sections, there are a few additional Web-related terms with which one should be familiar, and they are covered here.

Communication-Related Terms

- **IP address.** IP addresses are expressed as four numbers, ranging from 0 to 255, separated by periods, or decimal points. An example of an IP address is 131.247.152.18. IP addresses are difficult to remember, but each is mapped to a unique domain name that has more meaning and is easier to remember. Examples of domain names are www.usf.edu , www.udayton.edu, or www.prenhall.com. Domain name servers maintain an index of IP addresses and their matching domain names.

- **Hypertext Transfer Protocol (HTTP).** Communication protocol used to transfer browser requests to a Web server and to transfer pages from the Web server back to the browser. However, this protocol is not particularly secure, but another protocol, **HTTPS**, provides for encryption and transmission through a secure port.

- **Uniform Resource Locator (URL).** A Web address used to specify the communication protocol and IP address of a Web server. Optionally, the folder path and file name of the HTML file being requested may also be specified. Figure 10-2 shows a typical URL. HTTP is assumed as the default communication protocol if not specified with a URL. The Web server's root document folder is assumed as the starting location if the folder path and file name are not specified.

Figure 10-2
A typical URL

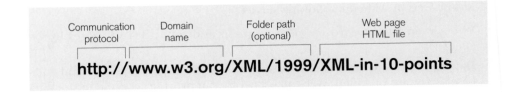

Communication protocol   Domain name   Folder path (optional)   Web page HTML file

http://www.w3.org/XML/1999/XML-in-10-points

Web-Related Terms

- **Static Web pages.** Web pages whose content is established at the time they are written. The same information is displayed whenever the page is accessed.
- **Dynamic Web Pages.** Web pages that display the data requested or input by the client station. Creation of a dynamic Web page generally requires that a database be attached to the page by an open database connectivity connection. ODBC connections were discussed in Chapter 9.

COMMON INTERNET ARCHITECTURE COMPONENTS

A bewildering array of technologies and tools, many identified by acronyms, has come together to create the Internet environment. This section discusses the most common components of that environment. We begin with the various languages that are used, sometimes in tandem, to create Web pages. Several resources operate as Web server middleware. These process requests either going to or coming from the Web server. We classify them into server-side extensions and Web server interfaces. Web servers and client-side extensions are also discussed.

Although Figure 10-1 gives an overview of the architecture required, there is no one right way to take the components and put them together. Rather, there are many possible configurations, using redundant tools. Often, Web technologies within the same category can be used interchangeably. One given tool may solve the same problem as well as another tool. An example that we will show at the end of the chapter is the use of ASP or ColdFusion to attach a database to a Website. The need to adhere to organizational development standards may determine the tool selected. Begin by being sure that you understand the category in which each tool is useful, so that you know when you should be considering it. After that, a good reference manual for the product will provide you with its syntax and guide you through the interface issues that surface.

Internet-Related Languages

The **World Wide Web Consortium**, known as **W3C**, is the chief standards body for HTTP and HTML. Founded in 1994 by Tim Berners-Lee, W3C is an international consortium of companies. W3C's intent is to develop open standards that foster the development of Web conventions so that Web documents can be consistently displayed across all platforms. They have also issued specifications for XML and XHTML. Their most current draft is a complete set of XML Schema modules for XHTML, and a framework for extending and modifying XHTML, issued March 22, 2001.

The fundamental authoring language used to create documents for the Web is **HTML**, an acronym for **Hypertext Markup Language**. HTML is similar to **SGML**, or **Standard Generalized Markup Language**, which states the rules for tagging elements of a document so that they can be formatted in a standard way. HTML tag conventions are based on SGML rules.

World Wide Web Consortium (W3C): An international consortium of companies intending to develop open standards that foster the development of Web conventions so that Web documents can be consistently displayed across all platforms.

Hypertext Markup Language (HTML): The scripting language used for documents displayed through browsers on the Web. HTML is similar to SGML, a more comprehensive information management standard.

Standard Generalized Markup Language (SGML): An information management standard adopted in 1986 by the International Organization for Standardization to script documents so that formatting, indexing, and linked information is defined across platforms and applications.

HTML is a scripting language, intended to define Web document structure and layout for display purposes, using a variety of tags and attributes. For example, an HTML document starts with the tags <HTML><HEAD>(document subject is entered here)</HEAD><BODY>. The information to be displayed and additional formatting tags follow, and the document will end with the tags, </BODY></HTML>.

XML is a rapidly developing scripting language, also based on SGML, that may, in conjunction with XHTML, replace HTML. XML is an acronym for **Extensible Markup Language**, a specification developed by the W3C. Designed especially for Web documents, XML allows the creation of customized tags. These tags can be used across organizations, enabling the definition, transmission, validation, and interpretation of data between applications and between organizations. XML has also proved useful for attaching legacy data to the Web, because the XML tags can be used to define data as it is formatted in the legacy data store, thus eliminating the need to reformat it.

Extensible Markup Language (XML): A scripting language based on SGML that allows the creation of customized tags, which enable easier transmission and sharing of data across organizations.

W3C has issued specifications for a hybrid scripting language, **XHTML**, which extends HTML code to make it XML compliant. XHTML uses three XML namespaces that correspond to three HTML 4.0 data type definitions (DTDs). These are Strict, Transitional, and Frameset. Because the modules used in XHTML conform to certain standards, layout and presentation remain consistent over any platform. The W3C wants XHTML to replace HTML as the standard scripting language. It is recommended that the reader visit the W3C Website to learn how close they are to accomplishing this objective.

XHTML: A hybrid scripting language that extends HTML code to make it XML compliant.

The languages mentioned thus far have been scripting or markup languages, intended for handling layout and display of documents, rather than to program functions or activities. A general-purpose programming language, **Java**, is well suited for use on the Web. Small Java programs, Java applets, download from a Web server to the client and run in a Java-compatible Web browser, such as Netscape Navigator or Microsoft Internet Explorer.

Java is an object-oriented language. It is simpler than C++, and was designed by Sun Microsytems with the intention of creating a language that caused fewer common programming errors. Java source code files compile into a format called *bytecode* that are executed by a Java interpreter. Java interpreters and runtime environments, known as *Java Virtual Machines (VMs)*, exist for most operating systems, allowing compiled Java code to run on most systems. Bytecode can also be converted directly into machine language instructions.

Java: A general-purpose, object-oriented programming language that is well suited to use on the Web. Small Java programs, called Java applets, download from a Web server to the client and run in a Java-compatible Web browser.

Although **JavaScript** shares many of the features and structures of the full Java language, Netscape developed it independently. Web authors use JavaScript to achieve interactivity and introduce dynamic content. For example, mouse rollovers, automatic notices that content has been updated, and error handling can be accomplished through JavaScripting embedded in the HTML code. When an event occurs, such as the mouse rolling over a button, the JavaScript will be activated. JavaScript is an open language and does not require a license. It is supported by current Netscape and Microsoft browsers.

JavaScript: A scripting language based on Java, but easier to learn, that is used to achieve interactivity on Web pages.

VBScript is similar to JavaScript. Just as JavaScript is based on Java but is simpler, so is VBScript based on Visual Basic, but it also is simpler. VBScript can be used to add buttons, scrollbars, and other interactive controls to a Web page. Microsoft developed this scripting language and the Microsoft Explorer browser supports it.

VBScript: A scripting language based on Microsoft Visual Basic and similar to JavaScript.

Cascading Style Sheets (CSS) are another feature developed by the W3C and being added to HTML. With CSS, designers *and* users create style sheets that define the appearance of different elements, such as headers and links. A style sheet can then be applied to any Web page. In fact, multiple style sheets can be applied to a Web page. Two W3C recommendations (CSS1 and CSS2) have been published. These recommendations are now implemented in most browsers, but they are not consistently implemented.

Cascading Style Sheets (CSS): Developed by the W3C, style sheets define the appearance of different elements and can be applied to any Web page. They are called cascading style sheets because more than one can be applied to a Web page.

Server-Side Extensions

Server-side extension: A software program that interacts directly with a Web server to handle requests.

In order to handle a request from a client that requires accessing a database, the Web server's capabilities must be increased or extended, because Web servers understand only HTML-formatted pages. A **server-side extension** is a program that interacts directly with a Web server to handle requests. For example, the Web server's capabilities must be extended so that it can support database requests. The process is shown in Figure 10-3. Initially, a request for information is submitted from a browser via the Web to the Web server. The SQL query will be included in the script, but cannot be directly interpreted by the Web server. Instead, the Web-to-database middleware identifies the query and prepares it to be passed to the database management system and the database, where the data items are stored. The result set returned by the query is returned back to the middleware, which converts the result so that it will display correctly when the Web page is returned to the client browser.

Server-side extensions allow for a high degree of flexibility. The network administrator can select any Web server, perhaps Netscape Fast Track Server or Microsoft Internet Information Server. Any ODBC compliant database that has SQL capability, such as Oracle, Sybase, or MS Access can be used, and the middleware will connect them both. ColdFusion and Netscape Application Server are examples of middleware. Detailed examples of the use of ColdFusion and ASP are included near the end of this chapter.

Web Server Interfaces

In order for a Web server to interact with an external program, a mechanism to establish the interface must be in place. Whether one uses the term interface, interoperability, or interactivity, this need to be able to communicate between the Web server and the client or the database is often necessary. Static Web pages do not require this type of interface because all of the information to be displayed is contained in the HTML document that will be shown. However, dynamic Web pages determine some of their content at the time that the client browser requests a page. For example, displaying updated information of some sort, such as the current inventory level for a product, will require a Web server interface. Two common Web server interfaces are:

Common Gateway Interface (CGI): A Web server interface that specifies the transfer of information between a Web server and a CGI program.

- **Common Gateway Interface (CGI)**
- Application Program Interface (API)

CGI specifies the transfer of information between a Web server and a CGI program. CGI programs are designed to accept and return data and may be written in any language that produces executable files, including C or C++, Perl, Java, or Visual

Figure 10-3
Web-to-database middleware

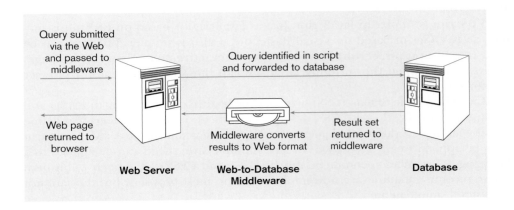

Basic. The data must conform to the CGI specification. CGI programs are commonly used to accept data from forms that are displayed in a browser and filled in by the user. They may also be used to accept data from a legacy system, perhaps from an existing database or other body of documents. Remember, the gateway programs are executable programs and can be run under different information servers interchangeably.

CGI programs are a common way for Web servers to interact dynamically with user requests. Some other client-side approaches will be covered shortly. CGI scripts are stored on the Web server and must be executed each time a user makes a request that uses that CGI script. In a situation where many users are sending requests that require the CGI scripts, performance can be slowed noticeably. Therefore, some server-side solutions such as Java scripts and applets and ActiveX controls have been devised, and they will be discussed later in the Client-Side Extensions section.

Java servlets are used as an alternative to CGI programs. Like applets, servlets are programs that execute from within another application rather than from the operating system, but they are stored on the server rather than with an application on a client. Servlets allow a client program to upload additional program code to a server, where it executes. Since servlets are small in file size and cross-platform compatible, they are ideal for small Internet applications accessible from a browser. Java servlets are persistent; once started, they remain in active memory and can fulfill multiple requests. A CGI program closes after it runs. Thus, Java servlets are more efficient because they are persistent, and server performance is less likely to be noticeably affected.

Application Programming Interfaces (APIs) are also more efficient than CGI scripts. They are implemented as shared code or dynamic link libraries (DLLs). This means that the code is resident in memory and can be called dynamically as needed. No external program need be executed for each request. An API is a set of routines, protocols, and tools that an application program uses to direct the operating system's performance of procedures. APIs can also use a shared connection to a database, rather than having to establish a new link each time a connection is requested. APIs do have some negatives, too. Because it resides on the Web server, an API error can cause a server to crash. APIs are specific to the operating system and Web server on which they reside, and must be rewritten to run with other systems.

Java servlet: A small program that executes from within another application rather than from the operating system and is stored on the server rather than with an application on a client.

Web Servers

There is an interesting Website (www.netcraft.com/survey/) that provides a monthly survey of the Web servers on the Internet that it can identify. In 1995, its first survey located 3,428 sites. In April 2001, it located 28,669,939 sites. This exponential growth of sites has been supported by the ability to communicate with databases and offer dynamic pages that contain current information. Each of these sites provides an HTTP service, the protocol that allows Web browsers and Web servers to communicate. HTTP is a relatively simple protocol, passing plain text via a TCP connection. Originally, a new HTTP connection had to be established to the Web server for each object to be downloaded to a browser. Newer versions of HTTP support a persistent connection so that multiple objects can be transmitted in packets over a single TCP connection.

A Web server must be able to serve many users at a time, and this is accomplished by multithreading or multiprocessing. Web servers running on Unix tend to use a form of multiprocessing. Others use multithreading, multiprocessing, or a hybrid of multiprocessing and multithreading. Multiprocessing uses multiple processors working in tandem to achieve faster processing. A thread is a process that is part of a larger program. Multithreading is the simultaneous running of processes that comprise more than one thread.

DNS (domain name server) balancing: A load-balancing approach where the DNS server for the hostname of the site returns multiple IP addresses for the site.

Popular Websites receive more hits than can be managed by a single server and multiple servers must be installed. Balancing the load to take advantage of the additional servers can be a challenge. Some sites use **DNS (domain name server) balancing** to handle more hits, placing multiple copies of the site on separate but identical physical servers. The DNS server for the hostname of the site returns multiple IP addresses for the site, either by returning more than one IP address for the hostname or by returning a different IP address for each DNS request received. While this approach is simple, it does not guarantee that the load on the servers will be balanced because the IP addresses chosen may not be balanced.

Software and hardware load balancing: A load-balancing approach where requests to one IP address are distributed among the multiple servers hosting the Website at the TCP/IP routing level.

Software and hardware load balancing can distribute the requests more evenly across the Web servers. Only one IP address is published for the site. Requests to this one IP address are distributed among the multiple servers hosting the Website at the TCP/IP routing level. The load balancing achieved by using software and hardware load balancing is usually better than the DNS method. Some load balancers detect a Web server in the pool that is down, and dynamically redirect the request to another Web server.

Reverse proxy: A load-balancing approach that intercepts requests from clients and caches the response on the Web server that sends it back to the client.

A third method reduces the load on a Website by intercepting requests from clients and caching the response on the Web server that sends it back to the client. This approach is called **reverse proxying**. The result is that the proxy can often serve a request from its own local cache rather than contacting the Web server, reducing the load on the Web server.

Some companies use global load-balancing techniques that distribute the work of sending data files all over the world. Typically, they use both DNS load balancing and software–hardware-based load balancing. By determining where a client is located, files located closest to the user are served to that user.

The distinction between Web servers and application servers is now becoming somewhat blurred, as Web servers turn into application servers that serve XML data and HTML data. Moreover, application servers are configured to act as a simple Web server while still performing as an application server. Decisions about configuration will be determined by the expectations being placed on the Website. Websites that are closely involved with delivering results from an application may find that it works best to have both a Web server and an application server. A site that delivers HTML pages without frequent reliance on an application may be very satisfied with a Web server approach with application server capabilities.

Client-Side Extensions

Extensions to the client-side add functionality to the browser. A few of the most popular are discussed briefly here, to give the reader a sense of client-side extensions. Plug-ins, ActiveX controls, and cookies reside on the client-side and are discussed here.

Plug-ins: Hardware or software modules that extend the capabilities of a browser by adding a specific feature, such as encryption, animation, or wireless access.

Plug-ins are hardware or software modules that add a specific feature or service, extending the original capabilities of a browser. Downloading and installing a specific plug-in in a browser's plug-in folder provides the extension: For example, RealAudio creates the ability to listen to audio broadcasts over the Web. Shockwave plays animation files. Other capabilities include palmtop PC synchronization, wireless access, and encryption. Although plug-ins were originally devised to conform to Netscape Navigator specifications, they also work with Microsoft Internet Explorer and other browsers. Microsoft Explorer supports many Netscape Navigator plug-ins, but it also uses a different software standard, ActiveX, instead of plug-ins. ActiveX controls are discussed next. Netscape Navigator also supports some ActiveX controls.

Most plug-ins are free and download quickly because they are small files. Even so, users can be resistant to adding a plug-in program that may cause their browser or machine to behave in unexpected ways. Companies may opt not to use plug-ins on their site because of this resistance, or because plug-ins may interfere with a company's ability to get their site selected by a search engine. As has happened with other externally developed functionality, the most popular plug-ins will probably be incorporated into future versions of the browsers.

ActiveX is a loosely defined set of technologies developed by Microsoft. ActiveX follows from two other Microsoft technologies called *OLE (Object Linking and Embedding)* and *COM (Component Object Model)*. ActiveX controls extend browsers, allowing the manipulation of data inside the browser. They are the third version of OLE controls presented by Microsoft, and use COM technologies to provide interoperability with other types of COM components and services. For example, they allow users to identify the authors of controls before allowing them to execute, an important Web security feature. COM architecture works across all Microsoft products, and creates objects that have a standard interface, so that they can be used by any COM-aware program. ActiveX controls are most commonly written in C++ or Visual Basic.

Cookies are used to identify a user when that user returns to a Website. Often a Website will request that a visitor fill out a form that includes name and e-mail, and may ask for other information such as mailing address, phone, and interests related to the site. The information provided will be stored in a cookie and sent to the Web browser. When the user returns to the site later, the contents of the cookie are sent back to the server and may be used to customize the Web page that is returned. Cookies are persistent, as they may be stored on the browser for a lengthy time. Users who object to providing such information may disable the storage of cookies in their Web browsers.

ActiveX: A loosely defined set of technologies developed by Microsoft that extends browser capabilities and allows the manipulation of data inside the browser.

Cookie: A block of data stored on a client by a Web server. When a user returns to the site later, the contents of the cookie are sent back to the Web server and may be used to identify the user and return a customized Web page.

WEB-TO-DATABASE TOOLS: COLDFUSION AND ASP

Many middleware applications that ease the connection of databases to Web applications now exist. ColdFusion and Microsoft Active Server Pages (ASP) are among the more popular. Other products receiving notice in mid 2001 include Cocoon, Element Construction Set (ECS), eXtensible Markup Language Compiler (XMLC), extensible Stylesheet Language Transformation (XSLT), and Java Server Pages (JSP). The merits of the various products are widely discussed, and center on the amount and nature of coding required, portability, and compiler requirements.

To aid understanding of connecting a database to a Web page, a simple shopping cart application follows. You can use either ASP or ColdFusion 4.0. A shopping cart is an application that allows you to select items and place an order from a Website. Code necessary to understand the connection process follows. The complete script files and instructions for setting up identical working shopping carts using ASP or ColdFusion are available from the text Website www.prenhall.com/hoffer. These sample files demonstrate pulling data from an attached database and do not actually store the order information or accept credit card information.

Both ASP and ColdFusion allow for the coding of custom tags within an HTML file. ColdFusion pages are stored in script files with a *.cfm* file extension. ASP pages are stored in script files with an *.asp* file extension. The custom tags enable server-side scripting that allows the creation of dynamic Web pages.

Active Server Pages (ASP) Example

ASP consists of text files that contain text, HTML, and scripting language commands, typically JavaScript or VBScript. Because these files are executed on the server, it is not necessary that the programmer be concerned about the client platform that will display the results of the server-side processing. Active Server Pages are identified by their extension, *.asp*. They may be accessed like other URLs through Web browsers, including Microsoft Internet Explorer and Netscape Navigator.

The request for an Active Server Page file results in the server processing any script commands that have been embedded in the page, generation of an HTML document, and transmission of that HTML document back to the client to be displayed.

Our simple ASP shopping cart example has one global file and six *.asp* files:

- global.asa—Every ASP application must have a *global.asa* file. It is generally used to manage both the application and any sessions that are started from a client.
- cart.asp—Displays the shopping cart contents and allows the addition and subtraction of items from the shopping cart.
- checkout.asp—Accepts shopper information and completes the order, but is incomplete with regard to storing the order and processing the credit card.
- item.asp—Displays information about a particular item (furniture piece) and provides an option to link to the search box and the main area.
- line.asp—Displays a list of all products that are available in a certain finish and gives access to the search box.
- search.asp—Displays a list of all products that match in Product_t.Product_ Description the search parameter specified from the FormField searchval.
- store.asp—Home page of the Pine Valley Furniture Store ColdFusion shopping cart demo. Provides access to a search tool to search for a specific item. It also lists all the different finish lines available for purchase.

Global.asa is a file where event scripts are specified and session and application objects that can be accessed by every page in an ASP application are declared. The *global.asa* file used in our shopping cart application is shown in Figure 10-4. It must be stored in the root directory of the ASP application. Each application can only have one *global.asa* file. Instructions for starting and ending applications and/or sessions can be placed here. In our example, starting a new session will start a shopping cart for the client requesting a session and a variable in which to keep track of the quantity ordered.

Of the six *.asp* files included in the simple shopping cart, *store.asp* has been reproduced in Figure 10-5. The remaining five files are available from the text Website

Figure 10-4
global.asa

```
<SCRIPT LANGUAGE=VBScript RUNAT=Server>

'You can add special event handlers in this file that will get run automatically when
'special Active Server Pages events occur. To create these handlers, just create a
'subroutine with a name from the list below that corresponds to the event you want to
'use. For example, to create an event handler for Session_OnStart, you would put the
'following code into this file (without the comments):

Sub Session_OnStart
'**Put your code here **
        Session("Cart") ' Tracks what they want to order
        Session("Count") ' Tracks the quantity that they want
End Sub

'EventName          Description
'Session_OnStart    Runs the first time a user runs any page in your application
'Session_OnEnd      Runs when a user's session times out or quits your application
'Application_OnStart Runs once when the first page of your application is run for the first
                    time by any user
'Application_OnEnd  Runs once when the web server shuts down

</SCRIPT>
```

Box A

```
<%@ language=VBScript %>
```

Box B

```
<%
option explicit
REM designed by: Michael Alexander
REM Project: Pine Valley Furniture Demo, ASP
REM Purpose: Store Entrance

REM This page provides entrance to the Pine Valley Furniture Store
REM asp demo version. It provides the user with a search tool to
REM search for a specific item. It also has a listing of all the
REM different Finish "Lines" available for purchase.
%>
```

Box C

```
<%
Dim conn
Dim rsRes
Dim strSQL
REM Set up Database connection
set conn = server.CreateObject ("adodb.connection")
conn.Open "PVFMDB"
%>
```

```
<HTML>
<HEAD>
<META NAME="GENERATOR" Content="Microsoft Visual Studio 6.0">
<TITLE>Pine Valley Furniture Company Web Store</TITLE>
</HEAD>
<BODY bgcolor=#ffffcc text=#00008b>
<TABLE align=center>
        <TR>
                <TD><STRONG><FONT size=6>Welcome to the Pine Valley Furniture Store
                        </FONT></STRONG></TD>
        </TR>
</TABLE>
<HR><BR><BR>
<TABLE>
        <TR>
                <TD valign=top align=center>
                        <B>Search for a product such as bookcase, nightstand, or table:</B><BR>

                        <FORM action="search.asp" method=post>
                                <INPUT Name="searchval" type=text width=20><BR><BR>
                                <INPUT Value="SEARCH!" type=submit><BR>
                        </FORM>
```

Box D

```
                        <% If Session("Cart") <> "" Then %>

                        <FORM method=post action=cart.asp>
                                <INPUT type=Hidden name=Quantity value=0>
                                <INPUT type=Hidden name=item value=0>
                                <INPUT type=Hidden name=none value=0>
                                <INPUT type=Submit value="Go to Cart">
                        </FORM><BR>
                        <% End If %>
```

```
                </TD>
                <TD align = center valign=top width=100>
                <B>Or, search by product finish:</B><BR><BR>
```

Figure 10-5
store.asp
(continues)

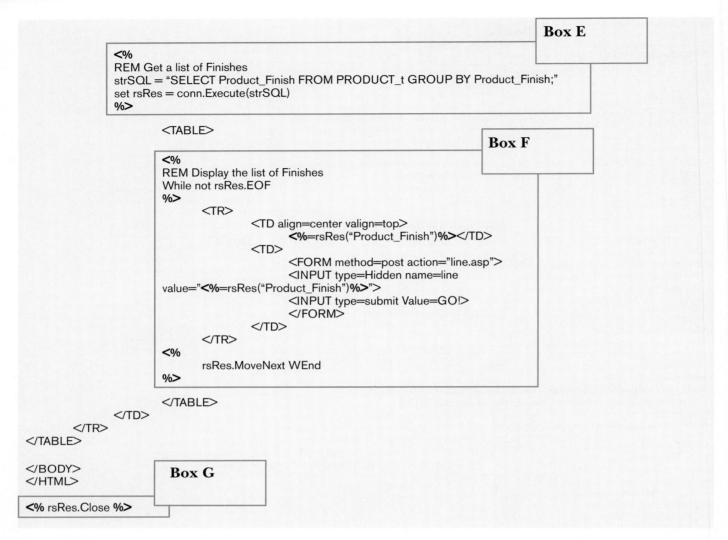

Box E

```
<%
REM Get a list of Finishes
strSQL = "SELECT Product_Finish FROM PRODUCT_t GROUP BY Product_Finish;"
set rsRes = conn.Execute(strSQL)
%>
```

```
<TABLE>
```

Box F

```
<%
REM Display the list of Finishes
While not rsRes.EOF
%>
        <TR>
                <TD align=center valign=top>
                        <%=rsRes("Product_Finish")%></TD>
                <TD>
                        <FORM method=post action="line.asp">
                        <INPUT type=Hidden name=line
value="<%=rsRes("Product_Finish")%>">
                        <INPUT type=submit Value=GO!>
                        </FORM>
                </TD>
        </TR>
<%
        rsRes.MoveNext WEnd
%>
```

```
</TABLE>
    </TD>
  </TR>
</TABLE>

</BODY>
</HTML>
```

Box G

```
<% rsRes.Close %>
```

Figure 10-5
(continued)

www.prenhall.com/hoffer, along with instructions for installation on a PC. *Store.asp* is the home page of the Pine Valley Furniture Company sample shopping cart and demonstrates enough different ASP capabilities to provide a general understanding of how an ASP application is used to attach a database to an application. Use the Personal Web server (PWS) to set up a test environment within which to run the shopping cart, if using a pc running Windows.

The following comments refer to Figure 10-5:

Box A uses the ASP tag (<% %>) to indicate to the server that the ASP application will be using VBScript and should be interpreted accordingly. **Box B** contains one command: *option explicit*. This simply means that all variables will be explicitly declared via a Dim statement. Using Option Explicit allows you to easily catch misspelled variable names. **Box C** declares variables explicitly and sets up the database connection. Note that the database name is described as "PVFMDB" and that the ODBC connection must use that name when it is set up.

Box D shows that ASP can handle conditional logic. In this case, if a client has chosen a product, it will be submitted to the cart to be tracked until final purchase is completed. **Box E** shows how ASP is used to connect to a database and send a query. In this case, the query will select the furniture finishes in which a particular product line is made. **Box F** shows the combination of HTML and ASP necessary to display the results of the query requested in Box E to be displayed on the client. **Box G**

closes the variable rsRes, which has been used to move through all of the finishes for a particular product line.

This short review of ASP coding makes it clear that anyone with experience in HTML and VBScript or JavaScript will be comfortable very quickly with using ASP to create a dynamic Website. Those with less familiarity with VBScript or JavaScript may find ColdFusion to be easier to understand and use quickly. We encourage you to set up both shopping carts and compare them on your own machine.

ColdFusion Example

ColdFusion requires the use of a server-side markup language, **ColdFusion Markup Language (CFML)**, to create ColdFusion application page scripts. These scripts are identified by their extension, *.cfm*. When a client browser requests a *.cfm* page from the Web server, it is passed to the ColdFusion application server where the script is executed, the result formatted in HTML and returned to the Web server. The Web server returns that result to the client where it is displayed.

CFML is modeled after HTML, and includes tags for reading and updating database tables, generating and retrieving e-mail messages, performing HTTP and FTP operations, credit card verifications and authorizations, and reading and writing client-side cookies. These capabilities allow the creation of dynamic pages, the use of live data to populate forms, the ability to process form submissions, and to interact with local files.

The simple ColdFusion shopping cart has seven *.cfm* files:

- application.cfm—This file sets the status of an application, client and session scope variables, and how long they are active. This file is automatically included by the ColdFusion server at the top of each page.

- cart.cfm—Displays the shopping cart contents and allows the addition and subtraction of items from the shopping cart.

- checkout.cfm—Accepts shopper information and completes the order, but is incomplete with regard to storing the order and processing the credit card.

- item.cfm—Displays information about a particular item (furniture piece) and provides an option to link to the search box and the main area.

- line.cfm—Displays a list of all products that are available in a certain finish and gives access to the search box.

- search.cfm—Displays a list of all products that match in Product_t.Product_Description the search parameter specified from the FormField searchval.

- store.cfm—Home page of the Pine Valley Furniture Store ColdFusion shopping cart demo. Provides access to a search tool to search for a specific item. It also lists all the different finish lines available for purchase.

The complete file *application.cfm* is shown in Figure 10-6. Notice that the <CFAPPLICATION> tag is used to assign an application name of *PVFC*. Client and session management are also set to "TRUE." Enabling client and session management makes it possible for a Web application to maintain a virtual state for each client, necessary for the shopping cart to remember each shopper's contents. These options make it possible to keep sessions distinguished and secure, with or without the use of cookies, and they work with virtually all browsers.

The database that will be accessed to get data is named here, and will have to be used when the shopping cart demo is installed on your own machine. In this case the ODBC data source is named "PVFMDB." The <CFIF> tag is used for conditional logic. In this case, if *Session.cart* is not defined, the client is starting a new session, and *session.cart* needs to be defined. If *session.cart* is already defined, no action will be taken. While not demonstrated in this simple sample code, it is also possible to set an

ColdFusion Markup Language (CFML): The language used to create ColdFusion application page scripts. The language is modeled after HTML and includes tags for performing operations such as reading and updating database tables.

```
<!---Name application--->
<CFAPPLICATION NAME="PVFC" CLIENTMANAGEMENT="TRUE" SESSIONMANAGEMENT="TRUE">
<!---Set application constants--->
<CFSET ODBC_DataSource = "PVFMDB">
<CFSET BG_Color = "ffffcc">
<CFSET Text = "00008b">
<!---Set application variables--->
<CFIF not isDefined("Session.cart")>
        <CFSET Session.cart=ArrayNew(2)>
</CFIF>
```

Figure 10-6
application.cfm

allowable time span for application scope variables and session scope variables here so that abandoned shopping carts will be automatically cancelled out.

One other file, *item.cfm*, is shown in Figure 10-7. Each use of a CFML tag has been bolded and marked by a box. Thus, it is easy to see how the CFML tags are similar in concept to the HTML tags. When the Web server encounters each of the CFML tags, it will contact the ColdFusion server to get the tag interpreted. We will consider each of the five sets of CFML tags to gain a general understanding of the nature of the CFML tags. The other five files included in the ColdFusion shopping cart may be explored also, but are not included in the text here.

Box A in Figure 10-7 demonstrates several CFML tags. The first, <**CFPARAM**>, is used to specify default values for parameters or to specify required parameters. Here a default value of "" is set for the *item* parameter. Then, the next CFML tag, <**CFIF**>, begins a conditional logic loop by determining whether *item* has taken on a value other than the default value specified in <**CFPARAM**>. When *item's* value is not the default value, "", there is a product to be displayed, and it will be put into the variable *strItem* using the CFML tag <**CFSET**>, which is used to assign values to variables.

<**CFIF**> is one of a set of tags used to establish conditional logic, and is one of the most common tags used. Every <**CFIF**> tag must have its matching </**CFIF**> tag. The tags used for comparisons are <**CFELSEIF**> and <**CFELSE**>. As many <**CFELSEIF**> tags may be used as needed, but only one <**CFELSE**> tag may be used within a <**CFIF**> loop. **Box C** contains another example of conditional logic that moves information about a desired item into the shopping cart (*cart.cfm*).

One tag remains in Box A, and that is <**CFLOCATION**>, which is used to redirect the browser to a different URL. In this case, the browser is redirected to the application's home page.

Box B contains the CFML tag that controls display, <**CFOUTPUT**>. The BODY statement has been placed within the CFOUTPUT block of code. Because of this, the values of each declared variable (those surrounded by # signs) will be used. The values of these variables were set as application constants in the *application.cfm* file.

Box D demonstrates the use of <**CFQUERY**> to connect to the database and select the desired information about an item. Note that the specified data source was identified in *application.cfm* and the value of *item* was determined in *search.cfm*. The SQL query that will return the product information to be displayed is also included in this code block. It uses the value of *item* returned by *search.cfm* and used as the value for *strItem*. The output from the query is displayed as a result of the code module in **Box E**. The <**CFOUTPUT**> tag formats the results of the query named *Item*. HTML code is used within the module to format the output of the query.

This short review of ColdFusion coding makes it clear that CFML tags are very similar to HTML tags and that they are easily put together to create a dynamic Web-enabled application that attaches to a database. There are nearly 100 CFML tags available that support traditional programming constructs and techniques. However, coding in traditional programming languages is not required, only an understanding

```
<!---
Designed by: Michael Alexander
Project: Pine Valley Furniture Demo, ASP
Purpose: Display a specific Product.

This page displays a specific item in its main area.
It also provides an option to link to the search box, and the main area.

Check to see if the user has gotten to this page correctly.
--->
```

Box A

```
<CFPARAM NAME="item" DEFAULT="">
<CFIF item IS NOT "">
<!--- We do have a Product, so put it into strItem.--->
        <CFSET #strItem# = #item#>
<CFELSE>
<!---We don't have a Product, so kick back out to main store page.--->
        <CFLOCATION url="store.cfm" addtoken="NO">
</CFIF>
```

```
<HTML>
<HEAD>
<META NAME="GENERATOR" Content="Microsoft Visual Studio 6.0">
<TITLE>Pine Valley Furniture Company Web Store</TITLE>
</HEAD>
```

Box B

```
<CFOUTPUT>
<BODY bgcolor=#BG_Color# text=#Text# link=#Text# vlink=#Text# alink=#Text# >
</CFOUTPUT>
```

```
<TABLE align=center>
        <TR>
                <TD><STRONG><FONT size=6>Pine Valley Furniture Store
                        </FONT></STRONG></TD>
        </TR>
</TABLE>
<HR>
<TABLE>
        <TR align=right>
                <TD valign=top align=center>
                        <B>Search for a product such as bookcase, nightstand, or table:</B><BR>

                        <FORM action="search.cfm" method=post>
                                <INPUT Name="searchval" type=text width=20><BR><BR>
                                <INPUT Value="SEARCH!" type=submit><BR>
                        </FORM>
                        <BR>
                        <A href="store.cfm">Return to Store Front</A><BR>
```

Box C

```
<CFIF not ArrayIsEmpty(Session.cart)>
        <FORM method=post action=cart.cfm>
                <INPUT type=Hidden name=Quantity value=0>
                <INPUT type=Hidden name=item value=0>
                <INPUT type=Hidden name=none value=0>
                <INPUT type=Submit value="Go to Cart">
        </FORM><BR>
</CFIF>
```

Figure 10-7
item.cfm
(continues)

```
            </TD>
            <TD valign=top width=75%>
                    <TABLE align=center>
                    <!---REM Get the information about the Product--->
```

Box D

```
<CFQUERY DATASOURCE=#ODBC_DataSource# Name="Item">
SELECT *
FROM PRODUCT_t
WHERE Product_ID = #strItem#
</CFQUERY>
```

Box E

```
        <CFOUTPUT query="Item">
        <tr>
                <td>Product: </td>
                <td width=75% align=left>#Product_Description#</td>
        </tr>
        <tr>

                <td>Finish: </td>
                <td width=75% align=left>#Product_Finish#</td>
        </tr>
        <tr>

                <td>Cost: </td>
                <td width=75%
                align=left>#DecimalFormat (Standard_Price) #</td>
        </tr>
        <tr>

                <FORM method=post action="cart.cfm">
                <INPUT type=Hidden Name=Item Value=#Product_Id#>
                <td colspan=2 align=center>
                        <INPUT type=Submit Value="Buy It!">
                </td>
                </FORM>
        </tr>
        <tr>

                <FORM method=post action="line.cfm">
                        <INPUT type=Hidden Name=line
                        Value="#Product_Finish#">
                <td colspan=2 align=center>
                        <INPUT type=Submit Value="Go to
                        #Product_Finish# Finish">
                </td>
                </FORM>
        </tr>
        </CFOUTPUT>

                    </TABLE>
            </TD>
        </TR>
</TABLE>


</BODY>
</HTML>
```

Figure 10-7
(continued)

of HTML is needed. ColdFusion is an example of products that have made writing custom Web-based applications much faster and simpler.

In both of the previous sections, examples of using SQL code embedded within code using other languages was demonstrated. Refer to Figure 10-5, Box E and Figure 10-7, Box D, to find SQL embedded within VBScript for an ASP Web-enabled database and inside CFML for a ColdFusion Web-enabled database. In each case, the SQL code is passed to the database by either the ASP server or the ColdFusion server, where it is interpreted and a result returned. This form of "embedded SQL" does not involve the more complicated syntax generally associated with embedded SQL within a third generation language (3GL) such as C. A more complete explanation of embedded SQL when used with 3GLs follows.

Embedded SQL

In Chapters 7 and 8 we used the interactive, or direct, form of SQL. In that case one SQL command is entered and executed at a time. It constitutes a logical unit of work, or transaction. The commands necessary to maintain a valid database, such as ROLLBACK and COMMIT, are transparent to the user in most interactive SQL situations. Another form of SQL is widely used in creating applications on both clients and servers; it is referred to as embedded SQL. SQL commands are embedded into 3GLs (Third Generation Languages) such as ADA, COBOL, C, Fortran, M, Pascal, or PL/I by placing them at appropriate locations in a 3GL host program. Oracle also offers PL/SQL, or Procedural Language SQL, a proprietary language that extends SQL by adding some procedural language features such as variables, types, control structures (including IF-THEN-ELSE loops), functions, and procedures. PL/SQL blocks of code can also be embedded in 3GL programs.

There are several reasons to consider embedding SQL in a 3GL. The first is the possibility of creating a more flexible, accessible interface for the user. Using interactive SQL effectively requires a good understanding of both SQL and the database structure, understanding the typical application user may not have. While many of the RDBMs come with form, report, and application generators (or such capabilities are available as add-ons), developers frequently envision capabilities that are not easily accomplished with these tools but that can be easily accomplished using a 3GL. Large, complex programs that require access to a relational database may best be programmed in a 3GL, with embedded SQL calls to an SQL database.

Also, it may be possible to improve performance by using embedded SQL. Using interactive SQL requires that each query be converted to executable machine code each time the query is processed. Or, the query optimizer, which runs automatically in a direct SQL situation, may not successfully optimize the query, causing it to run slowly. With embedded SQL the developer has more control of database access and may be able to create significant performance improvements. Knowing when to rely on the SQL translator and optimizer and when to control it through the program depends on the nature of the problem, and making this trade-off is best accomplished through experience and testing.

A third reason to use embedded SQL would be to improve database security. Restricted access can be achieved by a DBA through the GRANT and REVOKE permissions in SQL and by creating views. These same restrictions can also be invoked in the embedded SQL application, thus providing another layer of protection. Complex data integrity checks may be more easily accomplished, including cross-field consistency checks.

A program that is using embedded SQL will consist of the *host* program written in a 3GL such as C or COBOL, but there will also be sections of SQL code sprinkled throughout. Each section of SQL code will begin with EXEC SQL, keywords used to indicate an embedded SQL command that will be converted to the host source code when run through the precompiler. You will need a separate precompiler for each host language that you plan to use. Be sure to determine that the 3GL compiler is

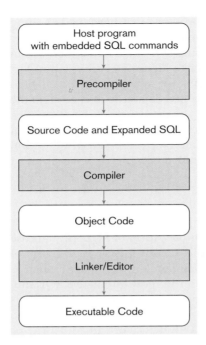

Figure 10-8
Processing an embedded SQL
program

compatible with your RDBMS's precompiler for each language. Figure 10-8 shows the steps that an embedded SQL program goes through as it is processed.

When the precompiler encounter an EXEC SQL statement, it will translate that SQL command into the host program language. Some, but not all, precompilers will check for correct SQL syntax and generate any required error messages at this point. Others will not generate an error message until the SQL statement actually attempts to execute. Some products' precompilers (DB2, SQL/DS, Ingres) create a separate file of SQL statements that is then processed by a separate utility called a binder, which determines that the referenced objects exist, that the user possesses sufficient privileges to run the statement, and the processing approach that will be used. Other products (Oracle, Informix) interpret the statements at run time rather than compiling them. In either case, the resulting program will contain calls to DMS routines and the link/editor programs will link them in.

Here is a simple example using C as the host language that will give an idea of what embedded SQL looks like in a program. This example uses a prepared SQL statement, named 'getcust,' which will be compiled and stored as executable code in the database. Cust_ID is the primary key of the customer table. Getcust, the prepared SQL statement, returns customer information (c_name, c_address, city, state, postcode) for an order number. A placeholder is used for the order information, which is an input parameter. Customer information is output from the SQL query and stored into host variables using the into-clause. This example assumes that only one row is returned from the query.

```
exec sql prepare getcust from
       "select c_name, c_address, city, state, postcode
       from customer_t, order_t
       where customer_t.cust_id = order_t.cust_id and order_id = ?";
       .

       .
       ./* code to get proper value in theOrder */
exec sql execute getcust into :c_name, :c_address, :city, :state,
       :postcode using theOrder;
       .

       .

       .
```

If a prepared statement returns multiple rows, it is necessary to write a program loop using cursors to return a tuple at a time to be stored. Cursors help to eliminate the impedance mismatch between SQL's set-at-a-time processing and procedural languages' record-at-a-time processing.

MANAGING WEBSITE DATA

The importance of databases to the Internet is clear. Some traditional database issues have taken on additional significance as databases have become more important to Internet applications. The first issue is that of security; Web applications establish connectivity and access with users outside of the company in ways that were unheard of just a few years ago. The second issue is privacy; companies are able to collect information about those who access their Websites. If they are conducting e-commerce activities, selling products over the Web, they can collect information about their customers that has value to other businesses. If a company sells customer information without those customers' knowledge, or if a customer believes that may happen, ethical and privacy issues are raised that must be addressed. The last issue considered is the rapidity with which Internet technology changes occur. The pace of technological change has accelerated, challenging database administrators to master frequent updates of existing products and identify and evaluate new products for their importance to business operations. Each of these issues is covered in the following sections.

Web Security Issues

One of the most significant inhibitors to the growth of e-commerce is the lack of user confidence in the security associated with those transactions. Web-related database security issues must be addressed so that sensitive information is protected and the risk of compromising the data is controlled. Hooking a business application to a public network such as the Internet requires that all identified vulnerabilities be handled. While database information needs to be returned to the client for display when a request is handled, obtaining that information must be carefully restricted. A client sending a request through an Internet connection should not be able to access the database directly.

Security measures may be taken throughout the system, at the network level, operating system level, Web server level, and database level. Precautions should be taken in each area, so that layers of security must be breached in order to reach sensitive data. Regular monitoring and security testing procedures should also be in place because frequent changes in the business and/or security environment can make a previously secure site vulnerable to intrusion. Figure 10-9 takes a closer look at hardware security that can be put in place in addition to the firewall that stands as a first line of defense against unwanted intrusions from the public.

In addition to the firewall discussed earlier and included in Figure 10-1, **router** symbols and an **intrusion detection system (IDS)** symbol have been added. Routers are intermediate devices placed on communications networks. They are used to transmit message packets and forward them to the correct destination over the most efficient pathway available. Intrusion detection systems try to identify attempts to hack or break into a computer system or to misuse it. IDSs may monitor packets passing over the network, monitor system files, monitor log files, or set up deception systems that attempt to trap hackers by luring them through well-known security holes. In addition, it should be noted that the Web servers are isolated from the business or internal host computers. And, the database server should be isolated from the Web server.

Router: An intermediate device on a communications network used to transmit message packets and forward them to the correct destination over the most efficient pathway.

Intrusion detection system (IDS): A system that tries to identify attempts to hack or break into a computer system or to misuse it. IDSs may monitor packets passing over the network, monitor system files, monitor log files, or set up deception systems that attempt to trap hackers.

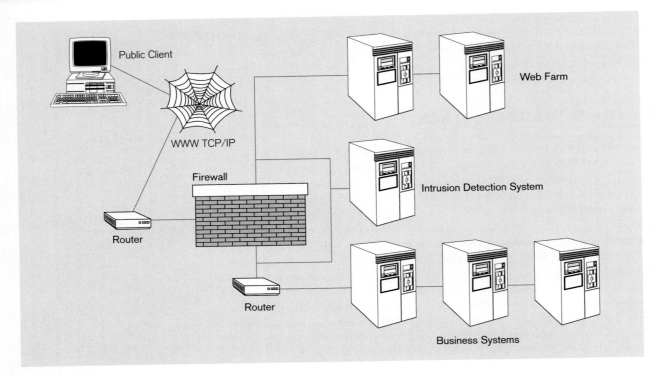

Figure 10-9
Establishing Internet security

Planning for Web Security Begin planning to establish security for a Web-enabled database application by performing a formal, written risk assessment that is approved by management. A risk assessment should consider at least the following factors:

- The nature of the risk
- The likelihood of the risk
- Potential operational, financial, and legal impact on the organization
- Existing circumstances that might lead someone to attempt to breach the security

The database administrator should not attempt to conduct the risk assessment without input from other involved employees. Any assignment to complete the risk assessment should be taken on by someone with the authority to complete the risk assessment successfully and the ability to convey the contents of the risk assessment to the appropriate level of management. Doing so will protect the database administrator because responsibility for addressing the risks will be assumed by management rather than by the database administrator.

Network Level Security Adequately securing a database for an Internet environment requires securing the network through which it communicates.

- The Web server and database server should be on a separate LAN from the other business systems, and there should be a firewall between them and the business systems if there must be a connection to the internal systems. The firewalls set up between the Web server and the database server and between them and the business systems should function only as firewalls and be password protected.
- Sharing of hard disks among the networked servers should also be kept to a minimum.

- Network and firewall logs, permitted so that modifications are not easy to accomplish, should be regularly monitored to discover any unauthorized or unusual activity.

- Software that monitors probes and attacks from external sources should be installed and regularly monitored. The person who is doing this monitoring may also be assigned to regularly check vendor sites and security Websites so that any newly discovered vulnerabilities can be patched as soon as possible.

Operating System Level Security Just as network level security must be established in order to protect the database and internal business systems, so must adequate operating system level security be established.

- Patch all known operating system vulnerabilities, again monitoring vendor and security Websites so that patches for newly discovered vulnerabilities can be applied as soon as they are available.

- Install anti-virus software that automatically checks for a virus whenever the machine is booted, a file is downloaded, or e-mail is received.

- Monitor server logs just as network logs are monitored for unauthorized activity. Install and monitor IDS software that detects external probes and attacks.

- In an Internet-enabled environment, disable any services that are not required but may provide access to an unauthorized user. For example, send-mail, an e-mail utility that has been superceded by newer e-mail programs, is still embedded in operating systems and should be disabled.

Web Server Security Each Web server should be configured in such a way that unauthorized access is very difficult. It would be best to make unauthorized access impossible, but the steady stream of new viruses and hacker access to machines makes one realize that complete system security cannot be attained. Attention to setting up Web servers so that access is as restricted as possible is suggested.

- Restrict the number of users on the Web server as much as possible. Of those users, give as few as possible superuser or administrator rights. Only those given these privileges should also be allowed to load software, edit files, or add files.

- Restrict access to the Web server, keeping a minimum number of ports open. Try to open a minimum number of ports, and preferably only *http* and *https*.

- Remove any unneeded programs that load automatically when setting up the server. Demo programs are sometimes included that can provide a hacker with the access desired. Compilers and interpreters such as Perl should not be on a path that is directly accessible from the Internet. CGI has potential security issues and should only be run if necessary. Restrict all CGI scripts to one subdirectory.

- If running on UNIX, be sure that the default operating system install as *root* was not used. Instead, install from a user's account that has only the minimum access necessary to run the Web server software.

Database level security is discussed in detail in Chapter 12.

Privacy Issues

Protection of individual privacy when using the Internet has become an important issue. E-mail, e-commerce and marketing, and other on-line resources have created new computer-mediated communication paths. New opportunities for impinging on individuals' privacy have developed right alongside. Many groups have an interest in people's Internet behavior, including employers, governments, and businesses. Applications that return individualized responses require that information be collected about the individual, but at the same time proper respect for the privacy and dignity of employees, citizens, and customers should be observed. This is a simple concept that is difficult to operationalize.

Individuals must guard their privacy rights, and need to be aware of the privacy implications of the tools they are using. For example, when using a browser they may elect to allow cookies to be placed on their machines or they may reject that option. In order to make a decision with which they would be comfortable, they must have learned several things. They must be aware of cookies, understand what they are, evaluate their own desire to receive customized information versus their wish to keep their browsing behavior to themselves, and learn how to set their machine to accept or reject cookies. Browsers and Websites have not been quick to help users understand all of these aspects. Abuses of privacy such as selling customer information collected in cookies has helped to increase general awareness of the privacy issues that have developed as use of the Web for communication, shopping, and other uses has developed.

At work, the individual needs to realize that communication executed through their employer's machines and networks is not private. Courts have upheld the rights of employers to monitor all employee electronic communication.

On the Internet itself, privacy of communication is not guaranteed. Encryption products, anonymous remailers, and built-in security mechanisms in commonly used software help to preserve privacy. Protecting the privately owned and operated computer networks that now make up a very critical part of our information infrastructure is essential to the further development of electronic commerce, banking, health care, and transportation applications over the Web.

The World Wide Web Consortium has created a standard, the Platform for Privacy Preferences (P3P), that will result in the communication of a Website's stated privacy policies and a comparison of that statement with the user's own policy preferences. P3P uses XML code on Website servers that can be fetched automatically by any browser or plug-in equipped for P3P. The client browser or plug-in can then compare the site's privacy policy with the user's privacy preferences and inform the user of any discrepancies. P3P addresses the following aspects of on-line privacy:

- Who is collecting the data?
- What information is being collected and for what purpose?
- Which information will be shared with others and who are those others?
- Can users make changes in how their data will be used by the collector?
- How are disputes resolved?
- What policies are followed for retaining data?
- Where can the site's detailed policies be found in readable form?

Anonymity is another important facet of Internet communication that has come under pressure. While U.S. law protects a right to anonymity, chat rooms and e-mail forums have been required to reveal the names of people who have posted messages anonymously. A 1995 European Parliament directive that would cut off data exchanges with any country lacking adequate privacy safeguards has led to an agreement that the United States will provide the same protection to European customers as European businesses do. This may lead Congress to establish legislation that is more protective than previously enacted legislation.

DCS-1000 (Carnivore): Device developed by the FBI to monitor e-mail traffic by tracking e-mail headers.

The FBI's e-mail monitoring device, **DCS-1000** (formerly named **Carnivore**) is a device that is installed on an e-mail server. It tracks e-mail headers, but not the content of the e-mail. Concerns have been expressed that DCS-1000 may open security holes, damage a company's technology infrastructure, or compromise privacy. The American Civil Liberties Union is trying to draw the attention of the United States

Congress to privacy laws that it considers outdated for Internet communication. While the government moves slowly toward revising privacy regulations to Internet communications issues, individuals and businesses should be sure that they understand their present rights and responsibilities with regard to establishing desired privacy levels.

Internet Technology Rate-of-Change Issues

As you have seen in this chapter, changes in hardware, software, and telecommunication technologies are playing a major role in the way the Information Age is developing. Rarely in the last two decades have companies had opportunities to implement an information system and rely on it for an extended period. The rate and breadth of change have caught many companies off guard. As planning horizons shorten, competing in such a dynamic environment has been very challenging, and companies have had to reinvent themselves and attempt to equip their employees with the environment, experiences, and skills required to thrive in a transformed economy and culture.

Over the last two decades, the rate of change in information technology has accelerated. Throughout, implementing the conceptually simple and elegant vision of integrated but distributed systems has been elusive. The phrase "the devil is in the details" comes to mind. Information technology planning has moved from being an independent tactical activity to being central to organizations' strategic planning processes. Expectations of both employees and customers for relevant, easy-to-use systems have risen dramatically. Effective IT systems are now seen as a critical success factor in the marketplace. Database technology has been fundamental to meeting these expectations and supporting business strategy.

Progress toward creating a more integrated data management environment began when databases replaced flat files. Relational database technology made it possible to record an item of data in one place but use it in different applications. Object-oriented databases hold the promise of improving response time because objects do not have to be reconstituted when they are requested.

Now the long anticipated integration of computing and telecommunications is transforming the way people acquire and share information. Traditional technology boundaries are becoming blurred. Cell phones and personal digital assistants (PDAs) connect to the Internet. People answer their e-mail through their pagers, sometimes while sitting in meetings. Television is delivered over airwaves, cables, and satellites. These integrations of traditionally separate technologies create new business opportunities and the need for new policies and laws to control public services such as airwaves and public networks. As new methods and locations for database access are established, database security issues come to the fore.

Concurrently, changes in organizational relationships also pressure database administrators to deal with new business forms. Models of competition have been supplemented by models of cooperation. As companies come together to work on a project, only to move apart when the project is completed, issues of shared database access never before raised must now be addressed.

Globalization of business is also increasing faster than ever before. Companies place work teams strategically around the world so that at least one team is always working. IT managers are assigned global management responsibilities, such as managing teams in upstate New York, Melbourne, and London. No longer is there available downtime for backing up and tuning databases; the database is expected to always be available.

In the face of this ever-increasing rate of change, database administrators must participate actively in accomplishing the alignment of organizational (IT) structure with business strategy. This requires an understanding of the business in addition to understanding the technology infrastructure and database architecture. Leadership skills, (including communication and listening skills), upward influence techniques, and employee management techniques must be highly developed. The successful IT manager can no longer depend on technical depth alone to navigate the rapid changes occurring in the business environment.

Summary

This chapter builds an understanding of the fit of databases with Internet applications, covers various Internet database architectures, illustrates the use of ASP and ColdFusion to Web-enabled databases, and discusses management issues associated with these topics. Several characteristics of the Web environment have supported the rapid adoption and implementation of Internet and intranet business applications, including the simplicity and functional similarities of the browser interfaces. The hardware and software independence of the browsers has eased the sharing of information across platforms. Development costs and time have been reduced.

The Internet environment includes a network that connects the client workstations, Web server, and database server, following TCP/IP protocols. Every computer connected to the Internet must have a distinct IP address. In a simple architecture, a request from a client browser is sent through the network to the Web server. If the request requires that data be obtained from the database, the Web server constructs a query and sends it to the database server, which processes the query and returns the results set. Firewalls are used to limit external access to the company's data.

Common components of Internet architecture are certain programming and markup languages, Web server middleware, including server-side extensions and Web server interfaces, Web servers, and client-side extensions. To aid understanding of connecting a database to a Web page, a simple shopping cart application has been included, using either ASP or ColdFusion.

Some traditional database issues have taken on additional significance as databases have become more important to Internet applications. These issues include security, privacy, and handling the increasingly rapid rate of change in both business and technology practices. Security measures must be placed at the network level, operating system level, Web server level, and database level. Individuals must guard their privacy rights, and need to be aware of the privacy implications of the tools they are using. The issues of anonymity must still be resolved.

Last, the rate of change in information technology has accelerated, and all of us must struggle with keeping those changes strategically aligned with changes in business practices.

While in some respects databases have matured, their fundamental importance to development of the Internet and electronic commerce have kept them in the forefront of technological change. This chapter has presented basic concepts of Web-enabled databases; the informed reader must turn to current outside reading to be completely abreast of recent opportunities in this area.

CHAPTER REVIEW

Key Terms

ActiveX
Browser
Business to business (B2B)
Business to consumer (B2C)
Cascading Style Sheets (CSS)
ColdFusion Markup Language (CFML)
Common Gateway Interface (CGI)
Cookie
DCS-1000 (Carnivore)
DNS (domain name server) balancing

Electronic business (e-business)
Electronic commerce (e-commerce)
Extensible Markup Language (XML)
Firewall
Hypertext Markup Language (HTML)
Intrusion detection system (IDS)
Java
Java servlet
JavaScript
Plug-ins

Proxy server
Reverse proxy
Router
Server-side extension
Software and hardware load balancing
Standard Generalized Markup Language (SGML)
VBScript
World Wide Web (WWW or Web)
World Wide Web Consortium (W3C)
XHTML

Review Questions

1. Define each of the following key terms:
   a. ColdFusion Markup Language (CFML)
   b. Cookie
   c. DNS balancing
   d. Electronic business
   e. Firewall
   f. Server-side extension
   g. W3C

2. Match the following terms and definitions:

____	browser	a.____	load-balancing approach for multiple Web servers
____	e-business		
____	firewall	b.____	World Wide Web Consortium
____	URL	c.____	hardware/software that limits access to company data
____	W3C		
____	XHTML	d.____	software that displays HTML documents
____	servlet		
____	reverse proxy	e.____	small program that executes from within another application and is stored on a server

   f.____ Web address that specifies IP address and communication protocol of a Web server

   g.____ technology-enabled business that uses Internet technology

   h.____ scripting language that extends HTML to make it XML compliant

3. Contrast the following terms:
   a. Electronic commerce; electronic business
   i. Internet; intranet; extranet
   c. HTML; XML; XHTML
   d. DNS balancing; software and hardware load balancing; reverse proxy
   e. HTML; SGML

4. Explain why attaching a database to a Web page is important in the facilitation of e-business.

5. What are the components of an environment needed to establish Internet database-enabled connectivity?

6. Explain the purpose and accomplishments of the World Wide Web Consortium.

7. What is the purpose of database middleware, such as ColdFusion and ASP?

8. Compare and contrast Web server interfaces, including CGI, API, and Java servlets.

9. Describe three methods for balancing Web server loads.

10. Explain what a cookie, as used in Internet terminology, is and how it can be used.

11. Explain how ASP or ColdFusion are used.

12. Describe security measures that should be taken to secure a Web-enabled database at the network level, the operating system level, and the Web server level.

13. Describe in general the proposed Platform for Privacy Preferences (P3P).

Problems and Exercises

1. Explain the difference between a static Website and a dynamic Website. What are the characteristics of a dynamic Website that enable it to better support the development of e-business?

2. The chapter lists nine commonly provided intranet services. Identify those services that you feel are essential to any Intranet. Identify those services that could be optional. Defend your reasoning for each service.

3. What does each set of numbers in an IP address mean? Discuss this in terms of the following address: 24.24.27.15. *Note:* You will need to research this question because the details to answer this are not in the chapter.

4. Discuss some of the languages that are associated with Internet application development. Classify these languages according to the functionality they provide for each application. It is not necessary that you use the same classification scheme used in the chapter.

5. After reviewing and testing the ASP and ColdFusion shopping carts available with the text, write a short comparison of your experiences with setting up and using each of them. Consider your programming background as you write the comparison.

6. Why is it necessary to establish security measures at four levels (network, operating system, Web server, and database levels) when Web-enabling a database?

7. Discuss the pros and cons of anonymity of users on the Internet.

Field Exercises

1. Consider your own personal computer. Determine the plug-ins you have downloaded and for what each is used. Are any of these plug-ins related to manipulating or presenting data that is being returned from a database?

2. Find where cookies have been saved on your personal computer. Review them and organize them by categories for this question. Describe your decision process if you decide to delete any of the cookies. Were you surprised by the number of cookies stored on your machine?

3. Determine what you would have to do to use ColdFusion or ASP on a public Website owned either by yourself or by the organization for which you work.

4. Conduct a risk assessment for your Website if you attach a database to it.

5. Outline the steps you would take to conduct a risk assessment for your place of employment with regard to attaching a database to the public site. If possible, help with the actual implementation of the risk assessment.

6. According to your own personal interests, use your demonstration copy of ColdFusion or ASP to attach a database to your personal Website. First, test it locally and then move it to your public site.

7. Obtain a printed copy of the privacy policy for computer use at your place of employment. Are there any changes in your use of computers at work that you need to make in order to comply with the policy?

References

Forta, B. 1998. *The ColdFusion 4.0 Web Application Construction Kit.* Indianapolis, IN: Que.

Merkow, M. S., and J. Breithaupt. 2000. *The Complete Guide to Internet Security.* Detroit, MI: AMACON Books.

Morrison, M., and J. Morrison. 2000. *Database-Driven Web Sites.* Cambridge, MA: Course Technology.

Prague, C. N., and M. R. Irwin. 1999. *Microsoft Access 2000 Bible.* Foster City, CA: IDG Books Worldwide, Inc.

Schneier, B. 2000. *Applied Cryptography: Protocols, Algorithms, and Source Code in C,* 2nd Edition. New York: John Wiley & Sons.

Zwicky, E. D., D. Russell, S. Cooper, and D. B. Chapman. 2000. *Building Internet Firewalls,* 2nd Edition. Sebastopol, CA: O'Reilly & Associates.

Web Resources

http://hoohoo.ncsa.uiuc.edu/cgi/ Information about and the complete CGI specification from NCSA.

http://www.w3.org/CGI/ W3C page about CGI.

http://www.w3.org/MarkUp/ W3C's homepage for HTML and XHTML.

http://www.netcraft.com/survey/ The Netcraft Web Server Survey tracks Web servers' market shares and SSL site operating systems.

http://webservercompare.internet.com/webbasics/index.html Tutorial about Web servers

http://staff.plugged.net.au/dwood/xmlc/index.html Tutorial about XMLC, a Java-based compiler that creates Java classes from a document written in HTML or XML, and allows the document to be faithfully recreated.

http://xml.apache.org/cocoon/ Java Web publishing framework that separates document content, style and logic, allowing independent design, creation, and management of each.

http://www.vbxml.com/xsl/tutorials/intro/default.asp Tutorial about XSLT, which allows the transformation of an XML file into an HTML file or another text-based format.

http://www.cve.mitre.org/ Common Vulnerabilities and Exposures (CVE) is a list of standardized names for vulnerabilities and other information security exposures that have been identified by the CVE Editorial Board and monitored by MITRE Corporation. CVE aims to standardize the names for all publicly known vulnerabilities and security exposures.

http://www.computerprivacy.org/who/ Americans for Computer Privacy (ACP), a group of more than 100 companies and 40 associations representing financial services, manufacturing, telecommunications, high-tech and transportation, as well as law enforcement, civil-liberty, pro-family, and taxpayer groups who are concerned about computer privacy.

http://www.cpsr.org/ Computer Professionals for Social Responsibility (CPSR), a public-interest alliance of computer scientists and others concerned about the impact of computer technology on society.

http://www.epic.org/ Electronic Privacy Information Center (EPIC).

MOUNTAIN VIEW COMMUNITY HOSPITAL

Project Case

Health care institutions moved to maintaining their records in electronic form more slowly than other business sectors. Results that are routinely generated by computerized processing, such as lab results, are now generally electronically accessible. However, for most hospitals, much information is still not captured electronically. For example, results from physical examinations, doctors' and nurses' notes, and patient and family histories are not captured electronically in most hospitals. Development of information systems that capture this data is fragmented across institutions and vendors, and the development of systems that can be easily shared is hindered as a result. Where health care systems are developed, the benefits can be readily observed. A recent system that recorded prescriptions electronically resulted in 55 percent fewer problems with incorrect medicines, dosages, or drug interactions.

PROJECT DESCRIPTION

Mountain View Community Hospital's planning committee believes that the hospital may be able to improve its operations by adopting Web-based solutions. They have read of exciting systems that have been demonstrated in localized settings, but have found that the systems are not readily available for them to adopt, and that information about costs and benefits of the systems is difficult to obtain.

In considering where a browser interface could be developed for Mountain View's health care systems, several issues have been raised.

- First, security is a primary concern. Patient health information requires high levels of confidentiality because it is so sensitive by nature.
- Data entry questions are also significant. Doctors, nurses, and other health care workers must be able and willing to enter the data into any system that is provided.
- System availability will also be crucial if a decision is made to implement a Web-enabled system.

- How difficult would it be to integrate a browser-based system with existing or planned systems?
- How will Mountain View demonstrate to the Health Care Financing Administration (HCFA) that the proposed system is cost-effective?
- How will Mountain View predict changes in work patterns that may occur?
- What organizational policies and procedures will need to be changed or modified as system changes are implemented?

PROJECT QUESTIONS

1. Discuss the extent and nature of privacy issues that the planning committee should consider when evaluating any decisions to provide more information that is critical to patients over the Web.

2. Discuss data entry issues that the planning committee should consider. Be sure to consider data entry by physicians, nurses, and other health care workers and propose possible approaches to address the issues you have raised.

3. Health care professionals want to engage patients more actively in their own health care. Locate at least five health care Websites that individuals can access. Compare and contrast the information and/or services that are available through each site. Suggest a possible service that Mountain View could consider for their Website that would involve patients more actively in their own health care.

4. What advantages of constructing a computer-based patient record can you list? Are there disadvantages to computer-based patient records, too? Please list both the advantages and disadvantages that you can identify.

PROJECT EXERCISES

The Mountain View planning committee is considering three business functions that could be moved to an on-line interface. For each option being considered below, address the following:

A. Security and confidentiality concerns: who would need to access the data, how would access be restricted, how likely is the proposed security system to be compromised?

B. Data entry requirements: which job functions would enter data, how much resistance is expected from each function, and how is this resistance to be handled?

C. The benefits that Mountain View could expect. The costs.

Here are the three possibilities that are being considered:

1. Submitting insurance claims on-line

2. Providing clinical information to patients on-line

3. Implementing supply chain management on-line

Which of these three possibilities do you recommend implementing first? Support your recommendation.

Chapter 11

Data Warehousing

LEARNING OBJECTIVES

After studying this chapter, you should be able to:

- Define the following key terms: **data warehouse, operational system, informational system, data mart, independent data mart, dependent data mart, enterprise data warehouse, operational data store, @ctive warehouse, reconciled data, derived data, event, transient data, periodic data, static extract, incremental extract, data scrubbing, refresh mode, update mode, data transformation, selection, joining, aggregation, star schema, grain, market basket analysis, conformed dimension, snowflake schema, OLAP, ROLAP, MOLAP, data mining,** and **data visualization.**

- Give two important reasons why an "information gap" often exists between the information manager's need and the information generally available.

- List two major reasons why most organizations today need data warehousing.

- Name and briefly describe the three levels in a data warehouse architecture.

- List the four main steps of data reconciliation.

- Describe the two major components of a star schema.

- Estimate the number of rows and total size in bytes of a fact table, given reasonable assumptions concerning the database dimensions.

- Design a data mart using various schemes to normalize and denormalize dimensions and to account for fact history and changing dimension attribute values.

INTRODUCTION

Everyone agrees that readily available high-quality information is vital in business today. Consider the recent comments of two data management experts:

> Information is pivotal in today's business environment. Success is dependent on its early and decisive use. A lack of information is a sure sign for failure. The rapidly changing environment in which business operates demands ever more immediate access to data. (Devlin, 1997)

Many corporations are actively looking for new technologies that will assist them in becoming more profitable and competitive. Gaining competitive advantage requires that companies accelerate their decision making process so that they can respond quickly to change. One key to this accelerated decision making is having the right information, at the right time, easily accessible. (Poe, 1996)

In light of this strong emphasis on information and the recent advances in information technology, you might expect most organizations to have highly developed systems for delivering information to managers and other users. Yet this is seldom the case. In fact, despite having mountains of data, and often many databases, few organizations have more than a fraction of the information they need. Managers are often frustrated by their inability to access or use the data and information they need.

Modern organizations are said to be drowning in data but starving for information. Despite the mixed metaphor, this statement seems to portray quite accurately the situation in many organizations. What is the reason for this state of affairs? Let's examine two important (and related) reasons why an information gap has been created in most organizations.

The first reason for the information gap is the fragmented way in which organizations have developed information systems—and their supporting databases—for many years. The emphasis in this text is on a carefully planned, architectural approach to systems development that should produce an integrated set of databases. However, in reality constraints on time and resources cause most organizations to resort to a "one-thing-at-a-time" approach to developing islands of information systems. This approach inevitably produces a hodgepodge of uncoordinated and often inconsistent databases. Usually databases are based on a variety of hardware and software platforms. In this environment it is extremely difficult if not impossible for managers to locate and use accurate information, which must be synthesized across these various systems of record.

The second reason for the information gap is that most systems are developed to support operational processing, with little or no thought given to the information or analytical tools needed for decision making. *Operational processing*, also called transaction processing, captures, stores, and manipulates data to support daily operations of the organization. *Informational processing* is the analysis of data or other forms of information to support decision making. The processing that is performed and the types of data required are very different for these two types of processing, as explained in the following section. Most systems that are developed internally or purchased from outside vendors are designed to support operational processing, with little thought given to informational processing.

Bridging the information gap are *data warehouses* that consolidate and integrate information from many internal and external sources and arrange it in a meaningful format for making accurate business decisions (Martin, 1997a). They support executives, managers, and business analysts in making complex business decisions through applications such as the analysis of trends, target marketing, competitive analysis, customer relationship management, and so on. Data warehousing has evolved to meet these needs without disturbing existing operational processing.

This chapter provides an overview of data warehousing. This exceptionally broad topic normally requires an entire text. In fact, most texts on the topic are devoted to just a single aspect, such as data warehouse design or administration. We focus on the two areas relevant to a text on database management: data architecture and database design. You will learn first how the data warehouse relates to existing operational systems. Described next is the three-tier data architecture, which is most appropriate for most data warehouse environments. Then we address the problem of extracting data from existing operational systems and loading them into a data warehouse. Next we show special database design elements frequently used in data warehousing. Finally, you will see how users interact with the data warehouse including on-line analytical processing, data mining, and data visualization.

BASIC CONCEPTS OF DATA WAREHOUSING

Data warehouse: A subject-oriented, integrated, time-variant, nonupdatable collection of data used in support of management decision-making processes.

A **data warehouse** is a subject-oriented, integrated, time-variant, nonupdatable collection of data used in support of management decision-making processes and business intelligence (Inmon and Hackathorn, 1994). The meaning of each of the key terms in this definition follows:

1. *Subject-oriented*   A data warehouse is organized around the key subjects (or high-level entities) of the enterprise. Major subjects may include customers, patients, students, products, and time.

2. *Integrated*   The data housed in the data warehouse are defined using consistent naming conventions, formats, encoding structures, and related characteristics gathered from several internal systems of record and also often from sources external to the organization.

3. *Time-variant*   Data in the data warehouse contain a time dimension so that they may be used to study trends and changes.

4. *Nonupdatable*   Data in the data warehouse are loaded and refreshed from operational systems, but cannot be updated by end users.

A data warehouse is not just a consolidation of all the operational databases in an organization. Because of its focus on business intelligence, external data, and time-variant data (not just current status), a data warehouse is a unique kind of database.

Data warehousing is the process whereby organizations extract meaning and inform decision making from their informational assets through the use of data warehouses (Barquin, 1996). Data warehousing is a recent initiative in information technology. Since it began about 15 years ago, it has evolved so rapidly that data warehousing is now one of the hottest topics in information systems. Studies repeatedly show that over 90 percent of larger companies either have a data warehouse or are starting one. A 1996 study of 62 data warehousing projects showed an average return on investment of 321 percent, with an average payback period of 2.73 years.

A Brief History

Data warehousing emerged as a result of advances in the field of information systems over several decades. Some key advances were the following:

- Improvements in database technology, particularly the development of the relational data model and relational database management systems (RDBMS)

- Advances in computer hardware, particularly the emergence of affordable mass storage and parallel computer architectures

- The emergence of end-user computing, facilitated by powerful, intuitive computer interfaces and tools

- Advances in middleware products that enable enterprise database connectivity across heterogeneous platforms (Hackathorn, 1993)

The key discovery that triggered the development of data warehousing was the recognition (and subsequent definition) of the fundamental differences between operational (or transaction processing) systems (sometimes called systems of record because their role is to keep the official, legal record of the organization) and informational (or decision support) systems. In 1988 Devlin and Murphy published the first article describing the architecture of a data warehouse, based on this distinction. In 1992 Inmon published the first book describing data warehousing and has subsequently become one of the most prolific authors in this field.

The Need for Data Warehousing

Two major factors drive the need for data warehousing in most organizations today:

1. A business requires an integrated, company-wide view of high-quality information.

2. The information systems department must separate informational from operational systems in order to dramatically improve performance in managing company data.

Need for a Company-Wide View Data in operational systems are typically fragmented and inconsistent. They are also generally distributed on a variety of incompatible hardware and software platforms. For example, one file containing customer data may be located on a Unix-based server running an Oracle DBMS, while another is located on an IBM mainframe running the DB2 DBMS. Yet for decision-making purposes it is often necessary to provide a single, corporate view of that information.

To better understand the difficulty of deriving a single corporate view, look at the simple example shown in Figure 11-1. This figure shows three tables from three separate systems of record, each containing some student data. There is a STUDENT_DATA table from the class registration system, a STUDENT_EMPLOYEE table from the personnel system, and a STUDENT_HEALTH table from a health center system. Each table contains some unique data concerning students, but even common data (such as student names) are stored using different formats.

Suppose you want to develop a profile for each student, consolidating all data in a single file format. Some of the issues that you must resolve are as follows:

- *Inconsistent key structures* The primary key of the first two tables is some version of the student social security number, while the primary key of STUDENT_HEALTH is Student_Name.

- *Synonyms* In STUDENT_DATA the primary key is named Student_No, while in STUDENT_EMPLOYEE it is named Student_ID (we discussed how to deal with synonyms in Chapter 5).

Figure 11-1
Examples of heterogeneous data

STUDENT_DATA

Student_No	Last_Name	MI	First_Name	Telephone	Status	•••
123-45-6789	Enright	T	Mark	483-1967	Soph	
389-21-4062	Smith	R	Elaine	283-4195	Jr	

STUDENT_EMPLOYEE

Student_ID	Address	Dept	Hours	•••
123-45-6789	1218 Elk Drive, Phoenix, AZ 91304	Soc	8	
389-21-4062	134 Mesa Road, Tempe, AZ 90142	Math	10	

STUDENT_HEALTH

Name	Telephone	Insurance	ID	•••
Mark T. Enright	483-1967	Blue Cross	123-45-6789	
Elaine R. Smith	555-7828	?	389-21-4062	

- *Free-form fields versus structured fields*   In STUDENT_HEALTH, Student_Name is a single field. In STUDENT_DATA, Student_Name (a composite attribute) is broken into its component parts: Last_Name, MI, and First_Name.

- *Inconsistent data values*   Elaine Smith has one telephone number in STUDENT_DATA, but a different number in STUDENT_HEALTH. Is this an error, or does this person have two telephone numbers?

- *Missing data*   The value for Insurance is missing (or null) for Elaine Smith in the STUDENT_HEALTH table. How will this value be located?

This simple example illustrates the nature of the problem of developing a single corporate view but fails to capture the complexity of that task. A real-life scenario would likely have dozens (if not hundreds) of files, and thousands (or millions!) of records. We will return to the issue of complexity and size later in this chapter.

Why do organizations need to bring data together from various systems of record? Ultimately, of course, the reason is to be more profitable, to be more competitive, or to grow by adding value for customers. This can be accomplished by increasing the speed and flexibility of decision making, improving business processes, or gaining a clearer understanding of customer behavior. For the previous student example, university administrators may want to investigate if the health or number of hours students work on campus are related their academic performance, if taking certain courses is related to the health of students, or whether poor academic performers cost more to support, for example, due to increased health care as well as other costs. In general, certain trends in organizations encourage the need for data warehousing; these trends include the following:

- *No single system of record*   Almost no organization has one database. Seems odd, doesn't it? Remember our discussion in Chapter 1 about the reasons for a database compared to separate file-processing systems? Because of the heterogeneous needs for data in different operational settings, because of corporate mergers and acquisitions, and due to the sheer size of many organizations, multiple operational databases exist.

- *Multiple systems are not synchronized*   It is difficult, if not impossible, to make separate databases consistent. Even if the metadata are controlled and made the same by one data administrator (see Chapter 13), the data values for the same attributes will not agree. This is because of different update cycles and separate places where the same data are captured for each system. Thus, to get one view of the organization, the data from the separate systems must be periodically consolidated and synchronized into one additional database. We will see that there can be actually two such consolidated databases—one called an operational data store and the other called an enterprise data warehouse, both of which we include under the topic of data warehousing.

- *Organizations want to analyze the activities in a balanced way*   Many organizations have implemented some form of a balanced scorecard—metrics that show organization results in financial, human, customer satisfaction, product quality, and other terms simultaneously. To ensure that this multidimensional view of the organization shows consistent results, a data warehouse is necessary. When questions arise in the balanced scorecard, analytical software working with the data warehouse can be used to "drill down," "slice and dice," visualize, and in other ways mine business intelligence.

- *Customer relationship management*   Organizations in all sectors are realizing that there is value in having a total picture of their interactions with customers across all touch points. Different touch points (e.g., for a bank, these touch points include ATM, teller, electronic funds transfers, investment portfolio management, and loans) are supported by separate operational systems. Thus, without a data warehouse, a teller may not know to try to cross-sell a customer one of the bank's mutual funds if a large, atypical automatic deposit transaction appears on the teller's screen. Or, an information technology company may want to prioritize in-bound calls to a help desk based on customer profitability, and sales staff may want to establish customer contact plans based on customer profitability. A total picture of the activity with a given customer requires a consolidation of data from various operational systems.

- *Supplier relationship management* Managing the supply chain has also become a critical element in reducing costs and raising product quality for many organizations. Organizations want to create strategic supplier partnerships based on a total picture of their activities with suppliers, from billing, to meeting delivery dates, to quality control, to pricing, to support. Data about these different activities can be locked inside separate operational systems (e.g., accounts payable, shipping and receiving, production scheduling, and maintenance). Enterprise resource planning systems have improved this situation by bringing many of these data into one database. However, ERP systems tend to be designed to optimize operational, not informational or analytical processing, which we discuss next.

Operational system: A system that is used to run a business in real time, based on current data. Also called system of record.

Need to Separate Operational and Informational Systems An **operational system** is a system that is used to run a business in real time, based on current data. Examples of operational systems are sales order processing, reservation systems, and patient registration. Operational systems must process large volumes of relatively simple read/write transactions, while providing fast response. Operational systems are also called systems of record.

Informational systems: Systems designed to support decision making based on historical point-in-time and prediction data for complex queries or data-mining applications.

Informational systems are designed to support decision making based on historical point-in-time and prediction data. They are also designed for complex queries or data-mining applications. Examples of informational systems are sales trend analysis, customer segmentation, and human resources planning.

The key differences between operational and informational systems are shown in Table 11-1. These two types of processing have very different characteristics in nearly every category of comparison. In particular, notice that they have quite different communities of users. Operational systems are used by clerks, administrators, salespersons, and others who must process business transactions. Informational systems are used by managers, executives, business analysts, and (increasingly) by customers who are searching for status information or who are decision makers.

The reason to separate operational and informational systems are based on three primary factors:

1. A data warehouse centralizes data that are scattered throughout disparate operational systems and makes them readily available for decision support applications.

Table 11-1 Comparison of Operational and Informational Systems

Characteristic	Operational Systems	Informational Systems
Primary purpose	Run the business on a current basis	Support managerial decision making
Type of data	Current representation of state of the business	Historical point-in-time (snapshots) and predictions
Primary users	Clerks, salespersons, administrators	Managers, business analysts, customers
Scope of usage	Narrow, planned, and simple updates and queries	Broad, ad hoc, complex queries and analysis
Design goal	Performance throughput, availability	Ease of flexible access and use
Volume	Many, constant updates and queries on one or a few table rows	Periodic batch updates and queries requiring many or all rows

2. A properly designed data warehouse adds value to data by improving their quality and consistency.

3. A separate data warehouse eliminates much of the contention for resources that results when informational applications are confounded with operational processing.

DATA WAREHOUSE ARCHITECTURES

The basic architectures used most often with data warehouses are first, a generic two-level physical architecture for entry-level data warehouses; second, an expanded three-level architecture that is increasingly used in more complex environments; and finally, the three-level data architecture that is associated with a three-level physical architecture.

Generic Two-Level Architecture

A generic architecture for a data warehouse is shown in Figure 11-2. Building this architecture requires four basic steps:

1. Data are extracted from the various internal and external source system files and databases. In a large organization there may be dozens or even hundreds of such files and databases.

2. The data from the various source systems are transformed and integrated before being loaded into the data warehouse. Transactions may be sent to the source systems to correct errors discovered in data staging.

3. The data warehouse is a database organized for decision support. It contains both detailed and summary data.

4. Users access the data warehouse by means of a variety of query languages and analytical tools. Results (e.g., predictions, forecasts) may be fed back to data warehouse and operational databases.

Figure 11-2
Generic two-level data warehousing architecture

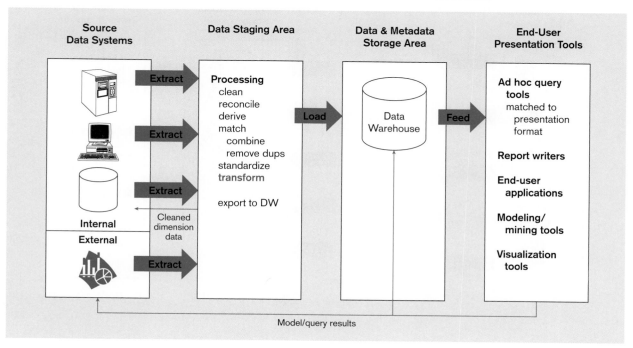

We will discuss in more detail in subsequent sections the important processes of extracting, transforming, and loading (ETL) data from the source systems into the data warehouse. We also overview in a subsequent section various end-user presentation tools.

Extraction and loading happens on a periodic basis, sometimes daily, weekly, or monthly. Thus, the data warehouse often does not have, nor does it need to have, current data. Remember, the data warehouse is not supporting operational transaction processing, although it may contain transactional data (but more often summaries of transactions and snapshots of status variables such as account balances and inventory levels). For most data warehousing applications, users are not looking for a reaction to an individual transaction, rather to trends and patterns in the state of the organization across a large subset of the data warehouse. At a minimum, five fiscal quarters of data are kept in a data warehouse so that at least annual trends and patterns can be discerned. Older data may be purged or archived. We will see later that one advanced data warehousing architecture, @ctive data warehousing, is based on a different assumption about the need for current data.

Independent Data Mart Data Warehousing Environment

Data mart: A data warehouse that is limited in scope, whose data are obtained by selecting and summarizing data from a data warehouse or from separate extract, transform, and load processes from source data systems.

Independent data mart: A data mart filled with data extracted from the operational environment, without benefit of a data warehouse.

Contrary to many of the principles discussed so far in this chapter, some organizations do not create one data warehouse. Instead, they create many separate data marts, each based on data warehousing, not transactional processing, database technologies. A **data mart** is a data warehouse that is limited in scope. Its contents are obtained either from independent ETL processes, as shown in Figure 11-3 for an **independent data mart**, or are derived from the data warehouse, which we will discuss in the next two sections. A data mart is customized for the decision-making applications of a particular end-user group. Thus, a data mart is designed to optimize the performance for well-defined and predicable uses, sometimes as few as a single or a couple of queries. For example, an organization may have a marketing data

Figure 11-3
Independent data mart data warehousing architecture

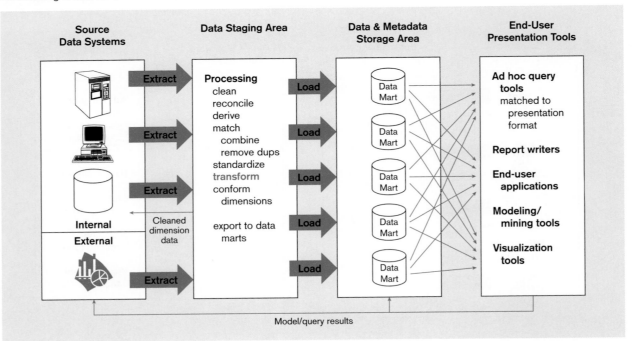

mart, a finance data mart, a supply chain data mart, and so on, to support known analytical processing.

We will provide a comparison of the various data warehousing architectures later, but you can see one obvious characteristic of the independent data mart strategy—the complexity for end users when they need to access data in separate data marts (evidenced by the criss-crossed lines connecting all the data marts to the end-user presentation tools). This complexity comes not only from having to access data from separate data mart databases, but also from possibly a new generation of inconsistent data systems—the data marts. If there is one set of metadata across all the data marts and if data are made consistent across the data marts through the activities in the data staging area (for example, by what is called "conform dimensions" in the data staging area box in Figure 11-3), then the complexity for users is reduced. Not so obvious in Figure 11-3 is the complexity for the ETL processes, because separate transformation and loads need to be built for each independent data mart.

The reason why organizations adopt this architecture is expediency. It can be organizationally and politically easier to have separate, small data warehouses than to get all organizational parties to agree to one view of the organization in a central data warehouse. Also, some data warehousing technologies have technical limitations for the size of the data warehouse they can support—what we will call later a scalability issue. Thus, technology, rather than the business, may dictate a data warehousing architecture if you first lock yourself into a particular data warehousing set of technologies before you understand your data warehousing requirements. We discuss the pros and cons of the independent data mart architecture compared to its prime competing architecture in the next section.

Dependent Data Mart and Operational Data Store Architecture

The independent data mart architecture in Figure 11-3 has several important limitations (Meyer, 1997), including:

1. A separate ETL processes is developed for each data mart, which can yield costly redundant data and efforts.

2. Data marts may not be consistent with one another, thus not providing a clear enterprise-wide view of data concerning important subjects such as customers, suppliers, and products.

3. There is no capability to drill down into greater detail or into related facts in other data marts or a shared data repository, so analysis is limited, or at best very difficult (e.g., doing joins across separate platforms for different data marts).

The value of independent data marts has been hotly debated. Kimball (1997) strongly supports the development of independent data marts as a viable strategy for a phased development of decision support systems. Armstrong (1997) and Inmon (1997 and 2000) point out these fallacies and many more. There actually are two debates around independent data marts:

1. One debate deals with the nature of the phased approach to implementing a data warehousing environment. The essence of this debate is whether each data mart should or should not evolve as a subset of an enterprise-wide definition of decision support data.

2. The other debate deals with a suitable database architecture for analytical processing. This debate centers on the extent to which a data mart database should be normalized.

The essences of these two debates are addressed throughout this chapter. We provide an exercise at the end of the chapter for you to explore these debates in more depth.

Dependent data mart: A data mart filled exclusively from the enterprise data warehouse and its reconciled data.

Enterprise data warehouse (EDW): A centralized, integrated data warehouse that is the control point and single source of all data made available to end users for decision support applications.

Operational data store (ODS): An integrated, subject-oriented, updatable, current-valued, detailed database designed to serve operational users as they do decision support processing.

One of the most popular approaches to address the independent data mart limitations raised earlier is to use the dependent data mart and operational data store architecture (see Figure 11-4). The first and second limitations are addressed by loading the **dependent data marts** from an **enterprise data warehouse (EDW)**, which is a central, integrated data warehouse that is the control point and single "version of the truth" made available to end users for decision support applications. Dependent data marts still have a purpose to provide a simplified and high-performance environment tuned to the decision-making needs of user groups. A user group can access its data mart, and then when other data are needed, users can access the EDW. Redundancy across dependent data marts is planned and redundant data are consistent because each data mart is loaded in a synchronized way from one common source of data. Integration of data is the responsibility of the IT staff managing the enterprise data warehouse, not end users who have to integrate data across independent data marts for each query or application. The dependent data mart and operational data store architecture is often called a "hub and spoke" approach, in which the EDW is the hub and the source data systems and the data marts are at the ends of input and output spokes.

The third limitation is addressed by providing an integrated source of all the operational data in an operational data store. An **operational data store (ODS)** is an integrated, subject-oriented, updatable, current-valued, detailed database designed to serve operational users as they do decision support processing (Imhoff, 1998; Inmon, 1998). An ODS is typically a relational database and normalized like databases in the systems of record, but it is tuned for decision-making applications. For example, indexes and other relational database design elements are tuned for queries that retrieve broad groups of data, rather than for transaction processing or querying individual and directly related records (e.g., a customer order). An ODS has a current picture of all activities, enterprise-wide. Because it has volatile, current data, the same query against an ODS very likely will yield different results at different times. An ODS typically does not contain history, whereas a EDW holds a history of snapshots of the state of the organization. An ODS may be fed from the database of an enterprise resource planning application, but because most organizations do not

Figure 11-4
Dependent data mart and operational data store architecture

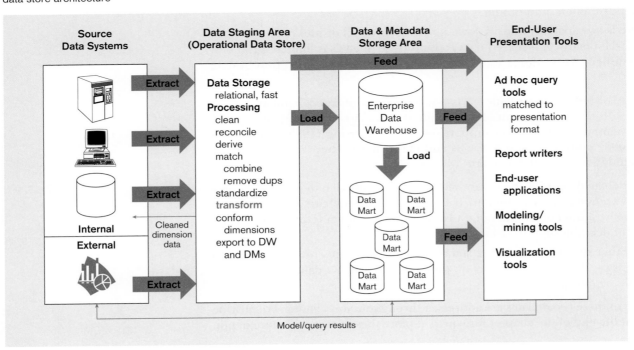

have only one enterprise resource planning (ERP) database and do not run all operations against one ERP, an ODS is usually different from an ERP database. Also, an
ODS is not designed for high-volume transaction processing, but rather for decision
support. The ODS also serves the role of the staging area for loading data into the
EDW. The ODS may receive data immediately or with some delay from the systems of
record, whichever is practical and acceptable for the decision-making requirements
that it supports.

The dependent data mart and operational data store architecture is also called a
corporate information factory (CIF) (see Imhoff, 1999). It is considered a comprehensive view of organizational data in support of all user data requirements.

There are definitely different approaches to data warehousing endorsed by different leaders of the field. Those that endorse the independent data mart approach
argue that this approach has two significant benefits:

1. It allows for the concept of a data warehouse to be proved by working on a
   series of small projects.

2. The length of time until there is some benefit from data warehousing is
   reduced because the organization is not delayed until all data is centralized.

The advocates of the corporate information factory view raise serious issues with
the independent approach; these issues include (Inmon, 1999; Armstrong, 2000) the
following:

1. Redundancy across data marts

2. The need for the users themselves to provide the integrated perspective of
   the organization across data marts

3. The extra work of many ETL processes

4. The likely use of data warehouse technologies for each data mart that does
   not scale up to an EDW because of technical limitations or because different
   technologies are used for different marts

5. The high cost to keep the data marts synchronized

Armstrong (2000) and others go further to argue that the benefits claimed by the
independent data mart advocates really are benefits of taking a phased approach to
data warehouse development. A phased approach can be accomplished within the
CIF framework as well, and is facilitated by the final data warehousing architecture
we review in the next section.

Logical Data Mart and @ctive Warehouse Architecture

The logical data mart and @ctive warehouse architecture is practical for only
moderate-sized data warehouses or when using high-performance data warehousing
technology, such as the NCR Teradata system. As can be seen in Figure 11-5, this
architecture has the following unique characteristics:

1. **Logical data marts** are not physically separate databases, but rather different
   relational views of one physical, slightly denormalized relational data warehouse (refer to Chapter 7 to review the concept of views).

2. Data are moved into the data warehouse rather than a separate staging area
   to utilize the high-performance computing power of the warehouse technology to perform the cleansing and transformation steps.

3. New data marts can be created quickly because no physical database or database
   technology needs to be created or acquired and no loading routines written.

4. Data marts are always up-to-date since data in a view is created when the view
   is referenced; views can be materialized if a user has a series of queries and
   analysis that need to work off the same instantiation of the data mart.

Logical data mart: A data mart created by a relational view of a data
warehouse.

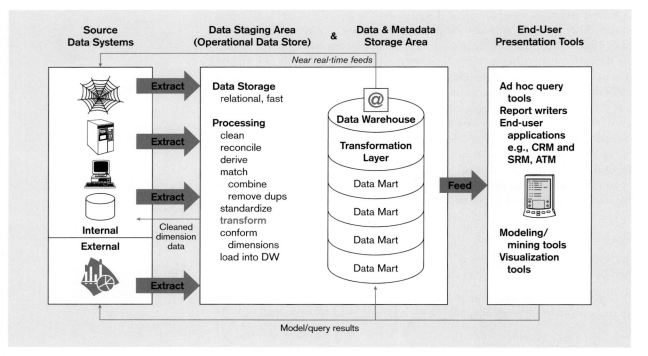

Figure 11-5
Logical data mart and @ctive warehouse architecture

Whether logical or physical, data marts and data warehouses play different roles in a data warehousing environment; these different roles are summarized in Table 11-2. Although limited in scope, a data mart may not be small. Thus, scalable technology is often critical. Although less complex to build because of its limited scope, you still face challenging issues for the ETL processes for data marts. Also, a significant burden and cost is placed on users when they themselves need to integrate the data across separate physical data marts (if this is even possible). As data marts are added, a data warehouse can be built in phases; the easiest way for this to happen is to follow the logical data mart and @ctive warehouse architecture.

Table 11-2 Data Warehouse Versus Data Mart

Data Warehouse	Data Mart
Scope	*Scope*
• Application independent	• Specific DSS application
• Centralized, possibly enterprise-wide	• Decentralized by user area
• Planned	• Organic, possibly not planned
Data	*Data*
• Historical, detailed, and summarized	• Some history, detailed, and summarized
• Lightly denormalized	• Highly denormalized
Subjects	*Subjects*
• Multiple subjects	• One central subject of concern to users
Sources	*Sources*
• Many internal and external sources	• Few internal and external sources
Other Characteristics	*Other Characteristics*
• Flexible	• Restrictive
• Data-oriented	• Project-oriented
• Long life	• Short life
• Large	• Start small, becomes large
• Single complex structure	• Multi, semi-complex structures, together complex

Adapted from Strange (1997)

The **@ctive data warehouse** aspect of the architecture in Figure 11-5 means that the source data systems and the data warehouse exchange data at a near-real-time pace because there is a need for rapid response to a current, comprehensive picture of the organization. For example, a help desk professional answering questions and logging problem tickets will have a total picture of the customer's most recent sales contacts, billing and payment transactions, maintenance activities, and orders. With this information, the system supporting the help desk can automatically generate a script for the professional to sell a maintenance contract, an upgraded product, or another product bought by customers with a similar profile. A critical event, such as entry of a new product order, can be considered immediately so that the organization knows at least as much about the relationship with its customer as does the customer. The orientation is that each event, with say a customer, is a potential opportunity for a customized and personalized communication based on a strategic decision of how to respond to a customer with a particular profile. Some beneficial applications for @ctive data warehousing include

- Just-in-time transportation for rerouting deliveries based on up-to-date inventory levels
- E-commerce where, for instance, an abandoned shopping cart can trigger an e-mail promotional message before the user signs off
- Fraud detection in credit card transactions, where an unusual pattern of transactions could alert a sales clerk or on-line shopping cart routine to take extra precautions

Such applications are often characterized by on-line, 7 days × 24 hours × 365 days user access. For any of the data warehousing architectures, users may be employees, customers, or business partners.

With high-performance computers and data warehousing technologies, there may not be a need for a separate ODS from the enterprise data warehouse. When the ODS and EDW are one and the same, then it is much easier for users to drill-down and drill-up when working through a series of ad hoc questions in which one question leads to another. It is also a simpler architecture, because one layer of the dependent data mart and operational data store architecture has been eliminated.

Three-Layer Data Architecture

Figure 11-6 shows a three-layer data architecture for a data warehouse:

1. Operational data are stored in the various operational systems of record throughout the organization (and sometimes in external systems).

2. Reconciled data are the type of data stored in the enterprise data warehouse and an operational data store.

3. Derived data are the type of data stored in each of the data marts.

Reconciled data are detailed, current data intended to be the single, authoritative source for all decision support applications. **Derived data** are data that have been selected, formatted, and aggregated for end-user decision support applications.

We discuss reconciled data and derived data in the next two sections. Two components shown in Figure 11-6 play critical roles in the data architecture; they are the enterprise data model and metadata.

Role of the Enterprise Data Model In Figure 11-6 we show the reconciled data layer linked to the enterprise data model. Recall from Chapter 2 that the enterprise data model presents a total picture explaining the data required by an organization. If the reconciled data layer is to be the single, authoritative source for all data required for decision support, it must conform to the design specified in the enterprise data model. Thus the enterprise data model controls the phased evolution of

@ctive data warehouse: An enterprise data warehouse that accepts near-real-time feeds of transactional data from the systems of record, immediately transforms and loads the appropriate data into the warehouse, and provides near-real-time access for the transaction processing systems to an enterprise data warehouse.

Reconciled data: Detailed, current data intended to be the single, authoritative source for all decision support applications.

Derived data: Data that have been selected, formatted, and aggregated for end-user decision support applications.

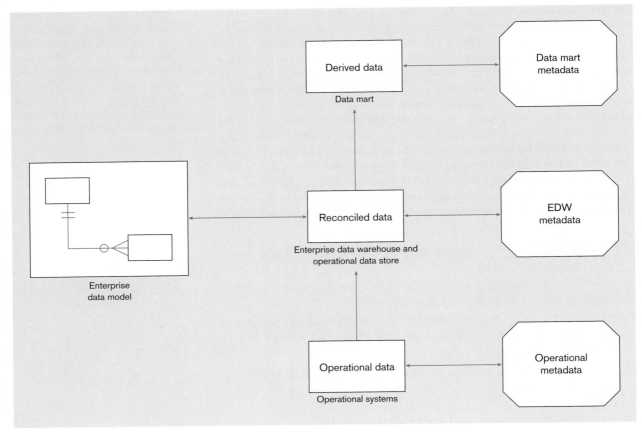

Figure 11-6
Three-layer data architecture

the data warehouse. Usually the enterprise data model evolves as new problems and decision applications are addressed. It takes too long to develop the enterprise data model in one step, and the dynamic needs for decision making will change before the warehouse is built.

Role of Metadata Figure 11-6 also shows a layer of metadata linked to each of the three data layers. Recall from Chapter 1 that metadata are data that describe the properties or characteristics of other data. Following is a brief description of the three types of metadata shown in Figure 11-6.

1. *Operational metadata* describe the data in the various operational systems (as well as external data) that feed the enterprise data warehouse. Operational metadata typically exist in a number of different formats and unfortunately are often of poor quality.

2. *Enterprise data warehouse (EDW) metadata* are derived from (or at least consistent with) the enterprise data model. EDW metadata describe the reconciled data layer as well as the rules for transforming operational data to reconciled data.

3. *Data mart metadata* describe the derived data layer and the rules for transforming reconciled data to derived data.

SOME CHARACTERISTICS OF DATA WAREHOUSE DATA

In order to better understand the data in each of these layers, you need to learn some basic characteristics of data as they are stored in data warehouse databases.

Status Versus Event Data

The difference between status data and event data is shown in Figure 11-7. The figure shows a typical log entry recorded by a database management system when processing a business transaction for a banking application. This log entry contains both status and event data: The "before image" and "after image" represent the *status* of the bank account before and then after a withdrawal. Data representing the withdrawal (or update event) are shown in the middle of the figure.

Transactions, which are discussed further in Chapter 12, are business activities that cause one or more business events to occur at a database level (Devlin, 1997). An **event** is a database action (create, update, or delete) that results from a transaction. Notice that a transaction may lead to one or more events. The withdrawal transaction in Figure 11-7 leads to a single event, which is the reduction in the account balance from 750 to 700. On the other hand, the transfer of money from one account to another would lead to two events: a withdrawal event and a deposit event. Sometimes nontransactions, such as an abandoned on-line shopping cart, busy signal or dropped network connection, or an item put in a shopping cart and then taken out before checkout, can also be important events.

Both status data and event data can be stored in a database. However, in practice most of the data stored in databases (including data warehouses) are status data. A data warehouse likely contains a history of snapshots of status data or a summary (say, an hourly total) of transaction or event data. Event data, which represent transactions, may be stored for a defined period but are then deleted or archived to save storage space. Both status and event data are typically stored in database logs (such as represented in Figure 11-7) for backup and recovery purposes. As will be explained below, the database log plays an important role in filling the data warehouse.

Transient Versus Periodic Data

In data warehouses it is often necessary to maintain a record of when events occurred in the past. This is necessary, for example, to compare sales or inventory levels on a particular date or during a particular period with the previous year's sales on the same date or during the same period.

Event: A database action (create, update, or delete) that results from a transaction.

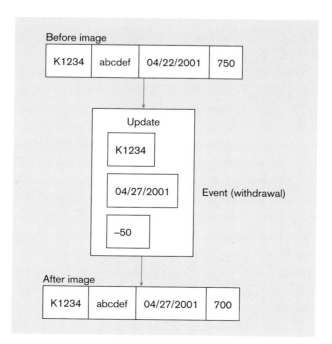

Figure 11-7
Example of DBMS log entry

Transient data: Data in which changes to existing records are written over previous records, thus destroying the previous data content.

Most operational systems are based on the use of transient data. **Transient data** are data in which changes to existing records are written over previous records, thus destroying the previous data content. Records are deleted without preserving the previous contents of those records.

You can easily visualize transient data by again referring to Figure 11-7. If the after image is written over the before image, the before image (containing the previous balance) is lost. However, since this is a database log both images are normally preserved.

Periodic data: Data that are never physically altered or deleted, once they have been added to the store.

Periodic data are data that are never physically altered or deleted once added to the store. The before and after images in Figure 11-7 represent periodic data. Notice that each record contains a timestamp that indicates the date (and time, if needed) when the most recent update event occurred (we introduced the use of timestamps in Chapter 3).

An Example of Transient and Periodic Data

A more detailed example comparing transient and periodic data is shown in Figures 11-8 and 11-9.

Figure 11-8
Transient operational data

Table X (10/01)

Key	A	B
001	a	b
002	c	d
003	e	f
004	g	h

Table X (10/02)

Key	A	B
001	a	b
002	r	d
003	e	f
004	y	h
005	m	n

Table X (10/03)

Key	A	B
001	a	b
002	r	d
C03	e	t
005	m	n

Transient Data   Figure 11-8 shows a relation (Table X) that initially contains four records. The table has three attributes: a primary key and two nonkey attributes *A* and *B*. The values for each of these attributes on the date 10/01 are shown in the figure. For example, for record 001 the value of attribute *A* on this date is *a*.

On date 10/02 three changes are made to the table (changes to rows are indicated by arrows to the left of the table). Record 002 is updated, so that the value of *A* is changed from *c* to *r*. Record 004 is also updated, so the value of *A* is changed from *g* to *y*. Finally, a new record (with key 005) is inserted into the table.

Figure 11-9
Periodic warehouse data

Table X (10/01)

Key	Date	A	B	Action
001	10/01	a	b	C
002	10/01	c	d	C
003	10/01	e	f	C
004	10/01	g	h	C

Table X (10/02)

Key	Date	A	B	Action
001	10/01	a	b	C
002	10/01	c	d	C
002	10/02	r	d	U
003	10/01	e	f	C
004	10/01	g	h	C
004	10/02	y	h	U
005	10/02	m	n	C

Table X (10/03)

Key	Date	A	B	Action
001	10/01	a	b	C
002	10/01	c	d	C
002	10/02	r	d	U
003	10/01	e	f	C
003	10/03	e	t	U
004	10/01	g	h	C
004	10/02	y	h	U
004	10/03	y	h	D
005	10/02	m	n	C

Notice that when records 002 and 004 are updated, the new records replace the previous records. Therefore the previous values are lost—there is no historical record of these values. This is characteristic of transient data.

More changes are made to the records on date 10/03 (to simplify the discussion, we assume that only one change can be made to a given record on a given date). Record 003 is updated, and record 004 is deleted. Notice that there is no record to indicate that record 004 was ever stored in the database. The way the data are processed in Figure 11-7 is characteristic of the transient data typical in operational systems.

Periodic Data One typical objective for a data warehouse is to maintain a historical record of key events or to create a time series for particular variables such as sales. This often requires storing periodic data, rather than transient data. Figure 11-9 shows the table used in 11-8, now modified to represent periodic data. The following changes have been made in Figure 11-9:

1. Two new columns have been added to Table X.
   a. The column named Date is a timestamp that records the most recent date when a row has been modified.
   b. The column named Action is used to record the type of change that occurred. Possible values for this attribute are C (Create), U (Update), and D (Delete).
2. Once a record has been stored in the table, that record is never changed. When a record is changed, both the before image and the after image are stored in the table. Although a record may be *logically* deleted, a historical version of the deleted record is maintained in the database for as much history (at least five quarters) as needed to analyze trends.

Now let's examine the same set of actions that occurred in Figure 11-8. Assume that all four records were created on the date 10/01, as shown in the first table.

In the second table (for 10/02), rows 002 and 004 have been updated. The table now contains both the old version (for 10/01) and the new version (for 10/02) for these rows. The table also contains the new row (005) that was created on 10/02.

The third table (for 10/03) shows the update to row 003, with both the old and new versions. Also, row 004 is deleted in this table. This table now contains *three* versions of row 004: the original version (from 10/01), the updated version (from 10/02), and the deleted version (from 10/03). The D in the last row for record 004 indicates that this record has been logically deleted, so that it is no longer available to users or their applications.

If you examine Figure 11-9 you can see why data warehouses tend to grow very rapidly. Storing periodic data can impose large storage requirements. A corollary is that users must choose very carefully the key data that require this form of processing.

THE RECONCILED DATA LAYER

As indicated in Figure 11-6, we use the term *reconciled data* to refer to the data layer associated with the operational data store and enterprise data warehouse. This is the term used by IBM in a 1993 paper describing data warehouse architectures. Although the term is not widely used, it accurately describes the nature of the data that should appear in the enterprise data warehouse and the way they are derived. More commonly, reconciled data are referred to as the result of the ETL process. An EDW or ODS usually is a normalized, relational database, because it needs the flexibility to support a wide variety of decision support needs.

Characteristics of Data after ETL

Extract, transform, and load is intended to provide a single, authoritative source for data that support decision making. Ideally, this data layer is detailed, historical, normalized, comprehensive, timely, and quality controlled.

1. *Detailed* The data are detailed (rather than summarized), providing maximum flexibility for various user communities to structure the data to best suit their needs.

2. *Historical* The data are periodic (or point-in-time) to provide a historical perspective.

3. *Normalized* The data are fully normalized (that is, third normal form or higher). (We discussed normalization in Chapter 5.) Normalized data provide greater integrity and flexibility of use than denormalized data. Denormalization is not necessary to improve performance, since reconciled data are usually accessed periodically using batch processes. We will see, however, that some popular data warehouse data structures are denormalized.

4. *Comprehensive* Reconciled data reflect an enterprise-wide perspective, whose design conforms to the enterprise data model.

5. *Timely* Except for @ctive warehousing, data need not be real-time, however, data must be current enough so that decision making can react in time.

6. *Quality controlled* Reconciled data must be of unquestioned quality and integrity, since they are summarized into the data marts and used for decision making.

Notice that these characteristics of reconciled data are quite different from the typical operational data from which they are derived. Operational data are typically detailed, but they differ strongly in the other four dimensions described above.

1. Operational data are transient, rather than historical.

2. They are not normalized. Depending on their roots, operational data may never have been normalized or may have been denormalized for performance reasons.

3. Rather than being comprehensive, operational data are generally restricted in scope to a particular application.

4. Operational data are often of poor quality, with numerous types of inconsistencies and errors.

The data reconciliation process is responsible for transforming operational data to reconciled data. Because of the sharp differences between these two types of data, clearly data reconciliation is the most difficult and technically challenging part of building a data warehouse. Fortunately several sophisticated software products are available to assist with this activity.

The ETL Process

Data reconciliation occurs in two stages during the process of filling the enterprise data warehouse.

1. An initial load, when the EDW is first created

2. Subsequent updates (normally performed on a periodic basis) to keep the EDW current and/or to expand it

Data reconciliation can be visualized as a process shown in Figure 11-10, consisting of four steps: capture, scrub, transform, and load and index. In reality, the steps may be combined in different ways. For example, data capture and scrub might be

Figure 11-10
Steps in data reconciliation

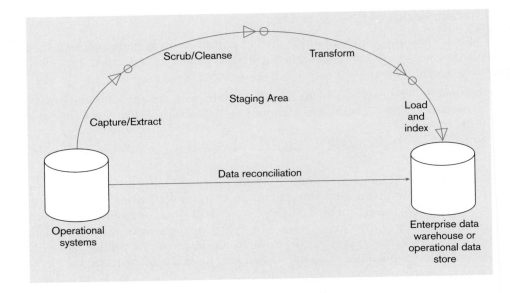

combined as a single process, or scrub and transform might be combined. We discuss capture, scrub, and load and index next, followed by a thorough discussion of transform.

Extract Capturing the relevant data from the source files and databases used to fill the EDW is typically called extracting. Usually, not all of the data contained in the various operational systems are required, but just a subset. Extracting the subset of data is based on an extensive analysis of both the source and target systems, which is best performed by a team directed by data administration and composed of both end users and data warehouse professionals.

The two generic types of data extracts are static extract and incremental extract. Static extract is used to fill the data warehouse initially, and incremental extract is used for ongoing warehouse maintenance.

Static extract is a method of capturing a snapshot of the required source data at a point in time. The view of the source data is independent of the time when it was created.

Incremental extract captures only the changes that have occurred in the source data since the last capture. The most common method is log capture. Recall that the database log contains after images that record the most recent changes to database records (see Figure 11-7). With log capture, only after images that are logged after the last capture are selected from the log.

English (1999) and White (2000) address in detail the careful steps necessary to qualify which systems of record and other data sources to use for extraction into the staging area. A major criteria is quality of the data in source systems. Quality depends on the following:

- Clarity of data naming, so the warehouse designers know exactly what data exist in a source system
- Completeness and accuracy of business rules enforced by a source system, which directly affects the accuracy of data; also, the business rules in the source should match the rules to be used in the data warehouse
- Format of data (common formats across sources help to match related data)

It is also important to have agreements with the owners of source systems so that they will inform the data warehouse administrators when changes are made in the metadata for the source system. Because transaction systems frequently change to meet

---

Static extract: A method of capturing a snapshot of the required source data at a point in time.

Incremental extract: A method of capturing only the changes that have occurred in the source data since the last capture.

new business needs and to utilize new and better software and hardware technologies, managing changes in the source systems is one of the biggest challenges of the extraction process. Changes in the source system require a reassessment of data quality and the procedures for extracting and transforming data. These procedures map data in the source systems to data in the target data warehouse (or data marts). A map says for each data element in the data warehouse which data from which source systems to use to derive that data; transformation rules, which we address in a separate section, then state how to perform the derivation. For custom-built source systems, a data warehouse administrator has to develop customized maps and extraction routines; predefined map templates can be purchased for some packaged application software, such as enterprise resource planning systems.

Extraction may be done by routines written with tools associated with the source system, say, a tool to export data. Data are usually extracted in a neutral data format, such as ANSI, comma delimited. Sometimes the SQL command SELECT . . . INTO can be used to create a table that can be brought into the staging area.

Once the data sources have been selected and extraction routines written, data can be moved into the staging area, where the cleansing process begins.

Cleanse Data in the qualified operational systems are often of poor quality. Some of the errors and inconsistencies typical of these data are as follows:

1. Misspelled names and addresses
2. Impossible or erroneous dates of birth
3. Fields used for purposes for which they were never intended
4. Mismatched addresses and area codes
5. Missing data
6. Duplicate data
7. Inconsistencies (e.g., different addresses) across sources

Let's consider some examples of such errors. Customer names are often used as primary keys or as search criteria in customer files. However, these names are often misspelled or spelled in various ways in these files. For example, the name "The Coca-Cola Company" is the correct name for the soft-drink company. This name may be entered in customer records as "Coca-Cola," "Coca Cola," "TCCC," and so on. In one study, a company found that the name "McDonald's" could be spelled 100 different ways!

Another type of data pollution occurs when a field is used for purposes not intended. For example, in one bank a record field was designed to hold a telephone number. However, branch managers who had no such use for this field instead stored the interest rate in it. Another example, reported by a major UK bank, was even more bizarre. The data-scrubbing program turned up a customer on their files whose occupation was listed as "steward on the Titanic"! (Devlin, 1997).

You may wonder why such errors are so common in operational data. The quality of operational data is largely determined by their value to the organization responsible for gathering them. Unfortunately, it often happens that the data-gathering organization places a low value on some data whose accuracy is important to downstream applications, such as data warehousing.

Given the common occurrence of errors, the worst thing a company can do is simply to copy operational data to the data warehouse. Instead, it is important to improve the quality of the source data through a technique called data scrubbing. **Data scrubbing** (also called data cleansing) is a technique using pattern recognition and other techniques to upgrade the quality of raw data before transforming them and moving the data to the data warehouse.

Successful data warehousing requires that a formal program in total quality management (TQM) be implemented. Total quality management focuses on defect prevention, rather than defect correction. Although data scrubbing can help

Data scrubbing: A technique using pattern recognition and other artificial intelligence techniques to upgrade the quality of raw data before transforming and moving the data to the data warehouse. Also called data cleansing.

upgrade data quality, it is not a long-term solution to the data quality problem. For a good discussion of TQM applied to data management, see English (1999).

The type of data cleansing required depends on the quality of data in the source system. Besides fixing the types of problems identified earlier, other common cleansing tasks include the following:

- Decoding data to make them understandable for data warehousing applications
- Reformatting and changing data types and performing other functions to put data from each source into the standard data warehouse format ready for transformation
- Adding time stamps to distinguish values for the same attribute over time
- Converting between different units of measure
- Generating primary keys for each row of a table (we discuss the formation of data warehouse table primary and foreign keys later in this chapter)
- Matching and merging separate extractions into one table or file and matching data to go into the same row of the generated table (this can be a very difficult process when different keys are used in different source systems, when naming conventions are different, and when the data in the source systems are erroneous)
- Logging errors detected, fixing those errors, and reprocessing corrected data without creating duplicate entries
- Finding missing data to complete the batch of data necessary for subsequent loading

The order in which different data sources are processed may matter. For example, it may be necessary to process customer data from a sales system before new customer demographic data from an external system can be matched to customers.

Once the data are cleansed in the staging area, data are ready for transformation. Before we discuss the transformation process in some detail, however, we briefly review in the next section the procedures used to load data into the data warehouse or data marts.

Load and Index The last step in filling the enterprise data warehouse is to load the selected data into the target data warehouse and to create the necessary indexes. The two basic modes for loading data to the target EDW are refresh and update.

Refresh mode: An approach to filling the data warehouse that employs bulk rewriting of the target data at periodic intervals.

Update mode: An approach in which only changes in the source data are written to the data warehouse.

Refresh mode is an approach to filling the data warehouse that employs bulk rewriting of the target data at periodic intervals. That is, the target data are written initially to fill the warehouse. Then at periodic intervals the warehouse is rewritten, replacing the previous contents. This mode has become less popular.

Update mode is an approach in which only changes in the source data are written to the data warehouse. To support the periodic nature of warehouse data, these new records are usually written to the data warehouse without overwriting or deleting previous records (see Figure 11-9).

As you would expect, refresh mode is generally used to fill the warehouse when it is first created. Update mode is then generally used for ongoing maintenance of the target warehouse. Refresh mode is used in conjunction with static data capture, while update mode is used in conjunction with incremental data capture.

With both the refresh and update modes, it is necessary to create and maintain the indexes that are used to manage the warehouse data. A type of indexing called *bit-mapped indexing* is often used in a data warehouse environment. Indexing was discussed in Chapter 6. We discuss indexing again later in this chapter when we address database design for data warehouses and marts.

Westerman (2001), based on the highly publicized and successful data warehousing at Wal-Mart Corporation, discusses factors in determining how frequently to update the data warehouse. His guideline is to update the data warehouse as frequently as is practical. Infrequent updating causes massive loads and users to wait for new data. Near-real-time loads are necessary for @ctive data warehousing, but may be inefficient and unnecessary for most data mining and analysis applications. Westerman suggests that daily updates are sufficient for most organizations. However, daily updates make it impossible to react to some changing conditions, such as repricing or changing purchase orders for slow-moving items. Wal-Mart updates the data warehouse continuously, which is practical given the massively parallel data warehouse technology they use.

Loading data into the warehouse typically means appending new rows to tables in the warehouse. It may also mean updating existing rows with new data (e.g., to fill in missing values from an additional data source), and it may mean purging identified data from the warehouse that have become obsolete due to age or that were incorrectly loaded in a prior load operation. Data may be loaded from the staging area into the warehouse by

- SQL commands (e.g., INSERT or UPDATE)
- special load utilities provided by the data warehouse or third-party vendor
- custom-written routines coded by the warehouse administrators

In any case, these routines must not only update the data warehouse but must also generate error reports to show rejected data (e.g., attempting to append a row with a duplicate key or updating a row that does not exist in a table of the data warehouse).

Load utilities may work in batch or continuous mode. With a utility, you write a script that defines the format of the data in the staging area and which staging area data map to which data warehouse fields. The utility may be able to convert data types for a field in the staging area to the target field in the warehouse, and may be able to perform IF...THEN...ELSE logic to handle staging area data in various formats or to direct input data to different data warehouse tables. The utility can purge all data in a warehouse table (DROP TABLE) before data loading (refresh mode) or can append new rows (update mode). The utility may be able to sort input data so that rows are appended before they are updated. The utility program runs as would any stored procedure for the DBMS, and ideally all the controls of the DBMS for concurrency control as well as restart and recovery in case of a DBMS failure during loading will work. Because the execution of a load can be very time-consuming, it is critical to be able to restart a load from a checkpoint in case the DBMS crashes in the middle of executing a load. See Chapter 12 for a thorough discussion of restart and recovery of databases.

DATA TRANSFORMATION

Data transformation (or transform) is at the very center of the data reconciliation process. **Data transformation** is the component of data reconciliation that converts data from the format of the source operational systems to the format of the enterprise data warehouse. Data transformation accepts data from the data capture component (after data scrubbing, if it applies), then maps the data to the format of the reconciled data layer, and then passes them to the load and index component.

Data transformation may range from a simple change in data format or representation to a highly complex exercise in data integration. Following are three examples that illustrate this range:

1. A salesperson requires a download of customer data from a mainframe database to her laptop computer. In this case the transformation required is simply mapping the data from EBCDIC to ASCII representation, which can easily be performed by off-the-shelf software.

Data transformation: The component of data reconciliation that converts data from the format of the source operational systems to the format of the enterprise data warehouse.

2. A manufacturing company has product data stored in three different legacy systems—a manufacturing system, a marketing system, and an engineering application. The company needs to develop a consolidated view of these product data. Data transformation involves several different functions, including resolving different key structures, converting to a common set of codes, and integrating data from different sources. These functions are quite straightforward, and most of the necessary software can be generated using a standard commercial software package with a graphical interface.

3. A large health care organization manages a geographically dispersed group of hospitals, clinics, and other care centers. Because many of the units have been acquired through acquisition over time, the data are heterogeneous and uncoordinated. For a number of important reasons, the organization needs to develop a data warehouse to provide a single corporate view of the enterprise. This effort will require the full range of transformation functions described below, including some custom software development.

The functions performed in data scrubbing and the functions performed in data transformation blend together. In general, the goal of data scrubbing is to correct errors in data *values* in the source data, whereas the goal of data transformation is to convert the data *format* from the source to the target system. Note that it is essential to scrub the data before they are transformed since, if there are errors in the data before they are transformed, the errors will remain in the data after transformation.

Data Transformation Functions

Data transformation encompasses a variety of different functions. These functions may be classified broadly into two categories: record-level functions and field-level functions. In most data warehousing applications, a combination of some or even all of these functions is required.

Record-Level Functions Operating on a set of records, such as a file or table, are the record-level functions most important: selection, joining, normalization, and aggregation.

Selection: The process of partitioning data according to predefined criteria.

Selection (also called *subsetting*) is the process of partitioning data according to predefined criteria. For data warehouse applications, selection is used to extract the relevant data from the source systems that will be used to fill the data warehouse. In fact, selection is typically a part of the capture function discussed earlier.

When the source data are relational, SQL SELECT statements can be used for selection (see Chapter 7 for a detailed discussion). For example, recall that incremental capture is often implemented by selecting after images from the database log that have been created since the previous capture. A typical after image was shown in Figure 11-7. Suppose that the after images for this application are stored in a table named ACCOUNT_HISTORY. Then the after images that have been created after 12/31/2001 can be selected with the following statements:

```
SELECT *
FROM ACCOUNT_HISTORY
WHERE Create_Date > 12/31/2001;
```

Joining: The process of combining data from various sources into a single table or view.

Joining combines data from various sources into a single table or view. Joining data is an important function in data warehouse applications, since it is often necessary to consolidate data from various sources. For example, an insurance company may have client data spread throughout several different files and databases. When the source data are relational, SQL statements can be used to perform a join operation (see Chapter 7 for details).

Joining is often complicated by factors such as the following:

1. Often the source data are not relational, in which case SQL statements cannot be used. Instead, procedural language statements must be coded.

2. Even for relational data, primary keys for the tables to be joined are often from different domains (e.g., engineering part number versus catalog number). These keys must then be reconciled before a SQL join can be performed.

3. Source data may contain errors, which makes join operations hazardous.

Normalization is the process of decomposing relations with anomalies to produce smaller, well-structured relations (see Chapter 5 for a detailed discussion). As indicated earlier, source data in operational systems are often denormalized (or simply not normalized). The data must therefore be normalized as part of data transformation.

Aggregation is the process of transforming data from a detailed level to a summary level. For example, in a retail business, individual sales transactions can be summarized to produce total sales by store, product, date, and so on. Since (in our model) the enterprise data warehouse contains only detailed data, aggregation is not normally associated with this component. However, aggregation is an important function in filling the data marts, as explained below.

Because selection, joining, and aggregation can often be done in SQL, some data warehouse experts argue that transformation should be done in an operational data store or even in the data warehouse.

Aggregation: The process of transforming data from a detailed to a summary level.

Field-Level Functions   A field-level function converts data from a given format in a source record to a different format in a target record. Field-level functions are of two types: single-field and multifield.

A *single-field* transformation converts data from a single source field to a single target field. Figure 11-11a is a basic representation of this type of transformation (designated by the letter "T" in the diagram). An example of a single-field transformation is converting a measurement from imperial to metric representation.

As shown in Figures 11-11b and c, there are two basic methods for performing a single-field transformation: algorithmic and table lookup. An algorithmic transformation is performed using a formula or logical expression. Figure 11-11b shows a conversion from Fahrenheit to Celsius temperature using a formula. When a simple algorithm does not apply, a lookup table can be used instead. Figure 11-11c shows the use of a table to convert state codes to state names (this type of conversion is common in data warehouse applications).

A *multifield* transformation converts data from one or more source fields to one or more target fields. This type of transformation is very common in data warehouse applications. Two multifield transformations are shown in Figure 11-12.

Figure 11-12a is an example of an many-to-one transformation (in this case, two source fields are mapped to one target field). In the source record, the combination of employee name and telephone number is used as the primary key. This combination is awkward and may not uniquely identify a person. Therefore in creating a target record, the combination is mapped to a unique employee identification (Emp_ID). A lookup table would be created to support this transformation. A data scrubbing program might be employed to help identify duplicates in the source data.

Figure 11-12b is an example of a one-to-many transformation (in this case, one source field has been converted to two target fields). In the source record, a product code has been used to encode the combination of brand name and product name (the use of such codes is common in operational data). However, in the target record it is desired to display the full text describing product and brand names. Again, a lookup table would be employed for this purpose.

More Complex Transformations   In Figure 11-12, the multifield transformations both involve only one source record and one target record. More generally, multifield transformations may involve more than one source record and/or more than

Figure 11-11
Single-field transformation
(a) Basic representation

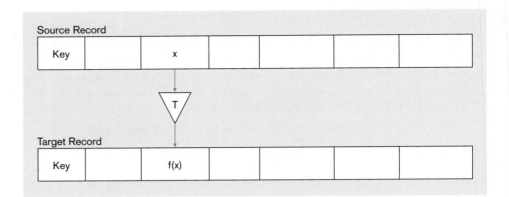

(b) Algorithmic transformation

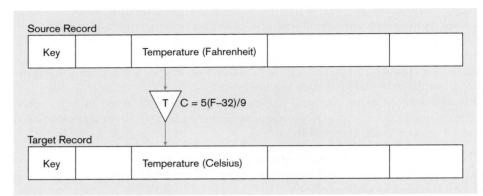

(c) Table look-up

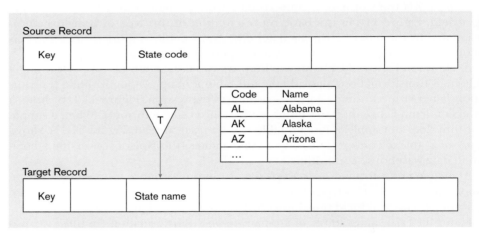

one target record. In the most complex cases, these records may even originate in different operational systems and in different time zones (Devlin, 1997).

Tools to Support Data Reconciliation

As you can readily see, data reconciliation is an extremely complex and challenging process. A variety of closely integrated software applications must be developed (or acquired) to support this process. Fortunately, a number of powerful software tools are available to assist organizations in developing these applications. In this section we describe three categories of such tools: data quality, data conversion, and data cleansing (for a more detailed discussion, see Williams, 1997). Table 11-3 summarizes the tools in each of these three categories.

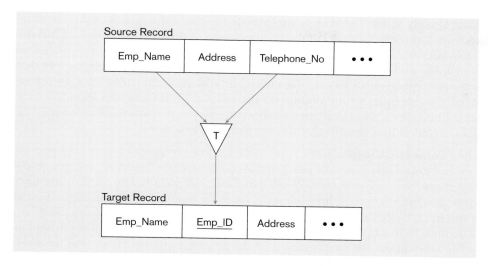

Figure 11-12
Multifield transformation
(a) A M:1 relationship

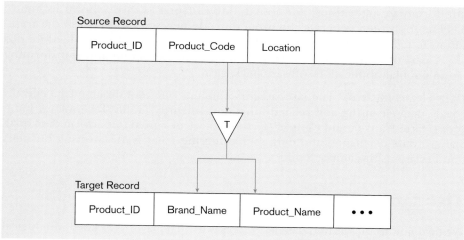

(b) A 1:M relationship

Table 11-3 Tools to Support Data Reconciliation

Product Name	Company	Description
WizRules	WizSoft, Inc. www.wizsoft.com	Rules discovery
Extract	Evolutionary Technologies International www.evtech.com	Extract, transform, load, and index
InfoRefiner	Computer Associates www.ca.com	Extract, transform, load, and index
DataBridge	Taurus Software, Inc. www.taurus.com	Extract, transform, load and index
Genio Suite	Hummingbird, Ltd. www.hummingbird.com	Extract, transform, enrich, load
Power Mart	Informatica www.informatica.com	Extract, transform, load, and index
Trillium	Harte-Hanks www.harte-hanks.com	Quality analysis and data cleansing
Centric	Firstlogic www.firstlogic.com	Quality analysis and data cleansing (see Information Quality Demo)
Integrity	Vality Technology, Inc. www.vality.com	Family of products for quality analysis, data scrubbing

Data Quality Tools These tools are intended to assess the quality of data in existing systems and compare them to the requirements of the data warehouse. Thus the tools are useful during an early stage of warehouse development. One such tool listed in Table 11-3 is WizRules (WizSoft, Inc.). WizRules is a rules discovery tool that searches through records in existing tables and discovers the rules associated with the data. For example, a rule might state the following: "If Customer_Name is Able or Baker, then City is San Diego; probability 0.95. This rule exists in 50 records." The product also identifies records that deviate from the established rules.

Data Conversion Tools The next set of tools shown in Table 11-3 are data conversion tools. These tools generally perform three mainstream functions: extract, transform, and load and index. Such tools listed in Table 11-3 include Extract (Evolutionary Technologies International), InfoRefiner (Computer Associates), DataBridge (Taurus Software, Inc.), Genio Suite (Hummingbird Ltd.), and Power Mart (Informatica).

The tools in this category are basically program-generation tools. They accept as input the schema (or file descriptions) of the source and target files, and the business rules that are to be used for data transformation. Typical business rules would include formulas, algorithms, and lookup tables (such as those shown in Figure 11-11). The tools then generate the program code necessary to perform the transformation functions on an ongoing basis. Some tools, such as Genio MetaLink for SAP R/3, part of Genio Suite, provide templates for extracting and transforming data from popular application software packages.

Data-Cleansing Tools The last category contains one tool designed specifically to provide data cleansing and related functions. Integrity (Vality Technology, Inc.), Trillium (Harte-Hanks), and Centric (Firstlogic) are designed to perform data quality analysis, data cleansing, and data reengineering (that is, discovering business rules and relationships among entities).

THE DERIVED DATA LAYER

We turn now to the derived data layer. This is the data layer associated with logical or physical data marts (see Figure 11-6). It is the layer with which users normally interact for their decision-support applications. Ideally, the reconciled data level is designed first and is the basis for the derived layer, whether data marts are dependent, independent, or virtual. In this section we first discuss the characteristics of the derived data layer and the way that it is derived from the reconciled data layer. We then introduce the star schema (or dimensional model), which is the data model most commonly used today to implement this data layer. A star schema is a specially designed denormalized relational data model. We emphasize that the derived data layer can use normalized relations; however, most organizations build many data marts, each optimized around one business object of interest to one user group (Moriarity, 1995).

Characteristics of Derived Data

Earlier we defined derived data as data that have been selected, formatted, and aggregated for end-user decision-support applications. As shown in Figure 11-6, the source of the derived data is the reconciled data described earlier. Derived data in a data mart are generally optimized for the needs of particular user groups such as departments, work groups, or even individuals. A common mode of operation is to select the relevant data from the enterprise data warehouse on a daily basis, format and aggregate those data as needed, then load and index those data in the target data marts.

The objectives that are sought with derived data are quite different from the objectives of reconciled data. Typical objectives are the following:

1. Provide ease of use for decision support applications.
2. Provide fast response for predefined user queries or requests for information.

3. Customize data for particular target user groups.

4. Support ad-hoc queries and data-mining applications.

To satisfy these needs, we usually find the following characteristics in derived data:

1. Both detailed data and aggregate data are present.

    a. Detailed data are often (but not always) periodic—that is, they provide a historical record.

    b. Aggregate data are formatted to respond quickly to predetermined (or common) queries.

2. Data are distributed to departmental servers.

3. The data model that is most commonly used for a data mart is the star schema, which is a relational-like model. Proprietary models are also sometimes used.

The Star Schema

A **star schema** is a simple database design (particularly suited to ad-hoc queries) in which dimensional data (describing how data are commonly aggregated) are separated from fact or event data (describing individual business transactions) (Devlin, 1997). Another name that is often used is the dimensional model (Kimball, 1996). Although the star schema is suited to ad-hoc queries (and other forms of informational processing), it is not suited to on-line transaction processing and therefore is not generally used in operational systems, operational data stores, or an EDW.

Star schema: A simple database design in which dimensional data are separated from fact or event data. A dimensional model is another name for star schema.

Fact Tables and Dimension Tables A star schema consists of two types of tables: fact tables and dimension tables. *Fact tables* contain factual or quantitative data about a business such as units sold, orders booked, and so on. *Dimension tables* hold descriptive data about the subjects of the business. The dimension tables are usually the source of attributes used to qualify, categorize, or summarize facts in queries, reports, or graphs. The simplest star schema consists of one fact table, surrounded by several dimension tables. Typical business dimensions (subjects) are Product, Customer, and Period. Period, or time, is always one of the dimensions. This structure is shown in Figure 11-13, which contains four dimension tables.

Each dimension table has a one-to-many relationship to the central fact table. Each dimension table generally has a simple primary key, as well as several nonkey attributes. The primary key in turn is a foreign key in the fact table (as shown in Figure 11-13). The primary key of the fact table is a composite key that consists of the concatenation of all of the foreign keys (four keys in Figure 11-13), plus possibly other components that do not correspond to dimensions. The relationship between each dimension table and the fact table provides a join path that allows users to query the database easily, using SQL statements for either predefined or ad-hoc queries. Nonkey attributes are generally called data columns, as shown in Figure 11-13.

By now you have probably recognized that the star schema is not a new data model, but instead a denormalized implementation of the relational data model. The fact table plays the role of an *n*-ary associative entity that links the instances of the various dimensions. To review associative entities see Chapter 3, and for an example of the use of an associative entity see Figure 3-11. The dimension tables are denormalized. Most experts view this denormalization as acceptable because dimensions are not updated and void costly joins; thus the star is optimized around certain facts and business objects.

Example Star Schema A simple example of a star schema is shown in Figure 11-14. This example has three dimension tables: PRODUCT, PERIOD, and STORE, and one fact table, named SALES. The fact table is used to record three business facts: total units sold, total dollars sold, and total dollars cost. These totals are recorded for each possible value of product, period, and store.

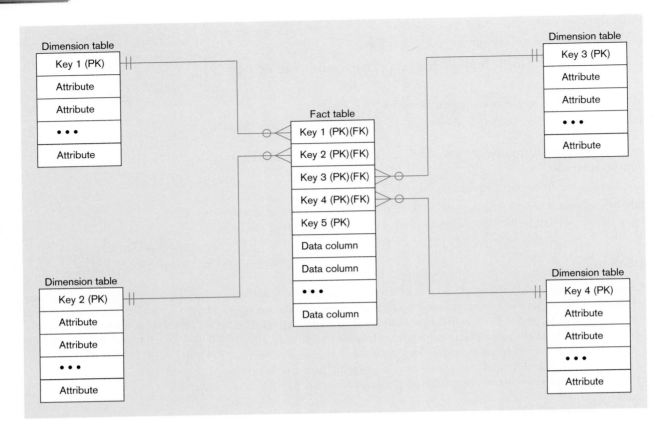

Figure 11-13
Components of a star schema

Figure 11-14
Star schema example

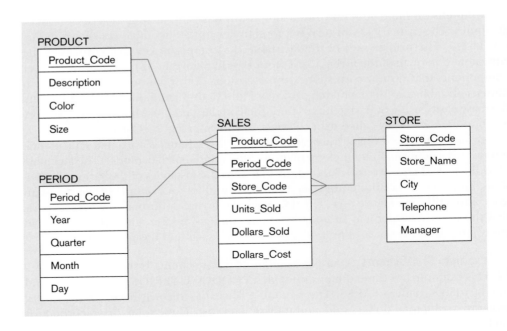

Some sample data for this schema are shown in Figure 11-15. From the fact table we find (for example) the following facts for product number 110 during period 002:

1. Thirty units were sold in store S1. The total dollar sales was 1500, and total dollar cost was 1200.

2. Forty units were sold in store S3. The total dollar sales was 2000, and total dollar cost was 1200.

Additional detail concerning the dimensions for this example can be obtained from the dimension tables. For example, in the PERIOD table we find that period 002 corresponds to year 2001, quarter 1, month 5. Try tracing the other dimensions in a similar manner.

Figure 11-15
Star schema with sample data

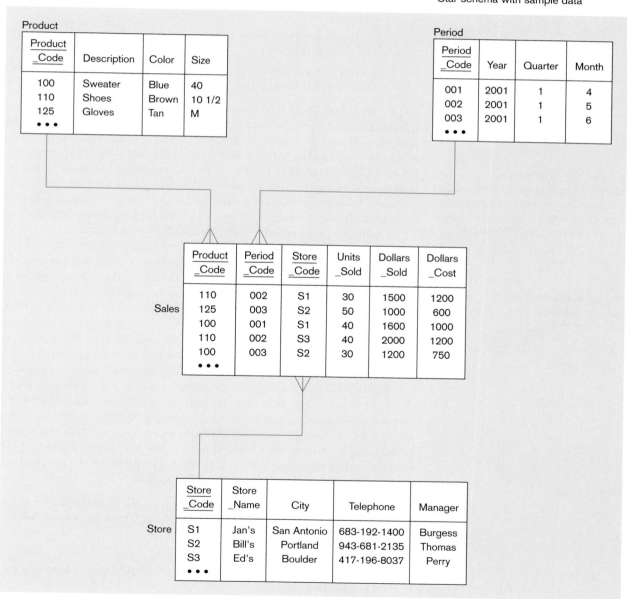

Surrogate Key Every key used to join the fact table with a dimension table should be a surrogate (nonintelligent or system assigned) key, not a key that uses a business value (sometimes called a smart key or a production key). That is, in Figure 11-15, Product_Code, Store_Code, and Period_Code should all be surrogate keys in both the fact and dimension tables. If, for example, it is necessary to know the product catalog number, engineering number, or inventory item number for a product, these attributes would be stored along with Description, Color, and Size as attributes of the product dimension table. The following are the main reasons for this surrogate key rule (Kimball, 1998):

- Business keys change, often slowly, over time, and we need to remember old and new business key values for the same business object. As we will see in a later section on slowing changing dimensions, a surrogate key allows us to handle changing and unknown keys with ease.

- Using a surrogate key also allows us to keep track of different nonkey attribute values for the same production key over time. Thus, if a product package changes in size, we can associate the same product production key with several surrogate keys, each for the different package sizes.

- Surrogate keys are often simpler and shorter, especially when the production key is a composite key.

- Surrogate keys can be of the same length and format for all keys, no matter what business dimensions are involved in the database, even dates.

Grain of Fact Table The raw data of a star schema are kept in the fact table. Determining the lowest level of detailed fact data stored is arguably the most important data mart design step. The level of detail of this data is determined by the intersection of all of the components of the primary key of the fact table. This intersection of primary keys is called the **grain** of the fact table. Determining the grain is critical and must be determined from business decision-making needs. There is always a way to summarize fact data by aggregating using dimension attributes, but there is no way in the data mart to understand business activity at a level of detail finer than the fact table grain.

Grain: The level of detail in a fact table determined by the intersection of all the components of the primary key, including all foreign keys and any other primary key elements.

The finest grain possible would be each business transaction, such as an individual line item or an individual scanned item on a product sales receipt, a personnel change order, a line item on a material receipt, a claim against an insurance policy, or an individual ATM transaction. A transactional grain allows users to perform **market basket analysis**, which is the study of buying behavior of individual customers. A grain higher than the transaction level might be all sales of a product on a given day, all receipts of a raw material in a given month at a specific warehouse, or the net effect of all ATM transactions for one ATM session. The finer the grain of the fact table, the more dimensions exist, the more fact rows that exist, and often, the closer the data mart model is to a data model for the operational data store.

Market basket analysis: The study of buying behavior of individual customers.

Kimball (2001) and others recommend using the smallest grain possible, given the limitations of the data mart technology. Even when data mart user information requirements imply a certain level of aggregated grain, often after some use, users ask more detailed questions (drill down) as a way to explain why certain aggregated patterns exist. You cannot "drill down" below the grain of the fact tables (without going to other data sources, such as the EDW, ODS, or the original source systems, which may add considerable effort to the analysis).

Size of the Fact Table As you would expect, the grain of the fact table has a direct impact on the size of that table. We can estimate the number of rows in the fact table as follows:

1. Estimate the number of possible values for each dimension associated with the fact table (in other words, the number of possible values for each foreign key in the fact table).

2. Multiply the values obtained in (1) after making any necessary adjustments.

Let's apply this approach to the star schema shown in Figure 11-15. Assume the following values for the dimensions:

total number of stores: 1000

total number of products: 10,000

total number of periods: 24 (two years' worth of monthly data)

Although there are 10,000 total products, only a fraction of these products are likely to record sales during a given month. Since item totals appear in the fact table only for items that record sales during a given month, we need to adjust this figure. Suppose that on average 50 percent (or 5,000) items record sales during a given month. Then an estimate of the number of rows in the fact table is computed as follows:

total rows = 1000 stores × 5000 active products × 24 months

$\qquad$ = 120,000,000 rows (!)

Thus in our relatively small example, the fact table that contains two years' worth of monthly totals can be expected to have well over 100 million rows. This example clearly illustrates that the size of the fact table is many times larger than the dimension tables. For example, the STORE table has 1000 rows, the PRODUCT table 10,000 rows, and the PERIOD table 24 rows.

If we know the size of each field in the fact table, we can further estimate the size (in bytes) of that table. The fact table (named SALES) in Figure 11-15 has six fields. If each of these fields averages four bytes in length, we can estimate the total size of the fact table as follows:

total size = 120,000,000 rows × 6 fields × 4 bytes/field

$\qquad$ = 2,880,000,000 bytes or 2.88 gigabytes

The size of the fact table depends on both the number of dimensions and the grain of the fact table. Suppose that after using the database shown in Figure 11-15 for a short period of time, the marketing department requests that *daily* totals be accumulated in the fact table (this is a typical evolution of a data mart). With the grain of the table changed to daily item totals, the number of rows is computed as follows:

total rows = 1000 stores × 2000 active products × 720 days (two years)

$\qquad$ = 1,440,000,000 rows

In the preceding calculation we have assumed that 20 percent of all products record sales on a given day. The database can now be expected to contain well over 1 *billion* rows. The database size is calculated as follows:

total size = 1,440,000,000 rows × 6 fields × 4 bytes/field

$\qquad$ = 34,560,000,000 bytes (or 34.56 gigabytes)

Many large retailers (such as Wal-Mart, Kmart, and Sears) and e-businesses (such as Travelocity.com and MatchLogic.com) now have data warehouses (or data marts). The size of most of these data warehouses is in the multiple-terabyte range, and growing rapidly as marketing people continue to press for more dimensions and an ever-finer grain in the fact table.

Modeling Date and Time Because data marts record facts about dimensions over time, date and time (henceforth simply called date) is always a dimension table and a date surrogate key is always one of the components of the primary key of any fact table. Because a user may want to aggregate facts on many different aspects of date, a date dimension may have many nonkey attributes. Also, because some characteristics of dates are country or event specific (e.g., whether the date is a holiday or there is some standard event on a given day, such as a festival or football game), modeling the date dimension can be more complex than illustrated so far.

Figure 11-16 shows a typical design for the date dimension. As we have seen before, a date surrogate key appears as part of the primary key of the fact table and

Figure 11-16
Modeling dates

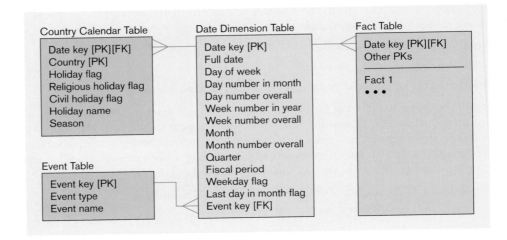

is the primary key of the date dimension table. The nonkey attributes of the date dimension table include all of the characteristics of dates that users use to categorize, summarize, and group facts that do not vary by country or event. For an organization doing business in several countries (or several geographical units in which dates have different characteristics), we have added a Country Calendar table to hold the characteristics of each date *in each country*. Thus, the Date key is a foreign key in the Country Calendar table, and each row of the Country Calendar table is unique by the combination of Date key and Country, which form the composite primary key for this table. A special event may occur on a given date (we assume here, for simplicity, no more than one special event may occur on a given date). We have normalized the Event data by creating an event table, so descriptive data on each event (e.g., the "Strawberry Festival" or the "Homecoming Game") are stored only once.

Variations of the Star Schema

The simple star schema introduced above is adequate for many applications. However, various extensions to this schema are often required to cope with more complex modeling problems. In this section we briefly describe two such extensions: multiple fact tables and the snowflake schema. For a discussion of additional extensions and variations, see Poe (1996) and www.ralphkimball.com.

Multiple Fact Tables It is often desirable for performance or other reasons to define more than one fact table in a given star schema. For example, suppose that various users require different levels of aggregation (in other words, a different table grain). Performance can be improved by defining a different fact table for each level of aggregation. The obvious trade-off is that storage requirements may increase dramatically with each new fact table. More commonly, multiple fact tables are needed to store facts for different combinations of dimensions.

Figure 11-17 illustrates a typical situation of multiple fact tables with two related star schemas. In this example, there are two fact tables, one at the center of each star:

1. Sales—facts about the sale of a product to a customer in a store on a date

2. Receipts—facts about the receipt of a product from a vendor to a warehouse on a date

As is common in this situation, data about one or more business subjects (in this case, Product and Date) need to be stored in dimension tables for each fact table. Two approaches have been adopted in this design to handle shared dimension

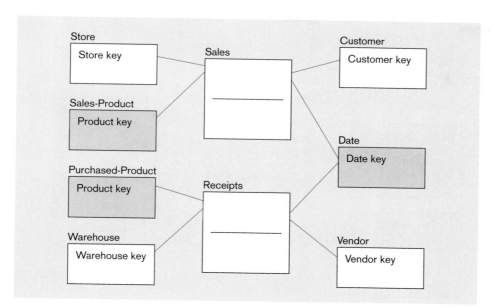

Figure 11-17
Conformed dimensions

tables. In one case, because the description of product is quite different for sales and receipts, two separate product dimension tables have been created. On the other hand, since users want the same descriptions of dates, one date dimension table is used. In each case, we have created a **conformed dimension**, meaning that the dimension means the same thing with each fact table, and hence, uses the same surrogate primary keys. Even when the two star schemas are stored in separate physical data marts, if dimensions are conformed, there is a potential for asking questions across the data marts (e.g., do certain vendors recognize sales more quickly and are they able to supply replenishments with less lead time). In general, conformed dimensions allow users to:

- Share nonkey dimension data
- Query across fact tables with consistency
- Work on facts and business subjects for which all users have the same meaning

Conformed dimension: One or more dimension tables associated with two or more fact tables for which the dimension tables have the same business meaning and primary key with each fact table.

Factless Fact Tables   There are applications for fact tables without any nonkey data, only the foreign keys for the associated dimensions. The two general situations in which factless fact tables may apply are to track events (see Figure 11-18a) and to inventory the set of possible occurrences (called coverage) (see Figure 11-18b). The star schema in Figure 11-18a tracks which students attend which courses at which time in which facilities with which instructors. All that needs to be known is whether this event occurs, represented by the intersection of the five foreign keys. The star schema in Figure 11-18b shows the set of possible sales of a product in a store at a particular time under a given promotion. A second sales fact table, not shown for Figure 11-18b, could contain the dollar and unit sales (facts) for this same combination of dimensions (i.e., with the same four foreign keys as the Promotion fact table plus these two nonkey facts). With these two fact tables and four conformed dimensions, it is possible to discover which products that were on a specific promotion at a given time in a specific store did not sell (i.e., had zero sales), which can be discovered by finding a combination of the four key values in the promotion fact table, which are not in the sales fact table. The sales fact table, alone, is not sufficient to answer this question since it is missing rows for a combination of the four key values, which has zero sales.

Figure 11-18
Factless fact table
(a) Factless fact table showing occurrence of an event

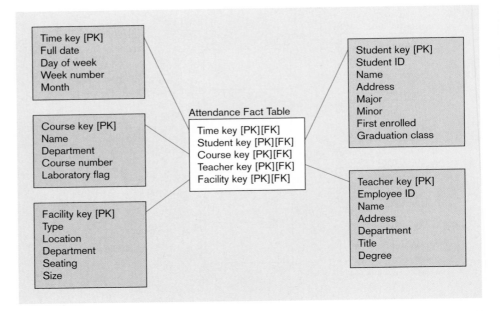

(b) Factless fact table showing coverage

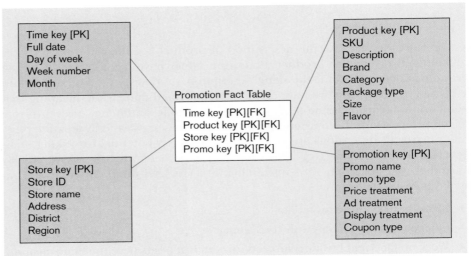

Normalizing Dimension Tables

Fact tables are fully normalized because each fact depends on the whole composite primary key and nothing but the composite key. On the other hand, dimension tables may not be normalized. Most data warehouse experts find this acceptable for a data mart optimized and simplified for a given user group, so that all of the dimension data are only one join away from associated facts. Sometimes, as with any relational database, the anomalies of a denormalized dimension table cause add, update, and delete problems. In this section, we address various situations in which it makes sense or is essential to further normalize dimension tables.

Multivalued Dimensions There may be a need for facts to be qualified by a set of values for the same business subject. For example, consider the hospital example in Figure 11-19. In this situation, a particular hospital charge and payment for a patient on a date (e.g., for all foreign keys in the Finances table) is associated with one or more diagnoses (we indicate this with a dashed M:N relationship line between the Diagnosis and Finances tables). We could pick the most important diagnosis as a

Figure 11-19
Multivalued dimension

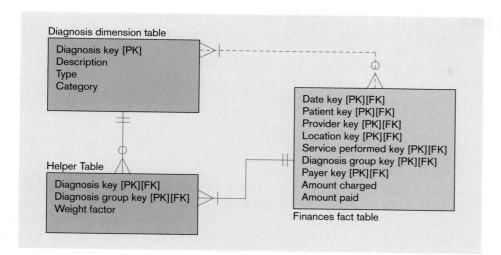

component key for the Finances table; but that would mean we lose potentially important information about other diagnoses associated with a row. Or, we could design the Finances table with a fixed number of diagnosis keys, more than we think is ever possible to associate with one row of the Finances table; but, this would create null components of the primary key for many rows, which violates a property of relational databases. The best approach (the normalization approach) is to create a table for an associative entity between Diagnosis and Finances. In the data warehouse database world such a table is called a "helper table," and we will see more examples of helper tables as we progress through subsequent sections. A helper table may have nonkey attributes (as can any table for an associative entity); for example, the weight factor in the Diagnosis group table of Figure 11-19 indicates the relative role each diagnosis plays in each group, presumably normalized to a total of 100 percent for all the diagnoses in a group. Also note that it is possible for more than one Finances row to be associated with the same Diagnosis group.

Hierarchies   Many times a dimension in a star schema forms a natural hierarchy. For example, there are geographical hierarchies (e.g., markets with a state, states within a region, and regions within a country) and product hierarchies (packages within a product, packages within bundles, and bundles within product groups). When a dimension participates in a hierarchy, the database designer has two basic choices:

1.   Include all the information for each level of the hierarchy in a single denormalized dimension table, thus creating considerable redundancy and update anomalies.

2.   Normalize the dimension into a nested set of tables with 1:M relationships between them. It will still be possible to aggregate the fact data at any level of the hierarchy, but now the user will have to either perform nested joins along the hierarchy or the user can be given a view of the hierarchy that is prejoined.

Consider the example of a typical consulting company that invoices customers for specified time periods on projects. A revenue fact table in this situation might show how much revenue is billed for how many hours on each invoice, which is for a particular time period, customer, service, employee, and project. Because consulting work may be done for different divisions of the same organization, if we want to understand the total role of our consulting in any level of a customer organization, we need a customer hierarchy. This hierarchy is a recursive relationship between organizational units; as shown in Figure 5-17, the standard way to represent this in a normalized database is to put into the company row a foreign key of the Company key for its parent unit.

Recursive relationships implemented in this way are difficult for the typical decision maker end user because specifying how to aggregate at any level of the hierarchy requires complex SQL programming. A simpler alternative appears in Figure 11-20. Figure 11-20a shows how this hierarchy is typically modeled in a data warehouse using a helper table (Kimball, 1998b; Chisholm, 2000). Each customer organizational unit the consulting firm serves is assigned a different surrogate customer key and row in the Customer dimension table, and the customer surrogate key is used as the foreign key in the Revenue fact table. The problem with joining in a recursive relationship of arbitrary depth is that the user has to write code to join an arbitrary number of times (once for each level of subordination) and these joins in a data warehouse, because of its massive size, can be very time-consuming (except for some high-performance data warehouse technologies using parallel processing). To avoid this problem, the helper table flattens out the hierarchy by recording a row for each organizational subunit and each of its superior organizational units (including itself) all the way up to the top unit of the customer organization. Each row of this helper table has three descriptors—the number of levels the subunit is from the superior unit for that table row, a flag indicating whether this subunit is the lowest in the hier-

Figure 11-20
Representing hierarchical relationships within a dimension
(a) Use of a helper table

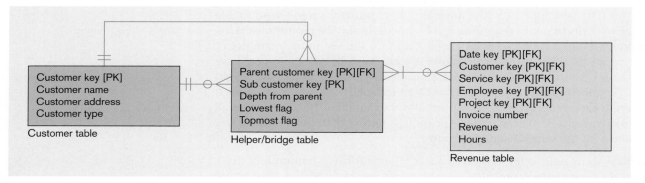

(b) Example hierarchy with customer and helper tables

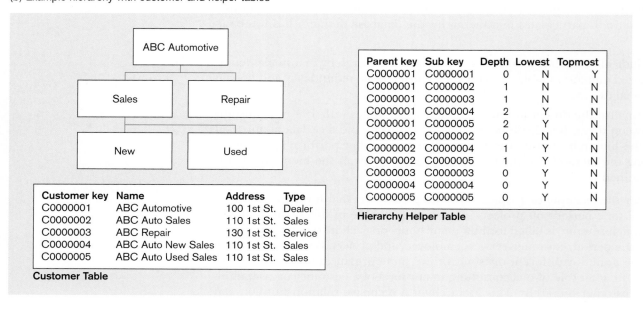

Parent key	Sub key	Depth	Lowest	Topmost
C0000001	C0000001	0	N	Y
C0000001	C0000002	1	N	N
C0000001	C0000003	1	N	N
C0000001	C0000004	2	Y	N
C0000001	C0000005	2	Y	N
C0000002	C0000002	0	N	N
C0000002	C0000004	1	Y	N
C0000002	C0000005	1	Y	N
C0000003	C0000003	0	Y	N
C0000004	C0000004	0	Y	N
C0000005	C0000005	0	Y	N

Hierarchy Helper Table

Customer key	Name	Address	Type
C0000001	ABC Automotive	100 1st St.	Dealer
C0000002	ABC Auto Sales	110 1st St.	Sales
C0000003	ABC Repair	130 1st St.	Service
C0000004	ABC Auto New Sales	110 1st St.	Sales
C0000005	ABC Auto Used Sales	110 1st St.	Sales

Customer Table

archy, and a flag indicating whether this subunit is the highest in the hierarchy. Figure 11-20b depicts an example customer organizational hierarchy and the rows that would be in the helper table to represent that total organization (there would be other rows in the helper table for the subunit-parent unit relationships within other customer organizations).

The Revenue fact table in Figure 11-20a includes a nonkey attribute of Invoice number. Invoice number is an example of what is called a "generative dimension," which has no interesting dimension attributes (so no dimension table exists and Invoice number is not part of the table's primary key) but it also is not a fact that will be used for aggregation. This attribute may be helpful if there is a need to explore an ODS or source systems to find additional details about the invoice transaction.

When the dimension tables are further normalized by using helper tables (sometimes called bridge or reference tables), the simple star schema turns into a **snowflake schema**. A snowflake schema resembles a segment of an ODS or source database centered on the transaction tables summarized into the fact table and all of the tables directly and indirectly related to these transaction tables. Many data warehouse experts discourage the use of snowflake schemas because they are more complex for users and require more joins to bring the results together into one table. A snowflake may be desirable if the normalization saves significant redundant space (e.g., when there are many redundant, long textual attributes) or when users may find browsing through the normalized tables themselves useful.

Snowflake schema: An expanded version of a star schema in which dimension tables are normalized into several related tables.

Slowly Changing Dimensions

As you recall, data warehouses and data marts track business activities over time. The business does not remain static over time—products change size and weight, customers relocate, stores change layouts, and sales staff are assigned to different locations. Most systems of record keep only the current values for business subjects (e.g., the current customer address). But in a data warehouse or data mart, we need to know the history of values to match the history of facts with the correct dimensional descriptions at the time the facts happened. For example, we need to associate a sales fact with the description of the associated customer during the time period of the sales fact, which may not be the description of that customer today. Of course, business subjects change slowly compared to most operational transactions. Thus, dimensional data change, but change slowly.

We might handle changing dimension attributes in one of three ways (Kimball, 1996b and 1999):

1. Overwrite the current value with the new value, but this is unacceptable because it eliminates the description of the past we need to interpret historical facts.

2. For each dimension attribute that changes, create a current value field and as many old value fields as we wish (i.e., a multivalued attribute with a fixed number of occurrences). This scheme might work if there were a predictable number of changes over the length of history retained in the data warehouse (e.g., if we keep 24 months of history and an attribute may change value at most monthly). However, this works only under this kind of restrictive assumption, and is not generalizable to any slowly changing dimension attribute.

3. Create a new dimension table row (with a new key) each time the dimension object changes; this new row contains all the dimension characteristics. A fact row is associated with the key whose attributes apply at the time of the fact. We may also want to store the date/time the change occurred and a reason code for the change. This approach allows us to create as many dimensional object changes as necessary. It, however, becomes unwieldy if rows frequently change or for very long rows.

Figure 11-21
Dimension segmentation

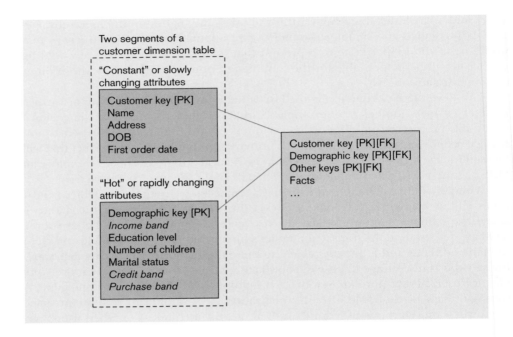

The third scheme is the most frequently used approach to handling slowly changing dimensions. Under this scheme, we may also store in a dimension row the surrogate key value for the original object; this way, we can relate all changes to their origin.

As noted above, however, this scheme can cause an excessive number of dimension table rows when dimension objects frequently change or when dimension rows are large, "monster dimensions." Figure 11-21 illustrates one approach, dimension segmentation, which handles this situation as well as the more general case of subsets of dimension attributes that change at different frequencies. In this example, the Customer dimension is segmented into two dimension tables; one segment may hold nearly constant or very slowly changing dimensions and other segments (we show only two in this example) hold clusters of attributes that change more rapidly and, for attributes in the same cluster, often change at the same time. These more rapidly changing attributes are often called "hot" attributes by data warehouse designers.

Another aspect of this segmentation is that for hot attributes, we changed individual dimension attributes, such as customer income (e.g., $75,400/year) into an attribute for a band, or range, of income values (e.g., $60,000–$89,999/year). Bands are defined as required by users and are as narrow or wide as can be useful, but certainly some precision is lost. Bands make the hot attributes less hot, because a change within a band does not cause a new row to be written. This design is more complex for users because they now may have to join facts with multiple dimension segments, depending on the analysis.

THE USER INTERFACE

"Build it and they will come" is a strategy that may work in some contexts but cannot be relied upon with data warehouses and data marts. Even a well-designed data mart, loaded with relevant data, may not be used unless users are provided with a powerful, intuitive interface that allows them to easily access and analyze those data. In this section we provide a brief introduction to contemporary interfaces for data warehouses.

A variety of tools are available to query and analyze data stored in data warehouses and data marts. These tools may be classified as follows:

1. Traditional query and reporting tools
2. On-line analytical processing (OLAP), MOLAP, and ROLAP tools
3. Data-mining tools
4. Data-visualization tools

Traditional query and reporting tools include spreadsheets, personal computer databases, and report writers and generators. For reasons of space (and since they are covered elsewhere) we do not describe these tools in this chapter. We describe the remaining three categories of tools after discussing the role of metadata.

Role of Metadata

The first requirement for building a user-friendly interface is a set of metadata that describes the data in the data mart in business terms that users can easily understand. We show the association of metadata with data marts in the overall three-level data architecture in Figure 11-6.

The metadata associated with data marts are often referred to as a "data catalog," "data directory," or some similar term. Metadata serve as kind of a "yellow pages" directory to the data in the data marts. The metadata should allow users to easily answer questions such as the following:

1. What subjects are described in the data mart? (Typical subjects are customers, patients, students, products, courses, and so on.)
2. What dimensions and facts are included in the data mart? What is the grain of the fact table?
3. How are the data in the data mart derived from the enterprise data warehouse data? What rules are used in the derivation?
4. How are the data in the enterprise data warehouse derived from operational data? What rules are used in this derivation?
5. What reports and predefined queries are available to view the data?
6. What drill-down and other data analysis techniques are available?
7. Who is responsible for the quality of data in the data marts, and to whom are requests for changes made?

Querying Tools

The most common database query language, SQL (see Chapters 7 and 8), is being extended to support some types of calculations and querying needed for a data warehousing environment. In general, however, SQL is not an analytical language (Mundy, 2001). SQL-99 does include some data warehousing extensions. Because many data warehousing operations deal with categories of objects, possibly ordered by date, SQL-99 includes a WINDOW clause to define dynamic sets of rows. For example, a WINDOW clause can be used to define three adjacent days as the basis for calculating moving averages (think of a window moving between the bottom and top of its window frame, giving you a sliding view of rows of data). PARTITION within a WINDOW is similar to GROUP BY; PARTITION tells a WINDOW clause the basis for each set, an ORDER BY clause sequences the elements of a set, and the ROWS clause says how many rows in sequence to use in a calculation. The RANK windowing function calculates something that is very difficult to calculate in standard SQL, which is the row of a table in a specific relative position based on some criteria (e.g., the customer with the third highest sales in a given period). See the section Proposed

Analytical Functions in Chapter 8 for an example of a WINDOW clause. SQL-99 still is not a full-featured data warehouse querying and analysis tool, but it is a start at recognizing the special querying needs of decision support systems.

On-Line Analytical Processing (OLAP) Tools

A specialized class of tools has been developed to provide users with multidimensional views of their data, then to easily analyze the data using a graphical interface. In the simplest case, data are viewed as a simple three-dimensional cube.

On-line analytical processing (OLAP): The use of a set of graphical tools that provides users with multidimensional views of their data and allows them to analyze the data using simple windowing techniques.

On-line analytical processing (or OLAP) is the use of a set of graphical tools that provides users with multidimensional views of their data and allows them to analyze the data using simple windowing techniques. The term on-line analytical processing is intended to contrast with the more traditional term *on-line transaction processing*. The differences between these two types of processing were summarized in Table 11-1. The term "multidimensional analysis" is often used as a synonym for OLAP.

An example of a "data cube" (or multidimensional view) of data that is typical of OLAP is shown in Figure 11-22. This view corresponds quite closely to the star schema introduced in Figure 11-14. Two of the dimensions in Figure 11-22 correspond to the dimension tables (PRODUCT and PERIOD) in Figure 11-14, while the third dimension (named measures) corresponds to the data in the fact table (named SALES) in Figure 11-14.

Relational OLAP (ROLAP): OLAP tools that view the database as a traditional relational database, in either a star schema or other normalized or denormalized set of tables.

Multidimensional OLAP (MOLAP): OLAP tools that load data into an intermediate structure, usually a three- or higher dimensional array.

OLAP is actually a general term for several categories of data warehouse and data mart access tools (Dyché, 2000). **Relational OLAP (ROLAP)** tools use variations of SQL and view the database as a traditional relational database, in either a star schema or other normalized or denormalized set of tables. ROLAP tools access the data warehouse or data mart directly. **Multidimensional OLAP (MOLAP)** load data into an intermediate structure, usually a three- or higher dimensional array. We illustrate MOLAP in the next few sections because of its popularity. It is important to note with MOLAP that the data are not simply viewed as a multidimensional array (cube for three dimensions), but rather a MOLAP data mart is created by extracting data from the data warehouse or data mart and then storing the data in a specialized separate

Figure 11-22
Slicing a data cube

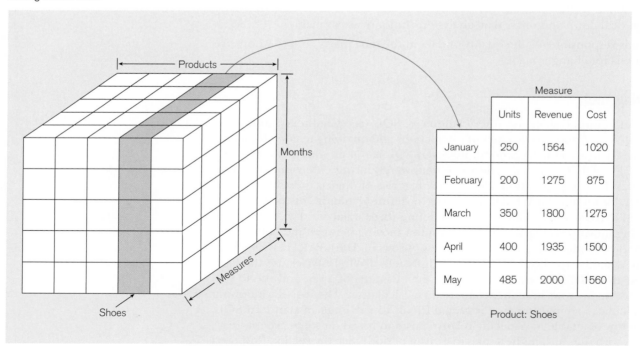

	Measure		
	Units	Revenue	Cost
January	250	1564	1020
February	200	1275	875
March	350	1800	1275
April	400	1935	1500
May	485	2000	1560

Product: Shoes

data store through which data can be viewed only through a multidimensional structure. Other, less-common categories of OLAP tools are DOLAP (database OLAP), which includes OLAP functionality in the DBMS query language (there are proprietary, non-ANSI standard SQL systems that do this), and HOLAP (hybrid OLAP), which allows access via both multidimensional cubes or relational query languages.

Slicing a Cube Figure 11-22 also shows a typical MOLAP operation—slicing the data cube to produce a simple two-dimensional table or view. In Figure 11-22, this slice is for the product named "shoes." The resulting table shows the three measures (units, revenues, and cost) for this product by period (or month). Other views can easily be developed by the user by means of simple "drag and drop" operations. This type of operation is often called "slicing and dicing" the cube.

Another operation closely related to slicing and dicing is data pivoting. This term refers to rotating the view for a particular data point, to obtain another perspective. For example, Figure 11-22 shows sales of 400 units of shoes for April. The analyst could pivot this view to obtain (for example) the sales of shoes by store for the same month.

Drill-Down Another type of operation often used in multidimensional analysis is *drill-down*—that is, analyzing a given set of data at a finer level of detail. An example of drill-down is shown in Figure 11-23. Figure 11-23a shows a summary report for the total sales of three package sizes for a given brand of paper towels—2-pack, 3-pack, and 6-pack. However, the towels come in different colors, and the analyst wants a further breakdown of sales by color within each of these package sizes. Using an OLAP

Figure 11-23
Example of drill-down
(a) Summary report

Brand	Package size	Sales
SofTowel	2-pack	$75
SofTowel	3-pack	$100
SofTowel	6-pack	$50

(b) Drill-down with color added

Brand	Package size	Color	Sales
SofTowel	2-pack	White	$30
SofTowel	2-pack	Yellow	$25
SofTowel	2-pack	Pink	$20
SofTowel	3-pack	White	$50
SofTowel	3-pack	Green	$25
SofTowel	3-pack	Yellow	$25
SofTowel	6-pack	White	$30
SofTowel	6-pack	Yellow	$20

tool, this breakdown can be easily obtained using a "point-and-click" approach with a mouse device.

The result of the drill-down is shown in Figure 11-23b. Notice that a drill-down presentation is equivalent to adding another column to the original report (in this case, a column was added for the attribute "color").

Executing a drill-down (as in this example) may require that the OLAP tool "reach back" to the data warehouse to obtain the detail data necessary for the drill-down. This type of operation can be performed by an OLAP tool (without user participation) only if an integrated set of metadata is available to that tool. Some tools even permit the OLAP tool to reach back to the operational data if necessary for a given query.

Data-Mining Tools

With on-line analytical processing, users are searching for answers to questions they have raised—for example, "Are health care costs greater for single or married persons?" With data mining, users are looking for patterns or trends in a collection of facts or observations. **Data mining** is knowledge discovery using a sophisticated blend of techniques from traditional statistics, artificial intelligence, and computer graphics (Weldon, 1996).

Data mining: Knowledge discovery using a sophisticated blend of techniques from traditional statistics, artificial intelligence, and computer graphics.

The goals of data mining are threefold:

1. *Explanatory.* To explain some observed event or condition, such as why sales of pickup trucks have increased in Colorado
2. *Confirmatory.* To confirm a hypothesis, such as whether two-income families are more likely to buy family medical coverage than single-income families
3. *Exploratory.* To analyze data for new or unexpected relationships, such as what spending patterns are likely to accompany credit card fraud.

Data-Mining Techniques Several different techniques are commonly used for data mining. See Table 11-4 for a summary of the most common of these techniques. The choice of an appropriate technique depends on the nature of the data to be analyzed, as well as the size of the data set. Data mining can be performed against either the data marts or the enterprise data warehouse (or both).

Data-Mining Applications Data-mining techniques have been successfully used for a wide range of real-world applications. A summary of some of the typical types of applications, with examples of each type, is presented in Table 11-5. Data-mining applications are growing rapidly, for the following reasons:

1. The amount of data in data warehouses and data marts is growing exponentially, so that users require the type of automated techniques provided by data-mining tools to mine the knowledge in these data.
2. New data-mining tools with expanded capabilities are continually being introduced.
3. Increasing competitive pressures are forcing companies to make better use of the information and knowledge contained in their data.

Table 11-4 Data-Mining Techniques

Technique	Function
Case-based reasoning	Derives rules from real-world case examples
Rule discovery	Searches for patterns and correlations in large data sets
Signal processing	Identifies clusters of observations with similar characteristics
Neural nets	Develops predictive models based on principles modeled after the human brain
Fractals	Compresses large databases without losing information

Table 11-5 Typical Data-Mining Applications (Adapted from Zaitz, 1997, and Dyché, 2000)

Type of Application	Example
Profiling populations	Developing profiles of high-value customers, credit risks, and credit-card fraud.
Analysis of business trends	Identifying markets with above average (or below average) growth.
Target marketing	Identifying customers (or customer segments) for promotional activity.
Usage analysis	Identifying usage patterns for products and services.
Campaign effectiveness	Comparing campaign strategies for effectiveness.
Product affinity	Identifying products that are purchased concurrently, or the characteristics of shoppers for certain product groups.
Customer retention and churn	Examining the behavior of customers who have left for competitors to prevent remaining customers from leaving.
Profitability analysis	Determining which customers are profitable given the total set of activities the customer has with the organization.
Customer value analysis	Determining where valuable customers are at different stages in their life.
Up-selling	Identifying new products or services to sell to a customer based upon critical events and life-style changes.

Data Visualization

Often the human eye can best discern patterns when data are represented graphically. **Data visualization** is the representation of data in graphical and multimedia formats for human analysis. Benefits of data visualization include the ability to better observe trends and patterns, and to identify correlations and clusters. Data visualization is often used in conjunction with data mining and other analytical techniques.

Data visualization: The representation of data in graphical and multimedia formats for human analysis.

Summary

Despite the vast quantities of data collected in organizations today, most managers have difficulty obtaining the information they need for decision making. Two major factors contribute to this "information gap." First, data are often heterogeneous and inconsistent as a result of the piecemeal system development approaches that have commonly been used. Second, systems are developed (or acquired) primarily to satisfy operational objectives, with little thought given to the information needs of managers.

There are major differences between operational and informational systems, and between the data that appear in those systems. Operational systems are used to run the business on a current basis, and the primary design goal is to provide high performance to users who process transactions and update databases. Informational systems are used to support managerial decision making, and the primary design goal is to provide ease of access and use for information workers.

The purpose of a data warehouse is to consolidate and integrate data from a variety of sources, and to format those data in a context for making accurate business decisions. A data warehouse is an integrated and consistent store of subject-oriented data obtained from a variety of sources and formatted into a meaningful context to support decision making in an organization.

Most data warehouses today follow a three-layer architecture. The first layer consists of data distributed throughout the various operational systems. The second layer is an enterprise data warehouse, which is a centralized, integrated data warehouse that is the control point and single source of all data made available to end users for decision support applications. The third layer is a series of data marts. A data mart is a data warehouse whose data are limited in scope for the decision-making needs of a particular user group. A data mart can be independent of an enterprise data warehouse (EDW), derived from the EDW, or a logical subset of the EDW.

The data layer in the enterprise data warehouse is called the reconciled data layer. The characteristics of this data layer (ideally) are the following: it is detailed, historical, normalized, comprehensive, and quality-controlled. Reconciled data are obtained by filling the enterprise data warehouse or operational data store from the various operational systems. Reconciling the data requires four steps: capturing the data from the source systems; scrubbing the data (to remove inconsistencies); transforming the data (to convert it to the format required in the data warehouse); and loading and indexing the data in the data warehouse. Reconciled data are not normally accessed directly by end users.

The data layer in the data marts is referred to as the derived data layer. These are the data that are accessed by end users for their decision support applications.

Data are most often stored in a data mart using a variation of the relational model called the star schema, or dimensional model. A star schema is a simple database design where dimensional data are separated from fact or event data. A star schema consists of two types of tables: dimension tables and fact tables. The size of a fact table depends in part on the grain (or level of detail) in that table. Fact tables with over one billion rows are common in data warehouse applications today. There are several variations of the star schema, including models with multiple fact tables, and snowflake schemas that arise when one or more dimensions have a hierarchical structure.

A variety of end-user interfaces are available to access and analyze decision support data. On-line analytical processing (or OLAP) is the use of a set of graphical tools that provides users with multidimensional views of their data (data are normally viewed as a cube). OLAP facilitates data analysis operations such as slice-and-dice, data pivoting, and drill-down. Data mining is a form of knowledge discovery that uses a sophisticated blend of techniques from traditional statistics, artificial intelligence, and computer graphics.

CHAPTER REVIEW

Key Terms

Aggregation
Conformed dimension
Data mart
Data mining
Data scrubbing
Data transformation
Data visualization
Data warehouse
Dependent data mart
Derived data
Enterprise data warehouse (EDW)
Event

Grain
Incremental extract
Independent data mart
Informational systems
Joining
Logical data mart
Market basket analysis
Multidimensional OLAP
On-line analytical processing (OLAP)
Operational data store (ODS)
Operational system

Periodic data
Reconciled data
Refresh mode
Relational OLAP
Selection
Snowflake schema
Star schema
Static extract
Transient data
Update mode
@ctive warehouse

Review Questions

1. Define each of the following terms:
   a. data warehouse
   b. data mart
   c. reconciled data
   d. derived data
   e. on-line analytical processing
   f. data mining
   g. star schema
   h. snowflake schema
   i. grain
   j. static extract
   k. incremental extract
   l. event

2. Match the following terms and definitions:

   _____ event
   _____ periodic data
   _____ data mart
   _____ star schema
   _____ data mining
   _____ reconciled data
   _____ dependent data mart
   _____ data visualization
   _____ transient data
   _____ snowflake schema
   _____ data transformation
   _____ data scrubbing

   a. previous data content is lost
   b. detailed, historical data
   c. converts data formats
   d. corrects errors in source data
   e. data are not altered or deleted
   f. a database action (e.g., create)
   g. limited scope data warehouse
   h. dimension and fact tables
   i. form of knowledge discovery
   j. filled from data warehouse
   k. results from hierarchical dimensions
   l. data represented in graphical formats

3. Contrast the following terms:
   a. static extract; incremental extract
   b. transient data; periodic data
   c. data warehouse; data mart; operational data store
   d. data scrubbing; data transformation
   e. reconciled data; derived data
   f. fact table; dimension table
   g. star schema; snowflake schema
   h. independent data mart; dependent data mart; logical data mart

4. Name the five major trends that necessitate data warehousing in many organizations today.

5. Briefly describe the major components of a data warehouse architecture.

6. List three types of metadata that appear in a three-layer data warehouse architecture, and briefly describe the purpose of each type.

7. List five typical characteristics of reconciled data.

8. List and briefly describe four steps in the data reconciliation process.

9. List five errors and inconsistencies that are commonly found in operational data.

10. Briefly describe three types of operations that can easily be performed with OLAP tools.

11. Explain how the phrase extract, transform, and load relates to the data reconciliaton process.

12. Explain the pros and cons/limitations of independent data marts.

13. Explain how the volatility of a data warehouse is different from the volatility of a database for an operational information system.

14. Explain the pros and cons of logical data marts.

15. List common tasks performed during data cleansing.

16. Describe the characteristics of a surrogate key as used in a data warehouse or data mart.

17. Why is time almost always a dimension in a data warehouse or data mart?

18. What is the purpose of conformed dimensions for different star schemas within the same data warehousing environment?

19. Can a fact table have no nonkey attributes? Why, or why not?

20. In what ways are dimension tables often not normalized?

21. What is a hierarchy as it relates to a dimension table?

22. What is the meaning of the phrase "slowing changing dimension"?

23. Explain the most common approach used to handle slowly changing dimensions.

Problems and Exercises

1. Examine the three tables with student data shown in Figure 11-1. Design a single table format that will hold all of the data (nonredundantly) that are contained in these three tables. Choose column names that you believe are most appropriate for these data.

2. The table below shows some simple student data as of the date 06/20/2001:

Key	Name	Major
001	Amy	Music
002	Tom	Business
003	Sue	Art
004	Joe	Math
005	Ann	Engineering

The following transactions occur on 06/21/2001:
1. Student 004 changes major from 'Math' to 'Business'.
2. Student 005 is deleted from the file.
3. New student 006 is added to the file. Name is 'Jim', Major is 'Phys Ed'.

The following transactions occur on 06/22/2001:
1. Student 003 changes major from 'Art' to 'History'.
2. Student 006 changes major from 'Phys Ed' to 'Basket Weaving'.

Your assignment is in two parts:
   a. Construct tables for 06/21/2001 and 06/22/2001 reflecting the above transactions, assuming that the data are transient (refer to Figure 11-8).
   b. Construct tables for 06/21/2001 and 06/22/2001 reflecting the above transactions, assuming that the data are periodic (refer to Figure 11-9).

3. Millennium College wants you to help design a star schema to record grades for courses completed by students. There are four dimension tables, with attributes as follows:
   - Course_Section. Attributes: Course_ID, Section_Number, Course_Name, Units, Room_ID, Room_Capacity. During a given semester the college offers an average of 500 course sections.
   - Professor. Attributes: Prof_ID, Prof_Name, Title, Department_ID, Department_Name.
   - Student. Attributes: Student_ID, Student_Name, Major. Each course section has an average of 40 students.
   - Period. Attributes: Semester_ID, Year. The database will contain data for 30 periods (a total of 10 years).

   The only fact that is to be recorded in the fact table is Course_Grade.
   a. Design a star schema for this problem. See Figure 11-14 for the format you should follow.
   b. Estimate the number of rows in the fact table, using the assumptions stated above.

c. Estimate the total size of the fact table (in bytes), assuming that each field has an average of 5 bytes.

d. Various characteristics of sections, professors and students change over time. How do you propose designing the star schema to allow for these changes? Why?

4. Having mastered the principles of normalization described in Chapter 5, you recognize immediately that the star schema you developed for Millennium College (Problem and Exercise 3) is not in third normal form. Using these principles, convert the star schema to a snowflake schema. What impact (if any) does this have on the size of the fact table for this problem?

5. You are to construct a star schema for Simplified Automobile Insurance Company (see Kimball, 1996 for a more realistic example). The relevant dimensions, dimension attributes, and dimension sizes are as follows:

- Insured Party. Attributes: Insured_Party_ID, Name. There is an average of two insured parties for each policy and covered item.
- Coverage Item. Attributes: Coverage_Key, Description. There is an average of 10 covered items per policy.
- Agent. Attributes: Agent_ID, Agent_Name. There is one agent for each policy and covered item.
- Policy. Attributes: Policy_ID, Type. The company has approximately one million policies at the present time.
- Period. Attributes: Date_Key, Fiscal_Period.

Facts to be recorded for each combination of these dimensions are: Policy_Premium, Deductible, and Number_of_Transactions.

a. Design a star schema for this problem. See Figure 11-14 for the format you should follow.

b. Estimate the number of rows in the fact table, using the assumptions stated above.

c. Estimate the total size of the fact table (in bytes), assuming an average of 5 bytes per field.

6. Simplified Automobile Insurance Company would like to add a Claims dimension to its star schema (see Problem and Exercise 5). Attributes of Claim are: Claim_ID, Claim_Description, and Claim_Type. Attributes of the fact table are now: Policy_Premium, Deductible, and Monthly_Claim_Total.

a. Extend the star schema from Problem and Exercise 5 to include these new data.

b. Calculate the estimated number of rows in the fact table, assuming that the company experiences an average of 2000 claims per month.

7. Millennium College (see Problem and Exercise 3) now wants to include new data about course sections: the department offering the course, the academic unit to which the department reports, and the budget unit to which the department is assigned. Change your answer to Problem and Exercise 3 to accommodate these new data requirements. Explain why you implemented the changes in the star schema the way you did.

8. As mentioned in the chapter, Kimball (1997), Inmon (1997 and 2000), and Armstrong (2000) have debated the merits of independent and dependent data marts and normalized versus denormalized data marts. Obtain copies of these articles from your library or from on-line sources and summarize the arguments made by each side of this debate.

Field Exercises

1. Visit an organization that has developed a data warehouse, and interview the data administrator or other key participant. Discuss the following issues:

a. How satisfied are users with the data warehouse? In what ways has it improved their decision making?

b. Does the warehouse employ a two-tier or three-tier architecture?

c. Does the architecture employ one or more data marts? If so, are they dependent or independent?

d. What end-user tools are employed? Is data mining used?

e. What were the main obstacles or difficulties overcome in developing the data warehouse environment?

2. Visit the following Internet Websites. Browse these sites for additional information on data warehouse topics, including case examples of warehouse implementations, descriptions of the latest warehouse-related products, and announcements of conferences and other events.

a. International Data Warehouse Association: http://www.idwa.com

b. The Data Warehousing Institute: http://www.dw-institute.com

c. Knowledge Discovery Mine: http://www.kdnuggets.com

d. Data Mining Institute: http://www.datamining.org

e. Data Warehousing Knowledge Center: http://www.datawarehousing.org

f. An electronic data warehousing journal: http://www.tdan.com

References

Armstrong, R. 1997. "A Rebuttal to the Dimensional Modeling Manifesto." A white paper produced by NCR Corporation.

Armstrong, R. 2000. "Avoiding Data Mart Traps." *Teradata Review* (Summer): 32–37.

Barquin, R. 1996. "On the First Issue of *The Journal of Data Warehousing*." *The Journal of Data Warehousing* 1 (July): 2–6.

Chisholm, M. 2000. "A New Understanding of Reference Data." *DM Review* (October): 60, 84–85.

Devlin, B. 1997. *Data Warehouse: From Architecture to Implementation*. Reading, MA: Addison Wesley Longman.

Devlin, B., and P. Murphy. 1988. "An Architecture for a Business Information System." *IBM Systems Journal* 27 (No. 1): 60–80.

Dyché, J. 2000. *e-Data: Turning Data into Information with Data Warehousing*. Reading, MA: Addison-Wesley.

English, L. P. 1999. *Improving Data Warehouse and Business Information Quality*. New York: John Wiley.

Griffin, J. 1997. "Fast Payback Projects." *DM Review* 7 (December): 10, 11.

Hackathorn, R. 1993. *Enterprise Database Connectivity*. New York: John Wiley & Sons.

IBM. 1993. "Information Warehouse Architecture." SC26–324–00. White Plains, NY: IBM Corp.

Imhoff, C. 1998. "The Operational Data Store: Hamering Away." *DM Review* (July): available from www.dmreview.com.

Imhoff, C. 1999. "The Corporate Information Factory." *DM Review* (December): available from www.dmreview.com.

Inmon, B. 1997. "Iterative Development in the Data Warehouse." *DM Review* 7 (November): 16, 17.

Inmon, W. 1992. *Building the Data Warehouse*. Wellesley, MA: QED Information Sciences.

Inmon, W. 1998. "The Operational Data Store: Designing the Operational Data Store." *DM Review* (July): available from www.dmreview.com.

Inmon, W. 1999. "What Happens When You Have Built the Data Mart First?" in TDAN, an electronic journal found at www.tdan.com.

Inmon, W. 2000. "The Problem with Dimensional Modeling." *DM Review* (May): 68–70.

Inmon, W. H., and R. D. Hackathorn. 1994. *Using the Data Warehouse*. New York: John Wiley & Sons.

Kimball, R. 1996a. *The Data Warehouse Toolkit*. New York: John Wiley & Sons.

Kimball, R. 1996b. "Slowly Changing Dimensions." *DBMS* (April): 18–20.

Kimball, R. 1997. "A Dimensional Modeling Manifesto." *DBMS* (August): available from www.dbmsmag.com.

Kimball, R. 1998a. "Pipelining Your Surrogates." *DBMS* (June): 18–22.

Kimball, R. 1998b. "Help for Hierarchies." *DBMS* (September) 12–16.

Kimball, R. 1999. "When a Slowly Changing Dimension Speeds Up." *Intelligent Enterprise* (August 3): 60–62.

Kimball, R. 2001. "Declaring the Grain." from Kimball University Design Tip #21 at www.ralphkimball.com, verified March 21, 2001.

Martin, J. 1997a. "New Tools for Decision Making." *DM Review* 7 (September): 80.

Martin, J. 1997b. "Web Warehousing." *DM Review* 7 (November): 10.

Meyer, A. 1997. "The Case for Dependent Data Marts." *DM Review* 7 (July/August): 17–24.

Moriarity, T. 1995. "Modeling Data Warehouses." *Database Programming & Design*, 8 (August): 61–65.

Mundy, J. 2001. "Smarter Data Warehouses." *Intelligent Enterprise* (February 16): 24–29.

Poe, V. 1996. *Building a Data Warehouse for Decision Support*. Upper Saddle River, NJ: Prentice-Hall.

Strange, K. 1997. "Can Data Marts Grow?" *CIO* (July): 34, 36.

Weldon, J. L. 1996. "Data Mining and Visualization." *Database Programming & Design* 9 (May): 21–24.

Westerman, P. 2001. *Data Warehousing: Using the Wal-Mart Model*. San Francisco, CA: Morgan Kaufmann.

White, C. 2000. "First Analysis." *Intelligent Enterprise* (June): available from www.intelligententerprise.com.

Williams, J. 1997. "Tools for Traveling Data." *DBMS* 10 (June): 69–76.

Zaitz, J. 1997. "Data Mining Neural Clusters." *DM Review* 7 (July/August): 91, 92.

Further Reading

Bischoff, J., and T. Alexander. 1997. *Data Warehouse: Practical Advice from the Experts*. Upper Saddle River, NJ: Prentice-Hall.

Goodhue, D., M. Mybo, and L. Kirsch. 1992. "The Impact of Data Integration on the Costs and Benefits of Information Systems." *MIS Quarterly* 16 (September): 293–311.

Jenks, B. 1997. "Tiered Data Warehouse." *DM Review* 7 (October): 54–57.

Web Resources

www.teradatareview.com *Teradata Review* magazine contains articles on the technology and application of the NCR Teradata data warehouse system. (This magazine recently changed its name and articles under the new and previous names can be found at www.teradatamagazine.com.)

www.dmreview.com *DM Review* is a monthly trade magazine that contains articles and columns about data warehousing.

www.tdan.com An electrical journal on data warehousing.

www.billinmon.com Bill Inmon is a leading authority on data management and data warehousing.

www.ralphkimball.com Ralph Kimball is a leading authority on data warehousing.

www.dw-institute.com Data warehousing Institute, an industry group that focuses on data warehousing methods and applications.

www.datawarehousing.org Data Warehousing Knowledge Center contains links to many vendors.

www.olapreport.com Detailed information about OLAP products and applications.

MOUNTAIN VIEW COMMUNITY HOSPITAL

Project Case

PROJECT DESCRIPTION

In most respects, Mountain View Community Hospital has followed a carefully planned approach to designing, selecting, and installing its information systems. The organization developed an enterprise data model to guide its database development (see Chapters 3 and 4). The hospital installed computer systems to support most of the routine operations in the organization. For example, there are systems for patient accounting, administrative services, and financial management. Most of these systems were acquired from outside vendors after a careful selection process.

Despite this careful planning, management is aware that there are some deficiencies and limitations in the present hospital information systems. Two typical problems that have been noted are the following:

1. Data are often duplicated in different files and databases, in different formats, and even in different media. For example, one set of patient data (used for billing purposes) resides in a patient accounting system based on a relational database. On the other hand, most patient medical records are maintained in a manual system (one folder per patient).

2. The systems are designed primarily to support operational (or transaction) processing, but are not generally well suited to provide management information or to support analytical studies that are increasingly required for modern hospital management.

The health care industry in general (including hospitals such as Mountain View Community) is being driven by the trend to managed care to gain better and more centralized access to its clinical, operational, and financial information (Griffin, 1997). A typical hospital data warehouse may contain four types of data: patient records; doctor, clinic, and hospital records; drug and pharmaceutical company records; and HMO and insurance company records (Martin, 1997b).

To address these concerns, managers at Mountain View Community Hospital would like to investigate whether the techniques of data warehousing might be successfully applied in their organization. Because the hospital is small, they realize that they could not justify a large-scale data warehouse development project. Nevertheless, they would like to develop a small prototype to test the concept. After some investigation they decide to develop two small prototype data marts:

1. A data mart that will record summary information regarding tests and procedures performed by physicians at the hospital.

2. A more detailed data mart that will record the details of tests and procedures performed by physicians for individual patients.

PROJECT QUESTIONS

1. What are some of the advantages that a hospital such as Mountain View Community might realize from a data warehouse and/or data mart?

2. Suppose that a hospital decides to develop a data mart using a star schema. List several dimensions that you would expect to find represented in this schema.

3. Should Mountain View Community Hospital consider developing a data mart (such as those proposed) without an established data warehouse? What are the risks associated with that approach? Do you think that an organization can develop a prototype data mart to investigate "proof-of-concept," without an established data warehouse? Discuss some of the likely advantages and disadvantages of this approach.

PROJECT EXERCISES

1. Summary data mart.
   a. Design a star schema:

   Physician dimension:
       Physician_ID (pk): 5 bytes
       Physician_Name: 10 bytes
       Specialty: 5 bytes
       Physician_Address: 10 bytes
       Physician_Telephone: 5 bytes

Treatment dimension:

>   Treatment_ID (pk): 3 bytes
>   Treatment_Description: 6 bytes

Period dimension:

>   Period_ID (pk): 2 bytes
>   Month: 1 byte
>   Year: 2 bytes

Treatment (fact) table:

>   Grain: monthly summary of treatments and average treatment costs, by physician and treatment
>   Monthly_Total: 3 bytes
>   Average_Cost: 5 bytes

b. Calculate the expected number of rows in the fact table and its estimated size (bytes).

Assumptions:

1. Treatments: approximately 500 *different* treatments are performed at the hospital. During a typical month, approximately 30 percent (or 150 different treatments) are performed.
2. Physicians: each treatment is performed by one physician.
3. Periods: If a full-scale data mart is developed, it is anticipated that 36 periods (or 3 years) of data will be accumulated.

2. Detailed data mart.

   a. Design a star schema.

   Physician dimension: same as above

   Treatment dimension: same as above

   Period dimension:

   >   Period_ID (pk): 3 bytes
   >   Date: 5 bytes

Patient dimension:

>   Patient_ID (pk): 5 bytes
>   Patient_Name: 10 bytes
>   Patient_Address: 10 bytes
>   Patient_Telephone: 5 bytes

Treatment (fact) table:

>   Grain: detail for each treatment occurrence administered to a patient by a physician
>   Treatment_Cost: 4 bytes
>   Treatment_Result: 20 bytes
>   Doctors_Order: 10 bytes

b. Calculate the expected number of rows in the fact table and its estimated size (bytes).

Assumptions:

1. Treatments. An average of 200 total treatments are performed for patients on a given day (this is based on an average patient census of 200, and an average of two treatments per patient per day).
2. Patients. Each treatment is performed for one patient. To simplify matters, assume that a given treatment may only be performed once by a given physician and for a particular patient on a given day.
3. Physicians. Each treatment is performed by one physician.
4. Periods. If a full-scale data mart is developed, it is anticipated that approximately 1000 days (nearly three years) of data will be collected.

c. Why is it necessary to assume that a given treatment may be performed only once by a given physician for a given patient on a given day? Suggest a way to overcome this limitation.

Part FIVE

Advanced Database Topics

An   Overview   of   Part   F I V E

Parts II through IV have prepared you to develop useful and efficient databases. Part V introduces some additional, important database design and management issues. These issues include database security, backup, and recovery; controlling concurrent access to data; preserving data quality; advanced topics in database performance tuning; and two of the most actively discussed database topics today—distributed databases and object-oriented databases. Following Part V are four appendices, covering alternative E-R notations, advanced normal forms (supplementing Chapter 5), data structures (supplementing Chapter 6), and the object-relational data model (complementing Chapters 5 and 14).

You are likely to conclude from reading this text that data are a corporate asset, just as personnel, physical resources, and financial resources are corporate assets. As such, data and information are resources that are too valuable to be managed casually. In Chapter 12 (Data and Database Administration) you will learn about the critical information resource management activities of data and database administration. You will learn the meaning of concurrency control, deadlock, encryption, information repository, locking, recovery, system catalog, transaction, and versioning. You will learn about the role of both

- a *data administrator*—the person who takes overall responsibility for data, metadata, and policies about data use, and

- a *database administrator*—the person who is responsible for physical database design and for dealing with the technical issues, such as security enforcement, database performance, and backup and recovery, associated with managing a database.

Data and database administration activities occur throughout the database development process. A data administrator plays a stronger role during early stages of database development and in the overall planning of data resources. A database administrator plays a stronger role during physical database design, implementation, and operation.

In larger organizations, databases may be distributed across multiple computers and locations. Special issues arise when an organization tries to manage distributed data as one database rather than many decentralized, separate databases. In Chapter 13 (Distributed Databases) you learn about homogeneous and heterogeneous distributed databases, the objectives and trade-offs for distributed databases, and several alternative architectures for such databases. You learn about the important concept of data replication and partitioning and how to synchronize multiple instances of the same data across a distributed database. You also study the special features of a distributed DBMS, including distributed transaction controls (such as commit protocols). There is a review of the evolution of distributed DBMSs and of the range of distributed DBMS products.

Chapter 14 (Object-Oriented Data Modeling) introduces an alternative to E-R modeling. Object-oriented models of data and other system aspects are becoming increasingly popular because of their ability to represent complex ideas using highly related modeling notations. This chapter uses the Unified Modeling Language (UML), a standard in this field. In the UML, an object is an entity that has three properties: state, behavior, and identity. The behavior of an object is determined by one or more operations that are encapsulated in the object. Associations, generalization, inheritance, and polymorphism are important concepts. This chapter presents an object-oriented version (in the form of a class diagram) of the Pine Valley Furniture case from Chapter 3.

Chapter 15 (Object-Oriented Database Development) demonstrates the transformation of class diagrams into schemas that can be implemented using object database management systems (ODBMSs). The object definition language (ODL) and object query language (OQL) are introduced. You learn how to create object-oriented database definitions in the ODL, including how to define objects, attributes, operations, and relationships; and the basics of the SQL-like OQL, including single- and multiple-table queries.

Chapter **12**

Data and Database Administration

LEARNING OBJECTIVES

After studying this chapter, you should be able to:

- Define the following key terms: **data administration, database administration, database security, encryption, database recovery, transaction, concurrency control, locking, deadlock, versioning, system catalog,** and **information repository**.

- List several major functions of data administration and of database administration.

- Describe the changing roles of the data administrator and database administrator in the current business environment.

- Describe the role of data dictionaries and information repositories and how they are used by data administration.

- Compare the optimistic and pessimistic systems of concurrency control.

- Describe the problem of database security, and list five techniques that are used to enhance security.

- Describe the problem of database recovery, and list four basic facilities that are included with a DBMS to recover databases.

- Describe the problem of tuning a database to achieve better performance, and list five areas where changes may be made when tuning a database.

INTRODUCTION

The critical importance of data to organizations is now recognized. Data are a corporate asset, just as personnel, physical resources, and financial resources are corporate assets. As such, data and information are resources that are too valuable to be managed casually. The development of information technology has made effective management of corporate data far more possible. Data administration activities have been developed to help achieve organizations' goals for the effective management of data. Effective data administration provides support for managerial decision making at all levels in the organization.

Ineffective data administration, on the other hand, leads to poor data utilization, and can be characterized by the following conditions, which are all too common in organizations:

1. Multiple definitions of the same data entity and/or inconsistent representations of the same data elements in separate databases, making integration of data across different databases hazardous.

2. Missing key data elements, whose loss eliminates the value of existing data.

3. Low data quality levels due to inappropriate sources of data or timing of data transfers from one system to another, thus reducing the reliability of the data.

4. Inadequate familiarity with existing data, including awareness of data location and meaning of stored data, thus reducing the capability to use the data to make effective strategic or planning decisions.

5. Poor and inconsistent query response time, excessive database downtime, and either stringent or inadequate controls to ensure agreed upon data privacy and security.

Organizations have responded to these data utilization issues with different strategies. Some have created a function called **data administration**. The person who heads this function is called the data administrator, or information resource manager, and takes responsibility for the overall management of data resources. A second function, that of **database administration**, has been regarded as responsible for physical database design and for dealing with the technical issues, such as security enforcement, database performance, and backup and recovery, associated with managing a database. Other organizations combine the data administration and database administration functions. The rapidly changing pace of business has caused the roles of the data administrator and the database administrator (DBA) to change, in ways that are discussed below.

Data administration: A high-level function that is responsible for the overall management of data resources in an organization, including maintaining corporate-wide definitions and standards.

Database administration: A technical function that is responsible for physical database design and for dealing with technical issues, such as security enforcement, database performance, and backup and recovery.

THE ROLES OF DATA AND DATABASE ADMINISTRATORS

Two factors are driving the changes in the data administration and database administration roles: the availability of more technologies and platforms that must be managed concurrently at many organizations, and the increased pace of business changes (Quinlan, 1996). Against the background of these changes, it is important to understand traditional role distinctions. This will help us to understand the ways in which the roles are being blended in organizations that have different information technology architectures.

Traditional Data Administration

Databases are shared resources that belong to the entire enterprise; they are not the property of a single function or individual within the organization. Data administration is the custodian of the organization's data, in much the same sense that the controller is custodian of the financial resources. Like the controller, the data administrator must develop procedures to protect and control the resource. Also, data administration must resolve disputes that may arise when data are centralized and shared among users, and must play a significant role in deciding where data will be stored and managed. Data administration is a high-level function that is responsible for the overall management of data resources in an organization, including maintaining corporate-wide data definitions and standards.

Data administration is responsible for a wide range of functions, including database planning, analysis, design, implementation, maintenance, and protection. Data administration is also responsible for establishing procedures for improving database performance and for providing education, training, and consulting support to users. The data administrator must interact with top management, users, and computer applications specialists.

Selecting the data administrator and organizing the function are extremely important. The data administrator must be a highly skilled manager capable of resolving differences that normally arise when significant change is introduced into an organization. The data administrator should be a respected, senior-level manager selected from within the organization, rather than a technical computer expert or a new individual hired for the position.

The manager of the data administration function requires a high level of both managerial and technical skills. On the one hand, this person must be capable of eliciting the cooperation of users, who may resist the idea of giving up their private data to a shared database. Also, these users must be convinced of the benefits of adhering to a set of standard definitions and procedures for accessing the database. On the other hand, the data administrator must be capable of managing a technical staff who deal with issues such as query optimization and concurrency control.

Traditional Database Administration

Typically, the role of database administration is taken to be a more hands-on, physical involvement with the management of a database or databases. Database administration is a technical function that is responsible for physical database design and for dealing with technical issues, such as security enforcement, database performance, and backup and recovery. The database administrator should be involved in every phase of database development, from database planning through the analysis, design, and implementation stages, and on through operation, maintenance, and modification. The DBA carries through the standards and procedures established by the data administrator, including enforcing programming standards, data standards, policies, and procedures. In organizations where there is not a separate database administration function, the DBA also assumes the responsibilities of the data administrator.

Just as the data administrator needs a wide variety of job skills, so does the DBA. A broad technical background, including a sound understanding of current hardware architectures and capabilities and a solid understanding of data processing, is essential. An understanding of the database development life cycle, including traditional and prototyping approaches, is also necessary. Strong design and data modeling skills are essential at the conceptual, logical, and physical levels. But managerial skills are also critical; the DBA must manage other information systems (IS) personnel as the database is analyzed, designed, and implemented, and the DBA must also interact with and provide support for the end users who are involved with the design and use of the database.

Evolving Approaches to Data and Database Administration

There are no universally accepted data administration and database administration structures, and organizations vary widely in their approaches to data administration. As business practices change, the roles are also changing within organizations. There is, however, a core set of data and database administration functions that must be met in every organization, regardless of the organization structure they have chosen. These functions may be spread across data administrators and database administrators, or at the other extreme, all of these functions may be handled by a single person. Some of the functions are organization-level functions, and those tend to be classed as data administration functions in organizations that distinguish between data administration and database administration. Other functions are much more specific to a database or application, and they tend to be classed as database administration functions. In any case, though, effective data and database administration today requires that the following functions be addressed:

- *Data policies, procedures, and standards*   Every database application requires protection established through consistent enforcement of data policies, procedures, and standards. Data policies are statements that make explicit the goals of data administration, such as, "Every user must have a password." Data procedures are written outlines of actions to be taken in order to perform a certain activity. Backup and recovery procedures, for example, should be communicated to all involved employees. Data standards are explicit conventions and behaviors that are to be followed and that can be used to help evaluate database quality. Naming conventions for database objects should be standardized for programmers, for example. Also, increased use of external data sources and increased access to organizational databases from outside the organization have increased the importance of employees' understanding of data policies, procedures, and standards.

- *Planning*   A key administration function is involvement with the development of the organization's information architecture. Effective administration requires both the understanding of the needs of the organization for information and the ability to contribute to the development of an information architecture that will meet the diverse needs of the typical organization. It is crucial that those involved in data and database administration understand the information requirements of the organization and be able to contribute to the development of the information architecture that will meet those needs.

- *Data conflict resolution*   Databases are intended to be shared, and usually involve data from several different departments of the organization. Ownership of data is a ticklish issue at least occasionally in every organization. Those in data and database administration are well placed to resolve data ownership issues because they are not typically associated with a certain department. Establishing procedures for resolving such conflicts is essential. If the administration function has been given sufficient authority to mediate and enforce the resolution of the conflict, they may be very effective in this capacity.

- *Internal marketing*   While the importance of data and information to the organization has become more widely recognized within the organization, it is not necessarily true that an appreciation for data standards has also evolved. The importance of following established procedures and policies must be proactively instituted through data and database administrators. Effective internal marketing may reduce resistance to change and data ownership problems.

- *Managing the information repository*   Repositories contain the metadata that describe an organization's data and data processing resources. Information repositories are replacing data dictionaries in many organizations. While data dictionaries are simple data-element documentation tools, information repositories are used by data administrators and other information specialists to manage the total information-processing environment. The repository is an essential tool for data and database administration and is used throughout the entire database system life cycle. An information repository serves as a source of information for each of the following:

  1. Users who must understand data definitions, business rules, and relationships among data objects

  2. Automated CASE tools that are used to specify and develop information systems

  3. Applications that access and manipulate data (or business information) in the corporate databases

  4. Database management systems, which maintain the repository and update system privileges, passwords, object definitions, etc.

- *Selection of hardware and software*   The evaluation and selection of hardware and software is critical to an organization's success. The increasingly rapid development of new hardware and software and the rapid change within organizations creates a very demanding situation. A vendor's database that is the most appropriate product available when the choice of platform is made may turn out to be an unfortunate choice if a competitor releases a new version that has different and more appropriate functionality. The current vendor may even go out of business, resulting in a production database that is a nightmare to maintain. Data and database administrators are being expected to know more about hardware architectures and to be able to administer both in-house-developed applications and off-the-shelf applications, as organizations strive to meet their information needs more rapidly.

- *Installing and upgrading the DBMS*   Once the DBMS is selected, it must be installed. Before installation, benchmarks of the workload against the database on a computer supplied by the DBMS vendor should be run. Benchmarking anticipates issues that must be addressed during the actual installation. (Benchmarking may also be used during hardware and software selection to compare competing products.) A DBMS installation can be a complex process of making sure all the correct versions of different modules are in place, all the proper device drivers are present, and the DBMS works correctly with any third-party software products. DBMS vendors periodically update package modules; planning for, testing, and installing upgrades to ensure existing applications still work properly can be time-consuming and intricate. Once the DBMS is installed, user accounts must be created and maintained.

- *Tuning database performance*   Because databases are dynamic, it is improbable that the initial design of the database will be sufficient to achieve the best processing performance for the life of the database. The performance of the database (query and update processing time as well as data storage utilization) needs to be constantly monitored. The design of a database must be frequently changed to meet new requirements and to overcome the degrading effects of many content updates. Periodically, the database must be rebuilt, reorganized, and reindexed to recover wasted space, to correct poor data allocation and fragmentation across storage devices, to allocate different buffer space for concurrent processing, and to reset parameters that define the best recovery procedures. Various system tables, needed by the DBMS but not containing business data, periodically need to be rebuilt to be consistent with the new size and use of the database.

- *Improving database query processing performance*   The workload against a database most certainly will expand over time as more users find more ways to use the growing amount of data in a database. Thus, some queries, which originally ran quickly against a small database, may need to be rewritten in a more efficient form to run in a satisfactory time against a fully populated database. Indexes may need to be added or deleted to balance performance across all queries. Data may need to be relocated to different devices to allow better concurrent processing of queries and updates. Arguably, the vast majority of the time spent by a DBA will be for tuning database performance and improving database query processing time.

- *Managing data security, privacy, and integrity*   Protecting the security, privacy, and integrity of the organizational databases rests with the database administration function. More detailed explanations of the ways in which privacy, security, and integrity are assured are included later in the chapter. Here it is important to realize that the advent of the Internet and intranets to which databases are attached, along with the possibilities for distributing data and databases to multiple sites, have complicated the management of data security, privacy, and integrity.

- *Data backup and recovery*   The DBA must ensure that backup procedures are established that will allow the recovery of all necessary data, should a loss occur through application failure, hardware failure, physical or electrical disaster, or human error or malfeasance. Common backup and recovery strategies are also discussed later in this chapter. These strategies must be fully tested and evaluated at regular intervals.

Reviewing these data and database administration functions should convince any reader of the importance of proper data administration, both at the organizational and the project level. Failure to take the proper steps can greatly reduce an organization's ability to operate effectively, and may even result in its going out of business. Pressures to reduce application development time must always be reviewed to be sure that necessary quality is not being forgone in order to react more quickly, for such shortcuts are likely to have very serious repercussions. Figure 12-1 shows how data and database administration functions are typically viewed with respect to systems development phases.

Evolving Approaches to Data Administration

Many organizations now have blended the data administration and database administration roles together. These organizations emphasize the capability to build a database quickly, tuning it for maximum performance, and being able to restore it to production quickly when problems develop. These databases are more likely to be departmental, client/server databases that are developed quickly using newer development approaches such as prototyping, which allow changes to be made more quickly. The blending of data administration and database administration roles also means that DBAs in such organizations must be able to create and enforce data standards and policies. DBAs in such environments are expected to deliver high-quality, robust systems quickly. Across all organizations, database administrators will be expected to maintain required quality levels while decreasing the time required to build a reliable system. Quinlan (1996) has suggested some changes in data administration and database administration practices that can be made at each stage of the traditional database development life cycle to accomplish these goals:

- *Database planning*   Improve selection of technology by selectively evaluating possible products. Be sure to consider each technology's fit with the enterprise data model, seeking to find ways to reduce time required in later stages as a result of careful selection of technology at the database planning stage.

- *Database analysis*   Try to work on physical design in parallel with development of the logical and physical models. Prototyping the application now may well lead to changes in the logical and physical data models earlier in the development process.

- *Database design*   Prioritize application transactions by volume, importance, and complexity. These transactions are going to be most critical to the application. Specifications for them should be reviewed as quickly as the transactions are developed. Logical data modeling, physical database modeling, and prototyping may occur in parallel. DBAs should strive to provide adequate control of the database environment while allowing the developers space and opportunity to experiment.

- *Database implementation*   Institute database change-control procedures so that development and implementation are supported rather than slowed. Wherever possible, segment the model into modules that can be analyzed and implemented more quickly. Find ways to test the system more quickly without compromising quality. Testing may be moved earlier in the development; use testing and change control tools to build and manage the test and production environments.

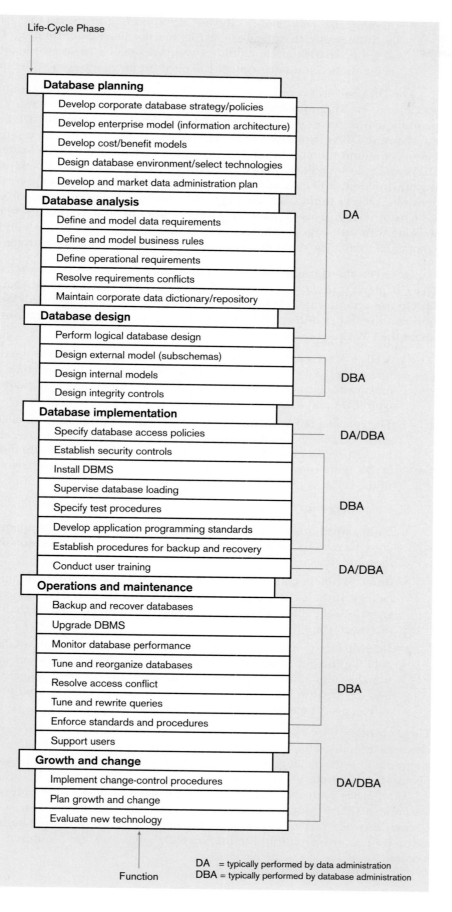

Figure 12-1
Functions of data administration and database administration

Life-Cycle Phase

Database planning
- Develop corporate database strategy/policies
- Develop enterprise model (information architecture)
- Develop cost/benefit models
- Design database environment/select technologies
- Develop and market data administration plan

Database analysis
- Define and model data requirements
- Define and model business rules
- Define operational requirements
- Resolve requirements conflicts
- Maintain corporate data dictionary/repository

Database design
- Perform logical database design
- Design external model (subschemas)
- Design internal models
- Design integrity controls

Database implementation
- Specify database access policies
- Establish security controls
- Install DBMS
- Supervise database loading
- Specify test procedures
- Develop application programming standards
- Establish procedures for backup and recovery
- Conduct user training

Operations and maintenance
- Backup and recover databases
- Upgrade DBMS
- Monitor database performance
- Tune and reorganize databases
- Resolve access conflict
- Tune and rewrite queries
- Enforce standards and procedures
- Support users

Growth and change
- Implement change-control procedures
- Plan growth and change
- Evaluate new technology

DA

DBA

DA/DBA

DBA

DA/DBA

DBA

DA/DBA

Function

DA = typically performed by data administration
DBA = typically performed by database administration

- *Operation and maintenance* Review all timesaving measures that have been taken to ensure that database quality has not been compromised. Consider using third-party tools and utilities wherever possible to save work; other tools such as Lotus Notes may reduce the need for meetings, thus saving time.

The DBA role will continue to evolve. Most see the DBA role as becoming more specialized, evolving into specialties such as distributed database/network capacity planning DBAs, server programming DBAs, off-the-shelf customizing DBAs, or data warehousing DBAs (Dowgiallo et al., 1997). The ability to work with multiple databases, communication protocols, and operating systems will be highly valued. Those DBAs who gain broad experience and develop the ability to adapt quickly to changing environments will have many opportunities. It is possible that some current DBA activities, such as tuning, will be replaced by decision support systems able to tune systems by analyzing usage patterns. Opportunities in large companies to continue working with very large databases (VLDBs) and opportunities in small and midsize companies to manage desktop and midrange servers should remain strong.

Data Warehouse Administration The significant growth in data warehousing (see Chapter 11) in the past five years has caused a new role to emerge, that of a data warehouse administrator (DWA). Inmon (1999) in several articles on his Website has outlined the duties of the DWA. As you might expect, two generalizations are true about the DWA role:

1. A DWA plays many of the same roles as do DAs and DBAs for the data warehouse and data mart databases for the purpose of supporting decision-making applications (rather than transaction-processing applications for the typical DA and DBA).

2. The role of a DWA emphasizes integration and coordination of metadata and data (extraction agreements, operational data stores, enterprise data warehouses) across many data sources, not necessarily the standardization of data across these separately managed data sources outside the control and scope of the DWA.

Specifically, Inmon suggests that a DWA has a unique charter to:

- Build and administer an environment supportive of decision-support applications; thus, a DWA is more concerned with time to make a decision than query response time.

- Build a stable architecture for the data warehouse—a corporate information factory; thus, a DWA is more concerned with the effect of data warehouse growth (scalability in the amount of data and number of users) than redesigning existing applications.

- Develop service level agreements with suppliers and consumers of data for the data warehouse; thus, a DWA works more closely with end users and operational system administrators to coordinate vastly different objectives and to oversee the development of new applications (data marts, ETL procedures, and analytical services) than do DAs and DBAs.

These responsibilities are in addition to the responsibilities typical of any data or database administrator, such as selecting technologies, communicating with users about data needs, making performance and capacity decisions, and budgeting and planning data warehouse requirements.

Inmon has estimated that every 100 gigabytes of data in the enterprise data warehouse (EDW) necessitates another DWA. Another metric is that a DWA is needed for each year of data kept in the EDW. The use of custom-built tools for extraction/transformation/loading usually increases the number of DWAs needed.

Data warehouse administrators typically report through the IT unit of an organization, but have strong relationships to marketing and other business areas that depend on the EDW for applications, such as customer or supplier relationship management, sales analysis, channel management, and other analytical applications. DWAs should not be part of traditional systems development organizations, as are many DBAs, because data warehousing applications are developed differently from operational systems and need to be viewed as independent from any particular operational system. Alternatively, DWAs can be placed in the primary end-user organization for the EDW, but this runs the risk of creating many data warehouses or marts, rather than leading to a true, scalable EDW.

MODELING ENTERPRISE DATA

In the current business environment DBAs are pressured to adapt to change while providing high-quality systems quickly. Key to achieving these expectations is developing an enterprise architecture or Information Systems Architecture, as described briefly in Chapter 2. The author of ISA (Zachman, 1987) sees the development of information systems to be similar to other complex product development and manufacturing processes. He has studied those processes in order to apply their principles and procedures to development of an information systems enterprise architecture. Building an enterprise architecture enables an organization to make the step from business strategy to implementation more effectively. Zachman (1997, p. 48) defines an enterprise architecture as "that set of descriptive representations (that is, models) that are relevant for describing an enterprise such that it (the enterprise) can be produced to management's requirements (quality) and maintained over the period of its useful life (change)."

All too often in systems development, the enterprise view has been de-emphasized as developers concentrated on building a piece of the enterprise system. It has often been problematic to fit these pieces together into a smoothly functioning enterprise system. Some systems are no longer relevant when completed, or do not remain relevant for long. System maintenance is a major portion of the overall cost of a new system. Problems such as the Year 2000 problem, estimated by the Gartner Group to have cost $400 billion worldwide, arise from past failures to address data element definitions within the enterprise architecture.

Ideally, every database development project should fit within the enterprise architecture. This means developing conceptual data models that are congruent with the needs of the business and that are then translated into logical data models, physical data models, and implemented systems. Such congruence has been clearly promoted and is a part of every database design life cycle. But the conceptual data models must also fit across Zachman's framework, meshing with the business process model, business network logistics, work flow models within the enterprise, the enterprise master schedule, and the enterprise business plan. Each component, such as the conceptual data model, has an architectural structure of its own, but it must also fit with the architectural structures of the other components of the framework. The enterprise-wide impacts of execution of each component must be considered, and problems and discontinuities resolved.

Organizations that articulate an enterprise architecture and develop standards and procedures to ensure that systems development projects fit within that enterprise architecture should experience benefits. Code can be reused, systems mesh together rather than conflicting with each other, and business objectives are met. As the articulation and incorporation of business rules becomes more sophisticated, those organizations with an articulated enterprise architecture should be able to implement those business rules more consistently and more quickly than similar organizations who have not developed an enterprise architecture. Such possibilities provide obvious strategic benefits to organizations in today's competitive environment.

PLANNING FOR DATABASES

The initial phase of the database development life cycle is planning. It is at this point that a proposed system should be carefully considered from the viewpoint of the enterprise architecture. Database design occurs within the constraints of the enterprise information system. During the planning phase, an initial assessment of the proposed database system is made. The proposed system should contribute to meeting the business's goals and strategies, which have been developed as part of the enterprise architecture. The other components of the Scope layer in the enterprise architecture are also important:

- What data will be included? Have they previously been identified as being important to the business?
- What processes will the system perform? Have these processes been identified as important organization processes?
- What business locations will the system affect? Should the locations identified be affected by such as system, or have some locations that will be unintentionally affected been identified?
- Which work units and people will use and be affected by the system, and what is the nature of these effects? What effects on work units beyond the work unit requesting the new system have been identified?
- How will the system fit with significant business events? Will the new system fit with existing schedules?
- How much data will be kept in the database? What is the size and capacity of the hardware needed to support the applications? Do candidate DBMS easily scale as the database grows after installation (i.e., will the DBMS support more users, more applications, larger files, etc., without significant database redesign or hardware changes)?

The initial assessment will also include consideration of continuing use of the existing system, modifying the existing system, or replacing the existing system. The decision will rest with the extent to which flaws in the current system exist, and the possibilities for correcting those flaws.

If a new system is a possibility, then a feasibility study should be conducted. The feasibility study should address the technical aspects of the project, including hardware and software purchase or development costs, operating environment, system size and complexity, and level of experience with similar systems. At this point it is not necessary to identify particular vendors or products, but classes of implementation, such as PC or mainframe hardware, database model, and programming language should be considered. The feasibility study should also address the estimated costs of the project, both tangible and intangible. Costs should be identified as one-time costs associated with the project or recurring costs that will continue throughout the life of the system. Operational feasibility, an assessment of the likelihood that the project will meet its expected objectives, should also be determined. The likelihood of completing the project within the expected time schedule should also be estimated. Any potential legal or contractual problems should be identified now. And, political implications of the project should be considered. Key stakeholder support for the project will greatly improve its prospects of success.

Once the feasibility information has been collected, a formal review of the project that includes all interested parties can be conducted. The focus of this review is to verify all information and assumptions in the baseline plan that has been developed before moving ahead with the project. After the project is approved, problems defined during the planning phase will be studied further during the analysis phase of the project.

MANAGING DATA SECURITY

The goal of **database security** is the protection of data from accidental or intentional threats to its integrity and access. The database environment has grown more complex, with distributed databases located on client/server architectures rather than mainframes. Access to data has become more open through the Internet and corporate intranets. As a result, managing data security effectively has become more difficult and time consuming. Some security procedures for client/server and Web-based systems were introduced in Chapter 9. Data administration is responsible for developing overall policies and procedures to protect databases. The facilities that data administrators have to use in establishing adequate data security are discussed below, but first it is important to review potential threats to data security.

Database security: Protection of the data against accidental or intentional loss, destruction, or misuse.

Threats to Data Security

Threats to data security may be direct threats to the database. For example, those who gain unauthorized access to a database may then browse, change, or even steal the data to which they have gained access. Focusing on database security alone, however, will not ensure a secure database. All parts of the system must be secure, including the database, the network, the operating system, the building(s) in which the database resides physically, and the personnel who have any opportunity to access the system. Figure 12-2 diagrams many of the possible locations for data security threats. Accomplishing this level of security requires careful review, establishment of

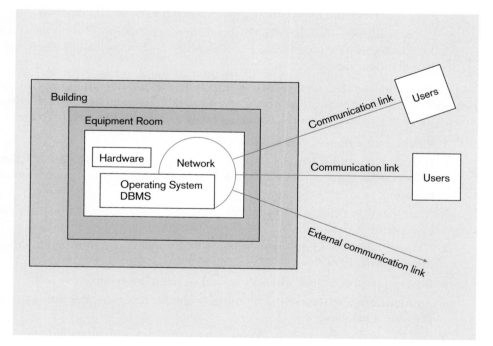

Figure 12-2
Possible locations of data security threats

security procedures and policies, and implementation and enforcement of those procedures and policies. The following threats must be addressed in a comprehensive data security plan:

- *Accidental losses, including human error, software, and hardware-caused breaches* Establishing operating procedures such as user authorization, uniform software installation procedures, and hardware maintenance schedules are examples of actions that may be taken to address threats from accidental losses. As in any effort that involves human beings, some losses are inevitable, but well thought out policies and procedures should reduce the amount and severity of losses. Of potentially more serious consequence are the threats that are not accidental.

- *Theft and fraud* These activities are going to be perpetrated by people, quite possibly through electronic means, and may or may not alter data. Attention here should focus on each possible location shown in Figure 12-2. For example, control of physical security, so that unauthorized personnel are not able to gain access to the machine room, should be established. Data access policies that restrict altering data immediately prior to a payroll run will help to secure the data. Establishment of a firewall to protect unauthorized access to inappropriate parts of the database through outside communication links is another example of a security procedure that will hamper people who are intent on theft or fraud.

- *Loss of privacy or confidentiality* Loss of privacy is usually taken to mean loss of protection of data about individuals, while loss of confidentiality is usually taken to mean loss of protection of critical organizational data, which may have strategic value to the organization. Failure to control privacy of information may lead to blackmail, bribery, public embarrassment, or stealing of user passwords. Failure to control confidentiality may lead to loss of competitiveness. State and federal laws now exist to require some types of organizations to create and communicate policies to ensure privacy of customer and client data. Security mechanisms must enforce these policies, and failure to do so can mean significant financial and reputation loss.

- *Loss of data integrity* When data integrity is compromised, data will be invalid or corrupted. Unless data integrity can be restored through established backup and recovery procedures, an organization may suffer serious losses or make incorrect and expensive decisions based on the invalid data.

- *Loss of availability* Sabotage of hardware, networks, or applications may cause the data to become unavailable to users, which again may lead to severe operational difficulties.

A comprehensive data security plan will include establishing administrative policies and procedures, physical protections, and data management software protections. The most important security features of data management software follow:

1. Views or subschemas, which restrict user views of the database
2. Domains, assertions, checks, and other integrity controls defined as database objects, which are enforced by the DBMS during database querying and updating
3. Authorization rules, which identify users and restrict the actions they may take against a database
4. User-defined procedures, which define additional constraints or limitations in using a database
5. Encryption procedures, which encode data in an unrecognizable form
6. Authentication schemes, which positively identify a person attempting to gain access to a database
7. Backup, journaling, and checkpointing capabilities, which facilitate recovery procedures

Views

In Chapter 7 we defined a view as a subset of the database that is presented to one or more users. A view is created by querying one or more of the base tables, producing a dynamic result table for the user at the time of the request. Thus, a view is always based on the current data in the base tables that it is built from. The advantage of a view is that it can be built to present only the data to which the user requires access, effectively preventing the user from viewing other data that may be private or confidential. The user may be granted the right to access the view, but not to access the base tables upon which the view is based. So, confining a user to a view may be more restrictive for that user than allowing him access to the involved base tables.

For example, we could build a view for a Pine Valley employee that provides information about materials needed to build a Pine Valley furniture product without providing other information, such as unit price, that is not relevant to the employee's work. This command creates a view that will list the wood required and the wood available for each product:

```
CREATE VIEW MATERIALS_V
     AS
     SELECT PRODUCT_T.PRODUCT_ID, PRODUCT_NAME, FOOTAGE,
     FOOTAGE_ON_HAND
          FROM PRODUCT_T, RAW_MATERIALS_T, USES_T
               WHERE PRODUCT_T.PRODUCT_ID = USES_T.PRODUCT_ID
               AND RAW_MATERIALS_T.MATERIAL_ID =
               USES_T.MATERIAL_ID;
```

The contents of the view created will be updated each time the view is accessed, but here are the current contents of the view, which can be accessed with the SQL command

```
SELECT * FROM MATERIALS_V;
```

PRODUCT_ID	PRODUCT_NAME	FOOTAGE	FOOTAGE_ON_HAND
1	End Table	4	1
2	Coffee Table	6	11
3	Computer Desk	15	11
4	Entertainment Center	20	84
5	Writer's Desk	13	68
6	8-Drawer Desk	16	66
7	Dining Table	16	11
8	Computer Desk	15	9

8 rows selected.

The user can write SELECT statements against the view, treating it as though it were a table. Although views promote security by restricting user access to data, they are not adequate security measures, because unauthorized persons may gain knowledge of or access to a particular view. Also, several persons may share a particular view; all may have authority to read the data, but only a restricted few may be authorized to update the data. Finally, with high-level query languages, an unauthorized person may gain access to data through simple experimentation. As a result, more sophisticated security measures are normally required.

Integrity Controls

Integrity controls protect data from unauthorized use and update. Often integrity controls limit the values a field may hold, limit the actions that can be performed on data, or trigger the execution of some procedure, such as placing an entry in a log to record which users have done what with which data.

One form of integrity control is a domain. In essence, a domain is a way to create a user-defined data type. Once a domain is defined, any field can be given that domain as its data type. For example, the following PriceChange domain (defined in SQL) can be used as the data type of any database field, such as PriceIncrease and PriceDiscount, to limit the amount standard prices can be augmented in one transaction:

```
CREATE DOMAIN PriceChange AS DECIMAL
    CHECK (VALUE BETWEEN .001 and .15);
```

Then, in the definition of, say, a pricing transaction table, we might have

```
PriceIncrease PriceChange NOT NULL,
```

One advantage of a domain is that, if it ever has to change, it can be changed in one place—the domain definition—and all fields with this domain will be changed automatically. Alternatively, the same CHECK clause could be included in a constraint on both the PriceIncrease and PriceDiscount fields, but in this case if the limits of the check were to change, a DBA would have to find every instance of this integrity control and change it in each place separately.

Assertions are powerful constraints that enforce certain desirable database conditions. Assertions are checked automatically by the DBMS when transactions are run involving tables or fields on which assertions exist. For example, assume that an employee table has fields of EmpID, EmpName, SupervisorID, and SpouseID. Suppose that a company rule is that no employee may supervise his or her spouse. The following assertion enforces this rule:

```
CREATE ASSERTION SpousalSupervision
    CHECK (SupervisorID <> SpouseID);
```

If the assertion fails, the DBMS will generate an error message.

Assertions can become rather complex. Suppose that Pine Valley Furniture has a rule that no two salespersons can be assigned to the same territory at the same time. Suppose a Salesperson table includes fields of SalespersonID and TerritoryID. This assertion can be written using a correlated subquery as

```
CREATE ASSERTION TerritoryAssignment
    CHECK (NOT EXISTS
        (SELECT * FROM Salesperson SP WHERE SP.TerritoryID IN
            (SELECT SPP.TerritoryID FROM Salesperson SSP WHERE
                SSP.SalespersonID <> SP.SalespersonID)));
```

Finally, triggers can be used for security purposes. Triggers were defined and illustrated in Chapter 8. A trigger, which includes an event, condition, and action, is potentially more complex than an assertion. For example, a trigger can do the following:

- Prohibit inappropriate actions (e.g., changing a salary value outside of the normal business day)
- Cause special handling procedures to be executed (e.g., if a customer invoice payment is received after some due date, a penalty can be added to the account balance for that customer)
- Cause a row to be written to a log file to echo important information about the user and a transaction being made to sensitive data, so that the log can be reviewed by human or automated procedures for possible inappropriate behavior (e.g., the log can record which user initiated a salary change for which employee)

As with domains, a powerful benefit of a trigger, like any stored procedure, is that the DBMS enforces these controls for all users and all database activities. The control does not have to be coded into each query or program. Thus, individual users and programs cannot circumvent the necessary controls.

Subject	Object	Action	Constraint
Sales Dept.	Customer record	Insert	Credit limit LE $5000
Order trans.	Customer record	Read	None
Terminal 12	Customer record	Modify	Balance due only
Acctg. Dept.	Order record	Delete	None
Ann Walker	Order record	Insert	Order amt LT $2000
Program AR4	Order record	Modify	None

Figure 12-3
Authorization matrix

Authorization Rules

Authorization rules are controls incorporated in the data management system that restrict access to data and also restrict the actions that people may take when they access data. For example, a person who can supply a particular password may be authorized to read any record in a database but cannot necessarily modify any of those records.

Fernandez, Summers, and Wood (1981) have developed a conceptual model of database security. Their model expresses authorization rules in the form of a table (or matrix) that includes subjects, objects, actions, and constraints. Each row of the table indicates that a particular subject is authorized to take a certain action on an object in the database, perhaps subject to some constraint. Figure 12-3 shows an example of such an authorization matrix. This table contains several entries pertaining to records in an accounting database. For example, the first row in the table indicates that anyone in the Sales Department is authorized to insert a new customer record in the database, provided that the customer's credit limit does not exceed $5,000. The last row indicates that the program AR4 is authorized to modify order records without restriction. Data administration is responsible for determining and implementing authorization rules that are implemented at the database level. Authorization schemes can also be implemented at the operating system level or the application level.

Most contemporary database management systems do not implement an authorization matrix such as the one shown in Figure 12-3; they normally use simplified versions. There are two principal types: authorization tables for subjects and authorization tables for objects. Figure 12-4 shows an example of each type. In Figure 12-4a, for example, we see that salespersons are allowed to modify customer records but not delete these records. In Figure 12-4b, we see that users in Order Entry or

Authorization rules: Controls incorporated in the data management systems that restrict access to data and also restrict the actions that people may take when they access data.

	Customer records	Order records
Read	Y	Y
Insert	Y	Y
Modify	Y	N
Delete	N	N

Figure 12-4
Implementing authorization rules
(a) Authorization table for subjects (salespersons)

	Salespersons (password BATMAN)	Order entry (password JOKER)	Accounting (password TRACY)
Read	Y	Y	Y
Insert	N	Y	N
Modify	N	Y	Y
Delete	N	N	Y

(b) Authorization table for objects (order records)

Figure 12-5
Oracle8i privileges

Privilege	Capability
SELECT	Query the object.
INSERT	Insert records into the table/view.
	Can be given for specific columns.
UPDATE	Update records in table/view.
	Can be given for specific columns.
DELETE	Delete records from table/view.
ALTER	Alter the table.
INDEX	Create indexes on the table.
REFERENCES	Create foreign keys that reference the table.
EXECUTE	Execute the procedure, package, or function.

Accounting can modify order records, but salespersons cannot. A given DBMS product may provide either one or both of these types of facilities.

Authorization tables such as those shown in Figure 12-4 are attributes of an organization's data and their environment; they are therefore properly viewed as metadata. Thus, the tables should be stored and maintained in the repository. Since authorization tables contain highly sensitive data, they themselves should be protected by stringent security rules. Normally, only selected persons in data administration have authority to access and modify these tables.

For example, in Oracle8i, the privileges included in Figure 12-5 can be granted to users at the database or table level. INSERT and UPDATE can be granted at the column level. Where many users, such as those in a particular job classification, need similar privileges, roles may be created that contain a set of privileges, and then all of the privileges can be granted to a user simply by granting the role. To grant the ability to read the product table and update prices to a user with the login ID of smith, the following SQL command may be given:

GRANT SELECT, UPDATE (unit_price) ON PRODUCT_T TO SMITH;

There are eight data dictionary views that contain information about privileges that have been granted. In this case, DBA_TAB_PRIVS contains users and objects for every user who has been granted privileges on objects, such as tables. DBA_COL_PRIVS contains users who have been granted privileges on columns of tables.

User-Defined Procedures

User-defined procedures: User exits (or interfaces) that allow system designers to define their own security procedures in addition to the authorization rules.

Some DBMS products provide user exits (or interfaces) that allow system designers or users to create their own **user-defined procedures** for security, in addition to the authorization rules we have just described. For example, a user procedure might be designed to provide positive user identification. In attempting to log on to the computer, the user might be required to supply a procedure name in addition to a simple password. If valid password and procedure names are supplied, the system then calls the procedure, which asks the user a series of questions whose answers should be known only to that password holder (such as mother's maiden name).

Encryption

Encryption: The coding or scrambling of data so that humans cannot read them.

For highly sensitive data such as company financial data, data encryption can be used. **Encryption** is the coding or scrambling of data so that humans cannot read them. Some DBMS products include encryption routines that automatically encode sensitive data when they are stored or transmitted over communications channels. For example, encryption is commonly used in electronic funds transfer (EFT) systems. Other DBMS products provide exits that allow users to code their own encryption routines.

Any system that provides encryption facilities must also provide complementary routines for decoding the data. These decoding routines must be protected by adequate security, or else the advantages of encryption are lost, and they also require significant computing resources.

Two common forms of encryption exist: one key and two key. With a *one-key* method, also called data encryption standard (DES), both the sender and the receiver need to know the key that is used to scramble the transmitted or stored data. A *two-key* method, also called a duel-key method, public-key method, or asymmetric encryption, employs a private and a public key. Two-key methods are especially popular in electronic commerce applications to provide secure transmission and database storage of payment data, such as credit card numbers. With this method, all users know each other's public keys, but only each individual knows the private key. A first-time user is assigned the pair of keys by the system of trust, for example, a DBMS or security system working with the DBMS. A message (such as a transaction to update the database) is encrypted using the sender's private key and the receiver's public key; this message can be decrypted using only the receiver's private key and the sender's public key. The sender and receiver may be two users (or user programs) or the DBMS and a user (or user program). A two-key method depends on the public key directory being secure and not able to be corrupted. Thus, the public keys must be maintained in a highly secure environment, possibly by a third party. Companies such as Verisign exist for the purpose of maintaining public keys and certifying new keys. A variation of the two-key method is digital signatures, which provide evidence, formalism, approval, efficiency, and authentication for electronic commerce (see Web Resource http://abanet.org/scitech/ec/isc/dsg-tutorial.html for an excellent tutorial on digital signatures and public key certificates).

Authentication Schemes

A long-standing problem in computer circles is how to positively identify persons who are trying to gain access to a computer or its resources. The first line of defense is the use of passwords, which provides some protection. However, people assigned passwords for different devices quickly devise ways to remember these passwords, ways that tend to decrease the effectiveness of the password scheme. The passwords get written down, where others may find them. They get shared with other users; it is not unusual for an entire department to use one common password for access. Passwords get included in automatic logon scripts, which removes the inconvenience of remembering them and typing them but also eliminates their effectiveness. And passwords usually traverse a network in cleartext, not encrypted, so if intercepted they may be easily interpreted. Also, passwords cannot, of themselves, ensure the security of a computer and its databases, because they give no indication of who is trying to gain access. The current distributed and networked environments require additional security measures. Different approaches and combinations of approaches are being tried to deal with this problem.

First, industry has developed devices and techniques to positively identify any prospective user. The most promising of these appear to be **biometric devices**, which measure or detect personal characteristics such as fingerprints, voiceprints, eye pictures, or signature dynamics. The use of retina prints has declined because of concerns about possible damaging effects to the eye by the laser optics used to capture a retina print. To implement the biometric approach, several companies have developed a smart card that embeds an individual's unique biometric data (such as fingerprints or hand geometry) permanently on the card. To access a computer, the user inserts the card into a reader device (a biometric device) that reads the person's fingerprint or other characteristic. The actual biometric data are then compared with data in a database, and the two must match for the user to gain computer access.

Biometric device: Techniques that measure or detect personal characteristics such as fingerprints, voiceprints, eye pictures, or signature dynamics.

A lost or stolen card would be useless to another person, since the biometric data would not match. Such a smart card is useful with an ATM, credit card purchasing, and even electronic commerce.

Another approach is the use of third-party mediated authentication systems, which establish user authenticity through a trusted authentication agent, such as Kerberos. Developed at MIT, Kerberos is primarily used in application-level protocols, such as TELNET or FTP, to provide user-to-host security. Kerberos works by providing a secret key (Kerberos ticket) to a user that can then be embedded in any other network protocol. Any process which implements that protocol can then be certain of the source of the request. Sun Microsystems also has an authentication mechanism, called DES Authentication, which is based on the sender encrypting a timestamp when the message is sent, which is then checked against the receiver's internal clock. This requires agreement between the agents as to the current time and both must be using the same encryption key. Liability issues have kept third-party authentication schemes from achieving widespread acceptance. Public key, certificate-based authentication schemes which issue to parties identification certificates that they can then exchange without further involvement of a third party are also being used. Such digital certificates will be used extensively in electronic commerce transactions involving credit card or digital cash purchases.

A last piece of the authentication problem is establishing nonrepudiation. That is, after a message has been sent, the user should not be able to repudiate having sent the message, or say that it was not sent. Biometric devices coupled with the sending of messages are used to establish nonrepudiation.

BACKING UP DATABASES

Database recovery: Mechanisms for restoring a database quickly and accurately after loss or damage.

Database recovery is data administration's response to Murphy's law. Inevitably, databases are damaged or lost because of some system problem that may be caused by human error, hardware failure, incorrect or invalid data, program errors, computer viruses, network failures, conflicting transactions, or natural catastrophes. Since the organization depends so heavily on its database, the database management system must provide mechanisms for restoring a database quickly and accurately after loss or damage.

Basic Recovery Facilities

A database management system should provide four basic facilities for backup and recovery of a database:

Backup facilities: An automatic dump facility that produces a backup copy (or *save*) of the entire database.

Journalizing facilities: An audit trail of transactions and database changes.

1. **Backup facilities**, which provide periodic backup copies of portions of or the entire database
2. **Journalizing facilities**, which maintain an audit trail of transactions and database changes
3. A *checkpoint facility*, by which the DBMS periodically suspends all processing and synchronizes its files and journals
4. A *recovery manager*, which allows the DBMS to restore the database to a correct condition and restart processing transactions

Backup Facilities The DBMS should provide backup facilities that produce a backup copy (or *save*) of the entire database plus control files and journals. Typically, a backup copy is produced at least once per day. The copy should be stored in a secured location where it is protected from loss or damage. The backup copy is used to restore the database in the event of hardware failure, catastrophic loss, or damage.

Some DBMSs provide backup utilities for the DBA to use to make backups; other systems assume the DBA will use the operating system commands, export commands, or SELECT . . . INTO SQL commands to perform backups. Since performing the nightly backup for a particular database is repetitive, creating a script that automates regular backups will save time and result in fewer backup errors.

With large databases, regular backups may be impractical, as the time required to perform the backup may exceed that available. Or, a database may be a critical system that must always remain available; so, a cold backup, where the database is shut down, is not practical. As a result, backups may be taken of dynamic data regularly (a so-called hot backup in which only a selected portion of the database is shut down from use) but backups of static data, which don't change frequently, may be taken less often. Incremental backups, which record changes made since the last full backup, but which do not take so much time to complete, may also be taken on an interim basis, allowing for longer periods of time between full backups. Determining backup strategies, thus, must be based on the demands being placed on the database systems.

Journalizing Facilities A DBMS must provide journalizing facilities to produce an audit trail of **transactions** and database changes. In the event of a failure, a consistent database state can be reestablished using the information in the journals together with the most recent complete backup. As Figure 12-6 shows, there are two basic journals, or logs. The first is the **transaction log**, which contains a record of the essential data for each transaction that is processed against the database. Data that are typically recorded for each transaction include the transaction code or identification, action or type of transaction (e.g., insert), time of the transaction, terminal number or user ID, input data values, table and records accessed, records modified, and possibly the old and new field values.

The second kind of log is the **database change log**, which contains before- and after-images of records that have been modified by transactions. A **before-image** is simply a copy of a record before it has been modified, and an **after-image** is a copy of the same record after it has been modified.

Transaction: A discrete unit of work that must be completely processed or not processed at all within a computer system. Entering a customer order is an example of a transaction.

Transaction log: A record of the essential data for each transaction that is processed against the database.

Database change log: Before- and after-images of records that have been modified by transactions.

Before-image: A copy of a record (or page of memory) before it has been modified.

After-image: A copy of a record (or page of memory) after it has been modified.

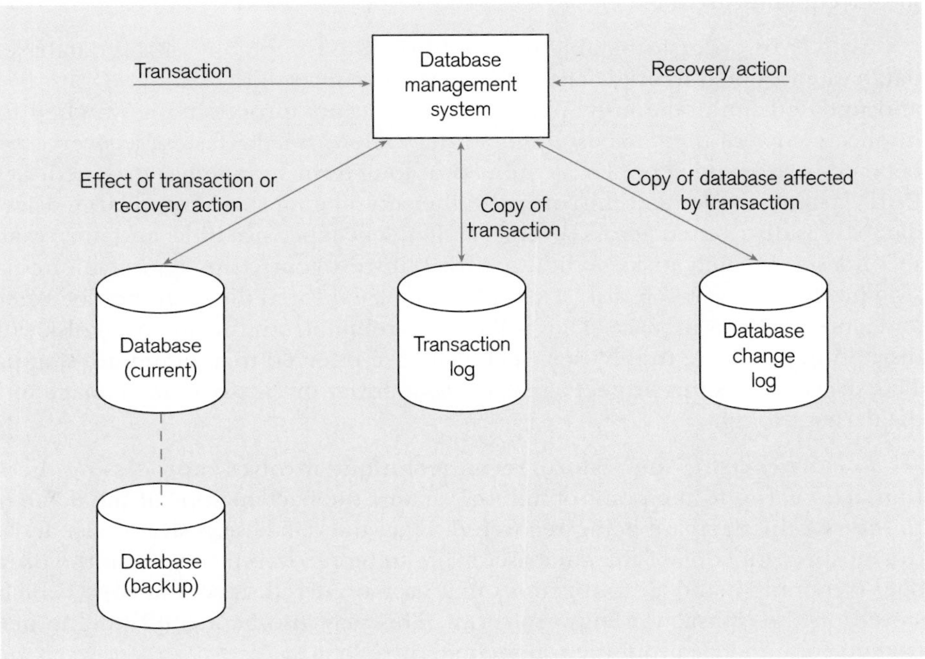

Figure 12-6
Database audit trail

Some systems also keep a security log, which can alert the DBA to any security violations that occur or are attempted.

The recovery manager uses these logs to undo and redo operations, which we explain later in this chapter. These logs may be kept on disk or tape; because they are critical to recovery, they, too, must be backed up.

Checkpoint facility: A facility by which the DBMS periodically refuses to accept any new transactions. The system is in a quiet state, and the database and transaction logs are synchronized.

Checkpoint Facility A **checkpoint facility** in a DBMS periodically refuses to accept any new transactions. All transactions in progress are completed, and the journal files are brought up to date. At this point, the system is in a quiet state, and the database and transaction logs are synchronized. The DBMS writes a special record (called a checkpoint record) to the log file, which is like a snapshot of the state of the database. The checkpoint record contains information necessary to restart the system. Any dirty data blocks (pages of memory that contain changes that have not yet been written out to disk) are written from memory to disk storage, thus ensuring that all changes made prior to taking the checkpoint have been written to long-term storage.

A DBMS may perform checkpoints automatically (which is preferred) or in response to commands in user application programs. Checkpoints should be taken frequently (say, several times an hour). When failures do occur, it is often possible to resume processing from the most recent checkpoint. Thus, only a few minutes of processing work must be repeated, compared with several hours for a complete restart of the day's processing.

Recovery manager: A module of the DBMS which restores the database to a correct condition when a failure occurs and which resumes processing user requests.

Recovery Manager The **recovery manager** is a module of the DBMS which restores the database to a correct condition when a failure occurs and which resumes processing user requests. The type of restart used depends on the nature of the failure. The recovery manager uses the logs shown in Figure 12-6 (as well as the backup copy, if necessary) to restore the database.

Recovery and Restart Procedures

The type of recovery procedure that is used in a given situation depends on the nature of the failure, the sophistication of the DBMS recovery facilities, and operational policies and procedures. Following is a discussion of the techniques that are most frequently used.

Switch In order to be able to switch to an existing copy of the database, the database must be mirrored. That is, at least two copies of the database must be kept and updated simultaneously. When a failure occurs, processing is switched to the duplicate copy of the database. This strategy allows for the fastest recovery and has become increasingly popular as the cost of long-term storage has dropped. Level 1 RAID systems implement mirroring. Rather than being stored on a large drive, the database is distributed across several smaller, less expensive disks and mirrored to a second set of such disks. When a disk failure occurs, the system immediately switches to the mirrored disk. The defective or damaged disk can then be removed and a new disk put in place. That disk can be rebuilt from the mirrored disk with no disruption in service to the user. Such disks are referred to as being hot-swappable. This strategy does not protect against loss of power or catastrophic damage to both databases, though.

Restore/rerun: A technique that involves reprocessing the day's transactions (up to the point of failure) against the backup copy of the database.

Restore/Rerun The **restore/rerun** technique involves reprocessing the day's transactions (up to the point of failure) against the backup copy of the database or portion of the database being recovered. First, the database is shut down and then the most recent copy of the database or file to be recovered (say, from the previous day) is mounted, and all transactions that have occurred since that copy (which are stored on the transaction log) are rerun. This may also be a good time to make a backup copy and clear out the transaction, or redo, log.

The advantage of restore/rerun is its simplicity. The DBMS does not need to create a database change journal, and no special restart procedures are required. However, there are two major disadvantages. First, the time to reprocess transactions may be prohibitive. Depending on the frequency of making backup copies, several hours of reprocessing may be required. Processing new transactions will have to be deferred until recovery is completed, and if the system is heavily loaded, it may be impossible to catch up. The second disadvantage is that the sequencing of transactions will often be different from when they were originally processed, which may lead to quite different results. For example, in the original run, a customer deposit may be posted before a withdrawal. In the rerun, the withdrawal transaction may be attempted first and may lead to sending an insufficient funds notice to the customer. For these reasons, restore/rerun is not a sufficient recovery procedure and is generally used only as a last resort in database processing.

Transaction Integrity A database is updated by processing transactions that result in changes to one or more database records. If an error occurs during the processing of a transaction, the database may be compromised, and some form of database recovery is required. Thus, to understand database recovery, we must first understand the concept of transaction integrity.

A business transaction is a sequence of steps that constitute some well-defined business activity. Examples of business transactions are "Admit Patient" in a hospital and "Enter Customer Order" in a manufacturing company. Normally, a business transaction requires several actions against the database. For example, consider the transaction "Enter Customer Order." When a new customer order is entered, the following steps may be performed by an application program:

1. Input order data (keyed by user).

2. Read CUSTOMER record (or insert record if a new customer).

3. Accept or reject the order. If Balance Due plus Order Amount does not exceed Credit Limit, accept the order; otherwise, reject it.

4. If the order is accepted, Increase Balance Due by Order Amount. Store the updated CUSTOMER record. Insert the accepted ORDER record in the database.

When processing transactions, the DBMS must ensure that the transactions follow four well-accepted properties, called the ACID properties:

- Atomic, meaning that the transaction cannot be subdivided, and hence, it must be processed in its entirety or not at all. Once the whole transaction is processed, we say that the changes are committed. If the transaction fails at any midpoint, we say that it has aborted. For example, suppose that the program accepts a new customer order, increases Balance Due, and stores the updated CUSTOMER record. However, suppose that the new ORDER record is not inserted successfully (perhaps there is a duplicate Order Number key, or perhaps there is insufficient physical file space). In this case, we want none of the parts of the transaction to affect the database.

- Consistent, meaning any database constraints that must be true before the transaction must also be true after the transaction. For example, if inventory on-hand balance must be the difference between total receipts minus total issues, this will be true both before and after an order transaction, which depletes on-hand balance to satisfy the order.

- Isolated, meaning changes to the database are not revealed to users until the transaction is committed. For example, this property means that other users don't know what on-hand inventory is until an inventory transaction is complete; this property then usually means that other users are prohibited from simultaneously updating and possibly even reading data that are in the process of being updated. We discuss this topic in more detail later under concurrency controls and locking. A consequence of transactions being isolated from one another is that concurrent transactions (i.e., several transactions in some partial state of completion) all affect the database as if they were presented to the DBMS in serial fashion.

- Durable, meaning changes are permanent. Thus, once a transaction is committed, no subsequent failure of the database can reverse the effect of the transaction.

Transaction boundaries: The logical beginning and end of transactions.

To maintain transaction integrity, the DBMS must provide facilities for the user or application program to define **transaction boundaries**—that is, the logical beginning and end of a transaction. In SQL, the BEGIN TRANSACTION statement is placed in front of the first SQL command within the transaction, and the COMMIT command is placed at the end of the transaction. Any number of SQL commands may come in between these two commands; these are the database processing steps that perform some well-defined business activity, as explained earlier. If a command such as ROLLBACK is processed after a BEGIN TRANSACTION is executed and before a COMMIT is executed, the DBMS aborts the transaction and undoes the effects of the SQL statements processed so far within the transaction boundaries. The application would likely be programmed to execute a ROLLBACK when the DBMS generates an error message performing an UPDATE or INSERT command in the middle of the transaction. The DBMS thus commits (makes durable) changes for successful transactions (those that reach the COMMIT statement) and effectively rejects changes from transactions that are aborted (those that encounter a ROLLBACK). Any SQL statement encountered after a COMMIT or ROLLBACK and before a BEGIN TRANSACTION is executed as a single statement transaction, automatically committed if it executed without error, aborted if any error occurs during its execution.

Although conceptually a transaction is a logical unit of business work, such as a customer order or receipt of new inventory from a supplier, you may decide to break the business unit of work into several database transactions for database processing reasons. For example, because of the isolation property, a transaction that takes many commands and a long time to process, may prohibit other uses of the same data at the same time, thus delaying other critical (possibly read-only) work. Some database data are used frequently, so it is important to complete transactional work on these so-called hotspot data as quickly as possible. For example, a primary key and its index for bank account numbers will likely need to be accessed by every ATM transaction, so the database transaction must be designed to use and release this data quickly. Also, remember, all the commands between the boundaries of a transaction must be executed, even those commands seeking input from an on-line user. If a user is slow to respond to input requests within the boundaries of a transaction, other users may encounter significant delays. Thus, if possible, collect all user input before beginning a transaction. Also, to minimize the length of a transaction, check for possible errors, such as duplicate keys or insufficient account balance, as early in the transaction as possible, so portions of the database can be released as soon as possible for other users if the transaction is going to be aborted. Some constraints (such as balancing the number of units of an item received with the number placed in inventory less returns) cannot be checked until many database commands are executed, so the transaction must be long to ensure database integrity. Thus, the general guideline is to make a database transaction as short as possible while still maintaining the integrity of the database.

Backward recovery (rollback): The back out, or undo, of unwanted changes to the database. Before-images of the records that have been changed are applied to the database, and the database is returned to an earlier state. Used to reverse the changes made by transactions that have been aborted or terminated abnormally.

Backward Recovery With **backward recovery** (also called **rollback**), the DBMS backs out of or undoes unwanted changes to the database. As Figure 12-7a shows, before-images of the records that have been changed are applied to the database.

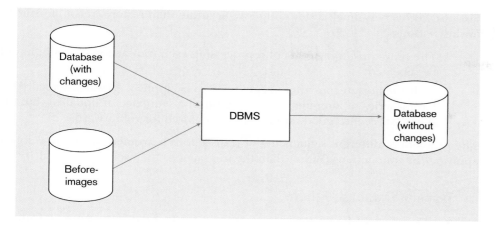

Figure 12-7
Basic recovery techniques
(a) Rollback

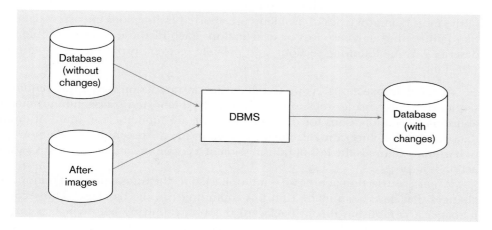

(b) Rollforward

As a result, the database is returned to an earlier state; the unwanted changes are eliminated.

Backward recovery is used to reverse the changes made by transactions that have aborted, or terminated abnormally. To illustrate the need for backward recovery (or UNDO), suppose that a banking transaction will transfer $100 in funds from the account for customer A to the account for customer B. These steps are performed:

1. The program reads the record for customer A and subtracts $100 from the account balance.

2. The program then reads the record for customer B and adds $100 to the account balance. Now the program writes the updated record for customer A to the database. However, in attempting to write the record for customer B, the program encounters an error condition (such as a disk fault) and cannot write the record. Now the database is inconsistent—record A has been updated but record B has not—and the transaction must be aborted. An UNDO command will cause the recovery manager to apply the before-image for record A to restore the account balance to its original value (the recovery manager may then restart the transaction and make another attempt).

Forward Recovery With **forward recovery** (also called **rollforward**), the DBMS starts with an earlier copy of the database. Applying after-images (the results of good transactions) quickly moves the database forward to a later state (see Figure 12-7b).

Forward recovery (rollforward): A technique that starts with an earlier copy of the database. After-images (the results of good transactions) are applied to the database, and the database is quickly moved forward to a later state.

Forward recovery is much faster and more accurate than restore/rerun, for the following reasons:

1. The time-consuming logic of reprocessing each transaction does not have to be repeated.

2. Only the most recent after-images need to be applied. A database record may have a series of after-images (as a result of a sequence of updates), but only the most recent, "good" after-image is required for rollforward.

The problem of different sequencing of transactions is avoided, since the results of applying the transactions (rather than the transactions themselves) are used.

Types of Database Failure

A wide variety of failures can occur in processing a database, ranging from the input of an incorrect data value to complete loss or destruction of the database. Four of the most common types of problems are aborted transactions, incorrect data, system failure, and database loss or destruction. Each of these types of problems is described in the following sections, and possible recovery procedures are indicated (see Table 12-1).

Aborted Transactions As we noted earlier, a transaction frequently requires a sequence of processing steps to be performed. An **aborted transaction** terminates abnormally. Some reasons for this type of failure are human error, input of invalid data, hardware failure, and deadlock (covered in the next section). A common type of hardware failure is the loss of transmission in a communications link when a transaction is in progress.

When a transaction aborts, we want to "back out" the transaction and remove any changes that have been made (but not committed) to the database. The recovery manager accomplishes this by backward recovery (applying before-images for the transaction in question). This function should be accomplished automatically by the DBMS, which then notifies the user to correct and resubmit the transaction. Other procedures, such as rollforward or transaction reprocessing, could be applied to bring the database to the state it was in just prior to the abort occurrence, but rollback is the preferred procedure in this case.

Incorrect Data A more complex situation arises when the database has been updated with incorrect, but valid, data. For example, an incorrect grade may be recorded for a student, or an incorrect amount input for a customer payment.

Incorrect data are difficult to detect and often lead to complications. To begin with, some time may elapse before an error is detected and the database record (or records) corrected. By this time, numerous other users may have used the erroneous data, and a

Aborted transaction: A transaction in progress that terminates abnormally.

Table 12-1 Responses to Database Failure

Type of Failure	Recovery Technique
Aborted transaction	Rollback (preferred) Rollforward/rerun transactions to state just prior to abort
Incorrect data (update inaccurate)	Rollback (preferred) Reprocess transactions without inaccurate data updates Compensating transactions
System failure (database intact)	Switch to duplicate database (preferred) Rollback Restart from checkpoint
Database destruction	Switch to duplicate database (preferred) Rollforward Reprocess transactions

chain reaction of errors may have occurred as various applications made use of the incorrect data. In addition, transaction outputs (such as documents and messages) based on the incorrect data may be transmitted to persons. An incorrect grade report, for example, may be sent to a student or an incorrect statement sent to a customer.

When incorrect data have been introduced, the database may be recovered in one of the following ways:

1. If the error is discovered soon enough, backward recovery may be used. (However, care must be taken to ensure that all subsequent errors have been reversed.)

2. If only a few errors have occurred, a series of compensating transactions may be introduced through human intervention to correct the errors.

3. If the first two measures are not feasible, it may be necessary to restart from the most recent checkpoint before the error occurred, and subsequent transactions processed without the error.

Any erroneous messages or documents that have been produced by the erroneous transaction will have to be corrected by appropriate human intervention (letters of explanation, telephone calls, etc.)

System Failure In a system failure, some component of the system fails, but the database is not damaged. Some causes of system failure are power loss, operator error, loss of communications transmission, and system software failure.

When the system crashes, some transactions may be in progress. The first step in recovery is to back out those transactions using before-images (backward recovery). Then, if the system is mirrored, it may be possible to switch to the mirrored data and rebuild the corrupted data on a new disk. If the system is not mirrored, it may not be possible to restart because status information in main memory has been lost or damaged. The safest approach is to restart from the most recent checkpoint before the system failure. The database is rolled forward by applying after-images for all transactions that were processed after that checkpoint.

Database Destruction In the case of **database destruction**, the database itself is lost, or destroyed, or cannot be read. A typical cause of database destruction is a disk drive failure (or head crash).

Again, using a mirrored copy of the database is the preferred strategy for recovering from such an event. If there is no mirrored copy, a backup copy of the database is required. Forward recovery is used to restore the database to its state immediately before the loss occurred. Any transactions that may have been in progress when the database was lost are restarted.

Database destruction: The database itself is lost, or destroyed, or cannot be read.

CONTROLLING CONCURRENT ACCESS

Databases are shared resources. Database administrators must expect and plan for the likelihood that several users will attempt to access and manipulate data at the same time. With concurrent processing involving updates, a database without **concurrency control** will be compromised due to interference between users. There are two basic approaches to concurrency control: a pessimistic approach (involving locking) and an optimistic approach (involving versioning). We summarize both of these approaches in the following sections.

Most DBMSs run in a multiuser environment, with the expectation that users will be able to share the data contained in the database. If users are only reading data, no data integrity problems will be encountered, because no changes will be made in the database. However, if one or more users are updating data, then potential problems with maintaining data integrity arise. When more than one transaction is being processed

Concurrency control: The process of managing simultaneous operations against a database so that data integrity is maintained and the operations do not interfere with each other in a multiuser environment.

against a database at the same time, the transactions are considered to be concurrent. The actions that must be taken to ensure that data integrity is maintained are called currency control actions. Remember that the CPU can process only one instruction at a time. As new transactions are submitted while other processing is occurring against the database, the transactions are usually interleaved, with the CPU switching among the transactions so that some portion of each transaction is performed as the CPU addresses each transaction in turn. Because the CPU is able to switch among transactions so quickly, most users will not notice that they are sharing CPU time with other users.

The Problem of Lost Updates

The most common problem encountered when multiple users attempt to update a database without adequate concurrency control is that of lost updates. Figure 12-8 shows a common situation. John and Marsha have a joint checking account and both want to withdraw some cash at the same time, each using an ATM terminal in a different location. Figure 12-8 shows the sequence of events that might occur, in the absence of a concurrency control mechanism. John's transaction reads the account balance (which is $1,000) and he proceeds to withdraw $200. Before the transaction writes the new account balance ($800), Marsha's transaction reads the account balance (which is still $1,000). She then withdraws $300, leaving a balance of $700. Her transaction then writes this account balance, which replaces the one written by John's transaction. The effect of John's update has been lost due to interference between the transactions, and the bank is unhappy.

Inconsistent read problem: An unrepeatable read, one that occurs when one user reads data that have been partially updated by another user.

Another, similar type of problem that may occur when concurrency control is not established is the **inconsistent read problem**. This problem occurs when one user reads data that have been partially updated by another user. The read will be incorrect, and is sometimes referred to as a dirty read or an unrepeatable read. The lost update and inconsistent read problems arise when the DBMS does not isolate transactions, part of the ACID transaction properties.

Figure 12-8
Lost update (no concurrency control in effect)

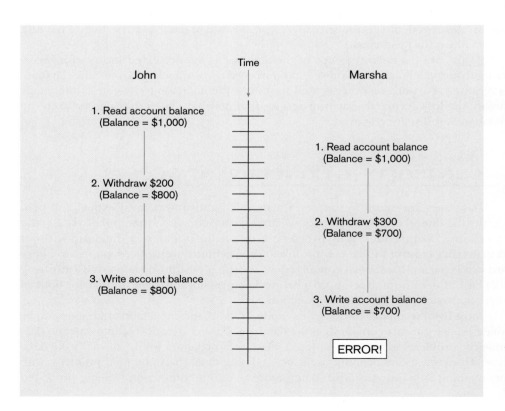

Serializability

Concurrent transactions need to be processed in isolation so that they do not interfere with each other. If one transaction were entirely processed at a time before another transaction, no interference would occur. Procedures that process transactions so that the outcome is the same as this are called serializable. Processing transactions using a serializable schedule will give the same results as if the transactions had been processed one after the other. Schedules are designed so that transactions that will not interfere with each other can still be run in parallel. For example, transactions that request data from different tables in a database will not conflict with each other and can be run concurrently without causing data integrity problems. Serializability is achieved by different means, but locking mechanisms are the most common type of concurrency control mechanism. With **locking**, any data that are retrieved by a user for updating must be locked, or denied to other users, until the update is complete or aborted. Locking data is much like checking a book out of the library—it is unavailable to others until the borrower returns it.

Locking: Any data that are retrieved by a user for updating must be locked, or denied to other users, until the update is completed or aborted.

Locking Mechanisms

Figure 12-9 shows the use of record locks to maintain data integrity. John initiates a withdrawal transaction from an ATM. Since John's transaction will update this record, the application program locks this record before reading it into main mem-

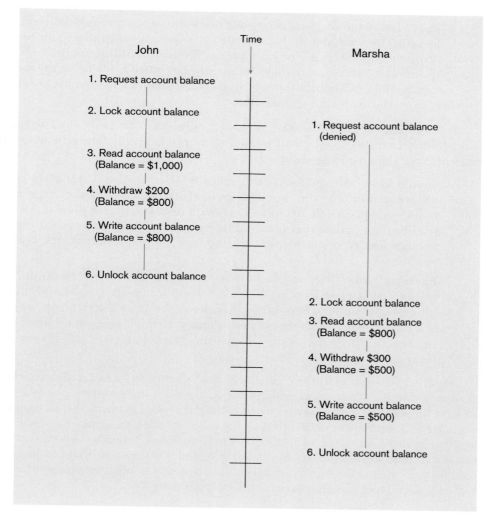

John

Time

Marsha

1. Request account balance

2. Lock account balance

    1. Request account balance (denied)

3. Read account balance (Balance = $1,000)

4. Withdraw $200 (Balance = $800)

5. Write account balance (Balance = $800)

6. Unlock account balance

    2. Lock account balance

    3. Read account balance (Balance = $800)

    4. Withdraw $300 (Balance = $500)

    5. Write account balance (Balance = $500)

    6. Unlock account balance

Figure 12-9
Updates with locking (concurrency control)

ory. John proceeds to withdraw $200, and the new balance ($800) is computed. Marsha has initiated a withdrawal transaction shortly after John, but her transaction cannot access the account record until John's transaction has returned the updated record to the database and unlocked the record. The locking mechanism thus enforces a sequential updating process that prevents erroneous updates.

Locking level (granularity): The extent of the database resource that is included with each lock.

Locking Level An important consideration in implementing concurrency control is choosing the locking level. The **locking level** (also called **granularity**) is the extent of the database resource that is included with each lock. Most commercial products implement locks at one of the following levels:

1. *Database*   The entire database is locked and becomes unavailable to other users. This level has limited application, such as during a backup of the entire database (Rodgers, 1989).

2. *Table*   The entire table containing a requested record is locked. This level is appropriate mainly for bulk updates that will update the entire table, such as giving all employees a 5 percent raise.

3. *Block or page*   The physical storage block (or page) containing a requested record is locked. This level is the most commonly implemented locking level. A page will be a fixed size (4K, 8K, etc.) and may contain records of more than one type.

4. *Record level*   Only the requested record (or row) is locked. All other records, even within a table, are available to other users. It does impose some overhead at run time when several records are involved in an update.

5. *Field level*   Only the particular field (or column) in a requested record is locked. This level may be appropriate when most updates affect only one or two fields in a record. For example, in inventory control applications the quantity-on-hand field changes frequently, but other fields (such as description and bin location) are rarely updated. Field-level locks require considerable overhead and are seldom used.

Types of Locks So far, we have discussed only locks that prevent all access to locked items. In reality, the database administrator can generally choose between two types of locks: shared and exclusive.

Shared lock (S lock or read lock): A technique that allows other transactions to read but not update a record or other resource.

1. **Shared locks**   Shared locks (also called S locks, or read locks) allow other transactions to read (but not update) a record or other resource. A transaction should place a shared lock on a record or data resource when it will only read but not update that record. Placing a shared lock on a record *prevents* another user from placing an exclusive lock, but not a shared lock, on that record.

Exclusive lock (X lock or write lock): A technique that prevents another transaction from reading and therefore updating a record until it is unlocked.

2. **Exclusive locks**   Exclusive locks (also called X locks, or write locks) prevent another transaction from reading (and therefore updating) a record until it is unlocked. A transaction should place an exclusive lock on a record when it is about to update that record (Descollonges, 1993). Placing an exclusive lock on a record prevents another user from placing any type of lock on that record.

Figure 12-10 shows the use of shared and exclusive locks for the checking account example. When John initiates his transaction, the program places a read lock on his account record, since he is reading the record to check the account balance. When John requests a withdrawal, the program attempts to place an exclusive lock (write lock) on the record, since this is an update operation. However, as you can see in the figure, Marsha has already initiated a transaction that has placed a read lock on the same record. As a result, his request is denied; remember that if a record is a read lock, another user cannot obtain a write lock.

Figure 12-10
The problem of deadlock

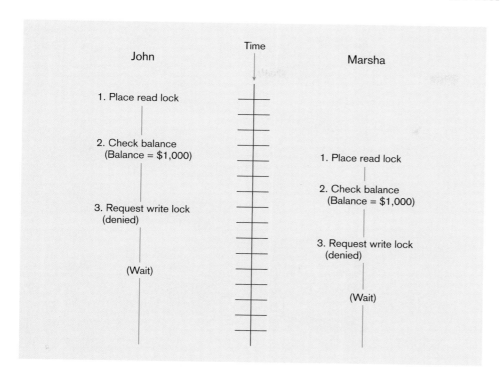

Deadlock   Locking solves the problem of erroneous updates but may lead to another problem, called **deadlock**: an impasse that results when two or more transactions have locked a common resource, and each must wait for the other to unlock that resource. Figure 12-10 shows a simple example of deadlock. John's transaction is waiting for Marsha's transaction to remove the read lock from the account record, and vice versa. Neither person can withdraw money from the account, even though the balance is more than adequate.

Figure 12-11 shows a slightly more complex example of deadlock. In this example, User A has locked record X and User B has locked record Y. User A then requests record Y (intending to update) and User B requests record X (also intending to update). Both requests are denied, since the requested records are already locked. Unless the DBMS intervenes, both users will wait indefinitely.

Managing Deadlock   There are two basic ways to resolve deadlocks: deadlock prevention and deadlock resolution. When **deadlock prevention** is employed, user programs must lock all records they will require at the beginning of a transaction, rather than one at a time. In Figure 12-11, User A would have to lock both records X and Y before processing the transaction. If either record is already locked the program must wait until it is released. Where all locking operations necessary for a transaction occur before any resources are unlocked, a **two-phase locking protocol** is being used. Once any lock obtained for the transaction is released, no more locks may be obtained. Thus, the phases in the two-phase locking protocol are often referred to as a growing phase (where all necessary locks are acquired) and a shrinking phase (where all locks are released). Locks do not have to be acquired simultaneously. Frequently some locks will be acquired, processing will occur, and then additional locks will be acquired as needed.

Locking all the required records at the beginning of the transaction (called conservative two-phase locking) prevents deadlock. Unfortunately, it is often difficult to predict in advance what records will be required to process a transaction. A typical program has many processing parts and may call other programs in varying sequences. As a result, deadlock prevention is not always practical.

Deadlock: An impasse that results when two or more transactions have locked a common resource, and each waits for the other to unlock that resource.

Deadlock prevention: User programs must lock all records they require at the beginning of a transaction (rather than one at a time).

Two-phase locking protocol: A procedure for acquiring the necessary locks for a transaction where all necessary locks are acquired before any locks are released, resulting in a growing phase, when locks are acquired, and a shrinking phase, when they are released.

Figure 12-11
Another example of deadlock

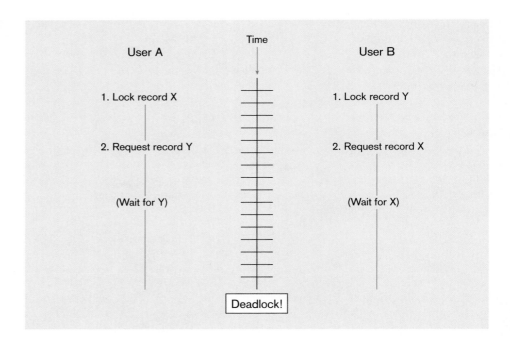

Two-phase locking in which each transaction must request records in the same sequence (i.e., serializing the resources) also prevents deadlock, but again this may not be practical.

The second, and more common, approach is to allow deadlocks to occur but to build mechanisms into the DBMS for detecting and breaking the deadlocks. Essentially, these **deadlock resolution** mechanisms work as follows. The DBMS maintains a matrix of resource usage, which, at a given instant, indicates what subjects (users) are using what objects (resources). By scanning this matrix, the computer can detect deadlocks as they occur. The DBMS then resolves the deadlocks by "backing out" one of the deadlocked transactions. Any changes made by that transaction up to the time of deadlock are removed, and the transaction is restarted when the required resources become available. We will describe the procedure for backing out shortly.

> **Deadlock resolution:** An approach that allows deadlocks to occur but builds mechanisms into the DBMS for detecting and breaking the deadlocks.

Versioning

Locking as described here is often referred to as a *pessimistic* concurrency control mechanism, because each time a record is required, the DBMS takes the highly cautious approach of locking the record so that other programs cannot use it. In reality, in most cases other users will not request the same documents, or they may only want to read them, which is not a problem (Celko, 1992). Thus, conflicts are rare.

A newer approach to concurrency control, called **versioning**, takes the *optimistic* approach that most of the time other users do not want the same record, or if they do, they only want to read (but not update) the record. With versioning, there is no form of locking. Each transaction is restricted to a view of the database as of the time that transaction started, and when a transaction modifies a record, the DBMS creates a new record version instead of overwriting the old record.

The best way to understand versioning is to imagine a central records room, corresponding to the database (Celko, 1992). The records room has a service window. Users (corresponding to transactions) arrive at the window and request documents (corresponding to database records). However, the original documents never leave

> **Versioning:** Each transaction is restricted to a view of the database as of the time that transaction started, and when a transaction modifies a record, the DBMS creates a new record version instead of overwriting the old record. Hence no form of locking is required.

the records room. Instead, the clerk (corresponding to the DBMS) makes copies of the requested documents and timestamps them. Users then take their private copies (or versions) of the documents to their own workplace and read them and/or make changes. When finished, they return their marked-up copies to the clerk. The clerk merges the changes from marked-up copies into the central database. When there is no conflict (for example, when only one user has made changes to a set of database records), that user's changes are merged directly into the public (or central) database.

Suppose instead that there is a conflict; for example, two users have made conflicting changes to their private copy of the database. In this case, the changes made by one of the users are committed to the database. (Remember that the transactions are timestamped, so that the earlier transaction can be given priority.) The other user must be told that there was a conflict, and his work cannot be committed (or incorporated into the central database). He must check out another copy of the data records and repeat the previous work. Under the optimistic assumption, this type of rework will be the exception rather than the rule.

Figure 12-12 shows a simple example of the use of versioning for the checking account example. John reads the record containing the account balance, successfully withdraws $200, and the new balance ($800) is posted to the account with a COMMIT statement. Meanwhile, Marsha has also read the account record and requested a withdrawal, which is posted to her local version of the account record. However, when the transaction attempts to COMMIT it discovers the update conflict, and her transaction is aborted (perhaps with a message such as, "Cannot complete transaction at this time"). She can then restart the transaction, working from the correct starting balance of $800.

The main advantage of versioning over locking is performance improvement. Read-only transactions can run concurrently with updating transactions, without loss of database consistency.

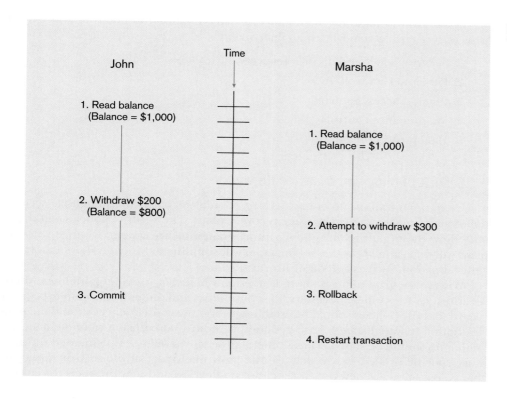

Figure 12-12
The use of versioning

Time

John

1. Read balance
   (Balance = $1,000)

2. Withdraw $200
   (Balance = $800)

3. Commit

Marsha

1. Read balance
   (Balance = $1,000)

2. Attempt to withdraw $300

3. Rollback

4. Restart transaction

MANAGING DATA QUALITY

High-quality data, that is, data that are accurate, consistent, and available in a timely fashion are essential to the management of organizations today. Organizations must strive to identify the data that are relevant to their decision making, to develop business policies and practices that ensure the accuracy and completeness of the data, and to facilitate enterprise-wide data sharing.

Establishment of a business information advisory committee consisting of representatives from each major business unit who have the authority to make business policy decisions can contribute to the establishment of high data quality (Moriarty, 1996). These committee members act as liaisons between IT and their business unit, and consider not only their functional unit's data needs but also enterprise-wide data needs. The members need to have a strong interest in managing information as a corporate resource, an in-depth understanding of the business of the organization, and good negotiation skills. Such members are sometimes referred to as **data stewards**, people who have the responsibility to ensure that organizational applications properly support the organization's enterprise goals. They must also ensure that the data that are captured are accurate and consistent throughout the organization, so that users throughout the organization can rely on the data.

Establishing enterprise-wide data quality standards is not easy, and there are even some business structures and practices that tend to inhibit data quality (Moriarty, 1996). Where organizations establish strategic business units that compete with each other within the enterprise, data sharing may be difficult as each strategic business unit strives to protect its competitive position. Regulated industries such as banking and telecommunications may be legally limited in the amount of data that can be shared. Another threat to maintaining high data quality may occur when data entry is conducted under an incentive plan or quota system that is based on volume of work completed. Then, achieving high speeds of data entry may override concerns about accuracy of data entry. Where data that need to be shared are collected from more than one business unit, the potential for inaccurate and inconsistent data skyrockets. Policies must be developed to handle each of the concerns listed above.

In addition to handling such concerns, any organization needs to address five areas with regard to achieving high data quality:

1. Security policy and disaster recovery
2. Personnel controls
3. Physical access controls
4. Maintenance controls
5. Data protection and privacy

Data steward: A person assigned the responsibility of ensuring that organizational applications properly support the organization's enterprise goals.

Security Policy and Disaster Recovery

Every organization, no matter its size, should establish comprehensive security policies and make detailed disaster recovery plans. The security policies will determine how the organization is going to maintain a secure system. Disaster recovery plans will determine how the organization will continue to function should an emergency situation, such as a flood or fire, arise.

Written security policies should be established that provide guidelines where security measures will be necessary. Responsibilities and duties of the employees with regard to those policies should be established, and the consequences should the policies not be followed stated. Last, general procedures to be taken to implement the guidelines should be stated. These general procedures will be implemented through more specific procedures, which are the most likely part of the security policy to change over time, as new uses for technology develop and new products for enforcing a secure environment are developed.

Disaster recovery plans should be worked out in detail prior to the occurrence of any disaster that may be foreseen, and if possible, tested. In 1993, for example, when Hurricane Andrew devastated the Miami area, many Tampa Bay organizations activated their hurricane disaster recovery plans. As a result, some organizations discovered that their plans to move data tapes to safer locations by using regularly scheduled airline flights would not be practical, and they used the opportunity to improve their hurricane disaster recovery plans. Contingency plans must consider data, equipment, personnel, and management issues involved in transferring operations to another location and safeguarding operations. Copies of the plans should be kept in multiple locations and reviewed periodically.

Larger organizations may arrange for space (a cold site) that can be used in the event of a disaster, either in the same general physical area, or in an area remote from the organization site being covered. Sometimes, an organization will invest in a warm site, which contains the equipment necessary to establish computer operations. And some organizations maintain a hot site, where their operations are conducted in duplicate, so that if one system encounters problems, an immediate switch can be made to the hot site.

The above discussion highlights several important general procedures and policies necessary to protect a database environment in the event of a security breach or disaster. Table 12-2 summarizes some specific procedures, which when coupled with the use of security commands provided by the DBMS (such as views, grants, user accounts, encryption, and biometric devices), lead to a comprehensive database protection plan.

Table 12-2 Database Protection Procedures

Backup and Development Environments

Tape Backups   Institute formal procedures for checking out backup tapes.

Disk Backups   Disk backup and redundant (e.g., RAID) copies need as much protection from unauthorized use as do active databases.

Development Databases   If these contain actual data, then there must be controls on programmers and developers, acceptance testers, and users involved in systems development so that data are not revealed to those who have no right or need to know.

System and Special-Use Accounts

These accounts (such system administration accounts as SYSMANAGER and DBA, possibly provided with the DBMS, and accounts used for database testing) often have greater privileges than typical user and developer accounts. These user IDs and passwords must be protected (and must be inventoried) so that they are used only for authorized purposes by the right people.

Database Names and Locations

It is advisable to use aliases for all physical database objects and hide the actual location of data as much as possible. This point emphasizes the value of user views, discussed earlier in the chapter.

System Files

These files contain sensitive database data, such as user IDs, data locations, field descriptions, and other data dictionary contents, and so forth. These must be protected from corruption and unauthorized use. One strategy is to store these files on devices other than the actual database, where extra levels of protection can be applied by the operating systems and physical access to the devices can be instituted.

Password Control

Make passwords expire in a fixed amount of time, thus forcing database users of all types to periodically change passwords. This can greatly limit the liability of stolen or inappropriately shared passwords.

Isolate Databases

Locate different production as well as production versus test databases in separate environments and apply separate server and operating system level security on each.

Adapted from Loney (2000).

Personnel Controls

Adequate controls of personnel must be developed and followed, for the greatest threat to business security is often internal rather than external. In addition to the security authorization and authentication procedures discussed earlier in this chapter, organizations should develop procedures to ensure a selective hiring process that validates potential employees' representations about their backgrounds and capabilities. Monitoring to ensure that personnel are following established practices, taking regular vacations, working with other employees, and so forth, should be followed. Employees should be trained in those aspects of security and quality that are relevant to their jobs, and be encouraged to be aware of and follow standard security and data quality measures. Standard job controls, such as separating duties so no one employee has responsibility for an entire business process, or keeping application developers from having access to production systems, should also be enforced. Should an employee need to be let go, there should be an orderly set of procedures to remove authorizations and authentications and to notify other employees of the status change.

Physical Access Controls

Limiting access to particular areas within a building is usually a part of controlling physical access. Sensitive equipment, including hardware and peripherals, such as printers (which may be used to print classified reports) can be controlled by placement in secure areas. Other equipment may be locked to a desk or cabinet, or may have an alarm attached. Backup data tapes should be kept in fireproof data safes and/or kept off-site at a safe location. Procedures that make explicit the schedules for moving media and disposing of media, and that establish labeling and indexing of all materials stored, and so forth, must be established.

Placement of computer screens so that they cannot be seen from outside the building may also be important. Control procedures for areas external to the office building should also be developed. Companies frequently use security guards to control access to their buildings, or use a card swipe system or handprint recognition system to automate employee access to the building. Visitors may be given an identification card and required to be accompanied throughout the building.

Maintenance Controls

An area of control that helps to maintain data quality but that is often overlooked is maintenance control. Organizations should review external maintenance agreements for all hardware and software they are using to ensure that appropriate response rates are agreed to for maintaining data quality. It is also important to consider reaching agreements with the developers of all critical software so that the organization can get access to source code should the developer go out of business or stop supporting the programs. One way to accomplish this is by having a third party hold the source code, with an agreement that it will be released if such a situation develops.

Data Protection and Privacy

Concerns about the rights of individuals to not have personal information collected and disseminated casually or recklessly have intensified as more of the population has become familiar with computers and as communications among computers have proliferated. Information privacy legislation generally gives individuals the right to know what data have been collected about them, and to correct any errors in those data. As the amount of data exchanged continues to grow, the need is also growing to develop adequate data protection. Also important are adequate provisions to allow the data to be used for legitimate legal purposes, so that organizations who need the data can access them and rely upon their quality.

DATA DICTIONARIES AND REPOSITORIES

An integral part of relational DBMSs is the **data dictionary**, which stores metadata, or information about the database, including attribute names and definitions for each table in the database. The data dictionary is usually a part of the **system catalog** that is generated for each database. The system catalog describes all database objects, including table-related data such as table names, table creators or owners, column names and data types, foreign keys and primary keys, index files, authorized users, user access privileges, and so forth. The system catalog is created by the database management system and the information is stored in systems tables, which may be queried in the same manner as any other data table, if the user has sufficient access privileges.

Data dictionaries may be either active or passive. An active data dictionary is managed automatically by the database management software. Active systems are always consistent with the current structure and definition of the database because they are maintained by the system itself. Most relational database management systems now contain active data dictionaries that can be derived from their system catalog. A passive data dictionary is managed by the user(s) of the system, and is modified whenever the structure of the database is changed. Since this modification must be performed manually by the user, it is possible that the data dictionary will not be current with the current structure of the database. However, the passive data dictionary may be maintained as a separate database. This may be desirable during the design phase, as it allows developers to remain independent from using a particular RDBMS for as long as possible. Also, passive data dictionaries are not limited to information that can be discerned by the database management system. Since passive data dictionaries are maintained by the user, they may be extended to contain information about organizational data that is not computerized.

Repositories

While data dictionaries are simple data-element documentation tools, information repositories are used by data administrators and other information specialists to manage the total information processing environment. The **information repository** is an essential component of both the development environment and the production environment. In the application development environment, people (either information specialists or end users) use CASE tools, high-level languages, and other tools to develop new applications. CASE tools may tie automatically to the information repository. In the production environment, people use applications to build databases, keep the data current, and extract data from databases. Each of these activities requires that the information repository be accessed and that it be current.

As indicated above, CASE tools often generate information that should be a part of the information repository, as do documentation tools, project management tools, and of course the database management software itself. When they were first developed, the information recorded by each of these products was not easily integrated. Now, however, there has been an attempt to make this information more accessible and shareable. The **Information Repository Dictionary System (IRDS)** is a computer software tool that is used to manage and control access to the information repository. It provides facilities for recording, storing, and processing descriptions of an organization's significant data and data processing resources (Lefkovitz, 1985). When sys-

Data dictionary: A repository of information about a database that documents data elements of a database.

System catalog: A system-created database that describes all database objects, including data dictionary information, and also includes user access information.

Information repository: A component that stores metadata which describes an organization's data and data processing resources, manages the total information processing environment, and combines information about an organization's business information and its application portfolio.

Information Repository Dictionary System (IRDS): A computer software tool that is used to manage and control access to the information repository.

tems are compliant with IRDS, it is possible to transfer data definitions among the data dictionaries generated by the various products. IRDS has been adopted as a standard by the International Standards Organization (1990), and includes a set of rules for storing data dictionary information and for accessing it.

Figure 12-13 shows the three components of a repository system architecture (Bernstein, 1996). First is an information model. This model is a schema of the information stored in the repository, which can then be used by the tools associated with the database to interpret the contents of the repository. Next is the repository engine, which manages the repository objects. Services such as reading and writing repository objects, browsing, and extending the information model are included. Last is the repository database, where the repository objects are actually stored. Notice that the repository engine supports five core functions (Bernstein, 1996):

- *Object management* Object-oriented repositories store information about objects. As databases become more object-oriented, developers will be able to use the information stored about database objects in the information repository. The repository can be based on an object-oriented database or it can add the capability to support objects.

- *Relationship management* The repository engine contains information about object relationships that can be used to facilitate the use of software tools that attach to the database.

- *Dynamic extensibility* The repository information model defines types, which should be easy to extend, that is, to add new types or to extend the definitions of those that already exist. This capability can make it easier to integrate a new software tool into the development process.

- *Version management* During development it is important to establish version control. The information repository can be used to facilitate version control for software design tools. Version control of objects is more difficult to manage than version control of files, since there are many more objects than files in an application, and each version of an object may have many relationships.

Figure 12-13
Three components of repository system architecture (Adapted from Bernstein, 1996)

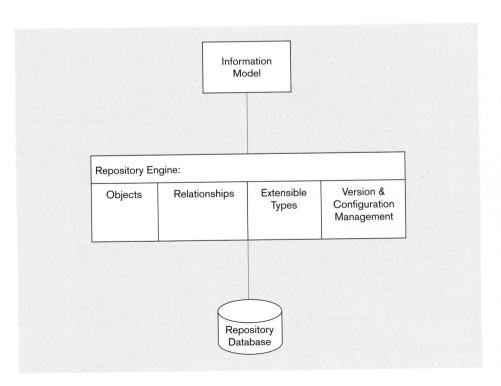

- *Configuration management*   It is also necessary to group the versioned objects into configurations that represent the entire system, which are also versioned. It may help you to think of a configuration as similar to a file directory, except configurations can be versioned and they contain objects rather than files. Repositories often use checkout systems to manage objects, versions, and configurations. A developer who wishes to use an object checks it out, makes the desired changes, and then checks the object back in. At that time, a new version of the object will be created and the object will become available to other developers.

As object-oriented database management systems become more available, and as object-oriented programming associated with relational databases increases, the importance of the information repository is also going to increase, since object-oriented development requires the use of the metadata contained in the information repository. Also, the metadata and application information generated by different software tools will be more easily integrated into the information repository now that the IRDS standard has been accepted. Although information repositories have already been included in the enterprise-level development tools, the increasing emphasis on object-oriented development should lead to more widespread use of information repositories.

OVERVIEW OF TUNING THE DATABASE FOR PERFORMANCE

Effective database support results in a reliable database where performance is not subject to interruption from hardware, software, or user problems and where optimal performance is achieved. Tuning a database is not an activity that is undertaken at the time of DBMS installation and/or at the time of implementation of a new application and then disregarded. Rather, performance analysis and tuning is an ongoing part of managing any database, as hardware and software configurations change, and as user activity changes. Five areas of DBMS management that should be addressed when trying to maintain a well-tuned database are addressed here: installation of the DBMS, memory usage, input/output contention, CPU usage, and application tuning. The extent to which the database administrator can affect each of these areas will vary across DBMS products. Oracle8i will be used as the exemplar DBMS throughout this section, but it should be noted that each product has its own set of tuning capabilities.

Tuning a database application requires familiarity with the system environment, the DBMS, the application, and the data used by the application. It is here that the skills of even an experienced database administrator are tested. Achieving a quiet environment, one that is reliable and allows users to secure desired information in a timely manner, requires skills and experience that are obtained by working with databases over time. The areas discussed below are quite general and are intended to provide an initial understanding of the scope of activities involved in tuning a database rather than providing the type of detailed understanding necessary to tune a particular database application.

Installation of the DBMS

Correct installation of the DBMS product is essential to any environment. Products often include README files, which may include detailed installation instructions, revisions of procedures, notification of increased disk space needed for installation, and so on. A quick review of any README files may save time during the installation process and result in a better installation. General installation instructions should also be reviewed. Failing to make such a review may result in default parameter values being set during installation that are not optimal for the situation. Some possible considerations are listed here.

Before beginning installation, the database administrator should ensure that adequate disk space is available. You will need to refer to manuals for the specific DBMS to be able to translate logical database size parameters (such as field length, number of table rows, and estimated growth) into actual physical space requirements. It is possible that the space allocation recommendations are low, as changes made to a DBMS tend to make it larger, but the documentation may not reflect that change. To be safe, allocate at least 20 percent more space than suggested by standard calculations. After installation, review any log files generated during the installation process. Their contents will reveal installation problems that were not noticed, or provide assurance that the installation proceeded as expected.

Allocation of disk space for the database should also receive consideration. For example, some UNIX backup systems have trouble with data files that exceed a gigabyte in size. Keeping data files under 1 gigabyte will avoid possible problems. Allocation of data files in standard sizes will make it easier to balance I/O, as data file locations can be swapped more easily should a bottleneck need to be resolved.

Memory Usage

Efficient usage of main memory involves understanding how the DBMS uses main memory, what buffers are being used, and what needs the programs in main memory have. For example, Oracle has many background processes that reside in memory when a database is running that handle database management functions. Some operating systems require a contiguous chunk of memory to be able to load Oracle, and a system with insufficient memory will have to free up memory space first. Oracle maintains in main memory a data dictionary cache that ideally should be large enough so that at least 90 percent of the requests to the data dictionary can be located in the cache rather than having to retrieve information from disk. Each of these is an example of typical memory management issues that should be considered when tuning a database.

Input/Output (I/O) Contention

Achieving maximum I/O performance is one of the most important aspects of tuning a database. Database applications are very I/O intensive—a production database will usually both read and write large amounts of data to disk as it works. While CPU clock speeds have increased dramatically, I/O speeds have not increased proportionately, and increasingly complex distributed database systems have further complicated I/O functioning.

Understanding how data are accessed by end users is critical to managing I/O contention. When hot spots, physical disk locations that are accessed repeatedly, develop, understanding the nature of the activity that is causing the hot spot affords the database administrator a much better chance of reducing the I/O contention being experienced. Oracle allows the DBA to control the placement of tablespaces, which contain data files. The DBA's in-depth understanding of user activity facilitates her ability to reduce I/O contention by separating datafiles that are being accessed together. Where possible, large database objects that will be accessed concurrently may be striped across disks to reduce I/O contention and improve performance. An overall objective of distributing I/O activity evenly across disks and controllers should guide the DBA in tuning I/O.

CPU Usage

Most database operations are going to require CPU work activity. Because of this, it is important to evaluate CPU usage when tuning a database. Using multiple CPUs allows query processing to be shared when the CPUs are working in parallel, and performance may be dramatically improved. DBAs need to maximize the performance of their existing CPUs while planning for the gains that may be achieved with each new generation of CPUs.

Monitoring CPU load so that typical load throughout a 24-hour period is known provides DBAs with basic information necessary to begin to rebalance CPU loading. The mixture of online and background processing may need to be adjusted for each environment. For example, establishing a rule that all jobs that can be run in off-hours *must* be run in off-hours will help to unload the machine during peak working hours. Establishing user accounts with limited space will help manage the CPU load also.

Application Tuning

The previous sections have concentrated on activities to tune the DBMS. Examining the applications that end users are using with the database may also increase performance. While normalization to at least 3NF is expected in many organizations that are using relational data models, carefully planned denormalization (see Chapter 6) may improve performance, often by reducing the number of tables that must be joined when running an SQL query.

Examination and modification of the SQL code in an application may also lead to performance improvement. Queries that do full table scans should be avoided, for example, because they are not selective and may not remain in memory very long. This necessitates more retrievals from long-term storage. Multitable joins should be actively managed when possible with the DBMS being used, as the type of join can dramatically affect performance, especially if a join requires a full table join.

Similarly, statements containing views and those containing subqueries should be actively reviewed. Tuning of such statements so that components are resolved in the most efficient manner possible may achieve significant performance gains. Chapter 6 discussed a variety of techniques a DBA could use to tune application processing speed and disk space utilization (such as reindexing, overriding automatic query plans, changing data block sizes, reallocating files across storage devices, and guidelines for more efficient query design). A DBA plays an important role in advising programmers and developers which techniques will be the most effective.

The preceding brief description of potential areas where database performance may be affected should convince the reader of the importance of effective database management and tuning. As a DBA achieves an in-depth understanding of a DBMS and the applications for which responsibility is assigned, the importance of tuning the database for performance should become apparent. Hopefully this brief section on database tuning will whet the reader's appetite for learning more about one or more database products in order to develop tuning skills.

Summary

The importance of managing data is emphasized in this chapter. The functions of data administration, which takes responsibility for the overall management of data resources, include developing procedures to protect and control data, resolving data ownership and use issues, and developing and maintaining corporate-wide data definitions and standards. The functions of database administration, on the other hand, are those associated with the direct management of a database or databases, including DBMS installation and upgrading, database design issues and technical issues such as security enforcement, database performance, and backup and recovery. The data administration and database administration roles are changing in today's business environment, with pressure being exerted to maintain data quality while building high-performing systems quickly. Key to achieving these expectations is developing an enterprise architecture (ISA) and performing adequate database planning.

Threats to data security include accidental losses, theft and fraud, loss of privacy, loss of data integrity, and loss of availability. A comprehensive data security plan will address all of these potential threats, partly through the establishment of views, authorization rules, user-defined procedures, and encryption procedures.

Database recovery and backup procedures are another set of essential data administration activities. Basic recovery facilities that should be in place include backup facilities, journalizing facilities, checkpoint facilities, and a recovery manager. Depending on the type of problem encountered, backward recovery (rollback) or forward recovery (rollforward) may be needed.

The problems of managing concurrent access in multiuser environments must also be addressed. The DBMS must ensure that database transactions possess the ACID properties: atomic, consistent, isolated, and durable. Proper transaction boundaries must be chosen to achieve these properties at an acceptable performance. If concurrency controls on transactions are not established,

lost updates may occur, which will cause data integrity to be impaired. Locking mechanisms, including shared and exclusive locks, can be used. Deadlocks may also occur in multiuser environments, and may be managed by various means, including using a two-phase locking protocol or other deadlock resolution mechanism. Versioning is an optimistic approach to concurrency control.

There are five areas of concern when maintaining high data quality: security policy and disaster recovery, personnel controls, physical access controls, maintenance controls, and data protection and privacy concerns.

Managing the data dictionary, which is part of the system catalog in most relational database management systems, and the information repository help the DBA maintain high-quality data and high-performing database systems. The establishment of the Information Repository Dictionary System (IRDS) standard has helped with the development of repository information that can be integrated from multiple sources, including the DBMS itself, CASE tools, and software development tools.

Effective data administration is not easy and encompasses all of the areas summarized above. Increasing emphasis on object-oriented development methods and rapid development are changing the data administration function, but better tools to achieve effective administration and database tuning are becoming available.

CHAPTER REVIEW

Key Terms

Aborted transaction
After-image
Authorization rules
Backup facilities
Backward recovery (rollback)
Before-image
Biometric device
Checkpoint facility
Concurrency control
Data administration
Data dictionary
Data steward
Database administration
Database change log

Database destruction
Database recovery
Database security
Deadlock
Deadlock prevention
Deadlock resolution
Encryption
Exclusive lock
Forward recovery (rollforward)
Inconsistent read problem
Information repository
Information Repository Dictionary System (IRDS)

Journalizing facilities
Locking
Locking level (granularity)
Recovery manager
Restore/rerun
Shared lock
System catalog
Transaction
Transaction boundaries
Transaction log
Two-phase locking protocol
User-defined procedures
Versioning

Review Questions

1. Define each of the following terms:
   a. Data administration
   b. Database administration
   c. Data steward
   d. Information repository

   e. Locking
   f. Versioning
   g. Deadlock
   h. Transaction
   i. Encryption

2. Match the following terms to the appropriate definitions.

_____ Backup facilities

_____ Biometric device

_____ Checkpoint facility

_____ Database recovery

_____ Database security

_____ Granularity

_____ Recovery manager

_____ Rollback

_____ Rollforward

_____ System catalog

a. protects data from loss or misuse

b. reversal of abnormal or aborted transactions

c. describes all database objects

d. automatically produce a saved copy of an entire database

e. application of after-images

f. might analyze your signature

g. restoring a database after a loss

h. DBMS module that restores a database after a failure

i. extent to which a database is locked for a transaction

j. records database state at moment of synchronization

3. Compare and contrast the following terms:
   a. data administration; database administration
   b. repository; data dictionary
   c. deadlock prevention; deadlock resolution
   d. backward recovery; forward recovery
   e. active data dictionary; passive data dictionary
   f. optimistic concurrency control; pessimistic concurrency control
   g. shared lock; exclusive lock
   h. before-image; after-image
   i. two-phase locking protocol; versioning
   j. authorization; authentication

4. What is the function of a data steward?

5. Briefly describe six stages in the life cycle of a typical database system.

6. Describe the changing roles of the data administrator and database administrator in the current business environment.

7. List four common problems of ineffective data administration.

8. List four job skills necessary for system data administration or data administrators. List four job skills necessary for project data administration or database administrators.

9. List and describe eleven functions that should be addressed in order to achieve effective database administration.

10. What changes can be made in data administration at each stage of the traditional database development life cycle in order to deliver high-quality, robust systems more quickly?

11. List and discuss five areas where threats to data security may occur.

12. Explain how creating a view may increase data security. Also explain why one should not rely completely on using views to enforce data security.

13. List and briefly explain how integrity controls can be used for database security.

14. What is the difference between an authentication scheme and an authorization scheme?

15. What is the advantage of optimistic concurrency control, compared with pessimistic concurrency control?

16. What is the difference between shared locks and exclusive locks?

17. What is the difference between deadlock prevention and deadlock resolution?

18. Briefly describe four DBMS facilities that are required for database backup and recovery.

19. What is transaction integrity? Why is it important?

20. List and describe four common types of database failure.

21. List and describe five areas that should be addressed in order to achieve high data quality.

22. What is an Information Resource Dictionary System (IRDS)?

23. List and briefly explain the ACID properties of a database transaction.

24. Explain the two common forms of encryption.

25. Outline six database protection procedures.

Problems and Exercises

1. Fill in the two authorization tables for Pine Valley Furniture Company below, based on the following assumptions (enter Y for yes or N for no):

Authorizations for Inventory Clerks

	Inventory Records	Receivables Records	Payroll Records	Customer Records
Read				
Insert				
Modify				
Delete				

Authorizations for Inventory Records

	Salespersons	A/R Personnel	Inventory Clerks	Carpenters
Read				
Insert				
Modify				
Delete				

(1) Salespersons, managers, and carpenters may read inventory records but may not perform any other operations on these records.

(2) Persons in Accounts Receivable and Accounts Payable may read and/or update (insert, modify, delete) receivables records and customer records.

(3) Inventory clerks may read and/or update (modify, delete) inventory records. They may not view receivables records or payroll records. They may read but not modify customer records.

2. Five recovery techniques are listed below. For each situation described, decide which recovery technique is most appropriate.

(1) Backward recovery

(2) Forward recovery (from latest checkpoint)

(3) Forward recovery (using backup copy of database)

(4) Reprocessing transactions

(5) Switch

a. A phone disconnection occurs while a user is entering a transaction.

b. A disk drive fails during regular operations.

c. A lightning storm causes a power failure.

d. An incorrect amount is entered and posted for a student tuition payment. The error is not discovered for several weeks.

e. Data entry clerks have entered transactions for two hours after a full database backup when the database becomes corrupted. It is discovered that the journalizing facility of the database has not been activated since the backup was made.

3. Whitlock Department Stores runs a multiuser DBMS on a local area network file server. Unfortunately, at the present time the DBMS does not enforce concurrency control. One Whitlock customer had a balance due of $250.00 when the following three transactions related to this customer were processed at about the same time:

(1) Payment of $250.00.

(2) Purchase on credit of $100.00.

(3) Merchandise return (credit) of $50.00.

Each of the three transactions read the customer record when the balance was $250.00 (that is, before any of the other transactions were completed). The updated customer record was returned to the database in the order shown above.

a. What balance will be included for the customer after the last transaction was completed?

b. What balance should be included for the customer after the three transactions have been processed?

4. For each of the situations described below, indicate which of the following security measures is most appropriate:

(1) authorization rules

(2) encryption

(3) authentication schemes

a. A national brokerage firm uses an electronic funds transfer (EFT) system to transmit sensitive financial data between locations.

b. An organization has set up an off-site computer-based training center. The organization wishes to restrict access to the site to authorized employees. Since each employee's use of the center is occasional, it does not wish to provide the employees with keys to access the center.

c. A manufacturing firm uses a simple password system to protect its database but finds it needs a more comprehensive system to grant different privileges (such as read, versus create or update) to different users.

d. A university has experienced considerable difficulty with unauthorized users who access files and databases by appropriating passwords from legitimate users.

5. Metro Marketers, Inc., wants to build a data warehouse for storing customer information that will be used for data marketing purposes. Building the data warehouse will require much more capacity and processing power than they have previously needed, and they are considering Oracle and Red Brick as their database and data warehousing products. As part of their implementation plan, Metro has decided to organize a data administration function. At present, they have four major candidates for the data administrator position:

a. Monica Lopez, a senior database administrator with five years of experience as an Oracle database administrator managing a financial database for a global banking firm, but no data warehousing experience.

b. Gerald Bruester, a senior database administrator with six years of experience as an Informix database administrator managing a marketing-oriented database for a Fortune 1000 food products firm. Gerald has been to several data warehousing seminars over the last twelve months and is interested in being involved with a data warehouse.

   c. Jim Reedy, currently project manager for Metro Marketers. Jim is very familiar with Metro's current systems environment and is well respected by his co-workers. He has been involved with Metro's current database system but has not had any data warehousing experience.

   d. Marie Weber, a data warehouse administrator with two years of experience using a Red Brick-based application that tracks accident information for an automobile insurance company.

Based on this limited information, rank the four candidates for the data administration position. Support your rankings by indicating your reasoning.

6. Referring to Problem and Exercise 5, rank the four candidates for the position of data warehouse administrator at Metro Marketing. Again, support your rankings.

7. Referring to Problem and Exercise 5, rank the four candidates for the position of database administrator at Metro Marketing. Again, support your rankings.

8. What concerns would you have if you accept a job as a database administrator and discover that the database users are entering one common password to log on to the database each morning when they arrive for work? You also learn that they leave their workstations connected to the database all day, even when they are away from their machines for an extended period of time.

9. An organization has a database server with three disk devices. The accounting and payroll applications share one of these disk devices and are experiencing performance problems. You have been asked to investigate the problem and tune the databases. What might you suggest to reduce I/O contention?

10. You take a new job as a database administrator at an organization that has a globally distributed database. You are asked to analyze the performance of the database and as part of your analysis discover that all of the processing for regional monthly sales reports is being conducted at the corporate headquarters location. Operations are categorized by five regions: Eastern United States, Western United States, Canada, South America, and Mexico. Data for each region are kept on a server located at the regional headquarters. What would you try to improve the time needed to create the monthly sales reports?

11. If a new version of a popular DBMS, such as Microsoft Access, is released while you are reading this text, perform an upgrade installation of this product from a previous version. What issues did you face? Did you need to convert the database? Why, or why not? If the database was converted, does it take more or less space than in the prior version? Why, or why not? Did all the existing queries and programs written for the prior version still work? Why, or why not? Can you run both the old version and the new version simultaneously on the same computer? Why, or why not?

12. Review your answer to Problem and Exercise 5 in Chapter 6. Is there an opportunity to create a domain for this database? If so, describe this domain. Also, are there any opportunities to define assertions to control the integrity of data for this database?

13. Review your answer to Problem and Exercise 5 in Chapter 6.

   a. Outline the steps in a business transaction to add a new card account for an existing customer. Define boundaries for one or more database transaction necessary to create ACID transactions. Justify your answer.

   b. Outline the steps in a business transaction to add a new card for a new customer. Define boundaries for one or more database transactions necessary to create ACID transactions. Justify your answer.

Field Exercises

1. Visit an organization that has implemented a database approach. Evaluate each of the following:

   a. The organizational placement of system data administration and project data administration

   b. The assignment of responsibilities for system data administration and project data administration

   c. The background and experience of the person chosen as head of data administration

   d. The status and usage of an information repository (passive, active-in-design, active-in-production)

2. Visit an organization that has implemented a database approach and interview an MIS department employee who has been involved in disaster recovery planning about the organization's disaster recovery plans. Before you go for the interview, think carefully about the relative probabilities of various disasters for the organization you are visiting. For example, is the area subject to earthquakes or other natural disasters? What type of damage might the physical plant be subject to? Or what is the background and training of the employees who must use the system? Find out about the organization's disaster recovery plans, and ask specifically about any potential problems you have identified.

3. Visit an organization that has implemented a database approach and interview them about the security measures that they take routinely. Evaluate each of the following:

   a. database security measures

   b. network security measures

   c. operating system security measures

   d. physical plant security measures

   e. personnel security measures

4. Identify an organization that handles large, sporadic data loads. For example, organizations that have implemented data warehouses may have large data loads as they populate their data warehouses. Determine what measures the organization has taken to handle these large loads as part of their capacity planning.

5. Databases tend to grow larger over time, not smaller, as new transaction data are added. Interview at least three compa-

nies who use databases extensively and identify their criteria and procedures for purging or archiving old data. Find out how often data are purged, and what type of data are purged. Identify the data each organization archives and how long those data are archived.

6. Visit http://tpc.org. Select a technical report article and relate what you read to this chapter. Write a report that outlines new ideas you find about at least one topic in this chapter.

References

Bernstein, P. A. 1996. "The Repository: A Modern Vision." *Database Programming & Design* 9:12 (December): 28–35.

Celko, J. 1992. "An Introduction to Concurrency Control." *DBMS* 5:9 (September): 70–83.

Descollonges, M. 1993. "Concurrency for Complex Processing." *Database Programming & Design* 6:1 (January): 66–71.

Dowgiallo, E., H. Fosdick, Y. Lirov, A. Langer, T. Quinlan, and C. Young. 1997. "DBA of the Future." *Database Programming & Design* (June): 33–41.

Fernandez, E. B., R. C. Summers, and C. Wood. 1981. *Database Security and Integrity*. Reading, MA: Addison-Wesley.

Inmon, W. H. 1999. "Data Warehouse Administration." www.billinmon.com/library/other/dwadmin.asp, verified July 25, 2001.

Lefkovitz, H. C. 1985. *Proposed American National Standards Information Resource Dictionary System*. Wellesley, MA: QED Information Sciences.

Loney, K. 2000. "Protecting Your Database." *Oracle Magazine* (May/June): 101–106.

Moriarty, T. 1996. "Better Business Practices." *Database Programming & Design* 9:7 (September): 59–61.

Rodgers, U. 1989. "Multiuser DBMS Under UNIX." *Database Programming & Design* 2:10 (October): 30–37.

Quinlan, T. 1996. "Time to Reengineer the DBA?" *Database Programming & Design* 9:3 (March): 29–34.

Zachman, J. A. 1987. "A Framework for Information Systems Architecture." *IBM Systems Journal* 26:3 (March): 276–92.

Zachman, J. A. 1997. "Enterprise Architecture: The Issue of the Century." *Database Programming & Design* 10:3 (March): 44–53.

 ## Web Resources

http://developer.netscape.com/docs/manuals/security/pkin/contents.htm This site provides a thorough explanation of a variety of modern encryption methods, including those mentioned in this chapter and a few others.

http://www.bionetrix.com, http://www.identicator.com, and http://www.keyware.com BioNetrix Systems, Identicator Technology, and Keyware Technologies are leaders in biometric technologies. Their Websites explain the diversity of biometric devices available for various applications.

http://www.isi.edu/gost/brian/security/kerberos.html This document is a guide to the Kerberos method of user authentication.

http://www.abanet.org/scitech/ec/isc/dsg-tutorial.html The American Bar Association Section of Science and Technology, Information Security Committee has prepared this excellent guide to digital signatures.

http://tpc.org The TPC is a nonprofit corporation founded to define transaction processing and database benchmarks and to disseminate objective, verifiable TPC performance data to the industry. This is an excellent site to learn more about evaluating DBMSs and database designs through technical articles on database benchmarking.

Project Case

At the end of Chapter 2, you learned of the Mountain View Community Hospital special study team that is developing a long-term business plan. You may remember that Mr. Heller, Mr. Lopez, Dr. Jefferson, and a consultant are the members of this team. They are trying to build a plan that will meet the hospital's goals of high-quality health care, cost containment, and expansion into new services, such as Dr. Browne's anticipated Geriatric Medicine department.

Mr. Heller, Director of Information Systems, regularly reads journals and magazines that he finds helpful, such as *Computerworld, Health Management Technology,* and *Healthcare Informatics.* His reading has made him aware of the movement toward implementing computer-based patient records (CPR) systems in leading hospitals in large metropolitan areas, and he is wondering if Mountain View should be planning now for future implementation of CPR. From his reading he has deduced that there are two perspectives on CPR. Until recently, CPR has been regarded as a way of replacing the existing manual systems of patient care record keeping, but use of the term is now changing. Many articles now refer to CPR as an integrated patient care information system to be accessible by hospital administrators, physicians, caregivers, and healthcare management organizations. A CPR system may well involve integrating health care information from diverse systems such as bedside terminals, laboratory systems, and administrative systems. Systems that achieve this degree of integration and accessibility are not expected to be available for several years.

Such systems will be a significant change in the way health care information is collected and used. Establishing CPR will provide an infrastructure for physicians to be able to access all medical records of their patients, even though those records are distributed over many locations, including various physician, hospital, laboratory, and insurance records. Eventually, if CPR integration is successful, nonredundant healthcare information across a patient's life will be available.

PROJECT QUESTIONS

1. Does CPR seem to have the potential to help Mountain View achieve its goals of achieving high-quality care and cost containment? Support your answers with examples of how you think these goals may or may not be achieved.

2. Establishing patient record security has always been a primary requirement of healthcare record keeping. What data security issues would you expect Mountain View to encounter if they decide to implement a CPR system that is accessible by physicians in the community, by laboratories, and by healthcare organizations?

3. Clinical decisions are the basis of over 70 percent of healthcare expenditures in the United States. In what ways could a CPR system aid clinical decision making and thus help to contain healthcare expenditures?

4. If CPR systems will not be widely available for several years, should Mr. Heller expend efforts now to consider such systems? Why or why not?

5. Is an integrated CPR system likely to be a good innovation for Mountain View to adopt, or do you think that it is an innovation that will be more suited to larger communities and larger hospitals? Are there any environmental situations, such as an agreement by physicians practicing at the hospital to adopt the system, that you would want to exist before you would advise Mountain View to adopt a CPR system?

PROJECT EXERCISES

1. If a CPR system were installed at Mountain View, list all the possible types of users that would need authorization to use the system. Include user groups external to the hospital that would be likely to be included in an integrated CPR system.

2. For each user type listed above, indicate what permissions (read, insert, delete, modify) you would grant.

3. In this case, Mr. Heller is beginning to engage in the planning activity described in the chapter as a typical data administration task. Outline briefly the issues that you feel he should include in his deliberations.

4. Legal questions such as data ownership, authentication, and admissibility have not yet been answered for CPR systems. If Mountain View decides to press ahead with plans for implementing a CPR system, what steps would they have to take in order to address each of these issues? Is there any way that they could press ahead if these issues have not been resolved? Does any one of these issues seem less important to you than the others? Why?

Chapter **13**

Distributed Databases

LEARNING OBJECTIVES

After studying this chapter, you should be able to:

- Define the following key terms: **distributed database, decentralized database, location transparency, local autonomy, synchronous distributed database, asynchronous distributed database, local transaction, global transaction, replication transparency, transaction manager, failure transparency, commit protocol, two-phase commit, concurrency transparency, timestamping,** and **semijoin.**

- Explain the business conditions that are drivers for the use of distributed databases in organizations.

- Describe the salient characteristics of the variety of distributed database environments.

- Explain the potential advantages and risks associated with distributed databases.

- Explain four strategies for the design of distributed databases, options within each strategy, and the factors to consider in selection among these strategies.

- State the relative advantages of synchronous and asynchronous data replication and partitioning as three major approaches for distributed database design.

- Outline the steps involved in processing a query in a distributed database and several approaches used to optimize distributed query processing.

- Explain the salient features of several distributed database management systems.

INTRODUCTION

When an organization is geographically dispersed, it may choose to store its databases on a central computer or to distribute them to local computers (or a combination of both). A **distributed database** is a single logical database that is spread physically across computers in multiple locations that are connected by a data communications network. We emphasize that a distributed database is truly a database, not a loose collection of files. The distributed database is still centrally adminis-tered as a corporate resource while providing local flexibility and customization. The network must allow the users to share the data; thus a user (or program) at location A must be able to access (and perhaps update) data at location B. The sites of a distributed system may be spread over a large area (such as the United States or the world), or over a small area (such as a building or campus). The computers may range from microcomputers to large-scale computers or even supercomputers.

Distributed database: A single logical database that is spread physically across computers in multiple locations that are connected by a data communications link.

A distributed database requires multiple database management systems, running at each remote site. The degree to which these different DBMSs cooperate, or work in partnership, and whether there is a master site that coordinates requests involving data from multiple sites distinguish different types of distributed database environments.

It is important to distinguish between distributed and decentralized databases. A **decentralized database** is also stored on computers at multiple locations; however, the computers are not interconnected by network and database software that make the data appear to be in one logical database. Thus users at the various sites cannot share data. A decentralized database is best regarded as a collection of independent databases, rather than having the geographical distribution of a single database.

Decentralized database: A database that is stored on computers at multiple locations; these computers are not interconnected by network and database software that make the data appear in one logical database.

Various business conditions encourage the use of distributed databases:

- *Distribution and autonomy of business units* Divisions, departments, and facilities in modern organizations are often geographically (and possibly internationally) distributed. Often each unit has the authority to create its own information systems, and often these units want local data over which they can have controls. Business mergers and acquisitions often create this environment.

- *Data sharing* Even moderately complex business decisions require sharing data across business units, so it must be convenient to consolidate data across local databases on demand.

- *Data communications costs and reliability* The cost to ship large quantities of data across a communications network or to handle a large volume of transactions from remote sources can be high. It is often more economical to locate data and applications close to where they are needed. Also, dependence on data communications can be risky, so keeping local copies or fragments of data can be a reliable way to support the need for rapid access to data across the organization.

- *Multiple application vendor environment* Today many organizations purchase packaged application software from several different vendors. Each "best in breed" package is designed to work with its own database, and possibly with different database management systems. A distributed database can possibly be defined to provide functionality that cuts across the separate applications.

- *Database recovery* Replicating data on separate computers is one strategy for insuring that a damaged database can be quickly recovered and users can have access to data while the primary site is being restored. Replicating data across multiple computer sites is one natural form of a distributed database.

- *Satisfying both transaction and analytical processing* As you learned in Chapter 11, the requirements for database management vary across OLTP and OLAP applications. Yet, the same data are in common between the two databases supporting each type of application. Distributed database technology can be helpful in synchronizing data across OLTP and OLAP platforms.

The ability to create a distributed database has existed since at least the 1980s. As you might expect, a variety of distributed database options exist (Bell and Grimson, 1992). Figure 13-1 outlines the range of distributed database environments. These environments are briefly explained by the following:

I. *Homogeneous* The same DBMS is used at each node.

    A. *Autonomous* Each DBMS works independently, passing messages back and forth to share data updates.

    B. *Nonautonomous* A central, or master, DBMS coordinates database access and update across the nodes.

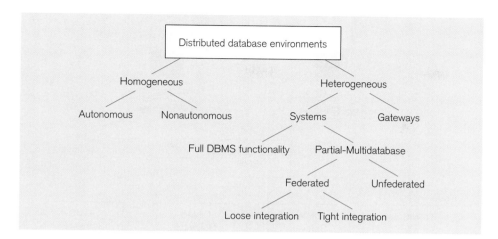

Figure 13-1
Distributed database environments
(adapted from Bell and Grimson, 1992)

II. *Heterogeneous*   Potentially different DBMSs are used at each node.

  A. *Systems*   Supports some or all of the functionality of one logical database.

   1. *Full DBMS Functionality*   Supports all of the functionality of a distributed database, as discussed in the remainder of this chapter.

   2. *Partial-Multidatabase*   Supports some features of a distributed database, as discussed in the remainder of this chapter.

    a. *Federated*   Supports local databases for unique data requests.

     i. *Loose Integration*   Many schemas exist, for each local database, and each local DBMS must communicate with all local schemas.

     ii. *Tight Integration*   One global schema exists that defines all the data across all local databases.

    b. *Unfederated*   Requires all access to go through a central coordinating module.

  B. *Gateways*   Simple paths are created to other databases, without the benefits of one logical database.

A homogeneous distributed database environment is depicted in Figure 13-2. This environment is typically defined by the following characteristics (related to the nonautonomous category described above):

- Data are distributed across all the nodes.
- The same DBMS is used at each location.
- All data are managed by the distributed DBMS (so there are no exclusively local data).
- All users access the database through one global schema or database definition.
- The global schema is simply the union of all the local database schemas.

It is difficult in most organizations to force a homogeneous environment, yet heterogeneous environments are much more difficult to manage.

As listed above, there are many variations of heterogeneous distributed database environments. In the remainder of the chapter, however, a heterogeneous environment will be defined by the following characteristics (as depicted in Figure 13-3):

- Data are distributed across all the nodes.
- Different DBMSs may be used at each node.
- Some users require only local access to databases, which can be accomplished by using only the local DBMS and schema.
- A global schema exists, which allows local users to access remote data.

Figure 13-2
Homogeneous distributed database environment (adapted from Bell and Grimson, 1992)

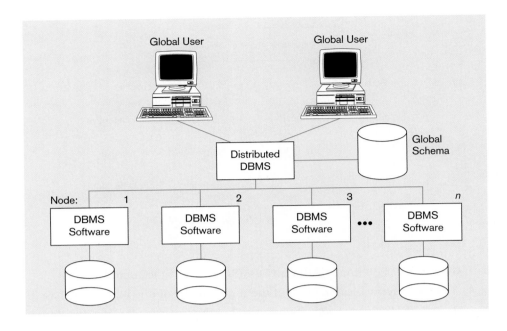

Objectives and Trade-offs

A major objective of distributed databases is to provide ease of access to data for users at many different locations. To meet this objective, the distributed database system must provide what is called **location transparency**, which means that a user (or user program) using data for querying or updating need not know the location of the data. Any request to retrieve or update data from any site is automatically forwarded by the system to the site or sites related to the processing request. Ideally, the user is unaware of the distribution of data, and all data in the network appear as a single logical database stored at one site. In this ideal case, a single query can join data from tables in multiple sites as if the data were all in one site.

Location transparency: A design goal for a distributed database, which says that a user (or user program) using data need not know the location of the data.

Figure 13-3
Heterogeneous distributed database environment (adapted from Bell and Grimson, 1992)

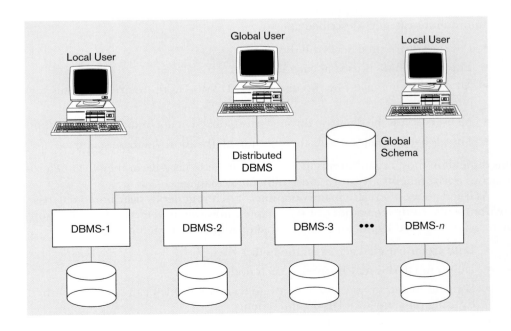

A second objective of distributed databases is **local autonomy**, which is the capability to administer a local database and to operate independently when connections to other nodes have failed (Date, 1995). With local autonomy, each site has the capability to control local data, administer security, log transactions, and recover when local failures occur, and provide full access to local data to local users when any central or coordinating site cannot operate. In this case, data are locally owned and managed, even though they are accessible from remote sites. This implies that there is no reliance on a central site.

A significant trade-off in designing a distributed database environment is whether to use synchronous or asynchronous distributed technology. With a **synchronous distributed database** technology, all data across the network are continuously kept up-to-date so that a user at any site can access data anywhere on the network at any time and get the same answer. With synchronous technology, if any copy of a data item is updated anywhere on the network, the same update is immediately applied to all other copies or aborted. Synchronous technology ensures data integrity and minimizes the complexity of knowing where the most recent copy of data are located. Synchronous technology can result in unsatisfactorily slow response time since the distributed DBMS is spending considerable time checking that an update is accurately and completely propagated across the network.

Asynchronous distributed database technology keeps copies of replicated data at different nodes so that local servers can access data without reaching out across the network. With asynchronous technology, there is usually some delay in propagating data updates across the remote databases, so some degree of at least temporary inconsistency is tolerated. Asynchronous technology tends to have acceptable response time since updates happen locally and data replicas are synchronized in batches and predetermined intervals, but may be more complex to plan and design to ensure exactly the right level of data integrity and consistency across the nodes.

Compared to centralized databases, there are numerous advantages to either form of a distributed database. The most important are the following:

- *Increased reliability and availability* When a centralized system fails, the database is unavailable to all users. A distributed system will continue to function at some reduced level, however, even when a component fails. The reliability and availability will depend (among other things) on how the data are distributed (discussed in the following sections).

- *Local control* Distributing the data encourages local groups to exercise greater control over "their" data, which promotes improved data integrity and administration. At the same time, users can access nonlocal data when necessary. Hardware can be chosen for the local site to match the local, not global, data processing work.

- *Modular growth* Suppose that an organization expands to a new location or adds a new work group. It is often easier and more economical to add a local computer and its associated data to the distributed network than to expand a large central computer. Also, there is less chance of disruption to existing users than is the case when a central computer system is modified or expanded.

- *Lower communication costs* With a distributed system, data can be located closer to their point of use. This can reduce communication costs, compared to a central system.

- *Faster response* Depending on how data are distributed, most requests for data by users at a particular site can be satisfied by data stored at that site. This speeds up query processing since communication and central computer delays are minimized. It may also be possible to split complex queries into subqueries that can be processed in parallel at several sites, providing even faster response.

Local autonomy: A design goal for a distributed database, which says that a site can independently administer and operate its database when connections to other nodes have failed.

Synchronous distributed database: A form of distributed database technology in which all data across the network are continuously kept up-to-date so that a user at any site can access data anywhere on the network at any time and get the same answer.

Asynchronous distributed database: A form of distributed database technology in which copies of replicated data are kept at different nodes so that local servers can access data without reaching out across the network.

A distributed database system also faces certain costs and disadvantages:

- *Software cost and complexity* More complex software (especially the DBMS) is required for a distributed database environment. We discuss this software later in the chapter.
- *Processing overhead* The various sites must exchange messages and perform additional calculations to ensure proper coordination among data at the different the sites.
- *Data integrity* A by-product of the increased complexity and need for coordination is the additional exposure to improper updating and other problems of data integrity.
- *Slow response* If the data are not distributed properly according to their usage, or if queries are not formulated correctly, response to requests for data can be extremely slow. These issues are discussed later in the chapter.

OPTIONS FOR DISTRIBUTING A DATABASE

How should a database be distributed among the sites (or nodes) of a network? We discussed this important issue of physical database design in Chapter 6, which introduced an analytical procedure for evaluating alternative distribution strategies. In that chapter we noted that there are four basic strategies for distributing databases:

1. Data replication
2. Horizontal partitioning
3. Vertical partitioning
4. Combinations of the above

We will explain and illustrate each of these approaches using relational databases. The same concepts apply (with some variations) for other data models, such as hierarchical and network.

Suppose that a bank has numerous branches located throughout a state. One of the base relations in the bank's database is the Customer relation. Figure 13-4 shows the format for an abbreviated version of this relation. For simplicity, the sample data in the relation apply to only two of the branches (Lakeview and Valley). The primary key in this relation is account number (Acct_Number). Branch_Name is the name of the branch where customers have opened their accounts (and therefore where they presumably perform most of their transactions).

Data Replication

An increasingly popular option for data distribution is to store a separate copy of the database at each of two or more sites. Replication may allow an IS organization to move a database off a centralized mainframe onto less expensive, departmental or

Figure 13-4
Customer relation for a bank

Acct_Number	Customer_Name	Branch_Name	Balance
200	Jones	Lakeview	1000
324	Smith	Valley	250
153	Gray	Valley	38
426	Dorman	Lakeview	796
500	Green	Valley	168
683	McIntyre	Lakeview	1500
252	Elmore	Lakeview	330

location-specific servers, close to end users (Koop, 1995). Replication may use either synchronous or asynchronous distributed database technologies, although asynchronous technologies are more typical in a replicated environment. The Customer relation in Figure 13-4 could be stored at Lakeview or Valley, for example. If a copy is stored at every site, we have the case of full replication (which may be impractical except for only relatively small databases).

There are five advantages to data replication:

1. *Reliability*   If one of the sites containing the relation (or database) fails, a copy can always be found at another site without network traffic delays. Also, available copies can all be updated as soon as possible as transactions occur, and unavailable nodes will be updated once they return to service.

2. *Fast response*   Each site that has a full copy can process queries locally, so queries can be processed rapidly.

3. *Possible avoidance of complicated distributed transaction integrity routines*   Replicated databases are usually refreshed at scheduled intervals, so most forms of replication are used when some relaxing of synchronization across database copies is acceptable.

4. *Node decoupling*   Each transaction may proceed without coordination across the network. Thus, if nodes are down, busy, or disconnected (e.g., in the case of mobile personal computers), a transaction is handled when the user desires. In the place of real-time synchronization of updates, a behind-the-scenes process coordinates all data copies.

5. *Reduced network traffic at prime time*   Often updating data happens during prime business hours, when network traffic is highest and the demands for rapid response greatest. Replication, with delayed updating of copies of data, moves network traffic for sending updates to other nodes to non–prime time hours.

Replication has two primary disadvantages:

1. *Storage requirements*   Each site that has a full copy must have the same storage capacity that would be required if the data were stored centrally. Each copy requires storage space (the cost for which is constantly decreasing), and processing time is required to update each copy on each node.

2. *Complexity and cost of updating*   Whenever a relation is updated, it must (eventually) be updated at each site that holds a copy. Synchronizing updating near real time can require careful coordination, as will be clear later under the topic of commit protocol.

For these reasons, data replication is favored where most process requests are read-only and where the data are relatively static, as in catalogs, telephone directories, train schedules, and so on. CD-ROM and DVD storage technology has promise as an economical medium for replicated databases. Replication is used for "noncollaborative data," where one location does not need a real-time update of data maintained by other locations (Thé, 1994). In these applications, data eventually need to be synchronized, as quickly as is practical. Replication is not a viable approach for online applications such as airline reservations, automated teller machine transactions, and other financial activities—applications for which each user wants data about the same, nonsharable resource.

Snapshot Replication   Different schemes exist for updating data copies. Some applications, like those for decision support and data warehousing or mining—which do not require current data—are supported by simple table copying or periodic snapshots. This might work as follows, assuming multiple sites are updating the same data. First, updates from all replicated sites are periodically collected at a master or primary site, where all the updates are made to form a consolidated record of all changes. With some distributed DBMSs, this list of changes is collected in a snapshot log, which is a table of row identifiers for the records to go into the snapshot. Then a read-only snapshot of the replicated portion of the database is taken at the master site. Finally, the snapshot is sent to each site where there is a copy (it is often said that these other sites "subscribe" to the data owned at the primary site). This is called a full refresh of the database (Edelstein, 1995a; Buretta, 1997). Alternatively, only those pages that have changed since the last snapshot can be sent, which is called a differential or incremental refresh. In this case, a snapshot log for each replicated table is joined with the associated base to form the set of changed rows to be sent to the replicated sites.

Some forms of replication management allow dynamic ownership of data, in which the right to update replicated data moves from site to site, but at any point in time, only one site owns the right. Dynamic ownership would be appropriate as business activities move across time zones, or where the processing of data follows a work flow across business units supported by different database servers.

A final form of replication management allows shared ownership of data. Shared updates introduces significant issues for managing update conflicts across sites. For example, what if tellers at two bank branches try to update a customer's address at the same time? Asynchronous technology will allow conflicts to exist temporarily. This may be fine as long as the updates are not critical to business operations, and such conflicts can be detected and resolved before real business problems arise.

The cost to perform a snapshot refresh may depend on whether the snapshot is simple or complex. A simple snapshot is one that references all or a portion of only one table. A complex snapshot involves multiple tables, usually from transactions that involve joins (such as the entry of a customer order and associated line items). With some distributed DBMSs, a simple snapshot can be handled by a differential refresh whereas complex snapshots require more time-consuming full refreshes. Some distributed DBMSs support only simple snapshots.

Near Real-Time Replication For near real-time requirements, store and forward messages for each completed transaction can be broadcast across the network informing all nodes to update data as soon as is possible, without forcing a confirmation to the originating node (as is the case with a coordinated commit protocol, discussed below) before the database at the originating node is updated (Schussel, 1994). One way to generate such messages is by using triggers (discussed in Chapter 8). A trigger can be stored at each local database so that when a piece of replicated data is updated, the trigger executes corresponding update commands against remote database replicas (Edelstein, 1993). With the use of triggers, each database update event can be handled individually and transparently to programs and users. If network connections to a node are down or the node is busy, these messages informing the node to update its database are held in a queue to be processed when possible.

Pull Replication The schemes explained above for synchronizing replicas are all examples of push strategies. Pull strategies also exist. In a pull strategy, the target, not the source node, controls when a local database is updated. With pull strategies, the local database determines when it needs to be refreshed, and requests a snapshot or the emptying of an update message queue. Pull strategies have the advantage that the local site controls when it needs and can handle updates. Thus, synchronization is less disruptive and occurs only when needed by each site, not when a central master site thinks it is best to update.

Database Integrity with Replication For both periodic and near real-time replication, consistency across the distributed, replicated database is compromised. Whether delayed or near real-time, the DBMS managing replicated databases still must ensure the integrity of the database. Decision support applications permit synchronization on a table-by-table basis, whereas near real-time applications require transaction-by-transaction synchronization. But in both cases, the DBMS must ensure that copies are synchronized per application requirements.

The difficulty of handling updates with a replicated database also depends on the number of nodes at which updates may occur (Froemming, 1996). In a single-updater environment, updates will usually be handled by periodically sending read-only database snapshots of updated database segments to the nonupdater nodes. In this case the effects of multiple updates are effectively batched for the read-only sites. This would be the situation for product catalogs, price lists, and other reference data for a mobile sales force. In a multiple-updater environment, the most obvious issue is data collisions. Data collisions arise when the independently operating updating nodes are each attempting to update the same data at the same time. In this case, the DBMS must include mechanisms to detect and handle data collisions. For example, the DBMS must decide if processing at nodes in conflict should be suspended until the collision is resolved.

When to Use Replication Whether replication is a viable alternative design for a distributed database depends on several factors (Froemming, 1996):

1. *Data timeliness* Applications that can tolerate out-of-date data (whether this be for a few seconds or a few hours) are better candidates for replication.

2. *DBMS capabilities* An important DBMS capability is whether it will support a query that references data from more than one node. If not, then replication is a better candidate than the partitioning schemes, which are discussed in the following sections.

3. *Performance implications* Replication means that each node is periodically refreshed. When this refreshing occurs, the distributed node may be very busy handling a large volume of updates. If the refreshing occurs by event triggers (for example, when a certain volume of changes accumulate), refreshing could occur at a time when the remote node is busy doing local work.

4. *Heterogeneity in the network* Replication can be complicated if different nodes use different operating systems and DBMSs, or, more commonly, use different database designs. Mapping changes from one site to *n* other sites could mean *n* different routines to translate the changes from the originating node into the scheme for processing at the other nodes.

5. *Communications network capabilities* Transmission speeds and capacity in a data communications network may prohibit frequent, complete refreshing of very large tables. Replication does not require a dedicated communications connection, however, so less expensive, shared networks could be used for database snapshot transmissions.

Horizontal Partitioning

With *horizontal partitioning* (see Chapter 6 for a description of different forms of table partitioning), some of the rows of a table (or relation) are put into a base relation at one site, and other rows are put into a base relation at another site. More generally, the rows of a relation are distributed to many sites.

Figure 13-5 shows the result of taking horizontal partitions of the Customer relation. Each row is now located at its home branch. If customers actually conduct most

Figure 13-5
Horizontal partitions
(a) Lakeview Branch

Acct_Number	Customer_Name	Branch_Name	Balance
200	Jones	Lakeview	1000
426	Dorman	Lakeview	796
683	McIntyre	Lakeview	1500
252	Elmore	Lakeview	330

(b) Valley Branch

Acct_Number	Customer_Name	Branch_Name	Balance
324	Smith	Valley	250
153	Gray	Valley	38
500	Green	Valley	168

of their transactions at the home branch, the transactions are processed locally and response times are minimized. When a customer initiates a transaction at another branch, the transaction must be transmitted to the home branch for processing and the response transmitted back to the initiating branch (this is the normal pattern for persons using automated teller machines, or ATMs). If a customer's usage pattern changes (perhaps because of a move), the system may be able to detect this change and dynamically move the record to the location where most transactions are being initiated. In summary, horizontal partitions for a distributed database have four major advantages:

1. *Efficiency* Data are stored close to where they are used and separate from other data used by other users or applications.
2. *Local optimization* Data can be stored to optimize performance for local access.
3. *Security* Data not relevant to usage at a particular site are not made available.
4. *Ease of querying* Combining data across horizontal partitions is easy since rows are simply merged by unions across the partitions.

Thus, horizontal partitions are usually used when an organizational function is distributed, but each site is concerned with only a subset of the entity instances (frequently based on geography).

Horizontal partitions also have two primary disadvantages:

1. *Inconsistent access speed* When data from several partitions are required, the access time can be significantly different from local-only data access.
2. *Backup vulnerability* Since data are not replicated, when data at one site become inaccessible or damaged, usage cannot switch to another site where a copy exists; data may be lost if proper backup is not performed at each site.

Vertical Partitioning

With the *vertical partitioning* approach (again, see Chapter 6), some of the columns of a relation are projected into a base relation at one of the sites, and other columns are projected into a base relation at another site (more generally, columns may be projected to several sites). The relations at each of the sites must share a common domain, so that the original table can be reconstructed.

To illustrate vertical partitioning, we use an application for the manufacturing company shown in Figure 13-6. Figure 13-7 shows the Part relation with Part_Number

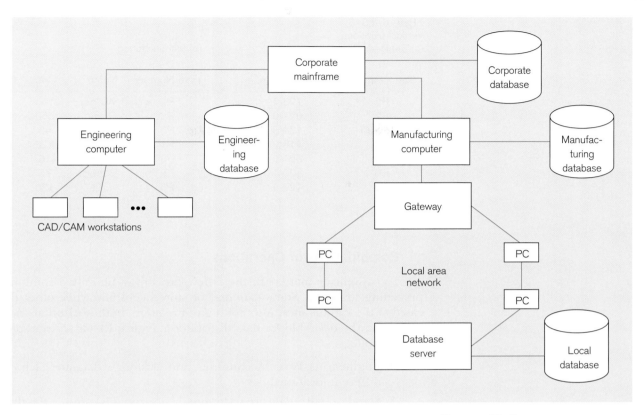

Figure 13-6
Distributed processing system for a manufacturing company

as the primary key. Some of these data are used primarily by manufacturing, while others are used mostly by engineering. The data are distributed to the respective departmental computers using vertical partitioning, as shown in Figure 13-8. Each of the partitions shown in Figure 13-8 is obtained by taking projections (that is, selected columns) of the original relation. The original relation in turn can be obtained by taking natural joins of the resulting partitions.

In summary, the advantages and disadvantages of vertical partitions are identical to those for horizontal partitions, with the exception that combining data across vertical partitions is more difficult than across horizontal partitions. This difficulty arises from the need to match primary keys or other qualifications to join rows across partitions. Horizontal partitions support an organizational design in which functions are replicated, often on a regional basis, while vertical partitions are typically applied across organizational functions with reasonably separate data requirements.

Part_Number	Name	Cost	Drawing_Number	Qty_on_Hand
P2	Widget	100	123-7	20
P7	Gizmo	550	621-0	100
P3	Thing	48	174-3	0
P1	Whatsit	220	416-2	16
P8	Thumzer	16	321-0	50
P9	Bobbit	75	400-1	0
P6	Nailit	125	129-4	200

Figure 13-7
Part relation

Figure 13-8
Vertical partitions
(a) Engineering (b) Manufacturing

Part_Number	Drawing_Number
P2	123-7
P7	621-0
P3	174-3
P1	416-2
P8	321-0
P9	400-1
P6	129-4

Part_Number	Name	Cost	Qty_On_Hand
P2	Widget	100	20
P7	Gizmo	550	100
P3	Thing	48	0
P1	Whatsit	220	16
P8	Thumzer	16	50
P9	Bobbit	75	0
P6	Nailit	125	200

Combinations of Operations

To complicate matters further, there are almost unlimited combinations of the preceding strategies. Some data may be stored centrally, while other data are replicated at the various sites. Also, for a given relation, both horizontal and vertical partitions may be desirable for data distribution. Figure 13-9 is an example of a combination strategy:

1. Engineering Parts, Accounting, and Customer data are each centralized at different locations.

2. Standard parts data are partitioned (horizontally) among the three locations.

3. The Standard Price List is replicated at all three locations.

The overriding principle in distributed database design is that data should be stored at the sites where they will be accessed most frequently (although other considerations, such as security, data integrity, and cost, are also likely to be important). The data administrator plays a critical and central role in organizing a distributed database in order to make it distributed, not decentralized.

Figure 13-9
Hybrid data distribution strategy
(Source: Copyright © *Database Programming & Design*, April 1989, Vol. 2, No. 4. Reprinted by permission of Miller Freeman Publications.)

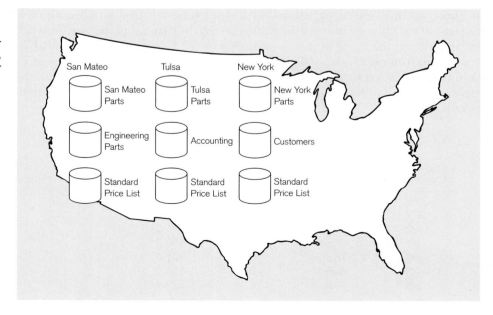

Selecting the Right Data Distribution Strategy

Based on the prior sections, a distributed database can be organized in five unique ways:

1. Totally centralized at one location accessed from many geographically distributed sites

2. Partially or totally replicated across geographically distributed sites, with each copy periodically updated with snapshots

3. Partially or totally replicated across geographically distributed sites, with near real-time synchronization of updates

4. Partitioned into segments at different geographically distributed sites, but still within one logical database and one distributed DBMS

5. Partitioned into independent, nonintegrated segments spanning multiple computers and database software

None of these five approaches is always best. Table 13-1 summarizes the comparative features of these five approaches using the key dimensions of reliability, expandability for adding nodes, communications overhead or demand on communications network, manageability, and data consistency. A distributed database designer needs to balance these factors to select a good strategy for a given distributed database environment. The choice of which strategy is best in a given situation depends on several factors.

- *Organizational forces* funding availability, autonomy of organizational units, and the need for security.

- *Frequency and locality or clustering of reference to data* In general, data should be located close to the applications that use those data.

Table 13-1 Comparison of Distributed Database Design Strategies

Strategy	Reliability	Expandability	Communications Overhead	Manageability	Data Consistency
Centralized	**POOR:** Highly dependent on central server	**POOR:** Limitations are barriers to performance	**VERY HIGH:** High traffic to one site	**VERY GOOD:** One, monolithic site requires little coordination	**EXCELLENT:** All users always have same data
Replicated with snapshots	**GOOD:** Redundancy and tolerated delays	**VERY GOOD:** Cost of additional copies may be less than linear	**LOW to MEDIUM:** Not constant, but periodic snapshots can cause bursts of network traffic	**VERY GOOD:** Each copy is like every other one	**MEDIUM:** Fine as long as delays are tolerated by business needs
Synchronized replication	**EXCELLENT:** Redundancy and minimal delays	**VERY GOOD:** Cost of additional copies may be low and synchronization work only linear	**MEDIUM:** Messages are constant, but some delays are tolerated	**MEDIUM:** Collisions add some complexity to manageability	**MEDIUM to VERY GOOD:** Close to precise consistency
Integrated partitions	**VERY GOOD:** Effective use of partitioning and redundancy	**VERY GOOD:** New nodes get only data they need without changes in overall database design	**LOW to MEDIUM:** Most queries are local but queries which require data from multiple sites can cause a temporary load	**DIFFICULT:** Especially difficult for queries that need data from distributed tables, and updates must be tightly coordinated	**VERY POOR:** Considerable effort, and inconsistencies not tolerated
Decentralized with independent partitions	**GOOD:** Depends on only local database availability	**GOOD:** New sites independent of existing ones	**LOW:** Little if any need to pass data or queries across the network (if one exists)	**VERY GOOD:** Easy for each site, until there is a need to share data across sites	**LOW:** No guarantees of consistency, in fact pretty sure of inconsistency

- *Need for growth and expansion*   The availability of processors on the network will influence where data may be located and applications can be run, and may indicate the need for expansion of the network.

- *Technological capabilities*   Capabilities at each node and for DBMSs, coupled with the costs for acquiring and managing technology, must be considered. Storage costs tend to be low, but the costs for managing complex technology can be great.

- *Need for reliable service*   Mission-critical applications and very frequently required data encourage replication schemes.

DISTRIBUTED DBMS

To have a distributed database, there must be a database management system that coordinates the access to data at the various nodes. We will call such a system a *distributed DBMS*. Although each site may have a DBMS managing the local database at that site, a distributed DBMS will perform the following functions (Elmasri and Navathe, 1989; Buretta, 1997):

1. Keep track of where data are located in a distributed data dictionary. This means, in part, presenting one logical database and schema to developers and users.

2. Determine the location from which to retrieve requested data and the location at which to process each part of a distributed query without any special actions by the developer or user.

3. If necessary, translate the request at one node using a local DBMS into the proper request to another node using a different DBMS and data model, and return data to the requesting node in the format accepted by that node.

4. Provide data management functions such as security, concurrency and deadlock control, global query optimization, and automatic failure recording and recovery.

5. Provide consistency among copies of data across the remote sites (e.g., by using multiphase commit protocols).

6. Present a single logical database that is physically distributed. One ramification of this view of data is global primary key control, meaning that data about the same business object is associated with the same primary key no matter where in the distributed database the data are stored, and different objects are associated with different primary keys.

7. Be scalable. Scalability is the ability to grow, reduce in size, and become more heterogeneous as the needs of the business change. Thus, a distributed database must be dynamic and be able to change within reasonable limits and without having to be redesigned. Scalability also means that there are easy ways for new sites to be added (or to subscribe) and to be initialized (e.g., with replicated data).

8. Replicate both data and stored procedures across the nodes of the distributed database. The need to distribute stored procedures is motivated by the same reasons for distributing data.

9. Transparently use residual computing power to improve the performance of database processing. This means, for example, the same database query may be processed at different sites and in different ways when submitted at different times, depending on the particular workload across the distributed database at the time of query submission.

10. Permit different nodes to run different DBMSs. Middleware (see Chapter 9) can be used by the distributed DBMS and each local DBMS to mask the differences in query languages and nuances of local data.

11. Allow different versions of application code to reside on different nodes of the distributed database. In a large organization with multiple, distributed servers, it may not be practical to have each server/node running the same version of software.

Not all distributed DBMSs are capable of performing all of the functions described above. The first six functions are present in almost every viable distributed DBMS. We have listed the remaining functions in approximately decreasing order of importance and how often they are provided by current technologies.

Conceptually, there could be different DBMSs running at each local site, with one master DBMS controlling the interaction across database parts. Such an environment is called a *heterogeneous distributed database*, as defined earlier in the chapter. Although ideal, complete heterogeneity is not practical today; limited capabilities exist with some products when each DBMS follows the same data architecture (for example, relational).

Figure 13-10 shows one popular architecture for a computer system with a distributed DBMS capability. Each site has a local DBMS that manages the database stored at that site. Also, each site has a copy of the distributed DBMS and the associated distributed data dictionary/directory (DD/D). The distributed DD/D contains the location of all data in the network, as well as data definitions. Requests for data by users or application programs are first processed by the distributed DBMS, which determines whether the transaction is local or global. A **local transaction** is one in which the required data are stored entirely at the local site. A **global transaction** requires reference to data at one or more nonlocal sites to satisfy the request. For local transactions, the distributed DBMS passes the request to the local DBMS; for global transactions, the distributed DBMS routes the request to other sites as necessary. The distributed DBMSs at the participating sites exchange messages as needed to coordinate the processing of the transaction until it is completed (or aborted, if necessary). This process may be quite complex, as we will see.

Local transaction: In a distributed database, a transaction that requires reference only to data that are stored at the site where the transaction originates.

Global transaction: In a distributed database, a transaction that requires reference to data at one or more nonlocal sites to satisfy the request.

Figure 13-10
Distributed DBMS architecture

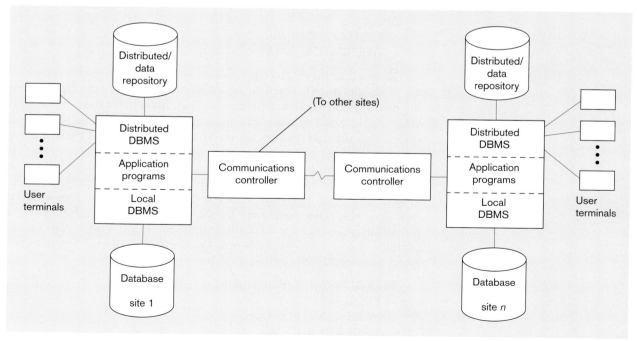

The DBMS (and its data model) at one site may be different from that at another site; for example, site A may have a relational DBMS, while site B has a network DBMS. In this case, the distributed DBMS must translate the request so that it can be processed by the local DBMS. The capability for handling mixed DBMSs and data models is a state-of-the-art development that is beginning to appear in some commercial DBMS products.

In our discussion of an architecture for a distributed system (Figure 13-10), we assumed that copies of the distributed DBMS and DD/D exist at each site (thus the DD/D is itself an example of data replication). An alternative is to locate the distributed DBMS and DD/D at a central site, and other strategies are also possible. However, the centralized solution is vulnerable to failure and therefore is less desirable.

A distributed DBMS should isolate users as much as possible from the complexities of distributed database management. Stated differently, the distributed DBMS should make transparent the location of data in the network as well as other features of a distributed database. Four key objectives of a distributed DBMS, when met, ease the construction of programs and the retrieval of data in a distributed system. These objectives, which are described below, are the following: location transparency, replication transparency, failure transparency, and concurrency transparency. To fully understand failure and concurrency transparency, we also discuss the concept of a commit protocol. Finally, we describe query optimization, which is an important function of a distributed DBMS.

Location Transparency

Although data are geographically distributed and may move from place to place, with *location transparency* users (including programmers) can act as if all the data were located at a single node. To illustrate location transparency, consider the distributed database in Figure 13-9. This company maintains warehouses and associated purchasing functions in San Mateo, California; Tulsa, Oklahoma; and New York City. The company's engineering offices are in San Mateo and sales offices in New York City. Suppose that a marketing manager in San Mateo, California, wanted a list of all company customers whose total purchases exceed $100,000. From a terminal in San Mateo, with location transparency the manager could enter the following request:

```
SELECT *
   FROM CUSTOMER
   WHERE TOTAL_SALES < l00,000;
```

Notice that this SQL request does not require the user to know where the data are physically stored. The distributed DBMS at the local site (San Mateo) will consult the distributed DD/D and determine that this request must be routed to New York. When the selected data are transmitted and displayed in San Mateo, it appears to the user at that site that the data were retrieved locally (unless there is a lengthy communications delay!).

Now consider a more complex request that requires retrieval of data from more than one site. For example, consider the Parts logical file in Figure 13-9, which is geographically partitioned into physically distributed database files stored on computers near their respective warehouse location: San Mateo parts, Tulsa parts, and New York parts. Suppose that an inventory manager in Tulsa wishes to construct a list of orange-colored parts (regardless of location). This manager could use the following query to assemble this information from the three sites:

```
SELECT DISTINCT PART_NUMBER, PART_NAME
   FROM PART
   WHERE COLOR = 'Orange'
   ORDER BY PART_NO;
```

In forming this query, the user need not be aware that the parts data exist at various sites (assuming location transparency) and that therefore this is a global transaction. Without location transparency, the user would have to reference the parts data at each site separately and then assemble the data (possibly using a UNION operation) to produce the desired results.

If the DBMS does not directly support location transparency, a database administrator can accomplish virtual location transparency for users by creating views (see Chapter 8 for a discussion of views in SQL). For the distributed database of Figure 13-9, the following view virtually consolidates part records into one table:

```
CREATE VIEW ALL_PART AS
    (SELECT PART_NUMBER, PART_NAME FROM SAN_MATEO_PART
    UNION
    SELECT PART_NUMBER, PART_NAME FROM TULSA_PART
    UNION
    SELECT PART_NUMBER, PART_NAME FROM NEW_YORK_PART);
```

where the three part table names are synonyms for the tables at three remote sites.

The preceding examples concern read-only transactions. Can a local user also update data at a remote site (or sites)? With today's distributed DBMS products, a user can certainly update data stored at one remote site, such as the Customer data in this example. Thus a user in Tulsa could update bill-of-material data stored in San Mateo. A more complex problem arises in updating data stored at multiple sites, such as the Vendor file. We discuss this problem in the next section.

To achieve location transparency, the distributed DBMS must have access to an accurate and current data dictionary/directory that indicates the location (or locations) of all data in the network. When the directories are distributed (as in the architecture shown in Figure 13-9), they must be synchronized so that each copy of the directory reflects the same information concerning the location of data. Although much progress has been made, true location transparency is not yet available in most systems today.

Replication Transparency

Although the same data item may be replicated at several nodes in a network, with **replication transparency** (sometimes called *fragmentation transparency*) the programmer (or other user) may treat the item as if it were a single item at a single node.

To illustrate replication transparency, see the Standard Price List file (Figure 13-9). An identical copy of this file is maintained at all three nodes (full replication). First, consider the problem of reading part (or all) of this file at any node. The distributed DBMS will consult the data directory and determine that this is a local transaction (that is, it can be completed using data at the local site only). Thus the user need not be aware that the same data are stored at other sites.

Now suppose that the data are replicated at some (but not all) sites (partial replication). If a read request originates at a site that does not contain the requested data, that request will have to be routed to another site. In this case the distributed DBMS should select the remote site that will provide the fastest response. The choice of site will probably depend on current conditions in the network (such as availability of communications lines). Thus the distributed DBMS (acting in concert with other network facilities) should dynamically select an optimum route. Again, with replication transparency the requesting user need not be aware that this is a global (rather than local) transaction.

A more complex problem arises when one or more users attempt to update replicated data. For example, suppose that a manager in New York wants to change the price of one of the parts. This change must be accomplished accurately and concurrently at all three sites, or the data will not be consistent. With replication trans-

Replication transparency: A design goal for a distributed database, which says that although a given data item may be replicated at several nodes in a network, a programmer or user may treat the data item as if it were a single item at a single node. Also called *fragmentation transparency*.

parency, the New York manager can enter the data as if this were a local transaction and be unaware that the same update is accomplished at all three sites. However, to guarantee that data integrity is maintained, the system must also provide concurrency transparency and failure transparency, which we discuss next.

Failure Transparency

Each site (or node) in a distributed system is subject to the same types of failure as in a centralized system (erroneous data, disk head crash, and so on). However, there is the additional risk of failure of a communications link (or loss of messages). For a system to be robust, it must be able to *detect* a failure, *reconfigure* the system so that computation may continue, and *recover* when a processor or link is repaired.

Error detection and system reconfiguration are probably the functions of the communications controller or processor, rather than the DBMS. However, the distributed DBMS is responsible for database recovery when a failure has occurred. The distributed DBMS at each site has a component called the **transaction manager** that performs the following functions:

Transaction manager: In a distributed database, a software module that maintains a log of all transactions and an appropriate concurrency control scheme.

1. Maintains a log of transactions and before and after database images.
2. Maintains an appropriate concurrency control scheme to ensure data integrity during parallel execution of transactions at that site.

For global transactions, the transaction managers at each participating site cooperate to ensure that all update operations are synchronized. Without such cooperation, data integrity can be lost when a failure occurs. To illustrate how this might happen, suppose (as we did earlier) that a manager in New York wants to change the price of a part in the Standard Price List file (Figure 13-9). This transaction is global: every copy of the record for that part (three sites) must be updated. Suppose that the price list records in New York and Tulsa are successfully updated; however, due to transmission failure, the price list record in San Mateo is not updated. Now the data records for this part are in disagreement, and an employee may access an inaccurate price for that part.

Failure transparency: A design goal for a distributed database, which guarantees that either all the actions of each transaction are committed or else none of them is committed.

With **failure transparency**, either all the actions of a transaction are committed or none of them are committed. Once a transaction occurs, its effects survive hardware and software failures. In the vendor example, when the transaction failed at one site, the effect of that transaction was not committed at the other sites. Thus the old vendor rating remains in effect at all sites until the transaction can be successfully completed.

Commit Protocol

Commit protocol: An algorithm to ensure that a transaction is successfully completed or else it is aborted.

Two-phase commit: An algorithm for coordinating updates in a distributed database.

To ensure data integrity for real-time, distributed update operations, the cooperating transaction managers execute a **commit protocol**, which is a well-defined procedure (involving an exchange of messages) to ensure that a global transaction is either successfully completed at each site or else aborted. The most widely used protocol is called a **two-phase commit**. A two-phase commit protocol ensures that concurrent transactions at multiple sites are processed as though they were executed in the same, serial order at all sites. A two-phase commit works something like arranging a meeting between many people. First, the site originating the global transaction or an overall coordinating site (like the person trying to schedule a meeting) sends a request to each of the sites that will process some portion of the transaction. In the case of scheduling a meeting, the message might be "Are you available at a given date and time?" Each site processes the subtransaction (if possible), but does not immediately commit (or store) the result to the local database. Instead, the result is stored in a temporary file. In our meeting analogy, each person writes the meeting on his or her calendar in pencil. Each site does, however, lock (prohibit other updating) its portion of the database being updated (as each person would prohibit other appointments at the same tentative meeting time). Each site notifies the originating site when it has completed its subtransaction. When all sites have responded, the originating site now initiates the two-phase commit protocol:

1. A message is broadcast to every participating site, asking whether that site is willing to commit its portion of the transaction at that site. Each site returns an "OK" or "not OK" message. This would be like a message that each person can or cannot attend the meeting. This is often called the prepare phase. An OK says that the remote site promises to allow the initiating request to govern the transaction at the remote database.

2. The originating site collects the messages from all sites. If all are "OK," it broadcasts a message to all sites to commit the portion of the transaction handled at each site. If one or more responses are "not OK," it broadcasts a message to all sites to abort the transaction. This is often called the commit phase. Again, our hypothetical meeting arranger would confirm or abort plans for the meeting depending on the response from each person. It is possible for a transaction to fail during the commit phase (that is, between commits among the remote sites), even though it passed the prepare phase; in this case, the transaction is said to be in limbo. A limbo transaction can be identified by a timeout or polling. With a timeout (no confirmation of commit for a specified time period), it is not possible to distinguish between a busy or failed site. Polling can be expensive in terms of network load and processing time.

This description of a two-phase commit protocol is highly simplified. For a more detailed discussion of this and other protocols, see Date (1995).

With a two-phase commit strategy for synchronizing distributed data, committing a transaction is slower than if the originating location were able to work alone. Recent improvements in this traditional approach to two-phase commit are aimed at reducing the delays caused by the extensive coordination inherent in this approach. Three improvement strategies have been developed (McGovern, 1993):

- *Read-only commit optimization*   This approach identifies read-only portions of a transaction and eliminates the need for confirmation messages on these portions. For example, a transaction might include checking an inventory balance before entering a new order. The reading of the inventory balance within the transaction boundaries can occur without the callback confirmation.

- *Lazy commit optimization*   This approach allows those sites which can update to proceed to update, and other sites which cannot immediately update are allowed to "catch up" later.

- *Linear commit optimization*   This approach permits each part of a transaction to be committed in sequence, rather than holding up a whole transaction when subtransaction parts are delayed from being processed.

Concurrency Transparency

The problem of concurrency control for a single (centralized) database is discussed in depth in Chapter 12. When multiple users access and update a database, data integrity may be lost unless locking mechanisms are used to protect the data from the effects of concurrent updates. The problem of concurrency control is more complex in a distributed database, since the multiple users are spread out among multiple sites and the data are often replicated at several sites, as well.

Concurrency transparency: A design goal for a distributed database, with the property that although a distributed system runs many transactions, it appears that a given transaction is the only activity in the system. Thus, when several transactions are processed concurrently, the results must be the same as if each transaction were processed in serial order.

The objective of concurrency management is easy to define but often difficult to implement in practice. Although the distributed system runs many transactions concurrently, **concurrency transparency** allows each transaction to appear as if it were the only activity in the system. Thus when several transactions are processed concurrently, the results must be the same as if each transaction were processed in serial order.

The transaction managers (introduced above) at each site must cooperate to provide concurrency control in a distributed database. Three basic approaches may be used: locking and versioning, which are explained in Chapter 12 as concurrency control methods in any database environment, and timestamping. A few special aspects of locking in a distributed database are discussed in Date (1995). The next section reviews the timestamping approach.

Timestamping: In distributed databases, a concurrency control mechanism that assigns a globally unique timestamp to each transaction. Timestamping is an alternative to the use of locks in distributed databases.

Timestamping With this approach, every transaction is given a globally unique timestamp, which generally consists of the clock time when the transaction occurred and the site ID. **Timestamping** ensures that even if two events occur simultaneously at different sites, each will have a unique timestamp.

The purpose of timestamping is to ensure that transactions are processed in serial order, thereby avoiding the use of locks (and the possibility of deadlocks). Every record in the database carries the timestamp of the transaction that last updated it. If a new transaction attempts to update that record and its timestamp is *earlier* than that carried in the record, the transaction is assigned a new timestamp and restarted. Thus, a transaction cannot process a record until its timestamp is *later* than that carried in the record, and therefore it cannot interfere with another transaction.

To illustrate timestamping, suppose that a database record carries the timestamp 168, which indicates that a transaction with timestamp 168 was the most recent transaction to successfully update that record. A new transaction with timestamp 170 attempts to update the same record. This update is permitted, since the transaction's timestamp is later than the record's current timestamp. When the update is committed, the record timestamp will be reset to 170. Now, suppose instead that a record with timestamp 165 attempts to update the record. This update will not be allowed, since the timestamp is earlier than that carried in the record. Instead, the transaction timestamp will be reset to that of the record (168), and the transaction will be restarted.

The major advantage of timestamping is that locking and deadlock detection (and the associated overhead) are avoided. The major disadvantage is that the approach is conservative, in that transactions are sometimes restarted even when there is no conflict with other transactions.

Query Optimization

With distributed databases, the response to a query may require the DBMS to assemble data from several different sites (although with location transparency, the user is unaware of this need). A major decision for the DBMS is how to process a query, which is affected by both the way a user formulates a query and the intelligence of the distributed DBMS to develop a sensible plan for processing. Date (1983) provides an excellent yet simple example of this problem. Consider the following situation adapted from Date. A simplified procurement (relational) database has the following three relations:

SUPPLIER (SUPPLIER_NUMBER, CITY)	10,000 records, stored in Detroit
PART (PART_NUMBER, COLOR)	100,000 records, stored in Chicago
SHIPMENT(SUPPLIER_NUMBER, PART_NUMBER)	1,000,000 records, stored in Detroit

and a query is made (in SQL) to list the supplier numbers for Cleveland suppliers of red parts:

```
SELECT      SUPPLIER.SUPPLIER_NUMBER
FROM        SUPPLIER, SHIPMENT, PART
WHERE       SUPPLIER.CITY = 'Cleveland'
    AND     SHIPMENT.PART_NUMBER = PART.PART_NUMBER
    AND     PART.COLOR = 'Red';
```

Each record in each relation is 100 characters long, there are 10 red parts, a history of 100,000 shipments from Cleveland, and a negligible query computation time compared with communication time. Also, there is a communication system with a data transmission rate of 10,000 characters per second and 1 second access delay to send a message from one node to another.

Date identifies six plausible query-processing strategies for this situation and develops the associated communication times; these strategies and times are summarized in Table 13-2. Depending on the choice of strategy, the time required to satisfy the query ranges from 1 second to 2.3 days! Although the last strategy is best, the fourth strategy is also acceptable.

In general, this example indicates that it is often advisable to break a query in a distributed database environment into components that are isolated at different sites, then determine which site has the potential to yield the fewest qualified records, and then move this result to another site where additional work is performed. Obviously, more than two sites require even more complex analyses and more complicated heuristics to guide query processing.

A distributed DBMS typically uses the following three steps to develop a query processing plan (Özsu and Valduriez, 1992):

1. *Query decomposition*   In this step, the query is simplified and rewritten into a structured, relational algebra form.

2. *Data localization*   Here, the query is transformed from a query referencing data across the network as if the database were in one location into one or more fragments which each explicitly reference data at only one site.

3. *Global optimization*   In this final step, decisions are made about the order in which to execute query fragments, where to move data between sites, and where parts of the query will be executed.

Table 13-2 Query-Processing Strategies in a Distributed Database Environment (Adapted from Date, 1983)

Method	Time
Move PART relation to Detroit, and process whole query at Detroit computer.	16.7 minutes
Move SUPPLIER and SHIPMENT relations to Chicago, and process whole query at Chicago computer.	28 hours
JOIN SUPPLIER and SHIPMENT at the Detroit computer, PROJECT these down to only tuples for Cleveland suppliers, and then for each of these, check at the Chicago computer to determine if associated PART is red.	2.3 days
PROJECT PART at the Chicago computer down to just the red items, and for each, check at the Detroit computer to see if there is some SHIPMENT involving that PART and a Cleveland SUPPLIER.	20 seconds
JOIN SUPPLIER and SHIPMENT at the Detroit computer, PROJECT just SUPPLIER_NUMBER and PART_NUMBER for only Cleveland SUPPLIERs, and move this qualified projection to Chicago for matching with red PARTs.	16.7 minutes
Select just red PARTs at the Chicago computer and move the result to Detroit for matching with Cleveland SUPPLIERs.	1 second

Certainly, the design of the database interacts with the sophistication of the distributed DBMS to yield the performance for queries. A distributed database will be designed based on the best possible understanding of how and where the data will be used. Given the database design (which allocates data partitions to one or more sites), however, all queries, whether anticipated or not, must be processed as efficiently as possible.

One technique used to make processing a distributed query more efficient is to use what is called a **semijoin** operation (Elmasri and Navathe, 1989). In a semijoin, only the joining attribute is sent from one site to another, and then only the required rows are returned. If only a small percentage of the rows participate in the join, then the amount of data being transferred is minimal.

For example, consider the distributed database in Figure 13-11. Suppose that a query at Site 1 asks to display the Cust_Name, SIC, and Order_Date for all customers in a particular Zip_Code range and an Order_Amount above a specified limit. Assume that 10 percent of the customers fall in the Zip_Code range and 2 percent of the orders are above the amount limit. A semijoin would work as follows:

1. A query is executed at Site 1 to create a list of the Cust_No values in the desired Zip_Code range. So 10,000 customers * .1, or 1,000 rows satisfy the Zip_Code qualification. Thus, 1,000 rows of 10 bytes each for the Cust_No attribute (the joining attribute), or 10,000 bytes, will be sent to Site 2.

2. A query is executed at Site 2 to create a list of the Cust_No and Order_Date values to be sent back to Site 1 to compose the final result. If we assume roughly the same number of orders for each customer, then 40,000 rows of the Order table will match with the customer numbers sent from Site 1. If we assume any customer order is equally likely to be above the amount limit, then 800 rows (40,000 * .02) of the Order table rows are relevant to this query. For each row, the Cust_No and Order_Date need to be sent to Site 1, or 14 bytes * 800 rows, thus 11,200 bytes.

The total data transferred is only 21,200 bytes using the semijoin just described. Compare this total to simply sending the subset of each table needed at one site to the other site:

- To send data from Site 1 to Site 2 would require sending the Cust_No, Cust_Name, and SIC (65 bytes) for 1000 rows of the Customer table (65,000 bytes) to Site 2.

- To send data from Site 2 to Site 1 would require sending Cust_No and Order_Date (14 bytes) for 8000 rows of the Order table (112,000 bytes).

Clearly, the semijoin approach saves network traffic, which can be a major contributing factor to the overall time to respond to a user's query.

A distributed DBMS uses a cost model to predict the execution time (for data processing and transmission) of alternative execution plans. The cost model is performed before the query is executed based on general network conditions; consequently the actual cost may be more or less, depending on the actual network and node loads, database reorganizations, and other dynamic factors. Thus, the parame-

Semijoin: A joining operation used with distributed databases in which only the joining attribute from one site is transmitted to the other site, rather than all the selected attributes from every qualified row.

Figure 13-11
Distributed database, one table at each of two sites

Site 1		Site 2	
Customer table		Order table	
Cust_No	10 bytes	Order_No	10 bytes
Cust_Name	50 bytes	Cust_No	10 bytes
Zip_Code	10 bytes	Order_Date	4 bytes
SIC	5 bytes	Order_Amount	6 bytes
10,000 rows		400,000 rows	

ters of the cost model should be periodically updated as general conditions change in the network (for example, as local databases are redesigned, network paths are changed, and DBMSs at local sites are replaced).

Evolution of Distributed DBMS

Distributed database management is still an emerging, rather than established technology. Current releases of distributed DBMS products do not provide all of the features described in the previous sections. For example, some products provide location transparency for read-only transactions but do not yet support global updates. To illustrate the evolution of distributed DBMS products, we briefly describe three stages in this evolution: remote unit of work, distributed unit of work, and distributed request. Then, in the next section, we summarize the major features of leading distributed DBMSs (present in these packages at the time of writing this text).

In the following discussion the term *unit of work* refers to the sequence of instructions required to process a transaction. That is, it consists of the instructions that begin with a "begin transaction" operation and end with either a "commit" or a "rollback" operation.

Remote Unit of Work The first stage allows multiple SQL statements to be originated at one location and executed as a single unit of work on a *single* remote DBMS. Both the originating and receiving computers must be running the same DBMS. The originating computer does not consult the data directory to locate the site containing the selected tables in the remote unit of work. Instead, the originating application must know where the data reside and connect to the remote DBMS prior to each remote unit of work. Thus the remote unit of work concept does not support location transparency.

A remote unit of work (also called a remote transaction) allows updates at the single remote computer. All updates within a unit of work are tentative until a commit operation makes them permanent or a rollback undoes them. Thus transaction integrity is maintained for a single remote site; however, an application cannot assure transaction integrity when more than one remote location is involved. Referring to the database in Figure 13-9, an application in San Mateo could update the Part file in Tulsa and transaction integrity would be maintained. However, that application could not simultaneously update the Part file in two or more locations and still be assured of maintaining transaction integrity. Thus the remote unit of work also does not provide failure transparency.

Distributed Unit of Work A distributed unit of work allows various statements within a unit of work to refer to *multiple* remote DBMS locations. This approach supports some location transparency, since the data directory is consulted to locate the DBMS containing the selected table in each statement. However, all tables in a *single* SQL statement must be at the same location. Thus, a distributed unit of work would not allow the following query, designed to assemble parts information from all three sites in Figure 13-9:

```
SELECT DISTINCT    PART_NUMBER, PART_NAME
FROM               PART
WHERE              COLOR = 'ORANGE'
ORDER BY           PART_NUMBER
```

Similarly, a distributed unit of work would not allow a single SQL statement that attempts to update data at more than one location. For example, the following SQL statement is intended to update the part file at three locations:

```
UPDATE    PART
SET       UNIT_PRICE = 127.49
WHERE     PART_NUMBER = 12345
```

This update (if executed) would set the unit price of part number 12345 to $127.49 at Tulsa, San Mateo, and New York (Figure 13-9). The statement would not be acceptable as a distributed unit of work, however, since the single SQL statement refers to data at more than one location. The distributed unit of work does support protected updates involving multiple sites, provided that each SQL statement refers to a table (or tables) at one site only. For example, suppose in Figure 13-9 we want to increase the balance of part number 12345 in Tulsa and at the same time decrease the balance of the same part in New York (perhaps to reflect an inventory adjustment). The following SQL statements could be used:

```
UPDATE      PART
SET         BALANCE = BALANCE – 50
WHERE       PART_NUMBER = 12345 AND LOCATION = 'TULSA'
UPDATE      PART
SET         BALANCE = BALANCE + 50
WHERE       PART_NUMBER = 12345 AND LOCATION = 'NEW YORK';
```

Under the distributed unit of work concept, either this update will be committed at both locations, or else it will be rolled back and (perhaps) attempted again. We conclude from these examples that the distributed unit of work supports some (but not all) of the transparency features described earlier in this section.

Distributed Request The distributed request allows a single SQL statement to refer to tables in more than one remote DBMS, overcoming a major limitation of the distributed unit of work. The distributed request supports true location transparency, since a single SQL statement can refer to tables at multiple sites. However, the distributed request may or may not support replication transparency or failure transparency. It will probably be some time before a true distributed DBMS, one that supports all of the transparency features we described earlier, appears on the market.

DISTRIBUTED DBMS PRODUCTS

Most of the leading vendors of database management systems have a distributed version. In most cases, to utilize all distributed database capabilities, one vendor's DBMS must be running at each node (a homogeneous distributed database environment). Client/server forms of a distributed database are arguably the most common form in existence today. In a client/server environment (see Chapter 9 for an explanation of client/server databases), it is very easy to define a database with tables on several nodes in a local or wide area network. Once a user program establishes a linkage with each remote site, and suitable database middleware is loaded, full location transparency is achieved. So, in a client/server database form, distributed databases are readily available to any information systems developer, and heterogeneity of DBMS is possible.

Although their approaches are constantly changing, it is illustrative to overview how different vendors address distributed database management. Probably the most interesting aspect is the differences across products. These differences (summarized in Table 13-3) suggest how difficult it is to select a distributed DBMS product, since the exact capabilities of the DBMS must be carefully matched with the needs of an organization. Also, with so many options, and with each product handling distributed data differently, it is almost impossible to outline general principles for managing a distributed database. The design of any distributed database requires careful analysis of both the business's needs and the intricacies of the DBMS. Thompson (1997) also recommends that a distributed DBMS product should be used only when you really need a distributed DBMS. Do not use a distributed DBMS to create a backup database for a mission-critical application; easier solutions, such as RAID (see Chapter 6), exist for simpler needs.

Table 13-3 Distributed DBMSs

Vendor	Product	Important Features
IBM	DataPropagator Relational (DPropR)	• Works with DB2 • Primary site and asynchronous updates • Read-only sites subscribe to primary site • Subscription to subset or query result
	Distributed Relational Database Architecture (DRDA)	• Heterogeneous databases
	DataJoiner	• Middleware to access non-IBM databases
Sybase	Replication Server	• Primary site and distributed read-only sites • Update to read-only site as one transaction • Hierarchical replication • Data and stored procedures replicated
	SQL Anywhere	• Mobile databases
	OmniSQL	• Heterogeneous databases
Oracle	Table Snapshot Option	• Periodic snapshots sent to read-only sites
	Symmetric Replication option	• Asynchronous and synchronous with multiple updatable copies and replication from any node to any other node (bidirectional) • Differential refresh • DBA controls replication • Two-phase commit
Computer Associates	CA-Ingres/Replicator	• All database copies updatable • Hierachical replication • DBA registers data for replication and other sites subscribe • Master/slave form allows slave to be an Ingres database
	Ingres/Net and Ingres/Star	• Decomposes query to distributed, homogeneous sites • Two-phase commit • Also used with non-Ingres databases
Microsoft	SQL Server	• Primary site and distributed read-only sites • Publish and subscribe, with articles and publications • One database can pass copies of publications to other sites • Mobile databases

Summary

This chapter covered various issues and technologies for distributed databases. We saw that a distributed database is a single logical database that is spread across computers in multiple locations connected by a data communications network. A distributed database is contrasted with a decentralized database, in which distributed data are not interconnected. In a distributed database, the network must allow users to share the data as transparently as possible, yet must allow each node to operate autonomously, especially when network linkages are broken or specific nodes fail. Business conditions today encourage the use of distributed databases: dispersion and autonomy of business units (including globalization of organizations), need for data sharing, and the costs and reliability of data communications. A distributed database environment may be homogeneous, involving the same DBMS at each node, or heterogeneous, with potentially different DBMSs at different nodes. Also, a distributed database environment may keep all copies of data and related data in immediate synchronization, or may tolerate planned delays in data updating through asynchronous methods.

There are numerous advantages to distributed databases. The most important of these are the following: increased reliability and availability of data, local control by users over their data, modular (or incremental) growth, reduced communications costs, and faster response to requests for data. There are also several costs and disadvantages of distributed databases: software is more costly and complex, processing overhead often increases, maintaining data integrity is often more difficult, and if data are not distributed properly, response to requests for data may be very slow.

There are several options for distributing data in a network: data replication, horizontal partitioning, vertical partitioning, and combinations of these approaches. With data replication, a separate copy of the database (or part of the database) is stored at each of two or more sites. Data replication can result in improved reliability and faster response, can be done simply under certain circumstances, allows nodes to operate more independently (yet coordinated) of each other, and reduces network traffic; however, additional storage capacity is required, and immediate updating at each of the sites may be difficult. Replicated data can be updated by taking periodic snapshots of an official record of data and sending the snapshots to replicated sites. These snapshots can involve all data or only the data that have changed since the last snapshot. With horizontal partitioning, some of the rows of a relation are placed at one site, and other rows are placed in a relation at another site (or several sites). On the other hand, vertical partitioning distributes the columns of a relation among different sites. The objectives of data partitioning include improved performance and security. Combinations of data replication and horizontal and vertical partitioning are often used. Organizational factors, frequency and location of queries and transactions, possible growth of data and node, technology, and the need for reliability influence the choice of a data distribution design.

To have a distributed database, there must be a distributed DBMS that coordinates the access to data at the various nodes. Requests for data by users or application programs are first processed by the distributed DBMS, which determines whether the transaction is local (can be processed at the local site), remote (can be processed at some other site), or global (requires access to data at several nonlocal sites). For global transactions, the distributed DBMS consults the data directory and routes parts of the request as necessary, and then consolidates results from the remote sites.

A distributed DBMS should isolate users from the complexities of distributed database management. By location transparency, we mean that although data are geographically distributed, they appear to users as if all of the data were located at a single node. By replication transparency, we mean that although a data item may be stored at several different nodes, the user may treat the item as if it were a single item at a single node. With failure transparency, either all the actions of a transaction are completed at each site, or else none of them are committed. Distributed databases can be designed to allow temporary inconsistencies across the nodes, when immediate synchronization is not necessary. With concurrency transparency, each transaction appears to be the only activity in the system. Failure and concurrency transparency can be managed by commit protocols, which coordinate updates across nodes, locking data, and timestamping.

A key decision made by a distributed DBMS is how to process a global query. The time to process a global query can vary from a few seconds to many hours depending on how intelligent the DBMS is in producing an efficient query-processing plan. A query-processing plan involves decomposing the query into a structured set of steps, identifying different steps with local data at different nodes in the distributed database, and finally choosing a sequence and location for executing each step of the query.

Few (if any) distributed DBMS products provide all forms of transparency, all forms of data replication and partitioning, and the same level of intelligence in distributed query processing. These products are, however, improving rapidly as the business pressures for distributed systems increase. Leading vendors of relational database products have introduced distributed versions, with tools to help a database administrator design and manage a distributed database.

CHAPTER REVIEW

Key Terms

Asynchronous distributed database
Commit protocol
Concurrency transparency
Decentralized database
Distributed database
Failure transparency

Global transaction
Local autonomy
Local transaction
Location transparency
Replication transparency

Semijoin
Synchronous distributed database
Timestamping
Transaction manager
Two-phase commit

Review Questions

1. Define each of the following terms:
   a. distributed database
   b. location transparency
   c. two-phase commit
   d. global transaction
   e. local autonomy
   f. timestamping
   g. transaction manager

2. Match the following terms to the appropriate definition:

   _____ replication transparency
   _____ unit of work
   _____ global transaction
   _____ concurrency transparency
   _____ replication
   _____ failure transparency

   a. guarantees that all or none of the updates occur in a transaction across a distributed database
   b. the appearance that a given transaction is the only transaction running against a distributed database
   c. treating copies of data as if there were only one copy
   d. references data at more than one location
   e. sequence of instructions required to process a transaction
   f. a good database distribution strategy for read-only data

3. Contrast the following terms:
   a. distributed database; decentralized database
   b. homogeneous distributed database; heterogeneous distributed database
   c. location transparency; local autonomy
   d. asynchronous distributed database; synchronous distributed database
   e. horizontal partition; vertical partition
   f. publish; subscribe
   g. full refresh; differential refresh
   h. push replication; pull replication
   i. local transaction; global transaction

4. Briefly describe six business conditions which are encouraging the use of distributed databases.

5. Explain two types of homogeneous distributed databases.

6. Briefly describe five major characteristics of homogeneous distributed databases.

7. Briefly describe four major characteristics of heterogeneous distributed databases.

8. Briefly describe five advantages for distributed databases compared to centralized databases.

9. Briefly describe four costs and disadvantages for distributed databases.

10. Briefly describe five advantages to the data replication form of distributed databases.

11. Briefly describe two disadvantages to the data replication form of distributed databases.

12. Explain under what circumstances a snapshot replication approach appears to be best.

13. Explain under what circumstances a near real-time replication approach appears to be best.

14. Briefly describe five factors that influence whether data replication is a viable distributed database design strategy for an application.

15. Explain the advantages and disadvantages of horizontal partitioning for distributed databases.

16. Explain the advantages and disadvantages of vertical partitioning for distributed databases.

17. Briefly describe five factors that influence the selection of a distributed database design strategy.

18. Briefly describe six unique functions performed by a distributed database management system.

19. Briefly explain the effect of location transparency on an author of an ad hoc database query.

20. Briefly explain the effect of replication transparency on an author of an ad hoc database query.

21. Briefly explain in what way two-phase commit can still fail to create a completely consistent distributed database.

22. Briefly describe three improvements to the two-phase commit protocol.

23. Briefly describe the three steps in distributed query processing.

24. Briefly explain the conditions that suggest the use of a semi-join will result in faster distributed query processing.

Problems and Exercises

Problems and Exercises 1–3 refer to the distributed database shown in Figure 13-9.

1. Name the type of transparency (location, replication, failure, concurrency) that is indicated by each statement.

   a. End users in New York and Tulsa are updating the Engineering Parts database in San Mateo at the same time. Neither user is aware that the other is accessing the data, and the system protects the data from lost updates due to interference.

   b. An end user in Tulsa deletes an item from the Standard Price List at the site. Unknown to the user, the distributed DBMS also deletes that item from the Standard Price List in San Mateo and New York.

   c. A user in San Mateo initiates a transaction to delete a part from San Mateo parts and simultaneously to add that part to New York parts. The transaction is completed in San Mateo but due to transmission failure is not completed in New York. The distributed DBMS automatically reverses the transaction at San Mateo and notifies the user to retry the transaction.

d. An end user in New York requests the balance on hand for part number 33445. The user does not know where the record for this part is located. The distributed DBMS consults the directory and routes the request to San Mateo.

2. Consider the Standard Price List in Figure 13-9.

a. Write an SQL statement that will increase the Unit_Price of Part_Number 56789 by 10%.

b. Indicate whether the statement you wrote in part (a) is acceptable under each of the following protocols:
   i. Remote unit of work
   ii. Distributed unit of work
   iii. Distributed request

3. Consider the four parts databases in Figure 13-9.

a. Write an SQL statement that will increase the Balance in Part_Number 56789 in San Mateo Parts by 10 percent, and another SQL statement that will decrease the Balance in Part_Number 12345 in New York Parts by 10 percent.

b. Indicate whether the statement you wrote in part (a) is acceptable under each of the following protocols:
   i. Remote unit of work
   ii. Distributed unit of work
   iii. Distributed request

4. Speculate on why you think a truly heterogeneous distributed database environment is so difficult to achieve. What specific difficulties exist in this environment?

5. Explain the major factors at work in creating the drastically different results for the six query-processing strategies outlined in Table 13-2.

6. Do any of the six query-processing strategies in Table 13-2 utilize a semijoin? If so, explain how a semijoin is used. If not, explain how you might use a semijoin to create an efficient query-processing strategy or why the use of a semijoin will not work in this situation.

7. Consider the SUPPLIER, PART, and SHIPMENT relations and distributed database mentioned in the section on Query Optimization in this chapter.

a. Write a global SQL query (submitted in Chicago) to display the Part_Number and Color for every part that is not supplied by a supplier in Columbus.

b. Design three alternative query-processing strategies for your answer to part (a).

c. Develop a table similar to Table 13-2 to compare the processing times for these three strategies.

d. Which of your three strategies was best and why?

e. Would data replication or horizontal or vertical partitioning of the database allow you to create an even more efficient query-processing strategy? Why or why not?

8. Consider the following normalized relations for a database in a large retail store chain:

STORE (Store_ID, Region, Manager_ID, Square_Feet)

EMPLOYEE (Employee_ID, Where_Work, Employee_Name, Employee_Address)

DEPARTMENT (Department_ID, Manager_ID, Sales_Goal)

SCHEDULE (Department_ID, Employee_ID, Date)

Assume that a data communications network links a computer at corporate headquarters with a computer in each retail outlet. The chain includes 50 stores with an average of 75 employees per store. There are 10 departments in each store. A daily schedule is maintained for 5 months (the previous 2 months, the current month, and next 2 months). Further assume that

• Each store manager updates the employee work schedule for her or his store roughly five times per hour.

• The corporation generates all payroll checks, employee notices, and other mailings for all employees for all stores.

• The corporation establishes a new sales goal each month for each department.

• The corporation hires and fires store managers and controls all information about store managers; store managers hire and fire all store employees and control all information about employees in that store.

a. Would you recommend a distributed database, a centralized database, or a set of decentralized databases for this retail store chain?

b. Assuming that some form of distributed database is justified, what would you recommend as a data distribution strategy for this retail store chain?

Field Exercises

1. Visit an organization that has installed a distributed database management system. Explore the following questions:

a. Does the organization have a truly distributed database? If so, how are the data distributed: replication, horizontal partitioning, vertical partitioning?

b. What commercial distributed DBMS products are used? What were the reasons the organization selected these products? What problems or limitations has the organization found with these products?

c. To what extent does this system provide each of the following:
   i. Location transparency
   ii. Replication transparency
   iii. Concurrency transparency
   iv. Failure transparency
   v. Query optimization

d. What are the organization's plans for future evolution of distributed databases?

e. Talk with a database administrator in the organization to explore how decisions are made concerning the location of data in the network. What factors are considered in this decision? Are any analytical tools used? If so, is the database administrator satisfied that the tools help to make the processing of queries efficient?

2. Using the World Wide Web, investigate the latest distributed database product offerings from the DBMS vendors mentioned in this chapter. Update the description of the features for one of the distributed DBMS products listed.

Search for distributed DBMS products from other vendors and include information about these products in your answer.

3. Visit an organization that has installed a client/server database environment. Explore the following questions:

a. What distributed database features do the client/server DBMSs in use offer?

b. Is the organization attempting to achieve the same benefits from a client/server environment as are outlined in this chapter for distributed databases? Which of these benefits are they achieving? Which cannot be achieved with client/server technologies?

References

Bell, D. and J. Grimson. 1992. *Distributed Database Systems*. Reading, MA: Addison-Wesley.

Buretta, M. 1997. *Data Replication: Tools and Techniques for Managing Distributed Information*. New York: John Wiley & Sons, Inc.

Date, C. J. 1983. *An Introduction to Database Systems*. Vol. 2. Reading, MA: Addison-Wesley.

Date, C. J. 1995. *An Introduction to Database Systems*. 6th ed. Reading, MA: Addison-Wesley.

Edelstein, H. 1993. "Replicating Data." *DBMS* 6 (June): 59–64.

Edelstein, H. 1995a. "The Challenge of Replication, Part I." *DBMS* 8 (March): 46–52.

Edelstein, H. 1995b. "The Challenge of Replication, Part II." *DBMS* 8 (April): 62–70, 103.

Elmasri, R., and S. B. Navathe. 1989. *Fundamentals of Database Systems*. Menlo Park, CA: Benjamin/Cummings.

Froemming, G. 1996. "Design and Replication: Issues with Mobile Applications—Part 1." *DBMS* 9 (March): 48–56.

Koop, P. 1995. "Replication at Work." *DBMS* 8 (March): 54–60.

McGovern, D. 1993. "Two-Phased Commit or Replication." *Database Programming & Design* 6 (May): 35–44.

Özsu, M. T., and P. Valduriez. 1992. "Distributed Database Systems: Where Were We?" *Database Programming & Design* 5 (April): 49–55.

Schussel, G. 1994. "Database Replication: Watch the Data Fly." *Client/Server Today* (October): 80–90.

Thé, L. 1994. "Distribute Data Without Choking the Net." *Datamation* (January 7): 35–38.

Thompson, C. 1997. "Database Replication: Comparing Three Leading DBMS Vendors' Approaches to Replication." *DBMS* 10 (May): 76–84.

Web Resources

http://dis.sema.es/projects/WIDE/ The WIDE project is a research and development project which is concerned with extending the technology of distributed and active databases, in order to provide added value to advanced, application-oriented software products implementing workflow techniques. These problems have been tackled by a consortium involving partners from organizations in Spain, Italy, and The Netherlands.

http://www.compapp.dcu.ie/databases/f449.html The Dublin City University maintains this Website, which is one of several con-

cerning databases and hypermedia. This site has an understandable tutorial on several important aspects of distributed databases.

http://databases.about.com/compute/databases/ This Website contains a variety of news and reviews about various database technologies, including distributed databases.

MOUNTAIN VIEW COMMUNITY HOSPITAL

Project Case

In the Mountain View Community Hospital case in Chapter 6, you made some physical database design decisions for a centralized database. Refer to your answers to Project Questions and Project Exercises in that case segment.

PROJECT DESCRIPTION

Mountain View Community Hospital is growing in several ways. First, the hospital will be opening its first satellite outpatient surgical unit in the Golf Estates suburb. Second, the hospital has been acquiring the practices of several doctor groups in the community and will be providing all patient recordkeeping and billing services for these offices and clinics. Given these significant changes, the hospital information systems staff members are considering using distributed computing and databases.

PROJECT QUESTIONS

1. What additional kinds of information, besides the information collected to make the physical database design decisions in the case in Chapter 6, do you need to decide if Mountain View Community should use distributed database technology?

2. What additional kinds of information, besides the information collected to make the physical database design decisions in the case in Chapter 6, do you need to design a distributed database for Mountain View Community?

3. Are there opportunities for data replication, horizontal partitioning, and vertical partitioning of a distributed database for Mountain View Community? If you are not sure, what other information would you need to answer this question?

PROJECT EXERCISES

Most of the data maintenance for the Mountain View Community Hospital database is local at the site of patient activity. For example, over 80 percent of changes to data represented in Case Figure 1 in Chapter 6 are made from doctor offices, 10 percent will be made at the main hospital, and 10 percent at the satellite surgical unit. Also, most queries are local (for example, a physician at a doctor's office will look up what treatments have been performed on a patient when that patient is in the office). But, because medical service questions usually require rapid response, the doctors are concerned about the performance of a distributed database.

On the other hand, administrative queries are almost exclusively centralized at the administrative offices located at the main hospital. Queries to produce statements, summaries of treatment statistics for state health agency inquiries, and physician productivity and profitability questions all are submitted by administrative staff at the hospital.

One proposal for the design of Mountain View's distributed database is to horizontally partition physician, patient, procedure, and consumption data and distribute these to the local physician office computer. For example, records for all the physicians in one practice, all the patients for whom any of these doctors are the primary care physician, and all the associated activity data will be stored on one computer at the doctors' office. Treatment and Item data are to be replicated across the sites. The main hospital computer and the surgical unit's computer are to maintain a copy of all data, since all the data need to be accessible when a patient is being treated at the hospital or surgical unit and data links to the offices are down.

1. What form of data replication integrity control would you recommend for this distributed database and why?

2. What would you recommend as a global query optimization plan for each of the following queries:
   a. What is the total number of units consumed of each Item during the last month?
   b. How many patients has each physician treated in each of the following categories over the past month: doctor offices, surgical unit, main hospital?
   c. Grouped by physician medical specialty, how many of each kind of treatment has each physician prescribed?

Chapter **14**

Object-Oriented Data Modeling

LEARNING OBJECTIVES

After studying this chapter, you should be able to:

- Define the following key terms: **object, state, behavior, object class, class diagram, object diagram, operation, encapsulation, constructor operation, query operation, update operation, scope operation, association, association role, multiplicity, association class, abstract class, concrete class, class-scope attribute, abstract operation, method, polymorphism, overriding, multiple classification, aggregation,** and **composition.**

- Describe the activities in the different phases of the object-oriented development life cycle.

- State the advantages of object-oriented modeling vis-à-vis structured approaches.

- Compare and contrast the object-oriented model with the E-R and EER models.

- Model a real-world application by using a UML class diagram.

- Provide a snapshot of the detailed state of a system at a point in time using a UML (Unified Modeling Language) object diagram.

- Recognize when to use generalization, aggregation, and composition relationships.

- Specify different types of business rules in a class diagram.

INTRODUCTION

In Chapters 3 and 4, you learned about data modeling using the E-R and EER models. In those chapters you learned how to model the data needs of an organization using entities, attributes, and a wide variety of relationships. In this chapter, you will be introduced to the object-oriented model, which is becoming increasingly popular because of its ability to thoroughly represent complex relationships, as well as to represent data and data processing in a consistent notation. Fortunately, most of the concepts you learned in those chapters correspond to concepts in object-oriented modeling, but as you will see, the object-oriented model has even more features than the EER model.

As you learned in Chapters 3 and 4, a data model is an abstraction of the real world. It allows you to deal with the complexity inherent in a real-world problem

---

The original version of this chapter was written by Professor Atish P. Sinha, University of Wisconsin–Milwaukee.

by focusing on the essential and interesting features of the data an organization needs. An object-oriented model is built around *objects,* just as the E-R model is built around entities. However, as we shall see later, an object *encapsulates* both data and *behavior,* implying that we can use the object-oriented approach not only for data modeling, but also for process modeling. To thoroughly model any real-world application, you need to model both the data and the processes that act on the data (recall the discussion in Chapter 2 about information planning objects). By allowing you to capture them together within a common representation, and by offering benefits such as *inheritance* and code reuse, the object-oriented modeling approach provides a powerful environment for developing complex systems.

The object-oriented development life cycle, depicted in Figure 14-1, consists of progressively developing object representation through three phases—analysis, design, and implementation—similar to the heart of the systems development life cycle explained in Chapter 2. In the early stages of development, the model you develop is abstract, focusing on external qualities of the system. As the model evolves, it becomes more and more detailed, the focus shifting to how the system will be built and how it should function. The emphasis in modeling should be on analysis and design, focusing on front-end conceptual issues, rather than back-end implementation issues, which unnecessarily restrict design choices (Rumbaugh et al., 1991).

In the analysis phase, you develop a model of the real-world application showing its important properties. The model abstracts concepts from the application domain and describes *what* the intended system must do, rather than *how* it will be done. It specifies the functional behavior of the system, independently of concerns relating to the environment in which it is to be finally implemented. You need to devote sufficient time to clearly understand the requirements of the problem. The analysis model should capture those requirements completely and accurately. Remember that it is much easier and cheaper to make changes or fix flaws during analysis than during the later phases.

In the object-oriented design phase, you define *how* the application-oriented analysis model will be realized in the implementation environment. Jacobson et al. (1992) cite three reasons for using object-oriented design. These three reasons are:

1. The analysis model is not formal enough to be implemented directly in a programming language. To move seamlessly into the source code requires refining the objects by making decisions on what operations an object will provide, what the communication between objects should look like, what messages are to be passed, and so forth.

Figure 14-1

Phases of object-oriented systems development cycle

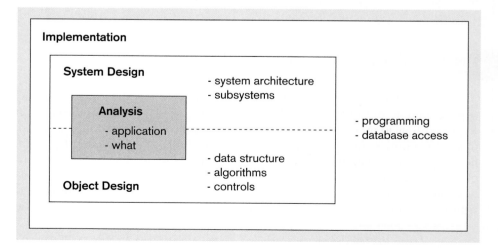

2. The actual system must be adapted to the environment in which the system will actually be implemented. To accomplish that, the analysis model has to be transformed into a design model, considering different factors such as performance requirements, real-time requirements and concurrency, the target hardware and systems software, the DBMS and programming language to be adopted, and so forth.

3. The analysis results can be validated using object-oriented design. At this stage, you can verify whether the results from the analysis are appropriate for building the system, and make any necessary changes to the analysis model.

To develop the design model, you must identify and investigate the consequences that the implementation environment will have on the design (Jacobson et al., 1992). All strategic design decisions—such as how the DBMS is to be incorporated, how process communications and error handling are to be achieved, what component libraries are to be reused—are made. Next, you incorporate those decisions into a first-cut design model that adapts to the implementation environment. Finally, you formalize the design model to describe how the objects interact with one another for each conceivable scenario (use case).

Rumbaugh et al. (1991) separate the design activity into two stages: system design and *object design*. As the system designer, you propose an overall system architecture, which organizes the system into components called subsystems and provides the context to make decisions such as identifying concurrency; allocation of subsystems to processors and tasks; handling access to global resources; selecting the implementation of control in software; and more.

During object design, you build a design model by adding implementation details—such as restructuring classes for efficiency, internal data structures and algorithms to implement each class, implementation of control, implementation of associations, and packaging into physical modules—to the analysis model in accordance with the strategy established during system design. The application-domain object classes from the analysis model still remain, but they are augmented with computer-domain constructs, with a view toward optimizing important performance measures.

The design phase is followed by the implementation phase. In this phase, you implement the design using a programming language and/or a database management system. Translating the design into program code is a relatively straightforward process, given that the design model already incorporates the nuances of the programming language and the DBMS.

Coad and Yourdon (1991b) identify several motivations and benefits of object-oriented modeling, which follow:

- The ability to tackle more challenging problem domains.
- Improved communication between the users, analysts, designers, and programmers.
- Increased consistency among analysis, design, and programming activities.
- Explicit representation of commonality among system components.
- Robustness of systems.
- Reusability of analysis, design, and programming results.
- Increased consistency among all the models developed during object-oriented analysis, design, and programming.

The last point needs further elaboration. In other modeling approaches, such as structured analysis and design (described in Chapter 2), the models that are developed (e.g., data flow diagrams during analysis and structure charts during design) lack a common underlying representation and, therefore, are very weakly connected. In contrast to the abrupt and disjoint transitions that those approaches suffer from, the object-oriented approach provides a continuum of representation from analysis to design to implementation (Coad and Yourdon, 1991a), engendering a seamless transition from one model to another (Jacobson et al., 1992). For instance, moving from object-oriented analysis to object-oriented design entails expanding the analysis model with implementation-related details, not developing a whole new representation.

In this chapter, we present object-oriented data modeling as a high-level conceptual activity. As you will learn in Chapter 15, a good conceptual model is invaluable for designing and implementing an object-oriented database application.

THE UNIFIED MODELING LANGUAGE

The Unified Modeling Language (UML) is "a language for specifying, visualizing, and constructing the artifacts of software systems, as well as for business modeling" (*UML Document Set*, 1997). It culminated from the efforts of three leading experts, Grady Booch, Ivar Jacobson, and James Rumbaugh, who have defined an object-oriented modeling language that is expected to become an industry standard in the near future. The UML builds upon and unifies the semantics and notations of the Booch (Booch, 1994), OOSE (Jacobson et al., 1992), and OMT (Rumbaugh et al., 1991) methods, as well as those of other leading methods.

The UML notation is useful for graphically depicting an object-oriented analysis or design model. It not only allows you to specify the requirements of a system and capture the design decisions, but it also promotes communication among key persons involved in the development effort. A developer can use an analysis or design model expressed in the UML notation as a means to communicate with domain experts, users, and other stakeholders.

For representing a complex system effectively, it is necessary that the model you develop has a small set of independent views or perspectives. UML allows you to represent multiple perspectives of a system by providing different types of graphical diagrams, such as the use-case diagram, class diagram, state diagram, interaction diagram, component diagram, and deployment diagram. The underlying model integrates those views so that the system can be analyzed, designed, and implemented in a complete and consistent fashion.

Because this text is about databases, we will describe only the *class diagram*, which addresses the data, as well some behavioral, aspects of a system. We will not describe the other diagrams because they provide perspectives that are not directly related to a database system, for example, the dynamic aspects of a system. But keep in mind that a database system is usually part of an overall system, whose underlying model should encompass all the different perspectives. For a discussion of other UML diagrams, see Hoffer, George, and Valacich (2002).

OBJECT-ORIENTED DATA MODELING

In this section, we introduce you to object-oriented data modeling. We describe the main concepts and techniques involved in object-oriented modeling, including: objects and classes; encapsulation of attributes and operations; association, generalization, and aggregation relationships; cardinalities and other types of constraints; polymorphism; and inheritance. We show how you can develop class diagrams, using the UML notation, to provide a conceptual view of the system being modeled.

Representing Objects and Classes

Object: An entity that has a well-defined role in the application domain as well as state, behavior, and identity.

In the object-oriented approach, we model the world in objects. Before applying the approach to a real-world problem, therefore, we need to understand what an object really is. An **object** is an entity that has a well-defined role in the application domain as well as state, behavior, and identity. An object is a concept, abstraction, or thing that makes sense in an application context (Rumbaugh et al., 1991). An object could be a tangible or visible entity (e.g., a person, place, or thing); it could be a concept or event (e.g., Department, Performance, Marriage, Registration, etc.); or it could be an artifact of the design process (e.g., User Interface, Controller, Scheduler, etc.).

You might be wondering how objects are different from entities in the E-R model you studied in Chapter 3. Clearly, entities in the E-R model can be represented as objects in the object model. But, in addition to storing a state (information), an object also exhibits behavior, through operations that can examine or affect its state.

The **state** of an object encompasses its properties (attributes and relationships) and the values those properties have, and its **behavior** represents how an object acts and reacts (Booch, 1994). An object's state is determined by its attribute values and links to other objects. An object's behavior depends on its state and the operation being performed. An operation is simply an action that one object performs upon another in order to get a response. You can think of an operation as a service provided by an object (supplier) to its clients. A client sends a message to a supplier, which delivers the desired service by executing the corresponding operation.

Consider an example of a student, Mary Jones, represented as an object. The state of this object is characterized by its attributes, say, name, date of birth, year, address, and phone, and the values these attributes currently have. For example, name is "Mary Jones," year is "junior," and so on. Its behavior is expressed through operations such as calc-gpa, which is used to calculate a student's current grade point average. The Mary Jones object, therefore, packages both its state and its behavior together.

All objects have an identity; that is, no two objects are the same. For example, if there are two Student instances with the same name and date of birth, they are essentially two different objects. Even if those two instances have identical values for all the attributes, the objects maintain their separate identities. At the same time, an object maintains its own identity over its life. For example, if Mary Jones gets married and changes her name, address, and phone, she will still be represented by the same object.

The term "object" is sometimes used to refer to a group of objects, rather than an individual object. The ambiguity can be usually resolved from the context. In the strict sense of the term, however, "object" refers to an individual object, not to a class of objects. That is the interpretation we follow in this text. If you want to eliminate any possible confusion altogether, you can use "object instance" to refer to an individual object, and **object class** (or simply **class**) to refer to a set of objects that share a common structure and a common behavior (just as we used entity type and entity instance in Chapter 3). In our example, therefore, *Mary Jones* is an object instance, while Student is an object class.

You can depict the classes graphically in a class diagram as in Figure 14-2a. A **class diagram** shows the static structure of an object-oriented model: the object classes, their internal structure, and the relationships in which they participate. In UML, a class is represented by a rectangle with three compartments separated by horizontal lines. The class name appears in the top compartment, the list of attributes in the middle compartment, and the list of operations in the bottom compartment of a box. The figure shows two classes, Student and Course, along with their attributes and operations.

The Student class is a group of Student objects that share a common structure and a common behavior. All students have in common the properties of name, date of birth, year, address, and phone. They also exhibit common behavior by sharing the calc-age, calc-gpa, and register-for(course) operations. A class, therefore, provides a template or schema for its instances. Each object knows to which class it belongs; for example, the Mary Jones object knows that it belongs to the Student class. Objects belonging to the same class may also participate in similar relationships with other objects; for example, all students register for courses and, therefore, the

State: Encompasses an object's properties (attributes and relationships) and the values those properties have.

Behavior: Represents how an object acts and reacts.

Object class: A set of objects that share a common structure and a common behavior.

Class diagram: Shows the static structure of an object-oriented model: the object classes, their internal structure, and the relationships in which they participate.

Figure 14-2
UML class and object diagrams
(a) Class diagram showing two classes

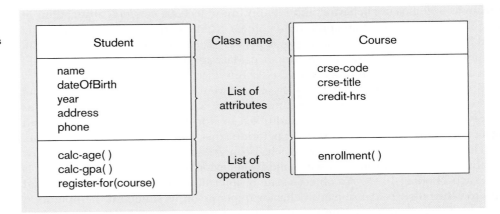

(b) Object diagram with two instances

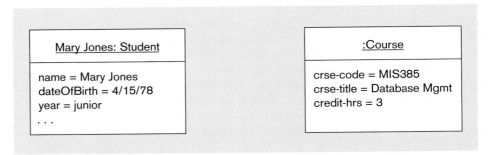

Student class can participate in a relationship called 'registers-for' with another class called Course (see the later section on Association).

An **object diagram**, also known as instance diagram, is a graph of instances that are compatible with a given class diagram. In Figure 14-2b, we have shown an object diagram with two instances, one for each of the two classes that appear in Figure 14-2a. A static object diagram, such as the one shown in the figure, is an instance of a class diagram, providing a snapshot of the detailed state of a system at a point in time (*UML Notation Guide,* 1997). We will provide examples of only static object diagrams, and not dynamic object diagrams (known as collaboration diagrams).

In an object diagram, an object is represented as a rectangle with two compartments. The names of the object and its class are underlined and shown in the top compartment using the following syntax:

> objectname : classname

The object's attributes and their values are shown in the second compartment. For example, we have an object called Mary Jones that belongs to the Student class. The values of the name, dateOfBirth, and year attributes are also shown. Attributes whose values are not of interest to you may be suppressed; for example, we have not shown the address and phone attributes for Mary Jones. If none of the attributes are of interest, the entire second compartment may be suppressed. The name of the object may also be omitted, in which case the colon should be kept with the class name as we have done with the instance of Course. If the name of the object is shown, the class name, together with the colon, may be suppressed.

An **operation**, such as calc-gpa in Student (see Figure 14-2a), is a function or a service that is provided by all the instances of a class. It is only through such operations that other objects can access or manipulate the information stored in an object. The operations, therefore, provide an external interface to a class; the interface presents the outside view of the class without showing its internal structure or how its operations are implemented. This technique of hiding the internal implementation

Object diagram: A graph of instances that are compatible with a given class diagram.

Operation: A function or a service that is provided by all the instances of a class.

details of an object from its external view is known as **encapsulation** or information hiding (Booch, 1994; Rumbaugh et al., 1991). So while we provide the abstraction of the behavior common to all instances of a class in its interface, we encapsulate within the class its structure and the secrets of the desired behavior.

Encapsulation: The technique of hiding the internal implementation details of an object from its external view.

Types of Operations

Operations can be classified into four types, depending on the kind of service requested by clients: (1) constructor, (2) query, (3) update, and (4) scope (*UML Notation Guide*, 1997). A **constructor operation** creates a new instance of a class. For example, you can have an operation called create-student within Student that creates a new student and initializes its state. Such constructor operations are available to all classes and are therefore not explicitly shown in the class diagram.

Constructor operation: An operation that creates a new instance of a class.

A **query operation** is an operation without any side effects; it accesses the state of an object but does not alter the state (Fowler, 2000; Rumbaugh et al., 1991). For example, the Student class can have an operation called get-year (not shown), which simply retrieves the year (freshman, sophomore, junior, or senior) of the Student object specified in the query. Note that there is no need to explicitly show a query such as get-year in the class diagram since it retrieves the value of an independent, base attribute. Consider, however, the calc-age operation within Student. This is also a query operation because it does not have any side effects. Note that the only argument for this query is the target Student object. Such a query can be represented as a derived attribute (Rumbaugh et al., 1991); for example, we can represent "age" as a derived attribute of Student. Because the target object is always an implicit argument of an operation, there is no need to show it explicitly in the operation declaration.

Query operation: An operation that accesses the state of an object but does not alter the state.

An **update operation** has side effects; it alters the state of an object. For example, consider an operation of Student called promote-student (not shown). The operation promotes a student to a new year, say, from junior to senior, thereby changing the Student object's state (value of the year attribute). Another example of an update operation is register-for(course), which, when invoked, has the effect of establishing a connection from a Student object to a specific Course object. Note that, in addition to having the target Student object as an implicit argument, the operation has an explicit argument called "course," which specifies the course for which the student wants to register. Explicit arguments are shown within parentheses.

Update operation: An operation that alters the state of an object.

A **scope operation** is an operation that applies to a class rather than an object instance. For example, avg_gpa for the Student class (not shown with the other operations for this class in Figure 14-2) calculates the average gpa across all students (the operation name is underlined to indicate it is a scope operation).

Scope operation: An operation that applies to a class rather than an object instance.

Representing Associations

Parallel to the definition of a relationship for the E-R model, an **association** is a named relationship between or among instances of object classes. As in the E-R model, the degree of an association relationship may be one (unary), two (binary), three (ternary), or higher (*n*-ary). In Figure 14-3, we use the examples from Figure 3-12 to illustrate how the object-oriented model can be used to represent association relationships of different degrees. An association is shown as a solid line between the participating classes. The end of an association where it connects to a class is called an **association role** (*UML Notation Guide*, 1997). Each association has two or more roles. A role may be explicitly named with a label near the end of an association (see the "manager" role in Figure 14-3a). The role name indicates the role played by the class attached to the end near which the name appears. Use of role names is optional. You can specify role names in place of, or in addition to, an association name.

Association: A named relationship between or among object classes.

Association role: The end of an association where it connects to a class.

Figure 14-3
Examples of association relationships of
different degrees
(a) Unary relationships

(b) Binary relationships

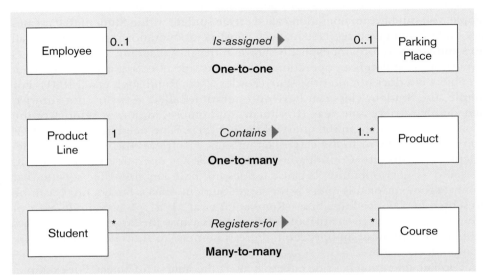

(c) Ternary relationship

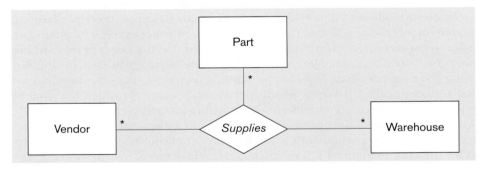

Figure 14-3a shows two unary relationships, *Is-married-to* and *Manages*. At one end of the *Manages* relationship, we have named the role as "manager," implying that an employee can play the role of a manager. We have not named the other roles, but we have named the associations. When the role name does not appear, you may think of the role name as being that of the class attached to that end (Fowler, 2000). For example, you may call the role for the right end of the *Is-assigned* relationship in Figure 14-3b as Parking Place.

Multiplicity: A specification that indicates how many objects participate in a given relationship.

Each role has a **multiplicity**, which indicates how many objects participate in a given relationship. In a class diagram, a multiplicity specification is shown as a text string representing an interval (or intervals) of integers in the following format:

lower-bound..upper-bound

The interval is considered to be closed, which means that the range includes both the lower and upper bounds. For example, a multiplicity of 2..5 denotes that a minimum of 2 and a maximum of 5 objects can participate in a given relationship. Multiplicities, therefore, are nothing but cardinality constraints that were discussed in Chapter 3. In addition to integer values, the upper bound of a multiplicity can be a star character (*), which denotes an infinite upper bound. If a single integer value is specified, it means that the range includes only that value.

The most common multiplicities in practice are 0..1, *, and 1. The 0..1 multiplicity indicates a minimum of 0 and a maximum of 1 (optional one), while * (or equivalently, 0..*) represents the range from 0 to infinity (optional many). A single 1 stands for 1..1, implying that exactly one object participates in the relationship (mandatory one).

The multiplicities for both roles in the *Is-married-to* relationship are 0..1, indicating that a person may be single or married to one person. The multiplicity for the manager role in the *Manages* relationship is 0..1 and that for the other role is *, implying that an employee may be managed by only one manager, but a manager may manage many employees.

Figure 14-3b shows three binary relationships: *Is-assigned* (one-to-one), *Contains* (one-to-many), and *Registers-for* (many-to-many). A binary association is inherently bidirectional, though in a class diagram, the association name can be read in only one direction (Rumbaugh et al., 1991). For example, the *Contains* association is read from Product Line to Product. (*Note:* As in this example, you may show the direction explicitly by using a solid triangle next to the association name.) Implicit, however, is an inverse traversal of *Contains,* say, *Belongs-to,* which denotes that a product belongs to a particular product line. Both directions of traversal refer to the same underlying association; the name simply establishes a direction.

The diagram for the *Is-assigned* relationship shows that an employee is assigned a parking place or not assigned at all (optional one). Reading in the other direction, we say that a parking place has either been allocated for a single employee or not allocated at all (optional one again). Similarly, we say that a product line contains many products, but at least one, whereas a given product belongs to exactly one product line (mandatory one). The diagram for the third binary association states that a student registers for multiple courses, but it is possible that he or she does not register at all, and a course, in general, has multiple students enrolled in it (optional many in both directions).

In Figure 14-3c, we show a ternary relationship called *Supplies* among Vendor, Part, and Warehouse. As in the E-R diagram, we represent a ternary relationship using a diamond symbol and place the name of the relationship there. The relationship is many-to-many-to-many, and as discussed in Chapter 3, it cannot be replaced by three binary relationships without loss of information.

The class diagram in Figure 14-4a shows binary associations between Student and Faculty, between Course and Course Offering, between Student and Course Offering, and between Faculty and Course Offering. The diagram shows that a student may have an advisor, while a faculty member may advise up to a maximum of 10 students. Also, while a course may have multiple offerings, a given course offering is scheduled for exactly one course. UML allows you to numerically specify any multiplicity. For example, the diagram shows that a course offering may be taught by one or two instructors (1, 2). You can specify a single number (e.g., 2 for the members of a bridge team), a range (e.g., 11..14 for the players of a soccer team who participated in a particular game), or a discrete set of numbers and ranges (e.g., 3, 5, 7 for the number of committee members, and 20..32, 35..40 for the workload in hours per week of the employees of a company).

Figure 14-4a also shows that a faculty member plays the role of an instructor, as well as that of an advisor. While the advisor role identifies the Faculty object associated with a Student object, the advisees role identifies the set of Student objects associated with a Faculty object. We could have named the association as, say, *Advises,* but, in this case, the role names are sufficiently meaningful to convey the semantics of the relationship.

Figure 14-4
Examples of binary association relationships
(a) University example

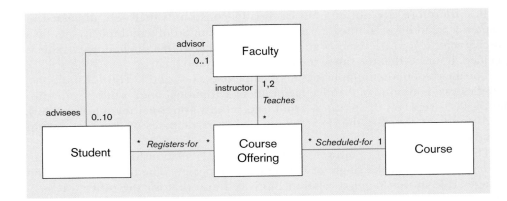

(b) Customer order example

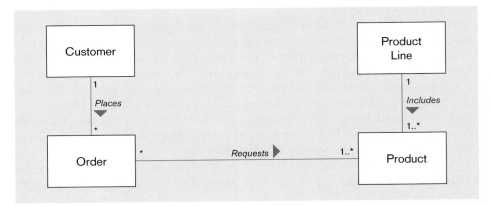

Figure 14-4b shows another class diagram for a customer order. The corresponding object diagram is presented in Figure 14-5; it shows some of the instances of the classes and the links among them. (*Note:* Just as an instance corresponds to a class, a link corresponds to a relationship.) In this example, we see the orders placed by two customers, Joe and Jane. Joe has placed two orders, Ord 20 and Ord 56. In Ord 20, Joe has ordered product P93 from the sports product line. In Ord 56, he has ordered the same sports product again, as well as product P50 from the hardware product line. Notice that Jane has ordered the same hardware product as Joe, in addition to two other products (P9 and P10) from the cosmetics product line.

Representing Association Classes

Association class: An association that has attributes or operations of its own or that participates in relationships with other classes.

When an association itself has attributes or operations of its own, or when it participates in relationships with other classes, it is useful to model the association as an **association class** (just as we used an "associative entity" in Chapter 3). For example, in Figure 14-6a, the attributes term and grade really belong to the many-to-many association between Student and Course. The grade of a student for a course cannot be determined unless both the student and the course are known. Similarly, to find the term(s) in which the student took the course, both student and course must be known. The checkEligibility operation, which determines if a student is eligible to register for a given course, also belongs to the association, rather than to any of the two participating classes. We have also captured the fact that, for some course registrations, a computer account is issued to a student. For these reasons, we model Registration as an association class, having its own set of features and an association with another class (Computer Account). Similarly, for the unary *Tutors* association, beginDate and numberOfHrs (number of hours tutored) really belong to the association, and, therefore, appear in a separate association class.

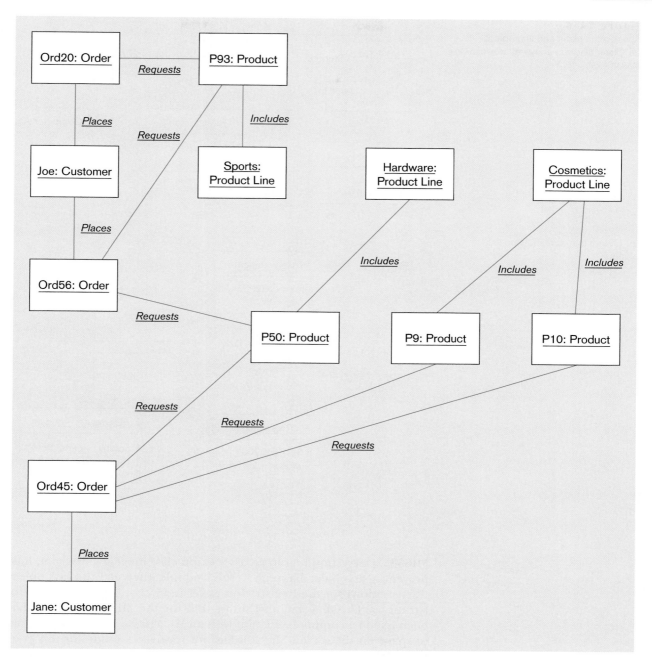

Figure 14-5
Object diagram for customer order example

You have the option of showing the name of an association class on the association path, or the class symbol, or both. When an association has only attributes, but does not have any operations or does not participate in other associations, the recommended option is to show the name on the association path, but to omit it from the association class symbol, to emphasize its "association nature" (*UML Notation Guide,* 1997). That is how we have shown the *Tutors* association. On the other hand, we have displayed the name of the Registration association—which has two attributes and one operation of its own, as well as an association called *Issues* with Computer Account—within the class rectangle to emphasize its "class nature."

Figure 14-6b shows a part of the object diagram representing a student, Mary Jones, and the courses she has registered for in the fall 2001 term: MKT350 and

Figure 14-6
Association class and link object
(a) Class diagram showing association classes

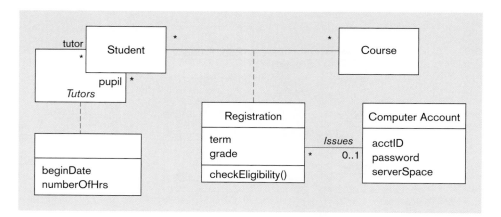

(b) Object diagram showing link objects

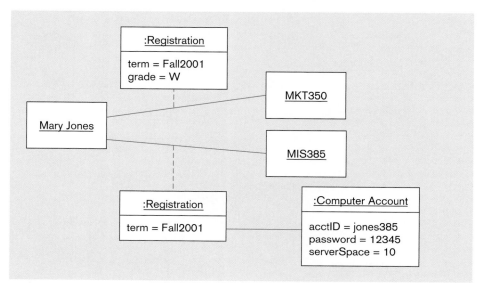

MIS385. Corresponding to an association class in a class diagram, link objects are present in an object diagram. In this example, there are two link objects (shown as :Registration) for the Registration association class, capturing the two course registrations. The diagram also shows that for the MIS385 course, Mary Jones has been issued a computer account with an ID, a password, and a designated amount of space on the server. She still has not received a grade for this course, but, for the MKT350 course, she received a grade of W because she withdrew from the course.

Figure 14-7 shows a ternary relationship among the Student, Software, and Course classes. It captures the fact that students use various software tools for different courses. For example, we could store the information that Mary Jones used Microsoft Access and Oracle for the Database Management course, Rational Rose and Visual C + + for the Object-Oriented Modeling course, and Level5 Object for the Expert Systems Course. Now suppose we want to estimate the number of hours per week Mary will spend using Oracle for the Database Management course. This process really belongs to the ternary association, and not to any of the individual classes. Hence we have created an association class called Log, within which we have declared an operation called estimateUsage. In addition to this operation, we have specified three attributes that belong to the association: beginDate, expiryDate, and hoursLogged.

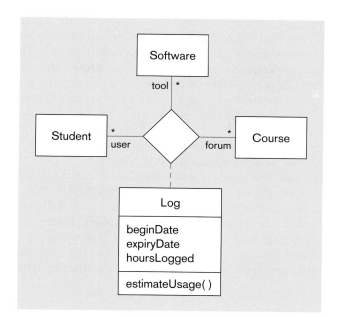

Figure 14-7
Ternary relationship with association class

Representing Derived Attributes, Derived Associations, and Derived Roles

A derived attribute, association, or role is one that can be computed or derived from other attributes, associations, and roles, respectively (the concept of a derived attribute was introduced in Chapter 3). A derived element (attribute, association, or role) is shown by placing a slash (/) before the name of the element. For instance, in Figure 14-8, age is a derived attribute of Student, because it can be calculated from the date of birth and the current date. Because the calculation is a constraint on the object class, the calculation is shown on this diagram within {} above the Student object class. Also, the *Takes* relationship between Student and Course is derived, because it can be inferred from the *Registers-for* and *Scheduled-for* relationships. By the same token, participants is a derived role because it can be derived from other roles.

Representing Generalization

You were introduced to *generalization* and *specialization* in Chapter 4. Using the enhanced E-R model, you learned how to abstract the common attributes of two or more entities, as well as the common relationships in which they participate, into a more general entity supertype, while keeping the attributes and relationships that are not common in the entities (subtypes) themselves. In the object-oriented model,

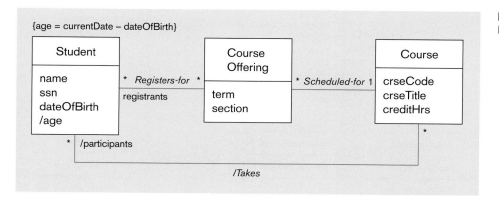

Figure 14-8
Derived attribute, association, and role

we apply the same notion, but with one difference. In generalizing a set of object classes into a more general class, we abstract not only the common attributes and relationships, but the common operations as well. The attributes and operations of a class are collectively known as the features of the class. The classes that are generalized are called subclasses, and the class they are generalized into is called a superclass, in perfect correspondence to subtypes and supertype for EER diagramming.

Consider the example shown in Figure 14-9a (see Figure 4-8 for the corresponding EER diagram). There are three types of employees: hourly employees, salaried employees, and consultants. The features that are shared by all employees—empName, empNumber, address, dateHired, and printLabel—are stored in the Employee superclass, while the features that are peculiar to a particular employee type are stored in the corresponding subclass (e.g., hourlyRate and computeWages of Hourly Employee). A generalization path is shown as a solid line from the subclass to the superclass, with a hollow triangle at the end of, and pointing toward, the superclass. You can show a group of generalization paths for a given superclass as a tree with multiple branches connecting the individual subclasses, and a shared segment with a hollow triangle pointing toward the superclass. In Figure 14-9b (corre-

Figure 14-9
Examples of generalization, inheritance, and constraints
(a) Employee superclass with three subclasses

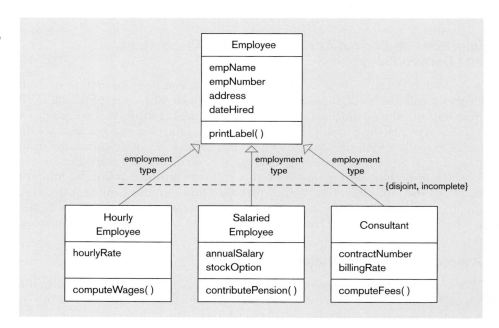

(b) Abstract Patient class with two concrete subclasses

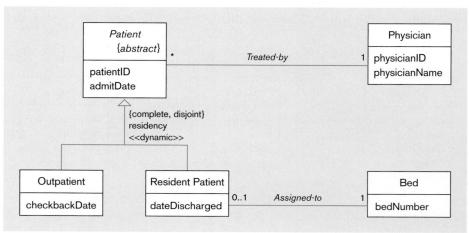

sponding to Figure 4-3), for instance, we have combined the generalization paths from Outpatient to Patient, and from Resident Patient to Patient, into a shared segment with a triangle pointing toward Patient. We also specify that this generalization is dynamic, meaning that an object may change subtypes.

You can indicate the basis of a generalization by specifying a discriminator next to the path. A discriminator (corresponding to the subtype discriminator defined in Chapter 4) shows which property of an object class is being abstracted by a particular generalization relationship (Rumbaugh et al., 1991). You can discriminate on only one property at a time. For example, in Figure 14-9a, we discriminate the Employee class on the basis of employment type (hourly, salaried, consultant). To disseminate a group of generalization relationships as in Figure 14-9b, we need to specify the discriminator only once. Although we discriminate the Patient class into two subclasses, Outpatient and Resident Patient, based on residency, we show the discriminator label only once next to the shared line.

An instance of a subclass is also an instance of its superclass. For example in Figure 14-9b, an Outpatient instance is also a Patient instance. For that reason, a generalization is also referred to as an *Is-a* relationship. Also, a subclass inherits all the features from its superclass. For example in Figure 14-9a, in addition to its own special features—hourlyRate and computeWages—the Hourly Employee subclass inherits empName, empNumber, address, dateHired, and printLabel from Employee. An instance of Hourly Employee will store values for the attributes of Employee and Hourly Employee, and, when requested, will apply the printLabel and computeWages operations.

Generalization and inheritance are transitive across any number of levels of a superclass/subclass hierarchy. For instance, we could have a subclass of Consultant called Computer Consultant, which would inherit the features of Employee and Consultant. An instance of Computer Consultant would be an instance of Consultant and, therefore, an instance of Employee too. Employee is an ancestor of Computer Consultant, while Computer Consultant is a descendant of Employee; these terms are used to refer to generalization of classes across multiple levels (Rumbaugh et al., 1991).

Inheritance is one of the major advantages of using the object-oriented model. It allows code reuse: There is no need for a programmer to write code that has already been written for a superclass. The programmer only writes code that is unique to the new, refined subclass of an existing class. In actual practice, object-oriented programmers typically have access to large collections of class libraries in their respective domains. They identify those classes that may be reused and refined to meet the demands of new applications. Proponents of the object-oriented model claim that code reuse results in productivity gains of several orders of magnitude.

Notice that in Figure 14-9b the *Patient* class is in italics, implying that it is an abstract class. An **abstract class** is a class that has no direct instances, but whose descendants may have direct instances (Booch, 1994; Rumbaugh et al., 1991). (*Note:* You can additionally write the word *abstract* within braces just below the class name. This is especially useful when you generate a class diagram by hand.) A class that can have direct instances (e.g., Outpatient or Resident Patient) is called a **concrete class**. In this example, therefore, Outpatient and Resident Patient can have direct instances, but *Patient* cannot have any direct instances of its own.

The *Patient* abstract class participates in a relationship called *Treated-by* with Physician, implying that all patients, outpatients and resident patients alike, are treated by physicians. In addition to this inherited relationship, the Resident Patient class has its own special relationship called *Assigned-to* with Bed, implying that only resident patients may be assigned to beds. So, in addition to refining the attributes and operations of a class, a subclass can also specialize the relationships in which it participates.

In Figure 14-9a and 14-9b, the words "complete," "incomplete," and "disjoint" have been placed within braces, next to the generalization. They indicate semantic constraints among the subclasses (complete corresponds to total specialization in the

Abstract class: A class that has no direct instances, but whose descendants may have direct instances.

Concrete class: A class that can have direct instances.

EER notation, whereas incomplete corresponds to partial specialization). In UML, a comma-separated list of keywords is placed either near the shared triangle as in Figure 14-9b, or near a dashed line that crosses all of the generalization lines involved as in Figure 14-9a (*UML Notation Guide,* 1997). Any of the following UML keywords may be used: overlapping, disjoint, complete, and incomplete. According to the UML Notation Guide (1997), these terms have the following meanings:

- *Overlapping*   A descendant may be descended from more than one of the subclasses (same as the overlapping rule in EER diagramming).
- *Disjoint*   A descendant may not be descended from more than one of the subclasses (same as the disjoint rule in EER diagramming).
- *Complete*   All subclasses have been specified (whether or not shown). No additional subclasses are expected (same as the total specialization rule in EER diagramming).
- *Incomplete*   Some subclasses have been specified, but the list is known to be incomplete. There are additional subclasses that are not yet in the model (same as the partial specialization rule in EER diagramming).

Both the generalizations in Figures 14-9a and 14-9b are disjoint. An employee can be an hourly employee, a salaried employee, or a consultant, but cannot, say, be both a salaried employee and a consultant at the same time. Similarly, a patient can be an outpatient or a resident patient, but not both. The generalization in Figure 14-9a is incomplete (a departure from what was shown in Figure 4-8), specifying that an employee might not belong to any of the three types. In such a case, an employee will be stored as an instance of Employee, a concrete class. In contrast, the generalization in Figure 14-9b is complete, implying that a patient has to be either an outpatient or a resident patient, and nothing else. For that reason, *Patient* has been specified as an abstract class.

In Figure 14-10, we show an example of an overlapping constraint. The diagram shows that research assistants and teaching assistants are graduate students. The

Figure 14-10
Example of overlapping constraint

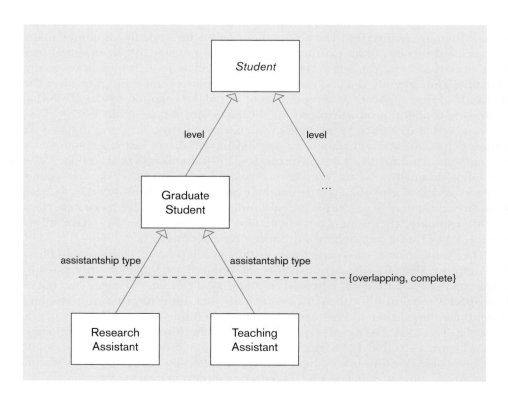

overlapping constraint indicates that it is possible for a graduate student to serve as both a research assistant and a teaching assistant. For example, Sean Bailey, a graduate student, has a research assistantship of 12 hours/week and a teaching assistantship of 8 hours/week. Also notice that Graduate Student has been specified as a concrete class so that graduate students without an assistantship can be represented. The ellipsis (. . .) under the generalization line based on the "level" discriminator does not represent an incomplete constraint. It simply indicates that there are other subclasses in the model that have not been shown in the diagram. For example, although Undergrad Student is in the model, we have opted not to show it in the diagram since the focus is on assistantships. You may also use an ellipsis when there are space limitations.

In Figure 14-11, we represent both graduate and undergraduate students in a model developed for student billing. The calc-tuition operation computes the tuition a student has to pay; this sum depends on the tuition per credit hour (tuitionPer-Cred), the courses taken, and the number of credit hours (creditHrs) for each of those courses. The tuition per credit hour, in turn, depends on whether the student is a graduate or an undergraduate student. In this example, that amount is $300 for all graduate students, and $250 for all undergraduate students. To denote that, we have underlined the tuitionPerCred attribute in each of the two subclasses, along with its value. Such an attribute is called a **class-scope attribute**, which specifies a value common to an entire class, rather than a specific value for an instance (Rumbaugh et al, 1991).

You can also specify an initial default value of an attribute using an " =" sign after the attribute name. This is the initial attribute value of a newly created object instance. For example, in Figure 14-11, the creditHrs attribute has an initial value of 3, implying that when a new instance of Course is created, the value of creditHrs is set to 3 by default. You can write an explicit constructor operation to modify the initial default value. The value may also be modified later through other operations. The difference between an initial value specification and a class-scope attribute is

Class-scope attribute: An attribute of a class that specifies a value common to an entire class, rather than a specific value for an instance.

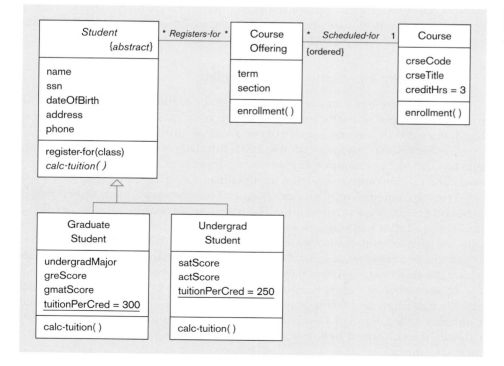

Figure 14-11
Polymorphism, abstract operation, class-scope attribute, and ordering

that while the former allows the possibility of different attribute values for the instances of a class, the latter forces all the instances to share a common value.

In addition to specifying the multiplicity of an association role, you can also specify other properties, for example, if the objects playing the role are ordered or not. In the figure, we placed the keyword constraint "{ordered}" next to the Course Offering end of the *Scheduled-for* relationship to denote the fact that the offerings for a given course are ordered into a list—say, according to term and section. It is obvious that it makes sense to specify an ordering only when the multiplicity of the role is greater than one. The default constraint on a role is "{unordered}"; that is, if you do not specify the keyword "{ordered}" next to the role, it is assumed that the related elements form an unordered set. For example, the course offerings are not related to a student who registers for those offerings in any specific order.

The Graduate Student subclass specializes the abstract Student class by adding four attributes—undergradMajor, greScore, gmatScore, and tuitionPerCred—and by refining the inherited *calc-tuition* operation. Notice that the operation is shown in italics within the Student class, indicating that it is an abstract operation. An **abstract operation** defines the form or protocol of the operation, but not its implementation (Rumbaugh et al., 1991). In this example, the Student class defines the protocol of the *calc-tuition* operation, without providing the corresponding **method** (the actual implementation of the operation). The protocol includes the number and types of the arguments, the result type, and the intended semantics of the operation. The two concrete subclasses, Graduate Student and Undergrad Student, supply their own implementations of the calc-tuition operation. Note that because these classes are concrete, they cannot store abstract operations.

It is important to note that although the Graduate Student and Undergraduate Student classes share the same calc-tuition operation, they might implement the operation in quite different ways. For example, the method that implements the operation for a graduate student might add a special graduate fee for each course the student takes. The fact that the same operation may apply to two or more classes in different ways is known as **polymorphism**, a key concept in object-oriented systems (Booch, 1994; Rumbaugh et al., 1991). The enrollment operation in Figure 14-11 illustrates another example of polymorphism. While the enrollment operation within Course Offering computes the enrollment for a particular course offering or section, an operation with the same name within Course computes the combined enrollment for all sections of a given course.

Interpreting Inheritance and Overriding

We have seen how a subclass can augment the features inherited from its ancestors. In such cases, the subclass is said to use *inheritance for extension*. On the other hand, if a subclass constrains some of the ancestor attributes or operations, it is said to use *inheritance for restriction* (Booch, 1994; Rumbaugh et al., 1991). For example, a subclass called Tax-Exempt Company may suppress or block the inheritance of an operation called compute-tax from its superclass, Company.

The implementation of an operation can also be overridden. **Overriding** is the process of replacing a method inherited from a superclass by a more specific implementation of that method in a subclass. The reasons for overriding include extension, restriction, and optimization (Rumbaugh et al., 1991). The name of the new operation remains the same as the inherited one, but it has to be explicitly shown within the subclass to indicate that the operation is overridden.

In *overriding for extension,* an operation inherited by a subclass from its superclass is extended by adding some behavior (code). For example, a subclass of Company called Foreign Company inherits an operation called compute-tax but extends the inherited behavior by adding a foreign surcharge to compute the total tax amount.

Abstract operation: Defines the form or protocol of the operation, but not its implementation.

Method: The implementation of an operation.

Polymorphism: The same operation may apply to two or more classes in different ways.

Overriding: The process of replacing a method inherited from a superclass by a more specific implementation of that method in a subclass.

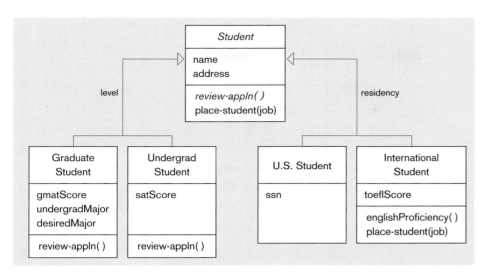

Figure 14-12
Overriding inheritance

In *overriding for restriction,* the protocol of the new operation in the subclass is restricted. For example, an operation called place-student(job) in Student may be restricted in the International Student subclass by tightening the argument job (see Figure 14-12). While students in general may be placed in all types of jobs during the summer, international students may be limited to only on-campus jobs because of visa restrictions. The new operation overrides the inherited operation by tightening the job argument, restricting its values to only a small subset of all possible jobs. This example also illustrates the use of multiple discriminators. While the basis for one set of generalizations is a student's "level" (graduate or undergraduate), that for the other set is his or her "residency" status (U.S. or international).

In *overriding for optimization,* the new operation is implemented with improved code by exploiting the restrictions imposed by a subclass. Consider, for example, a subclass of Student called Dean's List Student, which represents all those students who are on the Dean's List. To qualify for the Dean's List, a student must have a grade point average greater than or equal to 3.50. Suppose Student has an operation called mailScholApps, which mails applications for merit- and means-tested scholarships to students who have a gpa greater than or equal to 3.00, and whose family's total gross income is less than $20,000. The method for the operation in Student will have to check the conditions, whereas the method for the same operation in the Dean's List Student subclass can improve upon the speed of execution by removing the first condition from its code. Consider another operation called findMinGpa, which finds the minimum gpa among the students. Suppose the Dean's List Student class is sorted in ascending order of the gpa, but the Student class is not. The method for findMinGpa in Student must perform a sequential search through all the students. In contrast, the same operation in Dean's List Student can be implemented with a method that simply retrieves the gpa of the first student in the list, thereby obviating the need for a time-consuming search.

Representing Multiple Inheritance

So far you have been exposed to single inheritance, where a class inherits from only one superclass. But sometimes, as we saw in the example with research and teaching assistants, an object may be an instance of more than one class. This is known as **multiple classification** (Fowler, 1997; *UML Notation Guide,* 1997). For instance, Sean Bailey, who has both types of assistantships, has two classifications: one as an instance of Research Assistant and the other as an instance of Teaching Assistant. Multiple classification, however, is discouraged by experts. It is not supported by the ordinary UML semantics and many object-oriented languages.

Multiple classification: An object is an instance of more than one class.

Figure 14-13
Multiple inheritance

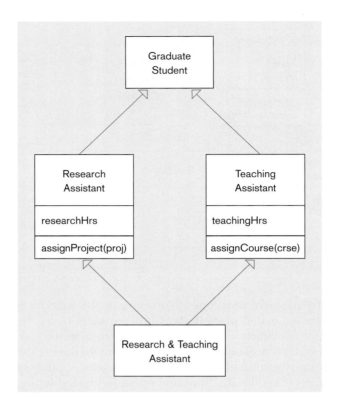

To get around the problem, we can use multiple inheritance, which allows a class to inherit features from more than one superclass. For example, in Figure 14-13, we have created Research & Teaching Assistant, which is a subclass of both Research Assistant and Teaching Assistant. All students who have both research and teaching assistantships may be stored under the new class. We may now represent Sean Bailey as an object belonging to only the Research & Teaching Assistant class, which inherits features from both its parents, such as researchHrs and assignProject(proj) from Research Assistant and teachingHrs and assignCourse(crse) from Teaching Assistant.

Representing Aggregation

Aggregation: A part-of relationship between a component object and an aggregate object.

An **aggregation** expresses a *Part-of* relationship between a component object and an aggregate object. It is a stronger form of association relationship (with the added "part-of" semantics) and is represented with a hollow diamond at the aggregate end. For example, Figure 14-14 shows a personal computer as an aggregate of CPU (up to four for multiprocessors), hard disks, monitor, keyboard, and other objects. Note that aggregation involves a set of distinct object instances, one of which contains or is composed of the others. For example, a Personal Computer object is related to (consists of) CPU objects, one of its parts. In contrast, generalization relates object classes: an object (e.g., Mary Jones) is simultaneously an instance of its class (e.g., Undergrad Student) and its superclass (e.g., Student). Only one object (e.g., Mary Jones) is involved in a generalization relationship. This is why multiplicities are indicated at the ends of aggregation lines, whereas there are no multiplicities for generalization relationships.

Figure 14-15a shows an aggregation structure of a university. The object diagram in Figure 14-15b shows how Riverside University, a University object instance, is related to its component objects, which represent administrative units (e.g., Admissions, Human Resources, etc.) and schools (e.g., Arts and Science, Business, etc.). A

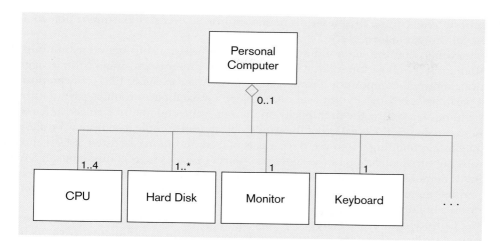

Figure 14-14
Example of aggregation

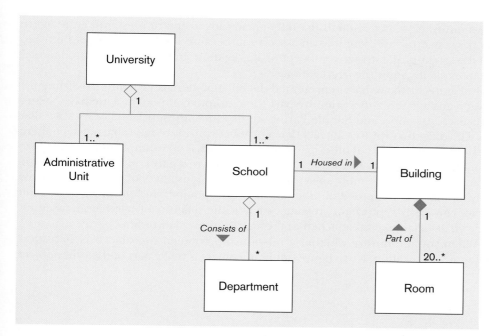

Figure 14-15
Aggregation and composition
(a) Class diagram

(b) Object diagram

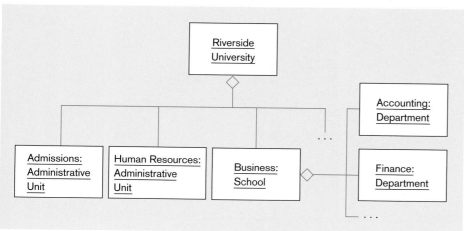

school object (e.g., Business), in turn, comprises several department objects (e.g., Accounting, Finance, etc.).

Composition: A part object that belongs to only one whole object and that lives and dies with the whole object.

Notice that the diamond at one end of the relationship between Building and Room is not hollow, but solid. A solid diamond represents a stronger form of aggregation, known as composition (Fowler, 2000; *UML Notation Guide*, 1997). In **composition**, a part object belongs to only one *whole* object; for example, a room is part of only one building. Therefore, the multiplicity on the aggregate end may not exceed 1. Parts may be created after the creation of the whole object; for example, rooms may be added to an existing building. However, once a part of a composition is created, it lives and dies with the whole; deletion of the aggregate object cascades to its components. If a building is demolished, for example, so are all its rooms. However, it is possible to delete a part before its aggregate dies, just as it is possible to demolish a room without bringing down a building.

Consider another example of aggregation, the bill-of-materials structure presented earlier in Chapter 3. Many manufactured products are made up of assemblies, which in turn are composed of subassemblies and parts, and so on. We saw how we could represent this type of structure as a many-to-many unary relationship (called Has_components) in an E-R diagram (see Figure 3–13). When the relationship has an attribute of its own, such as Quantity, the relationship can be converted to an associative entity. Note that though the bill-of-materials structure is essentially an aggregation, we had to represent it as an association because the E-R model does not support the semantically stronger concept of aggregation. In the object-oriented model, we can explicitly show the aggregation.

In Figure 14-16, we have represented the bill-of-materials structure. To distinguish between an assembly and a primitive part (one without components), we have created two classes, Assembly and Simple Part, both of which are subclasses of a class called Part. The diagram captures the fact that a product consists of many parts, which themselves can be assemblies of other parts, and so on; this is an example of *recursive* aggregation. Because Part is represented as an abstract class, a part is either an assembly or a primitive part. An Assembly object is an aggregate of instances of the Part superclass, implying that it is composed of other assemblies (optional) and primitive parts. Note that we can easily capture an attribute, such as the quantity of parts in an assembly, inside an association class attached to the aggregation relationship.

When you are unsure whether a relationship between two objects is an association or an aggregation, try to figure out if one object is really part of the other object.

Figure 14-16
Recursive aggregation

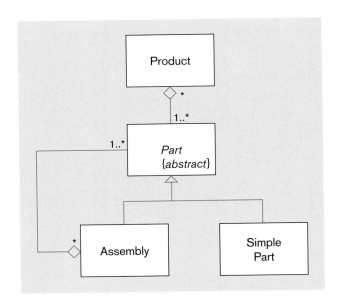

That is, is there a whole/part relationship? Note that an aggregation does not necessarily have to imply physical containment, such as that between Personal Computer and CPU. The whole/part relationship may be conceptual, for example, the one between a mutual fund and a certain stock that is part of the fund. In an aggregation, an object may or may not exist independently of an aggregate object. For example, a stock exists irrespective of whether it is part of a mutual fund or not, while a department does not exist independently of an organization. Also, an object may be part of several aggregate objects (e.g., many mutual funds may contain IBM stocks in their portfolios). Remember, however, that while this is possible in aggregation, composition does not allow an object to be part of more than one aggregate object.

Another characteristic of aggregation is that some of the operations on the whole automatically apply to its parts. For example, an operation called ship in the Personal Computer object class applies to CPU, Hard Disk, Monitor, etc., because whenever a computer is shipped, so are its parts. The ship operation on Personal Computer is said to *propagate* to its parts (Rumbaugh et al., 1991).

BUSINESS RULES

Business rules were discussed in detail earlier in Chapters 3 and 4. You saw how to express different types of rules in an E-R diagram. In the examples provided in this chapter, we captured many business rules as constraints—implicitly, as well as explicitly—on classes, instances, attributes, operations, relationships, etc. For example, you saw how to specify cardinality constraints and ordering constraints on association roles. You also saw how to represent semantic constraints (e.g., overlapping, disjoint, etc.) among subclasses. Many of the constraints that were discussed so far in this chapter were imposed by including a set of UML keywords within braces—for example, {disjoint, complete} and {ordered}—and placing them close to the elements the constraints apply to. For example, in Figure 14-11, we expressed a business rule that offerings for a given course are ordered. But if you cannot represent a business rule using such a predefined UML constraint, you can define the rule in plain English, or in some other language such as formal logic.

When you have to specify a business rule involving two graphical symbols (such as those representing two classes or two associations), you can show the constraint as a dashed arrow from one element to the other, labeled by the constraint name in braces (*UML Notation Guide,* 1997). In Figure 14-17, for example, we have stated the business rule that the chair of a department must be a member of the department by specifying the *Chair-of* association as a subset of the *Member-of* association.

When a business rule involves three or more graphical symbols, you can show the constraint as a note and attach the note to each of the symbols by a dashed line (*UML Notation Guide,* 1997). In Figure 14-17, we have captured the business rule that "each faculty member assigned to teach a section of a course must be qualified to teach that course" within a note symbol. Because this constraint involves all three association relationships, we have attached the note to each of the three association paths.

OBJECT MODELING EXAMPLE: PINE VALLEY FURNITURE COMPANY

In Chapter 3, you saw how to develop a high-level E-R diagram for the Pine Valley Furniture Company (see Figure 3-22). We identified the entity types, as well as their keys and other important attributes, based on a study of the business processes at the company. We will now show you how to develop a class diagram for the same

Figure 14-17
Representing business rules

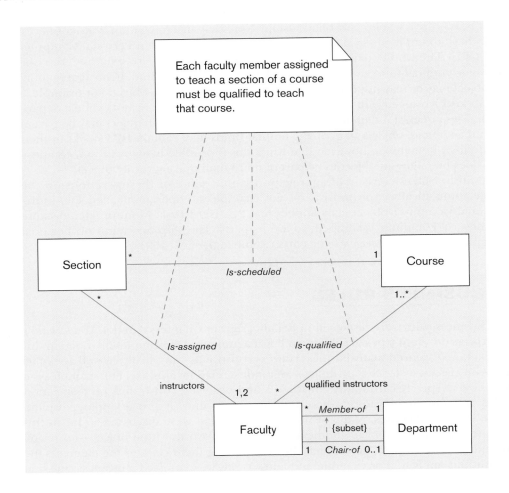

application using the object-oriented approach. The class diagram is shown in Figure 14-18. We discuss the commonalities, as well as the differences, between this diagram and the E-R diagram.

As you would expect, the entity types are represented as object classes and all the attributes are shown within the classes. Note, however, that you do not need to show explicit identifiers in the form of primary keys, because, by definition, each object has its own identity. The E-R model, as well as the relational data model (see Chapter 5), requires you to specify explicit identifiers because there is no other way of supporting the notion of identity. In the object-oriented model, the only identifiers you should represent are attributes that make sense in the real world, such as salespersonID, customerID, orderID, and productID, which are represented as keys in the class diagram. Notice that we have not shown an identifier for Product Line, based on the assumption that Product_Line_ID was merely included in the E-R diagram as an internal identifier, not as a real-world attribute such as orderID or productID. If Pine Valley Furniture Company does not actually use vendorID or, for that matter, any other attribute, to support its business processes, you should not include that attribute in the class diagram. For that reason, we have not shown identifiers for classes such as Vendor, Order Line, and Skill.

In the E-R diagram, "Skill" was shown as a multivalued attribute of Employee. In the class diagram, we have shown Skill as a separate object class, because, according to Fowler (2000), in a conceptual object-oriented model, an attribute should always be single-valued. Order Line is shown as an association class, as is *Supplies*. Note that while we have displayed the name of the Order Line association within the class sym-

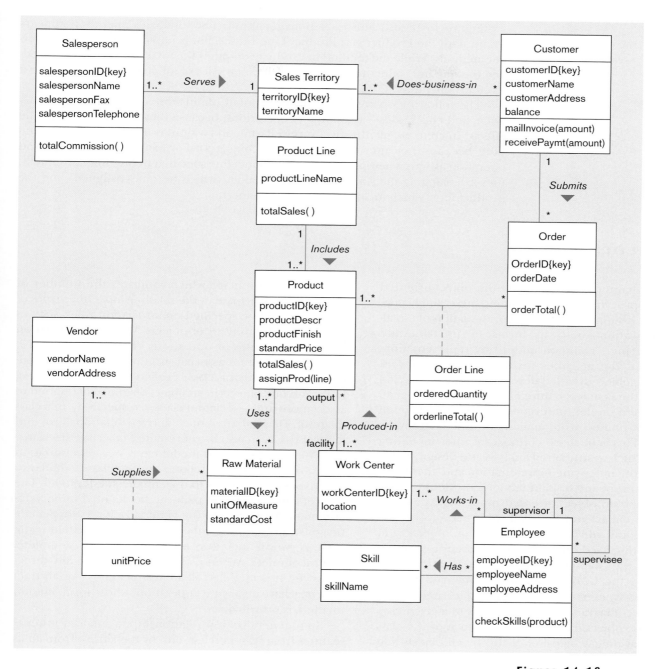

Figure 14-18
Class diagram for Pine Valley Furniture Company

bol to emphasize its "class nature," we have shown the name of the *Supplies* association on the association path to emphasize its "association nature."

The class diagram of Figure 14-18 shows several processes, represented as operations, that could not be captured in a E-R diagram. For example, Customer has an operation called mailInvoice, which, when executed, mails an invoice to a customer who has placed an order, specifying the total order amount in dollars, and increases the customer's outstanding balance by that amount. On receipt of payment from the customer, the receivePaymt operation adjusts the balance by the amount received. The orderlineTotal operation of Order Line computes the total dollar amount for a given order line of an order, whereas the orderTotal operation of Order computes the total amount for an entire order (i.e., the sum total of the amounts on all the order lines).

Figure 14-18 also illustrates polymorphism. The totalSales operation appears within both the Product and Product Line classes, but is implemented as two different methods. While the method in Product computes the total sales for a given product, the one in Product Line computes the total sales of all products belonging to a given product line.

The following operations—totalSales, totalCommission, orderTotal, orderlineTotal, and checkSkills—are all query operations, because they do not have any side effects. In contrast, mailInvoice, receivePaymt, and assignProd are all update operations because they alter the state of some object(s). For example, the assignProd operation assigns a new product to the product line specified in the "line" argument, thereby changing the state of both the product (which becomes assigned) and the product line (which includes one more product).

Summary

In this chapter, we introduced the object-oriented modeling approach, which is becoming increasingly popular because it supports effective representation of a real-world application—both in terms of its data and processes—using a common underlying representation. We described the activities involved in the different phases of the object-oriented development life cycle, and emphasized the seamless nature of the transitions that an object-oriented model undergoes as it evolves through the different phases, from analysis to design to implementation. This is in sharp contrast to other modeling approaches, such as structured analysis and design, which lack a common underlying representation and, therefore, suffer from abrupt and disjoint model transitions.

We presented object-oriented modeling as a high-level conceptual activity, especially as it pertains to data analysis. We introduced the concept of objects and classes, and discussed object identity and encapsulation. Throughout the chapter, we developed several class diagrams, using the UML notation, to show you how to model various types of situations. You also learned how to draw an object diagram that corresponds to a given class diagram. The object diagram is an instance of the class diagram, providing a snapshot of the actual objects and links present in a system at some point in time.

We showed how to model the processes underlying an application using operations. We discussed three types of operations: constructor, query, and update. The E-R model (as well as the enhanced E-R model) does not allow you to capture processes; it only allows you to model the data needs of an organization. In this chapter, we emphasized several similarities between the E-R model and the object-oriented model, but, at the same time, highlighted those features that make the latter more powerful than the former.

We showed how to represent association relationships of different degrees—unary, binary, and ternary—in a class diagram. An association has two or more roles; each role has a multiplicity, which indicates the number of objects that participate in the relationship. Other types of constraints can be specified on association roles, such as forming an ordered set of objects. When an association itself has attributes or operations of its own, or when it participates in other associations, the association is modeled as a class; such a class is called an association class. Links and link objects in an object diagram correspond to associations and association classes, respectively, in a class diagram. Derived attributes, derived relationships, and derived roles can also be represented in a class diagram.

The object-oriented model expresses generalization relationships using superclasses and subclasses, similar to supertypes and subtypes in the enhanced E-R model. The basis of a generalization path can be denoted using a discriminator label next to the generalization path. Semantic constraints among subclasses can be specified using UML keywords such as overlapping, disjoint, complete, and incomplete. When a class does not have any direct instances, it is modeled as an abstract class. An abstract class may have an abstract operation, whose form, but not method, is provided.

In a generalization relationship, a subclass inherits features from its superclass, and by transitivity, from all its ancestors. Inheritance is a very powerful mechanism because it supports code reuse in object-oriented systems. We discussed ways of applying inheritance of features, as well as reasons for overriding inheritance of operations in subclasses. We also introduced another key concept in object-oriented modeling, that of polymorphism, which means that an operation can apply in different ways across different classes. The concepts of encapsulation, inheritance, and polymorphism in object-oriented modeling provide system developers with powerful mechanisms for developing complex, robust, flexible, and maintainable business systems.

The object-oriented model supports aggregation, while the E-R or the enhanced E-R model does not. Aggregation is a semantically stronger form of association, expressing the *Part-of* relationship between a component object and an aggregate object. We distinguished between aggregation and generalization, and provided you with tips for choosing between association and aggregation in representing a relationship. We discussed a stronger form of aggregation, known as composition, in which a part object belongs to only one whole object, living and dying together with it.

In this chapter, you also learned how to state business rules implicitly, as well as explicitly, in a class diagram.

UML provides several keywords that can be used as constraints on classes, attributes, relationships, etc. In addition, user-defined constraints may be used to express business rules. When a business rule involves two or more elements, you saw how to express the rule in a class diagram, such as by using a note symbol. We concluded the chapter by developing a class diagram for Pine Valley Furniture Company, illustrating how to apply the object-oriented approach to model both the data and the processes underlying real-world business problems.

CHAPTER REVIEW

Key Terms

Abstract class
Abstract operation
Aggregation
Association
Association class
Association role
Behavior
Class diagram
Class-scope attribute

Composition
Concrete class
Constructor operation
Encapsulation
Method
Multiple classification
Multiplicity
Object
Object class (class)

Object diagram
Operation
Overriding
Polymorphism
Query operation
Scope operation
State
Update operation

Review Questions

1. Define each of the following terms:

a. object class
b. state
c. behavior
d. encapsulation
e. operation
f. method
g. constructor operation
h. query operation
i. update operation
j. abstract class

k. concrete class
l. abstract operation
m. multiplicity
n. class-scope attribute
o. association class
p. polymorphism
q. overriding
r. multiple classification
s. composition
t. recursive aggregation

2. Match the following terms to the appropriate definitions:

_____ concrete class
_____ abstract operation
_____ aggregation
_____ overriding
_____ polymorphism
_____ association class
_____ composition
_____ object class

a. operation applied in different ways
b. form, not implementation
c. direct instances
d. belongs to only one whole object
e. method replacement
f. part-of relationship
g. a set of objects
h. equivalent to associative entity

3. Contrast the following terms:

a. class; object
b. attribute; operation
c. state; behavior
d. operation; method
e. query operation; update operation
f. abstract class; concrete class
g. class diagram; object diagram
h. association; aggregation
i. generalization; aggregation
j. aggregation; composition
k. overriding for extension; overriding for restriction

4. State the activities involved in each of the following phases of the object-oriented development life cycle: object-oriented analysis, object-oriented design, and object-oriented implementation.

5. Compare and contrast the object-oriented model with the enhanced E-R model.

6. State the conditions under which a designer should model an association relationship as an association class.

7. Using a class diagram, give an example for each of the following types of relationships: unary, binary, and ternary. Specify the multiplicities for all the relationships.

8. Add role names to the association relationships you identified in Review Question 7.

9. Add operations to some of the classes you identified in Review Question 7.

10. Give an example of generalization. Your example should include at least one superclass and three subclasses, and a minimum of one attribute and one operation for each of the classes. Indicate the discriminator and specify the semantic constraints among the subclasses.

11. If the diagram you developed for Review Question 10 does not contain an abstract class, extend the diagram by adding an abstract class that contains at least one abstract operation. Also, indicate which features of a class are inherited by other classes.

12. Using (and, if necessary, extending) the diagram from your solution to Review Question 11, give an example of polymorphism.

13. Give an example of aggregation. Your example should include at least one aggregate object and three component objects. Specify the multiplicities at each end of all the aggregation relationships.

Problems and Exercises

1. Draw a class diagram, showing the relevant classes, attributes, operations, and relationships, for each of the following situations (if you believe that you need to make additional assumptions, clearly state them for each situation):

   a. A company has a number of employees. The attributes of Employee include employeeID (primary key), name, address, and birthdate. The company also has several projects. Attributes of Project include projectName and startDate. Each employee may be assigned to one or more projects, or may not be assigned to a project. A project must have at least one employee assigned, and may have any number of employees assigned. An employee's billing rate may vary by project, and the company wishes to record the applicable billing rate for each employee when assigned to a particular project. At the end of each month, the company mails a check to each employee who has worked on a project during that month. The amount of the check is based on the billing rate and the hours logged for each project assigned to the employee.

   b. A university has a large number of courses in its catalog. Attributes of Course include courseNumber (primary key), courseName, and units. Each course may have one or more different courses as prerequisites, or may have no prerequisites. Similarly, a particular course may be a prerequisite for any number of courses, or may not be prerequisite for any other course. The university adds or drops a prerequisite for a course only when the director for the course makes a formal request to that effect.

   c. A laboratory has several chemists who work on one or more projects. Chemists also may use certain kinds of equipment on each project. Attributes of Chemist include name and phoneNo. Attributes of Project include projectName and startDate. Attributes of Equipment include serialNo and cost. The organization wishes to record assignDate—that is, the date when a given equipment item was assigned to a particular chemist working on a specified project—as well as total-Hours, that is, the total number of hours the chemist has used the equipment for the project. The organiza-

   tion also wants to track the usage of each type of equipment by a chemist. It does so by computing the average number of hours the chemist has used that equipment on all assigned projects. A chemist must be assigned to at least one project and one equipment item. A given equipment item need not be assigned, and a given project need not be assigned either a chemist or an equipment item.

   d. A college course may have one or more scheduled sections, or may not have a scheduled section. Attributes of Course include courseID, courseName, and units. Attributes of Section include sectionNumber and semester. The value of sectionNumber is an integer (such as "1" or "2") that distinguishes one section from another for the same course, but does not uniquely identify a section. There is an operation called findNumSections that finds the number of sections offered for a given course in a given semester.

   e. A hospital has a large number of registered physicians. Attributes of Physician include physicianID (primary key) and specialty. Patients are admitted to the hospital by physicians. Attributes of Patient include patientID (primary key) and patientName. Any patient who is admitted must have exactly one admitting physician. A physician may optionally admit any number of patients. Once admitted, a given patient must be treated by at least one physician. A particular physician may treat any number of patients, or may not treat any patients. Whenever a patient is treated by a physician, the hospital wishes to record the details of the treatment, by including the date, time, and results of the treatment.

2. A student, whose attributes include studentName, address, phone, and age, may engage in multiple campus-based activities. The university keeps track of the number of years a given student has participated in a specific activity and, at the end of each academic year, mails an activity report to the student showing his participation in various activities. Draw a class diagram for this situation.

3. Prepare a class diagram for a real estate firm that lists property for sale. The following describes this organization:

   - The firm has a number of sales offices in several states; location is an attribute of sales office.
   - Each sales office is assigned one or more employees. Attributes of employee include employeeID and employeeName. An employee must be assigned to only one sales office.
   - For each sales office, there is always one employee assigned to manage that office. An employee may manage only the sales office to which she is assigned.
   - The firm lists property for sale. Attributes of property include propertyName and location.
   - Each unit of property must be listed with one (and only one) of the sales offices. A sales office may have any number of properties listed, or may have no properties listed.
   - Each unit of property has one or more owners. Attributes of owner are ownerName and address. An owner may own one or more units of property. For each property that an owner owns, an attribute called percentOwned indicates what percentage of the property is owned by the owner.

   Add a subset constraint between two of the associations you identified in your class diagram.

4. Draw a class diagram for some organization that you are familiar with—Boy Scouts/Girl Scouts, sports team, etc. In your diagram, indicate names for at least four association roles.

5. Draw a class diagram for the following situation (state any assumptions you believe you have to make in order to develop a complete diagram): Stillwater Antiques buys and sells one of a kind antiques of all kinds (for example, furniture, jewelry, china, and clothing). Each item is uniquely identified by an item number and is also characterized by a description, asking price, condition, and open-ended comments. Stillwater works with many different individuals, called clients, who sell items to and buy items from the store. Some clients only sell items to Stillwater, some only buy items, and some others both sell and buy. A client is identified by a client number, and is also described by a client name and client address. When Stillwater sells an item in stock to a client, the owners want to record the commission paid, the actual selling price, sales tax (tax of zero indicates a tax exempt sale), and date sold. When Stillwater buys an item from a client, the owners want to record the purchase cost, date purchased, and condition at time of purchase.

6. Draw a class diagram for the following situation (state any assumptions you believe you have to make in order to develop a complete diagram): The H. I. Topi School of Business operates international business programs in 10 locations throughout Europe. The School had its first class of 9000 graduates in 1965. The School keeps track of each graduate's student number, name, country of birth, current country of citizenship, current name, current address, and the name of each major the student completed (each student has one or two majors). In order to maintain strong ties to its alumni, the School holds various events around the world. Events have a title, date, location, and type (for example, reception, dinner, or seminar). The School needs to keep track of which graduates have attended which events. For an attendance by a graduate at an event, a comment is recorded about information School officials learned from that graduate at that event. The School also keeps in contact with graduates by mail, e-mail, telephone, and fax interactions. As with events, the School records information learned from the graduate from each of these contacts. When a School official knows that he or she will be meeting or talking to a graduate, a report is produced showing the latest information about that graduate and the information learned during the past two years from that graduate from all contacts and events the graduate attended.

7. Assume that at Pine Valley Furniture each product (described by product number, description, and cost) comprises at least three components (described by component number, description, and unit of measure) and components are used to make one or many products. In addition, assume that components are used to make other components and that raw materials are also considered to be components. In both cases of components, we need to keep track of how many components go into making something else. Draw a class diagram for this situation; indicate the multiplicities for all the relationships you identified in the diagram.

8. Draw a class diagram for the following problem. A nonprofit organization depends on a number of different types of persons for its successful operation. The organization is interested in the following attributes for all of these persons: ssn, name, address, and phone. There are three types of persons who are of greatest interest: employees, volunteers, and donors. In addition to the attributes for a person, an employee has an attribute called dateHired, and a volunteer has an attribute called skill. A donor is a person who has donated one or more items to the organization. An item, specified by a name, may have no donors, or one or more donors. When an item is donated, the organization records its price, so that at the end of the year, it can identify the top ten donors.

   There are persons other than employees, volunteers, and donors who are of interest to the organization, so that a person need not belong to any of these three groups. On the other hand, at a given time a person may belong to two or more of these groups (for example, employee and donor).

9. A bank has three types of accounts: checking, savings, and loan. Following are the attributes for each type of account:

   CHECKING: Acct_No, Date_Opened, Balance, Service_Charge

   SAVINGS: Acct_No, Date_Opened, Balance, Interest_Rate

   LOAN: Acct_No, Date_Opened, Balance, Interest_Rate, Payment

Assume that each bank account must be a member of exactly one of these subtypes. At the end of each month the bank computes the balance in each account and mails a statement to the customer holding that account. The balance computation depends on the type of the account. For example, a checking account balance may reflect a service charge, whereas a savings account balance may include an interest amount. Draw a class diagram to represent the situation. Your diagram should include an abstract class, as well as an abstract operation for computing balance.

10. Refer to the class diagram for hospital relationships (Figure 14-9b). Add notation to express the following business rule: A resident patient can be assigned a bed only if that patient has been assigned a physician who will assume responsibility for the patient's care.

11. An organization has been entrusted with developing a Registration and Title system that maintains information about all vehicles registered in a particular state. For each vehicle that is registered with the office, the system has to store the name, address, telephone number of the owner, the start date and end date of the registration, plate information (issuer, year, type, and number), sticker (year, type, and number), and registration fee. In addition, the following information is maintained about the vehicles themselves: the number, year, make, model, body style, gross weight, number of passengers, diesel-powered (yes/no), color, cost, and mileage. If the vehicle is a trailer, the parameters diesel-powered and number of passengers are not relevant. For travel trailers, the body number and length must be known. The system needs to maintain information on the luggage capacity for a car, maximum cargo capacity and maximum towing capacity for a truck, and horsepower for a motorcycle. The system issues registration notices to owners of vehicles whose registrations are due to expire after two months. When the owner renews the registration, the system updates the registration information on the vehicle.

a. Develop an object-oriented model by drawing a class diagram that shows all the object classes, attributes, operations, relationships, and multiplicities. For each operation, show its argument list.

b. Each vehicle consists of a drive train, which, in turn, consists of an engine and a transmission. (Ignore the fact that a trailer doesn't have an engine and a transmission.) Suppose that, for each vehicle, the system has to maintain the following information: the size and number of cylinders of its engine, and the type and weight of its transmission. Add classes, attributes, and relationships to the class diagram to capture this new information.

c. Give a realistic example (you may create one) of an operation that you override in a subclass or subclasses. Add the operation at appropriate places in the class diagram, and discuss the reasons for overriding.

Field Exercises

1. Interview a friend or family member to elicit from them common examples of superclass/subclass relationships. You will have to explain the meaning of this term and provide a common example, such as: PROPERTY: RESIDENTIAL, COMMERCIAL; or BONDS: CORPORATE, MUNICIPAL. Use the information they provide to construct a class diagram segment and present it to this person. Revise if necessary until it seems appropriate to you and your friend or family member.

2. Visit two local small businesses, one in the service sector and one in manufacturing. Interview employees from these organizations to obtain examples of both superclass/subclass relationships and operational business rules (such as "A customer can return merchandise only if the customer has a valid sales slip"). In which of these environments is it easier to find examples of these constructs? Why?

3. Ask a database administrator or database or systems analyst in a local company to show you an EER (or E-R) diagram for one of the organization's primary databases. Translate this diagram into a class diagram.

4. Interview a systems analyst in a local company who uses object-oriented programming and system development tools. Ask to see any analysis and design diagrams the analyst has drawn of the database and applications. Compare these diagrams to the ones in this chapter. What differences do you see? What additional features and notations are used and what are their purpose?

References

Booch, G. 1994. *Object-Oriented Analysis and Design with Applications,* 2nd ed. Redwood City, CA: Benjamin/Cummings.

Coad, P., and E. Yourdon. 1991a. *Object-Oriented Analysis,* 2nd ed. Englewood Cliffs, NJ: Prentice-Hall.

Coad, P., and E. Yourdon. 1991b. *Object-Oriented Design.* Englewood Cliffs, NJ: Prentice-Hall.

Fowler, M. 2000. *UML Distilled: A Brief Guide to the Standard Object Modeling Language,* 2nd ed. Reading, MA: Addison Wesley Longman.

Jacobson, I., M. Christerson, P. Jonsson, and G. Overgaard. 1992. *Object-Oriented Software Engineering: A Use Case Driven Approach.* Reading, MA: Addison-Wesley.

Rumbaugh, J., M. Blaha, W. Premerlani, F. Eddy, and W. Lorensen. 1991. *Object-Oriented Modeling and Design.* Englewood Cliffs, NJ: Prentice-Hall.

UML Document Set. 1997. Version 1.0 (January). Santa Clara, CA: Rational Software Corp.

UML Notation Guide. 1997. Version 1.0 (January). Santa Clara, CA: Rational Software Corp.

Web Resources

www.omg.org The Website for the Object Management Group, a leading industry association concerned with object-oriented analysis and design.

Project Case

PROJECT DESCRIPTION

This project description is similar to the project description included with Chapter 4. After you complete this project, it will be useful for you to compare the data models developed in each of the project cases from Chapters 3 and 4.

As a large service organization, Mountain View Community Hospital depends on a large number of persons for its continued success. There are four groups of persons on whom the hospital is most dependent: employees, physicians, patients, and volunteers. Of course there are some common attributes shared by all of these persons: personID (identifier), name, address, city-state-zip, dateOfBirth, and phone.

Each of the four groups of persons has at least one unique attribute. Employees have a dateHired, Volunteers have a skill, Physicians have a specialty and a pagerNumber, and Patients have a dateOfContact (date of first contact with the hospital) and calc-age. There are also unique methods for each of the four groups of persons. Employees have calc-benefits, Volunteers have assign-to-Center(CareCenter), Physicians have treats(Patient), and Patients have calc-age and assignToLocation(Bed). An Employee or a Physician who is also a Patient also has an attribute specialService.

There are other persons in the hospital community who do not belong to one of these four groups (although their numbers are relatively small). On the other hand, a particular person may belong to two (or more) of these groups at a given time (for example, Patient and Volunteer).

Each patient has one (and only one) physician who is responsible for that patient. A given physician may not be responsible for a patient at a given time, or may be responsible for one or more patients. Patients are divided into two groups: resident, and outpatient. Each resident patient has a dateOfAdmission attribute and a method of assignToBed(Bed), which overrides the assignToLocation method of all patients. Each outpatient is scheduled for zero or more visits. The entity visit has two attributes: date

(partial identifier) and comments. Notice that an instance of visit cannot exist without an outpatient owner entity.

Employees are subdivided into three groups: nurse, staff, and technician. Only nurse has the attribute certificate, which indicates the qualification (RN, LPN, etc.). Only staff has the attribute jobClass, while only technician has the attribute skill. Each nurse is assigned to one (and only one) care center. Examples of care centers are Maternity, Emergency, and Cardiology (care centers were formerly called wards). Attributes of care center are name (identifier) and location. A care center may have one or more nurses assigned to it. Also for each care center, one of the nurses assigned to that care center is appointed nurse_in_charge; however, a nurse cannot be appointed nurse_in_charge unless she or he has an RN certificate. Care centers are located in buildings, and a building is described by buildingNumber, buildingName, and buildingCode.

Each technician is assigned to one or more laboratories. Attributes of laboratory include name (identifier) and location. A laboratory must have at least one technician assigned to it and may have any number of technicians assigned. A laboratory is housed in one and only one building, and a building may house many laboratories. A laboratory includes equipment and the employees who work in that laboratory, and a laboratory also has a method numberOfEmployees.

There may be no beds assigned to a care center, or a care center may have one or more beds (up to any number) assigned to it. The only attribute of bed is bedID (identifier) and the only method of bed is utilization. bedID is a composite attribute, with components bedNumber and roomNumber. Each resident patient must be assigned to a bed. A bed may or may not have a resident patient assigned to it at a given time.

PROJECT QUESTIONS

1. Is the ability to model superclass/subclass relationships likely to be important in a hospital environment such as Mountain View Community Hospital? Why or why not?

2. Do there appear to be any link objects in the description of the data requirements in this project segment? If so, what are they?

3. Are there any abstract object classes in the description of this hospital? Why or why not?

PROJECT EXERCISES

1. Draw a class diagram to accurately represent this set of requirements, carefully following the notation from this chapter.

2. Develop definitions for each of the following types of objects in your class diagram from Project Exercise 1. Consult with some member of the hospital or health-care community if one is available; otherwise make reasonable assumptions based on your own knowledge and experience.

   a. Classes

   b. Attributes

   c. Relationships

   d. Methods

3. You should recognize the statement "A nurse cannot be appointed nurse_in_charge of a care center unless she or he has an RN certificate" as a statement of a business rule. How did you model this business rule differently from what you did in the project case in Chapter 4? What is the constrained object? Is it an entity, an attribute, a relationship, or some other object?

4. Compare the class diagram you developed in this chapter with the EER diagram that you developed in Chapter 4 and with the E-R diagram you developed in Chapter 3 in Project Exercise 2. What are the differences between these two diagrams? Why are there differences?

5. Did you find any examples of aggregation or composition in the description of the project in this chapter? Why or why not?

Chapter **15**

Object-Oriented Database Development

LEARNING OBJECTIVES

After studying this chapter, you should be able to:

- Concisely define each of the following key terms: **atomic literal, collection literal, set, bag, list, array, dictionary, structured literal,** and **extent**.

- Create logical object-oriented database schemas using the object definition language (ODL).

- Transform conceptual UML class diagrams to logical ODL schemas by mapping classes (abstract and concrete), attributes, operations (abstract and concrete), association relationships (one-to-one, one-to-many, and many-to-many), and generalization relationships.

- Identify the type specifications for attributes, operation arguments, and operation returns.

- Create objects and specify attribute values for those objects.

- Understand the steps involved in implementing object-oriented databases.

- Understand the syntax and semantics of the object query language (OQL).

- Use OQL commands to formulate various types of queries.

- Gain an understanding of the types of applications to which object-oriented databases have been applied.

INTRODUCTION

In Chapter 14, we introduced you to object-oriented data modeling. You learned how to conceptually model a database using UML class diagrams. In this chapter, we will describe how such conceptual object-oriented models can be transformed into logical schemas that can be directly implemented using an object database management system (ODBMS).

As you will learn later, although relational databases are effective for traditional business applications, they have severe limitations (in amount of programming

The original version of this chapter was written by Professor Atish P. Sinha, University of Wisconsin–Milwaukee.

required and DBMS performance) when it comes to storing and manipulating complex data and relationships. In this chapter, we will show how to implement applications within an object-oriented database environment.

In this chapter, we will adopt the Object Model proposed by the Object Database Management Group (ODMG) for defining and querying an object-oriented database (OODB). For developing logical schemas, we will specifically use the object definition language (ODL), a data definition language for OODBs specified in the ODMG 3.0 standard (Cattell et al., 2000). The object Database Management Group was formed in 1991 by OODB vendors to create standards, and hence make OODBs more viable. Just as an SQL data definition language (DDL) schema can be implemented in an SQL-compliant relational DBMS (see Chapter 7), a logical schema created using ODL can be implemented in an ODMG-compliant ODBMS.

We will use examples similar to the ones you saw earlier in Chapter 14 to show how to map conceptual UML class diagrams into logical ODL schemas. You will learn how to map classes (abstract and concrete), attributes, operations (abstract and concrete), association relationships (unary and binary), and generalization relationships from a UML class diagram into corresponding ODL constructs.

Recall from Chapter 7 that, in addition to the DDL component, SQL has a data manipulation language (DML) component that allows users to query or manipulate the data inside a relational database. A similar language, called object query language (OQL), has been specified in the ODMG 3.0 standard to query object databases (Cattell et al., 2000). We will describe how various types of queries can be formulated using OQL. The ODMG has prescribed versions of ODL and OQL for C++, Small talk, and Java. We use a generic version in our examples.

In Chapter 14, we showed a conceptual object-oriented model for the Pine Valley Furniture Company. In this chapter, we will transform this conceptual model into a logical ODL schema. Finally, we will discuss the types of applications for which ODBMSs are well suited and describe briefly some of the applications developed using existing ODBMS products.

OBJECT DEFINITION LANGUAGE

In Chapter 7, you learned how to use the SQL data definition language (DDL) to specify a logical schema for a relational database. Similarly, the object definition language (ODL) allows you to specify a logical schema for an object-oriented database. ODL is a programming language–independent specification language for defining OODB schemas. Just as an SQL DDL schema is portable across SQL-compliant relational DBMSs, an ODL schema is portable across ODMG-compliant ODBMSs.

Defining a Class

Figure 15-1 shows a conceptual UML class diagram (see Chapter 14 for an explanation of the notation for a class diagram) for a university database, an example with which all readers are familiar. For the time being, we will focus on the Student and Course classes, and their attribute properties. In ODL, a class is specified using the *class* keyword, and an attribute is specified using the *attribute* keyword. The Student and Course classes are defined as follows:

```
class Student {
    attribute string name;
    attribute Date dateOfBirth;
    attribute string address;
    attribute string phone;
// plus relationship and operations . . .
    };
```

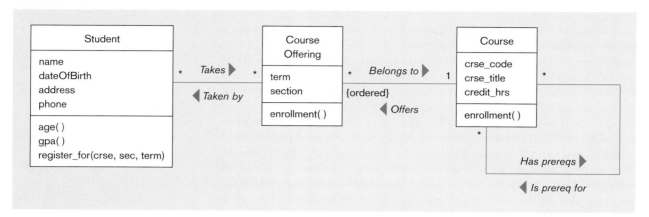

Figure 15-1
UML class diagram for a university database

```
class Course {
    attribute string crse_code;
    attribute string crse_title;
    attribute short credit_hrs;
// plus relationships and operation . . .
    };
```

We have highlighted the ODL keywords in bold. We have added comments (preceded by the "//" sign) to indicate that we need to add the relationships and operations (see Figure 15-1) to the classes at a later stage. Note that next to an attribute keyword, we have specified the type of the attribute followed by the attribute's name.

Defining an Attribute

An attribute's value is either a literal or an *object identifier*. As we discussed in Chapter 14 each object has a unique identifier. Because an object retains its identifier over its lifetime, the object remains the same despite changes in its state. In contrast, literals do not have identifiers and, therefore, cannot be individually referenced like objects. Literals are embedded inside objects. You can think of literal values as constants. For example, the string Mary Jones, the character C, and the integer 20 are all literal values.

The Object Model supports different literal types, including atomic literals, collection literals, and structured literals. Examples of **atomic literal** types are string, char (character), boolean (true or false), float (real number), short (short integer), and long (long integer).

A collection literal is a collection of elements, which themselves could be of any literal or object type. The collection literal types supported by the ODMG Object Model include *set, bag, list, array,* and *dictionary.* A **set** is an unordered collection of elements of the same type without any duplicates. A **bag** is an unordered collection of elements that may contain duplicates. In contrast to sets and bags, a **list** is an ordered collection of elements of the same type. An **array** is a dynamically sized ordered collection of elements that can be located by position. A **dictionary** is an unordered sequence of key-value pairs without any duplicates.

A **structured literal**, also known as *structure*, consists of a fixed number of named elements, each of which could be of literal or object type. The Object Model supports the following predefined structures: Date, Interval, Time, and Timestamp. In addition, it supports user-defined structures, examples of which will be given later.

Let us now go back to the ODL schema for the university database. The attributes name, address, and phone of Student, and crse_code and crse_title of Course are all of string type. A string attribute can store a string of alphanumeric characters enclosed

Atomic literal: A constant that cannot be decomposed into any further components.

Collection literal: A collection of literals or object types.

Set: An unordered collection of elements without any duplicates.

Bag: An unordered collection of elements that may contain duplicates.

List: An ordered collection of elements of the same type.

Array: A dynamically sized ordered collection of elements that can be located by position.

Dictionary: An unordered sequence of key-value pairs without any duplicates.

Structured literal: A fixed number of named elements, each of which could be of literal or object type.

within double quotes. The attribute credit_hrs of Course is short because its value is always an integer less than 2^{16}. In addition to these atomic literal types, the schema also specifies the structured literal type Date for the dateOfBirth attribute of Student.

Defining User Structures

In addition to the standard data types provided by ODL, you can define structures yourself by using the *struct* keyword. For example, you can define a structure called Address that consists of four components—street_address, city, state, and zip—all of which are string attributes.

```
struct Address {
    string street_address;
    string city;
    string state;
    string zip;
};
```

Similarly, you can define Phone as a structure consisting of an area code and a personal_number. Note that the latter is specified as a long integer, because it is more than 2^{16}.

```
struct Phone {
    short area_code;
    long personal_number;
};
```

There structures can now be used as the structure for elements of other structures. For example, if a student can have more than one phone number, the phone attribute could be defined by

```
attribute set ⟨ phone ⟩ phones;
```

Defining Operations

We can also define the operations for the two classes. In ODL, you specify an operation using parentheses after its name. The ODL definition for Student is now as follows:

```
class Student {
    attribute string name;
    attribute Date dateOfBirth;
//user-defined structured attributes
    attribute Address address;
    attribute Phone phone;
//plus relationship
//operations
    short age( );
    float gpa( );
    boolean register_for(string crse, short sec, string term);
};
```

We have defined all three operations shown in Figure 15-1: age, gpa, and register_for. The first two are query operations. The register_for operation is an update operation that registers a student for a section (sec) of a course (crse) in a given term. Each of these arguments, shown within parentheses, is preceded by its type.[1]

---

[1] If the strict ODL syntax is followed, the argument type has to be preceded by the keyword "in," "out," or "inout," specifying the argument as an input, output, or input/output, respectively. We have chosen not to show this specification for the sake of simplicity.

We also have to specify the return type for each operation. For example, the return types for age and gpa are short (short integer) and float (real number), respectively. The return type for the register_for operation is boolean (true or false), indicating if the registration was successfully completed or not. If the operation does not return any value, the return type is declared as void.

Each type of object has certain predefined operations. For example, a set object has a predefined "is_subset_of" operation and a data object (attribute) has a predefined boolean operation "days_in_year." See Cattell et al. (2000) for a thorough coverage of predefined object operations.

Defining a Range for an Attribute

If you know all the possible values that an attribute can have, you can enumerate those values in ODL. For example, if you know that the maximum number of sections for a course is 8, you can use the keyword *enum* before the attribute name (section) within the CourseOffering class and the possible values after the name.

```
class CourseOffering {
    attribute string term;
    attribute enum section {1, 2, 3, 4, 5, 6, 7, 8};
//operation
    short enrollment( );
};
```

Defining Relationships

Finally, we will add the relationships shown in Figure 15-1 to the ODL schema. The ODMG Object Model supports only unary and binary relationships. There are two binary relationships and one unary relationship in Figure 15-1. As discussed in Chapter 14, a relationship is inherently bidirectional. In Figure 15-1, we have provided names for both directions of a relationship. For example, we have named the relationship between Student and Course Offering *Takes* when traversing from the former to the latter, and *Taken by* when traversing in the reverse direction. We use the ODL keyword *relationship* to specify a relationship.

```
class Student {
    attribute string name;
    attribute Date dateOfBirth;
    attribute Address address;
    attribute Phone phone;
// relationship between Student and CourseOffering
    relationship set ⟨CourseOffering⟩ takes inverse CourseOffering::taken_by;
// operations
    short age( );
    float gpa( );
    boolean register_for(string crse, short sec, string term);
};
```

Within the Student class, we have defined the "takes" relationship, using the relationship keyword. The name of the relationship is preceded by the class the relationship targets: CourseOffering. Because a student can take multiple course offerings, we have used the keyword "set" to indicate that a Student object is related to a set of CourseOffering objects (and the set is unordered). This relationship specification represents the traversal path from Student to CourseOffering.

The ODMG Object Model requires that a relationship be specified in both directions. In ODL, the *inverse* keyword is used to specify the relationship in the reverse direction. The inverse of "takes" is "taken_by" from CourseOffering to Student. In the class definition for Student, we have named this traversal path (taken_by), preceded by the name of the class from where the path originates (CourseOffering), along with a double colon (::). In the class definition for CourseOffering shown below, the relationship is specified as "taken_by," with the inverse being "takes" from Student. Because a course offering can be taken by many students, the relationship links a set of Student objects to a given CourseOffering object. For a many-to-many relationship such as this, therefore, you must specify a collection (set, list, bag, or array) of objects on both sides.

```
class CourseOffering {
    attribute string term;
    attribute enum section {1, 2, 3, 4, 5, 6, 7, 8};
// many-to-many relationship between CourseOffering and Student
    relationship set ⟨Student⟩ taken_by inverse Student::takes;
// one-to-many relationship between CourseOffering and Course
    relationship Course belongs_to inverse Course::offers;
//operation
    short enrollment( );
};
```

The ODBMS would automatically enforce the *referential integrity* of the relationships you specify in an ODL schema (Bertino and Martino, 1993; Cattell et al., 2000). For instance, if you delete a Student object, the ODBMS will automatically dereference its links to all CourseOffering objects. It will also dereference links from all CourseOffering objects back to that Student object. If you link a Student object to a set of CourseOffering objects, the ODBMS will automatically create inverse links. That is, it will create a link from each of the CourseOffering objects back to the Student object in question.

We have specified another relationship, "belongs_to," for the CourseOffering class, with the inverse being "offers" from Course. Because a course offering belongs to exactly one course, the destination of the belongs_to traversal path is Course, implying that a CourseOffering object can be linked to only one Course object. In specifying the "one" side of an association relationship, therefore, you simply specify the destination object type, and not a collection (e.g., set) of an object type.

We show below how to specify the relationships and operation for Course. We have specified the offers relationship within Course, with the inverse being belongs_to. But because the course offerings are ordered within a course (according to section number within a given term), we have used *list*, as opposed to *set*, to denote the ordering within the collection. Both directions of the unary relationship shown in Figure 15-1, has_prereqs and is_prereq_for, begin and terminate in the Course class, as specified in the Course definition below.

```
class Course {
    attribute string crse_code;
    attribute string crse_title;
    attribute short credit_hrs;
// unary relationship for prerequisite courses
    relationship set ⟨Course⟩ has_prereqs inverse Course::is_prereq_for;
    relationship set ⟨Course⟩ is_prereq_for inverse Course::has_prereqs;
// binary relationship between Course and CourseOffering
    relationship list ⟨CourseOffering⟩ offers inverse CourseOffering::belongs_to;
//operation
    short enrollment( );
};
```

Figure 15-2
ODL schema for university database

```
class Student {
(      extent students)
       attribute string name;
       attribute Date dateOfBirth;
       attribute Address address;
       attribute Phone phone;
       relationship set ⟨CourseOffering⟩ takes inverse CourseOffering::taken_by;
       short age( );
       float gpa( );
       boolean register_for(string crse, short sec, string term);
};

class CourseOffering {
(      extent courseofferings)
       attribute string term;
       attribute enum section {1, 2, 3, 4, 5, 6, 7, 8};
       relationship set ⟨Student⟩ taken_by inverse Student::takes;
       relationship Course belongs_to inverse Course::offers;
       short enrollment( );
};

class Course {
(      extent courses)
       attribute string crse_code;
       attribute string crse_title;
       attribute short credit_hrs;
       relationship set ⟨Course⟩ has_prereqs inverse Course::is_prereq_for;
       relationship set ⟨Course⟩ is_prereq_for inverse Course::has_prereqs;
       relationship list ⟨CourseOffering⟩ offers inverse CourseOffering::belongs_to;
       short enrollment( );
};
```

Extent: The set of all instances of a class within the database.

The complete schema for the university database is shown in Figure 15-2. Notice that we have introduced the ODL keyword *extent* to specify the extents of the classes. The **extent** of a class is the set of all instances of the class within the database (Cattell et al., 2000). For example, the extent called students refers to all the Student instances in the database.

Defining an Attribute with an Object Identifier as Its Value

In all the examples that you have seen so far, an attribute's value is always a literal. Recall that we said that it could also be an object identifier. For instance, there could be an attribute called "dept" within Course that represents the department offering a course. Instead of storing the department's name, the attribute could store the identifier for a Department object. We need to make the following changes:

```
class Course {
// the dept attribute's value is an object identifier
       attribute Department dept;
// other attributes, operations, and relationships . . .
};

class Department {
       attribute short dept_number;
       attribute string dept_name;
       attribute string office_address;
};
```

The type of the dept attribute is Department, implying that the attribute's value is an object identifier for an instance of Department. This is akin to representing a unidirectional relationship, from Course to Department. The ODBMS, however, does not automatically maintain the referential integrity of such unidirectional relationships specified through attributes. If most of the references in user queries are from Course to Department (e.g., finding the name of the department offering a given course), not vice versa, and referential integrity is not an issue, then representing such a relationship in one direction using an attribute reference provides a more efficient alternative.

Defining Many-to-Many Relationships, Keys, and Multivalued Attributes

Figure 15-3a shows a many-to-many relationship between Employee and Project. To make an assignment, you need an Employee object, as well as a Project object. Hence we have modeled Assignment as an association class with features of its own. The features include the start_date, end_date, and hours attributes, and the assign operation. In Figure 15-3b, we have broken the many-to-many relationship between Employee and Project into two one-to-many relationships, one from Employee to

Figure 15-3
UML class diagram for an employee project database
(a) Many-to-many relationship with an association class

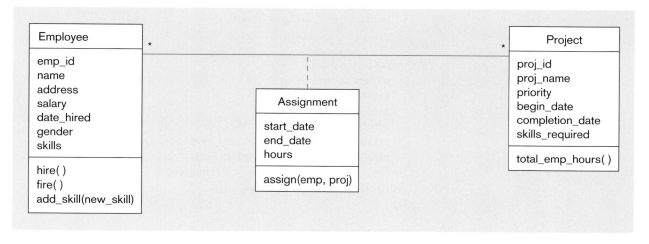

(b) Many-to-many relationship broken into two one-to-many relationships

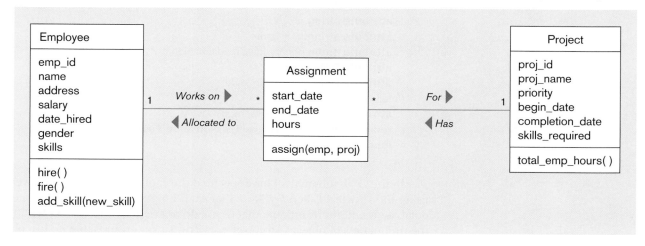

Assignment and the other from Project to Assignment. Although we could have specified the many-to-many relationship directly in ODL, we could not have captured the features special to Assignment unless we decomposed the relationship into two one-to-many relationships.

The class diagram shown in Figure 15-3b can now be transformed into the following ODL schema:

```
class Employee {
(   extent employees
// emp_id is the primary key for Employee
    key emp_id)
    attribute short emp_id;
    attribute string name;
    attribute Address address;
    attribute float salary;
    attribute Date date_hired;
    attribute enum gender {male, female};
// multivalued attribute
    attribute set ⟨string⟩ skills;
    relationship set ⟨Assignment ⟩ works_on inverse Assignment::allocated_to;
// the following operations don't return any values
    void hire( );
    void fire( );
    void add_skill(string new_skill);
};


class Assignment {
(   extent assignments)
    attribute Date start_date;
    attribute Date end_date;
    attribute short hours;
    relationship Employee allocated_to inverse Employee::works_on;
    relationship Project for inverse Project::has;
// the following operation assigns an employee to a project
void assign (short emp, string proj);
};


class Project {
(   extent projects
// proj_id is the primary key for Project
    key proj_id);
    attribute string proj_id;
    attribute string proj_name;
    attribute enum priority {low, medium, high};
    attribute Date begin_date;
    attribute Date completion_date;
//multivalued attribute
    attribute set ⟨string⟩ skills_required;
    relationship set ⟨Assignment⟩ has inverse Assignment::for;
    long total_emp_hours( );
};
```

In the ODL schema, we have specified the candidate keys for Employee and Project using the keyword called *key*. Note that each Employee or Project instance in an object database is inherently unique; that is, you do not require an explicit identifier to enforce the uniqueness of objects. However, specifying a key ensures that no two objects belonging to a class have the same value for the key attribute(s). The scope of uniqueness is confined to the extent of the class. Hence, before specifying a key for a class, you must specify its extent. The emp_id attribute must have a unique value for each Employee object; the same applies to proj_id of Project. ODL also supports compound keys, that is, keys consisting of more than one attribute. For example, if an employee is uniquely identified by name and address, then you could specify the key as follows:

keys {name, address}

The schema above also illustrates how to define a multivalued attribute, an attribute that may have multiple values at a given point in time. The skills attribute of Employee and the skills_required attribute of Project are each specified as a set of string values.

Defining Generalization

ODL supports unary and binary association relationships, but not relationships of higher degree. It allows you to represent generalization relationships using the *extends* keyword. In Figure 15-4, we have shown a UML class diagram you had seen earlier in Chapter 14. Three subclasses—Hourly Employee, Salaried Employee, and Consultant—are generalized into a superclass called Employee. The ODL schema corresponding to the class diagram is given below:

```
class Employee {
(    extent employees)
     attribute short emp_number;
     attribute string name;
     attribute Address address;
     attribute float salary;
     attribute Date date_hired;
     void print_label( );
};
```

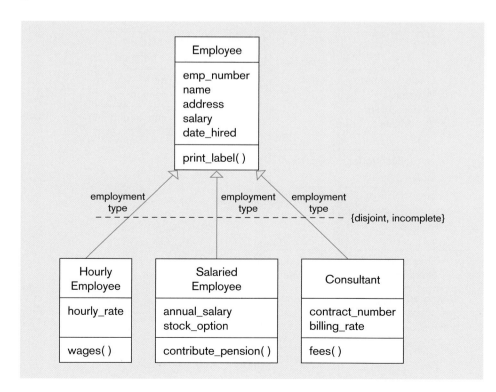

Figure 15-4
UML class diagram showing employee generalization

```
class HourlyEmployee extends Employee {
(     extent hrly_emps)
      attribute float hourly_rate;
      float wages( );
};

class SalariedEmployee extends Employee {
(     extent salaried_emps)
      attribute float annual_salary;
      attribute boolean stock_option;
      void contribute_pension( );
};

class Consultant extends Employee {
(     extent consultants)
      attribute short contract_number;
      attribute float billing_rate;
      float fees( );
};
```

The subclasses HourlyEmployee, SalariedEmployee, and Consultant extend the more general Employee class by introducing new features. For example, HourlyEmployee has two special features, hourly_rate and wages, in addition to the common set of features inherited from Employee. All the classes, including Employee, are concrete, implying that they can have direct instances. Employee is a concrete class because the subclasses are incomplete.

Defining an Abstract Class

Figure 15-5 shows an example of an abstract class called Student, which cannot have any direct instances. That is, a student has to be an instance of Graduate

Figure 15-5
UML class diagram showing student generalization

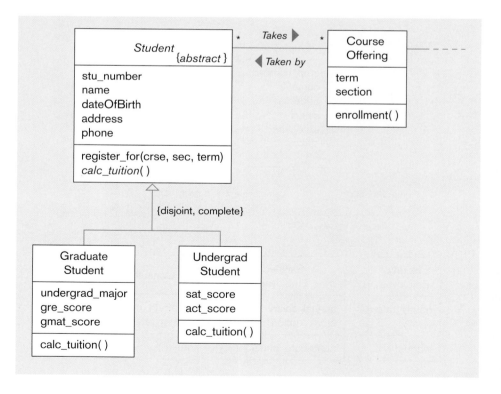

Student or of Undergraduate Student (note the "complete" constraint among the subclasses). In the logical schema, we specify Student as an abstract class as follows:

```
    abstract class Student {
(   extent students
    key stu_number)
    attribute long stu_number;
    attribute string name;
    attribute Date dateOfBirth;
    attribute Address address;
    attribute Phone phone;
    relationship set ⟨CourseOffering⟩ takes inverse CourseOffering::taken_by;
    boolean register_for(string crse, short section, string term);
// abstract operation
    abstract float calc_tuition( );
};
```

Notice that the calc_tuition operation of Student is abstract, implying that, at this level, the operation's form is specified but not its implementation. We have used the *abstract* keyword to specify both the abstract class and the abstract operation.[2] The subclasses are defined as follows:

```
    class GraduateStudent extends Student {
(   extent grads)
    attribute char undergrad_major;
    attribute GRE gre_score;
    attribute GMAT gmat_score;
    float calc_tuition( );
};
```

```
    class UndergradStudent extends Student {
(   extent undergrads)
    attribute SAT sat_score;
    attribute ACT act_score;
    float calc_tuition( );
};
```

Because both of the subclasses are concrete, the calc_tuition operations within them must also be concrete. Therefore, although each subclass inherits the form of the operation from Employee, it still has to provide the method. The calc_tuition operation is specified separately within each subclass, thereby illustrating polymorphism. The fact that it is concrete is indicated by the absence of the *abstract* keyword.

Defining Other User Structures

The schema definition contains user-defined structures such as GRE, GMAT, SAT, and ACT, which specify the types for the various test scores. While a predefined structure such as Date or Time allows you to readily use it for attribute specification,

---

[2]ODL does not currently support the "abstract" keyword for classes and operations. The syntax we have used parallels that of Java, which clearly differentiates an abstract class/operation from a concrete class/operation.

you can define additional structures that could be used for the same purpose. We define the structures for the test scores as follows:

```
struct GRE {
    Score verbal_score;
    Score quant_score;
    Score analytical_score;
};

struct GMAT {
    Score verbal_score;
    Score quant_score;
};

struct SCORE {
    short scaled_score;
    short percentile_score;
};

struct SAT { ... };

struct ACT { ... };
```

The GRE structure consists of a verbal score, a quantitative score, and an analytical score, while the GMAT structure does not have an analytical score. The type of each of these scores, in turn, is a structure called SCORE, which consists of a scaled score (e.g., 680) and a percentile score (e.g., 95%).

OODB DESIGN FOR PINE VALLEY FURNITURE COMPANY

In Chapter 14, we developed a conceptual object-oriented model for the Pine Valley Furniture Company in the form of a class diagram (see Figure 14-18). We will now transform this conceptual model into a logical ODL schema, which may be used to implement an object-oriented database system for the company.

The ODL schema is shown in Figure 15-6. By now you should be able to clearly understand how each class, attribute, operation, and relationship in the class diagram has been mapped to an equivalent ODL construct in the logical schema. A few points need some mention, however. The definitions of the Address and Phone structures are not shown in the figure because they were given previously. Notice that the type for the salespersonFax attribute of Salesperson is Phone, indicating that the attribute shares the same type as salesperson Telephone. Also, although the class diagram does not specify any of the collections as ordered, we ordered some of them in the ODL schema. For example, the collection of order lines contained within an Order object is specified as a list, implying that the order line objects are ordered or sorted.

Another thing to note is how we mapped the two many-to-many relationships, each with an association class, into two one-to-many relationships. The first one is between Order and Product with an association class called OrderLine. In the logical schema, we defined a class called OrderLine that participates in two one-to-many relationships, one with Order and the other with Product. The other many-to-many relationship with an association class is *Supplies,* which was similarly mapped into two one-to-many relationships, one between Vendor and Supply, and the other between RawMaterial and Supply.

```
class Salesperson {
(   extent salespersons
    key salespersonID)
    attribute string salespersonID;
    attribute string salespersonName;
    attribute Phone salespersonFax;
    attribute Phone salespersonTelephone;
    relationship SalesTerritory serves inverse
        SalesTerritory::represented_by;
    float totalCommission( );
};

class SalesTerritory {
(   extent salesterritories
    key territoryID)
    attribute char territoryID;
    attribute char territoryName;
    relationship set⟨Salesperson⟩ represented_by
        inverse Salesperson::serves;
    relationship set⟨Customer⟩ consists_of inverse
        Customer::does_business_in;
};

class Customer {
(   extent customers
    key customerID)
    attribute string customerID;
    attribute string customerName;
    attribute Address customerAddress;
    attribute float balance;
    relationship set⟨SalesTerritory⟩
        does_business_in inverse
        SalesTerritory::consists_of;
    relationship list⟨Order⟩ submits inverse
        Order::submitted_by;
    void mailInvoice(float amount);
    void receivePaymt(float amount);
};

class Order {
(   extent orders
    key orderID)
    attribute string orderID;
    attribute Date orderDate;
    relationship Customer submitted_by inverse
        Customer::submits;
    relationship list⟨OrderLine⟩ contains inverse
        OrderLine::contained_in;
    float orderTotal( );
};
```

```
class OrderLine {
(   extent orderlines)
    attribute short orderedQuantity;
    relationship Order contained_in inverse
        Order::contains;
    relationship Product specifies inverse
        Product::specified_in;
    long orderlineTotal( );
};

class Product {
(   extent products
    key productID)
    attribute string productID;
    attribute string productDescr;
    attribute char productFinish;
    attribute float standardPrice;
    relationship ProductLine belongs_to inverse
        ProductLine::includes;
    relationship set⟨OrderLine⟩ specified_in
        inverse OrderLine::specifies;
    relationship set⟨WorkCenter⟩ produced_at
        inverse WorkCenter::produces;
    relationship set⟨RawMaterial⟩ uses inverse
        RawMaterial::used_in;
    float totalSales( );
    boolean assignProd(string line);
};

class ProductLine {
(   extent productlines)
    attribute string productLineName;
    relationship list⟨Product⟩ includes inverse
        Product::belongs_to;
    float totalSales( );
};

class WorkCenter {
(   extent materialID
    key workCenterID)
    attribute char workCenterID;
    attribute string location;
    relationship set⟨Product⟩ produces inverse
        Product::produced_by;
    relationship list⟨Employee⟩ employs inverse
        Employee::works_in;
};
```

Figure 15-6
ODL schema for Pine Valley Furniture
Company database

(continues)

```
class RawMaterial {
(   extent rawmaterials
    key materialID)
    attribute string materialID;
    attribute enum unitOfMeasure {piece, box,
        carton, lb, oz, gallon, litre};
    attribute float standardCost;
    relationship set⟨Product⟩ used_in inverse Product::uses;
    relationship set⟨Supply⟩ listed_in inverse Supply::lists;
};

class Supply {
(   extent supplies)
    attribute float unitPrice;
    relationship RawMaterial lists inverse
        RawMaterial::listed_in;
    relationship Vendor provided_by inverse
        Vendor::provides;
};

class Vendor {
(   extent vendors)
    attribute string vendorName;
    attribute Address vendorAddress;
    relationship set⟨Supply⟩ provides inverse
        Supply::provided_by;
};
```

```
class Employee {
(   extent employees
    key employeeID)
    attribute string employeeID;
    attribute string employeeName;
    attribute Address employeeAddress;
    relationship set⟨WorkCenter⟩ works_in inverse
        WorkCenter::employs;
    relationship set⟨skill⟩ has inverse Skill::possessed_by;
    relationship Employee supervised_by inverse
        Employee::supervises;
    relationship set⟨Employee⟩ supervises inverse
        Employee::supervised_by;
    boolean checkSkills(string product);
};

class Skill {
(   extent skills);
    attribute string skillName;
    relationship set⟨Employee⟩ possessed_by inverse
        Employee::has;
};
```

Figure 15-6
(*continued*)

CREATING OBJECT INSTANCES

When a new instance of a class is created, a unique object identifier is assigned. You may specify an object identifier with one or more unique tag names. For example, we can create a new course object called MBA 669 as follows:

MBA669 **course** ( );

This creates a new instance of Course. The object tag name, MBA699, can be used to reference this object. We have not specified the attribute values for this object at this point. Suppose you want to create a new student object and initialize some of its attributes.

Cheryl **student** (**name:** "Cheryl Davis", **dateOfBirth:** 4/5/77);

This creates a new student object with a tag name of Cheryl and initializes the values of two attributes. You can also specify the values for the attributes within a structure as in the following example:

Jack **student** (
    name: "Jack Warner", dateOfBirth 2/12/74,
    address: {street_address "310 College Rd", city "Dayton", state "Ohio", zip 45468},
    phone: {area_code 937, personal_number 228–2252});

For a multivalued attribute, you can specify a set of values. For example, you can specify the skills for an employee called Dan Bellon as follows:

Dan **employee** (**emp_id:** 3678, **name:** "Dan Bellon",
    skills: {"Database design", "OO Modeling" });

Establishing links between objects for a given relationship is also easy. Suppose you want to store the fact that Cheryl took three courses in fall 1999. You can write:

Cheryl **student** (**takes:** {OOAD99F, Telecom99F, Java99F });

where OOAD99F, Telecom99F, and Java99F are tag names for three course offering objects. This definition creates three links for the "takes" relationship, from the object tagged Cheryl to each of the course offering objects.

Consider another example. To assign Dan to the TQM project, we write:

assignment (**start_date:** 2/15/2001, **allocated_to:** Dan, for TQM);

Notice that we have not specified a tag name for the assignment object. Such objects will be identified by the system-generated object identifiers. The assignment object has a link to an employee object (Dan) and another link to a project object (TQM).

When an object is created it is assigned a lifetime, either transient or persistent. A transient object exists only while some program or session is in operation. A persistent object exists until it is explicitly deleted. Database objects are almost always persistent.

OBJECT QUERY LANGUAGE

We will now describe the Object Query Language (OQL), which is similar to SQL-92 and has been set forth as an ODMG standard for querying OODBs. OQL allows you a lot of flexibility in formulating queries. You can write a simple query such as

Jack.dateOfBirth

which returns Jack's birth date, a literal value, or

Jack.address

which returns a structure with values for street address, city, state, and zip. If instead we want to simply find in which city Jack resides, we can write

Jack.address.city

Like SQL, OQL uses a select-from-where structure to write more complex queries. Consider, for example, the ODL schema for the university database given in Figure 15-2. We will see how to formulate OQL queries for this database. Because of the strong similarities between SQL and OQL, the explanations in the following sections are quite brief. For further explanations, you may want to review Chapters 7 and 8 on SQL and Chapter 14 on object modeling. The more interested reader is referred to the chapter on OQL in Cattell et al. (2000).

Basic Retrieval Command

Suppose we want to find the title and credit hours for MBA 664. Parallel to SQL, those attributes are specified in the select clause, and the *extent* of the class that has those attributes is specified in the from clause. In the where clause, we specify the condition that has to be satisfied. In the query shown below, we have specified the extent courses of the Course class and bound the extent to a variable called c in the from clause. We have specified the attributes crse_title and credit_hrs for the extent (i.e., set of all Course instances in the database) in the select clause, and stated the condition c.crse_code = "MBA 664" in the where clause.

```
select c.crse_title, c.credit_hrs
from courses c
where c.crse_code = "MBA 664"
```

Because we are dealing with only one extent, we could have left out the variable c without any loss in clarity. However, as with SQL, if you are dealing with multiple classes that have common attributes, you must bind the extents to variables so that the system can unambiguously identify the classes for the selected attributes. The result of this query is a bag with two attributes.

Including Operations in Select Clause

We can invoke operations in an OQL query similar to the way we specify attributes. For example, to find the age of John Marsh, a student, we invoke the "age" operation in the select clause.

```
select s.age
from students s
where s.name = "John Marsh"
```

The query returns an integer value, assuming that there is only one student with that name. In addition to literal values, a query can also return objects with identity. For example, the query

```
select s
from students s
where s.gpa >= 3.0
```

returns a collection (bag) of student objects for which the gpa is greater than or equal to 3.0. Notice that we have used the gpa operation in the where clause.

If we want to formulate the same query, but only for those students who do not reside in Dayton, we can use the *not* operator as in SQL:

```
select s
from students s
where s.gpa >= 3.0
and not (s.address.city = "Dayton")
```

Instead of using "not," we could have specified the new condition as follows:

```
s.address.city ! = "Dayton"
```

where ! is the inequality operator.

Now suppose that we want to find the ages of all students whose gpa is less than 3.0. This query is:

```
select s.age
from students s
where s.gpa < 3.0
```

Finding Distinct Values

The preceding query will return a collection of integers. It is possible that there is more than one student with the same age. If you want to eliminate duplicates, you can reformulate the query using the distinct keyword as shown below:

```
select distinct s.age
from students s
where s.gpa < 3.0
```

Querying Multiple Classes

In an OQL query, you can join classes in the where clause as in SQL. This is necessary when the relationship which is the basis for the join has not been defined in the object data model. When the relationship has been defined, then you can traverse the paths for the relationships defined in the schema. The following query finds the course codes of all courses that were offered in fall 2001.

```
select distinct y.crse_code
from courseofferings x,
        x.belongs_to y
where x.term = "Fall 2001"
```

We have used *distinct* in the select clause because a course may have had multiple offerings in the given term. In the *from* clause, we have specified a path from a CourseOffering object to a Course object using the "belongs_to" relationship between them. The variable "y" gets bound to the Course object where the path represented by x.belongs_to terminates.

Suppose that we want to find the number of students enrolled in section 1 of the MBA 664 course. The enrollment operation is available in CourseOffering, but the course code is available in Course. The query given below traverses from CourseOffering to Course using the belongs_to relationship. The variable "y" represents the destination object for the x.belongs_to path.

```
select x.enrollment
from courseofferings x,
        x.belongs_to y
where y.crse_code = "MBA 664"
and x.section = 1
```

The following query traverses two paths, one using the "takes" relationship and the other using the "belongs_to" relationship, to find the codes and titles of all courses taken by Mary Jones.

```
select c.crse_code, c.crse_title
from students s
        s.takes x,
        x.belongs_to c
where s.name = "Mary Jones"
```

We can also select a structure consisting of multiple components. For example, the following query returns a structure with age and gpa as its attributes.

```
select distinct struct(name: s.name, gpa: s.gpa)
from students s
where s.name = "Mary Jones"
```

Writing Subqueries

You can use a select statement within a select statement. To select course codes, course titles, and course offerings for which the enrollment is less than 20, you can write the following OQL command (see Figure 15-2 for the design of the database):

```
select distinct struct (code: c.crse_code, title: c_crse_title,
        (select x
        from c.offers x
        where x.enrollment < 20 ))
        from courses c
```

Recall that enrollment is an operation of a CourseOffering object and Course has a 1:M relationship offers with CourseOffering. This query returns a collection of distinct structures, each of which contains string values for course code and course title, and an object identifier for a CourseOffering object that has enrollment below 20.

You can also use a select statement within the from clause. In the example below, we have written a query that retrieves the names, addresses, and gpa's for those students over 30 with gpa more than or equal to 3.0.

```
select x.name, x.address, x.gpa
from (select s from students s where s.gpa >= 3.0) as x
where x.age > 30
```

Here *x* is the alias for the extent created by the select statement within the from clause.

Calculating Summary Values

OQL supports all the aggregate operators that SQL does: count, sum, avg, max, and min. For example, we can find the number of students in the university by using the count operator as follows:

```
count(students)
```

We could have also written this query as

```
select count (*)
from students s
```

Let us now consider the schema for the employee-project database that we saw earlier. Suppose we want to find the average salary of female employees in the company. We use the avg function to do that in the following query:

```
select avg_salary_female: avg (e.salary)
from employees e
where e.gender = female
```

To find the maximum salary paid to an employee, we use the max function:

```
max (select salary from employees)
```

To find the total of all employee salaries, we use the sum function:

```
sum (select salary from employees)
```

Calculating Group Summary Values

As in SQL, you can partition a query response into different groups. In the following query, we have used the group command to form two groups based on gender: male and female. The query calculates the minimum salary for each of the two groups.

```
select min (e.salary)
from employees e
group by e.gender
```

If we want to group the projects based on their priority levels, we can write the following query:

```
select *
from projects p
group by    low:       priority = low,
            medium:    priority = medium,
            high:      priority = high
```

This query returns three groups of project objects, labeled by the priority of the group: low, medium, and high.

Qualifying Groups As with SQL, we can use the *having* command to impose a condition or filter on each group as a whole. For example, in the following query, we filter only those groups for which a total of more than 50 hours have been logged in.

```
select *
from projects p
group by       low:         priority = low,
               medium:      priority = medium,
               high:        priority = high
having sum(select x.hours from p.has x) > 50
```

Using a Set in a Query

Sometimes you will have to find whether an element belongs to some set. To do that, you should use the *in* keyword. Suppose we want to find the IDs and names of those employees who are skilled in database design or object-oriented modeling. Note that skills is a multivalued attribute, implying that it stores a set of values. In the where clause, we have used "in" to check if database design or object-oriented modeling is one of the elements in an employee's skill set.

```
select emp_id, name
from employees
where "Database Design" in skills
or "OO Modeling" in skills
```

Similarly, we can find those employees who have worked in a project whose ID is TQM9.

```
select e.emp_id, e.name
from employees e,
     e.works_on a,
     a.for p
where "TQM9" in p.proj_id
```

To find those projects that do not require C ++ programming skills, we can write:

```
select *
from projects p
where not ("C ++ Programming" in p.skills_required)
```

Finally, you can use the existential quantifier *exists* and the universal quantifier *for all*. The following query finds those employees who have been assigned to at least one project.

```
select e.emp_id, e.name
from employees e
where exists e in (select x from assignments y
                   y.allocated_to x)
```

The select statement inside the where clause returns a set of employee objects (i.e., their identifiers) allocated to all the assignments. The exists quantifier then checks if an employee object bound in the from clause is in that set. If so, that employee's ID and name are included in the response, otherwise not.

If we want to find the employees who have worked only on projects starting since the beginning of 2001, we can use the *for all* quantifier as follows:

```
select e.emp_id, e.name
from employees e,
     e.works_on a
where for all a: a.start_date > = 1/1/2001
```

In the from clause, the query finds a set of assignment objects that an employee object is linked to through the "works_on" relationship. In the where clause, it applies the condition (start_date > = 1/1/2001) to all the objects in the set using the for all quantifier. Only if the condition is satisfied by all those objects are the employee's ID and name included in the query response.

Summary of OQL

We have illustrated in this section only a subset of the capabilities of OQL. See Cattell et al. (2000) and Chaudhri and Zicari (2001) for more standard OQL features and how OQL is implemented in various ODBMSs.

CURRENT ODBMS PRODUCTS AND THEIR APPLICATIONS

With the growing need in organizations to store and manipulate complex data (e.g., image, audio, and video) and relationships, in applications ranging from computer-aided design and manufacturing (CAD/CAM) to geographic information systems to multimedia, ODBMS products are gaining popularity. But more than anything else, industry analysts believe that Internet and Web-based applications are responsible for the sudden renewed interest in ODBMSs (King, 1997; Watterson, 1998). ODBMSs are certainly not overtaking RDBMSs, but they are viable products for selected appplications.

ODBMSs allow organizations to store diverse components (objects) associated with their Websites (Watterson, 1998). The proliferation of complex data types on the Web and the need to store, index, search, and manipulate such data have provided ODBMS technology an edge over other database technologies. To counter this emerging technology, major relational database vendors such as Oracle, Informix, IBM, and Sybase have come up with universal databases, also known as object-relational DBMSs (ORDBMSs), as a possible alternative. An ORDBMS is a hybrid relational DBMS that somehow incorporates complex data as objects (King, 1997; also see Appendix D). However, these systems raise concerns relating to performance and scalability. Moreover, the fundamental mismatch between relational and object technology may induce many firms to adopt the pure ODBMS option.

The types of applications for which ODBMSs are particularly useful include bill-of-materials data (see Figure 14-16), telecommunications data supporting navigational access, healthcare, engineering design, finance and trading, multimedia, and geographic information systems. Several commercial ODBMS products are currently available. Examples include ObjectStore (the current market leader), Versant, Gem-Stone, Objectivity, and Jasmine (see Table 15-1).

Watterson (1998) and Barry & Associates (www.odbmsfacts.com/faq.htm) provide several examples of real-world applications of ODBMSs. Lucent Technologies' Customer Support Division used GemStone to share information globally on customers' switches. Motorola used Objectivity to store complex celestial information for one of its satellite networks. Groupe Paradis, a retirement-plan management company in France, uses O_2 to access over 100 gigabytes of data spread across several databases. And companies like GTE, Southwest Airlines, and Time-Warner have used ObjectStore to develop dynamic Web applications that require integrating pieces of information from various sources on the fly. The Chicago Stock Exchange uses Versant ODBMS for its Internet-based trading system.

Industry experts predict that ODBMSs represent the most promising of the emerging database systems. While for traditional business applications, relational

Table 15-1 ODBMS Products

Company	Product	Web Site
Computer Associates	Jasmine	http://www.cai.com/products/jasmine.htm
Franz	AllegroSCL	http://www.franz.com
Gemstone Systems	GemStone	http://www.gemstone.com
neoLogic	neoAccess	http://neologic.com
Object Design	ObjectStore	http://www.odi.com
Objectivity	Objectivity/DB	http://www.objectivity.com
POET Software	POET Object Server	http://www.poet.com
Versant	Versant ODBMS	http://www.versant.com

Other Links Related to ODBMS Products

Barry & Associates	http://www.odbmsfacts.com
Doug Barry's *The Object Database Handbook*	http://wiley.com
Object database newsgroup	news://comp.databases.object
Rick Cattell's *The Object Database Standard ODMG 3.0*	http://www.mkp.com
Object Database Management Group	http://www.odmg.org
Chaudhri and and Zicari's *Succeeding with Object Databases*	http://www.wiley.com/compbooks/chaudhri

DBMSs are expected to maintain their hold on the market, the data for many applications, such as the ones described above, cannot be easily flattened to two-dimensional database tables. Also, accessing the data from various tables requires you to perform joins, which could become very costly.

Summary

In this chapter, you learned how to implement an object-oriented database system using the object definition language. We introduced you to the syntax and semantics of ODL. You learned how to transform a conceptual schema, represented in the form of a UML class diagram, to a logical schema, defined using ODL constructs. You further learned how to populate an OODB by creating new instances and specifying attribute values for those instances. We also introduced you to OQL, a language designed for querying OODBs. Using OQL, we showed you how to write various types of OODB queries.

The chapter also discussed the types of applications for which ODBMSs are well suited. It briefly described some of the applications for which current ODBMSs have been used.

While Chapter 14 provided you with the conceptual underpinnings of OODB design, this chapter provides you with the knowledge required to actually implement an object-oriented database system using an ODMG-compliant ODBMS.

CHAPTER REVIEW

Key Terms

Array
Atomic literal
Bag

Collection literal
Dictionary
Extent

List
Set
Structured literal

Review Questions

1. Define each of the following terms:
   a. object class
   b. relationship
   c. extent
   d. atomic literal
   e. structured literal

2. Contrast the following terms:
   a. list; bag; dictionary
   b. set; array
   c. collection literal; structured literal

3. Explain the concept of an object identifier. How is an object identifier different from a primary key in a relational system?

4. What is the purpose of the *struct* keyword in ODL?

5. What is the purpose of the *enum* keyword in ODL?

6. Explain the meaning of the term *relationship set* for many of the relationships in Figure 15-2.

7. Explain the hazards of representing a relationship in ODL by implying that an attribute's value is an object identifier rather by using the relationship clause.

8. Explain the meaning of the *extends* keyword in ODL.

9. Explain the parallels and differences between SQL and OQL.

Problems and Exercises

1. Develop an ODL schema for the following problem situation. A student, whose attributes include studentName, Address, phone, and age, may engage in multiple campus-based activities. The university keeps track of the number of years a given student has participated in a specific activity and, at the end of each academic year, mails an activity report to the student showing his participation in various activities.

2. Develop an ODL schema for a real estate firm that lists property for sale. The following describes this organization:
   • The firm has a number of sales offices in several states; location is an attribute of sales office.
   • Each sales office is assigned one or more employees. Attributes of employee include employeeID and employeeName. An employee must be assigned to only one sales office.
   • For each sales office, there is always one employee assigned to manage that office. An employee may manage only the sales office to which she is assigned.
   • The firm lists property for sale. Attributes of property include propertyName and location.
   • Each unit of property must be listed with one (and only one) of the sales offices. A sales office may have any number of properties listed, or may have no properties listed.
   • Each unit of property has one or more owners. Attributes of owner are ownerName and address. An owner may own one or more units of property. For each property that an owner owns, an attribute called percentOwned indicates what percentage of the property is owned by the owner.

3. Develop an ODL schema for some organization that you are familiar with—Boy Scouts/Girl Scouts, sports team, etc. Include at least four association relationships.

4. Develop an ODL schema for the following situation (state any assumptions you believe you have to make in order to develop the schema): Stillwater Antiques buys and sells one-of-a-kind antiques of all kinds (for example, furniture, jewelry, china, and clothing). Each item is uniquely identified by an item number and is also characterized by a description, asking price, condition, and open-ended comments. Stillwater works with many different individuals, called clients, who sell items to and buy items from the store. Some clients only sell items to Stillwater, some only buy items, and some others both sell and buy. A client is identified by a client number, and is also described by a client name and client address. When Stillwater sells an item in stock to a client, the owners want to record the commission paid, the actual selling price, sales tax (tax of zero indicates a tax exempt sale), and date sold. When Stillwater buys an item from a client, the owners want to record the purchase cost, date purchased, and condition at time of purchase.

Problems and Exercises 5–14 all pertain to the ODL schema in Figure 15-2. Write OQL queries for these exercises.

5. Find the names and phone numbers of all those students who took only one course in fall 2001.

6. Find the code and title of all courses that were offered in both the winter 2001 and fall 2001 terms.

7. Find the total enrollment for all sections of the MBA 664 course being offered in winter 2002.

8. Find the prerequisite courses (code and title) for the MIS 385 course.

9. Find all those students who reside in Cincinnati and who took the MBA 665 course in fall 2001.

10. Find the total credit hours for all prerequisite courses for the MIS 465 course.

11. Find the average age and gpa of students, grouped by the city they live in.

12. Find the courses (code and title) taken by Sean Chen in winter 2002.

13. Find the names and phone numbers of all students who are taking sections 1 and 2 of the MBA 665 course in winter 2002.

14. Find the minimum enrollment among all the sections of each 3 credit-hour course being offered in the winter 2002

term. The response should by grouped by course and the group label should be crse_code.

Field Exercises

1. Interview a database administrator in a company with which you are familiar. Ask this person to explain the potential benefits of an ODBMS for that organization. Are they planning to use an ODBMS? Why or why not?

2. Visit the World Wide Website for this textbook. From that site, visit several sites for vendors of ODBMSs. Prepare a

summary of one of the products you find. How does its DDL compare to the ODL in this chapter? How does its query language compare to the OQL explained in this chapter? What claims does the vendor make about the relative advantages of their product versus other ODBMS or relational products?

References

Bertino, E., and L. Martino. 1993. *Object-Oriented Database Systems: Concepts and Architectures.* Wokingham, England: Addison-Wesley.

Cattell, R. G. G., et al. (Eds.) 2000. *The Object Database Standard: ODMG 3.0.* San Francisco: Morgan Kaufmann.

Chaudhri, A. B., and R. Zicari. 2001. *Succeeding with Object Databases.* New York: Wiley.

King, N. H. 1997. "Object DBMSs: Now or Never." *DBMS* (July): 42–99.

Watterson, K. 1998. "When It Comes to Choosing a Database, the Object Is Value." *Datamation* (December/January): 100–107.

 Web Resources

See Table 15-1.

MOUNTAIN VIEW COMMUNITY HOSPITAL

Project Case

Review the project description found in the Project Case in Chapter 14. Refer to this description and your answer to Project Exercises for that case in responding to the following exercises.

PROJECT EXERCISES

1. Develop an ODL schema for your answer to Project Exercise 1 from Chapter 14.
2. Write three questions that would be typical of applications using this schema and develop OQL commands for each of these queries.

Appendix A

E-R Modeling Tools and Notation

Chapter 3 presents a notation for representing data models that is extended in Chapter 4 and followed throughout this textbook. Depending on the software tool available for depicting a data model, your ability to replicate this notation will vary. Just as business rules and policies are not universal, neither are the symbols and notation used in the various data modeling tools. Each uses different graphical constructs and methodologies that may or may not be able to convey the meaning of a particular business rule.

This appendix is intended to help you compare the book's notation with your modeling tool's notation. Four commonly used tools are covered: Visible Analyst 7.4, Platinum's ERwin 3.5.2, Microsoft's Access 2000, and Oracle Designer 6.0. Table A-1a and Table A-1b chart the notation used in each tool for entities, relationships, attributes, rules, constraints, and so forth. In addition, a screen capture for each tool is included in Figures A-3 through A-6, depicting each tool's interface.

Figure 3-22, an E-R diagram for Pine Valley Furniture Company (PVFC), is the basis for the examples pictured in this appendix. That figure shows the data model drawn from the narrative of PVFC business rules included in Chapter 3, using the text's notation system. Table A-1 allows a comparison of this notation with that available in the four software tools.

COMPARING E-R MODELING CONVENTIONS

As can be seen from Table A-1, modeling tools differ significantly in the notation available to create an entity-relationship diagram (ERD) that represents the logical data model. While not intended as an in-depth comparison of the various tools, the following explanation provides a means to analyze the tools' differences using the PVFC ERD depicted in Figure 3-22. Pay particular attention to differences in depicting many-to-many relationships, cardinalities and/or optionalities, foreign keys, and supertype/subtype relationships.

Visible Analyst Notation

This flexible tool provides the user with several choices for graphical depictions of data models. It has five notation possibilities from which to choose, including IDEF1X, Bachman, Crow's Foot, Arrow, and UML. Crow's Foot has been used in Table A-1 along with Gane & Sarson conventions, and in describing the tool. Choosing any other option gives different representation capabilities.

Entities Three entity symbols are available: fundamental, associative, or attributive. Detail level on the diagram is also flexible; for example, display only entity

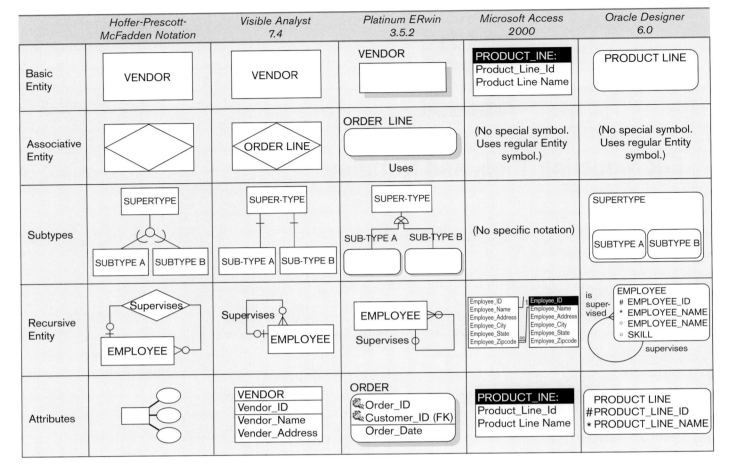

Table A-1
A Comparison of Hoffer, Prescott, and McFadden modeling notation with four software tools
(a) Common modeling tools notations

name, or entity name and primary key, or include all attributes, too. The symbol for an associative entity, for example, Order_Line, as shown in Table A-1a, automatically changes to a different symbol, with an [AS] indicator next to the entity name, when an attribute is placed on it, for example, Ordered_Quantity. Figure A-3 shows this.

Relationships Lines can be labeled in one or both directions and can have multiple segments, among several other options, allowing start and end points that are distant from each other. Depending on the notation chosen, relationship lines can display cardinality and can store the specific quantity of instances that one entity relates to another. Relationship lines can show 0:1, 1:1, 0:many, 1:many, or many:many. A dialog box allows cardinality to be changed for an existing relationship. A recursive relationship displays a parent and child as the same entity. The example in Table A-1a shows that an Employee may supervise many employees, but not all employees are supervisors; the notation indicates that nulls are allowed. The parent entity may have any number of children, but a child may have only one parent. The rule that an employee has exactly one supervisor cannot be shown—the optionality notation indicates that the employee *may* have no supervisor.

Platinum ERwin (CASE Tool) Notation

Here, one has the choice among IDEF1X, IE (Information Engineering), or DM (Dimensional Modeling) notations. The examples here demonstrate IE.

	Hoffer-Prescott-McFadden Notation	Visible Analyst 7.4	Platinum ERwin 3.5.2	Microsoft Access 2000	Oracle Designer 6.0
1:1	*(symbol)*	(Not available without cardinality)	(Not available without cardinality)	*(symbol)*	*(symbol)*
1:M	*(symbol)*	(Not available without cardinality)	(Not available without cardinality)	1 ∞ *(symbol)*	*(symbol)*
M:N	*(symbol)*	(Not available without cardinality)	*(symbol)*	(Not allowed)	*(symbol)*
Mandatory 1:1	*(symbol)*	*(symbol)*	*(symbol)* 1	(No optionality symbols)	*(symbol)*
Mandatory 1:M	*(symbol)*	*(symbol)*	*(symbol)* P	(No optionality symbols)	*(symbol)*
Optional 1:M	*(symbol)*	*(symbol)*	*(symbol)*	(No optionality symbols)	*(symbol)*

Table A-1
(*continued*)
(b) Common modeling tools cardinality/optionality notations

Entities If an entity is a child (weak) entity in an identifying relationship, it appears as a dependent entity, a box with rounded corners. Associative entity symbols are also represented this way. The user chooses to have keys migrate either to the primary or to the nonkey area of an entity box.

Relationships Cardinality options are flexible and may be specified unambiguously. A parent may be connected to "Zero, One, or More," signified by a blank space; "One or More," signified by a P; "Zero or One," signified by a Z; or "Exactly," some number of instances, which will appear on the ERD. Many-to-many relationships are automatically resolved—an associative entity is displayed in the logical model and the many-to-many relationship is eliminated. The recursive nonidentifying relationship, where parent and child are shown as the same entity, shows that an Employee (a Supervisor) may supervise many employees, but not all employees are supervisors. The notation indicates that nulls are allowed. The parent can have any number of children, but a child can only have one parent. Keys migrate automatically when the relationships are established, and foreign keys are notated "(FK)."

The chart captured from ERwin's on-line help and shown in Figure A-1 depicts the range of cardinality symbols that may be used from this product.

Microsoft Access 2000 Notation

Access cannot function as a diagramming tool used to build a logical model prior to the design of the database. Tables with attributes must have been defined in a database in order to depict them in a data model and to establish the relationships among entities. However, when the user is aware of this constraint, defining the table makes it available to be modeled on the relationships screen, and users of MS Access 2000 should be sure to take advantage of this capability to establish relationships.

Figure A-1
ERwin cardinality/optionality symbols

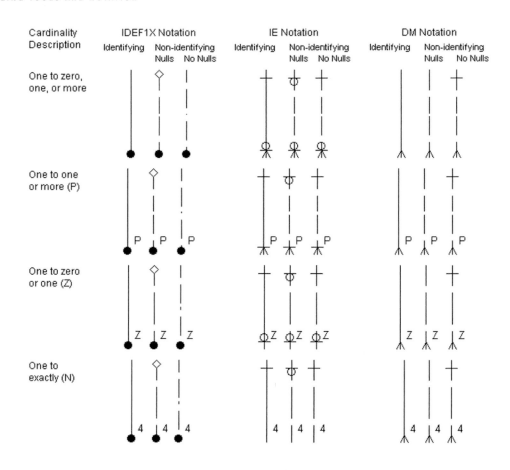

Entities Since Access's focus is on database design rather than database modeling, no specific symbols exist for the different entity types, including associative entities and supertypes or subtypes.

Relationships Depicted as lines, relationships are drawn by linking existing attributes between existing tables. Manipulation to arrange entities so that relationships can be shown clearly is limited. Relationship lines can be edited to change cardinality, but no distinction can be made to establish optionality. When relationships are established, there is no automatic migration of keys, as in ERwin, and the attributes must have been defined in order to be used as links. One-to-one or one-to-many recursive relationships are shown by placing two copies of a table on the workspace and establishing the link between the two copies of the table. In Table A-1a, two copies of EMPLOYEE, labeled automatically by Access as EMPLOYEE_t and EMPLOYEE_t_1, are shown. The recursive relationship is shown as a link between the two tables linking the primary key in the EMPLOYEE_t_1 table to the "Employee-supervisor" attribute in EMPLOYEE_t. The one-to-many nature of the recursive relationship is shown on the link between EMPLOYEE_t_1 and EMPLOYEE_t. Associative entities, such as Order_Line, are represented using the same notation as other entities. As in Figure 3-22, Order_Line is named in mixed case to distinguish it from other entities, which were named using capital letters. The many-to-many relationship between PRODUCT and ORDER is resolved by creating the associative entity Order_line that has a composite key, Order_ID and Product_ID.

Oracle Designer Notation

Diagrams drawn using the Entity Relationship Diagrammer tool can be set to show only the entity names, the entity names *and* the primary key, or the entity names and all of the attribute labels.

Entities No specific symbols exist for the different entity types, including associative entities and supertypes or subtypes. All entities are depicted as rounded rectangles, and attributes can be displayed within the box. Unique identifiers are preceded by a "#" sign and must be mandatory; mandatory attributes are tagged with "*" while optional attributes are tagged with "°."

Relationships Lines must be labeled in *both* directions, not just one direction, do not have multiple segments, and are challenging to manipulate and align. Relationship lines depict both cardinality and optionality and are drawn by first selecting the desired cardinality and optionality. These can be changed in a dialog box. Optionality is depicted using a solid line for mandatory relationships and a dotted line for optional relationships. In a binary relationship where optionality differs depending on the direction of the relationship, the line between the two entities will be bisected into a solid line and a dotted line. Read the relationship by starting at one entity and the line that is attached to that entity. Thus, in Figure A-6 a product must be made in a Work Center, but a Work Center is not required to manufacture a product in order to exist. Cardinality is read by picking up the cardinality sign attached to the other entity. Thus, a Customer *may* place an order or not, but when an order is placed, it must be related to a particular customer. Looking at the EMPLOYEE entity, the recursive supervisory relationship is depicted by the "pig's ear" attached to the entity. It shows that an Employee may supervise one or more employees and that an employee *must* be supervised by one employee, or supervisor. It is ambiguous as to whether the multiple cardinality is zero, one, or many. Figure A-2 shows the toolbar buttons available in Designer to establish a relationship—there is one button for each possible combination.

When working with Oracle Designer it is important to sketch out your data model carefully and completely before attempting to use the tool. Editing the model can be challenging and deleting an object from the diagram does not automatically delete it from the Repository.

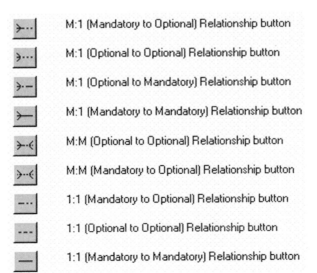

›–··	M:1 (Mandatory to Optional) Relationship button
›···	M:1 (Optional to Optional) Relationship button
›·–	M:1 (Optional to Mandatory) Relationship button
›	M:1 (Mandatory to Mandatory) Relationship button
›··‹	M:M (Optional to Optional) Relationship button
›··‹	M:M (Mandatory to Optional) Relationship button
–··	1:1 (Mandatory to Optional) Relationship button
···	1:1 (Optional to Optional) Relationship button
—	1:1 (Mandatory to Mandatory) Relationship button

Figure A-2
Oracle Designer 6.0 relationships toolbar

COMPARISON OF TOOL INTERFACES AND E-R DIAGRAMS

For each of the software modeling tools included in Table A-1, a screen capture of part of the entire data model for Figure 3-22 is included here. These figures should give you a better idea of what the symbol notation looks like in actual use. Figure A-3 was drawn using Visible Analyst 7.4, with the Crow's Foot and Gane & Sarson options selected. Figure A-4 was drawn using Platinum ERwin 3.5.2 and the Informa-

Figure A-3
Visible Analyst 7.4 interface

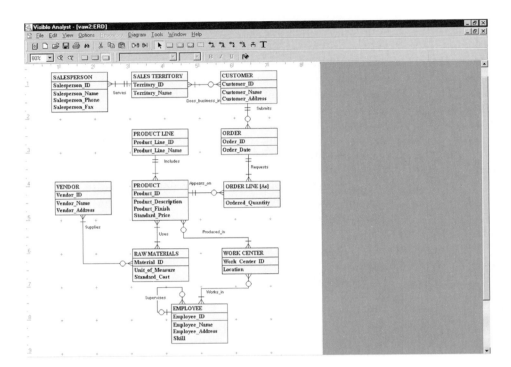

Figure A-4
Platinum ERwin 3.5.2 interface

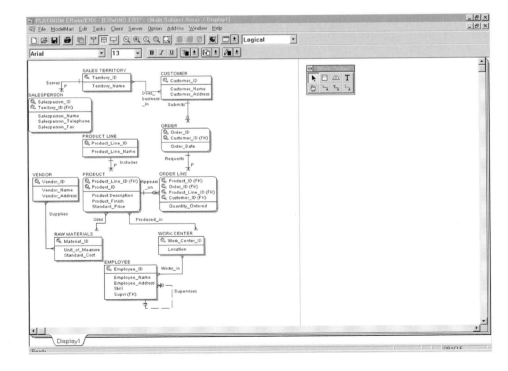

tion Engineering (IE) option. Referential integrity symbols may be optionally displayed, but were not included in this diagram. Figure A-5a is a screen capture of the relationships screen from MS ACCESS 2000, and Figure A-5b shows the printout that is generated from the screen using the "Print Relationships . . ." option under the File menu. Figure A-6 was drawn using Oracle Designer 6.0 with the Information Engineering (IE) option selected.

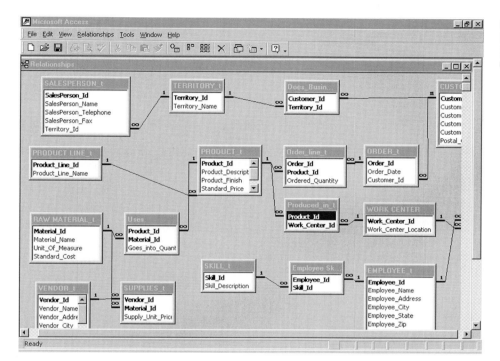

Figure A-5
Microsoft Access 2000
(a) Microsoft Access 2000 interface—
relationships screen

(b) MS Access 2000 interface—
relationships report

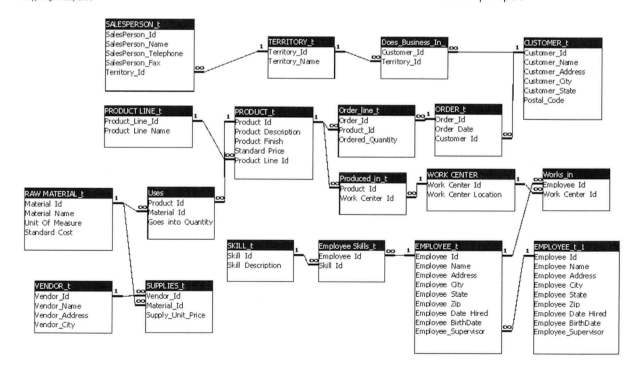

Figure A-6
Oracle Designer 6.0 interface

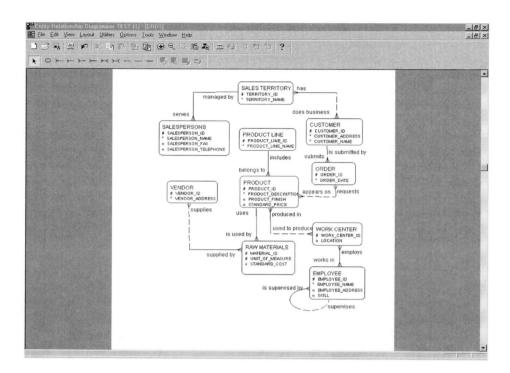

Appendix B

Advanced Normal Forms

In Chapter 5 we introduced the topic of normalization and described first through third normal forms in detail. Relations in third normal form (3NF) are sufficient for most practical database applications. However, 3NF does not guarantee that all anomalies have been removed. As indicated in Chapter 5, several additional normal forms are designed to remove these anomalies: Boyce-Codd normal form, fourth normal form, and fifth normal form (see Figure 5-22). We describe Boyce-Codd normal form and fourth normal form in this appendix.

BOYCE-CODD NORMAL FORM

When a relation has more than one candidate key, anomalies may result even though that relation is in 3NF. For example, consider the STUDENT_ADVISOR relation shown in Figure B-1. This relation has the following attributes: SID (student ID), Major, Advisor, and Maj_GPA. Sample data for this relation are shown in Figure B-1a, and the functional dependencies are shown in Figure B-1b.

Figure B-1
Relation in 3NF, but not BCNF
(a) Relation with sample data

STUDENT_ADVISOR

SID	Major	Advisor	Maj_GPA
123	Physics	Hawking	4.0
123	Music	Mahler	3.3
456	Literature	Michener	3.2
789	Music	Bach	3.7
678	Physics	Hawking	3.5

(b) Functional dependencies in STUDENT_ADVISOR

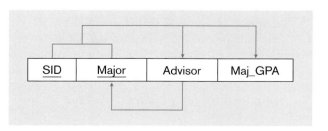

589

As shown in Figure B-1b, the primary key for this relation is the composite key consisting of SID and Major. Thus the two attributes Advisor and Maj_GPA are functionally dependent on this key. This reflects the constraint that although a given student may have more than one major, for each major a student has exactly one advisor and one GPA.

There is a second functional dependency in this relation: Major is functionally dependent on Advisor. That is, each advisor advises in exactly one major. Notice that this is *not* a transitive dependency. In Chapter 5 we defined a transitive dependency as a functional dependency between two nonkey attributes. In contrast, in this example a key attribute (Major) is functionally dependent on a nonkey attribute (Advisor).

Anomalies in STUDENT_ADVISOR

The STUDENT_ADVISOR relation is clearly in 3NF, since there are no partial functional dependencies and no transitive dependencies. Nevertheless, because of the functional dependency between Major and Advisor there are anomalies in this relation. Consider the following examples:

1. Suppose that in Physics the advisor Hawking is replaced by Einstein. This change must be made in two (or more) rows in the table (update anomaly).

2. Suppose we want to insert a row with the information that Babbage advises in Computer Science. This, of course, cannot be done until at least one student majoring in Computer Science is assigned Babbage as an advisor (insertion anomaly).

3. Finally, if student number 789 withdraws from school, we lose the information that Bach advises in Music (deletion anomaly).

Definition of Boyce-Codd Normal Form (BCNF)

Boyce-Codd normal form (BCNF): A relation in which every determinant is a candidate key.

The anomalies in STUDENT_ADVISOR result from the fact that there is a determinant (Advisor) that is not a candidate key in the relation. R. F. Boyce and E. F. Codd identified this deficiency and proposed a stronger definition of 3NF that remedies the problem. We say a relation is in **Boyce-Codd normal form (BCNF)** if and only if every determinant in the relation is a candidate key. STUDENT_ADVISOR is not in BCNF because although the attribute Advisor is a determinant, it is not a candidate key (only Major is functionally dependent on Advisor).

Converting a Relation to BCNF

A relation that is in 3NF (but not BCNF) can be converted to relations in BCNF using a simple two-step process. This process is shown in Figure B-2.

In this first step, the relation is modified so that the determinant in the relation that is not a candidate key becomes a component of the primary key of the revised relation. The attribute that is functionally dependent on that determinant becomes a nonkey attribute. This is a legitimate restructuring of the original relation because of the functional dependency.

The result of applying this rule to STUDENT_ADVISOR is shown in Figure B-2a. The determinant Advisor becomes part of the composite primary key. The attribute Major, which is functionally dependent on Advisor, becomes a nonkey attribute.

If you examine Figure B-2a, you will discover that the new relation has a partial functional dependency (Major is functionally dependent on Advisor, which is just one component of the primary key). Thus the new relation is in first (but not second) normal form.

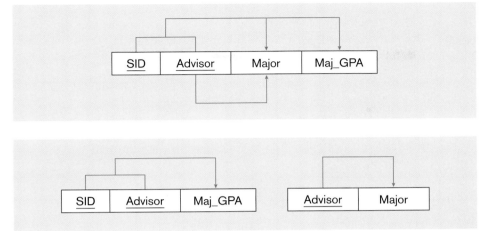

Figure B-2
Converting a relation to BCNF relations
(a) Revised STUDENT_ADVISOR relation (2NF)

(b) Two relations in BCNF

(c) Relations with sample data

STUDENT

SID	Advisor	Maj_GPA
123	Hawking	4.0
123	Mahler	3.3
456	Michener	3.2
789	Bach	3.7
678	Hawking	3.5

ADVISOR

Advisor	Major
Hawking	Physics
Mahler	Music
Michener	Literature
Bach	Music

The second step in the conversion process is to decompose the relation to eliminate the partial functional dependency, as we learned in Chapter 5. This results in two relations, as shown in Figure B-2b. These relations are in 3NF. In fact the relations are also in BCNF, since there is only one candidate key (the primary key) in each relation. Thus we see that if a relation has only one candidate key (which therefore becomes the primary key), then 3NF and BCNF are equivalent.

The two relations (now named STUDENT and ADVISOR) with sample data are shown in Figure B-2c. You should verify that these relations are free of the anomalies that were described for STUDENT_ADVISOR. You should also verify that you can re-create the STUDENT_ADVISOR relation by joining the two relations STUDENT and ADVISOR.

Another common situation in which BCNF is violated is when there are two (or more) overlapping candidate keys of the relation. Consider the relation in Figure B-3a. In this example, there are two candidate keys: (SID,COURSE_ID) and (SNAME,COURSE_ID), in which COURSE_ID appears in both candidate keys. The problem with this relationship is that we cannot record student data (SID and SNAME) unless the student has taken a course. Figure B-3b shows two possible solutions, each of which creates two relations that are in BCNF.

FOURTH NORMAL FORM

When a relation is in BCNF, there are no longer any anomalies that result from functional dependencies. However, there may still be anomalies that result from multivalued dependencies (defined below). For example, consider the table shown in

Figure B-3
Converting a relation with overlapping candidate keys to BCNF
(a) Relation with overlapping candidate keys

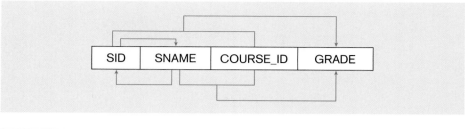

(b) Two alternative pairs of relations in BCNF

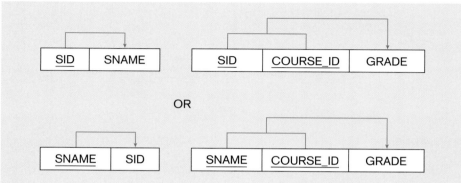

Figure B-4a. This user view shows for each course the instructors who teach that course, and the textbooks that are used (these appear as repeating groups in the table). In this table the following assumptions hold:

1. Each course has a well-defined set of instructors (for example, Management has three instructors).

2. Each course has a well-defined set of textbooks that are used (for example, Finance has two textbooks).

3. The textbooks that are used for a given course are independent of the instructor for that course. For example, the same two textbooks are used for Management regardless of which of the three instructors is teaching Management.

In Figure B-4b this table has been converted to a relation by filling in all of the empty cells. This relation (named OFFERING) is in first normal form. Thus, for each course, all possible combinations of instructor and text appear in OFFERING. Notice that the primary key of this relation consists of all three attributes (Course, Instructor, and Textbook). Since there are no determinants other than the primary key, the relation is actually in BCNF. Yet it does contain much redundant data that can easily lead to update anomalies. For example, suppose that we want to add a third textbook (author: Middleton) to the Management course. This change would require the addition of *three* new rows to the relation in Figure B-4b, one for each Instructor (otherwise that text would apply only to certain instructors).

Multivalued Dependencies

Multivalued dependency: The type of dependency that exists when there are at least three attributes (e.g., A, B, and C) in a relation, with a well-defined set of B and C values for each A value, but those B and C values are independent of each other.

The type of dependency shown in this example is called a **multivalued dependency**, which exists when there are at least three attributes (for example, A, B, and C) in a relation, and for each value of A there is a well-defined set of values of B and a well-defined set of values of C. However, the set of values of B is independent of set C, and vice versa.

OFFERING

Course	Instructor	Textbook
Management	White Green Black	Drucker Peters
Finance	Gray	Jones Chang

(a) Table of courses, instructors, and textbooks

OFFERING

Course	Instructor	Textbook
Management	White	Drucker
Management	White	Peters
Management	Green	Drucker
Management	Green	Peters
Management	Black	Drucker
Management	Black	Peters
Finance	Gray	Jones
Finance	Gray	Chang

(b) Relation in BCNF

Figure B-4
Data with multivalued dependencies

To remove the multivalued dependency from a relation, we divide the relation into two new relations. Each of these tables contains two attributes that have a multi-valued relationship in the original relation. Figure B-5 shows the result of this decomposition for the OFFERING relation of Figure B-4b. Notice that the relation called TEACHER contains the Course and Instructor attributes, since for each course there is a well-defined set of instructors. Also, for the same reason TEXT contains the attributes Course and Textbook. However, there is no relation containing the attributes Instructor and Course since these attributes are independent.

A relation is in **fourth normal form (4NF)** if it is in BCNF and contains no multi-valued dependencies. You can easily verify that the two relations in Figure B-5 are in 4NF and are free of the anomalies described earlier. Also, you can verify that you can reconstruct the original relation (OFFERING) by joining these two relations. In addition, notice that there are less data in Figure B-5 than in Figure B-4b. For simplicity, assume that Course, Instructor, and Textbook are all of equal length. Because there are 24 cells of data in Figure B-4b and 16 cells of data in Figure B-5, there is a space savings of 25 percent for the 4NF tables.

Fourth normal form: A relation in BCNF that contains no multivalued dependencies.

HIGHER NORMAL FORMS

At least two higher-level normal forms have been defined: fifth normal form (5NF) and domain-key normal form (DKNF). Fifth normal form deals with a property called "lossless joins." According to Elmasri and Navathe (2000), "these cases

Figure B-5
Relations in 4NF

TEACHER

Course	Instructor
Management	White
Management	Green
Management	Black
Finance	Gray

TEXT

Course	Textbook
Management	Drucker
Management	Peters
Finance	Jones
Finance	Chang

occur very rarely and are difficult to detect in practice." For this reason (and also because fifth normal form has a complex definition), we do not describe 5NF in this text.

Domain-key normal form (DKNF) is an attempt to define an "ultimate normal form" that takes into account all possible types of dependencies and constraints (Elmasri and Navathe, 2000). Although the definition of DKNF is quite simple, according to these authors "its practical utility is quite limited." For this reason we do not describe DKNF in this text.

For more information concerning these two higher normal forms see Elmasri and Navathe (2000) and Dutka and Hanson (1989).

References

Dutka, A., and H. Hanson. 1989. *Fundamentals of Data Normalization.* Reading, MA: Addison-Wesley.

Elmasri, R., and S. Navathe. 2000. *Fundamentals of Database Systems.* 3rd ed. Reading, MA: Addison-Wesley, pp. 440, 443.

Appendix C

Data Structures

Data structures are the basic building blocks of any physical database architecture. No matter what file organization or DBMS you use, data structures are used to connect related pieces of data. Although many modern DBMSs hide the underlying data structures, the tuning of a physical database requires understanding the choices a database designer can make about data structures. This appendix addresses the fundamental elements of all data structures and overviews some common schemes for storing and locating physical elements of data.

POINTERS

A pointer was introduced in Chapter 6. As described in that chapter, a pointer is used generically as any reference to the address of another piece of data. In fact, there are three types of pointers, as illustrated in Figure C-1:

1. *Physical address pointer* Contains the actual, fully resolved disk address (device, cylinder, track, and block number) of the referenced data. A physical pointer is the fastest way to locate another piece of data, but it is also the most restrictive: if the address of the referenced data changes, all pointers to it must also be changed. Physical pointers are commonly used in legacy database applications with network and hierarchical database architectures.

2. *Relative address pointer* Contains the relative position (or "offset") of the associated data from some base, or starting, point. The relative address could be a byte position, a record, or a row number. A relative pointer has the advantage that when the whole data structure changes location, all relative references to that structure are preserved. Relative pointers are used in a wide variety of DBMSs; a common use is in indexes in which index keys are matched with row identifiers (a type of relative pointer) for the record(s) with that key value.

3. *Logical key pointer* Contains meaningful data about the associated data element. A logical pointer must be transformed into a physical or relative pointer by some table lookup, index search, or mathematical calculation to actually locate the referenced data. Foreign keys in a relational database are often logical key pointers.

Table C-1 summarizes the salient features of each of these three types of pointers. A database designer may be able to choose which type of pointer to use in different situations in a database. For example, a foreign key in a relation can be imple-

Figure C-1
Types of pointers
(a) Physical address pointer

(b) Relative address pointer for *R*th record in file

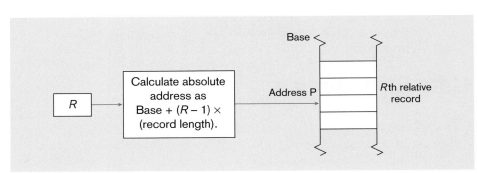

(c) Logical key pointer for record with key

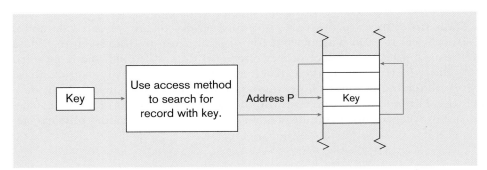

mented using any of these three types of pointers. In addition, when a database is damaged, a database administrator who understands what types of pointers are used may be able to rebuild broken links between database contents.

DATA STRUCTURE BUILDING BLOCKS

All data structures are built from several alternative basic building blocks for connecting and locating data. Connecting methods allow movement between related elements of data. Locating methods allow data within a structure to first be placed or stored and then found.

Table C-1 Comparison of Types of Pointers

Characteristic	Type of Pointer		
	Physical	**Relative**	**Logical**
Form	Actual secondary memory (disk) address	Offset from reference point (beginning of file)	Meaningful business data
Speed of access	Fastest	Medium	Slowest
Sensitivity to data movement	Most	Only sensitive to relative position changes	Least
Sensitivity to destruction	Very	Very	Often can be easily reconstructed
Space requirement	Fixed, usually short	Varies, usually shortest	Varies, usually longest

There are only two basic methods for *connecting* elements of data:

1. *Address sequential connection*   A successor (or related) element is placed and located in the physical memory space immediately following the current element (see Figures C-2a and c). Address sequential connections perform best for reading the entire set of data or reading the next record in the stored sequence. In contrast, address sequential structures are inefficient for retrieving arbitrary records and data update (add, delete, and change) operations. Update operations are also inefficient because the physical order must be constantly maintained, which usually requires immediate reorganization of the whole set of data.

2. *Pointer sequential connection*   A pointer (or pointers) is stored with one data element to identify the location of the successor (or related) data element (see Figures C-2b and d). Pointer sequential is more efficient for data update operations because data may be located anywhere as long as links between related data are maintained. Another major feature of pointer sequential schemes is the ability to maintain many different sequential linkages among the same set of data by using several pointers. We review various common forms of pointer sequential schemes (linear data structures) shortly.

Also, there are two basic methods for *placement* of data relative to the connection mechanism:

1. *Data direct placement*   The connection mechanism links an item of data directly with its successor (or related) item (see Figures C-2a and b). Direct placement has the advantage of immediately finding the data once a connection is traversed. The disadvantage is that the actual data are spread across large parts of disk storage because space for the actual data must be allocated among the connection elements.

2. *Data indirect placement*   The connection mechanism links pointers to the data, not the actual data (see Figures C-2c and d). The advantage of indirect placement is that scanning a data structure for data with specified characteristics is usually more efficient because the scanning can be done through compact entries of key characteristics and pointers to the associated data. Also, the connection and placement of data are decoupled, so the physical organization of the data records can follow the most desirable scheme (for example, physically sequential for a specified sorting order). The disadvantage is the extra access time required to retrieve both references to data and the data, and the extra space required for pointers.

Any data structure, file organization, or database architecture uses a combination of these four basic methods.

LINEAR DATA STRUCTURES

Pointer sequential data structures have been popular for storing highly volatile data, typical of what is found in operational databases. Transactional data (such as customer orders or personnel change requests) and historical data (such as product price quotes and student class registrations) make up a large portion of operational databases. Also, because users of operational databases want to view data in many different sequences (for example, customer orders in sequence by order date, product numbers, or customer numbers), the ability to maintain several chains of pointers running through the same data can support a range of user needs with one set of data.

The ability of a linear data structure to handle data updates is illustrated in Figure C-3. Figure C-3a shows how easy it is to insert a new record into a linear (or

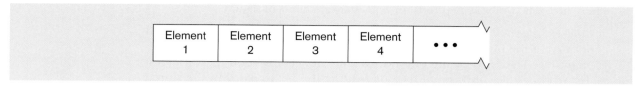

(a) Address sequential connection (sequential)

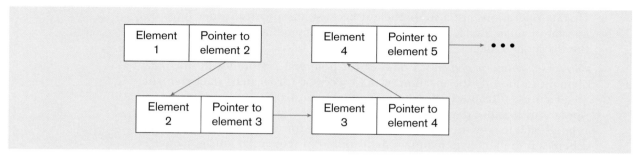

(b) Pointer sequential connection (simple chain or list)

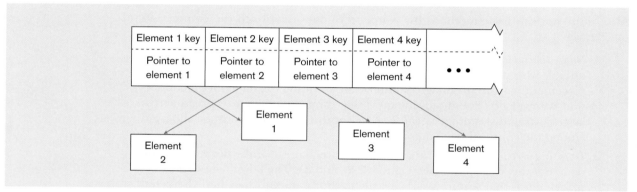

(c) Address sequential, data indirect connection (key index)

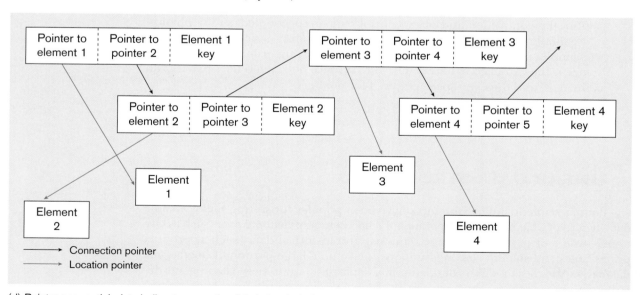

(d) Pointer sequential, data indirect connection (chain key index)

Figure C-2
Basic location methods

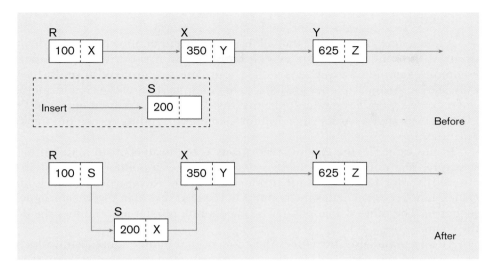

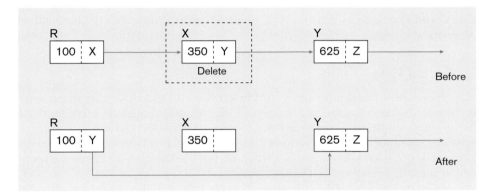

Figure C-3
Maintaining a pointer sequential data structure
(a) Insertion

(b) Deletion

chain) structure. This figure illustrates a file of product records. For simplicity, we represent each product record by only the product number and a pointer to the next product record in sequence by product number. A new record is stored in an available location (S) and patched into the chain by changing pointers associated with the records in locations R and S. In Figure C-3b the act of deleting a record is equally easy, as only the pointer for the record in location R is changed. Although there is extra space to store the pointers, this space is minimal compared to what may be hundreds of bytes needed to store all the product data (product number, description, quantity on hand, standard price, and so forth). It is easy to find records in product number order given this structure, but the actual time to retrieve records in sequence can be extensive if logically sequential records are stored far apart on disk.

With this simple introduction to linear data structures, we now consider four specific versions of such structures: stacks, queues, sorted lists, and multilists. We conclude this section with some cautions about linear, chain data structures.

Stacks

A stack has the property that all record insertions and deletions are made at the same end of the data structure. Stacks exhibit a last-in-first-out (LIFO) property. A common example of a stack is a vertical column of plates in a cafeteria. In business information systems, stacks are used to maintain unprioritized or unsorted records (for example, the line items associated with the same customer order).

Queues

A queue has the property that all insertions occur at one end and all deletions occur at the other end. A queue exhibits a first-in-first-out (FIFO) property. A common example of a queue is a check-out lane at a grocery store. In business information systems, queues are used to maintain lists of records in chronological order of insertion. For example, Figure C-4 illustrates a chained queue of Order Line records kept in order of arrival for a common Product record in Pine Valley Furniture.

In this example, the Product record acts as the head-of-chain node in the data structure. The value of the Oldest_order_line field is a pointer to the oldest (first entered) Order Line record for product 0100. The Next_order_line field in the Order_Line record contains the pointers to the next record in reverse chronological sequence. The value ∅ in a pointer is called a null pointer and signifies the end of the chain.

This example also introduces the concept of a bidirectional chain, which has both forward and backward pointers. The benefit of next and prior pointers is that data in the records can be retrieved and presented in either forward or backward order, and the code to maintain the chain is easier to implement than with single-directional chains.

Sorted Lists

A sorted list has the property that insertions and deletions may occur anywhere within the list; records are maintained in logical order based on a key field value. A common example of a sorted list is a telephone directory. In business information systems, sorted lists occur frequently. Figure C-5a illustrates a single-directional, pointer sequential sorted list of Order records related to a Customer record, in which records are sorted by Delivery_date.

Maintaining a sorted list is more complex than maintaining a stack or queue because insertion or deletion can occur anywhere in a chain which may have zero or many existing records. To guarantee that insertions and deletions always occur in the interior of the chain, "dummy" first and last records are often included (see

Figure C-4

Example of a queue with bidirectional pointers

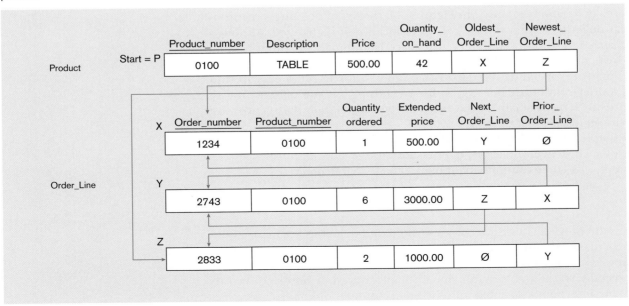

Figure C-5b). Figure C-5c shows the result of inserting a new Order into the sorted list of Figure C-5b. To perform the insertion, the list is scanned starting from the address in the pointer First_order. Once the proper position in the chain is found, there must be a rule for deciding where to store a record with a duplicate key value, if duplicates are allowed, as in this example. Usually this location for a duplicate record will be first among the duplicates because this requires the least scanning.

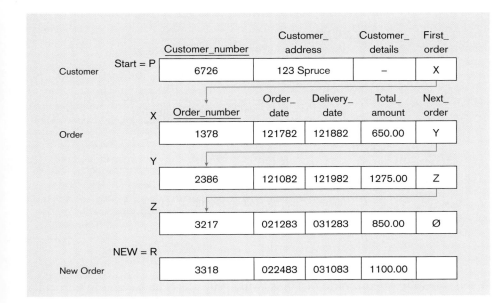

Figure C-5
Example of a sorted list
(a) Before new Order insertion and without dummy first and dummy last Orders

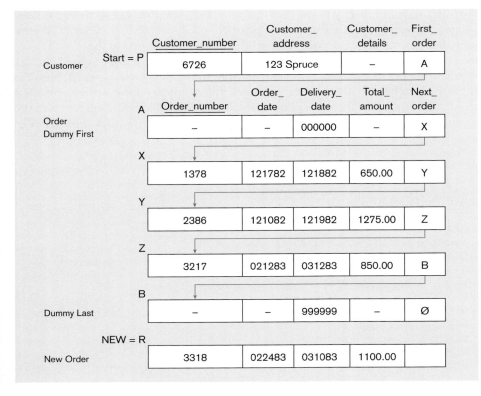

(b) Before new Order insertion and with dummy first and dummy last Orders

(continues)

Figure C-5

(*continued*)
(c) After new Order insertion (Circled numbers next to pointers indicate the step number in the associated maintenance procedure that changes pointer value.)

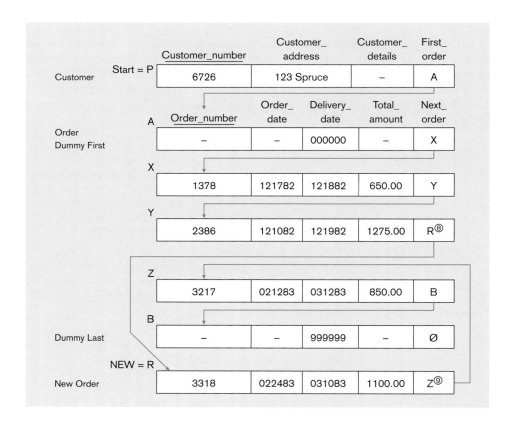

If you use a file organization or DBMS which supports chains, and in particular sorted lists, you will not have to write the code to maintain lists. Rather, this code will exist within the technology you use. Your program will simply issue an insert, delete, or update command, and the support software will do the chain maintenance. Figure C-6 contains an outline of the code needed to insert a new record in the sorted list of Figure C-5b. In this outline, position variables PRE and AFT are used to hold the values of the predecessor and successor, respectively, of the new Order record. Step 7 is included in brackets to show where a check for duplicate keys would appear if required. The symbol ← means replace the value of the variable on the left with the value of the variable on the right. Steps 8 and 9, which change pointer values, in Fig-

Figure C-6

Outline of record insertion code

```
/*   Establish position variables beginning values */
1    PRE ← First_order(START)
2    AFT ← Next_order(PRE)
/*   Skip/scan through chain until proper position is found */
3    DO WHILE Delivery_date(AFT) < Delivery_date(NEW)
     4   PRE ← AFT
     5   AFT ← Next_order(AFT)
6    ENDO
7    [If Delivery_date(AFT) = Delivery_date(NEW) then indicate a Duplicate Error and
     terminate procedure]
/*   Weld in new chain element */
8    Next_order(PRE) ← NEW
9    Next_order(NEW) ← AFT
```

ure C-5 show exactly which pointers would change for the example of this figure. You may want to desk check this routine by manually executing it to see how variables' values are set and changed.

Multilists

A multilist data structure is one for which more than one sequence is maintained among the same records. Thus, multiple chains are threaded through the same records, and records can be scanned in any of the maintained sequences without duplicating the data records. The trade-off for this flexible accessing is the extra storage space and maintenance for each chain. With a multilist, it is possible to walk through one association and in the middle decide to follow another. For example, while accessing the Order records for a given Customer (one list), we could find all the Orders to be delivered on the same day of delivery for a given Order record. Such a multilist is depicted in Figure C-7.

A multilist provides some of the same benefits of multiple indexes (see Chapter 6 for a discussion of primary and secondary key indexes). The major disadvantages of multilists, and the main reasons they are not used in relational DBMSs, is that the cost to scan a list is high compared to accessing an index, and there is no quick way to respond to multiple key qualifications with multilists (for example, find all the orders for customers in the Northwest region and products in the Paper product line). For this and other reasons, indexes have generally replaced linear data structures in modern database technologies. However, legacy applications may still use technologies employing single- and multilist structures.

Figure C-7
Example of multilist structures

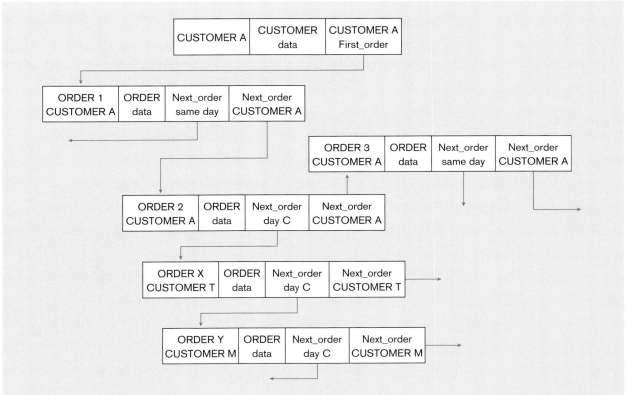

HAZARDS OF CHAIN STRUCTURES

Besides the limitation of chains that prohibits their use in quickly responding to multiple-key qualifications, chains also have the following hazards and limitations:

1. Long chains can take an enormous amount of time to scan because records in sequence are not necessarily stored physically close to one another.

2. Chains are vulnerable to being broken. If an abnormal event occurs in the middle of a chain maintenance routine, the chain can be partially updated and the chain becomes incomplete or inaccurate. Some safety measures can be taken to cope with such mistakes, but these measures add extra storage or processing overhead.

TREES

The problem that a linear data structure may become long and hence time consuming to scan is an inherent issue with any linear structure. Fortunately, nonlinear structures, which implement a divide-and-conquer strategy, have been developed. A popular type of nonlinear data structure is a tree. A tree (see Figure C-8) is a data structure that consists of a set of nodes that branch out from a node at the top of the tree (thus the tree is upside down!). The root node is the node at the top of a tree. Each node in the tree, except the root node, has exactly one parent and may have zero, one, or more than one child nodes. Nodes are defined in terms of levels: the root is level zero, and the children of this node are at level one, and so on.

A leaf node is a node in a tree that has no child nodes (e.g., nodes J, F, C, G, K, L, and I in Figure C-8). A subtree of a node consists of that node and all the descendants of that node.

Balanced Trees

The most common use of trees in database management systems today is as a way to organize the entries within a key index. As with linear data structures, the database programmer does not have to maintain the tree structure because this is done by the

Figure C-8
Example of a tree data structure

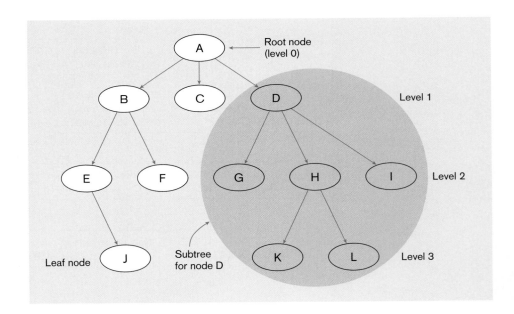

DBMS software. However, a database designer may have the opportunity to control the structure of an index tree to tune the performance of index processing.

The most common form of tree used to build key indexes is a balanced tree, or B-tree. In a B-tree, all leaves are the same distance from the root. For this reason, B-trees have a predictable efficiency. B-trees support both random and sequential retrieval of records. The most popular form of B-tree is the B+-tree. A B+-tree of degree m has the following special balanced tree property:

- Every node has between $m/2$ and m children (m is an integer greater than or equal to 3 and usually odd), except the root (which does not obey this *lower* bound)

It is this property that leads to the dynamic reorganization of nodes, which we illustrate later in this section.

VSAM (virtual sequential access method), a data access method supported by many operating systems, is based on the B+-tree data structure. VSAM is a more modern version of ISAM (indexed sequential access method). There are two primary differences between ISAM and VSAM: (1) the location of index entries under ISAM are limited by the physical boundaries of a disk drive, whereas in VSAM index entries may span the physical boundaries, and (2) an ISAM file needs to be occasionally rebuilt when its structure becomes inefficient after many key additions and deletions, whereas in VSAM the index is dynamically reorganized in incremental ways when segments of the index become unwieldy.

An example of a B+-tree (of degree 3) appears in Figure C-9 for the Product file of Pine Valley Furniture. In this diagram, each vertical arrow represents the path followed for values that are equal to the number to the left of the arrow, but less than the number to the right of the arrow. For example, in the nonleaf node that contains the values 625 and 1000, the middle arrow leaving the bottom of this node is the path followed for values equal to 625 but less than 1000. Horizontal arrows are used to connect the leaf nodes so that sequential processing can occur without having to move up and down through the levels of the tree.

Suppose you wanted to retrieve the data record for product number 1425. Notice that the value in the root node is 1250. Because 1425 is greater than 1250, you follow the arrow to the right of this node down to the next level. In this node you find

Figure C-9
Example of a B+-tree

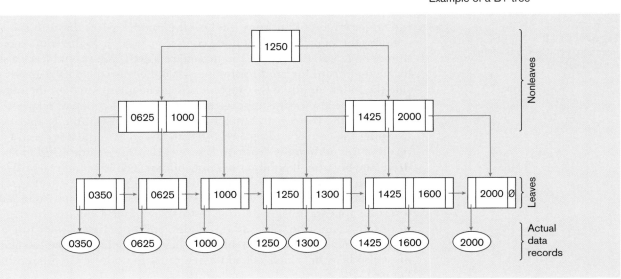

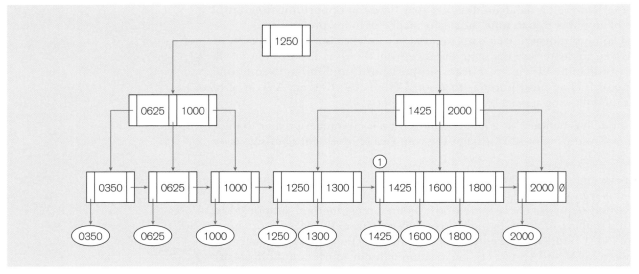

(a) Insertion of record 1800

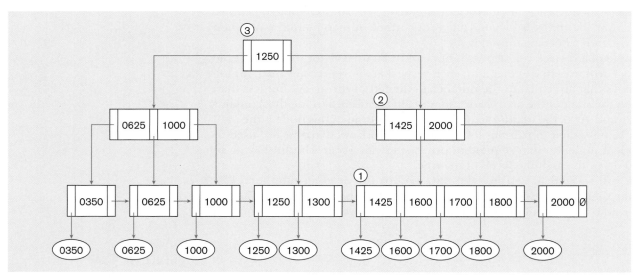

(b) Initial attempt to insert record 1700

Figure C-10
Inserting records in a B+-tree
(*continues*)

the target value (1425), so you follow the middle arrow down to the leaf node that contains the value 1425. This node contains a pointer to the data record for product number 1425, so this record can now be retrieved. You should trace a similar path to locate the record for product number 1000. Because the data records are stored outside the index, multiple B+-tree indexes can be maintained on the same data.

A B+-tree also easily supports the addition and deletion of records. Any necessary changes to the B+-tree structure are dynamic and retain the properties of a B+-tree. Consider the case of adding a record with key 1800 to the B+-tree in Figure C-9. The result of this addition is shown in Figure C-10a. Since node 1 still has only three children (the horizontal pointer does not count as a child pointer), the B+-tree in Figure C-10a still satisfies all B+-tree properties. Now consider the effect of adding another record, this time with key 1700, to the B+-tree in Figure C-10a. An initial result of this insertion appears in Figure C-10b. In this case, node 1 violates the degree limitation, so this node must be split into two nodes. Splitting node 1 will cause a new entry in node 2, which then will make this node have four children, one too many. So, node 2 must also be split, which will add a new entry to node 3. The final result is shown in Figure C-10c.

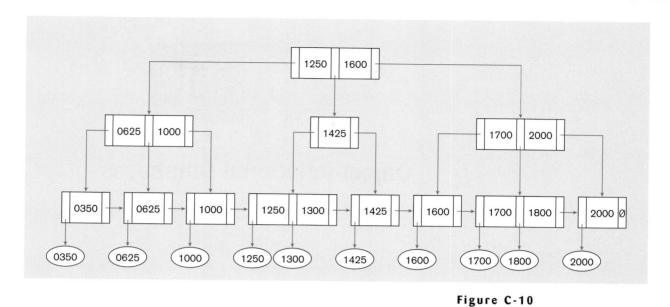

Figure C-10
(*continued*)
(c) Final B+-tree after insertion of record 1700

An interesting situation occurs when the root becomes too large (has more than *m* children). In this case, the root is split, which adds an additional level to the tree. The deletion of a record causes an entry in a leaf to be eliminated. If this elimination causes a leaf to have fewer than *m*/2 children, that leaf is then merged with an adjacent leaf; if the merged leaf is too large (more than *m* children), the merged leaf is split, resulting simply in a less skewed redistribution of keys across nodes. The result is that a B+-tree is dynamically reorganized to keep the tree balanced (equal depth along any path from the root) and with a limited number of entries per node (which controls the bushiness, or width, of the tree).

If you are interested in learning more about B-trees, see Comer (1979), a classic article on B-tree properties and design.

Reference

Comer, D. 1979. "The Ubiquitous B-tree." *ACM Computing Surveys* 11 (June): 121–37.

Appendix D

Object-Relational Databases

In this textbook we have described the two models most widely used for the design and implementation of databases: relational and object-oriented. The relational model (with its associated relational database management systems) is the model most often used for implementing mainstream business applications today. Some of the strengths of this model are the following:

- data independence, described in Chapter 1
- powerful query language (SQL), described in Chapter 7
- mature relational database management system technology, including features such as on-line backup and recovery and flexible concurrency control (described in Chapter 12)

Despite these strengths, we noted in Chapter 14 (as well as in other chapters) that the relational data model is not well suited to handling complex data types such as images, audio, video, and spatial (or geographical) data. Thus the object-oriented data model was introduced primarily to manage these complex data types (this model is described in Chapters 14 and 15). The market for object-oriented database management systems has grown slowly, yet the technology is extremely promising for applications such as Web servers that incorporate multimedia data types. The weaknesses of object-oriented database systems (at least until recently) have been the lack of important features found in relational systems such as query capability, on-line backup and recovery, and flexible concurrency control.

In summary, relational and object-oriented database systems each have certain strengths as well as certain weaknesses. In general the weaknesses of one type of system tend to be a strength of the other (and vice versa). This has led the industry to develop a new generation of hybrid database system—the object-relational system—that seeks to combine the best features of both models (Stonebraker, et al., 1990). Most of the major DBMS vendors have released a version of an object-relational database system. These systems handle objects and rules, encapsulation, polymorphism, and inheritance, and are compatible with RDBMSs. In this appendix we present a brief description of this type of system, including its advantages and disadvantages.

BASIC CONCEPTS AND DEFINITIONS

Object-relational database management system: A database engine that supports both relational and object-oriented features in an integrated fashion.

An **object-relational database management system** (or **ORDBMS**) is a database engine that supports both relational and object-oriented features in an integrated fashion (Frank, 1995). Thus the user can (at least ideally) define, manipulate, and

608

query both relational data and objects while using common interfaces (such as SQL). The underlying data model of the DBMS is relational. Thus, whereas the database may appear to a programmer to be object-oriented, the storage and process is relational; hence, there is an overhead to map between relational and objects.

Two other terms that are used for object-relational databases are extended relational and universal server. The term *extended relational* (an older term) derives from the fact that the first versions of these types of systems were developed by adding object-oriented features onto existing relational DBMSs. The term *universal server* (a more contemporary term) is based on the stated objective of managing *any* type of data (including user-defined data types) with the same server technology.

Features of an ORDBMS

As indicated above, the intent with ORDBMS is to combine the best features of the relational and object database models. Following are the main features usually included:

1. An enhanced version of SQL (similar to SQL3) that can be used to create and manipulate both relational tables and object types or classes

2. Support for traditional object-oriented functions including inheritance, polymorphism, user-defined (or abstract) data types, and navigational access

Complex Data Types

There are three main categories of data types in SQL: NUMERIC, CHARACTER, and TEMPORAL. NUMERIC types include DECIMAL and INTEGER, while TEMPORAL types include DATE and TIME (Celko, 1995).

Modern business applications often require storing and manipulating complex data types that are not easily handled by relational systems. Some of the more common of these complex data types are shown in Table D-1. For each data type, this table provides a brief description and one or more typical applications. For example, the Graphic data type consists of geometric objects such as points, lines, and circles; typical applications are for computer-assisted design (CAD), computer-assisted manufacturing (CAM), computer-assisted software engineering (CASE) tools, and presentation graphics (such as charts and graphs).

ENHANCED SQL

The most powerful feature of an ORDBMS is that it uses an extended version of a relational query language (such as SQL3) to define, fetch, and manipulate data (Cattell, 1994); Chaudhri and Zicari, 2001).

Table D-1 Complex Data Types

Data type	Description	Example applications
Image	Bit-mapped representation	Documents, photographs, medical images, fingerprints
Graphic	Geometric objects	CAD, CAM, CASE, presentation graphics
Spatial	Geographic objects	Maps
Recursive	Nested objects	Bills of materials
Audio	Sound clips	Music, animation, games
Video	Video segments, movies	Training films, product demonstrations, movies
Array	Subscripted variables	Time series, multidimensional data, multivalued attribute
Computational-intensive	Data requiring extensive computations	Data mining, financial instruments (e.g., derivatives)

A Simple Example

Suppose that an organization wants to create a relation named EMPLOYEE to record employee data (see Figure D-1). Traditional relational attributes in this table are the following: Emp_ID, Name, Address, and Date_of_Birth. In addition, the organization would like to store a photograph of each employee that will be used for identification purposes. This attribute (whose type is defined by an object) is named Emp_Photo in Figure D-1. When the data for a particular employee are retrieved, the employee photo will be displayed with the remaining data.

SQL3 will provide statements to create both tables and data types (or object classes). For example, the SQL CREATE TABLE statement for EMPLOYEE might appear as follows:

```
CREATE TABLE EMPLOYEE
    Emp_ID INTEGER NOT NULL,
    Name CHAR(20) NOT NULL,
    Address CHAR(20),
    Date_of_Birth DATE NOT NULL,
    Emp_Photo IMAGE);
```

In this example IMAGE is a data type (or class), and Emp_Photo is an object of that class. IMAGE may be either a predefined class or a user-defined class. If it is a user-defined class, a SQL CREATE CLASS statement is used to define the class. The user can also define methods that operate on the data defined in a class. For example, one method of IMAGE is Scale( ), which can be used to expand or reduce the size of the photograph. The method would be coded in Java, C ++, or Smalltalk and would be encapsulated with the IMAGE CLASS. Methods can be used in the select list of queries just like attributes.

Content Addressing

One of the most powerful features of the relational SQL language is the ability to select a subset of the records in a table that satisfy stated qualifications. For example, in the EMPLOYEE relation a simple SQL statement will select records for all employees whose date of birth is on or before 12/31/1940 (see Chapter 7 for examples). In contrast, "pure" object database systems do not have this query capability. Instead, access to objects is navigational—that is, each object has a unique object identifier (see Chapter 14).

Figure D-1
Relation with complex object

Emp_ID	Name	Address	Date_of_Birth	Emp_Photo
12345	Charles	112 Main	04/27/1973	
34567	Angela	840 Oak	08/12/1967	
56789	Thomas	520 Elm	10/13/1975	

The ORDBMS products extend relational's content addressibility to complex objects (Norman and Bloor, 1996). **Content addressing** is the facility that allows a user to query a database (or database table) to select all records and/or objects that satisfy a given set of qualifications.

SQL3 includes extensions for content addressing with complex data types. Let's see how content addressing might be applied in the EMPLOYEE table. Remember that each employee record contains (or is at least linked to) a photo of that employee. A user might want to pose the following query: given a photograph of a person, scan the EMPLOYEE table to determine if there is a close match for any employee to that photo, then display the data (including the photograph) of the employee or employees selected (if any). Suppose the electronic image of a photograph is stored in a location called My_Photo. Then a simple query for this situation might appear as follows:

```
SELECT *
    FROM EMPLOYEE
    WHERE My_Photo LIKE Emp_Photo;
```

Content addressing in an ORDBMS is a very powerful feature that allows users to search for matches to multimedia objects such as images, audio or video segments, and documents. One obvious application for this feature is searching databases for fingerprint or voiceprint matches.

Content addressing: The facility that allows a user to query a database to select all records and/or objects that satisfy a given set of qualifications.

ADVANTAGES OF THE OBJECT-RELATIONAL APPROACH

For applications that require complex processing or significant query activity on large datasets, the object-relational approach offers several advantages compared to relational database systems (Moxon, 1997):

1. *Reduced network traffic*   Queries that employ methods to scan data can be executed entirely on the server, without the need to send large quantities of data back to the clients.

2. *Application and query performance*   The methods that process large datasets can exploit large parallel servers to significantly improve performance.

3. *Software maintenance*   The fact that data and methods are stored together on the server greatly simplifies the task of software maintenance.

4. *Integrated data and transaction management*   All transaction integrity, concurrency, and backup and recovery are handled within the database engine.

ORDBMS VENDORS AND PRODUCTS

A list of the major vendors and the ORDBMS products they provide is shown in Table D-2. The table also shows the extender technology (or framework) that is provided by each vendor that allows users to define their own data types, as well as the methods that manipulate those data.

Table D-2 ORDBMS Vendors and Products

Vendor	ORDBMS Product	Extender technology	Website
IBM	DB2 Universal Database	DB2 Extenders	www_4.ibm.com/software/data/db2/udb/
Informix	Dynamic Server	Data Blades	www.informix.com/informix/products/integration/datablade/datablade_ds.htm
Oracle	Oracle 8	Data Cartridges	www.oracle.com/oramag/webcolums/ora8804.html
Computer Associates	ODB-II (Jasmine)	none	www.cai.com/products/jasmine.htm

References

Cattell, R. 1994. *Object Data Management: Object-Oriented and Extended Relational Database Systems.* Reading, MA: Addison-Wesley, pp. 303–304.

Celko, J. 1995. *Instant SQL Programming.* Chicago: Wrox Press, pp. 54–55.

Chaudhri, A.B., and R. Zicari. 2001. *Succeeding with Object Databases.* New York: Wiley.

Frank, M. 1995. "Object-Relational Hybrids." *DBMS* 8 (July): 46–56.

Melton, J. 1995. "A Case for SQL Conformance Testing." *Database Programming & Design* 10 (7): 66–69.

Moxon, B. 1997. "Database out of This Universe." *DB2 Magazine* 2 (Fall): 9–16.

Norman, M., and R. Bloor. 1996. "To Universally Serve." *Database Programming & Design* 9 (July): 26–35.

Stonebraker, M., et al. 1990. "Third-Generation Database System Manifesto—The Committee for Advanced DBMS Function." *SIGMOD Record* 19, 3: 31–44.

Web Resources

See Table D-2.

www.object-relational.com This site from Barry & Associates, Inc. compares the features of many object-relational DBMSs.

http://technet.oracle.com/products/oracle8/info/objwp3/x003t wp.htm. This paper is an overview of the object-relational features of Oracle 8.

Glossary of Acronyms

ACM	Association for Computing Machinery	**DDL**	Data Definition Language
AITP	Association of Information Technology Professionals	**DFD**	Data Flow Diagram
		DK/NF	Domain-Key Normal Form
ANSI	American National Standards Institute	**DML**	Data Manipulation Language
API	Application Program Interface	**DNS**	Domain Name Server
ASCII	American Standards Code for Information Interchange	**DSS**	Decision Support System
		EDI	Electronic Data Interchange
ASP	Active Server Pages	**EDW**	Enterprise Data Warehouse
BCNF	Boyce-Codd Normal Form	**EER**	Extended Entity-Relationship
BOM	Bill of Materials	**E-R**	Entity-Relationship
B2B	Business-to-Business	**ERD**	Entity-Relationship Diagram
B2C	Business-to-Consumer	**ERP**	Enterprise Resource Planning
CAD/CAM	Computer-Aided Design/Computer-Aided Manufacturing	**ETL**	Extract-Transform-Load
		FK	Foreign Key
CASE	Computer-Aided Software Engineering	**GUI**	Graphical User Interface
CD-ROM	Compact Disk-Read-Only Memory	**HTML**	Hypertext Markup Language
CFML	ColdFusion Markup Language	**HTTP**	Hypertext Transfer Protocol
CGI	Common Gateway Interface	**IBM**	International Business Machines
COM	Component Object Model	**I-CASE**	Integrated Computer-Aided Software Engineering
CPU	Central Processor Unit		
CRM	Customer Relationship Management	**ID**	Identifier
CRT	Cathode Ray Tube	**IDS**	Intrusion Detection System
C/S	Client/Server	**I/O**	Input/Output
CSF	Critical Success Factor	**IRDS**	Information Repository Dictionary System
CSS	Cascading Style Sheets	**IRM**	Information Resource Management
DA	Data Administrator (or Data Administration)	**IS**	Information System
		ISA	Information Systems Architecture
DBA	Database Administrator (or Database Administration)	**ISAM**	Indexed Sequential Access Method
		ISO	International Standards Organization
DBD	Database Description	**IT**	Information Technology
DBMS	Database Management System	**ITAA**	Information Technology Association of America
DB2	Data Base2 (an IBM Relational DBMS)		
DCL	Data Control Language		

613

JDBC	Java Database Connectivity		**RAID**	Redundant Array of Inexpensive Disks
JSP	Java Server Pages		**RDBMS**	Relational Database Management System
LAN	Local Area Network		**ROLAP**	Relational On-line Analytical Processing
LDB	Logical Database		**SDLC**	Systems Development Life Cycle
LDBR	Logical Database Record		**SGML**	Standard Generalized Markup Language
MB	Million Bytes		**SMP**	Symmetric Multiprocessing
MIS	Management Information System		**SQL**	Structured Query Language
M:N	Many-to-Many		**SQL/DS**	Structured Query Language/Data System (an IBM relational DBMS)
M:1	Many-to-One			
MOLAP	Multidimensional On-line Analytical Processing		**SSL**	Secure Sockets Layer
			TCP/IP	Transmission Control Protocol/Internet Protocol
MPP	Massively Parallel Processing			
MVCH	Mountain View Community Hospital		**TQM**	Total Quality Management
NUPI	Nonunique Primary Index		**UDF**	User-Defined Function
NUSI	Nonunique Secondary Index		**UDT**	User-Defined Datatype
ODBC	Open Database Connectivity		**UML**	Unified Modeling Language
ODBMS	Object Database Management System		**UPI**	Unique Primary Index
ODL	Object Definition Language		**URL**	Uniform Resource Locator
ODS	Operational Data Store		**USI**	Unique Secondary Index
OLAP	On-line Analytical Processing		**VBA**	Visual Basic for Applications
OLE	Object Linking and Embedding		**VLDB**	Very Large Database
OLTP	On-line Transaction Processing		**W3C**	World Wide Web Consortium
OO	Object-Oriented		**WWW**	World Wide Web
OODM	Object-Oriented Data Model		**XHTML**	Extensible Hypertext Markup Language
OQL	Object Query Language		**XML**	Extensible Markup Language
O/R	Object/Relational		**XSL**	Extensible Style Language
ORDBMS	Object-Relational Database Management System		**1:1**	One-to-One
			1:M	One-to-Many
OSAM	Overflow Sequential Access Method		**1NF**	First Normal Form
PC	Personal Computer		**2NF**	Second Normal Form
PK	Primary Key		**3NF**	Third Normal Form
PVF	Pine Valley Furniture		**4NF**	Fourth Normal Form
QBE	Query-by-Example		**5NF**	Fifth Normal Form

Glossary of Terms

Note: The chapter or appendix in which a term is defined is listed in parentheses after the definition.

Aborted transaction   A transaction in progress that terminates abnormally. (12)

Abstract class   A class that has no direct instances, but whose descendants may have direct instances. (14)

Abstract operation   Defines the form or protocol of the operation, but not its implementation. (14)

Action   An operation, such as create, delete, update, or read, which may be performed on data objects. (4)

Action assertion   A statement of a constraint or control on the actions of the organization. (4)

@ctive data warehouse   An enterprise data warehouse that accepts near-real-time feeds of transactional data from the systems of record, immediately transforms and loads the appropriate data into the warehouse, and provides near-real-time access for the transaction processing systems to an enterprise data warehouse. (11)

ActiveX   A loosely defined set of technologies developed by Microsoft that extends browser capabilities and allows the manipulation of data inside the browser. (10)

After-image   A copy of a record (or page of memory) after it has been modified. (12)

Aggregation   The process of transforming data from a detailed to a summary level. (11) A part-of relationship between a component object and an aggregate object. (14)

Alias   An alternative name used for an attribute. (5)

Anchor object   A business rule (a fact) on which actions are limited. (4)

Anomaly   An error or inconsistency that may result when a user attempts to update a table that contains redundant data. The three types of anomalies are insertion, deletion, and modification. (5)

Application partitioning   The process of assigning portions of application code to client or server partitions after it is written, in order to achieve better performance and interoperability (ability of a component to function on different platforms). (9)

Application Program Interface (API)   Sets of routines that an application program uses to direct the performance of procedures by the computer's operating system. (9)

Array   A dynamically sized ordered collection of elements that can be located by position. (15)

Association   A named relationship between or among object classes. (14)

Association class   An association that has attributes or operations of its own or that participates in relationships with other classes. (14)

Association role   The end of an association where it connects to a class. (14)

Associative entity   An entity type that associates the instances of one or more entity types and contains attributes that are peculiar to the relationship between those entity instances. (3)

Asynchronous distributed database   A form of distributed database technology in which copies of replicated data are kept at different nodes so that local servers can access data without reaching out across the network. (13)

Atomic literal   A constant that cannot be decomposed into any further components. (15)

Attribute   A property or characteristic of an entity type that is of interest to the organization. (3)

Attribute inheritance   A property by which subtype entities inherit values of all attributes of the supertype. (4)

Authorization rules   Controls incorporated in the data management systems that restrict access to data and also restrict the actions that people may take when they access data. (12)

Backup facilities   An automatic dump facility that produces a backup copy (or save) of the entire database. (12)

Backward recovery (rollback)   The back out, or undo, of unwanted changes to the database. Before-images of the records that have been changed are applied to the database, and the database is returned to an earlier state. Used to reverse the changes made by transactions that have been aborted or terminated abnormally. (12)

Bag An unordered collection of elements that may contain duplicates. (15)

Base table A table in the relational data model containing the inserted raw data. Base tables correspond to the relations that are identified in the database's conceptual schema. (7)

Before-image A copy of a record (or page of memory) before it has been modified. (12)

Behavior Represents how an object acts and reacts. (14)

Binary relationship A relationship between the instances of two entity types. (3)

Biometric device Techniques that measure or detect personal characteristics such as fingerprints, voiceprints, eye pictures, or signature dynamics. (12)

Bitmap index A table of bits in which each row represents the distinct values of a key and each column is a bit, which when on indicates that the record for that bit column position has the associated field value. (6)

Blocking factor The number of physical records per page. (6)

Boyce-Codd normal form (BCNF) A relation in which every determinant is a candidate key. (B)

Browser Software that displays HTML documents and allows users to access files and software related to the HTML documents. Browsers are based on the use of hyperlinks, which allow the user to jump to other documents by clicking on an object. Most also allow a user to download and transfer files, access news groups, play audio and video files, and execute small modules of code, such as Java applets or ActiveX controls. (10)

Business function A related group of business processes that support some aspect of the mission of an enterprise. (2)

Business rule A statement that defines or constrains some aspect of the business. It is intended to assert business structure or to control or influence the behavior of the business. (3)

Business to Business (B2B) Phrase used to describe electronic businesses that conduct e-commerce transactions with other businesses, including their suppliers and vendors. (10)

Business to Consumer (B2C) Phrase used to describe electronic businesses that conduct retail sales businesses to consumers. (10)

Candidate key An attribute, or combination of attributes, that uniquely identifies a row in a relation. (5)

Cardinality constraint Specifies the number of instances of one entity that can (or must) be associated with each instance of another entity. (3)

Cascading Style Sheets (CSS) Developed by the W3C, style sheets define the appearance of different elements and can be applied to any Web page. They are called cascading style sheets because more than one can be applied to a Web page. (10)

Catalog A set of schemas that, when put together, constitute a description of a database. (7)

Checkpoint facility A facility by which the DBMS periodically refuses to accept any new transactions. The system is in a quiet state, and the database and transaction logs are synchronized. (12)

Class diagram Shows the static structure of an object-oriented model: the object classes, their internal structure, and the relationships in which they participate. (14)

Class-scope attribute An attribute of a class that specifies a value common to an entire class, rather than a specific value for an instance. (14)

Client/server architecture *See* Client/server systems.

Client/server systems A networked computing model that distributes processes between clients and servers, which supply the requested services. In a database system, the database generally resides on a server that processes the DBMS. The clients may process the application systems or request services from another server that holds the application programs. (9)

ColdFusion Markup Language (CFML) The language used to create ColdFusion application page scripts. The language is modeled after HTML and includes tags for performing operations such as reading and updating database tables. (10)

Collection literal A collection of literals or object types. (15)

Commit protocol An algorithm to ensure that a transaction is successfully completed or else it is aborted. (13)

Common Gateway Interface (CGI) A Web server interface that specifies the transfer of information between a Web server and a CGI program. (10)

Completeness constraint A type of constraint that addresses the question whether an instance of a supertype must also be a member of at least one subtype. (4)

Composite attribute An attribute that can be broken down into component parts. (3)

Composite identifier An identifier that consists of a composite attribute. (3)

Composite key A primary key that consists of more than one attribute. (5)

Composition   A part object that belongs to only one whole object and that lives and dies with the whole object. (14)

Computer-aided software engineering (CASE)   Software tools that provide automated support for some portion of the systems development process. (2)

Conceptual schema   A detailed, technology independent specification of the overall structure of a database. (2)

Concrete class   A class that can have direct instances. (14)

Concurrency control   The process of managing simultaneous operations against a database so that data integrity is maintained and the operations do not interfere with each other in a multiuser environment. (12)

Concurrency transparency   A design goal for a distributed database, with the property that although a distributed system runs many transactions, it appears that a given transaction is the only activity in the system. Thus, when several transactions are processed concurrently, the results must be the same as if each transaction were processed in serial order. (13)

Conformed dimension   One or more dimension tables associated with two or more fact tables for which the dimension tables have the same business meaning and primary key with each fact table. (11)

Constraint   A rule that cannot be violated by database users. (1)

Constructor operation   An operation that creates a new instance of a class. (14)

Content addressing   The facility that allows a user to query a database to select all records and/or objects that satisfy a given set of qualifications. (15)

Cookie   A block of data stored on a client by a Web server. When a user returns to the site later, the contents of the cookie are sent back to the Web server and may be used to identify the user and return a customized Web page. (10)

Correlated subquery   In SQL, a subquery in which processing the inner query depends on data from the outer query. (8)

Corresponding object   A business rule (a fact) that influences the ability to perform an action on another business rule. (4)

Data   Facts, text, graphics, images, sound, and video segments that have meaning in the users' environment. (1)

Data administration   A high-level function that is responsible for the overall management of data resources in an organization, including maintaining corporate-wide definitions and standards. (12)

Data control language (DCL)   Commands used to control a database, including administering privileges and the committing (saving) of data. (7)

Data definition language (DDL)   Those commands used to define a database, including creating, altering, and dropping tables and establishing constraints. (7)

Data dictionary   A repository of information about a database that documents data elements of a database. (12)

Data independence   The separation of data descriptions from the application programs that use the data. (1)

Data manipulation language (DML)   Those commands used to maintain and query a database, including updating, inserting, modifying, and querying data. (7)

Data mart   A data warehouse that is limited in scope, whose data are obtained by selecting and summarizing data from a data warehouse or from separate extract, transform, and load processes from source data systems. (11)

Data mining   Knowledge discovery using a sophisticated blend of techniques from traditional statistics, artificial intelligence, and computer graphics. (11)

Data scrubbing   A technique using pattern recognition and other artificial intelligence techniques to upgrade the quality of raw data before transforming and moving the data to the data warehouse. Also called data cleansing. (11)

Data steward   A person assigned the responsibility of ensuring that organizational applications properly support the organization's enterprise goals. (12)

Data transformation   The component of data reconciliation that converts data from the format of the source operational systems to the format of the enterprise data warehouse. (11)

Data type   A detailed coding scheme recognized by system software, such as a DBMS, for representing organizational data. (6)

Data visualization   The representation of data in graphical and multimedia formats for human analysis. (11)

Data warehouse   An integrated decision support database whose content is derived from the various operational databases. (1) A subject-oriented, integrated, time-variant, nonupdatable collection of data used in support of management decision-making processes. (11)

Database   An organized collection of logically related data. (1)

Database administration   A technical function that is responsible for physical database design and for dealing with technical issues, such as security enforcement, database performance, and backup and recovery. (12)

Database application   An application program (or set of related programs) that is used to perform a series of database activities (create, read, update, and delete) on behalf of database users. (1)

Database change log   Before- and after-images of records that have been modified by transactions. (12)

Database destruction   The database itself is lost, or destroyed, or cannot be read. (12)

Database management system (DBMS)   A software application that is used to create, maintain, and provide controlled access to user databases. (1)

Database recovery   Mechanisms for restoring a database quickly and accurately after loss or damage. (12)

Database security   Protection of the data against accidental or intentional loss, destruction, or misuse. (12)

Database server   A computer that is responsible for database storage, access, and processing in a client/server environment. Some people also use this term to describe a two-tier client/server environment. (9)

DCS-1000 (Carnivore)   Device developed by the FBI to monitor e-mail traffic by tracking e-mail headers. (10)

Deadlock   An impasse that results when two or more transactions have locked a common resource, and each waits for the other to unlock that resource. (12)

Deadlock prevention   User programs must lock all records they require at the beginning of a transaction (rather than one at a time). (12)

Deadlock resolution   An approach that allows deadlocks to occur but builds mechanisms into the DBMS for detecting and breaking the deadlocks. (12)

Decentralized database   A database that is stored on computers at multiple locations; these computers are not interconnected by network and database software that make the data appear in one logical database. (13)

Degree   The number of entity types that participate in a relationship. (3)

Denormalization   The process of transforming normalized relations into unnormalized physical record specifications. (6)

Dependent data mart   A data mart filled exclusively from the enterprise data warehouse and its reconciled data. (11)

Derivation   A statement derived from other knowledge in the business. (4)

Derived attribute   An attribute whose values can be calculated from related attribute values. (3)

Derived data   Data that have been selected, formatted, and aggregated for end-user decision-support applications. (11)

Derived fact   A fact that is derived from business rules using an algorithm or inference. (4)

Determinant   The attribute on the left-hand side of the arrow in a functional dependency. (5)

Dictionary   An unordered sequence of key-value pairs without any duplicates. (15)

Disjoint rule   Specifies that if an entity instance (of the supertype) is a member of one subtype, it cannot simultaneously be a member of any other subtype. (4)

Disjointness constraint   A constraint that addresses the question whether an instance of a supertype may simultaneously be a member of two (or more) subtypes. (4)

Distributed database   A single logical database that is spread physically across computers in multiple locations that are connected by a data communications link. (13)

DNS (domain name server) balancing   A load-balancing approach where the DNS server for the hostname of the site returns multiple IP addresses for the site. (10)

Dynamic SQL   The process of making an application capable of generating specific SQL code on the fly, as the application is processing. (8)

Dynamic view   A virtual table that is created dynamically upon request by a user. A dynamic view is not a temporary table. Rather its definition is stored in the system catalog and the contents of the view are materialized as a result of an SQL query that uses the view. Distinguish from a materialized view, which may be stored on a disk and refreshed at intervals or when used, depending on the RDBMS. (7)

Electronic business (e-business)   A technology-enabled business that is using Internet-related technology to facilitate the development of more integrated relations with customers and suppliers. (10)

Electronic commerce (e-commerce)   Internet-based business transactions, including such activities as order processing and fulfillment, customer relationship management interactions, electronic data interchange (EDI), and bill payments. (10)

Embedded SQL   The process of including hard-coded SQL statements in a program written in another language, such as C or Java. (8)

Encapsulation   The technique of hiding the internal implementation details of an object from its external view. (14)

Encryption   The coding or scrambling of data so that humans cannot read them. (12)

Enhanced entity-relationship (ERR) model   The model that has resulted from extending the original E-R model with new modeling constructs. (4)

Enterprise data model   A graphical model that shows the high-level entities for the organization and the relationships among those entities. (1)

Enterprise data modeling   The first step in database development, in which the scope and general contents of organizational databases are specified. (2)

Enterprise data warehouse (EDW)   A centralized, integrated data warehouse that is the control point and single source of all data made available to end users for decision support applications. (11)

Enterprise key   A primary key whose value is unique across all relations. (5)

Enterprise resource planning (ERP) systems   A business management system that integrates all functions of the enterprise, such as manufacturing, sales, finance, marketing, inventory, accounting, and human resources. ERP systems are software applications that provide the data necessary for the enterprise to examine and manage its activities. (1)

Entity   A person, place, object, event, or concept in the user environment about which the organization wishes to maintain data. (3)

Entity cluster   A set of one or more entity types and associated relationships grouped into a single abstract entity type. (4)

Entity instance   A single occurrence of an entity type. (3)

Entity integrity rule   No primary key attribute (or component of a primary key attribute) can be null. (5)

Entity type   A collection of entities that share common properties or characteristics. (3)

Entity-relationship (E-R) diagram   A graphical representation of an entity-relationship model. (3)

Entity-relationship (E-R) model   A logical representation of the data for an organization or for a business. (3)

Equi-join   A join in which the joining condition is based on equality between values in the common columns. Common columns appear (redundantly) in the result table. (8)

Event   A database action (create, update, or delete) that results from a transaction. (11)

Event-driven   Nonprocedural programming that detects an event when it occurs and generates an appropriate response to that event. (9)

Exclusive lock (X lock or write lock)   A technique that prevents another transaction from reading and therefore updating a record until it is unlocked. (12)

Extensible Markup Language (XML)   A scripting language based on SGML that allows the creation of customized tags, which enable easier transmission and sharing of data across organizations. (10)

Extent   A contiguous section of disk storage space. (6) The set of all instances of a class within the database. (15)

Extranet   Use of Internet protocols to establish limited access to company data and information by the company's customers and suppliers. (1)

Fact   An association between two or more terms. (3)

Failure transparency   A design goal for a distributed database, which guarantees that either all the actions of each transaction are committed or else none of them is committed. (13)

Fat client   A client PC that is responsible for processing presentation logic, extensive application and business rules logic, and many DBMS functions. (9)

Field   The smallest unit of named application data recognized by system software. (6)

File organization   A technique for physically arranging the records of a file on secondary storage devices. (6)

File server   A device that manages file operations and is shared by each of the client PCs attached to the LAN. (9)

Firewall   A hardware/software security component that limits external access to company data. (10)

First normal form   A relation that contains no multivalued attributes. (5)

Foreign key   An attribute in a relation of a database that serves as the primary key of another relation in the same database. (5)

Forward recovery (rollforward)   A technique that starts with an earlier copy of the database. After-images (the results of good transactions) are applied to the database, and the database is quickly moved forward to a later state. (12)

Fourth normal form   A relation in BCNF that contains no multivalued dependencies. (B)

Function   A stored subroutine that returns one value and has only input parameters. (8)

Functional decomposition   An iterative process of breaking down the description of a system into finer and finer detail in which one function is described in greater detail by a set of other, supporting functions. (2)

Functional dependency   A constraint between two attributes or two sets of attributes. (5)

Generalization   The process of defining a more general entity type from a set of more specialized entity types. (4)

Global transaction   In a distributed database, a transaction that requires reference to data at one or more nonlocal sites to satisfy the request. (13)

Grain   The level of detail in a fact table determined by the intersection of all the components of the primary key, including foreign keys and any other primary key elements. (11)

Hash index table   A file organization that uses hashing to map a key into a location in an index, where there is a pointer to the actual data record matching the hash key. (6)

Hashed file organization   A storage system in which the address for each record is determined using a hashing algorithm. (6)

Hashing algorithm   A routine that converts a primary key value into a relative record number (or relative file address). (6)

Homonym   An attribute that may have more than one meaning. (5)

Horizontal partitioning   Distributing the rows of a table into several separate files. (6)

Hypertext Markup Language (HTML)   The scripting language used for documents displayed through browsers on the Web. HTML is similar to SGML, a more comprehensive information management standard. (10)

Identifier   An attribute (or combination of attributes) that uniquely identifies individual instances of an entity type. (3)

Identifying owner   The entity type on which the weak entity type depends. (3)

Identifying relationship   The relationship between a weak entity type and its owner. (3)

Inconsistent read problem   An unrepeatable read, one that occurs when one user reads data that have been partially updated by another user. (12)

Incremental commitment   A strategy in systems development projects in which the project is reviewed after each phase and continuation of the project is rejustified in each of these reviews. (2)

Incremental extract   A method of capturing only the changes that have occurred in the source data since the last capture. (11)

Independent data mart   A data mart filled with data extracted from the operational environment, without benefit of a data warehouse. (11)

Index   A table or other data structure used to determine the location of rows in a file that satisfy some condition. (6)

Indexed file organization   The storage of records either sequentially or nonsequentially with an index that allows software to locate individual records. (6)

Information   Data that have been processed in such a way as to increase the knowledge of the person who uses the data. (1)

Information engineering   A formal, top-down methodology that uses a data orientation to create and maintain information systems. (2)

Information repository   A component that stores metadata which describes an organization's data and data processing resources, manages the total information processing environment, and combines information about an organization's business information and its application portfolio. (12)

Information Repository Dictionary System (IRDS)   A computer software tool that is used to manage and control access to the information repository. (12)

Information systems architecture (ISA)   A conceptual blueprint or plan that expresses the desired future structure for the information systems in an organization. (2)

Informational systems   Systems designed to support decision making based on historical point-in-time and prediction data and for complex queries or data-mining applications. (11)

Intranet   Use of Internet protocols to establish access to company data and information that is limited to the organization. (1)

Intrusion detection system (IDS)   A system that tries to identify attempts to hack or break into a computer system or to misuse it. IDSs may monitor packets passing over the network, monitor system files, monitor log files, or set up deception systems that attempt to trap hackers. (10)

Java   A general-purpose, object-oriented programming language that is well suited to use on the Web. Small Java programs, called Java applets, download from a Web server to the client and run on a Java-compatible browser. (10)

Java servlet   A small program that executes from within another application rather than from the operating system and is stored on the server rather than with an application on a client. (10)

JavaScript   A scripting language based on Java, but easier to learn, that is used to achieve interactivity on Web pages. (10)

Join   A relational operation that causes two tables with a common domain to be combined into a single table or view. (8)

Join index   An index on columns from two or more tables that come from the same domain of values. (6)

Joining   The process of combining data from various sources into a single table or view. (11)

Journalizing facilities   An audit trail of transactions and database changes. (12)

Legacy data   Data contained by a system used prior to the installation of a new system. Often legacy data resides on mainframe systems, which may have been replaced by client/server systems or Web-enabled systems. (1)

List   An ordered collection of elements of the same type. (15)

Local autonomy   A design goal for a distributed database, which says that a site can independently administer and operate its database when connections to other nodes have failed. (13)

Local transaction   In a distributed database, a transaction that requires reference only to data that are stored at the site where the transaction originates. (13)

Location transparency   A design goal for a distributed database, which says that a user (or user program) using data need not know the location of the data. (13)

Locking   Any data that are retrieved by a user for updating must be locked, or denied to other users, until the update is completed or aborted. (12)

Locking level (granularity)   The extent of the database resource that is included with each lock. (12)

Logical data mart   A data mart created by a relational view of a data warehouse. (11)

Market basket analysis   The study of buying behavior of individual customers. (11)

Massively parallel processing (MPP)/shared nothing architecture   Massively parallel processing systems where each CPU has its own dedicated memory. (9)

Materialized view   Copies or replicas of data based on SQL queries created in the same manner as dynamic views. However, a materialized view exists as a table and thus care must be taken to keep it synchronized with its associated base tables. (7)

Maximum cardinality   The maximum number of instances of one entity that may be associated with each instance of another entity. (3)

Metadata   Data that describe the properties or characteristics of other data. (1)

Method   The implementation of an operation. (14)

Middleware   Software that allows an application to interoperate with other software without requiring the user to understand and code the low-level operations necessary to achieve interoperability. (9)

Minimum cardinality   The minimum number of instances of one entity that may be associated with each instance of another entity. (3)

Multidimensional OLAP (MOLAP)   OLAP tools that load data into an intermediate structure, usually a three- or higher dimensional array. (11)

Multiple classification   An object is an instance of more than one class. (14)

Multiplicity   A specification that indicates how many objects participate in a given relationship. (14)

Multivalued attribute   An attribute that may take on more than one value for a given entity instance. (3)

Multivalued dependency   The type of dependency that exists when there are at least three attributes (e.g., A, B, and C) in a relation, with a well-defined set of B and C values for each A value, but those B and C values are independent of each other. (B)

Natural join   Same as equi-join except one of the duplicate columns is eliminated in the result table. (8)

Normal form   A state of a relation that results from applying simple rules regarding functional dependencies (or relationships between attributes) to that relation. (5)

Normalization   The process of decomposing relations with anomalies to produce smaller, well-structured relations. (5)

Null   A value that may be assigned to an attribute when no other value applies or when the applicable value is unknown. (5)

Object   An entity that has a well-defined role in the application domain as well as state, behavior, and identity. (14)

Object class   A set of objects that share a common structure and a common behavior. (14)

Object diagram   A graph of instances that are compatible with a given class diagram. (14)

Object-relational database management system   A database engine that supports both relational and object-oriented features in an integrated fashion. (C)

On-line analytical processing (OLAP)   The use of a set of graphical tools that provides users with multidimensional views of their data and allows them to analyze the data using simple windowing techniques. (11)

Open database connectivity (ODBC) standard   An application programming interface that provides a common language for application programs to access and process SQL databases independent of the particular RDBMS that is accessed. (9)

Operation   A function or a service that is provided by all the instances of a class. (14)

Operational data store (ODS)   An integrated, subject-oriented, updatable, current-valued, detailed database designed to serve operational users as they do decision support processing. (11)

Operational system   A system that is used to run a business in real time, based on current data. Also called system of record. (11)

Outer join   A join in which rows that do not have matching values in common columns are nevertheless included in the result table. (8)

Overlap rule   Specifies that an entity instance can simultaneously be a member of two (or more) subtypes. (4)

Overriding   The process of replacing a method inherited from a superclass by a more specific implementation of that method in a subclass. (14)

Page   The amount of data read or written by an operating system in one secondary memory (disk) input or output operation. For I/O with a magnetic type, the equivalent term is record block. (6)

Partial functional dependency   A functional dependency in which one or more nonkey attributes are functionally dependent on part (but not all) of the primary key. (5)

Partial specialization rule   Specifies that an entity instance of the supertype is allowed not to belong to any subtype. (4)

Periodic data   Data that are never physically altered or deleted, once they have been added to the store. (11)

Persistent Stored Modules (SQL/PSM)   Extensions defined in SQL-99 that include the capability to create and drop modules of code stored in the database schema across user sessions. (8)

Physical file   A named portion of secondary memory (a magnetic tape or hard disk) allocated for the purpose of storing physical records. (6)

Physical record   A group of fields stored in adjacent memory locations and retrieved and written together as a unit by a DBMS. (6)

Physical schema   Specifications for how data from a conceptual schema are stored in a computer's secondary memory. (2)

Plug-ins   Hardware or software modules that extend the capabilities of a browser by adding a specific feature, such as encryption, animation, or wireless access. (10)

Pointer   A field of data that can be used to locate a related field or record of data. (6)

Polymorphism   The same operation may apply to two or more classes in different ways. (14)

Primary key   An attribute (or combination of attributes) that uniquely identifies each row in a relation. (5)

Procedure   A collection of procedural and SQL statements that are assigned a unique name within the schema and stored in the database. (8)

Project   A planned undertaking of related activities to reach an objective that has a beginning and an end. (2)

Prototyping   An iterative process of systems development in which requirements are converted to a working

system that is continually revised through close work between analysts and users. (2)

Proxy server   A firewall component that manages Internet traffic to and from a local area network. It can also handle access control and document caching. (10)

Query operation   An operation that accesses the state of an object but does not alter the state. (14)

Query-by-Example (QBE)   A direct manipulation database language that uses a graphical approach to query construction. (9)

Reconciled data   Detailed, current data intended to be the single, authoritative source for all decision support applications. (11)

Recovery manager   A module of the DBMS which restores the database to a correct condition when a failure occurs and which resumes processing user requests. (12)

Recursive foreign key   A foreign key in a relation that references the primary key values of that same relation. (5)

Redundant Array of Inexpensive Disks (RAID)   A set, or array, of physical disk drives that appear to the database user (and programs) as if they form one large logical storage unit. (6)

Referential integrity   An integrity constraint specifying that the value (or existence) of an attribute in one relation depends on the value (or existence) of a primary key in the same or another relation. (7)

Referential integrity constraint   A rule that states that either each foreign key value must match a primary key value in another relation or the foreign key value must be null. (5)

Refresh mode   An approach to filling the data warehouse that employs bulk rewriting of the target data at periodic intervals. (11)

Relation   A named two-dimensional table of data. (5)

Relational DBMS (RDBMS)   A database management system that manages data as a collection of tables in which all data relationships are represented by common values in related tables. (7)

Relational OLAP (ROLAP)   OLAP tools that view the database as a traditional relational database, in either a star schema or other normalized or denormalized set of tables. (11)

Relationship instance   An association between (or among) entity instances where each relationship instance includes exactly one entity from each participating entity type. (3)

Relationship type A meaningful association between (or among) entity types. (3)

Replication transparency A design goal for a distributed database, which says that although a given item may be replicated at several notes in a network, a programmer or user may treat the data item as if it were a single item at a single node. Also called *fragmentation transparency*. (13)

Repository A centralized knowledge base of all data definitions, data relationships, screen and report formats, and other system components. (1, 2)

Restore/rerun A technique that involves reprocessing the day's transactions (up to the point of failure) against the backup copy of the database. (12)

Reverse proxy A load-balancing approach that intercepts requests from clients and caches the response on the Web server that sends it back to the client. (10)

Router An intermediate device on a communications network used to transmit message packets and forward them to the correct destination over the most efficient pathway. (10)

Scalar aggregate A single value returned from an SQL query that includes an aggregate function. (7)

Schema That structure which contains descriptions of objects created by a user, such as base tables, views, and constraints, as part of a database. (7)

Scope operation An operation that applies to a class rather than an object instance. (14)

Second normal form A relation in first normal form in which every nonkey attribute is fully functionally dependent on the primary key. (5)

Secondary key One field or a combination of fields for which more than one record may have the same combination of values. Also called a nonunique key. (6)

Selection The process of partitioning data according to predefined criteria. (11)

Semijoin A joining operation used with distributed databases in which only the joining attribute from one site is transmitted to the other site, rather than all the selected attributes from every qualified row. (13)

Sequential file organization The storage of records in a file in sequence according to a primary key value. (6)

Server-side extension A software program that interacts directly with a Web server to handle requests. (10)

Set An unordered collection of elements without any duplicates. (15)

Shared lock (S lock or read lock) A technique that allows other transactions to read but not update a record or other resource. (12)

Simple attribute An attribute that cannot be broken down into smaller components. (3)

Snowflake schema An expanded version of a star schema in which dimension tables are normalized into several related tables. (11)

Software and hardware load balancing A load-balancing approach where requests to one IP address are distributed among the multiple servers hosting the Website at the TCP/IP routing level. (10)

Specialization The process of defining one or more subtypes of the supertype and forming supertype/subtype relationships. (4)

Standard Generalized Markup Language (SGML) An information management standard adopted in 1986 by the International Organization for Standardization to script documents so that formatting, indexing, and linked information is defined across platforms and applications. (10)

Star schema A simple database design in which dimensional data are separated from fact or event data. A dimensional model is another name for star schema. (11)

State Encompasses an object's properties (attributes and relationships) and the values those properties have. (14)

Static extract A method of capturing a snapshot of the required source data at a point in time. (11)

Stored procedure A module of code, usually written in a proprietary language such as Oracle's PL/SQL or Sybase's Transact-SQL, that implements application logic or a business rule and is stored on the server, where it runs when it is called. (9)

Stripe The set of pages on all disks in a RAID that are the same relative distance from the beginning of the disk drive. (6)

Strong entity type An entity that exists independently of other entity types. (3)

Structural assertion A statement that expresses some aspect of the static structure of the organization. (4)

Structured literal A fixed number of named elements, each of which could be of literal or object type. (15)

Subtype A subgrouping of the entities in an entity type that is meaningful to the organization and that shares common attributes or relationships distinct from other subgroupings. (4)

Subtype discriminator An attribute of the supertype whose values determine the target subtype or subtypes. (4)

Supertype A generic entity type that has a relationship with one or more subtypes. (4)

Supertype/subtype hierachy A hierarchical arrangement of supertypes and subtypes, where each subtype has only one supertype. (4)

Symmetric multiprocessing (SMP) A parallel processing architecture where the processors share a common shared memory. (9)

Synchronous distributed database A form of distributed database technology in which all data across the network are continuously kept up-to-date so that a user at any site can access data anywhere on the network at any time and get the same answer. (13)

Synonyms Two (or more) attributes having different names but the same meaning, as when they describe the same characteristics of an entity. (5)

System catalog A system-created database that describes all database objects, including data dictionary information, and also includes user access information. (12)

Systems development life cycle (SDLC) The traditional methodology used to develop, maintain, and replace information systems. (2)

Tablespace A named set of disk storage space in which physical files for database tables may be stored. (6)

Term A word or phrase that has a specific meaning for the business. (3)

Ternary relationship A simultaneous relationship among the instances of three entity types. (3)

Thin client A PC configured for handling user interfaces and some application processing, usually with no or limited local data storage. (9)

Third normal form A relation that is in second normal form and has no transitive dependencies present. (5)

Three-tier architecture A client/server configuration that includes three layers: a client layer and two server layers. While the nature of the server layers differs, a common configuration contains an application server. (9)

Time stamp A time value that is associated with a data value. (3)

Timestamping In distributed databases, a concurrency control mechanism that assigns a globally unique timestamp to each transaction. Timestamping is an alternative to the use of locks in distributed databases. (13)

Top-down planning A generic information systems planning methodology that attempts to gain a broad understanding of the information system needs of the entire organization. (2)

Total specialization rule Specifies that each entity instance of the supertype must be a member of some subtype in the relationship. (4)

Transaction A discrete unit of work that must be completely processed or not processed at all within a computer system. Entering a customer order is an example of a transaction. (12)

Transaction boundaries The logical beginning and end of transactions. (12)

Transaction log A record of the essential data for each transaction that is processed against the database. (12)

Transaction manager In a distributed database, a software module that maintains a log of all transactions and an appropriate concurrency control scheme. (13)

Transient data Data in which changes to existing records are written over previous records, thus destroying the previous data content. (11)

Transitive dependency A functional dependency between two (or more) nonkey attributes. (5)

Trigger A named set of SQL statements that are considered (triggered) when a data modification (INSERT, UPDATE, DELETE) occurs. If a condition stated within the trigger is met, then a prescribed action is taken. (8)

Two-phase commit An algorithm for coordinating updates in a distributed database. (13)

Two-phase locking protocol A procedure for acquiring the necessary locks for a transaction where all necessary locks are acquired before any locks are released, resulting in a growing phase, when locks are acquired, and a shrinking phase, when they are released. (12)

Unary relationship A relationship between the instances of a single entity type. (3)

Update mode An approach in which only changes in the source data are written to the data warehouse. (11)

Update operation An operation that alters the state of an object. (14)

User view A logical description of some portion of the database that is required by a user to perform some task. (1)

User-defined datatype (UDT) SQL-99 allows uers to define their own datatype by making it a subclass of a standard type or creating a type that behaves as an object. UDTs may also have defined functions and methods. (8)

User-defined procedures User exits (or interfaces) that allow system designers to define their own security procedures in addition to the authorization rules. (12)

VBScript A scripting language based on Microsoft Visual Basic and similar to JavaScript. (10)

Vector aggregate Multiple values returned from an SQL query that includes an aggregate function. (7)

Versioning Each transaction is restricted to a view of the database as of the time that transaction started, and when a transaction modifies a record, the DBMS creates a new record version instead of overwriting the old record. Hence no form of locking is required. (12)

Vertical partitioning Distributing the columns of a table into several separate physical records. (6)

Visual Basic for Applications (VBA) The programming language that accompanies Access 2000. (9)

Weak entity type An entity type whose existence depends on some other entity type. (3)

Well-structured relation A relation that contains minimal redundancy and allows users to insert, modify, and delete the rows in a table without errors or inconsistencies. (5)

World Wide Web (WWW) The total set of interlinked hypertext documents residing on special servers, called Web servers or HTTP servers, worldwide. The Web servers are configured to make the information they hold easily accessible to each other and to allow files to be accessed, transferred, and downloaded. Also referred to as W3 or the Web. (10)

World Wide Web Consortium (W3C) An international consortium of companies intending to develop open standards that foster the development of Web conventions so that Web documents can be consistently displayed across all platforms. (10)

XHTML A hybrid scripting language that extends HTML code to make it XML compliant. (10)

Credits

Microsoft Access and Access 2000 are registered trademarks of Microsoft Corporation in the United States and other countries.

Certain portions of copyrighted Oracle Corporation screen displays of software programs have been reproduced herein with the permission of Oracle Corporation.

Chapter 1 Page 20: Table 1-4, from "Database Technology: Sorting Out the Options" by C. White in *Supplement to Database Programing & Design 8* (December): 41–44, 46. Copyright © 1995 by C M P Media. Reproduced with permission of C M P Media via Copyright Clearance Center.

Chapter 3 Page 79: Table 3-1 from "Turning Rules into Requirements," by E. Gottesdiener in *Application Development Trends 6* (7): 37–60, 1999, and "Business Rules Everywhere," by D. Plotkin in *Intelligent Enterprise 2* (4): 37–44, 1999.

Chapter 4 Page 149: Figure 4-15 adapted from GUIDE Business Rules Project, 1997. Reprinted with permission of SHARE Inc.

Chapter 5 Page 183: Figure 5-16 adapted from GUIDE Business Rules Project, 1997. Reprinted with permission of SHARE Inc.

Chapter 7 Page 288: Figure 7-8 from *Introduction to SQL*, 3/e, by Rick F. van der Lans. Copyright © 2000. Reprinted by permission of the author.

Chapter 8 Page 300: Figure 8-1 from "The Extra Mile" by R. Winter in *Intelligent Enterprise,* June, 26, 2000, p. 63. Copyright © 2000 by C M P Media. Reproduced with permission of C M P Media via Copyright Clearance Center. Page 313: Figure 8-5 from "The Procedural DBA" by C.S. Mullins in *Database Programming & Design* 8 (12), pp. 40–45. Copyright © 1995 by C M P Media. Reproduced with permission of C M P Media via Copyright Clearance Center.

Chapter 9 Page 323: Figures 9-1, 9-2 adapted from "Client/Server: Where Are We Really?" by G. Anderson and B. Armstrong in *Health Management Technology,* May 1995, with permission of Nelson Publishing. Pages 331, 332: Figures 9-5, 9-6, 9-7 from "Parallel Database: The Shape of Things to Come" by M. Ferguson in *Database Programming & Design,* October 1994, pp. 32–44. Copyright © 1994 by C M P Media. Reproduced with permission of C M P Media via Copyright Clearance Center. Page 342: Figure 9-9 adapted from *Access 97 Bible,* by C. Prague and M. Irwin, Foster City, CA: IDG Books, 1997.

Chapter 11 Page 404: Table 11-2 adapted from "Can Data Marts Grow?," by K. Strange in *CIO* (July, 1997): 34, 36. Page 437: Table 11-5 adapted from "Data Mining Neural Clusters," by J. Zaitz in *DM Review* 7 (July/August, 1997): 91, 92, and *e-Data: Turning Data into Information with Data Warehousing* by J. Dyché, Reading, MA: Addison-Wesley, 2000.

Chapter 12 Page 461: Figure 12-13 adapted from "The Repository: A Modern Vision," by P.A. Bernstein in *Database Programming & Design* 9:12 (December, 1996): 28–35. Page 479: Table 12-2 adapted from "Protecting Your Database," by K. Loney in *Oracle Magazine* (May/June, 2000): 101–106.

Chapter 13 Page 495–496: Figures 13-1–13-3 adapted from *Distributed Database Systems* by D. Bell and J. Grimson, Reading, MA: Addison-Wesley, 1992. Page 504: Figure 13-9 Copyright © *Database Programming & Design* 2:4 (April, 1989). Reprinted by permission of Miller Freeman Publications. Page 513: Table 13-2 adapted from *An Introduction to Database Systems,* Vol. 2, by C.J. Date, Reading, MA: Addison-Wesley, 1983.

Index

Note: **Boldface** terms are defined on the page that is boldface.